Make not Marriage

THE MYTH AND REALITY OF LOVE, RELATIONSHIPS AND SEX

KHEL KALYAN

ISBN: 978-1-9196349-8-2 (paperback)
ISBN: 978-1-9196349-9-9 (ebook)

FIRST EDITION July 2025
Published by MW PUBLISHER
mwpublisher.com

In this book, you are the protagonist, though I have replaced your name with the word "love". Your new name appears over a thousand times; every time you see and read it, I would like you to identify with the feeling of love, accepting love as part of your selfhood...if only for the sake of experiment. You see: love is, above all things, an incarnation of your own essence. Love can only be known and defined through you, as you. You are the hero of this story, the only fairy tale which actually comes true, because in this case "love" truly will live happily ever after!

Contents

Preface

Who wrote this and why?

I was married, once and briefly, and I've had a good run of beautiful, inspiring relationships over the course of my 48 years on this planet. I also suffered a devastating heartbreak, which turned out to be the best thing that ever happened to me. Today, though, I am in a new relationship, one that I never imagined was even possible: I fell in love with being alone. As most people would agree, even while mindful of the irony, being with someone is often as difficult as finding someone to love. Strangely enough, though, seeking a partner and getting along with them both become much easier once you develop a talent for being content in your own company. Being comfortably alone affords you the perspective and distance needed to notice the romantic mistakes we continually repeat. Solitude allowed me to perceive how our supposedly loving relationships are often a source of misery rather than joy. Why should this be, where does this state of affairs come from?

In this book, I discuss the problem from first, and indeed spiritual, principles to shed some much-needed light on the matter. Along the way, I also make some suggestions anyone – single, married, or dating – can apply in their own life. This book is unique in the sense that it does not adhere to any conventional ideas, nor does it quite fit into the traditional "self-help" genre. Instead, I offer advice based on the perspective I've gained over decades of studying the human mind while forming a personal connection with the reality beyond the mind: infinite love witnessed through deep meditation. It is only from this personal experience I can write about love.

Fundamentally, the human mind, heart, and soul are the same in each of us; we're all cut from the same cloth. Though people can be fantastically interesting and diverse in one sense, there is nothing especially unique or enigmatic about any one individual. We are all driven by the same principles and follow the same rules. Consider your own mind, which is just one manifestation of a universal consciousness in which we all exist as one. From this vantage point, no one is truly separate: we all suffer the same fears and we all essentially chase after the same thrills. Therefore, if you approach and respect everyone as if they were a reflection and part of yourself, you will attain the highest connection possible with others. The separation between us is seen in its proper light: as an illusion generated by the egoic mind. It is because I've embraced this unified perspective that I can write about you, because the truth is: I am you. Love encompasses everyone, without any exception whatsoever. Nobody is estranged from this universal love, regardless of whether you're an atheist, nihilist, cynic, religious, or indifferent. Though we've twisted God into so many perverted interpretations, love is a different matter: it is an experience that's accessible to each of us. Though its existence can't be proven or refuted in a laboratory, we need only gaze inward to find it.

Though all who sincerely seek love may find it unambiguously, its true nature is often hidden underneath a mass of extrinsic influences. Accordingly, I invite you to reassess the way you approach love, marriage, relationships, and sex. Specifically, I want you to question how and why we follow convention, tradition, and culture so blindly. Without any deeper inquiry, slaves to custom only end up suffering in the name of love rather than finding the joy they so desperately seek. Love is, in fact, an act of rebellion, because truly sampling love requires one to break a few rules, be brave enough to escape the herd, and stand alone. We all know, deep down even though we won't admit it, that the well-worn path to love doesn't exactly come easy and for so many perhaps not at all! It requires courage to chart a new course.

The negative effects of marriage are mostly kept hidden compared to the obvious human failings people love to complain about. Traditional marriage can be compared to a diet high in sugar: a slow, drawn-out death that allows you to live what you believe is a normal life without ever knowing the harm it causes...or even becoming aware of the alternative way to live and love. To know the real detriment of marriage would cause you to discover how love actually works. This would require you to deviate from the conventional and descend into this infinite mystery, and this is a task that must be undertaken all by yourself.

Marriage ultimately erects walls between lovers, it enforces conditions, and is wholly restrictive. Love, on the other hand, knows no boundaries; love is total freedom. Therefore, marriage fundamentally works against human nature. Marriage is not a spiritual affair, nor is it ordained by God as you may have been led to believe, it is strictly a manmade institution that attempts to control love, confine it, extend it beyond its natural course. Love is a preternatural law onto itself, it cannot be contained within a shell of vows and duties.

Having said all this, I will not harp on matrimony's obvious defects too much. My aim is not to discourage you from ever getting married, in fact, it really doesn't make much difference to your evolution and happiness. Instead, this is a book about what love really is, my task is only to bring you closer and closer to experiencing love. Love doesn't exist without someone to feel it, and beauty simply cannot be without someone to see it. Love is created by the observer. You are what makes all the difference in the world. Nothing is beautiful without your perception and there is no love unless you are involved.

Introduction

Love isn't supposed to hurt!

I ask you to keep an open mind while I share my thoughts on the mysterious, immense, inexhaustible reality of love. If something I say contradicts your existing ideas about romance or derides a tried and trusted recipe for happy relationships, take a deep breath and ask yourself whether your reaction originates in principle or prejudice. My greatest hope in writing this book is that you will be totally honest with yourself while reading it. In many cases, I believe, there is the capacity within you to agree with much of what I say; however, your mind simply won't allow you to awaken that intrinsic, inalienable, yet neglected part of yourself.

If this book has any credibility, it is because of you as the reader, not myself as the writer. Without you, these words are dead and lifeless. Until you read them, they are only flat, two-dimensional squiggles on a page that really amount to nothing valuable without your insight applied to them. You are what will bring this book to life. However, this does not mean that everyone who reads this book will discover what love really is, the ultimate responsibility rests with you.

Unlike many other love and relationship books out there, this book does not give you a ten-step agenda to fix a failing marriage or reassure you that everything is actually all your exes' fault. I have deliberately avoided trying to teach you formulas and stratagems to improve your relationship...or simply allow it to survive. These kinds of games are only superficial aspects of love. Whatever effort and compromises we end up making, we somehow continue falling short of what we innately seek. Most of us are stuck believing the "perfect" relationship, literally "as seen on TV", is what defines true love, but this is a facile and naïve impression of romance. This book will examine love and relationships as separate realities, as only from this perspective can you discover what truly matters. Let's be clear about this: finding your soul mate does not teach you what love is. Such, apparently healthy, relationships are simply a case of good chemistry; that's all.

The truth is that nobody just automatically knows what love is. In the first place, it is not a physical or emotional desire, so one must take pains to learn the true, unbounded nature of love. Having a spouse or lover is only tangentially relevant to this search, as we are all ultimately alone, even while signing a contract that permanently ties you to another's destiny. Though this truth has no place in fairy tales, it's exactly this realisation that sets you on the path to finding love. Before we start inflicting our loneliness on others, we must come to recognise aloneness as our greatest quality, as your relationship with yourself will be the most wondrous you will ever come to experience. Your solitude is the only company you can rely on and, in the end, it will become your greatest love. You cannot love anyone until you know peace while being alone. It's hard to overstate the importance of this discovery: once you know and love yourself, you naturally love everything in the universe. Indeed, love is intimately connected with spiritual enlightenment: both bridge the gap between self and other.

It's possible that my emphasis on spiritual principles will make you doubt me at times; that's okay. Most books on relationships, marriage, and divorce try to speak from a place of rational pragmatism and like to use statistics to support their arguments. For example, one convenient fact authors enjoy flaunting is that marriages fail 56% of the time. Is the information that more than half of marriages end in divorce useful news for anyone but divorce lawyers, though?

In the first place, this kind of superficial and misleading data has not discouraged people from getting married, even multiple times. Secondly, using that kind of starting point doesn't lend much credibility to the spurious, arbitrary reasoning people like to tack onto it. But, most importantly of all, let's set the record straight: divorce is not equivalent to failure! In fact, the ever-rising divorce rate is a positive signal; it indicates that society is gradually evolving out of a redundant, invidious tradition. Though often uncomfortable, divorce is how we regain control of our lives and break free of awkward, unchecked loyalties that do more harm than good. If we prove strong enough, divorce can be the moment we begin thinking for ourselves and cease allowing another to hold our happiness hostage.

What Is Love, Truly?

You are not a statistic, and I won't treat you like one. By my estimate, though, the vast majority of people never actually experience what love truly is. This great tragedy is the result of our tendency to mindless herd behaviour: the mainstream maintains the trend and presents any other way of living as absurd or unimaginable. Treating loveless marriage as the norm also just happens to conveniently support the global economy and all those who profit from it: expendable purchases are our unconscious substitute for love we lack.

I greatly desire to help you join the small minority of people who constantly experience the inner light and buoyancy that comes from knowing love. The fundamental reason for so few people being happy is precisely because they haven't discarded their egos. Love is the absence of ego, and this is a key component of becoming one of the blessed few who eventually find true love. Before you can reach this happy state, however, we need to discuss who you truly are. Specifically, your ego – the outer, false part of yourself – is a product of its surroundings, an imitation of what we see. As a result of all the images, marketing, social media, and other influences we can avoid only with difficulty, nothing about us is original. Even knowledge is borrowed this way, including the only way we know how to love, the way we practice relationships, and what we demand of them.

Romantic relationships (so we're told and believe unquestioningly) are meant to nurture love. Once you study them objectively, however, they are the very thing that draws us further away from the feeling of connection we so desperately seek. This is because, without exception, all human associations have become a crutch for love and affection, simulating these superficially without ever magically bringing them into existence. Relationships exist as a unit of co-dependency: the complete opposite of love. Instead of liberating both of you, as genuine devotion to another person does, dependency holds you hostage to another's affection. Is it any wonder marriage makes so many couples miserable, when we think of this as the normal way to relate to another person?

Sooner or later, every relationship is pushed to a breaking point because we rely on them as our salvation and the source of what we lack in ourselves. We are conditioned to believe that love is found outside of our own being, beyond our own reality. This imposes an unfair obligation on our partners. The desire to be loved, the impulse to see it as a commodity to be traded, is the very reason we never find what we seek. This is because no one can give you love, nor is loving you anyone's responsibility.

Love and learning

As children, we learn our first lessons about what affection, comfort, and the warmth of love are from our families. Through that foundation of experience, we become imbued with love. Whatever initial idea of love we established from our parent's touch, understanding love continues to be a process of discovery well beyond those early years, a growth, and an expansion of one's own being. Love is your own currency; love will only ever radiate from you at its centre. This is how love works. When you have found self-love, you become self-sufficient, because true love needs no other; two independent lovers don't trade love but rather merge and melt into each other.

The pain in any relationship always originates from possessive attachment, which is the only way most of us know how to connect and demonstrate love. Thus all our supposedly positive, loving traits are expressed in the form of control, jealousy and ownership – all of which come from fear. Love is non-possessive and knows no attachment; love arises from and expresses freedom.

Of course, this mindset is quite incompatible with the conventional approach to love, which encourages us to accept love as something as hurtful as it is blissful, a bizarre amalgam of joy and sorrow. It is typically out of fear that animals attack, yet what we call love causes us to become just as vicious, proving we are closer to our feral origins than we'd like to think.

By contrast, when you are bursting with authentic love, you fear nothing and are free of any pain. Your love demonstrates that you have evolved into a spiritual being and left your more primitive impulses behind. The nature of this metamorphosis has been described as chakra transformation. (Chakras are nerve clusters and glands within the body; each is also a spiritual centre.) These nexuses of energy can either remain in their primal, animalistic state or can be elevated to a higher essence. When this happens, lust advances to love, anger becomes compassion, hate turns into affection, attachment into non-possessiveness, and so on.

Ignoring the spiritual nature of this process means the nature of the love we exchange is mostly dependent on how the other responds. We calibrate love on the premise of giving and receiving, love is always a transaction. Love has even become a business measured in terms of profit and loss. When a relationship begins, we hide away our true feelings until we know they will be reciprocated, in order to ensure our effort and sincerity will be rewarded. Should there ever be an imbalance in the scales of affection, we attack our sweethearts as if we're being robbed: love is considered a commodity that we spend only grudgingly.

Marriage is established solely based on these conditions; they are actually written down on paper and endorsed by law. This is precisely what makes traditional matrimony such a farcical imitation of love: because no person can justifiably support a relationship based on emotional transactions, just like conditional love is not real love. That is why the love contained within a marriage immediately comes to an end as soon as divorce rears its head – even though the same two people still possess the same reasons for cherishing one another, their feelings change irrevocably once the contract is breached. Should we dare to unreservedly love someone, regardless of what we can obtain from the relationship, marriages would succeed a lot better than they actually do (and divorce, if necessary, would be seen not as the end of a relationship but just another stage in its evolution).

Discarding False Notions of Love

Instead of accepting the spiritual, selfless nature of love, we continue to love selfishly. Howsoever hard we try to compromise and coexist with the ones we believe we love, in relationship after relationship, romance only proves to be a source of suffering, every time. And this has been going on for so long that we aren't even aware of the pain any more, as if it's meant to be there. A type of love that hurts is all we have sampled, it is all we know. Every love story, song, poem, and romantic film would seem incomplete without this travesty – we celebrate love on the altar of pain and challenge.

My approach to love is entirely unlike anything else you've read on the subject. Perhaps this isn't the kind of book you were looking for, which may well mean it's the one you really need to read. The facts contained here aren't founded on my opinions or religious suppositions, nor even based on the dating and romantic experiences I've had. Instead, everything I share with you pertains to existential and physical laws that govern our existence, spiritual truths that pertain to all of us, generally without our knowing. Nothing in this book is speculation or conjecture. As you will see, it is only by merging into infinite love. the highest peak of human emotion, that I can even begin to share a love story: anything less would render this book on love incomplete or prejudiced.

For the majority of people, love is only experienced and understood as two separate parts, with different individuals playing the parts of the lover and the beloved. This exchange will always burden both people in the relationship, as each will (either voluntarily or by submitting to the other's expectations) make compromises and forbearances just to live in relative harmony with another human being. These situations end up being a kind of theatre of differences and conflict – this shortcoming doesn't make romantic relationships or marriages a bad thing, but you should accept that they are not conducive environments for the expression of love. In particular, a marriage is a prolonged association based on obligation instead of freedom, and that means the seed of personal evolution perishes. What marriages claim to be love really amounts to loyalty, attachment and familiarity.

This does not, however, mean we should simply give up on the whole idea of romance. Sometimes, if you're very fortunate, you will experience a rare moment in life, when love takes on a new dimension, one that cannot be explained, translated, or reduced to any one concept. When your eyes are opened in this way, love is no longer an restrictive relationship as much it is an inclusive acceptance and reverence for everything, all at once. This experience, which words can't define or describe with any degree of precision, is the greatest part of life, the mysterious path to love that I am pointing out to you.

Love is something we all seek, and we all have different ways of striving to encounter it. I, for instance, once searched it out through travel, friends, money, ambitions, and even a string of somewhat meaningful relationships. Yet, I never quite gained the connection that satisfied me, the thing I imagined love to be. Once I had lost faith in the whole notion, I realised relationships are a counterfeit of what love really is. This was, in fact, a complete epiphany, which led me to experience love in a different, extraordinary way. I realised that I was never on a voyage with love as the destination, because any such search for love would be counterproductive. Once you've embraced the right attitude, love just happens to you: suddenly, you are enveloped by a force beyond your control or expectation. This kind of love is the effect of becoming liberated, being free of the constraints you previously believed to be so essential to what love is.

Finding True Connection

You see, relationships are some of the best things in life, but that doesn't mean they are where love comes from. Human connection and genuine love are entirely separate experiences. Relationships don't incubate love, people do. When you come to appreciate the difference, you're much less likely to go and ruin what could be a good relationship just because you didn't find that ineffable joy you imagined love to be. An enjoyable relationship is simply a connection, nothing more than good chemistry. Love is a separate phenomenon, which comes from you regardless of how well your relationships perform.

If you are scouring the world for the perfect relationship, you might want to consider whether you've already met the right person but weren't ready. Perhaps you weren't yet worthy of their affection or you couldn't see their value, thus you either corrupted the relationship or allowed the opportunity to pass you by without even noticing what you were giving up. The truth is that, outside of fairy tales, love doesn't depend on finding the right person to spend your life with. Rather, love is your own journey into your own being. Who accompanies you on the road is almost inconsequential compared to your own willingness to love.

Like all spiritual realisations, this lesson can be difficult and painful to learn. It often requires something going devastatingly wrong for us before we wake up to a better way of living. In my case, everything in my life came to a grinding halt in 2017 due to a monumental heartbreak arising from a failed relationship. Yet, as I gradually discovered, my breakdown had nothing to do with the woman in question or the relationship I had lost. The source of my pain was all internal, it was all about me. The core issue was not that I suddenly found myself alone, but that there was a deeper wound within me; one that no relationship could heal or any person should be expected to soothe. In the end, my sadness turned out to be a lifeline, driving me to ponder the larger problem of my ego's fragile nature. Now, deep melancholy can be as excruciating as a physical injury and will cause most people to re-evaluate their lifestyles in favour of some soul-searching. For me, it created a chance for deep reflection; it created a mirror, allowing me to see exactly who I was trying so hard to be.

What happened along the way was something I never expected. I found love without wanting or looking for it, I experience it without having a special someone by my side, something I never imagined was even possible, never mind so profoundly rewarding. Many would agree: the challenge of being with someone special is no less intricate than the quest to find them. And yet, both paths open to you once you've made peace with solitude and learned to find fullness in your own presence.

In my case (and unlike anyone else I know of) moving beyond the desire to be with someone was something I couldn't plan for and didn't actively pursue. Yet, that is what love really feels like, the miracle I had been vainly seeking in others. One accurate, though unconventional, definition of love is that it's the absence of desire, the absence of needing anyone or anything – even while, perhaps, being with someone and sharing a life. It seems to me that almost everyone today spends a great deal of time scurrying around, chasing after some kind of change in their romantic situation. Sometimes, it takes a huge setback to realise that the alternative isn't another relationship or pinning your hopes on a different person. Hopefully, by writing this book, I can make the road to this awareness a little smoother for you.

I am talking about the direct path to love itself and how to expand your consciousness so that love becomes the basis of your existence, so that love engulfs you all around. It so happens, that once you have found this love, when you're overflowing and radiating it, you'll realise that you're truly free to do whatever you want: marry, don't marry, or be single for the rest of your life. All these things become non-essential, inconsequential to your happiness.

Are you ready to know what love really is?

Chapter One

Make love not ~~war~~ *marriage*

The path from ego to love

Chances are that you picked up this book because the title intrigued, or perhaps even startled, you. What, you're probably wondering, could be going through the author's mind? In case you hadn't noticed, "Make love, not marriage" is a nod to the famous Hippy slogan: "Make love, not war" – in fact, to me, they mean essentially the same thing!

Indeed, marriage is like war, for all practical purposes, complete with manoeuvres, tactics, retreats, attacks, victories and defeats. A relationship between two lovers is a battle of minds...although this kind of tussle is a natural, intrinsic, and colourful part of being a human, not a curse. Without psychological conflict, we wouldn't learn nearly as much about ourselves and others. Aside from the entertainment these skirmishes afford, they are a means for us to transform and evolve: we learn more through intimacy than at any university.

However, this kind of war is not without its casualties. Maintaining a relationship forces us into submission to another person's desires, and in most cases succeeds in hammering us into something we are not meant to be. As soon as the wedding cake is cut, we're expected to take on the part of being a husband or wife, often based on the characters you saw your parents act out in marriage's theatre of conflict. No one should be reduced to playing these roles: they not only impose an unfair obligation on you, but the emphasis on dutiful commitment, self-denial, and forbearance impedes the growth of love. Love does not thrive in such an environment; love truly is an unpredictable force of nature and can't be controlled.

The battle that inevitably ensues when two people decide to remain together for the rest of their lives has brought about a ridiculous amount of literature over the decades. These books aim to make you believe that there is a code to dating, rules of engagement that govern the couple's coming battles. Then, they set out even more standards and guidelines about the mind games you'll play to ensure your feelings are protected and you get what you want. Such manipulation, the most superficial and meaningless embodiment of love, will only divide the two of you, even while giving the impression you are getting along and working things out.

To be clear, I am not against marriage. Though it does have an undeniably negative effect on how we live, you can say much the same thing about the Hippy concept of "free love". Unlike the original slogan, "make love" is not actually an invitation to indulge the sensual part of human nature – when I use it, it stands as a spur to find love. Love is infinitely more than we know; it is only from the metaphysical and spiritual perspective that one can uncover its magic and come to experience it. I

Make love not war marriage

simply encourage you to love; that's all, make what you will out of that statement. More specifically, I acknowledge that romance, relationships, and sex are all integral parts of human existence and therefore spirituality, an aspect of ourselves that should pervade all parts of life. In fact, we should all strive to cultivate a certain kind of awareness of everything we do – including by how we choose to love.

Relationships Vs Love

Despite the best (and presumably most sincere) efforts of thousands of authors, almost every piece of relationship advice out there today shares one important flaw: love is not spoken of as a raw material, it is only ever identified and discussed as part of a relationship. In fact, popular self-help books tend to avoid the subject of fundamental, profound love as much as possible, preferring to talk about related concepts like affection, cooperation, respect, and physical attraction. In many cases, they don't even touch on what should be the central theme; instead, their advice lingers on the periphery and doesn't approach the core of what love really is. If you were to read a book on gardening that never mentions watering plants, you'd find it absurd...but here we are. Yet their instructions for happy marriages are bound in red book covers cheerfully festooned with heart-shaped symbols, often making bestseller lists due to the specious encouragement they offer. If you want to keep thinking of romance as war, if you want to see your lover as your subtle, revered enemy, then these are the books for you.

Now, no relationship can ever truly be peaceful all the time – if it were, it would be stagnant, unsatisfying, and sterile as far as personal growth is concerned. Anyone who tries to sell you "a happily ever after" philosophy is deceiving you. It is exactly these kinds of optimistic untruths that cause real love to be so rarely experienced, because true love barely resembles the fairy-tale. Love is continually marketed as being all about idealised relationships, yet relationships are just associations that can be formed either out of love or in its absence. Two people with wildly differing conceptions of love can easily end up together; for emotional comfort, for financial security, because society expects it – all reasons unrelated to love. The facade of romance is in no way the source of love, yet the outward forms of relationships have been given enormous precedence. If you buy into this, you will never get to the fountainhead of genuine love.

Once you discard this conditioning, though, the true nature of love becomes much more apparent and accessible. To give one example, I can direct my love to a deer, a flower, a perfect sunset, another human being, or just about anything. Everything I relate to in this way joins me in a communion or meeting of two energies, and that is exactly what a loving relationship is. Love is an unconditional and inclusive connection with everything you see, touch and experience; love is not ruled by choice nor motivated by expectation.

Unconditional love will probably sound like an unreachable ideal, because we've become strangely adept at switching our willingness to love on and off as we choose. That is why discovering real love is nothing less than transformative, a life-changing event. When you have found the kind of love that lies beyond physical attraction, emotional resonance, or simple self-interest, you will never be the same person again. Can many of us claim to have achieved such a lofty plateau? We use all the lingo associated with love, but mostly in order to imitate the shallow concept that's been shown to us. We expend a great deal of energy pretending we're loving but, in actuality, the relationships we have simply don't touch the core of our souls. Our counterfeit connections don't rock our world enough to transform us, liberate us from our egoic shell. Love, in contrast, will demolish the old you; love initiates everyone into a new way of thinking, living and being.

The human connections we expend so much of our effort on are not exemplars of love and peace – these must come from your own being. All ordinary, generic relationships represent nothing but friction; this is a natural consequence of how energy and chemistry work when two individual forces collide and meet. People who maintain successful relationships, who might end up proving the reality of "happily ever after", aren't necessarily good lovers as such. Instead, they are merely two adults who happen to be emotionally mature. They both know how to handle conflict without breaking down emotionally, they've learned how to practice transparency, friendship and open communication, and (unlike many) they have developed the ability to deepen their emotional connection. These are the basic and essential traits that make an intimate relationship work and endure, and we see many couples around the world achieve a lifetime of happiness together. But this doesn't prove these couples have found anything close to the experiential bliss of what love really is. Still, relationships are an essential joy in the life that allows us to evolve. Every romantic encounter occurs only in order to make us grow, but you mustn't take a happy, lifelong relationship as your model for what love really is!

Attracting Your Soulmate

Soulmates are mistakenly considered to be your perfect match, perhaps made in heaven. In truth, though, there isn't anything about a relationship which resembles perfection. All love relationships are inherently flawed; that's the whole point of them and precisely why they are beautiful. They are what they are: an opportunity to grow, learn and consciously evolve. More often than not, the people who mistreat us, take advantage of us and get on our last raw nerve turn out to be our greatest teachers. They are invaluable because they expose all our weaknesses and bring our hidden traumas into the light. With this in mind, do you still think soulmates are always the "right people" for us? If your goal is to expand your awareness and insight, can't soulmates often be the "wrong people" instead? The people who infuriate us and trigger all our bad traits can easily be said to be wrong for us...but this may only be because we take too narrow a view of love's role in our journey through life.

Very many people on the planet won't openly admit it, but believe they married the wrong person and imagine they would have had a better love life with someone more like them. Some run from imperfect relationships, consumed with bitter regret, in search of a true soulmate connection. Regardless of prior experiences, we are convinced that we are wise enough to create the connection we want with someone who is supposedly right for us. Practically every single person today exhausts themselves hunting for the famed soulmate. They do this in ignorance of the fact that we are all someone's soulmate. We have the capacity to become healers and teachers for each other, even when we bring out the worst parts in one another. Every person, no matter how they behave and treat us, is a divine signal, someone placed in our path to help us learn who we are.

Equally, it could well be that many of us have previously dated and even shared a life with the right person, an individual that was in fact perfect for us, but one who we overlooked and neglected. Therefore, we must expand our views on who is right and who is wrong for us, what differentiates a bad relationship from a good one. This is not a matter of pleasure, comfort, or apparent harmony. Every encounter is purposefully suited to our spiritual maturity at any given time, sent our way by the mysterious workings of the universe.

Some relationships are short-lived, as people who are not meant to stay long come into your life. Nevertheless, they sometimes teach us more in a few months than people we know for a lifetime. These are the fleeting strangers who say and do exactly what you need to hear and experience, then they quietly drift away out of your life. To put this another way: some relationships aren't about living happily ever after, but have a great deal of impact on our lives, presenting us with a short burst of realisation. As we become more self-aware, we come to accept all our love affairs (good or bad, short or long) as our teachers. In the process, we also improve our ability to attract better people into our lives. Every relationship is a divine connection, so you could say we are all in a soulmate relationship right now. Every love affair raises our consciousness, most especially if we are receptive to its lessons. I hope, now that you've heard this thought stated, you will be inspired to look at all your exes and your current lover differently. Perhaps, you'll even want to silently thank them for their teaching – even if it wasn't pleasant at the time.

It certainly doesn't help to chase after your soulmate. If you have a few decades behind you in this lifetime, you will have observed a noticeable change in the landscape of how couples and singles alike behave: the popularity of marriage has been steadily declining while divorce rates are increasing across different cultures. Whereas people used to consider "settling down" as a prime goal of early adulthood, having numerous sexual partners in your 20s is now the norm. Meanwhile, a small but rising number of individuals have become so disillusioned with the transactional, image-obsessed nature of modern relationships that they've given up on dating altogether. Many others only secure their best chance at a relationship way beyond their 40s, after many failed attempts.

Although it is certainly possible to eventually find the relationship that works out for you, this has little to do with stumbling upon the right person but everything to do with your maturity. You see, the people we date and connect with on an intimate level are those who mirror who we are at that given time. We attract our equals, but I don't necessarily mean people of similar social and financial status: rather, those who resonate with us in ways beyond physical appearance and emotional compatibility. These individuals, mysteriously steered to us, are impeccably matched to our needs (though often not our desires). This includes their flaws, too, which may form a counterpoint to your own. Have you ever wondered why someone special came into your life? It was because they were, in one way or another, your soul's reflection; they are part of your karmic journey.

This realisation implies that expanding your social circle or trying internet dating is not the answer to your loneliness. Instead, you'll find that working on your own development and intentionally raising your consciousness (by reading this book, for example!) improves the calibre of the potential lovers who cross your path. As you deliberately grow, the people you date will reflect your increasing spiritual maturity. Every person you intimately engage with should be regarded as your soul's reflection, an opportunity to learn.

This means that, as you refine and expand your awareness, you will automatically meet and date the type of people you've always wanted to. Previously, you may have thought you lacked the charisma and confidence to attract desirable partners, but there were really more profound forces at work. For example, if you have consistently been dating self-absorbed fools or people who took advantage of you, this only indicates something about the person you were at that time. There was a lesson for you to absorb, or a pattern of behaviour you needed to discard; these cycles repeat only until you succeed. Therefore, the solution here is for you to improve the spiritual echo you send out into the world. Perhaps, this could also mean temporarily withdrawing and not reflecting anything back at all – this happens to be my current situation and one which I am wholeheartedly embracing.

I'd very much like for this book to be useful to as many people as possible. However, all the guidance I provide has to be adapted to your situation, and the change you need will have to come entirely from you. The cornerstone of the approach to love I want you to follow is, in essence, to become the person worthy of the one who you really long for.

I am reminded of the ancient fable of Rama and Sita, a deeply loving couple who embody the greatest Hindu love story. Every Indian woman wants to find her Rama and every man seeks to marry his Sita. However, as many of us learn too late, mere desire doesn't get you anywhere; as a few discover, the act of searching for the perfect mate is equally futile. The only

Make love not war marriage

reliable method is to become an attractor for the one you seek. Therefore, since I'm male, I must become Rama, the archetype of strength, integrity, devotion, and other quintessentially desirable masculine qualities. Then, Sita will naturally appear in the guise of any woman I choose to be with. It is not that I must chase after her, especially since she is an idealised role model; instead, I must actualise the Rama within me.

But, while this approach definitely works, it will prove horribly frustrating for so many people while they are still trapped in their old habits. To find the perfect love means devoting time towards inner self-awareness and perhaps shattering your current worldview. I admit, it seems simpler to just carry on with the old routine and take your chances. But ask yourself: has what you've been doing all along been working? Have you, perhaps, noticed that you keep following the same behavioural patterns in each new relationship you enter? On deeper examination, you'll also come to see that you've been dating the same kind of people all your life. This is entirely because of your own nature; the kind of love you're able to experience remains the same purely because you yourself have not changed.

Breaking Free

Though this dilemma – of naturally attracting the "wrong" people, time after time – manifests clearly in the area of romance, it's actually indicative of a deeper, spiritual problem. It's a sign that you're stuck, you've become stagnant, in defiance of life's only purpose: to keep evolving, ascending upwards. The reason why almost every relationship you see lacks any sign of authentic love is that people ignore this fundamental human truth.

It could be that you're reading this while you're in a relationship; if so, your seeking out this book could be a sign that something in your life needs improving (in fact, this is probably true for all of us!). However, change is only ever realised when we break free of old habits, and these unconscious actions etched into our subconscious minds go deeper than you may think. Anger, jealousy, possessiveness, dependency, and attachment are all learned behaviours, not immutable emotional reactions from which we can never hope to escape. In fact, breaking the chains of habit is essential if we hope to experience romantic fulfilment, as our unreasoning routines all tend to manifest as exploitation, not love.

Unfortunately, these kinds of attitudes have become an accepted and normalised part of how we love each other. We've lost sight of the fact that relationships don't need to be a vehicle for control. Pleasant coexistence can only be grounded in freedom, and that means freedom *for* others as well as freedom *from* others. Love is the subtle and elusive experience that results from these two expressions of liberty. (I'll be examining the critical importance of freedom in depth, just a little further on in the book.)

We're all told that love is of the heart, and this is true as far as it goes. But...we are too afraid to explore this territory too deeply, too afraid to risk seeing what the heart may show us. We find it more comforting to linger in our inherently selfish, egoic minds, which do most of the work of convincing us that what we have really is love. Everyone believes they want to experience love, but they aren't genuinely prepared to go as far as is needed. Instead, we remain stuck in celebrating a mediocre impression of what love can be.

The truth is that love terrifies people, as if, deep down, they all know where it may lead them. You see, love is not an experience that happens without changing you, love is a transformation of the self. You cannot truly love without becoming an embodiment of love. Love is a death, as it marks the end of the old you and brings forth a new way of life entirely. You become that love song you always enjoyed, the melody you once heard and never forgot, you start living your favourite poem. Are we actually ready for that kind of life? Fundamental change, the threat of losing yourself in the unknown, is always scary. It's no surprise that love is frightening, because it means the absence of

Make love not war marriage

the ego's defences, love is total vulnerability; moreover, a lover is always fearless of what may come. Don't be afraid, though: we feel that way only because we have become too acquainted with distrust. There have certainly been moments in your life when you have felt vulnerable enough to fall in love. This "fall" represents the collapse of the ego that occurs when you drop your guard enough to risk love penetrating your being. In those unencumbered moments, you forget who you are, because you become love itself! I'm confident that you do know what I speak of, you've been there, you have sampled a glimpse of it. Love requires the courage needed to surrender; love is a devotion, a worship, a celebration and, at its highest peak, love is nothing less than divine.

However, this tremendous event is always short-lived, often subsiding because we end up being hurt or deceived, because we dared to be a child again and the world took advantage of our innocence. It is often women who suffer most after opening their hearts, then become deeply distrustful of loving again. Men, too, start to become hesitant to dive in (as it were), to surrender to another human once more, because of those one, two or maybe several occasions when bliss ended in pain. This has happened to almost all of us. Now, we are all too afraid to love, or we love imperfectly and half-heartedly because we're too busy guarding ourselves – our false, egoic selves, at least. I would like to introduce you to a more forthright way to trust, namely not to trust a single person but trusting the whole universe instead. It has not been a lack of caution that's been your problem, but your refusal to embrace a more expansive confidence that transcends particular outcomes. When you no longer care whether you win, it becomes impossible for you to lose.

This comes with one caveat you should be prepared for, namely that finding what you're really looking for may require you to let go of someone you think you love. These kinds of decisive moments, when you break free of unwarranted attachments and misplaced loyalty, will transform you in ways beyond what you ever believed were possible. This is when you realise that it is not specific human connections, but freedom from commitments to people, that overwhelms you with true love. I am all for relationships, but they only become worthwhile and meaningful once we've become capable of experiencing love without anyone's assistance or company. An interesting sign of our times is the rising number of people who voluntarily choose to remain single. Pessimists see this as the death of romance, without realising that thoughtful solitude helps us evolve into better lovers.

Similarly, if you are reading this book in hopes of mending a broken heart, consider the great advantage this temporary sadness blesses you with. Heartache was my path to finding love; the grief of loneliness can mark the advent of enlightenment. You only need to accept your pain as a friend, welcome it in, and we'll move through this gloomy landscape together as I show you what comes after.

You are love

You, dear reader, are the subject of this book. However, since I do not know your name, I have replaced it with the word "love". Whenever you see it, I'd like you to become love, if only for a moment, not as something you chase, but as something you are. Love, after all, is not something external to be grasped at. It is the shape of your own soul made visible. It speaks in your voice, moves with your breath. It only remains for you to discover this part of your essence.

What, indeed, is the purpose of knowing anything about love if you don't understand who you are? There is no better example of ignorance than neglecting yourself in favour of your outer life, yet all we ever do is give our attention to things, to others. Recognising yourself as love will not inflate your ego; in fact, the

Make love not war marriage

selfish, disconnected part of you will pale into insignificance. It is only egos and their narrow limits that desire to be special and significant – love is happy to be the most ordinary person in the world.

All those who have never become love themselves are simply imitating an idea of what they think love ought to be, parroting the word without understanding what it means. For many people, love is a part-time job, something which they switch on to twist delicate situations in their favour. You see, we are quite cunning when it comes to love, a cloak we mostly use to tell lies and deceive people. Love has become a cynical tool to get what you want, as cold-blooded as any political or business tactic.

Since this book is fundamentally about you, it's purposely designed to be a mirror that will allow you to see your true reflection for the first time. This image of yourself goes way deeper than your physical appearance, or in fact what you currently think of as your personality. When you know yourself in your greatest aspect, as love, the world becomes divine simply because you've become capable of viewing it through that lens. As you'll then discover, love and hate, hell and heaven, exist only as our own psychological projections, they are of your own making.

Your mistaken identity (ego)

Any book grappling with the meaning of love would be incomplete without paying equal attention to ego, too. This may seem like a contradiction: though I want to encourage you to embrace love as your true self, you will also find that I occasionally refer to you as an ego! These two identities are easily confused with one another; not just because of the way we misunderstand love but because "ego" and "love" are curiously connected yet entirely distinct. Consider this: if loving someone has ever proved to hurt you in any way whatsoever, then you were acting as an ego instead of as love. A romance that incited heartache, loss, anguish, possessiveness, jealousy, or vengeance in you was essentially doomed from the start, because it was based on egotism rather than love. Love, by contrast, imparts freedom, is painless, nonaggressive, and blissful. The perennial question: "Who am I?" is answered by walking the corridor that leads from ego to love. Incidentally, the "I" that you think you are, the ego, is strident in its identification with your physical body, your wealth, your pride in your achievements, even the traumas you've suffered – all of these typically lay the foundations for a relationship, they are the superficial aspects of ourselves we like to share. Love, by comparison, makes its presence known through silence, powerfully yet unobtrusively. The love that represents who you truly are is transcendental.

Ego is the part of you which you associate with your personality. It has to be defended constantly – any thoughts of humility, powerlessness, or vulnerability are poison to it. However, even though your instincts will oppose you, it's this part of you that I want you to seek out and destroy. This is the only battle worth fighting and winning in life; the surest path to finding what love really is. Always remember: love can only ensue when the ego's defences are down. Your ego may seem like an asset, but it's really nothing but a burden. Your inner reality is love, while the ego is an imposter, a kind of shell surrounding our true selves.

However, ego is also not to be regarded as a bad thing. It was a necessity while we were at an earlier stage of our evolution. Ego remains a necessary tool for functioning within a complex, confusing world. A child only begins to act as an independent person once they develop an ego. Ego is a persona we take on naturally as a kind of defence mechanism. We cultivate it, and often to an unnecessary degree, but it's also part of what makes us human. Secondly, a negative approach will only create a conflict within you.

Trying to deny the ego is futile and counterproductive. However, there comes a time when we realise that a greater wisdom exists,

Make love not war marriage

beyond the mostly rational events and level of existence the ego is skilled at dealing with. Eventually, the ego becomes like an old article of clothing that no longer fits, such as when we try and attempt to experience what love really is. Once we understand that ego keeps us trapped in a reoccurring pattern of painful experiences, it is time to finally shed this psychic skin. This breakthrough represents a major peak on the road of human evolution.

Ego is a purely psychological construct, made up of layers of experiences and thoughts. Over time, these perceptions and projections become engrained and solidify into an identity that takes on a life of its own. Mistakenly, or at least superficially, we call this our personality. This personality has now become a cherished possession, yet it is constructed entirely out of the influences of others and the environment we live in. In that sense, your personality is not really yours at all, it amounts to nothing more than an agglomeration of information we have been exposed to over the years.

Experiencing love becomes a possibility when we begin breaking free of our egoic shell. Though I hate to crush your fantasy, I have to tell you again that finding love really doesn't have much to do with finding your soul mate! Romantic relationships are just extensions of who we are as people, they are not what ultimately defines love. When love comes from within you, on the other hand, every detail in life can define love. Indeed, love is an evolutionary breakthrough, a major milestone on the way to spiritual enlightenment. My approach to finding it is primarily to shatter all your illusions about love. Love is not as most people imagine it, realising what it really entails is the consequence of unlearning, a deconditioning process. Many of you, I imagine, are reading this book because you have started to wake up from the ego-fulfilling fairy tale; you've finally given up hope that someone must honour and love you, because you've realised the idea that love sought from others is an illusion produced by the ego.

We live in an egocentric world, and its influence inevitably fortifies our false sense of self. The ego is forever lacking, wanting, desiring; its poverty means it only knows to win at all costs. This is why the phrase "make love, not war" so aptly applies to the way we handle romantic relationships: they are mostly a battle of two egos, rarely a meeting of two hearts. The ego is driven to win in every situation and always has to be right. Of course, in business, work, and other practical matters it is important to prove our credibility and watch out for our interests. However, when we come home and aim to win petty victories over our partners, we lose a part of our soul every time. It is only love that makes us lower our defences, put down the weapons of manipulation and stubbornness, and dare to lose. Think about what you truly gain while trying to prove you are right to your spouse: is it anything more than a brief, smug thrill? Now, consider the distance you create between yourselves every time you fight to win an argument...there is no victory in battling with your beloved. Couples will inevitably clash, there is really no escaping conflict. But the deeper issue rears its head when you wrangle to win every dispute, to prove you are superior to the other. This means you are not acting from love but from your ego, because the ego's natural defence mechanism is to never admit to losing or being proven wrong. Yet, as we all know from experience, there is no lasting satisfaction in winning a quarrel with someone you love, regardless of whether you're right. You're left only with remorse, winning pulls you further away from them – and, nevertheless, we're just as willing to take up arms next time. It's a peculiar kind of neurosis. I am not suggesting a relationship should avoid disagreement, especially when this is the result of one partner automatically submitting to the other. The key thing to understand is that winning at all costs epitomises failure. The sooner you realise this, the sooner you will rise from the ego.

The ego loves winning games that are ultimately designed for us to lose. That part of ourselves isn't excited by what comes easily, so it isn't all that attracted to an authentic person who is reliable,

Make love not war marriage

consistent and clearly proves they love us. No, instead we are thrilled to be chasing after someone who keeps us up all night guessing about their motivations. Your mind craves occasional attention from someone who is untrustworthy and erratic, much more than it values actual affection. We relish a glance from someone who is clearly "hard to get" and hard to please because this feels like winning something bigger than the love of someone who genuinely appreciates you. This is the painful difference between the ego and love. It's obvious for everyone to see, in the context of romance as elsewhere. Yet we wilfully blind ourselves to how badly we are in thrall to our false selves.

Our ego craves external validation, it seeks relevance and importance, sometimes even from people who don't like us. Unlike love, it is always vulnerable to what people may think or do. It's not hard to recognise your ego by these characteristics, but most of us never come to know it. Instead, we mistake our psychological stratagems and emotional hedging for love, as something deep and meaningful. We believe our romantic gestures are unselfish and fuelled by love, even when we are only attempting to secure our importance in the other's mind, feeding the ego's need for approval. But, as we gradually become aware of our egos, we simultaneously learn to spot this psychological pattern. After this point, by and by, we stop playing these old tricks on ourselves and others, as seeking out proof that we are worthy of love becomes less important. You see, the relationships you're used to aren't built on love but instead exist on the invisible foundation of dominance and power dynamics. By design and starting from childhood, the ego knows little but how to manipulate others, finding it natural to behave in a transactional way. It is only when we drop our defences that we become the alternative: not just people who try to avoid exploiting others but what we are born to be; we become love itself.

It is no surprise that all relationships, being subject to the same spiritual and psychological laws, suffer from the exact same problems. There's really nothing unique or puzzling about any couple's dirty laundry or what happens behind every closed door. Everyone who's had a partner has had to put up with the same kind of power struggle, all because we attempt to know love through the ego mind. It's why I wrote this book, which is fundamentally about bringing the power of awareness to whatever you are doing (whether in a relationship or any other sphere of life). When it comes to romance, this means becoming aware of how hard we are working for something we vainly believe will make us happy. This realisation reveals the stupidity of how we've been undertaking relationships: trying to force love to work is blinding us from love itself.

More significantly, the love I speak of is capable of transporting you to a reality beyond that of the body and the thinking mind. In that sense, it is comparable to meditation and other techniques of self-inquiry and self-development. To put this another way, love is just another word for consciousness; it's an alternative description of the mental state you can also obtain by deliberately remaining in silence and stillness. Love is the expression of a form of enlightenment. In the guise of a relationship, love is a merging of two separate parts, when the lover and your beloved combine into one experiential reality.

This is the love I know and want to share with you.

Chapter Two

The power of freedom

The foundation of love

Love is always in the social spotlight and has, because of the way it's traditionally talked about, created a lot of hype and expectations about relationships. You can hardly watch a few minutes of television or read a page in a magazine without seeing it mentioned a dozen times. But, for love to even exist, there must first be freedom. This book isn't, in fact, aimed at delivering love to you at all, it exists only to set you free. Love just happens to be the by-product of freedom. I could have chosen to title this book: "The Power of Freedom", but I realised that people are more acquainted with the idea of love. Frankly, love (in its many forms) is a merchandisable concept, adored by artists and advertising executives alike. "Freedom", on the other hand, is easily misinterpreted, especially when we think of freedom as something we already have!

The kind of freedom we're talking about here is not the Braveheart, William Wallace kind of patriotic idealism or even the type of political propaganda that pacifies you with permission to do something you want. That is not freedom, because it is not yours, it is given to you. Thinking of one common interpretation, freedom from being enslaved or oppressed is not the genuine article, because your thoughts and actions are still controlled to some degree. The ability to do whatever things you want without consequences is also not the freedom I am referring to, because your longing to do them is only another form of entrapment. One thing that meditation and self-examination teach us is that our desires are never our own: they are largely a consequence of social and cultural conditioning (not to mention marketing). The kind of freedom I would like to inspire you to embrace is the only true liberty that exists. All other concepts of freedom are counterfeit, since anything that is granted to you from outside is just a different kind of slavery.

True freedom, in a word, is to be yourself; it simply does not relate to doing something or having anything. Freedom is the natural yet extraordinary human state of being yourself. In order to be real, freedom must be effortless; this means it has become embodied within you. It is an intrinsic faculty you were originally born with: every child is born free. If you accept this, it follows that nobody can be awarded freedom as if it were some kind of special prize, nor can it be taken from them like a commodity that's bought and sold and stolen. However, this essential, priceless gift can be and is concealed from us. With the best of intentions, parents initiate their babies into a religion, impose cultural beliefs on them, and expose them to the multifarious influences the world has to offer. After a little time has passed, the resulting adult cannot comprehend what true freedom is, let alone what it feels like.

The seed of love grows out of freedom. Howsoever badly we want it, unadulterated love doesn't come to us automatically, or even at all if we do not also embrace freedom. So many people go through life without ever experiencing love's raw material, the undiluted, unalloyed stuff of which relationships should be made. Instead, we have been reconciled to a synthetic version which only provides a bittersweet experience. True love is hidden somewhere beneath the pain we attribute to romance and our ignorance of freedom.

Genuine love makes itself known by the absence of pain. The thread of freedom is woven into every part of its fabric – indeed, it is treasured more than even love, because it is recognised as larger than love. Freedom is your existential reality underlying all the more obvious traits and things you surround yourself with. To be free is to be all that you are and reject all you are not. True freedom does not relate to the world of having and doing, nor is it about pleasure: it transcends all the things we are typically ruled over instead of fighting against them. Freedom is a state of consciousness, an existence beyond choice and consequence. Most significantly while talking about relationships, this kind of freedom exempts us from the continual effort we apply to experience happiness and to find love.

Effortlessness' essence

The blunt truth is that life can be experienced either as enslavement or freedom. "Enslavement" sounds like an exaggerated description of how the vast majority of people live, doesn't it? Still, once you start to observe the impressionable nature of your own mind and how it induces you to blindly follow social norms, you will notice how mechanically we perform most duties in life, including long-term relationships.

In general, we don't even know that we are suffering or lacking something of great importance, especially within the theatrics of love relationships. We are unable to conceive of an alternative. This is because true freedom remains an unknown phenomenon, so we can't protest its absence or desire something which we don't even know exists. Yet freedom is surprisingly easy to achieve once you cast off your chains and begin living freely and spontaneously. For example, relationships can be experienced as either burdensome or effortless, in fact, every relationship begins as an effortless and blissful experience. In the beginning, you can hardly believe how good life is; you enter this state of effortlessness because you are immersed, you are lost in the moment. But then, through no fault of anyone, maintaining the relationship becomes a struggle, and you exert yourself ever more in the hope of achieving the same effortless that you once had. This mental and spiritual phenomenon can't be forced, though, yet it is always happening when we aren't trying, in those moments when you are truly happy.

Effort is always a "means to an end", implying that we do what we must to support a greater purpose, even while the task may not be enjoyable. This way of living, we're told from an early age, is the only way to achieve anything worthwhile. At the same time, though, your purpose, intention, or reason for doing anything becomes your enslavement, because the task at hand becomes a chore. Because you are tied to the end goal, your action – working, learning, playing, or loving – is not freely flowing from within you.

Freedom arrives when an action is performed unconditionally, without restraint, and carries no seed of intention for the future. This detached state of being is where love for whatever you are doing arises effortlessly. When an artist simply paints for the joy of painting, when a musician, a dancer or a chef performs their craft for no reason other than for pleasure itself and the purpose and the goal have disappeared, they have totally dissolved in freedom. Therefore, careers, hobbies, and relationships which awaken your purposeless creativity will always generate love in you; working in this "flow state" is an expression of freedom.

For the vast majority, though, jobs are considered a means to an end, a necessary evil, not an opportunity to be creative without purpose or ambition. It's not surprising that almost all 9-to-5 duties feel like slavery and almost everyone hates their job. What is surprising is that any job can be loved if only you feel free while doing it, which relies on forgetting why you are doing it. Almost everyone has experienced moments when they've totally forgotten why they work, even while doing the most boring job. When you have forgotten the reason and purpose behind your task, you suddenly begin to love what you do because you are momentarily free of enslavement. Unfortunately, this usually lasts only a short while, until you are reminded of unpaid bills and all the reasons why you have to work.

The law of freedom applies to relationships, too. At first, this goes without saying: both partners are so buoyed up by a wave of enthusiasm and energy that they allow the future to take care of itself. In long-term couplings, though, the joy of being together, the freedom that was once there, has evaporated and we've become enslaved by the effort to make love work again. Whether we are motivated by the need to gain love from our partners or in order to feel good about ourselves, the chores of behaving appropriately and winning approval become exhausting. Over time, this shift from effortlessness to drudgery quietly chips away at your soul and we secretly come to hate the ones we love. Because the effort involved begins to outweigh the reward, we start drawing up emotional profit-and-loss statements and become disillusioned with the relationship. Meanwhile, single people seeking love become frustrated with the search, exhausted by the process of sorting through potential mates to find "the one". The demoralising chore of discovering love renders you enslaved to the effort of forging your own happiness, something that has become a kind of necessary burden instead of a path to love.

Many couples think that a successful marriage is invariably "a labour of love". The idea is that the effort we apply to make a relationship work is a sign of virtue, but every ounce of sweat we expend only adds to our enslavement. Ordinarily, we must do X to achieve Y, this is simply the law of cause and effect. However, while this principle works for almost everything else in the physical universe, love does not follow the same laws; love is moved by freedom. This means that the course of love is not swayed by effort, love is fundamentally effortless. Unfortunately, our minds are chained to the idea of causality, we see relationships in the same way as business transactions or sports games. As a result, we believe love is the result of applying effort, of some kind of doing. We cultivate this attitude as children, learning to please only to gain praise and affection. As adults, we have become enslaved to a mechanistic way of life that doesn't take spiritual laws into account. The pursuit of love has become a form of slavery, so the search for love is never experienced as a joy but as drudgery.

Our vocabulary, too, is a shackle. It is important not to get misled by the words "effort" and "effortless": these refer to the mental strain our approach to work causes, not the work itself. Obviously, we cannot live without physical, mental, and emotional effort. But, whenever you experience internal resistance to doing something, you're applying a particular kind of wholly unnecessary psychological effort. It feels like you are under the spell of a kind of subconscious gravity, imprisoned by the action's intended reward. By contrast, when you don't notice any pressure or tension during an act, you feel weightless. In mystical terms, this kind of effortlessness indicates you are in tune with the divine realm and, in those moments, love will inevitably emerge within you.

This doesn't apply only to your career and relationships. Any action at all can produce love within you, even washing the dishes. Suddenly, there comes a moment when a chore becomes effortless, you are in flow and want to continue to the very end. It's as if every coincidence goes your way, you become more creative, and – despite the lack of struggle and exertion – you find your work is being performed perfectly, too. As long as you're in this mental state, you are free, regardless of outside circumstances. Then, suddenly and from nowhere, you feel love for the most unexciting task.

Even if you're not an artist who can get immersed in your work, You've almost certainly experienced this for yourself in relationships. Honeymoon periods are always effortless, because nothing has yet become forced, all your interactions flow naturally as both parties share a kind of harmony that precludes conflict. Where you are and what you're doing makes little difference as long as you're together, because whatever you both decide to do is always joyful. In these blessed, early days, romance is just about sharing each other's company. As the relationship continues beyond a certain point, though, you gradually start to yearn for this effortless synergy, but the gravity of effort starts to pervade every aspect of that which you share. Naturally, the acts of kindness needed to sustain a relationship should continue, but these just mustn't ever be experienced as an obligation. The effortlessness found amidst a loving connection isn't even a sensation; in fact, when you are genuinely happy, when life is good, you don't even realise it because you have dissolved in the moment, you have vanished in utter levity, and make no comparisons to other times and situations.

In the age of internet dating and increasing expectations fuelled by social media, the arduous search for partners has become the most dreadful part of romance. It's no wonder the number of anxious single people in the world is only increasing, though this would not be so if more people understood the value of effortlessness. This is one of those situations where the faster you run, the slower you move: adding more intention and exertion to dating is invariably counterproductive. Goal-orientated thinking just doesn't apply to relationships. Finding the right person to share your love with should only ever happen by accident; love should be neither a quest nor an expectation. The pursuit to find someone is just another form of enslavement – what I mean is that, when you identify with the search, when its success seems like the only thing that matters, you are pulled down by the gravity of effort and trying to find love turns into suffering.

The only way out of this misery is to carry on searching, but now without purpose. Act as if you have already found what you are looking for, because in reality you already are what you desire. So, if it's love that you want, become that love right now. By and by, you will forget you are looking, but the search will continue nonetheless. What used to be arduous is now effortless and the journey has become as pleasurable as the goal itself, intolerable frustration has now become an effortless joy. If you're single and desperately longing to find someone, the importance you assign to the search will only become more wearisome as time goes on. Not only will you encumber even straightforward tasks with unnecessary baggage, but your angst will also keep attracting the wrong type of people, leading you ever further away from finding what you want.

You will most certainly attract love by becoming love – try it. It is not a matter of luck, or optimism, or confidence, or presenting yourself differently, or some kind of magic. I promise: you will generate more of the right kind of attention than you ever did before in your entire life. Now that the constant pursuit of love has become one of acceptance rather than obsession, even your urgent need for love will slowly quieten. At this stage, you are dancing and bursting with love whether you're single or not; loneliness no longer burdens you.

Now, whoever you eventually share your life with, your relationship will come into being as if by itself, as if you didn't do anything to bring it about. Because you are living in freedom, not expecting anything, that which you think you deserve naturally comes to you. Remember: real romantic abundance, by which I mean the love that will sweep you off your feet and transform your life, will not arise from your expectations or desires but rather from a profound surrender to unknown possibilities.

When I talk about how our compulsion to think in terms of desires and results enslaves us, it's not an empty metaphor. As soon as you can think of a reason for you to be doing anything in life, that goal becomes your master. When you don't cling to an intention behind what you do, you are living in freedom, just being in the moment, with the action itself as all the motivation you need. Life becomes so much easier and more fruitful when you don't require any rationale beyond the deed itself and the experience of the moment.

I, for instance, write books for no reason at all other than that I enjoy expressing myself through literature. Some people find the same pleasure in preparing food, others through playing the violin, or whatever – but always without any expectation or thought of some far-distant reward. If I applied a reason or a purpose to my writing, it would change the whole tenor of the activity. I would suddenly be enslaved by expectation and the freedom of creativity itself would be gone. Life is about dissolving in the act, for no greater purpose than enjoying the moment you are in.

This misunderstood worldview isn't exactly popular in today's society, where we're all supposed to strive for goals, chase results, and always be rushing toward the next, greatest thing. Reasons are supposed to be everything; you're even supposed to get caught up in having a reason for loving someone (this is the kind of tripe we use to embellish wedding speeches). All of this suddenly goes out the window one day when you actually find true love and cannot explain why you love them, nor feel the need to justify your attraction. This is the purest love there ever can be; love for the sake of love is the only satisfactory basis for a relationship.

Think back to the moments in your life when you are doing without thinking, perhaps while dancing, creating, loving, laughing, cooking, or eating. At these times, you are totally dissolved in freedom, you are lost in the moment and the act itself. Within you, there is no doer as such because the ego has disappeared, and this brings you to the realisation that your ego was the means of your enslavement all along. When you diligently pursue this awareness, freedom eventually brings you to a point of total oneness with existence. A free-spirited action will always bring you love – romantic or otherwise.

Marriage Vs Change

"You're not the person I married!" is a common complaint, often shouted at great volume. What did you expect, though?

Marriage is a binding contractual agreement to stay together in the name of love, regardless of whatever might happen in the future. Getting married appeals to our ideas about morality as the honourable thing to do, but this attitude requires us to ignore the insupportable nature of this feat. Because, while marriage may begin from a place of freedom, it by nature does little to retain it.

Marriage is a custom that eventually requires two people to make constant compromises to find peace. Have you noticed that such compromises were never required in the beginning? Where there was freedom, there was love, and the connection was effortless. Marriage is a promise to grow old together, but the bonds of matrimony are not conducive to the process of growing into one's true self. Marriage is unsustainable because we are never the same person from one day to the next. Humans are constantly changing and evolving organisms, both in terms of how we feel and who we are in our ever-changing environment.

There are many colours to your character, just like there are many dimensions to each person's life. Sadly, the best part of yourself is rarely discovered because of our inhibition to change, our fear of progressing according to natural forces within ourselves. All this is only reinforced by a legal agreement that obliges one to stay loyal to a promise, to stay rooted in a character you once were.

This is not love; love is a free-flowing energy that cannot be contained and, as such, love welcomes and even demands change. This is part and parcel of the understanding that every bit of life is an evolution, an unveiling of new layers. Any intimate connection should inspire you to change, even if this means becoming an entirely different person from who you were at the wedding. The decision to get married shouldn't be the end of your evolution and cannot forestall the emergence of your higher intelligence, even if your partner doesn't glimpse the same new horizon as you. Marriage can certainly work and exemplify what it means to enjoy a great union, but only if both spouses are permitted to grow (and often in divergent ways). True love does not hamper or inhibit another's freedom, within matrimony or elsewhere. Indeed, in some marriages, the love is so pure that one partner insists the other leave and find another life in which they can attain their potential. To an outside observer, this may seem incredibly callous, yet the exact opposite is true. It takes genuine love not to hold on to someone purely for your own advantage. Love is not an attachment or obligation but an honest duty towards another's happiness, which sometimes means letting someone go.

If you're convinced marrying your lover is the right path for you, I say: go for it! Nonetheless, I insist that you update your wedding vows, rewrite the obsolete script, and let all of us together change the customs of matrimony to reflect what love really is. Marriage should be a testimony to each individual's freedom rather than a plethora of restrictive compromises. Marriage should be a sharing, a collaborative way of remaining two distinct individuals without each trying to possess the other as property. Marriage should elevate independence above control, acknowledging that freedom takes precedence even over love. Let your example inspire the rest of us to believe that a union of two lovers is forged by the hand of mysterious forces, beyond the covenants of legal obligations. Love cannot be controlled or twisted into whatever thing we deem or desire it to be. But the shape of matrimony is something we can and should alter, until we can indeed all celebrate and worship love within the bounds of marriage.

What should wedding vows that acknowledge both love and freedom look like? This is a question that can only be adequately answered by each pair of imminent spouses; in fact, I would highly encourage you to write your own even if you're not William Butler Yeats. I can share one beautiful template with you, though. Though it's the work of modern-day writer Morgan Llywelyn, it incorporates elements from Celtic tradition stretching back to before Catholicism was common in Ireland:

You cannot possess me, for I belong to myself,
But while we both wish it, I give you that which is mine to give.
You cannot command me, for I am a free person,
But I shall serve you in those ways you require.
And the honeycomb will taste sweeter coming from my hand.
I pledge to you that yours will be the name I cry aloud in the night.
And the eyes into which I smile in the morning.
I pledge to you the first bite from my meat,
And the first drink from my cup.
I pledge to you my living and dying, equally in your care,
This is my wedding vow to you.
This is a marriage of equals.

Proponents of traditional marriage need to acknowledge that love cannot be forced or commanded into being. No one ever finds true love through determination and willpower, love is just the echo of something else entirely, a small part of a greater reality we can barely comprehend. We've just been running after the wrong thing all this time, thinking that marriage should restrict our scope for development instead of expanding it. Love is an experience of tremendous freedom, and, without freedom, the alchemy of love cannot occur. Alchemy, or transmutation, is an essential part of love as it's talked about in this book: an evolutionary transformation, something more significant than your physical birth – finding love can amount to a spiritual rebirth. You see, the love we typically apply to human connections, relationships and marriages doesn't shift your consciousness far

The power of freedom

enough to induce a metamorphosis. "In love" or not, you're still very much the same person. Relationships on this level have never redefined anyone's perception of the world. True love, on the other hand, is transformative: it will change your life and thus change the world, but it must begin with you – not marriage, finding your "soulmate", or by limiting their self-expression.

You see, we are all born with the capacity to expand our consciousness, but a vast number of people still fail due to blindly submitting to society, culture, or passing trends. Love, the kind that comes from the heart and soul, is such a rarity these days that most people can't recognise it anymore. If you are lucky enough to ever meet one of the few who are free, someone who personifies love, you're likely to conclude that person is either high on drugs, childishly naive, or pointlessly profound. You could be forgiven if you ignored such a person. However, those who love deeply and completely aren't crazy; they are simply an anomaly when compared to the vulgar world we have somehow created.

Without the boundless love that can be mistaken for insanity when brought to its ultimate expression, relationships are mostly an antagonistic, warlike kind of thing. They're supposedly designed to kindle love, but mostly end up destroying what genuine affection there used to be. Love ends where formal associations begin; what ensues is simply a battle that compels either or both parties to compromise more and more until neither is recognisable as the person they once were. If we want to sustain the love we initially felt for our partners, we should avoid the conventional ideal of preserving a relationship at all costs, no matter how widely this is seen as something to aspire to. This manner of co-existing means assaulting each other's freedom, but freedom is more marvellous than love and must always, if you have to choose one or the other, come first. Both as spiritual beings and caring partners, we should accept that the true path to love starts by revering our own freedom, which causes us to instinctively respect the freedom of others. Freedom must never be curtailed for the sake of love; on those unhappy occasions when these two values come into conflict, we have to prioritise freedom, always. But...this simply isn't the way of the world. Relationships are mostly a restraint, they restrict a person's individuality for the sake of tolerable coexistence. We have no right to prevent people from being who they are: "live and let live" must be the tenet of your relationship. Don't base your whole shared existence on conceding to another's demands or insisting that they concede to yours.

Avoiding the formalisms of marriage ultimately upholds your independence and individualism. Any longstanding relationship that isn't based on a contract demonstrates love better than any marriage, simply by acknowledging that love is ultimately such a powerful yet precarious force of nature. Love has nothing to do with loyalty, nor can it be enforced by the covenants of a legal document. Therefore, we should first seek to know what love really is before rushing to get married. Marriage, by its nature and regardless of your intentions, eventually leads you into a world of continual effort and kills your hope of experiencing the effortless nature of true love. In time, honouring love above marriage will help to create a better world, but it will take generations for that to happen. Perhaps, in another century or so, we will view marriage as a relic of the past and breathe a sigh of relief.

Right now, though, you don't need to worry about changing the world. "Make love, not marriage" is fundamentally a selfish maxim; it is all about protecting the individuality of each person involved. For the sake of my own inner peace, I don't care about building a better society and neither should you. Such an effort will only distract you from the most important part of life. You need to focus your energy on yourself and your evolution – all worthwhile benevolence begins with being selfish. In a sense, we are all born loners; we just don't get to ever explore that part of us as long as we constantly hanker for love outside of our own being. We create attachments here and there, hoping to find what we ourselves lack in another person, but the wonderful experience of discovering the true essence of love only begins to transpire once you begin to express your inner hermit. Embracing this facet of yourself will enhance your love life, relationships, connections, and level of awareness. Through self-love, you come to know the greatest part of being human: to be complete without needing anyone to complete you.

If the purpose of life had to be reduced to one word, it would be "freedom", because anything of real value is only possible when you are free. The freedom I talk about in this chapter is nothing less than a state of higher consciousness. One must be yourself, to know yourself. Learning to understand your true nature is the greatest of all discoveries, as well as a quest even the irreligious can adopt. The path requires no allegiance or commitment to anything outside of your own reality and existence. But, however simple this may sound, becoming yourself is also life's biggest challenge, especially in a world that is only out to exploit you. This is the unvarnished truth: even the people closest to you, the ones you share your whole life with, are unknowingly keeping you from your greatest discovery. It is only through insisting on our right to evolve that we become free and, thereby, become better lovers for those around us.

Chapter Three

Love vs relationships

The infinite and the limiting

Love is limitless, which means it goes way further than our biological urges, emotions and psychology...and, indeed, beyond the boundaries of the one person you've chosen to love. However, even within these confines, a relationship is a sacred connection because it gives you your first glimpses of the vastness of what love actually is. Most people only understand love as a special bond between two people. So, ordinarily, the most common conception of love is restricted to searching for the right person or nurturing an existing relationship.

In this chapter, I would like to distil the contrast between love and relationships. Love transcends anything we objectify or relate to in the world, love is an entity that pervades the universe without needing anyone or anything to experience it. Only the foolish limit it to the feelings created and exchanged between two people. Love exists as a personal, serene experience within you, no matter who or what comes and goes. The search for love begins within yourself, not in the outside world. If you've become disillusioned with romance, it's not a better dating website or new hairstyle you need, but an entirely new way of living and loving.

We are mentally conditioned to believe that we need people, that we can't experience and know love without a special someone. Yet love is not an exchange of any kind; love is a private inner experience and a spiritual principle. Elemental love needs no other, it is a part of you and comes only from you. Absorb this thought for a moment: you are the source, the light, the beacon of all the love in the world. Without you, love remains formless instead of manifest and, as a lodestone and focal point for love, you are always there and you will always be in spite of all change. Your love is one incarnation of the deathless, the eternal unbounded source of all creation.

I want to crush any preconception that love has anything to do with a Romeo-and-Juliet kind of romance. Love is certainly not defined by how much you struggle or are willing to fight to get what you want. Nor has love much to do with any social construct based on nurturing children and security, or anything that somehow involves compromising your entire life. There's no great honour in simply doing the best you can for your family just because it's morally expected of you. Love is also not a specific state of being between two people. Relationships can be built on love, but they can just as well exist (and often do) independently of love; love is a separate entity.

Most people are utterly confused about what relationships are supposed to be. They're trapped between obsolete notions from the past, influences from the media, and their own amorphous desires. There used to be conventional rules about dating and marriage: in some cultures, your parents would simply tell you who your spouse would be. In others, you were restricted to romancing within your social class; today, people are supposed

Love vs relationships

to date those of a similar level of physical attractiveness and income. It's hard to tell which of these is most ridiculous!

There was once a time when a man was supposed to express his interest through material gifts and emotional investment with the woman he desired; she would either reciprocate or not. These rules no longer entirely apply, but their influence lingers on. It is past time for a rational discussion on relationships, one that's rooted in actual human experience while being open to a spiritual perspective on what love really is.

The genuine connections that are formed and enjoyed between two people is life's greatest experience. Finding a partner and creating a life in which to enjoy affection, trust, sharing, children, and security comprises a wonderful vision and, truthfully, this attainment isn't beyond anyone's reach. However, we wrongly regard this as the culmination and end of love. A relationship is certainly a respectable quest worthy of pursuing, but knowing love is entirely a separate discovery. All species on this planet are inherently coded to relate to and bond with one another, to protect and carry out a biological imperative: to procreate and provide comfort. We are programmed to bond with one another, our instincts destine us to engage in the ritual of human contact. Forming relationships is entirely beyond our control, it's not even a choice. In contrast, love is a radical and mysterious energy that we can at best hint at with our love songs, wedding rings, and 50th-anniversary parties. You can engage in all these traditions wholeheartedly even while having no inkling of the real experience of love.

Love has often been described as the electricity created between the lover and the beloved, a feeling you can experience but not understand. However, when love is truly manifest, it embodies the capacity to be happy with yourself, totally contented in your own company. Despite all the games we play in our human interactions, in the end, the joy of freedom is what we eventually come to understand love to be. It is, ironically, your ache for affection and the temporary discomfort of loneliness that preclude you from ever coming to know true love.

The comfort, elation, purpose, and validation we're all vainly looking for in a relationship already exist in you, right now. We're all overflowing with love, happiness and orgasmic energy, however darkly these are veiled from your awareness right now. The ancient path that's hinted at in every spiritual tradition has always directed us inward on a quest in search of that abundant energy.

Love is oceanic

Understanding something as unfathomable as the origin and nature of love is hard; fortunately, there is a useful parallel in how the ocean behaves. Just like the ocean, love is unsympathetic and even oblivious to your desires and your objectives. Love is indifferent to our external realities; it dwells in a world of its own, but that does not stop us from enjoying it. Like fishermen, we can easily make use of it to enrich our lives, but most of the vast ocean (like love) does not directly have your interests at heart, other than simply existing for you. Most people, if suddenly dropped into the ocean, would panic and soon die as a result of not knowing how to survive amidst the swirling waves. If one learns how to ride the swells like a dexterous surfer, though, you can play with the forces of nature and move in harmony with them. By understanding and embracing the surges and currents, you will find sheer pleasure in their apparent chaos and become one with the universal ocean, making it a friend.

Love works in much the same way: we are all swirling in an ocean of love, we've just become too insensitive to notice. Our callousness and blindness, along with our fixation on control, are the reason love hurts us all. Love can ruin you in an instant and often does, turning your whole life upside down and perhaps destroying you in the process. Unless you've overcome your need to dictate the course of your life, love does not come naturally; loving is a skill to be learned, love is a divine insight and the key to our evolution. We must embrace the indefinable, impetuous nature of love in order not to be wounded by it.

Beginning as children, we've each cultivated strategies for trying to win love by any means possible. Love is not susceptible to tricks, though, so we grow up mostly disenchanted by these cruel games we play. Some of us, consumed by the need for love but incapable of fulfilling it, come to secretly hate life and eventually die feeling miserable, never having experienced what they desired the most. In exceptional cases, we hear of someone taking their own life, love having turned into bitter tragedy instead of the fountain of joy.

The cosmic joke behind all this is that what we long for so fervently is freely accessible, but the path to find it is hidden: love requires a deeper form of inquiry than most people are comfortable with. The love I speak of is not the familial love you relate to or the romance you have tried to acquire. True love has no voice, no agenda, no direction; it does not diminish, nor does it discriminate between good or bad. Love is a universal force beyond this world, and this book is meant to help you tune in to that frequency so that every experience of life is infused by it.

Love vs romance

Once we are under the spell of romance, it's nothing short of madness. Intense passion is something we can't control; insanity is something we do not always recognise, and that's the way it is with infatuation. We are led to believe it is love, but let's be clear: romance is not love.

However, deep love is a special kind of madness. Spiritually awakened lovers are mad, they are glazed-eyed drunkards high on love, but in their case it is a controlled, conscious insanity. They experience a deep devotion that shines a spotlight on every moment. The difference is that, unlike puppy love, their love isn't a force that's bottled up waiting for someone to arrive and release it; love is a constantly flowing energy. Romance, by contrast, depends on someone coming along to allow you to project your passion.

To put it another way, repressed sexual energy manifests itself as romance. From a Tantric perspective, sexual energy is generated in the genitals and ascends into other areas of the body; once it reaches the heart and brain, it is transformed into romance. This is the most beautiful way of enjoying sexual pleasure – all sex should at the very least contain a romantic component – but we should recognise that this kind of pleasure is only short-lived.

Have you noticed, by the way, that the world is lacking in romance these days? Once upon a time, sex was not as easily available; since the urges that fuel romance were repressed for one reason or another, this sexual energy was sublimated and manifested itself as art, poetry, and graceful courtship. Today, of course, sexual energy is easily discharged due to the ease of meeting eager partners through dating apps, not to mention pornography and prostitution. All these are to blame for killing old-fashioned romance and, along with it, refined expressions of a major part of what it means to be human. It's like having a magical battery of spiritual energy and then short-circuiting it just so we can watch the sparks: while I don't advocate sexual abstinence in general or for its own sake, sex without love is a tremendous waste.

Infatuation is really a sign of naivety, nothing more than a shadow of your hormones and not emblematic of your heart or authentic feelings. Eventually, a wise person becomes alert to this fact and guards themselves against these shallow romantic impulses. Observing that their emotions are often nothing more than brain chemistry, they perceive how these feelings will only cheat you in the end. Physical attractions are deceptive: they promise joy at first but soon abandon you, leaving you feeling like you've fallen off a cliff instead of in love. Too often, we are duped into relationships and even marriages by the clamour of our own minds, fooling ourselves into mistaking romance for true love. I should know: that's exactly what happened to me! I met a beautiful young woman and, almost straight away, our hearts were so intensely aroused that we couldn't bear to be apart from one another. After only a few months of knowing her, I proposed, and we got married in a daze, without hesitation, as if it were all foretold in the stars. Only a week after the wedding, though, I felt my formerly compelling feelings suddenly disengaging. At the time, I thought it was just the jitters, the anxiety every new spouse expects, but that emotional withdrawal is what marked the end of our short-lived, doomed relationship (we became like strangers and divorced within the same year).

So, be on your guard against relationships that begin too intensely. I admit, they feel incredible, making the earth shake beneath your feet and the stars wander drunkenly around the heavens. Romances are there to be enjoyed, but remember: whatever is said, whatever is promised or felt, is mostly counterfeit. Because we are possessed by our emotions and not wholly conscious of what is happening to us, we can't distinguish between the superficial and the absolute in that state. Such grandiose passion will inevitably subside and that low tide, howsoever hard you try and resist it, will signal the end of the relationship. In a different context, the whole thing would be funny: two people suddenly coming to life and experiencing sensations they never knew existed, only to lapse into a sort of coma. All romances eventually die, leaving most of those involved believing that this is all that love is. Some bend all their efforts toward securing the next relationship high, just like a junkie, while others break apart and become disenchanted by the whole idea. Both kinds of people, however, never realise that they hadn't even come close to the true glory of love; a furnace, not a firework.

Discovering the more pervasive, patient, powerful kind of love does not depend on following the script of red roses, love songs, and candlelit dinners. Life is only a vehicle for experience, eventually leading to the mysteries that dwell beyond even our most subtle human emotions. Love must first be in place before "the one" is found; this is the entire premise of this book. Otherwise, we are building all our relationships on a foundation of sand, of changeable feelings that don't really stand up to much at all. It is because we have not sought to find the love within us that we so desperately seek out the ersatz substitute of human contact. Love is not a substance passed from one person to the next, nor can we truly share it. This is because love is a drug and, like any drug-induced experience, we can't give it to another, can't allow someone else to feel it. The majority of people claim to know love because they are loved by someone, but that gratifying sensation is not love, as love can only ever be a product of one's own being. The delusion that this back-to-front approach is even possible is why everyone holds someone else accountable for the way they feel. In reality and in the end, no one is responsible for us, no one can truly alter how we perceive existence.

Relationships follow no laws but their own. Without an awareness of how the groundswell of love re-writes these rules, they're always a bittersweet pleasure, a dualistic dance of kindness and animosity. Anyone seeking to find love in a relationship rather than creating it themselves will be inevitably, sorely disappointed. What most people see as love, what they're taught to expect, is not a continuous flow of affection and joy but rather a cat-and-mouse dance around the real thing. Whatever patience or tolerance or humility you use to brace yourself against the demands of a relationship will constantly be tested and often broken down sooner or later, leading you down the road of continuous apologies and compromise. This may continue for years, until the moment one person eventually tires of the effort involved in making love work every day.

So many of the temporary bonds we cultivate are the result of some irrepressible impulse, they are a natural expression of desires we simply can't explore without experiencing them. But,

Love vs relationships

as much as these connections rock our world, every emotion that originates from outside of our own being soon dwindles into an anticlimactic descent into boredom and staleness, which we prolong past what's meaningful out of a false sense of duty or fear of being alone.

When you inquire more deeply into any human connection, observing what truly binds people together, our relationships (however loving or passionate) are always clouding something innate and magical that links us all. This divine spark, obscured by carnal and emotional neediness, is nothing less than our own impetus towards freedom, including the freedom from needing anyone. After reading this book, you will understand that freedom and love are equivalent and, when you finally come to know this truth, you will do whatever it takes to preserve both in a way that disparages neither. When, in time, you truly find your spiritual sense of "home", you will soar to such an altitude that no human contact can influence you for better or for worse. When you approach any relationship from this stance, love will flourish automatically, because both of you are free people, free to stay and free to leave.

I was fortunate enough to wake up to this mode of effortless existence after years of practising meditation. I realised that romance is mostly deceptive and the relationships that eventually ensue are merely an imitation of what love really should be. A book like this shouldn't have to catalogue a ton of platitudes on how to revive a failed relationship or give you advice on how to be a better lover. Any guidance you need only has to outline what a relationship is and what it will never be. This, I know, will be debated, but relationships are completely overhyped as a source of love and happiness. Those two attributes must come from you, entirely; nobody else can fill these voids – and expecting them to will only result in frustration for you both. Today, I know that being happy and filled with love has nothing to do with the world we live in or even the people that roam it. When you finally come to learn this, you have already unearthed the treasure of true love.

If we aren't brave enough to inquire into love's true nature, we end up willingly deceiving ourselves about the way we practice relationships. People are desperate to demonstrate, both to themselves and others, how happy they are because of being entwined with someone else. This is a game we all play, without ever admitting that we are living a farce, feigning that it's our romantic efforts that are generating love. Only unhappy people try to prove they are happy; their own contentment depends on convincing the world that everything in their lives is great. The greater their insecurity, the greater their unsatisfied desire, and the more firmly they're trapped by a made-up, flawed, and harmful interpretation of love.

The nature of love

Accepting life "as it is", instead of wasting your energy dreaming about how it should be, is both a consequence of love and a precursor to it. The conflict between what we desire and what actually happens is the only reason we are continually disappointed with life. The way we allow wishful thinking to outweigh reality also explains why love keeps eluding us because love is, in part, the ability to embrace whatever happens in our lives. It is a sublime kind of indifference: when you cease to think of events as "good" or "bad", they each reveal themselves in their proper light. Love doesn't spontaneously spring from finding the right person; if anything, that's looking at things backwards. If you yearn to fall in love, if you desperately want to find a beautiful soul to spend your life with, you're only increasing your chances of experiencing a run of hapless relationships. On the other hand, once you have found love, independently of any particular person, love will continue to exist before, during and after any given relationship.

If you keep failing at the romance game, though, don't hold on to the resulting resentment. Instead of trying to alter your dating tactics, accept that your apparent failure is itself a beautiful

Love vs relationships

reality. Christians like to say that: "God moves in mysterious ways", but the principle holds even if you aren't religious: our day-to-day trials and tribulations are really reflective of a deeper reality whose only aim is evolution. No experience in life is genuinely unfortunate, everything that happens is glorious even if the purpose behind it remains obscure. The person who can laugh and gain joy from every human encounter has found love, because only through love does every experience become a thing of beauty that needn't be explained. Incidentally, it's highly likely that you've already met the right person several times over, but were not yet ready to profit from the opportunity. Part of preparing yourself for the next such occasion is learning that love empowers you to be impartial to how reality unfolds. It does not care whether you're alone or married, richer or poorer, or whether your partner conforms to some kind of romantic ideal. Attaining this kind of equanimous acceptance of the world is the surest way to happiness in life and love alike. You see, attachment to a certain situation or fantasy only draws us further away from happiness. Everyone has a dream of what their reality should look like, but clinging to this only leads to a psychological conflict that achieves exactly nothing except to destroy the bliss of whatever you have right now and whatever else may come to pass.

I'm not talking about settling for an unsatisfying relationship or managing your expectations, lowering the bar for what you hope for in a relationship. Instead, I'd like you to consider what life would be like if victory and defeat, romance and solitude, wealth or poverty were all the same to you. Now, this is a pretty foundational, life-altering expansion in your perception of the world; it commonly requires years of self-development to master it as your everyday state of mind. However, the journey is worth it: you will live in constant tranquillity and contentment, even if your physical circumstances remain much the same. For now, though, you can make a start on this journey by, instead of always evaluating how happy or unhappy you are, trying to simply embrace life as if you were an actor playing a role.

The person who ceases to prefer one outcome over another lives a choiceless existence and becomes one with the universe, they become love itself. Because love has no partiality or prejudice, it abides without conflict; love is fundamentally choiceless, accepting instead of seizing and observing rather than possessing. Someone who has internalised this precept does not cling to any specific destiny, instead, they have taken up their rightful place in the universal flow, the joyful dance of the cosmos and all it contains. They are no longer separated from the whole by fighting against the currents of circumstance; rather, they are like a wave gliding through the ocean. Action continues, choice continues, life carries on as normal, but their happiness does not depend on any longed-for result. In consequence, life as well as love has now become effortless for them.

Contradictions can be found in all aspects of life, sometimes offering lessons for those willing to grasp them; sometimes, it seems, existing only to amuse or confound us. Even on the threshold of enlightenment, we encounter this kind of plot twist: in order to keep functioning in the world, we have to carry on choosing, but now while remaining innately choiceless. Reconciling these two opposites may seem like a tightrope walk and, in fact, cannot be done using the rational mind alone. Yet understanding the necessity of each of these complementary approaches, in meditative awareness, makes them function in harmony. Now, you are an instrument of the universal love itself, you can see yourself acting but the actor is no more. You will continue to live the same life, but you are now indifferent to what happens. Observe your life as if you are seeing a movie, notice the different faces you wear, enjoy the highs and the lows, but simply watch as if you are looking at someone else's life.

Knowing the paradox of love and hate

Whenever you notice a fascination, a pull towards your opposite sex, you are experiencing a kind of biological magnetism. In the language of physics, opposite polarities attract each other. In the language of sex, the same principle applies to the male and female essences; this is what triggers our romantic and sexual affairs.

We learn so much about our true selves through our relationships. Though the magnetism of sexual interest may provide the initial impulse, a profound spiritual metamorphosis is occurring beneath the surface; these encounters provide us with more fodder for evolution than our everyday minds are capable of perceiving – we may never even become aware of it. Our relationships are based not only on commonality but also on the clash and sharing of differences, and these contrasts naturally create a subtle combat between two minds. Conflict must never be considered a negative or even destructive part of a loving relationship, because disagreements are mostly inevitable. In fact, healthy, long-lasting relationships consist of couples that are mature enough to handle conflict without breaking down and running away from each other. The people we grow close to are necessarily mirrors to the part of us that is otherwise hidden from sight. Our partners and lovers reveal our wounds, our vices, they bring it all out in the open and, for that reason, they are unknowingly your guiding lights, your teachers. You'll find that small clashes never escalate as long as you reflect on divergence as an opportunity for learning and an essential part of a happy love life.

At the heart of every relationship, a delicate war is taking place, affection is underpinned by unspoken conflict. Hidden under a pantomime of loving gestures, beneath every sweet word, there is an ongoing tug of war: for control over the other, for greater closeness or space, and perhaps for each partner to establish their own freedom.

This may sound like a bleak romantic philosophy, but benign combat is really an endemic part of any relationship. No love affair is absent of discord, conflict, and even hatred. Hate, like dissimilarity, is a necessary part of love. Within hate, we unearth enormous passion; you can even say that we hate only the people we truly love. Deeply reflect on the person you desire most in the world, and you will surely notice the shadow of hatred lurking behind every loving act and every facet of them you admire. We secretly come to hate the ones we deeply love, because we are invisibly held hostage, we are enslaved by their love. Hate, when coupled with love, is not a negative emotion; in fact, no feeling, attitude, or action is fundamentally wrong or harmful until you become aware of it and characterise it as such. If you care about your partner and the world at large, you need to bring these obscure, objectionable parts of your character to light, without reviling or judging them, or trying to suppress them and thus giving them power. You see, it is only in unawareness that these emotions are destructive. As soon as we become aware of them, weighing them without sentiment, our demons are exposed and, in time, disappear.

A relationship comes alive in conflict. What I mean is that total, undisturbed, peaceful harmony would cause a relationship to cease to exist, it would be dead, empty of the vital ingredient needed to keep the flame alive. A human connection is a dynamic confluence of two forces: love and hate. These are like two colours in a painting that complement, overlap, and contrast each other in different areas. For a connection to endure, it must be moved by the right proportion of both conflict and harmony, just enough of both fuels the desire to remain together. Each side of the affection-animosity coin has its own purpose and beauty.

The evolutionary ascent to eternal love is born out of the dualistic paradox of love and hate. When we come to embrace conflict as an opportunity to learn and grow, without allowing our ego to seize the reins, we come to know hate as a bridge to love. Instead, we fight, then argue about why we fight. We clash and then get upset over the fact that we have differences. As a result, we spend much of our time feeling guilty and apologising for being ourselves, for being exactly who the other was attracted to in the first place. The course of relationships is always unpredictable

Love vs relationships

but, foolishly ignoring this fact, we continue to try to steer them and even change the other to suit our own interests better. We are always trying to force perfect harmony into being, which is mostly impossible.

The paradox between love and hate is really no contradiction at all. Both of these are only labels, names we assign to emotional impulses that are really complementary, not opposite. Respect your lover's differences and embrace your conflicts: the sparks between you add enormous colour to life. More importantly, life is not a challenge without them, they are a source of learning and thus part of fulfilling your life's goal.

Chemistry

A romantic relationship is an emotional dialogue of deep human passions, and feelings. These connections are truly magnificent events and each has its own unique beauty. But, ultimately, these connections are built purely on chemistry and animal attraction, and this is why romance and love are distinct entities. Relationships are a hormonally charged rush, a volatile cocktail of emotions, and that is why they are never stable.

Our mood is always turbulent: for the most part, we're not even truly sure what we're feeling in any given moment as it passes, never mind what our emotions were telling us in past days. All human contact that is based on fleeting sentiment deceives us by making the capricious seem permanent and the trivial important. This is why we can't ever be sure of how we may feel about someone in the future, why all marriage promises carry a grain of falsehood within them.

It is incredibly important to learn to distinguish between chemistry and love. Fortunately, there's a simple acid test for this: everything in you that changes is chemical, everything that is constant is love. So, intermittently loving someone really means that attraction is vying with loathing. If we claim to love someone today and later feel indifferent towards them, what we had wasn't love but simply good chemistry.

When you get right down to it, every aspect of life is experienced as a chemical reaction taking place within our bodies. Even happiness is just a chemical experience, no different to eating chocolate: both induce the same effect and release identical brain chemicals. Even without taking drugs, altered chemistries weave in and out of our lives, allowing us to be constantly entertained and stimulated by a variety of experiences.

There are, of course, many chemicals that influence our behaviours, but dopamine and oxytocin are the most influential when it comes to human intimacy. Weeping love songs, stirring love stories, and moving poetry speak only of the fables of oxytocin, assigning cosmic significance to a phenomenon that's really no more miraculous than the way in which our bodies digest food. However, we have chosen to call this "love" and continue to misconstrue its source and reason for being. Once we come to understand that we are only slaves of chemistry, we can begin to evolve and soar to greater heights.

When we feel happy and passionate in romantic encounters, we're under the influence of dopamine, which is why we feel pleasure in the company of certain people. This chemical high immediately becomes addictive, and we seek to regain that experience more and more; this is how and why we turn brief dalliances into long-term relationships. Both oxytocin and dopamine are sometimes referred to as "love hormones" because they are released in the body when we feel deep intimacy, pleasing physical contact, and affection. Oxytocin, in particular, is associated with sexual arousal and orgasm.

Whatever passion and fondness we possess for someone today, we must come to accept that this experience will eventually change, simply because chemistry is something we cannot control. Chemistry is the work of nature; it was chemistry that brought you and your partner together and it is chemistry that

Love vs relationships

will eventually shift your mood and drive you apart. Witness closely how events unfold: your apparent free will to choose whom you desire really has no part to play in your love affairs. Before you can even think about who to love or who to hate, the choice has already been made, you've already been steered by chemical forces transpiring within you. Chemistry is a free-flowing force of nature, so how we feel from one moment to the next is not driven by one's choice. Therefore, no one can rightly be held responsible for how they feel because our brain chemistry changes as often as the weather: both climates are beyond our control. As you inquire more deeply into this enigmatic insight into choice and free will, you will find yourself reaching a climactic breakthrough. You will discover that the egoic part of you is, in fact, powerless; neither it nor you choose anything in your life. Instead, everything is happening by itself, driven by forces beyond your control or understanding. You go through life as if you are watching a movie. Think about it for a moment: your birth and death happen without your say-so, what makes you think what happens in between these two milestones is dictated by you?

Breakups are experienced as deeply distressing because they rupture so many memories and insecurities within us. But these endings are mistakenly believed to be the result of conscious choice. We unfairly blame each other, assuming that our partners have decided to stop loving us and eventually chose to leave. In reality, people don't have a say in how they feel, because they are driven by the turbulent chemistry stirring in their brain. All our emotions are simply visitors: passion rises one day and soon subsides, all without our control. Feelings are not driven by our choice. If you become still and meditative and simply observe your inner life for a day, you will begin to notice that you are not actually in control of anything. Your thoughts, your physical actions, the words that come out of your mouth, and your emotions are all working together as a mechanical organism that is acting autonomously – you are just a passive witness being pulled along.

Love is an addictive rush, and the withdrawal symptoms of reduced dopamine and oxytocin are what we experience as heartache. This cycle of pain and pleasure is what we assume love to be: something that rips your world apart or builds it anew must surely be love! However, true love does not cause distress; conversely, where there is attachment, anxiety, or jealousy, there is no love. When you finally realise love does not come from relationships and has little to do with your transient feelings, you will have found what true love is.

"I love you"

"I love you" is a statement that we have come to acknowledge as the epitome of affection, a signal of virtue and an act of compassion. When we say "I love you" to people outside of romanticism, to a child, to a pet, or to a tree, it is mostly non-possessive. It is a moment when we feel compelled to voice the magnetic warmth at our heart centre. It's a free expression, one that carries no conditions or expectations for its recipient. However, when we use this phrase in a romantic context, it often transforms into something else entirely, a claim, a demand, a subtle attempt to bind the other person to us. It shifts from a simple, unguarded expression of warmth into a transaction, laden with expectations. When applied within a relationship or as a precursor to one, what is really meant is often: "I want to have you".

You see, we only know how to possess; we don't know how to love. Our eyes see something beautiful and we want to claim that beauty for ourselves. This is what normally lies behind telling someone "I love you". As soon as those words leave your mouth, you've possessed the other as yours, you've presented them with a contract. "I love you" is just another way to say: "I claim you". Strip away the moonbeams and violins, and you'll find that these words are only ever uttered out of desperation, by people who really have no love to give. They are either too busy, too lazy, or too ignorant to prove their feelings by demonstrating genuine love, so instead they try to imprison you with this seemingly benevolent gesture.

An assertion of love confines both the one who says it and the one who hears it. When we say: "I love you", love has immediately become an exchange, a transaction. "I love you" is a subtle question; it inadvertently means: "Do you love me?" You are, in fact, not offering your love at all, never mind with the freedom and generosity true love entails. Rather, you are demanding *their* love. "I love you" obligates the other, it carries such weight and baggage that it forces the listener to respond, to perform, to be appreciative. I personally never say "I love you" to anyone; it means nothing to me, it is a lifeless and empty phrase. In every respect, these words fall short of the real thing and are an overbearing gesture. It's a worn-out catchphrase we all use to claim someone's attention.

I promise you: if you quit using this assertion, real love will begin to illuminate you from within. Being more thoughtful with what we say prevents us from hiding behind words anymore. When you stop mindlessly pledging your love, you are required to become what love is meant to be. "I love you" is mostly used to sugar-coat an uncomfortable experience, when we need to apologise or reimburse the other for the comfort they provide us with. Without realising, we get hooked by these words and then, without us even realising it, our relationships exist only in those moments when we declare: "Do you know how much I love you", "You are my greatest love", "I cannot live without you" and all the rest of it. Worse, whenever someone adds "always" to these statements, they ring even more hollow; the result of transient chemistry being mistaken for eternal love. What used to be a formality has now become the entire framework of how we relate to our lovers.

True love is all-encompassing, while the possessive kind does nothing but draw boundaries. Have you ever considered that acclaiming one person as your greatest love also means excluding the whole rest of humanity? Such a seemingly innocent phrase limits your ability to experience infinite love, treating it as something that can only be apportioned to a chosen few.

So, if you really want to prove your undying love to one person, manifest it by living it. Your whole being must radiate love, otherwise, you are just hiding behind empty words signifying a shell of what can be the greatest human experience. Love cannot be turned on and off at your discretion, certainly not by saying or hearing some magical incantation. When you kiss your beloved and walk off to work each morning, is your love put on ice until you embrace your lover again? Instead, let your love spill beyond the boundaries of your romance, let it reveal itself with every face you encounter on your way to work, in every moment you inhabit. Love is too big and too inclusive to be held hostage within the walls of your romantic affair. Though I'm not talking about sleeping around, love is an open relationship with the whole cosmos: when you are overflowing with love like the sun pours out light, there'll be no way to control its direction.

Love is in the heart of the perceiver, it requires no logo or verbal emblem. When you choose to love someone special, show them through example what love really is and what it means. Love is a constant, everlasting expression, it exists in every breath, it can be seen in your walk, every word you utter is intensified and sweetened by love and, when the time comes to part ways, love will allow both of you to follow your own paths. Love does not attach or impede one's independence, love affords us the strength to let go without any lingering attachment or jealousy.

Love is already where you are, it exists even in the presence of two enemies, we just don't see it. Love arises and sustains itself effortlessly, it doesn't need to be worked for, nurtured or discovered, it is a causeless experience that is eternally present. It is only our fear-stricken behaviour that blinds us to what is already there. Indeed, all we do in our relationships is destroy the love that was there in the beginning, often through our possessive instincts trying to curtail the limitless. Then, we wonder where it all went wrong: love was once part of your life because you weren't trying to look for it, you weren't forcing love to happen, it simply was. When you have to look for it, it may be time to part ways.

Forgive yourself

Your life's purpose revolves solely around you, likewise, I have written this book only for you, whoever you are. Whatever journey this book takes you on, my allegiance will always reside with you. I am not here to comfort your beloved nor interested in saving your relationship (by the way, mending a relationship that's run its natural course is virtually impossible). If you think your relationship needs a reboot, your desire to rekindle its embers is actually a sign of its demise. Reviving such a relationship will only mean that both of you will have to make further compromises to make it last the distance. In the end, this kind of transactional give-and-take will only chip away at your freedom and make you resent the extra effort you're having to put in. Relationships that have to be forced into being aren't going to contribute anything to either party's happiness. It is incredibly noble to admit that a relationship should cease.

Relationships condition us to believe that we're somehow supposed to make others happy. However, life isn't about making anyone happy other than yourself. It is foolish and arrogant to even try to do this for someone else; you can't make a gift of something another person has to find for themself. Contrary to what you've been told, love and happiness are only found through being selfish, so go ahead and be the rebel that breaks this useless social dogma.

Love shouldn't be a sacrifice that infringes on your own happiness, but rather a joy that's shared freely. Love is about knowing who you are, and you will first experience it in your own company.

Learning to love is all about finding your inner self. You are the sole protagonist in your story: no one will afford you the time, the love and the affection that only you can give yourself. You must give your love to the most important person alive, and this is you. Once your inner light is lit, the fire of your being will warm the whole world, and this selfish route is the only one that leads to being truly selfless. Instead, what we're faced with is a world where people are so desperate to help others, hoping to appear moral and dutiful, that they completely neglect their own self-discovery.

Above all, this kind of benign selfishness means that you shouldn't sacrifice your freedom to make an unworkable relationship linger on a little longer. We give our relationships too much importance, destroying our independence and individuality in the process. Success in romance is unduly valued as the only measure of human happiness, but it isn't: each love affair is an ephemeral bubble that only the unwise are led on by. Be kind and forgive yourself, accept that relationships are hard work and sometimes not worth keeping alive – in fact, it's a wonder that any of them endure within the confines of social expectations.

Therefore, quit feeling remorseful for the hearts you break or for not living up to someone's ideal. Whether good or bad, all intimate encounters are there for you to grow as a person, with the ultimate goal of learning what love is. Only rarely does the flame of a relationship last a lifetime. In most cases, it is a fleeting joy, so know when it's time to let go and allow yourself and your beloved to be free again.

There is no relationship that can surpass the bliss you can find while being alone; love is an independent discovery, an inner journey you can only really undertake by yourself. One day, all of us finally come full circle, realising that what we spent a lifetime searching for something we already possessed. Regardless of what your television tells you, it's perfectly fine to spend large chunks of your life by yourself, growing instead of shackling yourself to another. It's not just acceptable, but essential, to put

Love vs relationships

your own happiness first – you cannot serve anyone else until you do.

An intimate connection between two lovers is a convenience, it means somebody to be cosy in bed with and help you do laundry. Without the spark of genuine love, it is nothing but a practical arrangement, and selecting a partner is no different to picking out a house in which to live. Just like any possession we accrue, relationships require maintenance and demand our constant attention...the point is: I want you to start viewing relationships as utilitarian. They shouldn't be considered bigger or more valuable than the two individual people inhabiting it.

I want you to, instead, reflect on how beautiful you are. Love is found through the mirror of self-knowledge, which allows us to see everyone as an image of love, not to mention as a reflection of ourselves. I want you to become the ultimate lover, which requires every part of your being to become a song, your life turning into a dance. When you embrace love, your company becomes a joy to be in, such a person naturally experiences an exemplary rapport with everyone they meet. What's more, their former impulses, whether to form meaningless attachments in the name of pleasure or alternatively build long-term relationships out of insecurity, will gracefully grow into the pursuit of lasting, meaningful lovemaking.

Most probably, you've encountered various people in life whom you've either adored or despised on sight. The reason for this is that every person is our mirror: we see our failings and our virtues through people, strangers as much as friends become our reflection – and every person is there to teach us something. And there is no greater teacher than the romantic connections we form; these can truly help us rise to our higher selves. I want to inspire you to revere your lover as your guru, let them be your light, become sacred in their company as if they are a bridge to another reality. Importantly, the same applies to you, you must become their guru and never stand in the path of their growth and evolution. The question is: can you both love one another in this way?

When you share a bed, a house, money, children, an entire lifetime with someone, you will be continually provoked, challenged, and seduced. In every moment together, your lover will expose your flaws and inadequacies – through them, you can recognise your reflection, warts and all. You'll see what you're ego would prefer not to see: your temper, your jealousy, your possessive streak, your happiness and your desperation all come alive in their presence. Never, in all other social interactions, are we so manipulative and generous all at once.

For all the virtues of solitude, it is only through the ones we love that we come to know who we really are. Most of the time, we ignore the falsity and emptiness of our ego, we are too cowardly to admit to our mind games; instead, we blame others. Relationships that do not allow for this kind of prevarication are a way for us to learn what love is and know who we are. Use your partner as a mirror, they will reveal your inadequacies better than any doctor or psychotherapist ever can. Use them as witness to the underhanded tactics you wield to gain the upper hand, the nuances of the ways you try to win and lie and pretend. How long are you going to maintain this subterfuge when there's always someone to call your bluff?

You are alive only to experience all the colours of life, you are here to act out all kinds of characters. Through meditation, through observing your inner self, you realise that there are no good people in the world, nor are there any bad people: everyone is playing a role, everyone is learning, each of us is moving closer and closer to the source of all creativity. Self-realisation is a continual process that requires going deeper and deeper into your own personality, unearthing every new layer of pretence. In this sense, all our interactions with other people, and romance especially, represent great opportunities for learning and evolving. Through loving relationships, we support one another as we each climb to a higher place within ourselves.

Love vs relationships

Every person we meet is broken; in absolute terms, this applies as much to you and me as to Idi Amin and Jeffrey Dahmer. However, we are all deceptive creatures, great storytellers; everyone is trying to be a better version of themselves but mostly winging it. The majority of what we say is untrue, we are masters at fooling people into believing us. Soon enough, every person is convinced of their own fabricated lie, their deception becomes their own reality.

A relationship is as precarious as it is pleasurable, but I am sure you'll agree that profound human connection is the one thing we are willing to risk everything for, no matter what the outcome. It's certainly an experience we can't live without as well as one that makes life worth living! The convergence of two lovers is life's most treasured experience, regardless of how it may end. My intention in writing this book is to let you elevate this connection to a supernatural culmination. When two lovers truly come together, they cease to exist as separate entities: what remains is unified love. This is the divine moment when the two egos vanish into each other and lover and beloved become indistinguishable. This is what "making love" really means; sex is only peripheral to the greater process.

Is this an ideal that inspires you, a goal to work toward? Such a relationship becomes a vehicle for ascension, a way of letting each other soar to a higher place within each of you. This meeting of spirits only becomes possible when we independently work on ourselves to manifest love in our own beings, not by crowing: "I love you!" or embracing the confines society has set for relationships.

Chapter Four

Marriage

A solution to yesteryear's problem

From a young age, we are taught that marriage is the thing that allows us to experience true love and the only respectable way to create a family and, crucially, that it entails endurance and discipline. Considering that most people in the world are products of marriage, it's understandable that virtually the whole world finds itself hoodwinked by this antiquated ritual. How many of us have actually examined these assumptions critically, or even delved into their origins?

Love and marriage were never equivalent. Marriage, which is really a component of property law, was invented by ancient cultures and intended only to control people, to keep parents together. It is a social and religious arrangement that served an important purpose in a bygone era: to protect people from themselves. The bonds of matrimony provided a structure that repressed our sexual instincts, discouraged gross negligence towards children, and determined who would inherit what from their parents. Along the way, though, the negative impact of marriage has quietly gone unquestioned even though it curtails our most basic life force: freedom. The freedom I constantly refer to isn't related to the ordinary human rights we take for granted each living day: it goes much deeper, reaching to the depth of eternity. When I say freedom, I am talking about that which pertains to your soul, your deathless, eternal reality. Freedom is your nature, like lustre is inherent to gold. When a human's inner flame is unencumbered, they are truly happy and reflect their true nature. Whatever seemingly reasonable restrictions are enforced on us by matrimonial law, religion, or simply your beloved's expectation, they infringe on our most innate quality and dull any hope of experiencing true love.

I do not advocate against marriage just because two lovers end up quarrelling and moving apart, as this always happens between two consenting adults regardless of what rules they follow. My argument against marriage is that it is fundamentally opposed to the laws of nature, even while the real impact is never discussed or detected – unless you begin going deeper into your inner reality. Whoever engages in the debate on marriage these days generally knocks it for all the obvious reasons but sadly fails to go to the heart of the matter. One simply cannot argue against marriage without addressing the impact it has on the existential freedom I speak of.

Today, people continue to willingly accept such restrictions and we gladly pledge monogamy. However, this is only because we don't genuinely trust ourselves or, in fact, know any other way to live. In terms of social behaviour, humans have practically evolved into a different species, but still we don't dare to question this old institution.

Marriage, by design, confines you within layers of costly and intricate impediments to breaking your vows. Should you ever want to regain your freedom, this would require a heart-rending legal scuffle that only hurts everyone involved. Given that we know that divorce is a common outcome, why do we this to ourselves? From a spiritual perspective, all our psychological miseries and emotional heartaches are born from the unnatural influences we fabricate for ourselves and others, from trying to subvert our true selves. Marriage is a prime example of this and the damage working against our inherent human nature causes.

Marriage has curtailed our sensitivity to what love really is. Without ever inquiring into our own needs and that which lies at the bedrock of a loving relationship, we pretend to love by being obedient and dutiful, we imitate a certain role without penetrating to its centre. Who you choose as lifelong lover and whether you feel affection for them may not even be all that pertinent: marriage is a status symbol we crave as a symbol of respect and accomplishment. The more responsibility you carry, the more hard work and years you've put in, the more children and possessions you've accumulated...the more others admire you. Between the expectations we lay upon ourselves, our partners' demands, and social norms, marriage is a form of human control; and the worst part is we don't even know this is happening to us. Instead, we believe it's what we chose to do with our life and that marriage – regardless of the strings attached – is what we wanted.

The traditions of marriage provide you with a script on how to live your life; most people have no other plan for happiness, so many can't imagine facing life's challenges without it. Doing so would force people to create their own paths, and most of us are accustomed to navigating unconsciously, going with society's flow. One needs considerable courage to challenge family tradition, break outdated rules, and risk pursuing a non-traditional lifestyle – even if that's what would make you happy. While many continue to dutifully praise the loyalty associated with marriage, they neglect to mention or even notice that they've accepted a life of restriction. Because this romantic contract is touted so zealously, the burden that marriage imposes upon you isn't considered carefully in the beginning, when we publicly declare "until death do us part" in front of hundreds of people. What is totally disregarded is that the weight marriage forces on you is inevitably felt about five years into the marriage, if not sooner, and all we can tell these disappointed couples is to "tough it out".

After ten years have passed, a married couple typically isn't in love any more. Intimacy has been replaced by familiarity. They are just two people sharing a home, sharing income and expenses, sharing responsibilities. The togetherness that was once there has turned into a convenient lifestyle, a system of coexistence and codependency, a way to get through the months and years. However comfortable, the encumbrance of marriage slowly erodes your identity and human potential. However, your deterioration as an individual goes completely unremarked and unchecked...until the day you suddenly and irrevocably become aware of what has happened to you. What you enjoyed in the beginning has been altered beyond recognition by the passage of time. At this point, your relationship becomes a dragging obligation rather than something you want to genuinely continue with. It drains your energy and curtails your horizons, causing you to sacrifice personal evolution in return for a fragile security.

If you married someone based purely on love, you've perhaps stumbled upon a wonderful and rare thing: a connection that supports without ensnaring, a relationship that allows both of you to exist as separate individuals as well as a unified whole. Such a relationship is a combination of great chemistry, self-love, and emotional maturity. But these unusual couples should not be mistaken for examples of a typical marriage. The vast majority don't ever experience such a relationship, and this chapter is intended to address the how and why.

Trust

Marriage is a legal contract that forces two parties to trust one another, even when there is really little or no trust between them. Though this is less common today, many women still tend to acquiesce to marriage largely because it offers financial security. There is an unspoken transaction in this kind of marriage: money for services rendered. Women are the creators of life, as those who bear and mostly raise children, they expect men to honour their sacrifice by way of financial support. In addition and to ensure that the deal endures even if the love affair does not, marriage offers women an assurance of monetary compensation in the case of separation. Without a legal contract, I suspect, many women would not choose to have children and, lacking the desire to have children, they would not so easily enter into marriage. Beneath the veneer of smiles, champagne and confetti, a wedding is just a business meeting after all. With many of the historical reasons for its existence no longer in force, it's become a game some women play purely for financial assurance and other tangible benefits. What this all comes down to is: a marriage certificate is little more than a warranty for a man's trustworthiness and a symbol of women's lack of trust in the men they claim to count on!

Men, too, have less-than-noble reasons for desiring marriage; for them, marriage provides the advantage of legal quasi-ownership of women. In the early days of their relationships, men like to awe their beloved with considerable effort and diligence, perhaps even keeping them rapt and entertained for years. However, the chemistry eventually fades and they are no longer willing to sustain the passion and intensity this kind of romance requires. For them, therefore, marriage promises the comfort of holding a permanent claim on a woman's loyalty and attention, regardless of any lack of passion and effort on his part in years to come. You don't need to look very far for examples of married women who pine for attention and passion, things that were abundantly available to them before they got married. The emotional security of marriage makes men lazy; the implied principle that their women are now their possessions removes the urgency to impress them. There's no chance of married women turning to anyone else for affection, at least without very harmful consequences, so married men don't feel the need to measure up to the standards they set before marriage.

We have become doubting and mistrustful people; we do not know how to believe in others. The clearest sign of this is that we expect a legal contract between two lovers, even though its necessity as a tool of social order has long since expired. It is not that we are anxious about the future, it's just that we don't trust the one we claim to love unconditionally. Have you ever wondered, after you were betrayed or let down, why you had trusted that person? This happens because your trust was based on your emotional state and attachment to your chosen outcome: this is not so much trust as an attempt to control something you have no control over. It's a case of believing in those promises you wanted to be true. Trust is a deeper and more expansive attitude to life, where you simply trust whatever happens, even if it isn't what you would have chosen for yourself. In this choiceless tranquillity, your trust in people and indeed life itself can never be broken, because you will always be at peace with whatever results turn up.

We often say: "I trust my spouse", "I believe in my best friend", and so on. These phrases really express wishes instead of stating facts; deep down, we all know that nobody is completely reliable. One should never place your trust in a person, because that trust may well be broken sooner or later. A breach of trust, one you invited by extending emotional credit, will only leave you mistrustful towards others and the universe at large, and that is a pretty glum way to go through life. In future, remember that suspicion exists only because we put our faith in people, but they are not bound to uphold our trust. People must be allowed to do as they choose, but the way we try to misrepresent our trust as their obligation is a form of captivity no one should be ensnared by – in marriage, friendship, or any other kind of relationship.

We don't know how to employ the true power of trust, which is closely related to love. Understanding this premise can easily be explained in words, though intensive self-reflection is required to truly understand it: instead of pinning your hopes on another person, learn to trust the entire universe. You see: when you assign your trust to your beloved, your connection with them becomes based on the condition they don't betray you. Under the terms stated in your marriage contract, your trust holds their freedom hostage and forbids them from enjoying any unforeseeable personal change. This is a sure road to unhappiness, for both of you. In reality, it is completely unnecessary to trust or distrust anyone. Instead, by removing that word from your mental vocabulary, you will begin to experience a deep sense of peace and satisfaction. When trust remains within you regardless of what anyone does or what happens in your life, disappointment becomes an impossibility. Trust, in this sense, is a matter of profound acceptance of the unknown, that which is ultimately out of your control, including other people's actions. "Faith" is another word that describes the same concept. When you trust life in its totality, you lose all expectations and fall deeply in love with all outcomes. When you don't demand anything from your lover or anybody else, you can perceive their choices in the proper light and without feeling any resentment. Therefore, by embracing a broader, more spiritual concept of trust, you bestow freedom on all those you claim to love. The only key is that you must trust reality as it happens, in its entirety. When your trust is total and your acceptance unconditional, you embrace whatever life throws at you, you trust all people to act according to their nature and not as if their purpose in life is to satisfy your desires, and your happiness no longer has any preconditions. Nothing has the power to affect you and you will be unshakable in all circumstances.

So, if it's really as easy as I make it sound, why does every love affair generate doubt? The answer is surprisingly simple: doubt is of the mind, while trust is of the heart. How, then, can doubt and love exist together? Love is truly naked, it is transparent, love comes only to those who are innocent, childlike and vulnerable in the company of their beloved ones. Such a lover has no care for the future, they have no fear of losing out to anyone or being taken advantage of; to them, trust in their partner is irrelevant. An all-embracing lover can never be subjugated or exploited by another, because love is invincible, love accepts all outcomes, love simply contains no fear.

There are no certainties when sharing a life with someone. There are too many unknowns, including love itself: it flows by its own will, one day it's directed at one person and the next it has moved on. That is what gives love its magical presence and indifference to the future. It cares nothing for your wedding vows; love exists only in an eternal now. It's simply not amenable to human thinking or analysis, as the mind cannot follow along with the carefree nature and changeable course of love. We invented marriage in an attempt to capture love, it's our way to control it by bringing it within a rational framework, confine it within a legal bond, and dress it up with diamond rings and name swaps.

Because love cannot be restrained in order to fit our preconceptions, marriage is full of hidden doubts and only pretends to embody the ideal of love. Each spouse quietly disguises their true feelings while purporting to trust the other. This doubt, that an unreasonable promise can stand the test of time, is the shroud that inhibits love in any relationship. Where there is even the tiniest iota of mistrust, there can be no space for love. I want to inspire you to be indifferent, uncaring, and let go of wanting anything more than simple love in your relationship. But we have all become so business-minded, so obsessed with agreements and trustworthiness, that this transactional attitude is carried over to the bedroom, to the altar, and to the grave.

It is true that fear arises from our rational intelligence and isn't a bad thing in itself – without the capacity for fear, we would remain helpless against many everyday perils. In matters of love, though, we must tread fearlessly. Our ineptitude at doing so is why love is such a rarity, seldom experienced because it requires one to abandon the warnings of their intellect, forgo what has previously guided us away from being hurt. With love, we must go blindly forth, we must become totally defenceless and even choiceless. But no marriage is devoid of fear, the other face of trust and often the reason for people getting married in the first place. We have never allowed ourselves to trust in the ineffable order behind events, so we cannot know the power that is granted to those who surrender to the will of the cosmos. This is the magic of love, the great joy that awaits all those who are willing to trust in life.

Adultery

Dogs bark even when we'd prefer them to be quiet, lions eat meat even if their brutality revolts us, birds crap where they will. In each case, we acknowledge the discomfort caused, but we don't make any moral judgments when animals act according to their nature. Why, then, do we apply such glaringly different standards to human beings? We tell ourselves that we, and others, have free will and therefore responsibility. In reality, though, our self-control is mostly an illusion invented by our ego. We justify our bad acts after performing them, when in reality we didn't truly choose to do what we did.

Another unpalatable truth is that marriage is what creates adultery; the latter word would be meaningless without the former. More specifically, betrayal can only exist if there are rules each person is trusted to uphold. However, no relationship should be based on a set of rules or agreements, because these cease to matter when love, emotions, and natural instincts are concerned. Love cannot be controlled, its growth and direction can't be predicted, and therefore love must never be punished, whatever form it takes. This would be similar to yelling at the sky for being cloudy. Adultery is a legal term, it's a man-made offence, it has no place in natural morality. Our marital dos and don'ts do not originate from love and consciousness, they come from the ego. Our ego, our thinking, judging mind, loves rules and definitions because these are all it comprehends; its nature is to limit and delineate. Unfortunately, its impulse to draw boundaries is of absolutely no help in comprehending the infinite, and that's where love comes from.

So, we say that adultery is perpetrated when a married person has sex outside the confines of their marriage. It may be committed either out of sexual frustration, or for pleasure, or purely out of love – all of these motivations are supposed to be equally unacceptable. Yet, any of them are permissible and free of blame when love is prioritised over tradition. Only injudicious, outdated doctrines claim otherwise. Fundamentally, everyone is free to do as they choose, everyone should follow their heart, pursue their desires, and embrace that which ultimately allows them to live as free people.

Saying: "I love you" does not give us the right to control another soul's destiny. Why is marriage the one modern instance in which slavery is allowed? Who are we to restrict another human being's ability to express themselves as they wish? If you're of a puritanical or authoritarian persuasion, you may choose to force your rules on another and argue that love and trust are part of your contract. This quickly leads to a paradox, though, as your love is riddled with conditions and stipulations. It would mean you believe that your commitment to another forms an unspoken promise on their part, which now allows you to decide what they can and can't do. This kind of logic comes from possessiveness and fear, not love, because true love only imparts freedom. The end result of trying to enforce an ersatz agreement on the ungovernable heart, by contrast, always involves misery and dependence.

There's a good chance that your knee-jerk response to what I am saying is to think that it's wrong, absurd, and an inconceivable way of loving someone. If so, this only proves how far we are from understanding spiritual love, which is unquestionably linked to freedom. If one is absent, the other is (at best) diminished to a mere shadow of its true essence. Love liberates, love does not possess the other. Yet the conventions of marriage only teach us how to control another person's life, they condition us to rule over our partners, and, when you examine it dispassionately, marriage really makes us all conniving and loveless distortions of the lovers we're supposed to be. All our heartaches and romantic tragedies come from our greed and attachment to another person. If we were willing to free our lovers to live as they choose, marriage would become irrelevant overnight.

Adultery is almost an inevitability. Howsoever one suppresses one's instincts, marriage will eventually frustrate everyone. It will disrupt our emotions and tempt our sexuality, because the concept of exclusivity to one person has been forced upon you instead of being willingly accepted. Even if you claim to be an Atheist, religious influences have conditioned everyone's mind into believing monogamy is natural and righteous, so we have been led to consider adultery is wrong. But it is quite the opposite, monogamy is incongruous, and polygamy consistent with the natural world.

To be clear: I'm not advocating sleeping around; I'm merely pointing out that the desire to do so is a natural consequence of marriage's shortcomings. When someone's freedom is artificially limited, they shouldn't be punished for the entirely predictable result. That is not to say that desiring to stay with one partner is impossible or unhealthy – it most certainly is achievable and, even stripped of moralistic baggage, more noble than the alternative. I believe that staying true to one partner is the best way to experience love and take pleasure in sex. However, an unwavering commitment to finding fulfilment in one relationship doesn't prove anything about the virtuousness of monogamy –

or marriage for that matter. When this happens of its own accord, it is an indication that one has proceeded beyond lust and found what love really is. Enforced monogamy, by contrast, is nothing more than mental programming, which falsely promises to transcend lust and the desire for sexual variety by clinging to societal principles or religious subjugation. Prohibitions against committing adultery do not destroy our instincts, they only cause them to manifest in our subconscious, ready to wreak all sorts of havoc in some unguarded moment or to re-emerge at some other time. To those who take a spiritual view of life, one can only evolve beyond our primal nature through freedom and practice. Simply adhering to some arbitrary moral code is no kind of victory: though your actions may be controlled, the desire behind them has only been repressed, not sublimated or overcome. An impulse to polygamy remains part of human nature and cannot be eradicated, no matter what sermons bigots attempt to brainwash us with. That is why monogamy, when imposed from outside, only causes sexual frustration, perversion, and adultery.

This also implies that monogamy or exclusivity to one person, however much it's seen as an integral part of the marriage pact, should never be an expectation. In fact, it shouldn't even be considered a principled way of life. Monogamy has made us prejudiced and judgmental of those acting from their natural instincts, as if this weren't the most dignified and authentic way to live. Marriage was created because people wanted to control our natural behaviour, which was necessary for social order in past centuries, but there is no feasible reason for monogamy to be enforced by law today. The closer we are to our primal instincts, the nearer we are to learning what love really is, while laws that run contrary to both our animal and spiritual natures turn us into unloving people.

Adulterous affairs are more common than most people realise. Those who play away from home have obviously, in their own minds, justified their actions in order to protect their sanity.

In a sense, adultery is what keeps married people together, because people would feel totally imprisoned if they could not at least dream of having an affair. The nature of this enslavement makes people dream of living without its bounds; without this possibility, even more would break free, and this applies to men in particular. Prostitution is called the oldest trade on the planet. Sadly, it exists at least in part to service married men who require the prospect of sexual escape to tolerate their marriages. In some perverse way, marriage and prostitution exist as collaborative institutions.

Monogamy brought prostitution into being because marriage aims to curb desires that are ultimately uncontrollable. Religion has traditionally frowned on women providing sex for payment, but this would never have become so prevalent without religious dominion and repression. Religious morals work against the forces of nature, but humans will naturally follow their primal instincts and no religion can stop this from ever happening. Every facet of prudish morality is entirely man-made, and this artificial disparagement of sex has caused our whole culture to become sexually stifled. Predictably, though, our sexual inclinations have not been subdued or elevated to a higher plane, but instead forced underground. The crass condemnation and subdual of sex resulted in pornography and corruption rather than romance and its artistic expression.

Pornography insults both our intelligence and our freedom to grow, the best parts of being human. Sex is one of our stairways to conscious evolution but, as long as we subjugate and repress it, lust remains capable of beguiling our senses and disrupting how we live as individuals, couples, and a society. Inasmuch as sex continues to be taboo, people continue to be persuaded down the road of perversion. The fact that adult men still behave like boys at the sight of a naked woman proves we have not sexually matured. Prurience and puritanism go hand in hand; the dichotomy between loftily sanctimonious values and human nature is just too great.

Marriage therapists should really encourage couples to visit a nudist gathering at least once during their life together (incidentally, this is also a great aid to meditation practice, as it bewilders and shakes your self-image and self-conscious ego). Spending time with other unclothed people in a non-sexual context reveals how bizarre our attitudes to simple human nakedness have become: we are ever so immaturely intrigued by something that is innately unremarkable and ordinary. If we'd simply engage with our natural desires on their own terms instead of declaring them sinful, we'd soon be able to move beyond our unhealthy concern with sexuality. It's such an entirely commonplace aspect of life, but as long as sex and nudity are still considered forbidden fruits, the mind remains unnaturally excited by it. It is common knowledge that men as well as women enjoy boasting and thinking about sex, but this is just another sign of how sexually immature we still are.

Because our sexual urges have been bottled up, they have never been allowed to express themselves naturally and in tandem with love. When it is seen as a route to consciousness expansion and love, sex soon begins to lose its abnormal appeal and fascination. Eventually, you will find sex for the sake of pleasure or ego fulfilment to indeed be an overrated pastime. Sex can be a door to liberation, it is a staircase to our higher intelligence. But as long as we are still a sexually repressed society, there is little chance of this happening anytime soon. Our egos remain mired in guilt, desire, pride, and jealousy, and these attitudes inevitably spill over in how we view sex.

In the language of love, sex is a sacred event. It is not lustful but divine; sex is a human's chance to experience what love is. Sex and love can be one and the same, but while sex is still considered indecent, it will never be recognised for its higher purpose. Sex has both primal and spiritual facets, but deprecating its primal side prevents it from becoming a bridge to spiritual evolution. As a result of our false, cherished values, including the taboo against nudity and adultery, we remain stuck exploring it only as an animal impulse, fuelled by nothing but lust and the need for procreation.

One by one, each of us can reintroduce the idea of sex as a communion of love. Admitting that it is only through love that we should create life, we come to realise that it is only through love that we should engage in sensual contact. Without love, we are using sex as an expression of base desires; we remain at the animalistic level without ever having tasted what true humanness amounts to.

Healing From Adultery

Imagine a lady called Maya, married with two children, who works hard at love, and who has remained faithful to her husband throughout their ten-year relationship. Everything seems great, or at least as good as it gets. Then, she receives the news that her partner has been seeing a secret lover. This affair, naturally, required her husband to lie about his whereabouts and much else; he carefully tried to hide the true nature of his devotion and their marriage from her – to save her feelings, perhaps. Yet, regardless of his motivation and intentions, all this was happening behind her back.

The most conventional assumption would be that Maya should surrender to the righteous pain of jealousy and betrayal; after all, she herself has remained loyal to her marriage and is entitled to her suffering. But this is precisely where the problem comes in! Maya's reactions are deemed a natural response, while her husband's affair is immediately condemned by prevailing thinking as heartless and disloyal. Additionally, he has sinned against her twice as adultery hurts in two ways: some might find it in them to forgive their partner for having sex with another person, but being deceived and lied to is what often cuts deeper.

Now, though, let's consider this story more closely (by the way, please feel free to switch the male and female roles around in your mind, because it makes no difference who has been unfaithful or remained loyal in a marriage). The point of this yarn is to examine the origins of our emotional reactions, how we judge and take revenge on our partners despite claiming we love them. Every moment, events are happening over which we have no control. To be more specific, illicit affairs within marriage are commonplace and something we tacitly knew was possible. Why else do we marry, but to put a leash on our lover?

So, if you are left shocked and hurt by learning about infidelity in your marriage, I'd like you to be dispassionate and accept that the event was mostly unavoidable. Even if your spouse had curbed their impulses, they would still be feeling lust for other men or women. The person from whom you demand loyalty is on their own trajectory, they are ultimately not under your control or, when you get right down to it, even their own. Humans are inherently free-spirited, which means we are independent, autonomous beings who cannot be constrained by mere convention. It is only under the pretext of relationships that we are required to struggle against our natural inclinations. Therefore, when a person is confined within a marriage, they find themselves in precisely the environment that was bound to create the event that they feared happening. Before choosing to confine someone by saying: "I do", one must come to accept that adultery is highly likely within the restrictions of marriage.

Love is a cosmic field. When we align ourselves with this ocean of consciousness, we access a higher intelligence that gives us the power to connect with and interpret life's events on a much deeper level. Among other things, this allows us to see life through the lens of another person's heart, and we become profoundly empathic. This greater insight allows us to avoid falling into the reactionary trap of resorting to emotions like betrayal, hurt and perhaps vengefulness.

More than anything, our condemnation of adultery is merely a matter of moralistic thinking, which is inherently unnatural and flawed. What we call morality rests on judgment and self-righteousness, which ensnares us into separating the events of life into right or wrong. When seen through loving eyes, this is absurd. Only the ego understands the world in terms of division, only the ego points the finger at what it deems good and bad. Love does not recognise the distinction between good and bad, it is all-embracing and inclusive.

Morality is purely a consequence of egoic thinking. No loving person is either immoral or moral, as their authentic way of being transcends such differences. Conversely, whatever the mind is applied to, its conclusions can't escape a dualistic worldview. Duality is how the mind perceives the physical world, as it can only identify things by way of contrast. The mind only knows love as the opposite of hate, it understands cold in terms of warmth, and so on. This means our minds are very poorly equipped to comprehend spiritual concepts like life and love, both of which fall into the domain of nonduality. From the vantage point higher intelligence provides, all categorisations lose their separateness and become part of one universal flow, and this is exactly what occurs when we see the world using the prism of consciousness – love.

Only through love can we rise beyond the ego and therefore beyond the need to judge. Love helps us ascend above the duality of good and bad, self and other, and even pleasure and pain. Love supersedes all divisions. judgment based on division, by contrast, judgment does not promote love but instead distances you from it, showing you a counterfeit version and demanding that you look no further. Ethics, too, arise from dualistic thinking. An obsession with them has not made everyone better behaved but rather quick to condemn others, if only to feel better about their own failings at living up to an impossible standard. It doesn't take much effort to notice this kind of hypocrisy: religious and self-righteous people are often the most shamelessly unspiritual, simply because they cannot ever perceive or accept their fellow man or the world as it is. "As it is", apart from its everyday meaning, has incredibly profound connotations. To a spiritually awakened person, this phrase can signify seeing without judgment or accepting life as you find it, allowing life to be, permitting everything to come as it may, and embodying receptivity and non-judgment as reflections of true love.

The ability to love engages our higher intelligence, a human faculty which the mind simply cannot equal. Love empowers one with a sense of connectivity and empathy, allowing us to see others as ourselves, almost as if part of our own bodies, and even to appreciate our lovers as much as one of our own limbs. The influences modern life throws at us, unfortunately, ensure that developing this way of looking at the world rarely happens naturally. Pandering to our ingrained notions of judgment and morality, the media often relishes the opportunity to disparage someone for misconduct. Sure enough, the mass of people are easily led astray into condemnation, making an attitude of inclusion that much more difficult to develop. Judgement is an indulgence the ego craves way too fervently. In our minds, judging purported wrongdoers creates an elevated distance from such people, making a pleasing feeling of righteousness transpire within us. When we were children, the ego's need for righteousness was gratified whenever our siblings stumbled or got into trouble – and we have not outgrown this pettiness. In days past, people would flock to town squares to gawk at public executions, and it's the same impulse that makes people today follow media scandals with great interest and why random people go and observe courtroom dramas. Fiction, too, panders to this egoic desire: we love nothing so much as a villain we're allowed to hate and distance ourselves from.

However, through love, you will see that no human is truly apart from you; we are all one and the same, we all share a certain dignity as inhabitants of this planet. No matter anyone's actions, someone who loves doesn't presume to judge them, recognising that it's just an accident of circumstance that we are not guilty of the same crimes. If you look deeper into your own mind, you will recognise that we all contain the same instincts and vices – who knows what we would be capable of if we were living out a different role. Someone's willingness to project judgment of any kind always indicates that they are deeply unloving – a flaw no amount of preaching can correct.

Choosing love instead of judgment changes your entire worldview. We have to ask, then, why we immediately choose to disregard our erstwhile love when a relationship ends due to infidelity. Why, when we claim to have formerly loved someone, do we fall into condemnation the moment they stray from monogamy? Just try it: using love as your starting point for questioning their actions and without falling into the trap of morality, you will discover a profound, unexpected ability to feel connection and empathy for them. Now, you will begin perceiving the other's actions without necessarily assigning blame and, instead, move into the serenity of understanding.

I'll give you an example: Emily, a close friend of mine, was extremely hurt after finding out John, her then-boyfriend of nine years (and also my close friend), was having an affair. Both were special to me, each in their own unique way. As a result of his adultery being revealed, John couldn't face or speak to me or any of his friends. He was torturing himself with the guilt he felt for hurting Emily and thereby letting everyone down. Because we were all part of a closely-knit friend circle, John felt he had betrayed all of us. The last I heard of him, he had left the country and built a new career and life elsewhere, all because of the overpowering remorse he felt. He cut ties with everyone he'd known, becoming an exile. Equally, the whole event devastated Emily, and it took a few years for her to regain her confidence and move on with her life.

A relationship that ends because of adultery, sadly, destroys two people's lives, leaving one saddled with enduring guilt and the other with the insecurity of having been lied to and perhaps discarded in favour of another. In a purely physical sense, though, neither Emily nor John were harmed: all their pain was psychological. But these commonplace emotional reactions and resentful feelings they'd been taught to harbour are toxic, they are unnatural, and they are unnecessary. Though they are deemed acceptable and seen as the inescapable inverse of love, these devastating emotional aftershocks are purely the result of its absence. To make matters worse, our friends and family generally add to the problem and give us the wrong advice, encouraging us to indulge in negative emotions, our need to punish or be punished, rather than inquiring into their nature. This kind of reinforcement gives us the validation we want to hear, but this only fuels our destructive reactions of pain and guilt.

Let's think, for a moment, how this kind of scenario might play out if possessiveness and loyalty were replaced with love. In this case, each experience – whatever its nature and regardless of the pain it elicits – becomes a learning, a growth, and something which you will, in time, appreciate as a blessing. Due to one of those apparent paradoxes that permeate the universe, all suffering leads us to salvation, to our own freedom. When you release yourself from attachment, your mind opens up like a flower as vast as the sky; you enter into the conscious energy field that is universal love. In that state, you feel no guilt and know no pain – nor will you wish to inflict these on another. It will then become obvious to you that love, when we truly love those close to us, is shared by giving total freedom to one another.

If you notice that your lover has gained some weight, does that entitle you to dictate what they may or may not eat? If some of their friends have opinions that don't align with yours, does that give you the right to demand that they no longer speak to them? Yet, somehow, we high-handedly apply different rules where affection and, especially, sex is concerned. Our knee-jerk emotional reactions prove that we have, in fact, not found true love. All we know about it stems from what we've learnt from others, whether by word or example, and that is why we can only understand love in terms of possession. Fear narrows our minds into imitating what we see others do, but love opens our hearts and immediately makes us larger than any situation. With love as our guide, healing from adultery is not so much a question of granting or seeking forgiveness, unburdening ourselves of guilt or recovering our pride, but of acknowledging the illusory, temporary nature of all of these concepts.

In other words, whatever hurt we may feel as a result of another's freedom of choice, we must rise to our higher intelligence to accept life's events without judgment. When we admit the fact that we neither can nor should control another's actions (any more than we can govern even our own), we're left with no choice but to allow people to be as they are. Judgment does not fix a broken heart but instead only magnifies the pain. Clinging to the duality of good and bad validates and reaffirms how you feel. This pleases the lesser part of yourself so much that your negative feelings, those memories that are causing you to suffer, will never leave, even long after the breakup. When judging others and justifying yourself have become linked, have become a part of your subconscious mind, you will carry these treasured, horrible scars for a lifetime.

The key to releasing yourself from the psychic injury of someone's behaviour towards you is to break free from moralistic thinking. That includes discarding forgiveness, which is also part of our flawed moral construct. The conceit of absolution is just another face of judgment; it grows out of self-righteousness. Reject what religious ideals have misled you into believing: that forgiveness is a virtue, a decision that will set you free of the past and provide emotional relief – it sure as hell doesn't! Don't fall into the trap of forgiving someone who has somehow wronged you. Forgiveness doesn't stem from love, instead, it is a subtle snare set by the ego. Love is of a substantially higher order than forgiveness and, in fact, makes it irrelevant. Love knows no wrong in others, love sees themselves in each and every one, love destroys the need for forgiveness. When we realise that no action is inherently good or bad, we instantly connect to life and love on a deeper level. This is the truth that genuinely sets you free, but in order to live as a free person, you must also acknowledge others' freedom to be as they are.

In a world where marriage is really just an unwelcome relic of a long-ago past, it is unconscionable that adultery continues to be an acceptable reason to punish someone. In an ideal world, our legal system and (more importantly) our individual attitudes based on independent thinking would spring from an understanding of our human instincts. However, being human, these aren't limited to fighting, fleeing, feeding, and mating, and thus such a view must also incorporate spiritual love and unifying empathy. As we learn more about the hows and whys of adultery, we come to see that such events are almost always unsurprising. Indeed, it is both shrewd and useful to think of the unfolding of all life's challenges as inevitable, as if our existence really is a continuum of unavoidable events determined by our past actions and choices. From this perspective, we can't help but compassionately tolerate the missteps of others and allow life to happen as it comes, without feeling remorse, blame or shock. To be more specific: if the principle of monogamy has been breached in your relationship, it is wise to reflect on the fact that you were trying to control the uncontrollable to begin with. Whatever happens in the moment, however trivial or momentous it appears, it is the result of tremendous forces you cannot possibly hope to control, and this fact of life is something we must ultimately come to accept.

Having said all that, we can certainly practice successful monogamy in our love lives, but this can only be achieved when we first acknowledge that we are a fundamentally polygamous species. My thoughts on adultery should not be misconstrued as encouragement to indulge in open relationships. The more wholesome approach is to see monogamy as something that develops as the result of two people's love for one another, not a way to forcibly bring this love into being. Nonetheless, I am totally indifferent to whatever particular way of life you choose; my attitude is that you should be just as you are. What I do want is to inspire you to embrace emotional openness and acquiesce to all varieties of human freedom.

When we personally reserve the right to be free, it automatically follows that we freely bestow that right on others, too. You may well find that you're prepared to accept the principle of freedom as an intrinsic part of your relationship, but find yourself unable to welcome the habit of total, impartial tolerance in your own life. Perhaps you understand, at some level, that all people are meant to be free, but can't quite put this into practice yet. This is okay; either is a sign that you're on the right path. It certainly required a huge shift in my life, not to mention a deeper level of awareness, for me to embrace this as the only reality and foundation of a loving relationship.

Divorce

Divorce is fundamentally the best part and high point of marriage – and for many different reasons. In fact, divorce is an event to look forward to with anticipation; in spite of the chorus of voices around you declaring it a moral failure, one should never associate divorce with disaster. Divorce should be celebrated as a more auspicious event than your wedding day. Since I've made my views on marriage clear, you're probably expecting to hear something like this from me, but the reasoning behind it may surprise you: the end of a marriage is a giant leap forward in your spiritual evolution simply because you had the courage to conclude a life chapter that was no longer working out. People naturally grow in different directions even while they're together and, in a healthy relationship, divorce just signifies that they've grown beyond the potential of the marriage.

So many loveless and unworkable unions continue to exist because of the fear of religious opprobrium, a desire to avoid legal and financial upheaval, concern about social censure, and – most of all – the fear of being alone. Ending such a marriage is a courageous act, not a surrender, and most of those brave enough to concede defeat eventually come to praise this step as the greatest turning point in their life. You see, after years of labouring under the constraints and control of marriage, divorce is the only way for them to rediscover their selfhood, a treasure they didn't fully appreciate when they were single. As soon as the dust of separation has settled, they find their voice again, whereas their authenticity used to be buried beneath the script one reads from while pretending to be the archetypical spouse.

We place such absurd importance on the permanence of our unions. We proclaim that they will continue until death parts us from this mortal coil, just like medieval peasants did. We make eternity a condition of bestowing our love, immediately forging the first shackle of marriage, and this has huge psychological consequences. This is because, when a marriage is dissolved by divorce instead of death (as they so often are) we assign all sorts of psychic cachet and assumptions to its end, thinking of it as a termination instead of a completion.

Divorce undoubtedly feels like failure, but how much of this is because of the mental baggage we've been saddled with without our consent? You have failed to do what you promised publicly... but those promises weren't written by you. A contract entered into under duress is legally invalid, and who among us can say they weren't somehow pressured into marriage? Even if the relationship does come to what others should be able to see as its natural conclusion, you can count on receiving condolences rather than congratulations; those who care about you anticipate you feeling broken and unwittingly help to make this a reality. Of course, even if divorce was unavoidable, you will already have invested a huge amount of psychological energy in sustaining the marriage, especially if you'd placed your hopes on its proclaimed everlasting quality. Yet the law ensures that what little stamina you have left will also be taxed, insisting that divorce usually becomes an incredibly stressful and acrimonious tug-of-war. Then, adding to the legal consequences of marriage, there is an expectation and even accepted rationales for each partner trying to destroy the other for their perceived betrayal, including through all manner of financial and familial wrangling. The realities of human nature and modern society may have forced tradition and law to accede to the necessity of divorce, but only grudgingly, and they make matters difficult wherever they can.

Maybe you've known a couple or two during the whole span of time between their wedding day and the day they instituted divorce proceedings. You will have noticed their transformation and growth over the years, but perhaps especially how their affection towards one another falls off a cliff the moment one of them talks to a divorce lawyer. The instant it hits you, that who you once thought your beloved is now your foe...that shift in perspective is devastating and embarrassing, but also laughable. So few people know what love is, so what most married couples have was never love in the first place. Why else would one, when the end of the relationship comes, try to seize whatever they can from their former lover, while they try their hardest to finagle out of any excessive burdens?

We should partly blame lawyers for evoking this bellicose mentality. They'll do their best to influence you to think only of your own interests, which is of course their job and purpose (which you pay them vast sums of money for). It's interesting to compare the role of the lawyer to that of the minister that married you: one ties you together while the other pries you apart, both considering themselves indispensable.

Marriage is a dirty business, a complete mockery of love. One day we claim to love, and the next we are left protecting ourselves from being fleeced by someone who we previously shared a bed with, looked deep in the eyes and made love with, the one you believed was your twin soul. We attack them not just as an enemy but with all the viciousness we would reserve for an ally who's betrayed us. It is primarily in the context of marriage that we prove how easily love can turn into war, and that affection ends with hate.

You may argue that certain marriages, especially faith-based ones, do indeed stand the test of time. For example, it's reported that Mormon temple marriages have a 90% success rate. Other Christian denominations typically claim a figure of somewhere over 75%, but what do these figures really tell us? In the first place, we should remember that there is no such thing as a successful marriage: there are only successful relationships, some of which involve marriage. Based on the figures I just stated, a large proportion of the people who manage to endure a marriage have toughed it out solely because of religious tradition and morality. They are afraid to even think about their own freedom; their conception of spirituality is rooted in loyalty and obedience instead. Religious people will rarely opt for divorce as a path to their own happiness, but it is precisely this ostensibly noble sacrifice that signifies an oppressive society. Ironically, this perspective on marriage – that it's designed to curb one's evolution instead of promoting your fulfilment – runs parallel to my own. The permanency of a relationship should be a matter of love and purely your own choice. There is no moral compass or preacher that has the right to tell you otherwise.

Breaking free from loyalty

Underlying the issues of mandatory trust, misconstrued betrayal, and the inevitable dissolution of marriage, there is another, unspoken question: the nature of our loyalty to those we love. Since this book is meant solely to benefit you, I want to highlight how your overindulged duty to the ancient tradition of family is causing you to lose out. Your marriage and your association with your children are typically perceived as a source of comfort and security, but I want you to re-examine how much these allegiances curtail your own freedom.

I want you to quantify the spiritual price you pay for your commitments to those you love. Whatever role you play in your family, your freedom and individuality are ultimately diminished. We all feel these bonds chafe, yet you have convinced yourself that family obligations provide you with all the love you need. You have to ask, though, who are you outside the bosom of your family? The roles we portray have superseded our own personalities, we lose our individuality because of our commitment to playing our parts within the family unit. Instead of being who we are, we become husbands or wives, we become mothers or fathers, indelibly burdening us with a sense of duty to which we are honour-bound. We have long forgotten the beauty of our own existence and forsaken our own freedom.

Statistics state that divorce is initiated by women over the age of forty 70% of the time, yet the reason such a person decides to end her marriage is never really known to her. She will normally find some excuse or rationalisation, blaming dwindling love, needy children, her failing sex life, her partner's annoying habits, her hormones, or her ageing body. But the truth is usually that she is daring to act selfishly for the first time. She is finally breaking free of her loyalty to others.

I want you to consider that your first and greatest duty is to yourself and rethink your duty to your children and your dearly beloved partner in this light. The role you've assumed in their lives is your own self-imposed imprisonment. Society, and we ourselves, have convinced us that this is part of life and love, a debt we must uphold no matter what. Certainly, taking care of those close to you is decent and natural, but the scope of our familial loyalty has quietly grown, unchecked, well beyond this, until it renders a person enslaved to a lifelong duty. Loyalty is an obligation that exists in many facets of life; however, like love or honesty or charity or forgiveness or selflessness or any dualistic concept, it can be applied for both good and evil purposes. All of these supposed virtues have historically been used to control people. An unthinking commitment to loyalty subdues a person's intelligence, like when soldiers kill other humans and risk their own lives because of an oath they've sworn. Loyalty makes you subservient, but love makes you rebellious and frees you from servitude.

Most husbands don't look for constant love in their marriage; this is to be expected because love is a dance, it is a passion, love is a spark that you must kindle anew every day. All that most men really want from their marriage is loyalty; we rarely ever see a husband complaining: "Where has all the love gone!?" They know that, with a wife who's loyal, they get everything they've come to expect from marriage: their food cooked, clothes cleaned, occasional sex, and so on. Loyalty allows them to be lazy because they know their relationship is safe. As long as loyalty is assured, there's no danger of his wife ever rising up, becoming selfish, speaking her mind, insisting on love, and eventually leaving for a better life. Because of the value placed on loyalty, and entirely without meaning to, he exploits her. Loyalty leads to robotic action; after a while, married life can become an unconscious existence, one in which we remain blithely obedient, accepting and enduring our duties without any deeper questioning while suppressing our instinct to pursue any other kind of happiness. Loyalty can be dressed up to resemble love, but it is never more than a mechanical act. Whatever allegiance doesn't come from your freedom of choice, doesn't come from your heart, is a man-made construct sadly masquerading as love and thus preventing you from experiencing the real thing!

There comes a point in almost all relationships where the passion that once existed cannot be revived, no matter how much you work at it, or what tricks you use to try to reignite your connection. This isn't someone's fault; it doesn't mean the relationship has died. On the contrary, it means the relationship has now matured and bloomed, it is the phase in which both of you have empowered the other's growth, allowed each to find their own voice. Now that you've grown, you are both ready to depart on your separate ways to the next horizon. Coming apart gracefully is akin to releasing each of your souls into the sky like a bird ready to take wing, this is the greatest example of love. This is what love really is: to be able to emancipate someone from your life, being able to let go of someone. Love comes from embracing and giving freedom, while loyalty is a form of obedience and control.

Marriages survive for decades largely because of loyalty; sadly, in such a marriage, love has become disregarded and no longer plays much of a role. Talk about love to such people, if you know some: the words they use will tell you that marriage and loyalty mean the same thing to them, and it is only loyalty that will take them to the grave together. When we structure our life around loyalty, we are not living for ourselves but remain with a loveless partner for the sake of our children, for the sake of not hurting anyone. We call this love; however, love is ultimately a selfish quality: anyone who has found eternal happiness achieved it by breaking all the rules.

It is incredibly important, not only for your physical welfare but your spiritual evolution, to break yourself free from the habit of searching for love in others. You are the master of your own happiness and destiny. Love cannot be forced to happen on demand, it cannot be compelled to endure the amount of time specified in a legal contract. There are few things so common and yet so damaging than how we all get caught up in our devotion; even when the love may be long gone, you hold on to some self-inflicted sense of fidelity.

Loyalty is not love; loyalty is psychological captivity. Love, on the other hand, is dangerous territory for those who possess each other though loyalty. This is because, when love is present, no one can be controlled and no one is reliable. Because love enables freedom, there will always be the risk of disloyalty where there is love. Love is inherently disloyal because love is ultimately transient, it can't be captured or held or seized. That is the magnificent nature of love, whoever it is experienced with. That is why detachment will remain the healthiest state of mind in all love affairs, and why letting go of a relationship that has run its course is the kindest thing to do.

Love transcends all our role models and traditions because to love is to be true to one's own self. Love breaks the pretence involved in acting out the roles of wife and husband. When there is love, there are no rules of engagement or obligation, only the right to just be – which is shared with one another. Both lovers have an equal claim to individuality and freedom; this is a natural spiritual law that no legal or religious construct can refute. Neither spouse is responsible for the other's happiness. Seeking your independence does not imply treachery, because we are ultimately alone, and only when we accept this reality do we find our true route to human evolution.

Chapter Five

Jealousy

Avarice masquerading as love

Jealousy, not love, is the dominant emotion in all of our relationships. Needless to say, jealousy is a poisonous attitude in any situation, but never more so than when we conflate it with love. Leaving aside the toxic behaviours it induces, it has a powerfully negative effect on our own mental health and inevitably leads to anxiety, insecurity and a lack of confidence.

We are made to believe the person we love automatically becomes our most precious possession. And, should the object of our affection become interested in or even momentarily distracted by another's company, we leap into action to protect what's ours. Jealousy is your automatic reaction to losing what you believe is yours. It is the emotion that exposes all our weaknesses and the flaws in our love connections. Jealousy and possessiveness are primal defence mechanisms that lead us to safeguard that which gives us pleasure, arising from a ruthlessly selfish conviction that whatever you desire rightly belongs to you and you only.

The propensity to jealousy is so ubiquitous that it's seen as a normal part of the human soul. According to the Old Testament, even God indulges in covetousness: "I am your jealous God" (Exodus 2:05 and Exodus 34:14). This is just one example of how religion has sullied everyone's mind to some extent, whether you believe in God or not. It is ordinary humans, incapable of conceiving of infinite divine greatness, who have shaped and formed our ideas about God, casting him in the image of human frailty and emotions. We then tell ourselves: "If God can be jealous, we might as well be too; why should we think we're doing anything wrong?" The Old Testament further says: "I am a very angry God". Where does this fictional character come from, if not out of our own human deficiencies? The deplorable end result is that we think that our egoic vices are a permissible part of how marriage should be approached.

At this point, it's only natural to ask: if jealousy is wrong, why is it such an unremarkable accompaniment to love? If you make an effort to observe your heart and mind more closely, though, you'll realise that this isn't the case. Jealousy is the ego, it arises from the absence of love, it is a shroud that hides you from love. Jealousy may behave somewhat like love, so it's easy to think you are in love just because you feel jealous. Seen in their proper light, however, they are polar opposites even if they sometimes manifest in similar ways. Jealousy has more to do with fear than love, it is based on exploitation rather than freedom.

Any relationship that involves intimacy endangers every ounce of our dignity. Loving someone is one of the few times in our lives that we create a bond of trust, forming a pact with one special person who knows our secrets and with whom we share our fondest memories. It is this sheltered, cherished, secret space that we'll fight to protect and keep off-limits to the rest of the world. And, should anything compromise it, we believe it is our right to protect what's ours, to defend our connection with our lover even at the cost of hurting them.

Admittedly, for me, jealousy was impossible to think beyond, let alone something I could envisage a love life without. I truly believed love and jealousy are interlinked, bound to coexist. As I understood things, not feeling jealous meant that I didn't really care for or love someone enough! This kind of thinking, though surprisingly common and generally accepted, does a great deal of harm. We've each seen more than enough cautionary examples of its effects, yet it's a tendency we all share and the poisonous sting of jealousy continues to exist in otherwise loving relationships. It's important to mention, however, that it's virtually impossible to simply stop yourself from feeling jealous. Trying to suppress this normal, though disagreeable, reaction would only amount to burying the discomfort under positive thoughts; the real issue would remain hidden in the subconscious and still cause you murmurs of uneasiness.

Howsoever you try to trick your mind, you cannot cause a negative thought to disappear or go away. The mind will always try to rationalise a situation and reassure you that everything is fine. It's programmed to try to make you feel confident about yourself. All of this simply disguises the fact that a negative thought can never be turned into a positive one; it continues to carry the same harmful momentum. (There are plenty of naïve books that claim otherwise, but these are typically based on a fairly narrow idea of how the mind works. I very much doubt that any qualified psychologist advises their clients to: *"Just think positive!"*)

Those who believe in the supposed power of mental positivity only allow their minds to trick themselves, expending a great deal of effort in the process. It's true that your mind can subdue a negative thought, convincing the conscious mind to be cheerful. However, the hidden, underlying issue invariably remains, a shadow behind whatever smile you are faking. Deep down, you will know that you have not transcended your bitterness, anger, or worry, no matter how hard you try to force the mind to be happy. There are very few shortcuts on the road to love.

The thinking mind is an invaluable tool; at the same time, it is your worst enemy. There is no crueller torturer than your own thoughts. It is by our own hand that we suffer in all parts of life. Pain is a given, a corollary of existence, but it is our minds that turn this into anguish and sorrow.

Despite our minds' shortcomings, jealousy and other negative thoughts can certainly be discarded. However, these leave by themselves, at the proper time, without any forced effort on your part. This is part of the mysterious way love operates: when you are touched by this subtle energy, you are left mystified about how you've been suddenly cured of your mental ills. Anxiety leaves you without its departure even being noticed; you won't even recall what having intransigent worries felt like. Love and its work will forever remain mysterious, the way it heals is completely unlike how the mind solves rational problems, and this enigma is part of love's magnificence. It's not something you can understand by thinking: all you must do is become open and vulnerable to it. Allow love to possess you, and the transformation happens by itself.

Formerly, I felt the sting of jealousy so intensely that I was sometimes barely able to sleep or function in my everyday role; whenever my romantic target seemed to be drifting into the arms of another, I would basically go to pieces. Jealously is a lethal yet subtle toxin, thus, once you're free of it, you will no longer recognise yourself. Discarding this inner burden, which we've somehow accepted as a normal part of love, is life-changing to say the least. I am sure the idea of being in a relationship without feeling jealous of the attention of "yours truly" will appear confusing or even absurd to many people. However, even the smallest amount of jealousy is an indication that what you feel for your partner is not love, but possessiveness. I know some of you will think that separating these two impulses is much too radical and far-fetched a concept, yet refusing to do so is precisely why we cannot experience what love really is.

Even when confronted by this thought, and knowing full well how destructive jealousy can be, most of us carry on with life as we're used to without ever inquiring into our reasons for resenting a lover's freedom, believing that jealousy is part of being human and impossible to live without. All relationships, we're told, require at least a tinge of jealousy to survive, a "healthy" amount of possessiveness. Because of this toxic emotion, we are weighed down by an undiagnosed illness that quietly goes on impoverishing our love lives.

Jealousy is a natural and inevitable instinct inasmuch as it is a by-product of the ego-mind. Our normal way of thinking, based on a mere projection of who we think we are, is at the root of all human misery. This means that, by coming to know the patterns and routines of your own psyche, the solution to all your problems (and the path to a better humanity) is revealed. It is through observing and understanding our own behaviour that we learn and evolve – human suffering is our route to higher intelligence. Therefore, thoughts that kindle unrest within you must be inquired into. Not doing so, hard as it may be, will only cause the same invidious habits to persist. If our hurtful traits and tendencies become accepted as normal, our vices become our encumbrance and bondage.

We have become so adjusted to jealousy that it has become entrenched in our personalities and deemed to have a meaningful purpose. Each of us is supposed to fight for what we love, but not just against external challenges: we end up taking up arms against love itself! Then again, most parts of human psychology are insane. Controversial as this statement may seem, anyone can prove it: you only need to observe your own mind for a few moments. You'll come to know the scary truth, namely that you have no control over what may pop into your head from one moment to the next. Anyone who explores the deeper facets of their inner life will come to know that a higher faculty than the rational mind is needed to attain sanity. Western psychology, despite all its advances, rarely acknowledges anything beyond the mind. Eastern spiritual disciplines, by contrast, have long revealed the reality of consciousness to the world. This message is now rapidly picking up momentum as the solution to all humanity's problems, either through the greater perspective afforded by meditative awareness or via the influence of love itself. Love, in its plainest description, amounts to conscious awareness; effectively, love and consciousness are no different. The paths of meditation and finding love converge in the end, and either allows us to effortlessly get rid of the burden of jealousy.

Even a tiny amount of jealousy taints an entire relationship. There can be no love where there is jealousy, and that is why virtually no one knows what love really feels like. In fact, we can only understand romantic attachment in terms of jealousy and possessiveness. We're all supposed to pander to this vice, behaving in a certain way so as not to hurt our partner: avoiding close connections with friends of the opposite sex, not lingering too long in conversations with them, being careful not to flirt or give the impression of doing so, and so on. On the other side of the coin, a deplorably large number of people actively play with their partner's insecurities, a nasty trick used to keep their lovers' attention engaged on them, exploiting their inclination to jealousy in order to feel more wanted. It seems that, in many cases, individuals feel overshadowed by their partner's success and desirability and thus resort to these kinds of tactics to keep the spotlight on them. Jealously is nothing less than a plague that blinds us to real love, that keeps us existing at lower levels of consciousness, and that brings harm to a relationship where none needed to exist.

The origin of jealousy

In matters relating to love, we devote a great deal of effort to holding on to jealousy. This serves no purpose; as a first step towards overcoming it, you have to realise that jealousy is a consequence of marriage. In their natural, original state, relationships and love are absent of envy and possessiveness. Marriage is an invented custom, it is a perversion of human nature and therefore not compatible with the way our mind, body and spirit work.

While we are strongly conditioned to believe that marriage is moral and it, for many, still remains a crucial religious rite, legal matrimony fundamentally opposes the edicts of nature and the laws that govern the changing landscape of your emotions. In fairness, humans have always been aware that love is a precarious force of nature, one we don't understand nor control nor can rely on – one day you love someone and the next day you hate them! So, because of these precipitous mood swings, marriage was created to capture the emotion we feel today so that both partners may feel secure regardless of what the future holds.

In order to investigate the origin of jealousy, we must think back to when humans were nomadic. Back then, as hunters and gatherers, we had to keep moving from place to place as resources – plants and prey – dwindled. We would only stay rooted to one location until we'd eaten all the easily accessible food, which kept humans constantly travelling to more fruitful hunting and foraging grounds.

Both men and women have made equal but diverse contributions to human civilisation. Hunting was predominantly a man's game, while women's sensibilities enabled them to excel in other areas. We have all heard the saying: "A woman makes a house into a home"; this is because she is naturally more sensitive and graceful than her male counterparts. She is responsive to the subtle signals of nature and her surroundings. While men searched far and wide for food, women exercised their talents closer to where their families sheltered. Knowledge and intuition of the cycles of nature became her tool for survival. It was women who discovered how to cultivate land. By learning how to produce vegetables and other crops, women curtailed nomadism. Men, certainly, don't possess the same instinct for nurturing and fostering life, so it was women who reduced the need for moving from place to place. It was them who made permanent settlements and, by extension, all human culture possible.

Slowly, wandering tribes and roaming bands found sanctuary in a new way of living. Instead of portable possessions, arable land, as the means to produce food and ensure long-term survival, became the source of wealth. As people began producing surpluses of food, the barter system came into being: having too much of one thing proved pointless, so the excess was exchanged for other varieties of food and whatever else was available. In time, many new, hitherto-impossible professions developed. However, most people were still occupied in farming and, as fertile ground became scarcer, farmland became the most valuable human commodity.

It was at this juncture that private property became an integral part of human culture and each family's heritage. Inheritances largely consisted of land; due to its value, it became important to pass it down to a rightful heir. Prior to this development, society was almost certainly matrilineal: who your mother was counted for a great deal (and could easily be established), while the identity of one's father played a comparatively small role in one's status. As economics began to play a central part in human life and the way land was passed down through generations started to play a major role in each clan's prospects, though, each person's paternity began to define their identity. It was against this backdrop, strictly on the basis of wealth, that marriage was created. Love had nothing to do with it: what mattered was creating trust, ensuring sexual fidelity, and securing private property.

Marriage offered women a certain degree of standing, security, and equality. Outside of this formalism, women mostly had little say in their families' financial decisions or any part in property ownership. The husband benefitted from the arrangement, too, by gaining the assurance that his children were indeed his own blood and therefore worthy to inherit his private property. Romantic attraction and concern for the welfare of your children had always existed. Promoting these wasn't the purpose of the new institution, though: marriage was not created out of deference for love but for the sake of protecting wealth.

You can hardly deny that marriage always has been and still is a reflection of our attitudes toward money. As part of the deal, because the pursuit of wealth means securing the ownership of property within the family, it means forfeiting individual freedom. Even today, men and women tie the knot, and some people even consider marriage to be part of a divine plan. This doesn't change the fact that marriage is far from sacred and totally unsuited to human nature. Getting married cannot guarantee your happiness, nor can it make your current feelings endure into the future. Freedom is part of our essence, and this includes the freedom to change.

It is precisely because marriage opposes the forces of nature that we have seen it fail on so many levels. One example of its abnormality is sexual infidelity and adultery, which have been an endemic part of marriage since its inception. Let's consider prostitution, which came into existence because of marriage. When accompanied by a prohibition against sex before wedlock, the tradition of marriage is hardly capable of withstanding one of our strongest animal impulses. After the wedding, monogamy removes the freedom to seek out sexual variety, ironically making it that much more appealing. It is often claimed that prostitution is the oldest profession and still remains a booming industry, but why such a trade exists in the first place is rarely scrutinised.

We all have our own ideas on this, but the real answer is very different from the obvious one. The core of the debate is frequently obscured by speculation on why sex workers choose to do what they do, which doesn't prove anything except our prejudices. If you want to rid the world of anything you dislike or feel is needless, you must eliminate the demand, the supply will then naturally disappear. All kinds of services are initiated by demand, the supply only comes later. This leaves us with the strange situation that, historically, prostitution has always been demonised and looked down upon, while the demand continues to go quietly unquestioned. For that matter and speaking of prejudices, men *per se* are not to blame for creating or sustaining prostitution – the real reason lies much, much deeper. Men are just acting according to their impulses as, to most men, a prostitute is no different from any other woman, with the sole distinction being that the meeting just happens to involve payment. Men's natural desire for sex is in no way enhanced because of the prevalence of prostitution. The availability of women for hire is only incidental to the underlying instinct to procreate, which has been warped and deformed as a result of marriage's unnatural constraints.

To understand what I mean, try to picture how humans lived before marriage was invented. The most important thing to appreciate is that humans loved one another long before marriage provided a structure for romance – prior to this development, neither love nor sex was expected to resemble servitude. Accordingly, at that time, prostitution didn't exist, but that doesn't mean that humans enjoyed sex any less than today. Men and women alike pursued pleasure, without betraying anyone's trust because there was no legal contract to mandate monogamy. Each person lived in freedom and imparted the same autonomy to others, realising that, when freedom exists, there can be no jealousy. As often as not, sharing your life with another in freedom rather than under obligation causes the desire to sleep with others to evaporate. However, acknowledging each other's ability to do what they choose is a necessary precondition for this state of happy, organic monogamy – it cannot be forced into being by laws, traditions, or wishful thinking.

It was marriage, not free-spirited love, that brought suspicion, deceit, and adultery into being. Suspicion, as an artificial construct, is toxic to relationships. Our reaction to this lethal poison is not to extract it but instead to impede the other and keep them captive. Women, as the ones who bear children, experience greater confinement than men under the rules of marriage. It was men who created marriage, after all, just like it was men who invented religion. Since the motives behind both weren't exactly free of self-interest, the result was to control women's freedom so that men could reign as masters of their families and society as a whole. Taken to its logical conclusion, this meant that women were barred from education and any other pursuit that might allow them to embrace a more independent role. Even today, in some countries, only men are allowed to learn, grow, and govern others' way of life. The lengths gone to in order to preserve this status quo are often bizarre, like when women who followed an alternative spirituality were demonised as witches and often killed during the 14th to 16th century in Christian Europe. Even Marie Curie, the first person ever to win two Nobel prizes, was barred from higher education due to her gender and had to attend "The Flying University", a secret society that catered to women like her. Yet, even after thousands of years of male dominance, we still live in a world where women are not treated as equals. All of this would have been quite different if the institution of marriage had never been established.

Marriage did indeed promote social stability in a bygone era; perhaps, even today, it has some benefits. However, its failings are far bigger than its merits. Couples that proceed into matrimony lose their friendships, unwittingly becoming silent enemies instead of lovers. Marriage plays a dirty trick on us, affecting us much more deeply than we care to notice. Being contractually tied to one person obligates us to become their jailer, as whatever open affection once existed shifts into secrecy and dishonesty. Intimate friendships contain no secrets; we freely share our most personal emotions without the fear of being judged or losing a friend due to opening up. By contrast, the typical husband is afraid of sharing his unvarnished opinions with his wife, nor is the average wife willing to tell her husband what she really thinks about. Marriages are full of secrets and lies, and the truly unsettling part is that we see this behaviour as normal. It is not that we ever intended to live this way, nor do relationships spontaneously gravitate to a place of reticence, furtiveness, and self-censorship. It is because of the lack of freedom that marriage imposes on us that we develop the habit of keeping secrets from our lovers.

Marriage is a form of captivity that we willingly accept in the beginning, without really considering its long-term implications and the deeper impact it has on our well-being. A contractual union in the name of love is an idealistic and harshly uncompromising notion, yet we have all been conditioned to believe that it is honourable, principled, and somehow a predestined way for all of us to live. People can't freely be themselves in a marriage: they are forced to live up to a role they don't quite know how to play, forever unable to share their true desires and feelings. Why can't we share the most intimate, private aspects of ourselves; isn't love about bearing all and having no secrets?

Lasting friendship should be all that a loving relationship aspires to be. A lot of married couples boast about being best friends, but these relationships still contain secrets. Aware of how fragile the marital bond actually is, spouses remain unable to share how they really feel about one another and what they genuinely want out of life. Good friends, by contrast, share and discuss everything, even if it's likely to be hurtful or contentious. Our friends are those with whom we can confidently be ourselves, secure in our mutual freedom and without fear of losing someone...because we don't harbour any delusions of possessing them in the first place!.

This is why a romantic relationship should also be a friendship, a meeting of minds and hearts that assumes each other's freedom to feel, think, and grow, even when the result may break your heart. The truth is that humans are not biologically destined to be monogamous; arguably, humans are the most sexually charged species on the planet and their need for variety in mates is built into their very genes. A man cannot help himself from sneaking a glance at a beautiful woman, even while in the company of his equally beautiful wife. He basically has no control over this action: he does not choose to be disloyal, he can at best choose to be honest! Women, used to being pursued instead of having to initiate their affairs, follow different tactics while acting from the same appetites. They typically spend an enormous amount of time and effort on looking their best and highlighting their most sexually provocative features. This custom is often described in terms of self-respect instead of merely trying to be alluring to new romantic partners, and this is true to some extent. Nevertheless, the driving motivation behind it isn't simple, abstract vanity but rather an instinctive rebellion against monogamy.

Yet, in spite of our natural programming, we try our best to conform to a rigidly exclusive mode of coupling. It is unnatural to insist that a loving relationship cannot allow diverse partners. A penchant for exploring sex and love with other partners should not be vilified but rather celebrated. A desire for variety, in sex as in other spheres of life, is a mark of intelligence, embracing diversity is a signature of your life force. Marriage forcibly narrows our minds and hearts to fixation on one person. In some cases, this mode of co-existence can certainly hold the possibility of a happily-ever-after scenario but, for the vast majority of people, enforced monogamy only compels us to constantly fight against our innate desires. The fact that we can often hide and suppress these urges, even from ourselves, does not reduce the amount of harm done: deep down, we feel split into two halves, demonising part of ourselves when the urge to sexual exploration is really no less noble than the inclination to faithfulness.

Romantic love is an evolutionary milestone; we are not animals who breed purely by compulsion. Nor do we stay with our mate out of instinct or just for the sake of our offspring. The human experience of love has the potential to be even greater than it is, though: genuine love is not what society and couples practice today. Once we come to experience the reality of love, we immediately break free of conventional principles; even though we've been persuaded to follow these all our lives, they simply become irrelevant once we discover our capacity to love. This kind of love nurtures your intelligence and, most of all, your freedom. If a relationship leaves you fighting your senses and impulses, then what you have is not love but captivity. If you are left feeling bitterly protective over your loved one, then your bond with them is not born out of love but possessiveness.

When two people come together under a commitment to share a life, they should build their love on unguarded friendship and transparency. As soon as lovers begin talking about marriage, their friendship shifts, the openness that was there now becomes reticent. The people involved are not to blame: marriage, as a result of its artificiality, causes us to become furtive about our own secrets and cautious of the other's hidden inner life.

Avoiding this trap is easier than you may think. It only takes one of you to know the art of love, the other will happily follow your example. After all, your partner, too, only seeks love and will mirror your actions. Loving is an art. Like any facet of our evolution, it is a learning and brings us closer to understanding the ultimate universal law. Sadly, its subtleties are lost on the majority of people, who rarely get to ever experience love in its purity. It requires an open-hearted and open-minded soul to discover its nature. Not being ready to embrace the true nature of love as individuals, couples are left consumed by jealousy and possessiveness. This causes a great deal of private unhappiness, but the real tragedy is how these and related feelings are translated into the whole of society, giving rise to a whole pantheon of evils.

Possessiveness

Marriage and, in fact, all conventional relationships are predicated on the idea that love is all about holding on to the other. This is to be expected: all of society's traditions and values, it seems, exist only to indulge our egos. The ego only knows how to possess and is happy to exploit another for its own comfort. Accordingly, all the kinds of love we exhibit are forms of human entrapment, because the pretext of love is what allows us to own a person as our property. Our relationships become mechanisms for using people, techniques for turning their time and energy to our own selfish purposes. Love, to us, means enjoying someone's undivided attention. If our lover's focus should suddenly be distracted towards another, we immediately respond with fear and fury and go about safeguarding that which we claim as our own.

Marriage shamelessly evokes a sense of ownership and entitlement over another human; you could even say that this is its fundamental characteristic. There's certainly a kind of predatory attraction to having and holding someone who we can rightly call our own, who will never let us down, a person who's bound to us and responsible for making us feel secure in an otherwise ruthless and unpredictable world. From childhood on, the way people discuss love misleads us about what marriage is: it's talked about as the culmination of all romantic love while, in reality, marriage is irrelevant to a loving relationship. At best, it's an incidental and insignificant adornment to such a bond. Marriage doesn't make relationships; it is only tolerated by them. Marriage is a game of endurance, not an endurance of love; love doesn't need to be endured and its course can't be controlled regardless of your hopes or determination. Wedding vows are an attempt to make permanent what is inherently fleeting. By contrast, love is wholly insecure, joyful in its complete unreliability. How can marriages hope to control this cosmic energy, this primal force that recognises only freedom as the ultimate law?

Humans are fundamentally greedy. Despite our best intentions and whatever code of ethics we claim to subscribe to, our basic selfishness often intrudes on those we love. Consequently, we have developed a keen instinct for guarding and protecting what belongs to us. In contexts other than romance, such as business, this is a positive thing, otherwise you would end up being robbed. Being possessive is a defence mechanism we need to survive, to avoid losing everything we've worked hard to establish. Unfortunately, very few of us are aware of our reasons for doing what we do so unconsciously. While our possessive streak may be a valid reaction to living in the social jungle, it is not an appropriate response to every situation. Our greed also mars our behaviour towards our lovers. In the attempt to keep hold of what's ours, we have reduced people into objects, assigned them the same status as a shirt or a toothbrush. You see, we can only possess items: a house, a car, a watch, but people are different from objects and do not easily submit to being claimed as possessions. Because of our inherent desire for freedom, any attempt at domination is inevitably harmful. Though being protective is commonly mistaken for love, it is really a more or less deliberate attempt to chain a lover's spirit.

Lust is certainly a passionate, driving instinct. When you look at the way everything from pop music to shampoo is advertised, you could easily conclude that the majority of people's decisions are made on the basis of sexual desire. Analysing this impulse a little more thoughtfully, we see that passion is always selective: it fixates on one single person, which makes it aggressive and dynamic. Passion can easily turn into obsession. Love, however, is not selective but inclusive. This simple acid test always enables you to distinguish between these two highly divergent impulses, even when they seem to overlap or resemble one another.

Love is simply radiated out into the world, available to all no matter who comes into your orbit. Even when no one else is present, love is nonetheless there; it is never directed by choice, so whoever comes near will be warmed by the roaring fire within you. At some level, you can sense whenever you're in the company of somebody who embodies love. It needn't be directed at you personally or be the result of any kind of intent, it simply emanates from these enlightened individuals, continually enriching all those around them without ever leaving them any poorer. This kind of love is never possessive, because it is all-encompassing. Through love, passion is transformed into compassion; passion confines, compassion liberates.

Shouldn't your love foster compassion and elevate others? Ask yourself: do you truly want your partner to be happy, regardless of whether they're with or without you? Most people will answer "yes", but this may just be a reflection of their self-image, sustained by the ego, of being a "good guy". In reality, the world is full of broken marriages that end in disgust, hatred, and indifference to the other's future. When someone decides to part ways with you, chooses to move in another direction with their life, love and compassion are immediately replaced with attempts to make them suffer: physically, financially, and emotionally.

A love that ends...was never love in the first place. Love is unbreakable because love is unconditional. When we love truly, we care for a person regardless of what they do for us or even to us. True love is boundless benevolence and ceaseless consideration for a person's happiness, no matter whether they remain with you or turn away from you. Think back over the failed relationships you've experienced yourself or observed from a distance: it will become obvious that jealousy is more closely linked with hate than it is with love. Let's imagine you love someone but later realise that they would be happier with someone else, or are told that they've decided they're better off with someone they admire more than you. Would you let them go, or would you do everything to keep hold of them, including making them feel guilty for breaking your heart? A superficial, rose-tinted glance at our relationships may give rise to the mistaken belief that we are very good at loving others. However, once we examine our true motives, the conditions we impose on others, and the mind games we play, we see that we lack any real compassion for those we claim to love. When we allow ourselves to be honest, we quickly realise how self-seeking and possessive we truly are. Worse, we portray our most vicious traits as virtues, all in the name of love.

Trying to cling to anything, including a person, is always futile in the end. Whenever you experience happiness, do you not also feel the insecurity underlying it, the spectre of time lurking behind the laughter? Whenever we find pleasure in the present moment, the mind inevitably desires to extend that delight into the future. However, time and reality do not conform to our self-centred desires, least of all those expressed in our marriage vows. The shadow of time falls over every aspect of life; we are all guilty of attempting to hold on to good things and we are all destined to lose them eventually. This emotional attachment to outcomes beyond our control is a major feature of the human condition; in fact, Buddhist philosophy considers attachment to be the origin of all pain.

The insecurity inherent in romantic relationships and the inexorable nature of time are not actually the tragedy they seem. Rather, these are lessons, examples enlightening you to the truth that nothing in life is dependable or subject to your desire. Instead of acceding to this reality, our ego tries to possess everything that comforts our senses, forging an attachment that really exists only in the mind. That is why every relationship motivated by the fear of losing someone will eventually proceed to marriage. For whatever reason, people believe that getting married will extend the love they have now – indefinitely. Of course, muttering some vows can't control love nor resolve the deeper existential riddle you face. When a man gets on his knees with a ring he can barely afford and asks a girl he thinks he loves to marry him, he is doing so out of fear of losing a good thing. Chances are, she will accept his proposal for equally selfish and short-sighted reasons. Really, hoping that marriage will endlessly prolong the happiness you provide each other today is vain in both senses of the word: both futile and conceited.

Life is fundamentally uncertain and variable. Knowing this is a hallmark of intelligence. It is important to discern how limited our control over other people and the world at large really is. All the happiness we can ever claim exists in the present moment: the future is beyond our grasp. The art of living in the moment is the greatest discovery you can make, a virtual doorway to another dimension, a way of experiencing total bliss, a place where anxiety and loss have no meaning. Love is not an everlasting experience but seems eternal when you fully embrace the power of living in the present. This isn't some poetic musing but rather a simple statement of fact – however, simply hearing about it does you no good at all unless you've comprehended life like this yourself, even if only briefly.

Sex and jealousy

Sexuality occupies a uniquely irrational place in human morality, somehow, when sex is involved, we become absurdly possessive, eager to resort to anger or hold a grudge.

Jealousy is just the tip of the iceberg, too. Why is it we become so territorial over the bodies of our loved ones? The fact is that we simply can't come to terms with someone else putting their hands on what we consider to be our property. Though Freud's psycho-sexual theories aren't taken very seriously nowadays, it's still true that copulation remains deeply symbolic of all other facets of romance. In the end, for anyone who hasn't learned to love truly, it all eventually comes down to sex! While sex remains a taboo facet of life, a sexual experience between two lovers is not just intimate and deeply private but desperately precious on a multitude of levels. Should anyone invade this close connection or compete with us in this sphere, it would devastate our self-worth and sense of attachment. Sex, when accompanied by deep emotions, is an act that heightens our sensitivity of another human's body, not just because of the pleasure we feel but because we connect with them on a subtler plane. We carry the memories of this merging with us long after the erotic experience has passed. These recollections, even when not fully understood or appreciated for what they are, confirm and intensify our bond to another's physical form. In effect, we use sex to mark them as our territory, brand a person as our possession.

Lust has a somewhat raw and depraved connotation in polite society; suspicious of its power, we hesitate to speak of it aloud. Yet lust is part of everything we do, it is as pervasive as it is subtle. A man chooses the car he drives, the words he utters, the work he does, and the ways in which he spends money largely because of lust. A woman carefully picks out the right dresses to wear, chooses the social settings in which she'll be seen, and even cultivates an entire character around being alluring – everything we do is, ultimately, aimed at appearing more attractive to our counterparts of the opposite sex. This doesn't make us shameless or wanton, it only means we are alive and energetic. Lust is a primal instinct, powerful enough to sweep you off your feet, as if some unknown force were momentarily possessing your soul. Yet as awesome and irresistible as this energy is, it is not love. Every relationship, without exception, is initiated by lust and mostly stays there, never to be elevated to a higher plane. Instead, we dress up our intimate affairs so that they resemble love. All the while, everything we do, say and experience comes from lust, turning our most prized connections into a form of make-believe. I know you'll think I am going too far in stating that relationships are not the real thing. However, you can easily observe, just like I do, that humans only pretend to be loving and relationships are a pantomime. This doesn't mean what we have isn't valuable in its own right or that we're deliberately deceptive, we just don't know what love really is. We have nothing to which we can compare our current style of relationships. If the thought of sex incites jealousy in you, then what you have for your lover is lust, not love. This will be a hard fact to swallow and, one way or another, you'll comfort yourself with the thought that I have got it all wrong. Only when you have tasted what love is and feel completely undisturbed in all aspects of life will you come to accept the central role of lust.

Having said all that, lust is an endemic part of human existence: it is interwoven into the fabric of our habits of thinking and living. On a spiritual level, lust is a stairway to a higher place. When we try to condemn lust as demonic or make any attempt to suppress or control it, we are really blaspheming against life itself. (Of course, this idea goes directly against all religious teachings, because they have always feared sex and never understood its divine power.)

Accordingly, what we call "love" is generally not love at all but only some version of lust. It doesn't take any great insight to chart this distinction for yourself: lust hurts, love does not, and as it happens we have all been hurt in the name of love. Instructive as this kind of pain can be, it mostly indicates that we have not found love at all but are still lingering at the level of lust. The life force I speak of has many different manifestations, of which physicality and lust are only one. The same energy, however, can be transmuted and applied in other, more rewarding ways...but only once we've freed ourselves of attachment to this kind of sensuality.

The same can be said about our attitudes to sex, too. The many facets of communing with another person's body are reflected by the number of different terms and euphemisms we have for it, from the clinical to the vulgar. For example, the way we ordinarily have sex is not "making love" at all. For millennia, we have been "doing it" like animals and not in our capacity as spiritual beings; this means that we have not yet experienced our humanness in all its splendour. When sex is based on attachment, it is little more than an expression of lust. However, when sex is enjoyed without any element of possessiveness, you have transcended lust and are now in love's domain.

Not many people have the will and ability to scale such a peak, and those who do often find themselves without any counterparts who share this unique perspective. This only proves the sad rarity of love in our world. Lust is a universal but also primal and animalistic trait; it takes effort and focus to rise beyond it and, until we do, we remain as animals until we have developed the capacity to love. Love is not a state of being you can take up and discard like an occasional hobby: love is an identity, love is a personification of the divine, love is you. Lust, by comparison, is aggressive, reckless, territorial, and all about seizing what you covet. Love is compassionate and thinks only about giving. Even when love involves sex, it simply does not occupy the same space as lust.

As we draw closer to love, something miraculous begins to happen deep within us. It cannot be rationally explained. Love dissipates the part of us that is insecure, it takes away our instinct to possess the other as ours or mistake the ephemeral for the permanent. Love allows us to connect with others on a new, deeper level, namely spiritual consciousness. Ironically and at the same time, it also disconnects us from old attachments, including to the less aware, more egotistical mind we normally use to navigate life and relationships. Love is the only energy that fuses all separate entities into one organic whole. Just to give you some perspective: when you look at your beloved and regard them as an entirely separate person from you, you are seeing through the eyes of lust. However, if you can look at them and see your own reflection, when you experience another person as your own reality, you have scaled the evolutionary ladder and are seeing from the highest point of view, which is love. Ultimately, it is love that allows us to ascend from the physical to a non-physical state of being, just like it shows us the way from lust to true connection. Love, romantic and otherwise, is fundamentally spiritual in nature, and transcending our current limitations is its essential purpose.

At its core, love is a mysterious force of nature. Scientists can describe gravity and quantum physics, but nobody has a handle on the workings of love. Even so, it's unmistakable when you are touched by it: it is a blessing, it is a benediction, you are simply left in tremendous levity and bliss. Maybe, the best things in life are meant only to be experienced and never to be understood.

Likewise, love is ultimately illogical, its nature is not amenable to rational analysis. The mind we are so proud of, the ability to think, reason, and weigh information, is indeed a sophisticated tool, the culmination of millions of years of evolution, but we shouldn't be blind to its limitations. Life is meant only to transcend each successive stage of our development, meaning that there's more to existence than can be comprehended through logic; love is a stepping stone towards something more sublime, beyond the reach of the mind. In our thoughts, for example, we confine our identity to that of a separate body-mind organism, but love allows us to perceive ourselves not just as a discrete entity but as the whole universe itself. Through love, all that exists becomes a part of your own existence – and this is a concept the mind simply cannot grapple with. This is how wonderful love really is! Love signifies the end of division and the beginning of a unified oneness. Along the way, you realise that separation is synonymous with attachment and limitation. Oneness allows a much broader range of experience and is indistinguishable from freedom; lust and love, attachment and freedom, are gradually transformed into one another as we grow and learn.

I don't mean to disparage our animal instincts, I only wish to place them in their proper context. Lust is the soil from which love grows; without this fertile earth, there can be no germination. Love is the carefully cultivated fruition of lust, like a flower that grows within you. This process can be nurtured but not rushed: lust cannot be suppressed. A lot of religious people try, straining to live within the bounds of their arbitrary proscriptions. Some even cover their bodies' beauty, others pray whenever they are tempted, begging their creator to deliver them from their own biology, but such efforts will always fail. Nature inevitably asserts itself; you'd have better luck running from your own shadow. Nobody can control or banish lust, and stifling this natural impulse only leads to perversion. You see, it is important to note that attachment has two faces: whether we decide to partake or choose to abstain, we remain stuck in the same trap, as both are manifestations of the very same attachment. Whether you indulge a vice or repudiate it, it remains part of your emotional makeup. People who are caught up in either attitude remain shackled to their attachment, and this only hinders them from transcending it. The approach to sex that I hope to inspire in you is neither one nor the other, but an invitation to simply discard the attitudes that don't serve your own evolution.

Sex is a celebration of our humanity, something which is eminently worth celebrating. Far from lowering us to the level of animals, sex allows us to germinate the seed of love within ourselves – with the important stipulation that its purpose is to help us ascend to a higher version of ourselves. I have always been charged with sexual energy, just like every healthy person. Why did nature equip humans, above all other species, with such an inexhaustible reserve of power? This fact alone proves that sex can open a doorway to a higher dimension, a sacred portal to our next stage of evolution. After we begin to refine the way we engage in sex, ideally through love but even while still driven by lust, there comes a priceless moment in time when those receptive to the truth begin to experience a certain indifference towards sex. This is a sign that their sexual energy has taken on a new form, preparing them for a new journey and transforming their inner geography. For them, sex is no longer an interaction with one person but with life in all its facets; in a sense, they are making love with existence itself.

The importance of graduating from lust to love, becoming free of jealousy and possessiveness, is not an indication that you and the world at large should reject monogamy in favour of casual sex, open relationships, and polyamorous behaviour. That said, there is nothing fundamentally wrong with either monogamy or polygamy. You are free to choose either depending on your predilections and circumstances, as both have a place in human society. Regardless, when your actions are ruled by love, you naturally prefer to engage in sexual relationships only with people you love and are deeply connected with. When we live life through love, we evolve from lust and naturally withdraw from frivolous affairs and search for more meaningful encounters.

Anyone who has undertaken the experiment can testify that love heightens a sexual experience beyond anything lust alone can ever achieve. While lust may prime us for an affair, it is through love that we experience sex in its truest form. Consequently, no sexual encounter should be devoid of love. Having sex solely for pleasure perverts the intention behind the act, as they really should be one and the same. Sex is not just a means for procreation or a form of entertainment but a sacred act of celebration between two lovers.

However, the fact that sex remains taboo in many societies across the world means we are hampering our own evolution. Humans are sexually immature and emotionally self-absorbed; this is the reason we'd feel so enraged and jealous if our partners should sleep with someone else. I do not wish to condone infidelity, especially when it's accompanied by deceit, but there's no denying that adultery is common within marriages. The point I really want to make is that, when we begin to spiritually mature, sex becomes trivial, and so our insecurities about it automatically dwindle. Whether someone has many sexual partners throughout their lives or restricts themselves to one is largely irrelevant to this process.

Sex is nothing extraordinary, it is the most natural and commonplace thing two lovers can enjoy. Instead of commending its virtues, society has driven sex into the basement of our subconscious, where it festers into repressed cravings, anxiety and perversions (all while advertisers make hay from our stifled sensuality). Sex must be allowed to become an ordinary part of life. As much as we celebrate it within the bounds of love, there must come a time when sex becomes unimportant. Sex is a rung on the evolutionary ladder, while lust ensnares us at the bottom, where we are unconsciously afflicted with possessiveness and jealousy. This is an entirely self-inflicted malady: through love, we can easily escape the grip of negative thoughts and begin to experience sex as a sacred encounter.

The flaw in honesty

Before we finish up this chapter, I need to discuss how we tend to misjudge people based on their intention and commitment to being honest. Often enough, the end of a relationship is precipitated by the discovery that one or the other partner has been dishonest, perhaps having broken their promise to be sexually faithful, perhaps in some other way. This is a common occurrence, yet it is very rare for people to intentionally deceive you while they're play-acting the part of a truthful person. The vast majority of us genuinely intend to remain honest in our relationships, but many unintentionally fail to uphold their promises due to circumstances they didn't expect or couldn't control. Does this make such a person heartless? We all endeavour to live up to our own standards of honesty, but the truth is that no one can guarantee their word beyond the present day. However devoted we may be to our beloved, in the context of relationships, a promise is simply a reflection of current intentions, not a guarantee of future behaviour.

Marriage is supposed to bridge the gaps caused by broken promises and survive the known flimsiness of human virtue. It is true that, in some cases, we find unbreakable trust and honesty between family members and longstanding friends, but any betrayal, no matter how small, begets an unspoken wariness. There is no doubt that this kind of suspicion endures for years where our love life is concerned. Yet this is almost inevitable, simply because every relationship involves two separate, independent individuals who are essentially free but also compelled by various forces they can't control. One of these is lust, which is the most treacherous of all human propensities because of how it operates at an instinctive, unconscious level. As a result, we're forced to restrain our sensibilities when we choose to get married. We don't really trust our partners as much as we claim to, just like we don't wholly trust ourselves: we are all intrinsically aware that lust is an unpredictable force of nature. That is why marriage is enforced by law, created only to save us from ourselves (or at least the parts of us we know we can't control).

Let's use an example: you've been in a relationship for a year when you discover that your partner is secretly on a dating app, possibly looking for something new in either the short or long term. At the same time, he or she has proven to have strong feelings for you. What do you do, how should you respond?

Though you may well deem this situation unfortunate, it is also an opportunity to learn things about your relationship that our superficial, emotional reactions don't allow us to notice. The truth is that we have a hand in every event and situation that finds its way into our lives; we are subtly responsible for everything that happens. Therefore, this is the time to deeply reflect on the events that led up to this event and consider how you might have unknowingly caused this to happen. Too often, we are reflexively unwilling to take an ounce of responsibility when someone else has been unfaithful. It's just easier (not to say ruthless) to blame the other entirely. If you have the courage to be completely honest with yourself and dispassionately examine the reality you both face, looking beyond the feelings of shame and anger, you may come to realise that you would have probably acted no differently had you found yourself in their shoes.

There are always enormous lessons to be learnt from being hurt, especially in relationships. There is no shame in admitting that you were simply living in a naive bubble and, perhaps, the relationship was never as straightforward and honest as you believed it to be. My point in telling you all this is that we mistakenly overvalue the reliability of human honesty. People may try their hardest to be the one you want them to be, but even that is mostly impossible. Consequently, it's wise to allow every person to fail at what they promise, because we humans really don't know what we are doing. Regardless of our intentions, we have no actual idea of what we may be incited to from one moment to the next. The future is always an unknown, and – as anyone may discover through meditation – our thoughts and actions truly aren't under our control.

Therefore, no person can rightly be called an honest person, though of course we all claim to be. At the end of the day, human integrity is not really a dependable quality. When you look at it even more closely, honesty can even be said to be an entrapment. As nothing in the world is certain, no one can truly be honest. Consider this: the universe itself doesn't deal honestly with you, reality is perennially full of shocks and plot twists. This doesn't mean I condone dishonesty, in fact, telling the truth and honouring commitments are part of my core values. Instead, I want to encourage you to be realistic about people's ability to do both within the bounds of love and within the laws of nature. Wedding vows, for instance, simply entice us to promise too much in the beginning, declaring that we will personify this exemplary lover who will never break another's heart. Such a lofty promise will only lead a fallible human into dishonesty at some level, at some point in the future.

So, in truth, all our claims to be honest in a relationship amount to nothing but a courteous act, the expected thing to say, a matter of good manners rather than a prediction of a fickle, capricious future. We are all merely actors playing different roles. The truest depiction of life is as a divine theatre performance, or *leela* as it is referred to in Eastern mysticism. When you're graceful and open-minded enough to embrace this reality, you come to notice how all of life's actions and occurrences playfully interweave and flow along patterns by themselves. This comprises a spiritual awakening: the line between all dualities becomes unclear and the differences between good and bad, love and hate, day and night, life and death, honesty and deceitfulness, all fade into irrelevance. You come to understand that nothing in life is wholly absolute, and interpreting it as such boils down to pettiness.

We each have many faces to the character we were assigned in this lifetime, we are all chameleons adapting to every new situation without even trying. We wear different masks around different people, in different situations, and you can notice this for yourself the next time you communicate with a young child, the postman, or your spouse. In each moment you find yourself in, you play a new role, what you say depends on the situation. If you probe more deeply into your day-to-day life, interpreting events as if they were projected on a screen you're merely watching, you'll come to realise that the words you speak originate from somewhere beyond your control or choosing. It's as if we are being passively pulled along by the lines in a script we haven't read. Think about it: are you really choosing what to say, think, or do in each passing moment? For the most part, you are only watching what happens, whether within yourself or outwardly, life is just a happening you take little active part in, you are witnessing the play as both actor and audience! Much of meditation and spiritual growth really add up to simply acknowledging this reality.

Life is a pantomime, and it includes moments in which we are honest as well as dishonest. This doesn't mean we're all bad people, it simply reflects the fact that our romantic affairs are just selfish games we play. Along the way, we say what needs to be heard while doing what we must to protect our own feelings. Once you see through the game, once you've seen that all relationships are a dishonest bit of fun, you soar beyond all the lies and all truths; you have become love itself! At that point, jealousy will be the furthest thing from your mind, an abstract concept you no longer have any attachment to or use for.

Chapter Six
The bliss found in aloneness

Love dwells in solitude

We have been conned into thinking that being single or ending up alone is quite possibly the worst thing that could ever happen to us. For some, this prospect is even more terrible than making a life-long commitment to the wrong person. Aside from the obvious reasons, including those we've talked about in previous chapters, have you ever thought about why people really get married? When you examine this question, you'll find that, more often than not, we don't marry because of love but rather out of fear, pretending to make a virtue of our dread of solitude. We end up sharing our lives with another person not because of our devotion to them but to soothe a deep, innate sense of loneliness.

I trust that, by now, you've noticed a certain theme in my views on relationships, namely that almost all the characteristics we commonly associate with intimacy actually stem from fear, not love at all. Fear and love are polar opposites, but most of us are so oblivious to our inner lives that we easily confuse one for the other. With so few examples of genuinely heartfelt relationships to learn from, we regard jealousy, attachment, possessiveness, and loneliness as natural parts of the way lovers relate to each other. We mistake the masquerade for the real thing and glorify fear instead of love, which is why it's so difficult to come to know the true face of the latter.

The truth is that we are all singular entities; isolation is our natural state of being. Aloneness is our existential identity. Even so, you share this planet with 8 billion other people, each with individual private lives, thoughts and dreams. This thought provides the ego with the necessary comfort that you are not alone. However, the ego only sees and relates to the world using the impression of separation. This is its flaw, because nothing is separate, everything is one unified organism. When you begin expanding your field of awareness, thereby enlarging your capacity to love, you will see that there are no distinct objects, there are no individual humans as such but rather an infinite oneness. In other words, you may be relieved to know that your aloneness does not exclude you from anyone but instead empowers universal connectivity.

Being in a relationship deepens our ignorance that's rooted in separation, masking our existential oneness. By becoming aware of the power that aloneness affords, we become better lovers as result, because we are in touch with a greater force within us to connect with humanity. However, as long as we continue to deny our true, solitary nature, we will forever remain ignorant of what love is. By compulsively forming new human attachments, we are running away from our roots. We come into life alone and we go beyond it without any company; whatever we may get up to in the time between these events does not negate our natural individuality. Happiness is known in the void of aloneness or not at all. Right now, though, loneliness probably appears like torture to you as you contemplate who you want to

The bliss found in aloneness

meet and date next. The idea of being single for the rest of your life may well fill you with horror. Yet there exists another, more rewarding way of living: the love that solitude furnishes you with has been completely overlooked as one of the advantages of giving up on romance, temporarily or even for good. Of course, this revolutionary outlook goes against everything society has taught you. Instead of looking for clarity and contentment by ourselves, we try our hardest to avoid being alone, incessantly searching for someone just so we won't be considered unloved.

When romance is a compulsion, you've lost the game before it has even started. Relationships don't succeed in filling the void you sense within you, they only distract us just enough to pretend that we're really whole. The more we indulge in the company of another, the more we escape – however temporarily – from ourselves, and the result is that we never discover love nor selfhood. Solitude and loneliness are not the same thing and shouldn't be conflated with each other; if you feel lonely, it only means you cannot bear your own company. The voiceless expanse within terrifies you. If this is the case, drawing closer to another person will not benefit you: your loneliness will remain no matter how well you cloak it with makeshift amusements. This chapter is meant to help you unearth and accept your fundamental aloneness, showing you that it is really a valued friend instead of a threatening stranger, celebrating it as a core part of your existence. Understanding and embracing the worth of solitude is a key step on the road to bringing your inner reality to light and consequently becoming the perfect lover for anyone you desire.

If you live in loneliness, welcome the experience and don't flee from it, ask it questions, look behind the veil of superficial feelings and impressions. Why are you afraid of being alone with your thoughts? Solitude is not an existential punishment but an opportunity for growth, and all that is needed to leverage it is sincere self-examination. You can gain an immense amount of understanding of why you feel so desolate without another person to hold and claim as your own: you'll find that there is no need to stop feeling lonely, because that's impossible. Instead, realising exactly why you can't stand solitude is all you need to conquer your fear of being alone.

If you can resist the mental discomfort that comes with being by yourself long enough to embrace loneliness as a friend, your unease will fade. The feeling will transform itself into something wonderful; when loneliness is not resisted but accepted, it flowers into a feeling of dominion and self-sufficiency you have never experienced before. Every part of this book is meant to disrupt your habitual thinking and push you out of your comfort zones, and there are few greater (or more invidious) comforts than being dependent on another person for solace. You are partly defined by the company you keep, and anything that bolsters this aspect of your identity is a huge reassurance to your ego. However, as we mature, so does our choice of partners. The character and direction of our evolution reflect the challenges we encounter in each new chapter of our lives. As we grow up, we begin to choose our partners consciously and then, one day, suddenly and unexpectedly, we prefer to experience the bliss found in being alone! Then, you'll notice that the presence of another becomes an option, not a compulsion.

Though we are all fundamentally alone, no one exists as a genuinely separate entity distinct from the rest of the universe. Whatever we can perceive is only an instance of the infinite consciousness that manifests as the physical universe and the objects it contains. You are not the limited, finite person you think you are: you are one exemplification of limitless love, who just happens to be localised within a body and habituated to thinking of itself as an individual. Solitude brings you to this incredible realisation by turning your devotion back to its source: you.

We are overly caught up in loving other people and hoping to gain their love in return. Unnatural as this may seem, I want you to temporarily eliminate them from your mental landscape, as

The bliss found in aloneness

if they simply do not exist. The mind portrays love as human connections, so the give and take between lover and beloved is the only embodiment of benevolence we know. That is why friends and lovers are revered as essential for experiencing love. But, despite our best efforts along these lines, love remains the most underutilised and rarely experienced human quality. The realisation that you are all that genuinely matters is the pathway to finding out what love truly consists of. I want you to actualise yourself as the most precious being on this planet – speaking from your point of view, this is perfectly true. Typically, we are fearful of evoking this sentiment for fear of inflating the ego. Nonetheless, it is essential that you acknowledge "the lover", namely you, as the source and creator of all the love in the world. From this perspective, you eliminate the need for a specific person to love. Along the way, you also do away with choice and discrimination: now everything and everyone becomes your beloved. Therefore, contrary to what you have been taught, self-elevation will not inflate the ego but destroy it. Love is you, not the other, love is a singular yet all-encompassing reality. It is not an exchange or even a connection, what you experience as love is nothing more than a reflection of yourself. This unifying, boundless love can only be found by turning your attention inward and allowing solitude to be your teacher.

Love is not a feeling that is engendered by the bonds between people. Instead, love is a quality beyond emotion that originates from your own independence and quietness. Learning to sample the greatest experience on earth requires the courage to step back from our habitual comforts. Only by withdrawing from people and breaking our habit of dependency on others can we ascend to a higher place, becoming able to accept the greater love found within the silence of our own company. The bliss you can only get to know in aloneness blooms when we withdraw into our own energy instead of allowing ourselves to be constantly distracted and overwhelmed by the company of others.

Being alone is your chance to find love

Being single is typically thought of as a pause between two relationships. Television, movies, and even the less insightful kind of novels reinforce this perception, painting romantic loneliness as something ill-fated and even shameful. Buying into this lie, everyone without a partner is left hoping for a reprieve from solitude, anticipating their next relationship. But why should anything need to change? Is being without that special someone, or perhaps just anyone you can at all tolerate, really such torture? It isn't; in fact, being single represents your chance to find out what love truly is. I would even go so far as to say that anyone who isn't comfortable with loneliness has no business attempting a relationship. The entire world is going about love backwards, confusing the journey with the destination, the effort with the reward, and the seed with the harvest. It is vitally important that we take a new look at "single life" because it is the ideal and perhaps the only opportunity to find love within. Contrary to what you've been doing your whole life, love is actually discovered while being alone. Love is not a by-product of being linked to another person. In other words, everyone should seek to find love long before they start looking for the perfect match, as this is the one and only route to romantic fulfilment. As long as you continue down the old path, no matter how perfect and beautiful your beloved may be, your relationship with them will be only mediocre, a close imitation of all your former heartbreak affairs.

Love is yours for the taking. It is your own special treasure, and you have unlimited amounts of it. It is radiating out from your soul and overflowing from within you. In fact, love is not contingent on anything other than what already exists within you. Only once you've discovered this fountain of inner love can you share it, only then do you become the ideal partner for someone.

Giving in to the anxiety associated with being single will only lead us to fall for the wrong kind of person, time and time again.

The bliss found in aloneness

After each failed relationship, we clearly realise that we were better off on our own, but somehow we never tire of our attempts to find the perfect partner by dating practically at random. As we continue searching for love outside ourselves, we are eventually left demoralised, coming to believe that the kind of love we desire simply doesn't exist outside of fiction.

We need to accept the reality that love is fortuitous, its reins are held by forces we can't influence or even perceive. The flowering of romance can't be anticipated or forced, and its arrival should be treated as a coincidence when it happens. This view isn't shared by many people, most of who believe that finding the right person and being in a relationship is either an inevitability or a task to be undertaken as systematically as repairing a washing machine. The approaches these forlorn souls use, like speed-dating events, smartphone dating apps, and matchmaking websites, are certainly a quick solution to finding someone these days, so it's no surprise that they experience one bitter disappointment after another. This is because the urgency to find someone coupled with the efficiency of online dating are actually symptoms of the problem. Despite all the evidence, we continue to believe that love will emerge on its own when two compatible people get together, even though this is basically impossible unless they already carry love within themselves.

There are billions of single people in the world, all hoping to find someone who will love them and accept their love in return, but these stories only rarely have happy endings. This is partly because most one-on-one relationships are a kind of psychological battle which constantly tests our affection and respect for one another. Being single does away with this constant drain on our mental and emotional resources; it is our chance to learn what love is. In time, and only by embracing self-love, do we learn how to communicate love for the other. Without self-love, our relationships with even supposedly perfect lovers will always be a challenge, an attempt to elicit the acceptance and affection we should be able to generate ourselves.

You can probably think of dozens of examples of people who've stayed in loveless partnerships because of their anxiety about being single. Though the fear of solitude looms large in our minds, realising that a relationship is going nowhere is a rarely exploited, golden opportunity which has to be seen for what it really is: your time to be selfish and explore who you are, experiencing total freedom and, more significantly, discovering that you are worthy of loving yourself.

When you find yourself unattached, you're tempted to jump at the first romantic opportunity just to avoid being alone again. I'm telling you: there is another way to live. Whether you're hesitantly testing the waters of a new relationship or thinking of giving up on a dying one, know that being alone is your chance to find real love. You will find that the seeds of that discovery are already within you. Though starting to love yourself is a singular experience and means altering much of your worldview, it becomes feasible when you don't have to take a partner's feelings into consideration. Embrace and rejoice in the liberty that comes with being unbound to anyone for the moment. Enjoy the levity found in being alone and free.

While all things in the universe are interconnected, at the same time we are also each ultimately alone. If you can, in addition, accept the cold, hard fact that you may never find your ideal lover or even someone who you imagine will make you happy, you will unearth a source of overwhelming love within you. It has always been there, yet it only becomes visible once you cease trying to control that which is ultimately out of your hands and realise that love is not dependent on others. Meanwhile, and most importantly, do not give up on romance just because of the possibility that it simply doesn't form part of your destiny. Love is not contingent on a human connection: love is everywhere. There are abundant opportunities to awaken love within you. It is found in everything. Love is subjective yet all-pervasive. It is not a one-size-fits-all experience, and this singular quality means that you can feel it within you without latching on to anything outside of yourself. Then, you will finally have become exactly what you were searching for all along. Loneliness will no longer be a burden, while connecting with others will cease to be a challenge.

Never lose sight of the fact that you are the star of this drama we call life. As soon as you fix the spotlight on yourself, without waiting for a supporting character to turn up, you will find everlasting love bursting from within. This is the significance of being single, a state that is often rejected as loveless and empty. But, regardless of whether you are single or in a relationship right now, you only need to look within yourself and you will find what you desire the most, even if you don't realise it yet: only by establishing self-love can you truly love others – and attract their love in turn.

Being dumped

Breakups are always painful, for both of the parties involved, but these experiences can be especially gruesome when they're not by your choice. To be rejected does indeed inflict excruciating, invisible wounds, certainly when a relationship which had endured for years ends but also if you've only known each other for a few weeks.

Most of us have lived through this kind of torment at least once in our lifetimes. The universal, unavoidable nature of these events doesn't diminish their impact, which can often take many years to overcome. Since this chapter is all about being alone, I thought it was important to write something about being dumped, a particularly unpleasant method of regaining your independence. In a sense, I'm even something of an expert in the field of breakups and the notorious heartache that accompanies them. The end of my relationship with the person I had assumed was going to be my life partner was the cruellest, darkest period of my life, but also ended up inducing the most dramatic and marvellous shift in my consciousness. The result was my being literally pushed into another life and mode of living.

However unpleasant, my grief turned out to be more significant and meaningful than any stretch of happiness I had ever experienced. You, too, can turn such an apparently tragic incident into the greatest thing that ever happens to you; misery, as you will come to learn, can be one's greatest teacher. It is both ruthless and compassionate in the way it imparts its lessons: the deeper the pain cuts, and the bleaker your sadness, the greater the possibility for transformation. Moderate gloominess and half-hearted tears only bring about mediocre insights and simply won't do; if you really want to cry, rend your garments and be impressively dramatic, go for it! Abandon control, embrace your sadness and disappointment, honour your melancholy, and embody what grief means to the world. Give vent to your feelings, freely, because what lies ahead is an opportunity for a tremendous breakthrough.

You cannot defeat sadness by distracting yourself from it, bravely resisting it, or simply hoping for it to go away. Though this is the advice many will offer you, it does not take the whole of your being into consideration and ignores the significance of experiencing both pain and pleasure in equal proportions. The suffering you've been contending with since being born is as important a part of your life as anything else. Buddhists sometimes claim that life is suffering and, indeed, human existence often seems to contain larger chunks of pain than happiness. This statement is usually misconstrued, though, especially when we ignore the illuminating nature of sorrow.

Perhaps you've recently broken up and, if it wasn't your decision to do so, you probably tried to fix things, tried to win them back. But everything we know is impermanent, and anything that is lost once is never worth seeking again. At best, you will only end up revisiting the same situation and would thus only be delaying the inevitable pain instead of feeling it now. For some, that may

The bliss found in aloneness

seem like a more pleasant solution than preparing yourself for getting over someone and learning how to live without them in your life. If you really can't do otherwise, if you're not ready to let go of the attachment that's causing you grief, by all means make the attempt. However, it is only once you have satisfied your sense of determination, proved your romantic tenacity, and given up on chasing what isn't meant for you that you can begin the process of transformation.

This starts by acknowledging one very important truth: that your heartache is all yours, it is a selfish and self-centred emotion. Your tears, your woes do not involve anyone but yourself, you are crying for your own sake. Heartache will only and ever be a consequence of self-pity, so you must brave the realisation that your feeling sorry for yourself isn't anyone else's fault or burden. Your dejection is purely and utterly an expression of your own egotism. You do not truly care for or love the one who got away from you because, if you did, you would be solely concerned for their future and happiness. If you weren't so caught up in your own ego, you would empathise and accept their decision to depart rather than resenting them for it. Yet it is often the case that we believe they are making a big mistake and we somehow know better. Accordingly, we try our hardest to convince them that their decision to leave us is wrong, selfishly trying to override their independence. This is incredibly short-sighted: even if they did take you back, you would be making so many changes to who you really are that the relationship wouldn't be authentic compared to the times when it was an effortless joy.

If you are feeling sad and can't stop thinking about the lover you've lost, direct your thoughts to wiser and more useful purposes. Visualising yourself as your loved one is a good first step. Try to understand their experience of the relationship and imagine their reasons for ending it. Here's the thing, though: while you do this, I want you to completely remove your own logic and rationalisations from the equation. Often, we are too cowardly to face painful realities head-on and without reservations. Even if we know that this method leads to finding relief, knowing that the truth will reveal us in a less-than-commendable light makes our minds veer away. Breakups habitually make us even more self-centred and self-absorbed than usual, so we rarely allow ourselves to decipher (and often don't even want to know) what our former partners truly needed and expected from us. Regardless, part of the healing process is to incorporate their experiences into your own, use your empathy to merge as one entity even now that you aren't in a relationship with them. Put yourself in their shoes, embody their view of the world without making excuses for yourself. You see, the eventual breakup is a pivotal part of every relationship; you often can't have one without the other. It is therefore important that we revere the ending with the same amount of respect as the inception. Remember, the cessation of a romance isn't the final end: you may have physically split apart, you are still tethered together on a subtler level even if you no longer see or speak to each other.

Pain, emotional or physical, doesn't have to mean suffering. Discomfort only turns into misery because you are resisting what hurts. Soon enough, you are sad about feeling sad, which adds another layer of grief. If you travel far enough down this spiral, melancholy can easily become depression, something that often takes years to shed.

There are many people who never quite leave their heartbreak behind, even if they believe they have. Deep sadness can be a terrific gift if we accept it as such. Like all strong, persistent emotions, it can have a powerfully uplifting effect on us, if we only allow it to be and accept the reality we are in. Some well-meaning but foolish people encourage us to let go of our past experiences and be free of our memories, but this advice runs counter to our nature as human beings. It is impossible to simply jettison your emotions or stop thinking about someone. The harder you try not to, the more energy you feed into the thought, so the effort to ignore your memories of someone carries the seeds of further discontent within itself. An entire industry has

The bliss found in aloneness

been established on the supposed efficacy of positive thinking, but it all rests on a lie: trying to erase an idea or replace it with its opposite will always prove counterproductive.

A much more worthwhile approach is to allow your ex-partners to remain a part of your thoughts, but without engaging your emotions. Simply watch these reflections as a passive, uninvolved observer. Rather than letting go of someone, let them be a part of you; don't try to pretend that they are not or that what you shared with them never happened. It is far easier and more soothing to recognise whatever has happened in your life and accept that these experiences, good and bad, influenced who you are today. When it comes to breakups recent or ancient, therefore, begin by resurrecting the same love you always had for those who were once part of your life. Permit yourself to feel gratitude for having had the chance to love them. Rather than trying to forcibly expel their memories from your mind or making a vague effort to let them go, allow them to settle into their proper place in your psyche. In time, you'll come to understand that, if you love someone, allowing them to follow their own path is the signature of your love for them. You must never impede someone else's destiny or hamper their future happiness, least of all someone you love. A loving relationship is graceful at every step of its development. If only you allow it to, the beginning, the middle, and the ending all culminate as a beautiful season of growth and discovery and not a pointless waste of your time.

This may hurt to hear, but if you feel even the slightest amount of loss and resentment towards someone you loved once they decide to leave you, then what you had for them was not love in the true sense of the word. If you delve beneath the surface and examine your feelings and impressions calmly, you'll realise that these emotions have more to do with hate than love! Allow yourself to feel your pain fully and inquire into its origins, probe into why you desire so desperately to reconnect with them. You will come to see how your agony springs from hatred, how, deep down, you bear a grudge against them for having the audacity to leave you and seek a better life for themselves. If you loved them, you would simply respect their decision. Regardless of whether it inconveniences or wounds you, you would want them to be happy both with and without you. Heartache is not reflective of love: without exception, it is a totally selfish reaction. Bitterness at being left behind only ever has to do with being possessive of another person's destiny, and this is something no one can claim as their property. Sadness may feel like love; after all, the pain you feel because of their departure is deeply emotional, but true love encompasses much more than emotions and desires.

Heartbreak, or any kind of suffering, is an invitation to evolve beyond it, and the darker the pain, the more vivid the teaching. Every ounce of life's agony is really a gift, alighting on you like a light from the heavens. Many people refuse to accept this truth, but wait a minute…did you really think spirituality is only about feeling good? As a result, almost no one listens to their pain, few people have the courage to face it. We ignore it, pretending that it's a glitch, as if it's not meant to be a part of life, as if it's not a part of the divine dance in which we all take part, as if it's karmic retribution for some unspecified thing you did wrong. Vainly hopeful, we want to run from it, discard it like yesterday's newspaper, and quickly and painlessly find refuge in happiness once more.

Our unwillingness to confront our inner turmoil explains why so many people are basically insane. Though the same kind of introspection can be used to untangle and heal all kinds of trauma, the breakthrough needed to overcome the loss of a loved one's departure from your life amounts to realising that what you had for them was not actually love. The way you feel about them is your own, self-created malady; the only way to cure it is to look inward.

If you are grieving, don't seek solace in drugs, mindless entertainment, superficial friendships and sexual liaisons, or trite platitudes about staying positive. Instead, take sadness by the

The bliss found in aloneness

hand and greet it warmly. It is just a visitor, the feeling will pass, providing that you don't leave your pain standing at the door, unrecognised and unacknowledged. Instead, welcome it in with a smile and watch, mindfully; pay attention to what it shows you. It's not here to hurt you but to guide you to a new way of living. However agonising it may be at first, this can be the start of something so much better, as long as you treat your pain with understanding and gratitude. Do we have it in us to feel thankful towards life even when the things we treasure are taken away from us? Indeed we do; love is a far, far deeper mystery than most of us care to know or ever come to experience.

If you now find yourself alone, don't compulsively start looking for anyone. Don't waste your breath talking about how you need a new beginning: you are already living it, so don't rush into another relationship out of the dread of being alone. You've been given a chance to take a break from the dating game, so take this opportunity to find out what love really is before you enter that world again. You are now in the most suitable place to discover self-love and prove that being comfortably alone is the greatest relationship you can have with anyone.

Self-love

You could be forgiven for thinking that developing affection for your own self is an absurd way of exploring the nature of love. However, this is only because, manipulated and misled by the stories society tells itself, you've lost touch with the concept of self-love. Ironically, you've never been encouraged to scrutinise this concept from a point of view that isn't hopelessly self-centred! In fact, you're probably far more used to disliking yourself than loving yourself. Religion is partly to blame for this epidemic of self-loathing, as it conditions people to continually feel unworthy and live in guilt – consequently, many devout people even come to accept shame as an act of righteousness!

Self-love can be described as the only true path to love, even though this means we've all been going about love the wrong way. Don't be confused: self-love does not require you to be selfish, but rather wholly altruistic. Legitimate self-love is the only path to loving others. Without the ability to love yourself, you have nothing to offer anyone aside from your pain.

You see, you can't share what you don't have and – let's be honest – loving others is a formidable endeavour. Love continually tests our serenity while obliging us to overlook other people's imperfections. I say: try the easier route first and find love by loving yourself instead! You are the nearest embodiment of the divine and the person closest to yourself; if you neglect self-love, your love for others will always be partial. Considering how many of us never find "the one", we can at least learn to love ourselves – and, as it turns out, this is not a consolation prize but the real answer to our romantic struggles. Self-love is more transformative even than genuine affection for another; it lets you expand into the infinite because the love that is awoken in you can extend to the whole universe. Self-love mustn't be confused with vanity. It doesn't involve becoming infatuated with your physical self nor is it about reckoning your achievements. Self-love is, instead, an unchanging atmosphere you retain in every moment you are in. Self-love is typically discouraged by parents, teachers, and society because of their fear of people becoming narcissists or egomaniacs. To be fair, we certainly see plenty of examples of both in the mainstream media today, but these are not examples of self-love. Self-love can indeed fester into egotism, but only if that love is distorted inward instead of expanding beyond the individual. When cultivated sincerely, self-love gradually and inadvertently, yet inevitably, leads one to becoming wholly selfless. A person who genuinely loves themselves soon starts overflowing with love. If love for yourself doesn't swell beyond your own space and being, then what you are dealing with is not love but only vanity.

The bliss found in aloneness

Self-love allows us to accept that we are each alone in the universe. Bleak as this may sound, that is the only reality that matters. Self-love is therefore a technique to bring you in touch with the truth of existence. It dispels the part of you that isn't truly innate to your being, the elements of your personality that amount to a facade and veneer over who you actually are. At the same time, it deepens your core self, that which really defines you, your spiritual being that essentially encompasses the whole cosmos. In this sense, self-love helps you separate the wheat from the chaff, leaving you acutely aware of the part of you that's most worthy of love. In the end, love for yourself brings you full circle to the ultimate truth accessible to those who dare to know it: that, despite appearances and our fundamental solitude, nothing really exists separately from you. It is all one entity manifested in countless different facets. In this sense, you are a reflection of all there is, and your self encompasses anything you relate to. Seen from this perspective, a romantic connection is really just a playful illusion that relies on the appearance of two separate individuals but, like any loving experience, basically adds up to a relationship with yourself. Whoever you love, relate to and connect with is only an unfamiliar part of you, because everything is an extension of your existence. Our experience of reality, at its most fundamental level, is equivalent to looking in a mirror, and everything you experience is a reflection of you, just like you are a reflection of the totality of the universe. Self-love is therefore a way of breaking through the filter of the egoic mind and becoming connected with the whole of existence on a deeper level.

We all start out thinking of ourselves as ordinary human beings: a person with a name, family, aspirations, assets, and so forth, but this is only a superficial reality. We are spiritual entities who just happen to be having a human experience in this lifetime. The spiritual part of you is interconnected with everything, it is only the human side of you that believes it is a separate entity. The spiritual organism, the true you – the "soul", if you will – is a deathless and eternal essence. Self-love is therefore a means to reclaim your spiritual aspect and, with it, total integration with all that exists, allowing us to be aware of the entire universe as one indispensable union. Self-love is infinite and, once you discover this unending reservoir within you, you will become eternal and immortal – this is the only love that lasts forever!

Self-love is your chance to nurture and cradle a blossoming life, which just happens to be the existence you are witnessing and the one flowering soul you can nurse into its full potential. Can you love yourself as you would love a small child, can you revere yourself as the most precious person alive? It is normal for parents to want children in order to enjoy the opportunity of loving someone more than the world itself, pouring all their love and attention into them in the hope of attentively observing a budding human grow into someone they are proud of. But I want you to think of yourself as that child, no less deserving of being cherished and encouraged than your own offspring.

You have forgotten your own worth: mistaken notions of love prevent you from considering the one life you're ultimately responsible for as the most significant feature of your existence. The truth is that the kindness you show to others isn't automatically reciprocated and no one will afford you the consideration which only you can give yourself. A useful meditation exercise in this regard is for you to observe and witness your human body as you would regard another person. This immediately takes crass egotism out of the equation, and only from that isolated perspective will you realise the significance of the life you have. Most people go through their whole lives without ever discovering themselves, without ever knowing who they are. Have you wondered why our mind is so keen to award love and attention to everything except itself? It is only because we don't realise that self-love is what anchors all other forms of genuine love. I want you to bring the mind's focus back to itself, back to you and back to reality!

This is not selfish. Finding the peace that exists in aloneness brings as much benefit to your future lovers as to yourself. If

The bliss found in aloneness

you demand that they furnish you with the love you're incapable of feeling for yourself, you're only harming them. It is far better for everyone if you abandon the tendency to keep searching for someone to fill your insufficiencies, hoping to find someone to fix your failure to love yourself, and instead choose to simply be alone. I should mention: the anxiety that accompanies sudden silence will be a stark contrast to the relationships you're so used to. You should be prepared for a mild shock, but I ask that you persevere: you will soon come to terms with aloneness and accept it as your natural state.

One of the things you will quickly notice is how much energy you used to expend on another person compared to the peacefulness of your own company. I admit that afterwards, when you're used to the tranquility and comfort of being alone, deciding to enter a new relationship takes a big leap of faith. I certainly have to think carefully before allowing someone into that treasured space. In many ways, being alone is still the best of all the relationships I have experienced and perhaps the only one that will allow me to live peacefully forever. All this is true – you probably glimpse this fact every time you're annoyed by your partner. Yet, amidst the incessant noise of relationships, we've become desensitised to the joys of simply existing in our own company. You may fear that there is no growth while you're alone. The human mind craves company, someone to focus on and provide a mirror to ourselves. Yet being alone offers immeasurable opportunities for evolution. In fact, at least in the beginning, solitude seems like a cruel lesson, simultaneously boring and terrifying in what it reveals about your true nature.

Being single forces you to extend yourself out into an incomprehensible void of nothingness. Your mind may jeer at you: "Are you able to cope without someone to distract you?" Yet, soon enough, you'll realise that what you thought was sterile barrenness is actually hushed tranquillity. It has always been all around you, you've just been refusing to let yourself hear it. Being by yourself, withdrawing from the constant banter that a relationship demands of you, allows you to explore the silence, stillness, and space that houses the spiritual being within you.

Above all, entering this new, noiseless territory is a courageous leap into the process of embracing love. In some respects, it is a new form of communication precisely because it is bereft of language, connection and company. There are no clear signposts to tell you what to expect in the silence of your own, unfiltered presence. Eventually, you will discover a mode of thinking beyond logic and reason, as the ineffable profundity of aloneness is made clear to you. Allowing yourself to experience prolonged gaps between relationships eventually reveals the true nature of life's textures, the enormous vitality and vibrancy contained within it, qualities which transcend the vocabulary of structured prose or rational thought. There are no words that can adequately express the sound of silence, just as there is no way to accurately describe the ache of a broken heart.

Sadness masquerades as hope

"Hope", like "love", is a beautiful word we like to misuse. We often say "I hope" when we really mean to express greed, using it as an excuse for wanting more than what is allotted to us. On an emotional level, we employ hope to hide our gloom and disappointment with reality. Hope is considered a virtue, but it really only stands between you and your happiness. Sadness disguises itself as hope: perhaps, right now, whatever you have or is going on in your life is disconcerting you, so you try to replace your present reality with an improbable vision of your future. So often, we pray, we daydream and blow out our birthday candles each year, wishing for something to change. If you're single at present, hope allows you to tolerate feeling alone because you hope to be connected with someone soon. Hope has a numbing effect, like mental anaesthesia; hope helps one brave the pain of whatever unsatisfying situation we find ourselves in.

Let me share a secret with you, one that ordinarily takes a lifetime to learn: today will always be the best that life will ever offer you. Like much of what I say, this sounds hopelessly depressing, but only until you grasp my true meaning. This takes time; a monumental shift in one's consciousness is required to experience this very moment as utter fulfilment. Once upon a time, religion extolled hope as an act of piety and something to aspire to. But, today, humans have evolved and so our approach to spirituality has matured along with our capacity to understand it. Many of those who are devoted meditators have completely eliminated the future from their minds: instead of deluding themselves about what may be, they focus all their attention on what they have in the here and now. Modern spirituality, freed of useless religious baggage, inspires us to embrace the precious "now" as the symbol of celebration. There are plenty of references to and descriptions of this state of bliss in writings dating back thousands of years. Today more than ever, though, the present moment has become the new altar on which we worship the divine. This fleeting, glorious moment is our only doorway to heaven. Hope, by contrast, is a sign of being in conflict with the divine course of events and refusing to accept that a cosmic plan governs our fate.

Discarding hope feels like seeing clouds suddenly depart, allowing the sun's rays to reveal its light and bestow its grandeur. Every single person keeps dreaming that they will find their ideal match, hopeful that they will get to know what love is, trying to remain enthusiastic about better times to come. Yet, however dearly we cling to our most cherished hopes, I say that every hope ultimately ends in vain. Reality does not obey your wishes, nor does it listen to our religious prayers. Destiny follows laws much greater than human logic. No doubt, the hopeful eventually find tolerable partners, but let's not be fooled by any of life's apparent victories: no win will ever quench your desire but will only leave you hoping for more. When all hope has ceased in you, however, you begin to accept the world as it is. You embrace life in its true majesty, without compulsively comparing it to what you'd wished for. Where does one retreat when all hope is abandoned? Only into reality, facing the situation we are in.

You don't, in fact, turn into a gloomy pessimist when all hope is lost. Something unimaginably grander transpires within you, bigger than any dream you can imagine. Unfortunately, almost no one dares to live without hope long enough to experience what I mean. When hope and its cousin, expectation, are abandoned, the future ceases to exist and all your dreams and wishes evaporate into nothingness. This may sound terrifying, like the end of everything you have to live for. Instead, what happens is that wisdom descends on the one who has no future, the one who lives with no goal or ambition in life. The nature of time changes for those who renounce hope and the present becomes intensified. Without hope for the future, you descend into the moment you are in, you become acutely and joyfully aware of your present reality. Depth of awareness is the path to happiness, heightened perception is the portal to understanding and enjoying reality. Ordinarily, the mind skips forwards, always hoping for better times to come, but the only direction to go for a fulfilling life is always to descend, go deeper into the reality you are in and see where it takes you. The ability to explore the profundity of each passing moment is what awaits all those who abandon hope.

What is so special about your hopes, what can you dare to hope for? Given your past experiences, what can possibly happen to you to make you truly happy instead of just leaving you pining for the next wonderful thing? Relying on hope is not innovative or original, you've simply never tried to live without it. At any given moment, you are either hoping for more of what you have or something you once had in the past. Hope doesn't offer anything new or transformative, it can only project a past or imagined experience into the future. Hope is always born out of sadness – it is the shadow of your misery. Think about it: a truly happy person does not hope for better times but gives their full attention to their delight in the present. When you're trapped in

The bliss found in aloneness

melancholy, your hope only becomes strengthened. The harder life becomes, the deeper your sadness grows and the more loftily your hopes rise, and the cycle only reinforces itself. Every sad person remains painfully hopeful, whereas every happy person knows nothing of hope.

I encourage you to forsake the future. Purge it from your mind and embrace a moment-to-moment lifestyle, a day-to-day existence. This becomes far easier when you recognise the power of today as opposed to the importance of tomorrow, the reality of your present experience versus the ambiguity of the future. In doing so, you will be able to harness the abundance to be found in each instant and enter your new life full of bountiful spontaneity, limitless gratitude, and magnanimous freedom.

Loneliness is only ever a state of mind. When people are alone, they pray for a miracle to change their destiny. Sometimes, they specify what they want from their imaginary future partner in considerable detail! But a far greater divine gift is obtained when we can accept whatever is happening rather than resisting it, uselessly demanding that things be different. Everyone desires something, sometimes to the point of obsession. Still, there are a few who dare to desire the unknown, trusting in the generosity of the universe instead of hoping for the expected and thus remaining open to the delights of surprise. Ultimately, being hopeful is a precarious game to play: what you think should bring you joy may not have the effect you want. Instead, allow yourself to walk ahead blindly and let the universe provide what is right for you. If you do this, you will experience the blissful sensation of being swept off your feet by each new gift the cosmos brings you. There is no greater feeling than to be uplifted by the arrival of something of which you had no expectation. The true nature of abundance is beyond hope and beyond your imagination.

There is a growing industry today cashing in by preying on people's desperate need to change their fate, known as "manifestation". While this method has proven results, it is an egocentric, shallow, New Age form of spirituality. The desire to change your destiny will keep you in the loop of time, always focussing on your future and caught in the snare of desire. The philosophy of manifestation is a trap! It closes the doorway to the present moment. I implore you to never get caught up in wishing, wanting or manifesting anything: always remember that your tiny logic cannot equal the illogical forces of cosmic play. A far greater fortune descends on those who accept the will of tomorrow.

Almost every prayer ever been spoken contains a want, a need, a desperate cry for help; all we know is to complain, all we desire is to be saved from the moment we are in. Lacking self-love, we neglect our own evolution in favour of momentary joy. Being single, especially for long periods, is a restorative and reflective period during which we can grow and self-inquire into the deeper meanings of life and love. Who, though, are we to decide what is right and wrong for us? What great wisdom do we possess that enables us to define what we need? Almost always, our desires lead us astray. The better course is to forget about hope and instead accept our past, present and future; this allows us to remain in continual peace.

Solitude

There are multitudes of people in the world who go through life alone; by choice or otherwise. Many have adapted, having been contentedly single for years but without ever experiencing the bliss found in solitude. Aloneness is not simply a question of spending more time away from people; instead, it is an entirely different alchemy. This kind of solitude is not even contingent on being alone or disconnected from society. Human contact is not something to despise but rather an opportunity to learn about yourself. A person who spends all their life meditating in a cave or living in nature surrounded by nothing but trees, mountains, greenery and animals could justifiably be branded as a coward: it requires real strength, tolerance and patience to maintain a connection with others. For this reason, I am not telling anyone

The bliss found in aloneness

to be a hermit or a recluse. Aloneness is not about renouncing the world; rather, aloneness is a prerequisite for self-inquiry and a path into your inner world. It is a state of mind, a condition of being, an attitude to reality: the reality that only you exist and everything you relate to is an extension of yourself.

Every human being should feel alone, should retain their sense of individuality, even while sharing a life with their partner. Solitude is an inner peace that remains with you no matter where you are or what company you keep. I could compare it to being in the comfort of home, where everything makes sense. In the end, aloneness and solitude are not lifestyle choices but threads that keep you connected to consciousness. Only from a position of self-love and self-awareness can we appreciate others in the same light, as unique individuals.

How, then, can we pursue greater self-love and awareness? With a growing number of people devoting time to inner development, the world contains an abundance of teachers and workshops offering effective tools for healing and resolving past trauma. These include therapeutic yoga, hypnotherapy and digression therapies that deal with painful memories, ecstatic dance events, sound healing, tai chi, meditation retreats, and many others. All of these are well worth looking into, as there is no greater or more effective gift we can bestow on the planet than the work we apply to ourselves. The harsh reality is that most people are neither mentally prepared nor spiritually qualified for relationships. Instead, we flippantly show up with our unresolved traumas and issues, hoping that each new partner will either ignore or repair these. When you meet someone, there is no way for them to prove and guarantee total transparency, sanity, and clearheadedness, nor are we usually able to detect the signs of unresolved issues that lurk in the subconscious mind of the one we are about to share our life with. The part of ourselves that is hidden only emerges after we're no longer able to pretend we're something we're not, that we have it together, after which the relationship may go speedily downhill.

In every relationship, we attract our equal and counterpart. Subtle, almost magnetic forces make them cross our paths and win our hearts. Too often, though, we try to force the laws of nature to bend to our will, and the results of this disrespect for the cosmos are rarely happy. For example, you might desire to be with someone who inspires you, someone you look up to, but who you're not ready to connect with at any kind of meaningful level. At best, they will only sympathise with your infatuation without being attracted to you, because you are not yet the kind of person they need in their life. This has nothing to do with wealth or physical attractiveness: once you have found the inner peace that solitude affords, you will attract what you once desired but couldn't previously draw into your life. People are expending all their energy looking for love when, really, they should already be generating spontaneous love from within, love should be your contribution to the world. Without love, we are all merely beggars, hoping for someone to give us something we ought to claim for ourselves, waiting for someone to cure our wounded pasts without striving to be worthy of them. Yet the spiritual laws that drive apparently random interactions are designed to promote our evolution and not necessarily our happiness. This means that romantic beggars, who hope to pry love from people instead of giving it away, consistently end up with each other. Naturally, two beggars in a relationship create more mutual misery than either would experience remaining on their own – and this keeps happening until they discover the inner origin of love.

So, the secret to being happy in a relationship lies in solitude; it has nothing to do with dyeing your hair, losing weight, learning to manipulate the opposite sex, or behaving in any way that doesn't come naturally to you. The first rule of love is to learn to experience happiness without being tied to another. If you can find ecstatic joy in the company of nothing but your own being, you will discover that people suddenly see you as the most attractive person on the planet. To achieve this, one must make time to be alone, welcome solitude, revere it as important even while in a relationship. Discover what it feels like to be content with just being alone, enjoy the moment without hoping for anything more, fall deeply in love with your own being. Aloneness is an ethereal and elusive experience because, in true, silent solitude, no one is present, not even you. The more time you spend alone, the more the part of you that isn't real, namely the ego, dwindles. This false, superficial, conditioned personality which we present to the world is always fortified in the company of others. Though you don't realise it, you've worked hard to build this persona, so discarding it seems like a great sacrifice. Consider, though, that the only reason you need to be around someone is to keep a counterfeit version of yourself alive, to sustain the mask which separates you from others!

When you are genuinely happy being alone, it's much easier to show your genuine face to those you love, making you that much more accessible to the right people. At the same time, you will become unconcerned with whether you meet someone or not, because both experiences (aloneness and connection) offer the same peace, love and happiness. For you, solitude will also be a relationship and space for learning. You will find that the beautiful irony of being indifferent to being single is that you become a magnet, and indeed only for your spiritual peers. You will, without any effort, meet another being who has discovered self-love and is also overflowing with it. Such a lover is abundantly wealthy, so they needn't beg anyone for love but instead have more than enough to share. Two people who've been liberated from the need to find love outside themselves are a divine match, as close to a perfect union as possible, because they join their souls without relinquishing their independence. Neither exploits nor depends on the other, they do not care to possess the other as their property, because true love submits to total freedom. Feelings like jealousy and possessiveness simply don't arise, as lovers only know how to live and let others live as they are meant to. Most significantly, their love is not confined to each other but rather felt as a tremendous celebration for all of existence.

Being alone amounts to a state of meditation, a condition of intensified awareness. In that tranquil space, the distinction between "self" and "other" vanishes and we become one with all that exists. When we have the courage to live as loners, we disconnect from our culture's harmful norms and society's restraints and thus become more open and welcoming. Aloneness is paradoxically synonymous with togetherness because, in deep solitude, our borders melt away and we merge into everything around us. When we have lost track of who we are, we have become part of everything. Then, there is no separation and love blooms. This is the reason we should embrace solitude: because being alone brings us closer together as one unified energy.

Learning to be alone

This chapter must not be read as a misanthropic plea to abandon your search for a life partner, because romantic love remains a beautiful and priceless experience. However, finding it only becomes possible once you possess the serenity discovered in aloneness. So, I want to encourage you to embrace the pauses, the empty gaps between relationships, and treat these opportunities as just as momentous as finding your perfect match. I don't value being single above being attached; I myself cherish both ways of living and would say that both have equal significance and beauty. As we come to know the peace and bliss found in our inner space, our compulsive need for connection becomes a distant memory. Freed from this harmful impulse, we release our lovers from all prior conditions and obligations. Therefore, once we discover the love within our own inner being, a relationship takes on a completely different character and suddenly becomes unforced and effortless.

For the most part, we learn to embrace detachment during a kind of detour in our lives, not as an intentional exercise in contemplation. This usually happens either when we've matured enough to become disenchanted with shallow relationships or when a younger person, frustrated and unfulfilled by the kind of partner they've been attracting, finds bliss in solitude. As a result, they may politely disengage from superficial conversations and start to respectfully decline invitations to events they used to enjoy. Looking from the outside, this can be mistaken for depression or snootiness, but it's really a shift in priorities and an opportunity to develop a new facet of themselves. Soon, they are fortunate enough to realise that being around people and keeping up social appearances isn't as essential as we are led to believe. They also expose another falsehood society tells us: that love is a consequence of sacrifice. It is only then, once they're freed of these burdensome preconceptions, that they become ready to enter a relationship that's based on love. Incidentally, a lot of people start to approach this realisation after having felt a certain amount of pain and pleasure at the hands of those they open their hearts to. They develop a vague idea that they've simply been assigning way too much importance to others, but this silent voice is usually overlooked as they rush off into the next unsatisfying coupling.

These numerous tragedies, these lost opportunities for growth, occur because we have all convinced ourselves that allowing people into our hearts is the one and only worthy thing we can do in life. However, there is a far greater discovery waiting for you, if only you are brave enough to accept the reality that the relationships we sacrifice everything for just aren't worth the effort. I would very much like for you to consider your alone space, your time for contemplation, your individuality, your silent peace, as the most treasured and reliable relationship available to you. Constantly remind yourself to avoid all those who distract you from your solitude and seek out those who allow you to be at peace even in their company. If you're not willing to indulge yourself in this way, every social connection you form takes away something far more valuable than whatever it promises you.

Guard your space with keen alertness and take a moment to reflect before you leap into a new relationship. Perhaps, you could reconsider the one you're in and ask yourself: "Is this worth the effort and energy? Would I be happier without them?". As soon as you begin to prioritise your solitude over the company of people, you will naturally attract more advanced souls into your orbit and, I promise, you will discover "the one" who is right for you.

There are relationships that are nothing but harmful and there exist some rare people that will uplift and nourish your spirit. Much of the dating advice you'll find out in the world revolves around ways of telling the difference between the two. But I can assure you: there is no person on this earth that can give you anything that surpasses the bliss found in aloneness.

Chapter Seven

The value of distance

Love deepens while being apart

In relationships, the tendency to share just about everything we have and grow ever more attached to our partners, more often than not, means we end up trampling on the very thing we're looking for. As I often say: love and freedom are inextricably intertwined. In this chapter, I hope to draw your attention to the necessity of preserving space between you and your partner. Distance, often in ample amounts, is as much an essential part of a loving relationship as affection. When we deliberately make time to be apart, we reignite the flames of attraction, respect, and commitment. It is generally accepted, but rarely examined, that marriage requires us to share everything we have: names, beds, car, house, friends, holidays, bathrooms. In some cases, this just makes practical sense. However, without thinking, we unwisely also lose the most precious aspect of ourselves: our space. We voluntarily surrender the empty space that contains the atmosphere in which we find true happiness.

Divorce isn't the only way in which a marriage can fail. Frequently, even couples who choose to remain together only do so by compromising too much. Along with their happiness, spouses sacrifice the last vestiges of their freedom and privacy (or demand that the other do so) and end up drifting apart due to their attempts to draw closer. By trying to make impossible concessions, the absurdity of the whole framework of marriage is revealed and it soon collapses. Contrary to widely espoused views on matrimony, and despite our inherent need for intimacy, relationships shouldn't impinge on your individuality...or your apparent closeness will only turn out to be counterfeit. In other words: if you want to live "happily ever after", start by preserving your personal space and liberty. This, not keeping your lover in a chokehold, is what makes for a successful marriage.

Regardless of how many people we're surrounded by, humans feel innately lonely until they form a strong bond with someone who's special to them. However, as we discussed in Chapter Six, no form of human connection can cure loneliness, nor are other people the place to look for love. When we've overcome loneliness by discovering inner solitude and have found love by coming to know self-love, by contrast, we realise the importance of space and distance as critical to preserving any kind of loving human connection. Think of this aspect of life as a dance: more satisfying with a partner, at least once you've learned the steps – but impossible to do successfully if you're clutching the other too tightly.

I ask you to keep an open mind, as this chapter may challenge your conventional ideas on how a couple should share their lives and create a family. When you examine the successful relationships you've seen, though, it's clear that the conventional template of marriage, which idealises obsession and ownership, is far from optimal simply because it's not aligned with human nature. Having been told that this is the only way, though, we copy and imitate, we conform to an outmoded practice. Many couples have indeed tried new formats for marriage but, due to not basing these on the spiritual principles that govern true love, these fail as often as they succeed. Seeing how conflict, whether open or hidden, is unavoidable in relationships, you can avoid many of the pitfalls that have trapped other couples by using distance to protect that which really matters. Every marriage entails friction, whether a cold war or one punctuated by bloody battles, so it's important to allow enough space for both of you to retreat instead of being overwhelmed. Very likely, you've heard the famous saying: "Absence makes the heart grow fonder". We can all attest to this being true whenever we are apart from our beloved for long stretches of time. When we reunite, we come together anew with a fresh appreciation for one another. Distance revives, stimulates and sustains love – in fact, periods of separation are just as important as the time we spend together. How strange that society continues to see couples who don't constantly cling to one another as failures, when anybody can disprove this myth with some simple experiments described in this chapter.

In addition to allowing ourselves physical space, we should guard against the temptation to continuously fixate on our lovers. When someone you love deeply and passionately is out of sight, it is incredibly important they also remain out of mind, too! At first glance, this may appear dangerously similar to becoming completely disconnected from one another. However, practising "out of sight, out of mind" will not only nourish your spirit but also feed energy back into your love life. Your beloved is like your home. Even when you are separated from your place of rest, you never forget where you find it. Not thinking constantly about someone you love doesn't weaken your connection to them. In fact, extraneous thoughts only clog the otherwise silent space you reserve for them. No one who isn't present should inhabit your mind when you are otherwise living in the current moment. I mean it: you should not think about the one you love at all! Before you recoil in disbelief, though, consider the fact that you are probably already banishing them from your thoughts while you're engrossed in work or spending time with your friends and family. Neither they nor you are poorer for not being on each other's minds all the time. I simply want you to deliberately stop when you find yourself mentally obsessing about someone you love. Of course, this is often the case at the beginning of a new relationship, when passion is blossoming and we tend to expect to occupy a large slice of each other's attention. Yet this is unhealthier than you may realise: both in the honeymoon period and within established relationships, staying out of each other's headspace is the secret to sustaining love. Lovers who constantly think about each other are like teenage couples who run up their parents' phone bills: useful fodder for romantic comedy movies, but ultimately pathetic and most certainly unsustainable.

The gift of emptiness

Let's address the issue of our needy attachment to those that we love. Some people view their relationships as the origin of all the love and security in their lives. For many of them, though, this is only a habitual assumption, one of the many beliefs I invite you to question because it normally remains untested. I want you to assess the weight a relationship bears down upon you, calculate how much it costs you in terms of your independence, and advocate the changes needed for your own freedom and mental sanity. We are all aware of the central importance of caring relationships; indeed, for many, it is the one thing that makes life worth living. My goal isn't to make you overturn these natural, positive feelings, but I would like you to see them in context.

In order to allow you to impartially evaluate the role you play in your relationship, think about how the associated responsibilities and attachments occupy a significant portion of your mind. As much as we believe life is always improved by having more, the truth is that your mind struggles under the weight of all the

The value of distance

responsibilities associated with owning more stuff and forging ever closer connections with others. Most people don't know or can't explain what they really desire in life beyond affection, wealth, respect, health, happiness, and all the money in the world. That unexplainable something happens to be an empty mind. An unburdened mind is the single most satisfying resource a human being can ever enjoy and possess, and this is what love leads you to. Within that emptiness exists all the pleasures of life and that which lies beyond it, and it is indeed the greatest wealth and prosperity one could ever achieve. In other words, the one thing we all desire, whether we realise it or not, is an empty mind – what we all crave most is nothing! However, as long as we are ensnared in the idea of attachment and possession, whether of objects or people, we simply have no idea of the value of emptiness, let alone how to achieve it. The whole concept seems absurd, especially when we're always tempted to go and chase after the latest shiny thing to catch our eye.

One of the results of finding love, and in fact the purpose of life, is to become aware of who you are as a transcendent individual and not a social creature forged by the influences and expectations of others. Therefore, I have to ask: outside the warm embrace of your relationship, who are you and what is it you really desire the most? We have become so inculcated with a sense of the importance of social roles and routines and responsible, honourable duty to our partners that we never come to know what we innately seek more than anything.

This thought may well be new to you. In fact, while many of my reflections on love and relationships may appear perplexing, it is because I've discovered what love really is, beyond our preconceptions, biology, and even emotions. Page by page, little by little, I am bringing you closer to what you desire above all else but can't yet define. Therefore, I ask only that you trust my approach long enough to try it for yourself, even if you find parts of it peculiar. Remember: a loving relationship, or in fact a connection we form with anything at all, is only a kind of trick the universe plays on us to let us achieve and realise something higher and bigger and perhaps beyond this world.

Above all things, love is levity, love is weightless, love is emptiness. Yet everything that we possess, including our loving relationships, labour under a certain mental gravity. Even our most comforting, loving thoughts and feelings impose inertia on us. Everything carries weight, and what your spirit truly desires above everything is to be free of this burden. We can do this by allowing our mind to remain empty and weightless as much as possible; this is essential for remaining in the space where love flourishes. In more practical terms, this means the next time you find yourself incessantly thinking, feeling and pining after someone, you should discard and banish those feelings. These are not signs you are experiencing love, but quite the opposite – actually, you're falling under the spell of gravity! When you observe your thoughts and emotions calmly and dispassionately, you'll realise that you are always experiencing love when you're not thinking or feeling anything about your lover. When such thoughts intrude upon your consciousness, you'll always find some other emotion behind them: lust, concern, anticipation, worry, or what have you. Love, however, is the expanse that is absent of thoughts and feelings. This thought, too, sounds absurd, but only because we have never sampled what love really is. What all of this comes down to, though, is that it's advisable and healthy for us to remain peacefully oblivious of our lovers whenever the two of you are apart.

Out of sight, out of mind

Don't forget this when you kiss your beloved goodbye each morning as you head to work: once you leave their physical presence, they should not exist in your inner reality and your headspace. Now, this is already true for most of us, even if we'd like to deny it. Life presents us with a plethora of other things to focus on while we're apart from our loved ones, so there's often

The value of distance

little time available for them to wander back into your mind. If you already exist this way, you'll find it reassuring to know you are practising something that promotes a loving relationship. You definitely don't need to feel guilty, especially as this habit also indicates that you are probably happy in your relationship yet no less content in the moments you are apart, wherever you may be. In fact, someone who has learned the art of happiness will not even miss their lover unduly or pine to be reconnected at all costs. This is not, however, a sign of indifference but only proof of a healthy mental balance, because a happy person doesn't waste a moment's thought or feeling on anything outside their present reality.

Missing someone only indicates that you are unhappy in the circumstances you happen to find yourself in. It has nothing to do with loving another. Of course, it has become a natural, expected part of life to regularly tell your lover: "I miss you", mostly out of courtesy. I don't, of course, mean that there's anything wrong with missing another's company while you're enjoying yourself, like when you find yourself watching a beautiful sunrise or enjoying a yummy dessert you would like to share with your partner. Most of the time, though, we miss someone out of boredom or discontent, and that's nothing to be proud of. Reminiscing is not a product of love, it's just a trick of the mind; a fantasy the ego uses to soothe you when you are lonely. We tend to recall pleasant memories of the past in the absence of joy. When we are unhappy, we lean on our imagination for comfort, but this results in the all-too-familiar anticlimax we often experience when seeing someone again after some time. You end up weirdly disappointed because you weren't really thinking of your lover when they were not with you. Rather, you were indulging yourself with a mental portrait you have of them, which is always a disservice to the real person.

So, the next time you feel like you're missing someone, be mindful and alert. Observe your thoughts and feelings and be honest, for a moment, about why you're craving their company.

Are you unhappy, lonely, or perhaps simply bored? Alternatively, could it be out of pure joy and a desire to share the moment you are in? Lovers should inspire one another to let go of them while being apart – it will only strengthen your relationship, regardless of any anxiety you might experience at first. Once we've had time to ourselves without the other lingering in our minds, we can come together as if for the first time and there will be an awesome freshness and sparkle between you. Every moment is a new beginning, but we don't see it this way, preferring to gauge the present by what we remember from the past. When you return to one another after time apart during which they occupied your thoughts, your mind projects what it remembers on the real person, and this often results in dissatisfaction.

Memory is a necessary tool, but we have become overly dependent on it, always dragging the past into each new reality. Change is the only constant in the universe, so each experience and human face actually exists as a new phenomenon in every new moment. Do you have the right to be angry at your lover because they're not as you remember them? Some people believe so, placing selfishness above love. Others, having learned meditation and mental discipline, manage to decouple from the chain of thoughts that continually run through our minds, leaving them free of the weight of memory. Being present in the moment makes us weightless, being free of memory allows us to experience our long-acquainted beloved as a new person every time we see them. Every day, waking up unveils a new reality, a new beginning. This is the most magnificent feature of the levity love brings: when you live in that state, awareness refreshes every moment as it happens. By living this way, you are less likely to become bored and tired of living with the same person for the rest of your life.

Nothing in the world hurts us more than our own thoughts. A relationship that consumes your mental energy, that remains within your field of perception even while your lover is far away, subtly undermines instead of strengthening itself. Such

The value of distance

relationships only make you feel insecure and unsure of yourself. Partners who stir you into constantly thinking about them aren't the ones for you. These people can't offer you any peace of mind; constant, obsessive concern about someone has nothing to do with love. The ego is addicted to overthinking, that is why we sadly obsess most over people who aren't emotionally available to us. When someone truly loves you, by contrast, you'll find your mind peacefully empty. There's no noise, no reason to worry about them and no guesswork required, except a deep, unspoken, unthinking connection between the two of you.

Therefore, you can forget about whatever magazine article you've read that encourages you to constantly long for and think about your lover. The secret to always being happy is to simply not think of anything or anyone which does not occupy your present reality. Instead, stay focused on the moment you're living. This will do your relationship no harm at all. Think about what makes you and your partner happy during the times you're actually together: women, in particular, want to lay claim to their men's undivided attention. Needless to say, this is a totally acceptable demand. We should all be fully absorbed, without exception, in the company of others, without daydreaming of other events outside of the domain you both occupy. But – and this is important – the exact same principle of awareness must also apply when we are apart: lovers should not be required to think about each other while enjoying their time and space alone. As a rule, women tend to think about their relationships more often, even while apart and usually when nothing is wrong, while men can switch off and find their required peace more easily. This is perfectly natural but is usually seen as uncaring and neglectful by women. The truth is, though, that the fairer sex is somewhat envious of how readily a man can enter his own private, serene headspace while being away from her (and even, sometimes, while being in the same room as her!)

Of course, if you are at work and your partner messages you or calls you, for that moment, they become present, alive, and part of your present reality once more. It's a fact of modern life and technology that another can spontaneously enter your space and time. As soon as the call has ended or the message has been responded to, however, let go of them, let go of the moment that has just passed and regain conscious awareness of where you are and what you are doing. Don't permit any residual feelings or thoughts to linger, even though this will prove frustratingly hard at first. This method of obtaining happiness is simply about retaining your present awareness wherever you are, it amounts to the habit of honouring every creative moment you experience. There is nothing more pressing or important than being immersed in where you are right now. This sense of awareness will keep you in a state of levity and persistent joy, wherever you are; this, in turn, makes you a charming and delightful person to be around. It's very hard to overstate the importance of being consciously present in every moment; in fact, it is the most essential part of the kind of spirituality I advocate.

Remember: even profound and pervasive feelings don't have all that much to do with loving another person. Falling in love doesn't mean that what you feel for another person is actually love. We often make this mistake, believing the heart and emotional desire to be the source of love, not realising that our feelings are still rooted firmly in the physical world. Like our minds, our hearts are still tied to the ego, and that is why our feelings are just as changeable and unreliable as our thoughts. Even so, the heart and its emotional impressions are subtler and more sensitive than the mind and its mental constructs, and therefore the heart is ever so much closer to experiencing love.

Being present in each moment is not the same as ignoring your lover. Don't worry: neither the memory of your beloved nor the connection you share will fade, as love itself will unexpectedly remind you of them throughout the day. It will leave you feeling like you've been caressed by an unfathomable force of energy; just welcome the sensation and let it pass. Don't pursue it, try to create more of it, or analyse it. Thinking too much on the subject or trying to elevate its significance will only take you on a rollercoaster journey made up of misleading thoughts and emotions. This is a trap laid by your ego that will only confuse you, because you are now adding weight to what should be a spontaneous sensation, you are tacking your own narrative onto something indefinable and weightless. Speaking of this, we must always be alert to our feelings as they have a way of disturbing our state of peace if we do not examine them consciously. Typically, we see whirlwind romances and honeymoon periods existing only on the strength of passion and excitement, burning brightly and briefly but soon flaming out. You will be able to see these feelings for what they are – deceptive and fleeting – if you pay attention. If you want something more meaningful and lasting, there is a place to find connection that lies beyond the heart. Even our most passionate feelings and most ardent emotions should be recognised as potentially barren and misleading, or they might well take you on a journey that ends sooner than you had hoped.

Strong emotions can literally drive you mad. They have a special capacity for torturing us, precisely because they originate from the ego. Feelings can consume you and often do just that when we are troubled about a relationship, trying to find a way forward or a way out. Even though they don't possess physical substance, we can be left exhausted and deeply anxious after a surge of unrelenting emotions. Thoughts and feelings are a part of love, so we must not deny ourselves their pleasure. None of them needs to be suppressed: even anger is an expression of love, just like all emotions are different shades of love...but they are valid and purposeful only once they become singular and intensely related to an experience in the present moment.

If you've never thought about it, it may come as a surprise that our need for attention and validation is the driving factor in all love connections. You may claim that it is love that motivates you, but only because you don't even know why you're battling for your lover's appreciation and approval; the power dynamics involved are all happening unconsciously. Observe your own life as if you were a third, uninvolved person, watch your ego objectively, and you will notice for the first time the silly games you play, all spurred by the need to win and maintain the advantage. In every romantic act, we are unknowingly seeking out proof that we matter. We instinctively fight for a place in our lover's mind and emotions, we need their recognition. Conversely, every time you call them or remember them, it reinforces their sense of importance, appeasing their deeply egoic need to remain relevant.

The ego is driven by fear, including the fear of being forgotten, the fear of being surpassed by someone else your lover might encounter while you are apart. For what other reason do we wear rings on our fingers if not due to jealousy and suspiciousness? But, if your partner really loves you, I can assure you that you will never be far from their mind and their emotions, even if you don't occupy a permanent space in them. You see, love is effortless above all things, it doesn't have to be reminded or strained. Love is all that you need, love is like knowing where home is, love is where you are most at ease. When you leave the house every day, you don't have to remind yourself where you live, the location of your home is an unshakable reality. The same applies to the ones we love and share our life with: they become an indivisible part of our lives.

What is the significance of remaining clear and empty whenever you are alone, temporarily forgetting about your relationship until you see your lover again? In the first place, consciously living in the moment will not inspire you to be unfaithful, nor will it disconnect you from them or reduce the passion you feel towards them. When we remain unconcerned with whatever does not exist in the moment, we become part of something bigger than life itself. In essence and despite everything you believe, love is simply an empty mind, it is a wordless silence and the part of us that's hidden beneath what we think and feel each day. A loving relationship is part of your spiritual evolution, but it is only a stepping stone to the real thing. When we abandon our reliance on the mind and emotions, however briefly, we are left free to touch another dimension within us, the presence of a nameless force, which is love. Love makes us wholesome and peaceful so that, when we are reunited with our loved ones, we are charged with abundant energy and life. Just remember that the levity love brings you in touch with is effectively a state of higher consciousness: levity is nothing less than a form of meditation, a union with the whole cosmos.

Living separately while coming closer together

Distance plays an existential role in our perception and relation with the world and the ones we love. It's true: the seen and unseen distance between us affects our relationships to a greater extent than we normally care to know. I'd like to draw your attention to the difference between these, the obvious and unnoticeable aspects of disconnection. You could be holding hands with your beloved right now, you may be physically close almost all the time, even while there remains a chasm-like inner distance between you. Conversely, two lovers can be in the habit of spending long stretches of time apart, even though the separation between their spirits is negligible compared to the former example. When looked at in this way, one of the traditional "proofs" of marriage's viability falls flat immediately: two people sharing a house and bedroom for the rest of their days doesn't mean they have found anything close to love.

There's a good chance you have personal experience of the value of distance. During the 2020-21 lockdown period, every relationship on the planet experienced added pressure and strain. When our freedom to travel or even leave home was taken away from us, we all quickly realised that the purpose of maintaining distance isn't only to prevent infection. In fact, it is the one feature that keeps relationships from blowing up! For many, circumstances during this time meant having to stay cooped up together as a family unit without breaks or pauses. In many cases, the result wasn't a strengthening of bonds but a huge number of relationships coming to a breaking point. Numerous couples parted ways and divorced, if not during the pandemic itself then shortly afterwards as the courts reopened. This was all the result of us being forcibly confined in our homes – the space between lovers, something we ordinarily take for granted or never saw as significant, was removed. The habitual act of leaving your loved one for eight hours of each day for work or pleasure turned out to be the very thing that makes relationships endure and keeps the flame of attraction alive.

Though there is no panacea when it comes to romance (other than love itself), I most certainly endorse distance as a remedy for a fading love life and a way to protect a blooming one. Still, we have to acknowledge that, during lockdown, some relationships thrived and deepened while others disintegrated. A relationship can indeed survive and even flourish without frequently spending time apart. However, such a bond is an indication that two individuals have acquired the ability to curb their egos. It is for this reason they don't feel the need to win every romantic battle in the ongoing war that is love. Their ego still exists in the background, as nobody becomes truly egoless short of achieving enlightenment, but they recognise the false self's voice and ignore it whenever prudent. When we experience love in these resplendent moments, we briefly become an egoless zero, a nobody, and obtain a glimpse of the next stage in human evolution. Instead of fighting to stake our claim and defend our case every day, instead of being mired in partialities and preferences about how our beloved should be, we lose the only part of us which leads us into altercations.

Until we're ready for that state of being, though, we need to shed some light on the times we come together and share our physical space as one: while we cook, eat, live, sleep, and enjoy a common existence together. I'd like to point out how we can create more space between us, thus enriching our attraction for

The value of distance

each other even while living under the same roof; we'll get to that in the following section. The value we assign to our personal space is nothing more or less than a mark of one's individuality – neither arbitrary nor, by itself, harmful. It still means that relationships will inevitably experience frustration as a result of elbow room being too scarce, but we can do a great deal to reduce this friction if not avoid it altogether. This idea seems so obvious in retrospect, one wonders why more couples don't practise this deliberately.

So many people complain about how exasperated they get because of spending too much time with their partners – you'd think there's something wrong with their relationships! This only happens because people try to pursue some kind of fairytale romance instead of listening to their hearts. Allowing distance should be seen as the hallmark of making love work. In today's world, space is palpably the missing ingredient in almost every marriage, not to mention its lack being the most common reason for two people either coexisting unhappily or ending up divorcing.

At the moment we think we've fallen in love, we want to be in each other's space constantly, oblivious to what we are actually sacrificing for the desire to share every waking minute. Still, this is quite acceptable as long as you don't ruin a budding romance by overstaying your welcome. Just recognise the verbal and other cues that it's time to postpone the fun for another day, listen to each other, and pull away despite the magnetic passion that draws you together. Coming apart and checking in with your own individuality, temporarily forgetting about your lover, is as meaningful as the times you jump into bed and make love. Spending time alone is a tactful move, not a prelude to splitting up, in every stage of a romantic relationship. Since love resembles war in so many ways, consider how soldiers and armies spend much more time manoeuvring and resting than fighting. This tactic mustn't be misread as "playing hard to get" or anything like those kinds of silly mind games. While we've all heard tons of relationship advice about capriciously withdrawing in order to make yourself more attractive, this is manipulative emotional trickery. Coming apart must always be a mutually shared occasion, allowing you both to heal, refresh, and finally reconnect with a flash of love like you felt the first time, every time you see each other.

If your relationship is in a challenging phase right now (assuming you haven't been totally neglecting each other), attempting to spend more time together isn't always the best solution. Instead of indulging this knee-jerk reaction, go away on separate holidays, spend time doing something in complete solitude, reflect on one another while being away, allow yourself to feel and remember what you have and, most of all, what you are lacking. Of course, embarking on this kind of uninterrupted contemplation may inspire you to choose another direction. You'll also risk losing your partner while they, too, consider their options. If this happens, it's probably for the best and unavoidable. Though such a realisation may come at the cost of your happiness, at the very least, your feelings and intentions will be authentic and carefully considered when you come back together.

Furthermore, if someone in a relationship asks for a break, this should never be resisted. If you try to talk them out of wanting some time without you, this will only ensure them leaving you for good. Allowing them their space will send them a strong signal that you're worth coming back to. A trial separation is something all relationships should encourage if the need ever surfaces. These may reveal a great solution other than divorce; or if you do end up breaking a time-honoured relationship, you can do so mindfully, without being overwhelmed by temporary emotions. Often, you'll find that you still deeply love and respect each other but simply need space to breathe, a break from the little frustrations that come with sharing a life with the same person every day. Considering the extra time you will have while on a break, you should be inspired to transform yourself, work on self-development, exercise, eat healthily, and embrace change. Alternatively, you could simply enjoy the beauty of being able to just do nothing and relax in your private, silent presence, whereas you would otherwise have to be obedient and answerable for just about everything you do.

The way to do this is to mutually agree on a prearranged span of time. If you're facing hardship, I would suggest pausing your relationship for a minimum of one year or even as long as three years, giving you both time to find your inner peace, happiness and well-being. Allow ample space for each of you to grow in different directions, and remember that permitting such an interval ultimately rests on an unbreakable bond between you that no amount of distance or time will dispel. If you like, you may agree to remain faithful during that period, but respecting monogamy during such a break has more to do with relishing your individual solitude and immersing yourself in your own private energy. On the other hand, having short flings can be equally restorative and healing, reminding you of the intimacy you already share with your spouse. As it turns out, a desire for sexual variety is often something that just needs to be gratified and then let go of so that we can go back to the one and only.

However, returning to one another, while the goal, shouldn't be seen as mandatory. If you manage to mutually arrange a pause in your relationship, it already proves that you have a mature, enduring friendship that stands stronger than that which most married couples enjoy. So, it may well serve you best to remain apart, yet stay deeply intimate, loving friends forever. Whatever happens, this is perhaps the best way to end a relationship without breaking your connection. The option to pause and the privilege of taking a break could even be written into a marriage contract, so that break-ups are dealt with through love and respect, not guilt and pain. Remember: love doesn't have to involve sharing a home or having sex, nor does a relationship require sharing a life. Love is whatever you make of it and every relationship is unique, so don't follow any prescribed script on what a loving connection should be like. You must cultivate and create your own private affair and inspire the world with the splendour you create through your signature union.

Changing how we sleep together

As we begin changing the way we act and express our feelings in a relationship, a new sense of space is cultivated, allowing both partners to reinstate their individuality. Adopting more physical space in an old relationship can be extremely valuable. Why, then, must two people share the same bed, every night and for the rest of their lives? In order to incorporate some distance between you, you can begin by keeping separate bedrooms, allowing you both to enjoy a more restful sleep. Many couples first try this only due to one snoring and are then surprised to find they're happier than ever. I believe a house should have two distinct, individual domains: one for her and the other for him. Each bedroom should reflect the male and female energy, respectively. A wife's bedroom will most likely be soothingly designed and furnished as if she were still a single and available woman, giving off an alluring atmosphere of seduction – the room should capture her as the husband will always remember her from their first meeting. Something similar applies to the husband's corner of the house: his room should exude masculinity, so when she enters his bed, she automatically feels comforted and excited by his fragrance and bold accents – she, too must be kept as intrigued by his energy as she was in the early days. While this is a perfectly valid approach to interior design, it's rarely put into practice. In any average married home, all these intimate details are somehow lost into oblivion, diluted by competing influences, yet it is periodic immersion in these qualities that keep our counterparts attractive and enigmatic and prevent us from becoming bored with each other.

In fact, I would suggest you retain separate homes, if you can, even after marriage. This is because all relationships start out with something resembling love in the early years and then, little by little, it begins to disappear. Have you ever wondered why? At first, you had something without even trying, then it gradually starts to slip away as soon as you try to hold on to it. I can assure you: the decline of passion has a lot to do with our eagerness to move in together and merge our individuality. While I know it seems like the most exciting thing to do at the time, constantly sharing the same space will cause any relationship to slowly lose its mystery and make each of you less appealing to your partner. Certainly, living together makes for a major financial saving and results in some special, treasured moments. However, having separate homes doesn't mean you can't enjoy all the comforts and pleasures you would have under a single roof: cooking and eating together, sex, entertaining, dancing, or whatever. The advantage of living apart is that you frequently have the chance to break away and keep renewing the relationship's energy. Of course, supporting the cost of two homes isn't always practical, but there are other ways of achieving the same result. For example, couples who are frequently separated by work requirements, in some cases for months at a time, are often called "brave" and "trusting". Really, they just enjoy the benefits of having physical space.

If you can afford it, though, I would suggest retaining both of your living spaces for as long as you can, even over the entire duration of your marriage. Holding on to your own home means you retain your essential detachment and identity, the same qualities which aroused your attraction in the beginning. It also allows the relationship to spread across two physical domains, serving as a formal recognition of each partner's individuality and freedom. Besides, both spouses have somewhere to retreat to if they're not capable of adequately supporting the other at any given moment. You can still share all the typical loving experiences except that, now, your love life will be on another level. She goes to his space and he enjoys her home from time to time, and each occasion remains special. The devoted romantic exchanges you kept up while dating go on while each tends their own garden and preserves their own property just how they like it. Living mostly separate lives doesn't take anything away from loving companionship; instead, it will retain or reawaken what you had in the beginning.

If you can't support two homes, then you should still strive to create the same kinds of boundaries under one roof, by having two separate bedrooms. This will also have a positive influence on any children you may have, demonstrating that space and freedom are natural and essential parts of love. Any concerns about the strength of your relationship will be instantly alleviated at the times you see one another in the parts of the house you share, as your love and connection will be visibly deepened and renewed. Your children learn their attitudes toward life and love primarily from such experiences, so you're benefiting them by pursuing your own happiness.

Sharing a home is, of course, more economical, but so much more can be jeopardised by the act of sharing the same physical space if you both, and your relationship, aren't ready for such a step. Too many people assume that the love will just keep flowing and they'll somehow discover a way to live in total harmony, but this rarely happens outside television shows. The family structure we still cling to today is a worn-out, antiquated system. In past centuries, for instance, children had to experience a tremendous amount of conflict growing up, witnessing every argument and battle between their parents. Divorce and domestic violence run in families; we imitate what we see our parents do however much we try and break the cycle. This is not really anyone's fault: the friction we see in family life is mostly inevitable as parents are placed under a huge amount of strain by living up to the demanding role that is expected of them. When family life can be spread across two homes, or even enjoyed in separate spaces under one roof, children can come to appreciate their father and mother as two separate yet deeply connected individuals. It is only when we have the space and freedom to be ourselves that we display our best qualities. Far too often, we see broken and loveless marriages struggling on for the sake of the children, but what good does this do anyone? If you want to divorce but hesitate because you're afraid of the effect this may have on your children, it is actually concern for their welfare that should inspire you to accept the end of the marriage. Whether there is true love or no affection at all between their parents, children should always enjoy a loving relationship with both. This can't easily happen if you force yourself to live up to a family structure that is only hurting everyone involved.

The way we continue to manage our relationships and marriages is, frankly, a primitive and outdated custom, ready to go the way of the top hat and smoking sections on aeroplanes. In particular, our strained efforts to share every item, every moment, and every room in the same house only serve to rot away the romance that brought a couple together in the first place. Space is often all that's needed to reawaken your love. You will regard the same person in a different light every time you reconnect, seeing their true self as if for the first time instead of falling back on the habitual image, the idealised memory, you've created of them. As your relationship grows and deepens, make sure to conserve the space you both need, as it will really be a major part of what's keeping you close. On those events when you come together, your love will be deepened, while your sexual experiences will also become renewed and elevated.

Wanting space is frequently mistaken for a desire to weaken a relationship, an attempt to begin decoupling from the other person. But the simple truth is that love needs space to breathe and survive. In fact, space is more important than time spent together. Most relationship difficulties can be resolved by creating space rather than jumping straight to divorce and breakup. My idea of a lasting, happy relationship is that two people should share a life in whatever imaginable way they choose, but without psychologically feeling tied to one another. Two people in love should feel innately single and unmarried even while they stand united. This will appear bizarre to you, but it is a pragmatic solution for troubled love relationships that runs far deeper than any conventional relationship advice out there. The value of feeling unattached even while deeply in love with someone is that it appeases your inner flame: freedom.

Individual freedom should not only be regarded as a remedy for a failing relationship but accepted as a matter of course, recognised as the only appropriate way to maintain the connection between you. If I should fall in love again, I will cherish the experience, so much so that I would want to keep it alive by renewing it every day. And I know that this is only possible within a structure that safeguards divergence and individuality even while the two of you share a life, totally in love with one another.

Chapter Eight

Sex as you don't know it

Beyond the pleasures of the flesh

Sex leads us to one another while also leading us astray more often than not, as we never understand its full potential and spiritual power. It is directly tied to the life force that powers not only our physical bodies but also our hearts, minds, and spirits. Our animal instinct is to squander this vital energy in frivolous sexual affairs; however, while sex is certainly enjoyable, it can also become a doorway into another dimension within yourself.

The pleasure and even the creation of life that sex affords us is only the threshold of its potential. There are many kinds of enjoyment and benefits that arise from the meeting of two opposites, though. To women, men will always remain a mystery; to men, women will always be an enigma. Neither can ever completely be understood by the other, we can only learn to love and be loved and delve deeper into the immense sexual magnetism between these two polarities.

We are irrepressibly fascinated with the other half of this universal duality. Regardless of any wilful decision on our part, we are pulled closer to our sexual counterparts, to a place where we can come together as one energy. In the title "Make love, not marriage", "make love" are the operative words. This phrase represents the meeting of two poles, with female as negative and male as positive. These two distinct essences are opposites but also complementary to each other. They each need the other in order to be fulfilled, and that is what creates the sexual attraction within and between us, just like when a magnetic force draws two objects towards each other.

We have all come to know the Taoist principle of "yin and yang" and perhaps also the Hindu concept of "Shiva and Shakti". Both signify the way all opposites converge to create one infinitely creative reality. All that exists does so through the meeting of opposites and, accordingly, the human species endures through the meeting of male and female. This generative union of two poles can be found on every level of creation. Haven't you ever pondered, at one time or another, how exactly the entire universe manages to exist? The whole foundation of reality provides a parallel to how a human being is created: the universe is born out of a kind of sexual interaction between negative and positive particles; this is what sparks the electric tension needed for an atom to exist.

Atoms, as unions of electrically charged opposites, are what constitute our physical universe. The behaviour of all matter arises from these tiny bundles of energy, infinitesimal loops created out of the interaction of positive and negative charges. This means that all observable reality consists of equal, complementary masculine and feminine contributions; at their meeting point, a vibration, is created. Everything we can see is neither solid nor static but really a vibrating assemblage of atoms. You can prove this yourself if you become frozen, still and motionless, in an unthinking state, in utter silence. You can actually see this energetic reality dancing all around you, feeling it at your

Sex as you don't know it

very core. You can even listen to this universal vibration as it happens: your own physical form, the ground which carries it, the walls and ceilings of the house that shelters it, the furniture that comforts it and the air that surrounds us…it is all vibrating. An endlessly oscillating universe also depends on the fact that atoms are actually winking in and out of existence. In other words, this cosmic sexual interplay also implies a continuum of life and death, as each atom goes through an endless loop of creation and destruction. The entire secret to the universe can thus be discerned in its smallest particle.

In more mundane terms, every relationship is initiated by a kind of magnetic pull. At this point, howsoever hard we try to convince ourselves we still have magnetism, marriages mostly extinguish our inner spark. This is the kind of tragedy that results from trying to interfere with the natural order. The ways in which we coexist in marriage slowly but surely evoke a fight over control and authority, which brings us closer to being rivals than fans of one another. Lifelong monogamy will always be a war, but our flawed marital strategy causes both armies to try to annihilate the other instead of merely clashing along their frontiers. Without ever thinking about it, we have killed our innate sensuality, we have lost that original passion, the tenderness and – most importantly – our esteem for each other that was once such an effortless part of the relationship. In this chapter, I will describe a different approach to sex that allows us to enjoy it on a higher plane. This involves reawakening our love lives and sexual experiences, but also becoming able to tap into that breathtaking climactic peak without engaging in physical intercourse and without even needing a partner to copulate with.

Sensuality

Nikola Tesla once famously said: "If you want to find the secrets to the universe, think in terms of energy, frequency and vibration." This is excellent advice, even though he himself couldn't go beyond contemplating the physical world and actually experience life as energy and vibration in the way I just explained. Incidentally, there are many people today seeking enlightenment using some technique or another that assumes it involves stepping beyond this dimension. All the while, they are totally oblivious to what is right in front of them: you are already there, you are always existing in enlightenment! The essential experience of enlightenment relies only on electricity and vibration, and this is the true purpose of sensuality. An awakened person is nothing more or less than a sensual being, a truly intelligent individual has simply mastered the ability to connect with sensations beyond thinking and feeling. They are therefore acutely perceptive and highly sensitive, by which I mean they relate to every experience through energy. Feeling the "energy" of someone or some place has become a phrase we often use flippantly, without ever bothering to define exactly what it entails, as if we vaguely know deep down that something exists beyond thinking and feeling. Love is energy and, in simple terms, energy is electricity. When an intelligent being can feel energy, they instinctively sense how, beneath the solid surface of all objects, there lies an illumination of electrically charged, trembling atoms. When you can sense this buzz, you are in fact feeling love: love is nothing more than experiencing life at its most profound level, at which time it offers us an ascent to a higher plane – love is simply heightened perceptivity.

The general tendency is to think of ourselves as bodies that just happen to have a few higher capacities, but it is more accurate to state we are beings of energy temporarily inhabiting bodies. This realisation is what transcendent sexuality evokes in us, and sexuality is implicit in any interaction where we are electrically attracted to something. Even if this statement makes you feel a little uncomfortable, your "electricity" – your life force – is always sexual in nature. Sexuality provides the fulcrum and leverage that allows us to become totally engaged and conscious. In our moments of greatest arousal, we feel the voltage of life running through us; the sexual pleasure we attain from an orgasm is

Sex as you don't know it

a taste of the divine. If you become truly liberated in your approach to love, if you are willing to completely let go of your inhibitions during your sexual encounters and experience these on a spiritual level, all your illusions about life will be shattered. A lover is essentially a rebel: their consciousness and behaviour cannot be controlled by any social or religious mandate: a lover is an anomaly, a social misfit. The pleasure you can attain through the touch of another human being can lift your spirits so far that you leave your past behind; sex allows you to discard all entrapments.

Love, and the physical act of love, makes you begin to vibrate more intensely. You become more aware of what you really are, which is an electric aura. Every time we become absorbed in anything, it is invariably a sexual experience; we can't deny our sensuality and we only limit ourselves by trying. Whether we adore music, dance, art and paintings, nature, food, people; our relationships with all these and more are experienced as a sexual encounter. If you dive more deeply into any entrancing experience while you are poised in inner stillness, perhaps looking at the moon on a velvet black sky or swimming in the ocean just as the sun descends into the horizon, you will feel the same deepened energy as is felt during an orgasm. We would all be acutely aware of this except for the fact that we can only use thoughts and emotions to communicate with the world. These are wholly inferior to the vivid comprehensiveness of actual experience: thoughts are unreliable, limited, and fearful, and often lead us into making mistakes. When you inhabit your inner space of love, though, you will always sense the electric and vibrational frequency of people, and your intelligence becomes one with whoever you are meeting.

Sensuality is just an electric frequency that resonates with and bolsters our attraction to every tiny detail of life. This means that, when we are sensually heightened, we become awestruck with every moment. This capacity exists in all of us, but is typically buried under mountains of mental and emotional noise: for example, we use our minds to make determinations about a person's goodwill instead of observing their essence directly. By comparison, awareness of the vibrational frequency within us lets us navigate through life with ease. An unwavering "yes, this is for me" or an assured "no, this is not for me" is felt deeply within you no matter the situation confronting you, furnished by a force bigger than thoughts and emotions.

Tantra – a branch of Indian mysticism that scientifically inquires into all aspects of human life through introspection – found parallels to the universe's fundamental laws practically everywhere; one facet of existence these mystics explored thoroughly is sex. When the male and female bodies come together in loving union, if their orgasmic climax is synchronised, that summit contains a divine meeting point. Two bodies become one electric organism, however briefly. In that moment, they both transcend their gender and individuality and become universal energy, which is love itself. Though the experience doesn't last long, we do not exist as an ego during an orgasm but instead touch another dimension within.

In the way we normally go about sex, when we only mate for pleasure, the sexual orgasm is only feeble and fleeting. As a result, sex is something humans continually desire, just so we can relive a tiny glimpse of that mysterious space every time we climax. Lacking any appreciation of the true significance of sex, our desire for it is also very crude, resting on the understanding that copulation is meant only for procreation or recreation. Both of these are valid and purposeful reasons for sleeping with someone. But, however much we desire sex, the reason we like it so much only crystallises when we become totally conscious and meditative during our sexual encounters. When we start to consider sex as an adjunct of love, we come to appreciate it as something more than just a lustful encounter. Accordingly, for those who seek to explore the deeper facets of humanity and life, sex becomes a sacred and spiritual practice: one which can not only heighten our experience of love but also enrich

Sex as you don't know it

our life energy, because sexuality is the supreme expression of our vitality. The orgasm obtained in this way can be compared to enlightenment, but a specific conjunction between masculine and feminine energy is required for that to ever occur.

Through getting in touch with love for ourselves, we begin to revere and practice sex only as an extension of love, not a mechanically self-indulgent act. All newly married couples make love but, after a decade or even much sooner, sex becomes a chore or something like physical exercise, a means to an end, something we do just before sleep. Anticipation and foreplay are given little importance.

The aim of exploring the deeper meaning of sex is not to turn you into a fanatic or nymphomaniac. Sex should never become a compulsion and, the more mindfully you practise sex, the further beyond it you go. Sooner or later, you begin to see past the bodily aspects and even that which most people would consider sexual. This allows you to escape the often-arduous effort of finding someone special and avoid the gymnastics that are necessary to find the orgasmic peak within us. Mystics reach a point in their study of sex where they naturally contain their life energy, which is otherwise lost at the moment of orgasm, within them. This means that this life energy is diverted and turned to higher purposes as opposed to the normal downward outflow during actual sex. Mystics have long learned how to guide their sexual life force upwards along the spine, channelling the energy of orgasm through their chakras, entailing an enlightenment that I can only refer to as the real orgasm.

There are, of course, people who try to emulate this mastery of sexual desire due to ill-conceived religious ideals. While they may fool others into thinking they are celibate, and may in fact physically refrain from sex, they are invariably in internal turmoil. Celibacy is not something that can be forced into being: it arises by itself without one's control or desire to give up sex. Celibacy is not something to applaud or even to work towards, as the effort is futile unless you have come to a comprehensive, spiritual understanding of love in all its facets. We should continue to enjoy sex as and when the passion arises, because abstinence is counterproductive and repressing the sexual impulse has more negative effects than we care to know. Specifically, repressed sexual desire does not leave you, nor is it transmuted into higher forms of life force; instead, it manifests in the mind in other ways, many of which can only be considered harmful and perverted.

The union of masculine and feminine

It is easy, on a somewhat mundane level, to understand the union of masculine and feminine as something that involves two different persons. However, in the search for love, the first meeting of these principles must always be made internally. On the surface, we are born as a member of either the male or female gender; that is clear. But inside, we are a compound of two aspects; we each have both masculine and feminine qualities. You could say that this is because both man and woman have contributed equally to your making, and their complementary characteristics continue on in you. Masculine and feminine cannot exist without one another, each contributes to every human's life regardless of what sex they are, and these two polarities are equally integral to human culture. Sadly, we have always lived in a world that has been dominated and even monopolised by masculinity, and that is one reason why human culture is so wracked with division and conflict. Because mankind's physical strength once allowed it to rule over womenkind (and the traditions based on this fact continue to endure), men have always managed to control and govern society in all matters. As a first step towards healing the world we live in, we have to recognise that both qualities have a purpose and are required in equal measure. Still, as much as the world desperately needs women to rise and take their rightful place, the real solution lies much deeper.

The problem doesn't result from having too many men in positions of power. Rather, the bigger issue is that men are excessively masculine, and women are inordinately feminine! The way to balance things out and allow us all to live in harmony has nothing to do with gender hiring quotas; if men would simply embrace their feminine side, the way they live and treat women would be completely transformed. Femininity is not strictly related to what genitalia you have, nor is it only found in womenkind: it is a form of greatness that exists within all of us. In fact, the universal energy (or Para Shakti as it is referred to in ancient mysticism) is itself feminine. Finding it is only a matter of gazing inwards, looking beyond the gender you were born with. In that mysterious place, you will see how you are an assemblage of both masculine and feminine. At the same time, the more deeply you descend within, you will become ever more aware of a dimension beyond gender and indeed the physical. What we find there is love, and when we've touched that core within us, a man will be more feminine and a woman will be better able to call on her masculine side when needed.

Love is like the unification of two hemispheres within you. While you should never be in doubt as to what primary gender you were born with, you can't neglect your other, more veiled half. If we don't find a place within us that helps us to think beyond our genitals' biases, we will only ever understand one part of our being, leaving us divided and incomplete. I am a heterosexual male, but my personality would be utterly warped if I didn't acknowledge both genders within me. I display broadly masculine characteristics only because my perceptions and behaviour are complemented by my inner femininity. Because of that, I'm aware that I am highly sensitive, emotional, empathic and patient – supposedly female traits which every man would do well to learn. For instance, I never feel awkward or alienated around women, while many of my male brethren come over as either arrogant or shy.

This inner union of both our masculine and feminine aspects creates a deep fulfilment, precisely because they create a completion within us. In the field of romance, as long as a human is divided, they typically remain stuck in the same pattern, forever searching externally for their counterpart, their soulmate, the one who's expected to redeem their deficiencies. This leaves them romantically powerless and unable to resist their sexual impulses, wherever these may lead them. This unfortunate behaviour isn't the result of them all being sex addicts but because they are vaguely aware of a deeply spiritual absence at the very root of their being. When a man cannot perceive his inner femininity or a woman refuses to recognise her masculinity, it's inevitable that they will search for this missing piece in the world outside themselves. In fact, even when we're perfectly in tune with our inner mirror image, the reason we desire sex is still because we all intensely desire to be whole. You've no doubt heard the adage "opposites attract": extroverts inevitably date introverts, analytical thinkers are always attracted to more empathetic personalities, and someone who's always prepared can't help but end up with a free spirit. These combinations work because they close a circle of energy deep within us. When two people make love, their inner circuit is complete, and both gender halves dissolve into each other. When you unite in sexual congress with another person, you are no longer a polarity: you have transcended all divisions, you are neither man nor woman, you have become the indivisible, which is love itself. Love is both all and nothing, it is the completion of a whole and the elimination of boundaries. The common expression, of course, is "to make love" but, on these occasions, it is more accurate to say you "become love". When the two sexes meld into each other, it means that love transcends all dualities, as love unifies. We can say then that sex, in its spiritual aspect, is the ability to "become love" through communion with the opposite sex.

However, love for ourselves already affords us a kind of completion. It allows a limited though entirely authentic union of masculine and feminine energies without the need to find your soulmate. Because self-love is itself a divine relationship, it implies an inner meeting of the male and female principles. When you have made friends with both polarities within you, the magnetic force you exert on others is enhanced, making you more attractive. Most of us have experienced something similar when we are in relationships: we attract more attention compared to when we are single and available, because our normal excess of male or female energy has been reconciled by its complement found in our partner. Observe carefully the next time you meet anyone you're immediately attracted to or inspired by: if you look closely, they tend to be individuals who don't represent any one gender utterly but are embodiments of both. This is, of course, very subtle, like when a woman is beautiful, gentle and quintessentially womanly, but also has a powerfully confident presence and a strong desire to prove herself. Conversely, when a man is characteristically manly but also unassuming, emotional and sensitive, others immediately see him as much more approachable. Wouldn't you naturally be interested in one or the other? The only sensible approach to becoming a magnet for someone new or reigniting your present lover's attraction is to integrate your two inner halves. When we are no longer divided, when we are made whole, the inner circuit is complete and you'll feel a strange sense of balance and power. This inner union makes us better lovers and more desirable sexual partners.

A man should allow himself to delve into his opposite side, normally hidden deep within him, just as a woman ought to let her masculine qualities come to the fore. Men must focus on making traditionally feminine qualities, like patience, submissiveness, sensitivity, and compassion, part of their being. Woman, embracing their masculinity, have to temper their normal intuitiveness with reason, their patience with an inclination to action, and their trust with scepticism. There are, of course, cases in which a person has drifted too far into their own antithesis. A woman's masculine energy may end up eclipsing her femininity; a man may lose touch with his gender's natural virtues. The important thing is to not have more of one than the other. Our ever-developing nature must include a harmonious balance of both masculinity and femininity because this is what makes us whole. Once we've accomplished this, we're able to switch between our divergent roles smoothly and with ease. Every day, there are times when a man behaves in a feminine manner, just like some situations demand that a woman act more masculinely. Even in our romantic relationships, we unknowingly switch roles from time to time. This allows us to understand and complement each other and also gives your lover the chance to counteract your imbalances.

Though our physical distinctions are important in our eyes, especially where sex is concerned, there is really very little difference between a man and a woman. In fact, the divergence is so minor that doctors can transform a man into a woman (or vice versa) simply by altering a person's hormonal system and performing surgery. However, nobody is inherently male or female; our spirits encompass both. Regardless of the existence of such extreme procedures for discovering your gender counterpoint, almost all of us relate to life according to the role assigned to us by our genitals. Nonetheless, a human being is a complex amalgamation of both sexes. If this were not so, we simply couldn't function, as this dualistic formation is part of the bedrock of nature itself.

Many of the problems that crop up in our relationships, romantic and otherwise, occur because men exaggerate while playing what they perceive to be the male role and women try to portray impossible paragons of femininity. This inevitably leads to internal clashes because we're unable to understand or accept our internal opposite. Instead, men are comfortable around their male friends and women generally feel more relaxed with the girls because, in these contexts, there is no division or friction between sexes, there is a special oneness and ease of communication. But in order to be part of a happy relationship between sexes, to experience and demonstrate love, we have to bridge the divergence between male and female within ourselves. This is complicated somewhat by the fact that

Sex as you don't know it

the mind is considered masculine: aggressive, proactive, and judgmental. The heart, by contrast, is seen as feminine because it is receptive, inclusive, and patient. In order to become who you are meant to be, these two must merge into one: both your thoughts and feelings have to work in harmony. This inner marriage of your inner man and woman will empower you to better understand the proper roles of your heart and head and, in time, become one with your lover in a way that transcends gender. This is where you will find true friendship and empathy: where your lover not only complements your being but your two inner halves support each other.

Observe your character more closely, either in meditation or as you go about your day: are you using all the faculties that are available to you, or are you limited to playing one gender role because you believe it's what's expected? If you're a man, are you sufficiently in touch with your emotions and subtler feelings to caress a woman when she needs your support; are you sensitive enough to cry when you feel deeply emotional? If you're a woman, are you also brave enough to feel secure in the world without a man to protect you; can you make snap judgments in an emergency without consulting your feelings? Before we make a start on forging a love connection with our ideal match, we should all first seek to know what is happening within us. Finding love is always primarily a matter of finding yourself by going inwards and bridging the union of masculine and feminine. Connecting with a soulmate can only come later.

Personally, I find speaking to women to be something of a spiritual experience as all women, without exception, are emotionally deeper and more sensitive creatures compared to men, many of whom are almost spiritually disabled. I can spend hours in the company of women as they discuss the finer, subtler details of life. It is common for women to bemoan the fact that men lack sensitivity and emotional intelligence;

women, above all things, just need to be heard. It is dull and crass for a man to intrude into a woman's space and praise her beauty, assuming that his attentions are welcome. However, when a man has the patience to find out how a woman's mind works, when he perseveres in the effort to touch the very core of her heart and soul, he pays her a high compliment. Because some women rarely, if ever, find someone who has the poise and patience to genuinely connect with them and appreciate them for their inner beauty, any man who makes the effort and displays awareness of his inner femininity becomes highly attractive. Once a man knows his inner woman, he transforms into the man that all women want.

Most importantly, you need to open your mind to the fact that there exists a kind of loophole in love, an opportunity to experience it that does not even have to involve another person. Nature has imparted all the faculties and tools each of us needs to experience happiness and love while remaining alone, without requiring anyone else to fulfil us. Consequently, on account of this inner union, we can even transcend the desire for sex. This doesn't necessarily mean becoming celibate or sexually impotent; instead, realising your inner union of male and female makes you completely free. You see, as a result of our attachment to everything in life that affords us pleasure, we run the risk of unknowingly becoming victims of that pleasure. However, liberating yourself from the urge to copulate by finding the inner balance between the two gender polarities within you makes it impossible for anyone to control you. Neither possessive relationships nor an obsession with sex will have any sway over you. This release affords incredible levity yet, ironically, finding self-love also makes us considerably more attractive to others, just in case you should ever decide to abandon a solitary existence. There is the capacity within you for an unending orgasmic experience, and such a peak can only be described as the greatest possible love affair because it involves you being in a relationship with the entire cosmos.

Sex as you don't know it

Head and heart

The head is masculine while the heart is feminine, so men tend to be somewhat calculating and women's motivations are more likely to stem from emotion. This is one reason why there is always misalignment in a relationship when partners haven't discovered the inner counterpart to their natural gender. Men think cerebrally about embarking on a relationship but, for women, relationships start in the heart. Men are, by and large, the pursuers and initiators of relationships. A woman usually welcomes a man taking on this role but, beneath his mannerly and polite facade, this approach is somewhat aggressive. Males are simply more assertive, as their instincts derive from their minds and not their hearts – stunningly, they're completely oblivious to this limitation!

When we scratch the surface of the mind, we find we are no different to animals. One of the functions of sex is to remind us of our animalistic nature: sex can only be aggressive, while love is accepting. When you are sexually attracted to someone, you can feel the beast in you come to life; this is the nature of lust, it compels us to want and possess, it is as primal as hunger or fear. Lust can be a frightening thing, but it mustn't be repressed: by embracing sexual desire, we can use it as a stepping stone to the place where love dwells, and I promise you that the view from there is magnificent.

A man will happily expend effort and money (often more than he actually can afford) to impress and delight his crush, but he is doing so mostly to win the prize of sex. Imagine a man approaching a girl he'd never met and telling her that he finds her attractive and would like to have sex with her sometime in the near future, skipping the usual weeks or months of courtship. He would almost certainly be considered rude and shameless because he hasn't fulfilled the customary obligations and performed the expected mating dance. I want you to be perfectly candid with yourself, though: is there any compelling difference between him and the guy who takes a girl on a journey into a fantasy land before he jumps into bed with her? Social norms aside, the first guy is at least honest.

This is why men often lose interest immediately after a sexual relationship has run its course and the initial passion has evaporated. The real kicker is that they don't even know why they're no longer attracted to the woman who seemed so alluring before. Men who aren't prone to introspection mostly begin a relationship for what they believe to be the right reasons – they've gone through the motions of romance, so their intentions must be pure, right? – but are rarely able to see it through to anything meaningful. As long as he is using only his head and not his heart, his mind cannot conceive of anything more significant than sex. He can honestly say the right things and sincerely act in a way that appears loving, but it's never wholly genuine or real because he was never acting from his heart.

The affection we simulate in our romantic meetups exists only so that both parties involved can make-believe that the relationship isn't all about sex when both of them know they are being driven by lust. Yet this charade, far from being a pointless waste of energy, is of fundamental importance. Think about it: before we engage in sexual intercourse, the verbal component of our foreplay is the only real difference from animals' pre-mating behaviour. The social aspect of the human mating dance – a process that starts well before anyone starts to take their clothes off – took nature millions of years of evolution to craft, and it is the yardstick by which we should measure the value of all our sexual encounters. Consider this: the longer a relationship lasts, the less important foreplay becomes. Then, one day, mostly out of boredom, we decide to kill the romantic aspect of the relationship entirely and get married; only then, after a few years, does sex become lifeless and robotic because foreplay has ceased to be a factor. Nor, for that matter, do we pay much attention to afterplay: once the job is done, both roll over to their side of the bed and go to sleep. Bish bosh bash!

The importance of foreplay

Let's be clear: the human brain is our principal sexual organ. Therefore, foreplay doesn't relate only to physical touch, though that part of the sexual dance is of course incredibly meaningful. For now, I want to focus on the kind of foreplay we engage in long before we've gotten anywhere near the bedroom, something we recognise as a kind of game we play not for physical pleasure but for our mutual emotional and mental amusement. It's a kind of theatre of the alluring that sets the stage for what follows and, more importantly, sharpens our anticipation and excitement to a fine edge. If you're in a long-standing relationship, I want to inspire you to reawaken the mystery and intrigue that was once there but may have gotten lost along the way. If you're in a marriage that's gone past a certain point, after which sex becomes a humdrum, short-lived event you only commit to an hour before you both go to sleep, then you have to break free of this cycle. Aside from containing an element of casual spontaneity, sex should also be intentional, cast in the shape of a seductive theme. Both of you should anticipate being physically together with great patience and expectancy, infusing the moment with the same forethought and vitality you once reserved for each other. We need to enhance the anticipation and savour the experience – if this takes time, so be it.

In matters of sex, quality rules over quantity. If your erotic experiences have become lacklustre, try making love only once a week or maybe even as infrequently as once per fortnight. "Making love" is something to be celebrated wholeheartedly and allowing ample time to help your anticipation build means it will be worth waiting for. When sex is not respected enough, on the other hand, it becomes something rushed and routine, often lacking true pleasure's essential prerequisites: physical foreplay and deep emotional contact. That is why, by making these precious moments scarce, we increase their value and learn to honour this time as something deeply sacred. Circle a date in your calendar, set a whole day aside just for the two of you, so that you mentally anticipate the event. Each of these occasions is about truly being together, so plan something as simple or elaborate as suits you. Perhaps you'd both like to spend time around the house gardening, cook something interesting together, take a short road trip to the countryside, or have a picnic in a scenic spot. These dates needn't involve a lot of expense or be weighed down with frills; excessive gaudiness will only get in the way of the natural simplicity of making love. Even if you do plan something special, the occasion should be something effortless, organic and within your financial means, so it can be repeated often without burdening your minds with worry. The point of spending an entire day together before you make love is that this allows you ample time to reconnect and rediscover one another without unnecessary distractions. Sensuality can be interweaved into every moment of your shared, special day; all your actions, your carefree interactions, and your dialogue are all part of the foreplay.

If you're married, you can take off your rings, symbolically removing your sense of being entitled to the other's body, so that you are obliged to seduce each other again, as strangers would. This isn't about role-playing, though: all that's needed is to be yourself yet remain an undiscovered country. To keep your sex life alive and your relationship vital, we must preserve the enigma. Spouses all begin as strangers. Even after living under the same roof for years, though, you should continue to honour the stranger who arrived in your life once upon a time. Knowing all there is to know about someone is impossible in any case; each of us contains additional mysteries to be unearthed and revered. We are never meant to be understood, only loved, and love, when it is pure, is what takes us into the labyrinth of another person's being – it has no other reason or rationale for existing. Sexual attraction, in its rawest state, is when our eyes land on something new and desirable. After all, we often can't help where our eyes take us when they sneak a peek at someone tempting. We must play by the rules of

Sex as you don't know it

nature and keep finding new ways to look at our partner. As soon as the mystery has died, the relationship and its passion die with it!

Alcohol

Whatever you decide to do on these special days, though, I implore you not to drink alcohol, a drug many people resort to in order to relax or somehow improve the experience. Aside from booze being largely incompatible with any kind of spiritual life, your relationship, your crucial attempt to seek out what love truly is, should be respected as sacred. Love does not need alcohol to intensify its splendour. Getting tipsy, as people tend to do on first dates to help break the ice, is a false high, a counterfeit love. It's for people who don't really like themselves sober. It also impairs your ability to gauge a person's credibility. The sensation of joy that alcohol offers you is not enduring or even real. Drinking even the smallest amount of alcohol taints the laughter, the elevated mood and confidence, the feelings of affection, and even the resulting expressions of love, thereby ruining your memories of these special days.

If you want to sample deep intimacy, then don't drink while you are together. Alcohol is a poison, not a reliable way of having fun on every social occasion, as I know from personal experience. The bitter truth is that we drink alcohol because we don't know how to be happy, we abuse it because we don't feel love. Alcohol, like any other drug, allows us to briefly escape reality and forget our miseries. A glass of wine seems much less romantic when viewed in this light. I'm not insisting that you stop drinking altogether, but do please avoid it whenever you are with your lover, as your time together is too valuable to spend with your senses dulled. Worse, drinking as a couple can easily become a pernicious habit, leading you to think you can only be intimate and affectionate to each other while intoxicated.

Love can easily be described as a drug, the ultimate high, one which no other drug can rival. This is why I don't drink: because I am now perpetually drunk, I am continually high because love provides me with overflowing ecstasy. The widespread, socially acceptable dependence on alcohol is the most certain proof that we haven't found love nor know what happiness feels like. Anyone who has discovered self-love and enjoys a loving relationship with life by being intensely connected to each moment does not need to drink or take drugs, though they can easily be mistaken for being stoned. For such a person, existence itself has become a drug and every one of their experiences is a song and dance. In other words, by abstaining from drinking, you will invite a new atmosphere into your relationship. If what you thought you had while being tipsy together turns out to be false, trying to connect while completely sober will be an awkward, but necessary, dose of cold reality. Alternatively, you will discover a deeper, more authentic sense of intimacy you never could have attained otherwise.

Use other means to beguile each other instead. Play enticing music, dress provocatively, apply evocative scents, and serve snacks you both find sensual. Above all, be genuine: think about what you'll say before you open your mouth, be attentive when your lover is speaking, consider every word between you to be a part of your dance. All this takes a lot of effort and it probably makes a major change from how you normally spend time together, but this is all to the good. If your relationship is stagnating, it's time to explore beyond the beaten path, so leave yesterday behind and embrace a new reality. Break free from your habits and comfort zone so that you can get in touch with a lover deep within you, a part of yourself you've never met before.

Silent foreplay

I'd like to suggest an unusual method for helping two lovers connect on a deeper level. Though the words you speak to

Sex as you don't know it

each other matter a great deal, in this case, the depth arises from silence. Words are of the head, influenced by the heart, but spiritual love is a silent entity. Above and beyond the hugs, kisses, and genteel words, silence is the direct path to knowing and experiencing love. This method is not the only way to forge a tender connection, and it will not be suited for every duo, but I trust you can come to appreciate at least some of its merits.

The origin of this exercise is that I knew two couples who had been together for eight and fourteen years respectively. Both married pairs still loved one another but were having frequent fights, something which had also affected their sex lives. Given that each couple had known each other for so long and had shared so many experiences together, it was no surprise that their familiarity had gradually removed all the magic they had once taken for granted.

It was time these two couples came together in a new way, using a method they had never tried before, and this was the sharing of silence. I asked both to try an exercise which they found a little weird at first, promising an experience that would permit them to harmonise on a level beyond language. In principle, it's simple: spend a day together without using language as a means of communication. With a little practice, it's easy enough to be silent while you're alone, muting your thoughts as an aid to deeper introspection. Being silent while in the company of someone you care for is quite a novel experience, though. Now, this will probably be difficult if you're in a new relationship, simply because it often takes people years to find a silent, comfortable contentment around another. In such a case, and in fact even if you thought you knew each other perfectly, it takes a certain amount of effort and patience. Doing this successfully will require you to dig deep and unearth your true commitment to each other. The rewards are great, though, as this exercise will be just as therapeutic for each of you on an individual level as it will benefit your relationship.

Each couple spent a day, from the moment they woke up to the moment they closed their eyes, in total silence. As an additional hurdle, the plan included having to do a practical task, which required them to work as a team, at a job that would have been easy had words been allowed. Remember: all this isn't a game but rather a form of foreplay. Approaching it sincerely and diligently, with an open mind, will lead to the two of you making love on a super-conscious level. If you have children or the phone rings, you can interact with these people as normal, but no dialogue can take place between you and your partner. One thing this teaches you is that you can indeed share a space without annoying each other. You see, words are the weapons we often use to subtly control, undermine, and hurt others. Now, for one day, we are laying those arms down, declaring a ceasefire, and sampling a new form of dialogue. Typically, silence in a relationship is itself a weapon. We are all far too familiar with "the silent treatment" we often suffer or inflict after having an argument. So we know the drill; it's not as if we've never sampled being silent together! But, this time, we're going to make a surprising discovery: silence can also be practised in total love, peace, and togetherness.

Besides, when you know someone thoroughly, there is often nothing more to talk about other than mundane events. Why not instead enjoy each other's energy without saying anything? Feeling uneasy during spells of silence means we're not entirely comfortable in each other's company, so we talk all kinds of nonsense just to fill those gaps. Soon, our dialogue becomes a bland repetition of what we said yesterday, when each word we say to our lover should really be meaningful. Learning to remain wordless and in a state of inner peace, without feeling uncomfortable or self-conscious because the person closest to you is present, is an emotional breakthrough on a personal level. If you can achieve this in tandem, you will have made love without even touching. If, at first, you can't manage going the whole day in silence, try the exercise for an hour or two at a time and increase the length on each occasion. What makes this harder is that, by shutting down your vocal cords, you will inescapably each turn to your own thoughts to keep you company, so at first you will both retreat into your own minds. No doubt, you'll be questioning the absurdity of this game and evaluating every detail of your partner's behaviour. Still, thoughts are just a dialogue with yourself. If you persist in staying speechless and simply begin watching your thoughts, you'll notice how insane and disjointed they all are. Once you come to this realisation – and uncover the important truth that you are actually an entity separate from your thoughts – you will begin to experience a sense of relief at not being controlled by them any longer. Don't try to force your mind to shut up; instead, just allow your thoughts to be. They will, in their own time, begin to disappear, leaving you alone and at peace in the company of your beloved.

When you set yourself a task to do together in silence, don't choose something that requires you to ask questions – crosswords are out, but building a jigsaw puzzle, gardening, painting a picture together, or cooking an unfamiliar recipe might be fun. You will come to understand how things can be done as a duo without resorting to words: soon, movement becomes a dance in which each partner knows the other's next step. Just be in flow with one another and refrain from criticising with frowns or the like; instead, pay close attention to what your lover is doing. If you want to withdraw from whatever you're busy with for a moment, your lover can simply notice this, acknowledge and respect what you're doing. If they like, they can follow along, allowing you both to be in touch on a deeper sensual level. With practice, you'll learn that you don't always need to communicate in words but can be in sync in a more visceral way. In fact, the purpose of this exercise is to heighten all your senses, drawing you closer together into a deep sensuality, with the aim of building up the tension required for making love.

Be aware: your mind will continue to dissuade you from persevering, questioning the validity of this method. This is, in fact, a sign that it's working, so you must ignore your thoughts, carry on, have faith in the goal, and trust that the positive effects of this exercise are worth the discomfort. Slowly and surely, you will discover a new convergence between the two of you like you've never experienced before, a sense of comfort that you had never realised could exist between two people. This moment can be compared to the sun abruptly breaking through on a cloudy day. Even while a couple is together, each partner should feel as if they are self-sufficiently alone, but this sense of seclusion is actually bolstered by melting into each other's energy. You'll know you've succeeded when you're not aware of your lover's presence nor even your own, but only observe the flow of an experience that's shared by you both. You see, as you each descend into your own individual silence while being together, you each come to lose your sense of "I am" as your egos dissipate. Suddenly, there will no longer be any separation between the two of you, as this will be replaced by a deep oneness. This is the highest form of connection, well beyond poetry or anything that can be accomplished by words; this is love.

As you refrain from speaking and thinking and indeed withdraw from your surface feelings, you will gradually become the experiencer and not the experience. This is actually the phenomenon this exercise is intended to let you sample: that of becoming a passive witness, as you would in meditation. It will seem like you've taken on the role of a third person in the room, viewing two people as they go about their business, without getting involved. This is a mode of perception that can only be known by living it; there are no words to adequately describe the nature of the mysterious encounter that awaits you both.

In future, the awkward silences that you otherwise rush to fill with pointless chatter will now become spaces in which you can both find not only individual peace but also a deeper connection. Silence is a precious medium, a bridge to connect with others and the world around us on a much deeper level; words only mask what it can reveal. Love blooms in this wordless space, but

Sex as you don't know it

we first have to become deeply sensitive in order to understand the subtle language of silence.

In case you don't yet feel up to spending a whole day with your partner in silence, another great technique you can try is to prepare for foreplay by centring yourself through meditation, spending the day in your own solitude, aiming to achieve a deep silence. Then, in the evening, come together in heightened awareness and radiating inner peace. In a sense, this solo method mirrors that described above, though it's not quite as effective at building a connection.

Meditation is a method of purifying and cleansing your being, it is the perfect preparation for accepting your beloved in your arms in a more profoundly sexual way. Light some candles, infuse the room with incense, make love in front of an open fire, create a sense of drama as if you are both ancient royalty, and elevate the shared occasion in whatever way you choose. You two are the most important people in the world. However you decide to spend your day, whether you choose to pass this time in dialogue or in silence, make sure it is a thing of beauty.

Orgasm

Orgasm is not, strictly speaking, restricted to the pleasurable moment that culminates sexual intercourse. Orgasm is a process that starts long before that, thus broadening the experience and enhancing the eventual climax. A woman may begin building up to her orgasm before a man has even touched her; her orgasm is naturally a prolonged and patient affair, grounded largely on her inner, deeper senses. Men, by contrast, are underdeveloped when it comes to sex. For them, sex is still an animal act, too fast and mostly furious. This is partly because the male attitude to sex arises from his mind, where it is seen as aggressive, kind of an onslaught even though it's overlaid with kindness. Men's instinctive approach to sex is all about speed and rushing to the desired outcome, often without caring or even realising that a woman's orgasm operates according to a completely different mechanism. Because of this discrepancy in timing, men tend to be selfish in sexual encounters, because they don't think in terms of savouring and slowing the whole process down enough for the women even to be fully ready for intercourse. Though foreplay occurs largely in the mind, the physical stage should not be overlooked: men mostly enter much too early. A man usually has only one shot at an orgasm, after which he has to rest before continuing. A woman, however, can have several during a single encounter, so men should pay attention to the importance of climaxing together – something that leaves both partners satisfied.

An additional difference between the sexes is that men are aroused by what they see and women by what they feel, physically as well as in the heart. These two senses impinge on our consciousness in completely different ways. It also explains why men invariably have their eyes open while making love and prefer the lights being left on; women instinctively keep their eyes closed so they can direct their attention inwards, where their experience is heightened.

Now, you may be surprised to learn that some men have never had a real orgasm! The confusion arises because orgasm has long been conflated with ejaculation, but while ejaculation is a soothing experience and provides essential physical relief, it is a very shallow and unsatisfying thing when compared to an orgasm. An ejaculation is only a physical phenomenon: moderately enjoyable, but not the real deal. A real orgasm can – and should – occur on multiple levels of your being, not just the body. A simple ejaculation doesn't arouse a man's centre, it hasn't made him transcend his mind and body. Ejaculation without orgasm is just a release; I would go so far as to say that making love just to ejaculate is a complete waste of effort. Moreover, ejaculation, either as masturbation or meaningless sex, is a waste of a man's precious life force: men lose huge amounts

Sex as you don't know it

of energy every time they experience one of these counterfeit orgasms.

In times past, everything in life took a long time, so patience was something people developed naturally. Today, we're all about instant gratification, but you should understand that some things just can't be rushed. We must seek to apply more of the critical virtue of patience in all our sexual connections. We have to re-learn how to savour the experience instead of rushing to its conclusion. There are, of course, occasions when sex must be brief for the sake of not having the time – spontaneous sex is often hurried, though briefness certainly affords its own kind of pleasure. Nevertheless, we should also schedule times and even entire days during which sex is not just limited to the bedroom or the actual act of penetration: sensuality must be part of every action in the lead-up to the physical stage of copulation. Only after a peak of passion has been generated, after hours of sexual tension and resistance, should we finally get to touch each other. By then, the passion between you is experienced as electricity, not just bodily need. Accordingly, allow your hands to become your eyes and feel the sculpture of your partner's body with great reverence, as if it's the first and only body you will ever admire, gently applying both strength and softness, massaging your fingers along their spine, neck, arms and legs until they surrender to a state of deep relaxation.

I am not suggesting a massage as such; this is merely an intimate way of caressing someone. A man should take the time to prepare a woman before he enters her because, the longer the foreplay, the greater the chance of climaxing together. Otherwise, the mismatched male and female tempos will not coincide. Finally, when the moment draws near, the women should lead from that point on. Taking position on top allows her to control the rhythm, thus making the man hold out longer in order for her to climax along with him. Too often, it's the case that the man climaxes too quickly, leaving the woman far behind and only half-finished. By then, his energy is lost and he will be too drained to satisfy her any further. The attempt to reach the final stage of orgasm together is all about being selfless, because a climax experienced in unison becomes a magnificent achievement in which you both find a deep synchronicity. This moment is incredibly special and allows one to know what it truly means to make love.

Women, both in and out of long-term relationships, have been forced to become accustomed to never experiencing a climax. They mostly have to be content with the build-up, sensing bliss approaching but rarely experiencing it. For that matter, most men also don't get to sample it, mistaking ejaculation for orgasm. In reality, an orgasm only occurs when your whole body becomes a sexual organ. The sensation is not confined only to the genitals but becomes a dynamic experience felt in every cell of your body; your entire anatomy quivers from head to toes as you submit completely to an overwhelming surge of energy. For precious moments, you are left in utter bafflement and speechlessness, caught in an abyss of your own serenity. The healing effects of this cosmic splendour have been proven many times over. A sense of peace and relaxation transpires after an authentic orgasm that confirms that the hours of build-up and anticipation were worth the effort. A mundane, uninspired ejaculation, by comparison, leaves a man with a hint of having been cheated because the end never lives up to his anticipation, while women are typically only partially satisfied.

Bad sex or, to be more exact, sexual incompatibility has ended many a relationship; in other cases, it sadly goes unquestioned. A mutually fulfilling sex life can keep a relationship going for a lifetime. Superconscious sex, however, will propel you both to a marvellous new level of connection, to a newfound levity. Experiencing shared orgasms should be the norm in any relationship, though it doesn't matter all that much if you never achieve these. It's worth the effort of at least trying. At the very least, laying the groundwork is a source of enormous fun and playfulness. An orgasm involves your whole being: mind, body and spirit, and only then does it become sacred. Sex becomes

Sex as you don't know it

a meditation, a worshipping of each other's existence in your life. If sex does not evoke immense gratitude to the one that aroused such a peak in you, it was not pursued to completion. Remember, too, that sex practised as an aspect of love should include afterplay. This is the moment of embrace, thankfulness, and deep connection to one another. It is essential that you make time after orgasm to be fully together, mind and spirit, to be comforted, to be grateful – appreciation is the essence of afterplay.

In the language of love, sex is a spiritual act, a shared gift that goes far beyond mere physical pleasure. However, as long as our approach to sex remains stranded at the primal level, its higher potentialities will never be known. Sex can be both physical and spiritual, it can be left mired in the lower animalistic stage or allowed to flower into something beyond this world. Those who make the necessary effort can count on experiencing something wonderful, something most of the world simply has no inkling of.

As you go through life, observe the games we play, how we pursue mates, and the way we talk about sex: it's not all that different to animal behaviour. When sex is taken to a spiritual plane, though, it becomes an extension of love, it turns into a merging of two energies far removed from what's necessary for procreation, a melding in which woman and man cease to exist. The fire of eternal love subsumes both. When you harness the power of love, you experience the triumph every orgasm is destined to achieve.

Far too often, men only play the role of a devoted lover just because this creates an amenable atmosphere for sex to take place. But, once he has ejaculated, his loving feelings quietly dissipate. This makes foreplay, when not practised in the sense I've discussed, a fairly dishonest business. It is therefore most important that whatever amount of loving foreplay you engage in doesn't become a pretence, a lackadaisical attempt to experience good sex. I want to inspire you to follow a new direction, one that acknowledges that sex is simply a concomitant of making love. Making love, I must add, is what comes before sex, and after sex, and everything in between. Love is the ultimate experience, and never too much effort to pursue.

Beyond sex

We can legitimately enjoy sex in any form; sex is whatever we want it to be. There are no spiritual rules or obligations that say sex should be either just a bit of fun lasting one night or part of something more meaningful and long-term. However, I want to invite you to undertake a journey that will enhance your experience of life by deepening your understanding of the vital energy that is ordinarily released in sexual intercourse. Our primitive need for sex is nothing but a holdover from our animal heritage. Unfortunately, humans in general have not sexually matured enough to look beyond these kinds of primal instincts. We mostly ignore the reality of our sexual energy being capable of much more than the obvious lust we all feel. In fact, this vital force is more powerful than your own mind when it is put to proper use. The same sexual life energy is also the source of all our creativity, but we want nothing more than to release it as soon as the urge arises in us. We remain sadly unaware of the phenomenal effect that takes place when we abide with this energy and allow it to accumulate without reacting to it, without being led astray. This spiritual essence, if allowed to remain in the body, can have tremendous effects far exceeding those any purely sexual orgasm could ever achieve.

I am not, however, suggesting you become celibate, partly because that is a dull kind of life; I mean something completely different. You will only truly understand what I am talking about after you've approached sex in a wholly new, profoundly intense way. You see, boredom is a sign of burgeoning intelligence, an indication that your spirit yearns for something more than you're used to. In fact, all humans are innately bored, but we refuse

Sex as you don't know it

to face it. Instead, we conceal our ennui beneath amusements, goals, and other distractions. We chase after love, enlightenment, sex, money and innumerable other fleeting pleasures. But, once you finally come to accept sex as boring, you are knocking on the door to a new dimension within you. You don't become averse to sex, nor does your desire for sex lessen, it's just that you become attuned to sex on a much higher level. While we live a bodily existence, we can't exactly transcend sex; no one can nor should. However, we can observe the changes sexual energy evokes as it transmutes into a higher form. There are many people with no particularly remarkable talents who exist in this state. This is because they have not resisted anything, they have not chosen to refrain from pleasure. In fact, such individuals are fundamentally choiceless, except that they are tuned into life on a higher frequency and allow love to guide their actions. They've realised that the vital force within us opens up a new way of existing and being in a relationship.

Love and sex don't have to exist together. Often, the paths of love and sex diverge in an otherwise healthy relationship. The connection between two lovers doesn't have to be severed just because the sexual dimension has shifted. There are many possible reasons for a person's appetite for sex diminishing; this isn't a choice we make but the result of our body changing regardless of our preferences. Some women's sex drive, for example, is significantly increased after menopause, whereas many women's sexual desire declines and sometimes disappears altogether. But if, for whatever reason, a person's desire for sex is reduced, it needn't be seen as a tragedy. As much as sex runs parallel to love, a loving connection can easily thrive in the absence of sex if both of you have soared to a greater space within you. In that inner space suffused with love, sex takes on a new form.

It is only once we have sampled the pinnacle of sexuality that we begin to see beyond the horizon into the space of nothingness, where only love has always been and always will be, the void out of which all experiences spring. There is a limitless space within us all that swallows all pleasurable experiences whole and, once you are done with fleeting delights, you are left desiring nothing more than to rest in the bliss of simply being. Being impartial and choiceless is the liberation we all seek but can't quite define. In this desireless state, love surmounts all lesser experiences. It is through sampling all stages of human development, every peak and trough of life, that one finally becomes needless of anything more than life itself, as its most ordinary details become marvellous to us. One does not need to discard anything: to a wise person, it soon becomes clear that having and not having amount to the same experience. What we once defiantly defended as important and essential will one day become meaningless to you, which means conflict, possessiveness and jealousies were all only a consequence of one's immaturity.

In the height of your self-development eventually everything falls away as unimportant, and only you and love remain.

Chapter Nine

The art of ~~war~~ *love*

When you finally accept a relationship as a clash of differences, you can focus on where love really exists.

Depending on your present state of mind and prior experiences of love, much of this book may have seemed a little questionable and, at times, even cynical towards relationships. This is by design: this book is fundamentally about bringing you closer to experiencing love, a kind of fulfilment which doesn't necessarily involve meeting the proverbial soulmate or lucking into the kind of relationship you've pinned your hopes on. Love is a reality separate from what we've been taught to think of as romance. In fact, love must come into being before a relationship does, as it is only then we can properly relate to and love others. Once you embrace this principle, it seems obvious, but most people require a lot of deprogramming before they can accept it.

Instead, romantic relationships are tirelessly endorsed as the only possible source and expression of love. At their best, our haphazard romances can indeed provide us with our first glimpse of something wonderful and mysteriously enchanting. Yet this secret transformation we find so hard to define takes place on a level well above and beyond any kind of love affair. As I said before: relationships are overvalued as a route to either pleasure or fulfilment. For starters, they are deeply unreliable as a source of joy, often transforming into misery. It is this very unreliability that spurs those who are ready for love to search for something more dependable, something everlasting. You see, relationships are just a bridge, not a final destination. We must each cross it and find ourselves on the other side. Before you attain this wisdom, you fervently desire to have a relationship, believing that the next person you find will be the jackpot. However, even after countless attempts and disappointments, you still don't know what you're really searching for or why you can't find it. You instinctively want to experience a love that's unmistakably true but sadly miss the mark every time. So, again and again, we take a leap of faith into whatever person comes along next, believing this is it: our greatest challenge. In reality, even a flourishing love relationship is only a prelude to something far, far greater.

I know that my approach to finding love isn't likely to resonate with the majority of people. It's utterly incompatible with mainstream advice on finding love: somehow attracting a soulmate and then putting in the effort needed to create the perfect synergy. That suggestion is actually far from the most pernicious recommendation you can find, but it is still not the path to love. Advice like this, which ignores the spiritual dimension of love, is invariably limiting and only undermines your potential to live a "happily ever after" fantasy. Every chapter of this book is meant to shatter conventional views on love and

The art of war love

relationships, demolish all your preconceptions about romance. In particular, I want to do away with the false idea that marriage or any romantic connection will somehow save you, make you happy, or show you the path to true love. If, for instance, you choose to build and nurture a loving connection with someone, you must be prepared to accept hatred, too, as relationships are founded on both.

Once you learn how to dispassionately observe your own mind and heart, you'll see how both hate and love evoke the other in equal measure. A relationship simply wouldn't survive if not for hate complimenting love. Love, as we normally perceive it, is defined by its opposite; that is why all lovers inevitably experience bitter fights as well as moments when they fall deeply in love all over again. Every romantic connection, without exception, is a "love-hate" relationship. No affair can sustain continuous love twenty-four hours of each day for the rest of our lives. A relationship requires both conflict and harmony: otherwise, there's nothing to fight for and the whole exercise becomes pointless! Grappling with the dynamic tension between love and hate has become a game we all know how to play; no abiding romance can exist without resembling a civil war.

Incidentally, there are tons of books and podcasts based on smoothing over this inescapable absurdity we find ourselves in. Countless "experts" (by their own lights, at least) make careers out of offering advice on how couples can be more cohesive, avoid conflict, and be better, more congenial partners. As you've probably noticed, I've avoided feeding you these kinds of tips and tricks. While those kinds of platitudes and suggestions are comforting and thus sell lots of books, they ignore the bigger picture, ask you to ignore the true nature of love, and thereby end up doing a great deal of harm. Your aunt, a good friend, and the old lady you happened to meet at the bus stop can all give you good relationship advice, but there's nothing ground-breaking about any of it, nor are their suggestions applicable to everyone and every situation. It's all wholly trite and only somewhat true. When you set out to find your one and only, being told you ought to learn what love is before you attempt to love someone probably doesn't sound very romantic. Make no mistake, though: you can learn all the hacks, rituals, stratagems, gambits, and tricks in the history of relationships, but they will not do you much good. As long as you remain obsessed with the superficial aspects of romance, you will stay trapped in the vast chasm that lies between your idea of the "perfect" relationship and the discovery of what love truly feels like.

The ego, the warmonger

Everyone would resent being called a narcissist and deny applying Machiavellian tactics in order to shift life in their favour. Even mentioning the possibility to somebody is likely to offend them deeply. Before we reject these tendencies entirely, though, one needs to examine how skilfully the ego plays its role in our marriages. No other type of human relationship is as manipulative. Indeed, it is in matrimony that we show our belligerent side, constantly reinforcing our defences and always remaining ready to attack. Children as young as four years old begin to learn that life is transactional, a constant see-saw of giving and taking. As a result of this realisation, we all automatically cultivate a sturdy ego as a weapon to defend and an instrument to get what we desire, especially other people's attention. The longing to be loved and, in fact, the desire for anything in life is driven by our insecurities.

Narcissism, far from being unusual, is fundamentally rooted in our egoic nature and is driven by our need for praise and fear of rejection. Since we're unable to recognise them for what they are, we continually soothe our selfish desires, especially by expecting compensation for the things we do for others – and we most certainly remember what kinds of actions get rewarded and cultivate these habits. As children, we are taught to always win, and so we learn that every argument has to be fought with

The art of war love

the intent to prove ourselves right and the other person wrong. Yet, seen from the spiritual perspective, you are not the culprit here: the ego is a natural and most cunning narcissist, and you are merely its victim. You don't have to feel guilty for something you didn't do, though it is nonetheless your responsibility to become aware of the sway your ego holds over your behaviour. Your unawareness is what makes you guilty.

If this book has relieved you of the burden of chasing after "the one" or made you re-evaluate the ceaseless effort you put in just to make love work in your relationship, then I've fulfilled my purpose. I want to make it clear that what you call "love" isn't love; most human relationships barely scratch the surface of what is really a profoundly spiritual emotion. The world has always been confused about how loving relationships work. Once you come to understand them more deeply, you can't help but laugh at the absurdity of our concept of romance. At the same time, whatever suffering and disappointment we endure in these affairs, these experiences are also invaluable, pointing us in the direction of something greater, a love that is entirely beyond this world.

Learning new psychological tricks to soothe daily marital conflict is analogous to being a good chess player: though it may seem selfish and devious, it's really just a matter of recognising the true nature of relationships. Our love connections are a form of benign combat: through the scuffle, we become better people. A relationship isn't the ultimate manifestation of love, in fact, our romantic ties are more like an essential tool to help us learn. The people we attract without even meaning to are mirrors to our weaknesses; through our associations with them, we heal and grow. Everyone, without exception, has a chance to evolve during each and every encounter. This is not always obvious and can often be unpleasant, however, when we look back on the battle, much later, we realise that the struggle was actually a blessing and a source of light.

Several people asked me a question while I was writing this book: "What is love?" I answer: "Love is that which does not relate to anything." If this answer derailed your train of thought, leaving your mind blank and somewhat bewildered, then you've stumbled upon the attitude this book has been guiding you towards. That uncertain, empty pause you wandered into is beyond the conventional, three-dimensional concept you normally understand as love. Ordinarily, we know love only in terms of objects and people we can relate with: their character, feelings, actions, substance, texture and appearance. For example, I love my Royal Enfield motorcycle, the music of Erik Satie, I love the sound of birds, I love my mum and even my neighbour's cat, too. However, these are all relationships, pertaining to my link with someone or something. Love, however, is the undying essence within all of us that is unrelated and unconnected to any particular thing.

Quitting the fairytale

In the end, the immutable fact is that all romantic relationships fail, even those between people who stay happily together. The failure is buried underneath your bravado and hidden by your optimistic smile, the disappointment amounts to simply being misinformed. Relationships are awfully different to what you are led to believe. Though they have huge value and merits that cannot be rivalled by any other source of joy, relationships are a bitter-sweet experience; just like all pleasures, they have their downsides. A new affair always seems magical. Very soon, though, you discover that you're expected to alter or suppress numerous facets of your character and casually abandon your most precious dreams. By making a daily effort to be "the one" your lover needs, you are left constantly swimming upstream, against the current, and eventually you are left completed washed out.

Worse, whenever we fail to live up to the version of ourselves someone else envisages, we either torture ourselves or blame the other. However, this kind of mutual disappointment is no one's fault: as evolving human beings, we are just not meant to live up to anyone's expectations. We simply demand too much from one another when we follow the societally accepted formula for what a love affair should be. In the beginning, it all feels ever so meaningful, changing yourself to suit your partner seems like the only right thing to do. We are somehow convinced that every relationship should be a test of our endurance and that suffering willingly is the only sincere evidence of our commitment and credibility. As a result of this mental inertia, it is incredibly poignant to finally come to learn that a relationship never truly fails nor succeeds: either outcome is just a useful environment in which we can alchemically grow. Nobody ever achieves anything resembling a victory over a lover; the only triumph you can hope for is within yourself. Of course, I understand that this message is hard to hear. Because we're taught to idealise romance and chase after soulmates, we eventually come to view its defects with bitterness, leaving us disillusioned and disappointed with love. Yet, in a profound sense, these are its best features: if marriages and relationships alike didn't deceive us, we would remain forever lost in a fairytale, never to awaken our higher faculties.

Almost all the relationship advice out there continues to string us along, playing to an old-age philosophy that claims that having a loving relationship and adoring family is a dream worth fighting for. As a result, many couples have children without thinking about the full extent of what this entails, having been blindly led to believe it's the best thing they'll ever do. Few people openly admit to regret becoming parents, but a large proportion are left in shock at the personal sacrifices raising children requires. Only rarely does anyone ever tell you what it's really like. What begins as an innocent kiss eventually leads you down the path of supporting a family and getting crushed by all the related commitments, leaving you completely stripped of your freedom, utterly exhausted and frustrated. However, the discontent we experience in every relationship isn't the result of us attracting the wrong people, since it actually doesn't make much difference who we end up with. When all is said and done, no one can furnish us with the love we were born to experience. I am fully aware that you probably don't tell anyone your deepest, truest feelings. However, I'd like to encourage you to carefully examine the part of ourselves that we all keep secret. What you'll discover is that all pleasurable experiences ultimately deceive, frustrate, and exhaust us. No matter how much you sacrifice, everything will come to bore you in the end. All love affairs are swamped in repetition, as each day consists of habitually doing the same thing over and over again with the same person. After a while, everyone quietly becomes bored with even the most perfect and desirable companion.

Along with the arrival of boredom, frustration overwhelms us, inducing us to leave the old in order to find the new. We break up and divorce with the optimistic hope that our soulmate is still out there somewhere, waiting to be discovered and wooed. Unfortunately, whoever you eventually find, nothing really changes and the same drama unfolds with a new cast of characters. Once upon a time, a love relationship provided us all a glimpse of something incredible, only for that vision to fade regardless of whatever efforts and compromises you made. Once it's lost, it never comes back as long as you keep searching for it in other people. Because we've all felt a moment of indescribable bliss at one time or another, we remain trapped in the hope of rediscovering it, falsely believing that happiness and love depend on finding a soulmate. As a result, we turn into serial daters, ploughing through one relationship after the other, miserably convinced that love lies in another's embrace instead of our own attitude towards life. Only after numerous failed attempts do you finally come to admit that it is not a new woman or a different man you so urgently need. In reality, what you're looking for is that ineffable, unbreakable bliss that lies within yourself; perhaps, now, you understand that you're craving something no other person can ever give you.

The art of war love

Romantic love is as habit-forming as any drug on this planet. How else can we explain how, even after numerous failed attempts, we are still bent on pursuing the love and hate, the give and take, the push and pull we find in every relationship? As much as we complain about life's innumerable pains, we have all seemingly become addicted to stress. We go out of our way to cultivate a life full of challenges: a strenuous relationship, a demanding career, a mountain of debt, and an exhausting social life to boot. All the while, throughout the struggle, you never cease hopelessly dreaming of finding love. Our dismay at never reaching this goal often leaves us feeling ashamed and inferior, and thus willing to do whatever we can to make another love us in the way we've always imagined love to be. Perhaps, today will be the day you come to accept that it is not a new person you so desperately seek. Strange as it may seem, your happiness is not dependent on the compromises and sacrifices you make for a lover but instead something that exists entirely beyond and separate from love affairs.

While we continue to succumb to the temptation of looking for love in relationships, we only attract affection based on whatever we can do for others and not simply for who we are. In time, we come to assume that love is always conditional, a transactional interplay of give and take, a zero-sum game. Clinging to this misunderstanding of what love can be, we neglect our true selves while living up to whatever version of us our highly critical partner deems worthy. Without consciously realising it, you're now held captive by your own need for love, not recognising that what you are actually receiving is not love at all. Instead, you and your lover just trade validation back and forth. After a while, our longing for acceptance and recognition swells to the point where we're forced to realise that no one can give us as much as we want. This is not a tragedy, though, but an opportunity for growth. As we peer more deeply into the charade our love relationships have become, we edge closer to a profound awakening, a chance to see that the prized relationship we desired so badly and worked so hard to sustain has quietly been deceiving us. Yes, we can all boast that we have been loved, some more than others, but at what cost?

We all begin exploring the path of love by pursuing relationships. Lacking any other frame of reference, we have no choice but to throw ourselves into whatever fairytale concept of love we care to feign. Along the way, of course, we realise that relationships provide many comforts that can facilitate a great life, such as being able to create a family, receiving financial support, and relying on companionship and affection. Despite these traditional advantages, though, we have to accept that marriage and relationships are just a practical utility, a tool, an imperfect but pragmatic instrument, equivalent to a house or a car or a washing machine. We can easily live without all of these, just like true love is not dependent on any of the things and people we relate to each day. Whatever grand romantic gestures we observe in the union of two suitably matched individuals, their shared happiness remains a brief and limited experience. This circumscribed version of love is all you're capable of until such time as you have expanded your perception to love all of life in its full range of colours: the good and the bad, the love and hate, aloneness and attachment. Remember: love that is driven by your choice is, after all, not real love at all but only a shoddy counterfeit.

People who don't love life in its entirety are discriminating against the fullness of existence. They prefer to divide life into what is suitable, what is worthy, and what is desirable – thereby isolating themselves from the totality of human experience. Love, however, does not discriminate; it is your internal flame, love is a choiceless demonstration, an invitation to dance, laugh and be totally unserious about whatever comes and goes. If you can sincerely boast of leading a wonderful life despite all the bullshit, misery and pain you've been through, you are already in love. You are in the bosom of a love so boundless that no soulmate or love relationship can ever equal its bliss. People who place their faith in others, insisting that they bring them joy, will always be left dissatisfied, with moments of hard-won contentment coming few and far between. People who lack self-love use the fairytale of soulmates as their template of love. Sadly, this steers them in entirely the wrong direction, considering that love does not relate to any one person. Life itself is meant to be loved in its fullness, so enjoying love may involve being single for the rest of your life or living out your days in a fiery, imperfect relationship. Love is not dependent on any particular destiny and it doesn't conform to any particular pattern; love simply is and always will be.

Loving life

In and out of season, we're all blithely told to "love life". By now, this phrase is something of an advertising cliché, not to mention slightly patronising (and entirely useless to anyone who isn't currently able to see the brighter side of things). Nonetheless, it remains a fact that gratitude for life is an evidence-based method for healing. Sincere thankfulness truly is a priceless tool for overcoming the lingering past and breaking through whatever is obstructing you from experiencing love right now. Love is inside you at this very moment, not in the future or out there somewhere. Most certainly, it doesn't arise in a relationship because it is something no one can give to you. Love already exists in all of us, but the caveat is that we can only experience love in the absence of pain. Everyone is bursting at the seams with love but our capacity to enjoy it is mostly impeded by our accumulated anguish. If you should ask someone why they are bitter or mistrusting instead of happy, they will probably blame their lack of love for life on past experiences. Family, childhood insecurities and memories, rough breakups, failure to attain our goals, addictions, and traumas burden us all. The good news is that overcoming fear is the path that leads directly to love! We all enter new relationships with unresolved issues, hoping no one will ever notice, expecting our relationship to resolve our hidden pains. Lo and behold, this plan never works out.

Mental and emotional pain is humanity's biggest crisis: almost everyone alive today can be diagnosed with a case of harbouring more fear than love. It's therefore no surprise that this is the reason we never come to experience happiness, bliss and ecstatic love. People's mental and emotional health is increasingly considered an issue, but is still approached from entirely the wrong angle: everyone carries on as if it's normal to be haunted by negative events that happened years and even decades ago. It is only once this inner pain becomes unbearable that we seek help. In the West, psychotherapy and prescription drugs have been the only treatments people can turn to. However, though both have shown some benefits, neither is an effective or permanent solution, as they only mask the problem. Psychoanalysis relies primarily on patients opening up and talking frankly about their innermost feelings. This both revives and appeases the issue but rarely takes us beyond it. Patients often become dependent on the process of therapy. Eventually, talking about issues old and new simply becomes a crutch that doesn't help to overcome the underlying problem.

Long ago, a far more effective and permanent treatment for the human condition was discovered in the East. We all carry our traumatic memories and pain within both the mind and body. As an antidote, ancient mystics inspired the world to meditate, a practice which takes a human beyond the limited reality of their thinking mind. Hatha yoga helps this process along through conscious breathing and having the body assume certain postures, contracting and stretching muscle tissue and aligning chakras, thereby releasing emotional pain that is normally hoarded within the body. I am an active proponent of both of these "holistic" treatments, but I'd also like to introduce you to a far simpler solution. You'll be glad to know that I am not requesting you to re-examine painful memories, organise your thoughts by journaling, forgive everyone who's wronged you, or force yourself to make peace with whatever may have happened to you in the past.

You see: we all consist of one energy which has many different manifestations, including fear and love. Therefore, if you constantly feel beset by fear, anguish, regret, or anger, you can simply trade that emotion for love. This sounds nigh-impossible because we expect it to be hard, but I'm simply asking you to exercise your gratitude "muscles". This means nothing more than feeling thankful for the life you have today, right now; nothing else is required to heal your inner being. I know how difficult it is for most of us to establish a habit of gratitude; we have become so identified with our pain and fear. Once you get started, however, you'll find the process remarkably easy. When we deliberately shift our attention from fear to love, something shifts deep within us, we resolve whatever happened in the past without having to batter it into submission, we are effortlessly released from the emotional and mental shackles of our memories. It is not that painful recollections somehow vanish, nor do we resolve issues logically by forgiving or forgetting anything. Overwhelming love for the moment you are in will simply drive out all past negative emotions, absorbing their energy and robbing them of their power.

Being thankful for and immersed in the present moment, nothing more, is the miracle formula to resolving your relationship with the past, present, and future, all at once. When your heart swells with gratitude, when you fall deeply in love with the life you have today, your consciousness expands, making you profoundly receptive to a higher frequency of existence. By learning to combine gratitude and love, we become more content and accepting of all of life's events. By extension, when we now look back at events which once seemed incredibly painful and regrettable, their emotional charge will have vanished. Instead, you will value these as essential episodes along the path that purposefully led you to this present moment. What's more, by reviewing our memories in this heightened state of consciousness, we begin to embrace our past actions and experiences with love instead of fear. From now on, if given the choice, you wouldn't change anything about your past. In general, feeling fearful only means that you are not living in the present, that your mind is tied to the past or the future. However, we can orchestrate a new reality: simply shift your focus so that you gratefully love the present moment, and your entire perspective will be turned on its head.

To descend into the simple pleasure of breathing, to adore life in whatever circumstances you find yourself in, is the greatest spiritual deed one could ever perform. It matters far more than any act of charity and is more effective than any religious prayer. Thankfulness is the only key you need to access the divine; learning grateful acceptance brings you into phenomenal bliss. The atomic, physical universe you see is only a narrow facet of reality, a screen for your perception, a creative yet illusory show made of energy. Yet each moment is still a gift of pure artistry, and even more so when you fall deeply in love with the celestial glory of each perceived moment, as this allows the eternal artist to respond. This means you instantly become connected to the source of all life and love, and anything is possible in that moment. All your past traumas and unresolved issues, existing outside the present, leave you, and you are no longer in fear of and in conflict with life.

People want to know what love is and expend a great deal of energy chasing it down all the wrong paths, when in reality love is nothing more than a higher level of sensitivity and perceptiveness. If you can discern love everywhere, right now, if you see yourself in all people including the ones you previously judged or looked down on, then you have found it, the genuine, everlasting article. It takes a delicately poised mind, body and heart to perceive love, so it's not something you can achieve casually or without effort. Even so, through the power of gratitude, love remains within everyone's grasp. To rejoice in your sorrows and joys alike is the only earnest religion. Without this thankful acceptance, your worship of the divine is only a hollow shell. Love is the only God that exists, there is no God other than pure love. Who needs a dogmatic interpretation of God, a statue or a painting to pray to, when you are already bursting with infinite love? When you finally become love itself, you realise that you are immortal, deathless, and begin to exist beyond the three-dimensional restrictions of space and time.

You may think this outlook is incompatible with loving a particular person, but nothing could be further from the truth. There is no finer or more apparent way to prove your love to someone than by showing your love for life. Without this, your love for your partner is just an act you turn on when it suits you, a laborious counterfeit you can only apportion to the one special individual you deem worthy to love, the unique person who deserves your effort more than anything in the world. That is not love, though, but discrimination, a selfish choice based on your judgment. Do you really think of love this way? Genuine love is an unending, unconditional pouring out of yourself, love really is choiceless. Have you ever given a thought to loving the chair you are seated on, or the bowl that cradles your food, the quilt that hugs you at night, the hook on which you hang your coat, or the distant sound of a police siren; are these not worthy of love? To state this another way: are these trivial, inconspicuous details of life not also a part of this divine theatre of life you find yourself in? Or do you reserve your attention only for those things that provoke delight in you: morning dew, sounds of birds, butterflies, waterfalls, a walk in nature, and fluffy-looking clouds? Do only things that give you pleasure merit your full consideration? Most people are oblivious to the many shades of love. For the majority of us, love can only be applied to the grand and the special, the things that spark joyful emotions. When you drop the armour of your ego and become a child once more, though, when you are innocent and defenceless, you become receptive enough to feel love for all the tiny, insignificant, imperfect details of life. Each of these is a manifestation of divinity, not just those things you choose to find attractive.

On the other hand, I understand how patronising it is for me to ask you to love all the shades of life, the bright and the grey alike, while you're also struggling to pay rent, raise kids, and get to work on time. How does one find the strength to feel thankful for the entirety of life when you're distracted each day by some new trouble that erodes any speck of joy? While a corrupt minority provoke wars only to sell weapons to both sides, while uncaring corporations pollute our oceans and hold us hostage in a multitude of ways? These irritations have probably convinced you that the entirety of life isn't deserving of love; that there is a firm boundary between what's good and what's evil. However, have you ever considered that you are the only reason there is no love in the world? Your perception is the only thing that is truly under your control; you are the one who creates hell and heaven, love and hate. These are just names we assign to different phenomena; they have no objective existence. If you wish to live in peace, love, and happiness, the obligation rests entirely with you; don't expect the world to become a utopia until you're able to perceive it as such.

The lover that I've been describing in this book is a lone warrior, a solitary soldier in the war of love, one who has found the courage to stand alone and defend themselves against all kinds of harmful societal influences and peer pressure. He or she is brave enough to live as themselves and love accordingly. More often than not, such an individual is thought of as a dropout from society – this is because a lover has lost faith in humanity. They know that, as a collective, we are lost: mobs, nations, and tribes will never manifest what love really is. Though learning to love is the only way of saving the world, it can only be done individually. An awakened person understands that love can only exist as a personal reality. It is impossible to simply elevate the mass of humanity to this level: it is only when we become free as individuals that we are enlightened and, one by one, bring about lasting change.

The art of war love

Fearmongers

Ever since the turn of the century, we have been continually bombarded with bad news that serves no purpose but to make us feel discouraged and fearful. By now, the media aren't even the obvious culprits anymore; instead our smartphones, friends, family, and well-intentioned strangers have come to feel that it's their duty to make sure everybody knows what's wrong with the world. Some people choose to spread negativity far and wide, not in the interest of saving the world or promoting justice but out of some macabre instinct. It seems that human beings enjoy having and expressing an opinion, especially when it comes to our species' failings. Being able to talk about "important issues" makes one feel well-informed and appear intelligent to others. All this serves no purpose at all: by paying attention to the circus, we simply help to support and justify the travesty that is public life. The single easiest way to learn more and become more intelligent is to reduce your news intake. Personally, I don't listen to the radio, watch television, or read newspapers; I certainly don't lend an ear to negative gossip. This hasn't made me heartless and ignorant. On the contrary, my deliberate ignorance of the world's affairs springs from a deep place of awareness, love, and acceptance of life as it is.

The only way to change the world is for you, personally, to allow yourself to drift away from the political bedlam and accept whatever is happening as part of the universe's creative flow, driven by infinite love. Chanting slogans and waving signs around, arguing with people who don't support your views, and even voting all come to exactly naught. The powers that be are invested in keeping society in perpetual fear, because fear is the opposite of love, fear is what obstructs our path to a state of heightened awareness. The people who run things, from individual companies to national governments, know all too well that love will change the world, so it's in their interest to keep us living in fear. Human unhappiness is the critical lubricant that keeps the system running smoothly. As long as you are afraid and hateful, you will never find love in your being.

Everyone knows that a "system" exists, though the suggestion that there is some sort of sinister organisation in control of the world is usually dismissed and ridiculed. But even those who laugh at the idea of a global conspiracy, who believe that today's power structures came together more or less by accident, have to acknowledge that contagious fear is our greatest enemy and a pervasive part of our lives. You really don't have any need for this drain on your energy, so don't fall into the trap of becoming a conspiracy theorist or even an expert on current affairs. Be brave enough to resist the allure of bad news; instead, choose to fear nothing and simply love life as it is. When you realise that you are merely a visitor passing through this world, the ills and flaws of humankind cease to affect your attitude of love and your ability to celebrate life. Only the ego, the source of our affection for vicarious tragedy, causes us to feel despair when, in fact, everything is exactly where it needs to be. There are many laudable activists attempting to make a positive change and we should all greatly admire these people's spirit, but without emulating their crusade. Let them carry on with what they believe to be their duty. However: think about how little you achieved yesterday, when you tried so hard to change the world. Today's priorities should be all about you. It is time to wake up!

Love is an enlightened capacity to view each moment as a divine event – yes, even war and disaster are part of love. I don't expect you to take my word for it, as this isn't something you can come to terms with rationally nor by simply thinking positively. Understanding what I mean requires first-hand experience of expanding your consciousness in order to see the world as it really is. When you access this awareness, you'll automatically view humanity's foibles without judgment, without the mind's unjust interpretation of events, and only then will you understand everything that happens as a divine play of polarities. All that we tend to ascribe to human wickedness or a pernicious universe

The art of war love

is seen in a new light. Once you consciously disconnect from mass and social media, you'll quickly realise that people have no new information to share with you, it's all borrowed old news magnified by being endlessly passed on from one person to the next. When we don't live in awareness, we unconsciously absorb all of this doom and gloom, even coming to believe that the state of the world is somehow our fault and the reason for our own failings. Love, by contrast, lets you appreciate every event in life as a necessary part of existence, an opportunity for growth. This makes a tremendous difference to your happiness: without love, we divide reality into what is good and bad or right and wrong, and this viewpoint will always keep you mired in internal conflict and confused about everything that happens to yourself and others.

Just imagine you're on a first date and the person sitting across you hates the world we live in, laments about their past, and holds a grudge against their parents. This would be a definitive sign that he or she doesn't have it in them to love themselves or anyone else. A person who clings to unresolved emotional issues about life or past experiences needs to discover self-love before they attempt any kind of relationship. Haters enjoy the company of other haters; they attract each other magnetically. Then, they sigh together about how wonderfully crap life has been, which their egos find immensely entertaining. Now, however, imagine that same date, but with someone who's been through pain, who hasn't been loved as much as they'd wanted, yet still adores every aspect of their life. Such a person loves their parents despite their shortcomings, doesn't resent former romantic partners, and doesn't waste energy bemoaning the latest news. You would choose that person above anyone else, wouldn't you? The same, of course, applies to how potential partners see you. So, let love always be your guide, because a person who radiates love in the face of anguish is invincible, no cloud can dampen their day. Such a lover will love you no matter what comes, and that is a priceless gift.

Incidentally, I've also noticed a tide of good news rising against the more prevalent trend of "doomscrolling". If you know what to look for, you'll see a conspicuous acceleration in human consciousness spreading all over the planet, person by person. This ignored development is far more significant than any political atrocity bemoaned on today's news. A growing number of people are waking up to a new way of living, thinking, and being. Humanity is gradually breaking free of the lies peddled by corrupt institutions and politicians and, as a result, we are gradually loosening the ties of slavery to a monetary system that is rigged against us.

People are casting guilt aside and finding the courage to discard their inherited religions in favour of independent self-inquiry. Facing the facts that everybody knows but most choose to ignore, more and more of us are choosing not to be poisoned by processed food anymore, choosing not to drink alcohol as an excuse to dance and be happy, choosing not to get stuck in marital contracts just to prove they can be trusted. The dreaded nine-to-five routine is being left behind as employees demand changes in the way we work, earn, and express our creativity. A growing club choose to retire early rather than simply accruing the maximum possible amount of money, all because we are beginning to realise how rich we are all once we truly recognise that we have enough! We are sleeping better and waking up earlier to meditate, dance, play and be creative. In many cases, whole alternative communities are being founded, some living off-grid, growing their own organic produce and home-schooling their children. Though this trend is obscured by the torrent of negative news we're inundated with every day, future generations will see these advancements in an entirely different light.

I promise you that there is plenty of love and abundance to be found everywhere around us as long as you're willing to go and search it out. Become a part of the flowering of human consciousness and love, or simply follow your own way and

The art of war love

inspire all around you. Gracefully embody the love that exists within you, and together we will change the ways of humanity.

Unconditional love

Loving freely, an attitude born out of sheer delight in life, is the only thing that ends the relationship war, signs a ceasefire of acceptance, ends all possessive conflict, and removes all strategy, calculation and scheming from the battle of romance. We enjoy claiming that we know our lover intimately, and that's probably true to some extent, but no one actually knows themselves. The pursuit of self-knowledge doesn't have to be a solemn spiritual journey inward, based on a formal system of meditation with incense and gongs and whatnot. In a relationship, it simply requires you to watch and listen to the psychological games you play: how you gather your forces for each skirmish, execute battle plans, and defend yourself in every confrontation. Of course, we don't bring artillery cannons into battle, but the metaphor of love as war is surprisingly apt. Our weapons are strictly psychological, and therefore winning is established on validation, control, and obtaining the upper hand. We are always measuring the outcome of everything we do; not even a kind word is free; everything we impart comes with a price and conditions attached.

Ironically, when we finally meet someone to call our own, we sincerely try to love them, to demonstrate what love means to us. Instead of sharing boundless affection with them, however, we unknowingly try to manipulate the other, causing the relationship to become purely transactional. If the scales don't swing in our favour for any reason, we react with defiance, holding the other accountable for not compensating us for our attachment to them. To love unconditionally represents the pinnacle of what love can ever be, yet the concept is alien to us: this kind of love is one-sided and cares about no reward, no remuneration. The love a mother imparts to her child, for example, is often cited as the perfect example of divine, unconditional love. Your mother has loved you from the moment you were born and she still does despite whomever you have become. Her love for you will never wane, even if you hate her in return. In romantic relationships, women are far more capable of loving freely; they are less fearful of expressing their love without it being reciprocated. This has as much as to do with her maternal predisposition as with the credibility of her lover.

However, this bit of conventional wisdom ignores the fact that motherliness is a quality that exists in all of us. Men, too, can be warm and nurturing without expecting anything in return. Unconditional love means lowering your guard and becoming vulnerable. Yes, this leaves you open to being taken advantage of, but allowing your love to flow without restriction yields a far greater reward than the risk of your love not being matched by your partners. When you love someone without expectation or attachment, your love becomes so pure it generates enormous joy just by existing, a sense of fulfilment that will make you feel grateful to your lover just for allowing you to love them. When you experience the simple joy of loving someone, you are left profoundly thankful.

You see, the one who dares to love openly just so happens to get more out of any relationship than the one being loved in such a way. Consider this carefully for a moment: would you prefer to be loved by someone or have the chance to love someone? Often enough, women favour being the lover rather than being the one who is loved, because they know how loving someone provides a greater joy than being loved. The giver benefits more than the receiver, on multiple levels. When you come to a point in your life where you are ready to love someone completely, no matter what and regardless of what happens between you, you will be uplifted by a force of nature that a mere recipient of love can ever experience. This is the hidden power of unconditional love.

In addition, when it comes to love that's given freely, the recipient needn't even know you love them. As one example of how this works, numerous people feel guilty or doubtful about why they still love their past companions, even though their exes will never be aware of their continuing feelings. This is a sign of unconditional love; felt purely for the benefit of the lover, it is strictly private, it imposes no responsibility on others and carries no strings of attachment. Because it is simply love for the sake of love, which is the greatest love there is, it elevates the donor without its recipient having to do a thing. Why not expand your circle of loved ones? If you can love everyone you have ever encountered and everyone who is present in your life today, you will harvest an abundance of joy and levity.

It's entirely possible that you can't find the right person to love; in that case, I implore you to love everyone. I mean every stranger and every friend you will ever meet – I promise you: you'll come to find that it's actually a whole lot easier to love the whole world indiscriminately than it is to focus your love on the one person you deem special! Love is the only resource that doesn't diminish when shared but instead accumulates. The more love you give, the more you will have left over. Try it: you'll see that loving all really isn't as difficult as you might imagine and you'll quickly come to know that loving is actually the only part of you that comes naturally. It is truly humanity's greatest, yet most underappreciated, instinct.

While some of the ideas you've read in this book may seem strange, its core message may well seem like an echo of your own thoughts, those which you never had the courage or the words to admit. I hope you feel inspired to follow an intention you could not express but felt in your bones. Perhaps, my words stimulated an awakening, a desire to explore your higher self through a sacred drug experience or some Tantric practices. These, along with several other techniques, provoke you into going where the mind normally can't, yank you out of your comfort zone, break you free of fixed ideas. I see my job as nothing more than divorcing you from what has been deceiving you; once you realise the falsity of the life most people live, finding a new path is up to you.

I will forever keep beating this drum: that your life is yours alone and in fact all you have. You must put yourself first, don't place your faith or happiness in another's hands. That is not how love works, as you are and always have been the source of the love you so badly desire, you are "the one" you've been searching for. Regardless of the depth of your desperation, I've shown you that there is a way out, even if this could mean losing what you have right now: breaking old promises, discarding what you once deemed so valuable but has only weighed you down, perhaps retiring from the dating life for a while. This could mean isolation and ridicule, but it will certainly be far more productive than anything else you have tried before, because finding yourself is ultimately the only battle worth fighting. When we dance and play our way through life, we are in tune with love and in sync with life's creative essence. Life and whatever you have achieved in it, or lost along the way, matters not at all; there is nothing important whatsoever about life except love and growth. If we take life seriously, then we are mistreating it and end up squandering what should be a joyous experience. Likewise, the world at large doesn't understand true love because almost everyone takes their love relationships far too seriously, we all demand way too much from each other.

Be kind to yourself, be kind to others, neither blame yourself for imperfect romances, nor hold anyone else accountable for your grief. If you haven't attained what you believed love to be, it only means you have something left to learn on the subject. The truth is that your case isn't unique; everyone has secretly failed at love but prefer to hide the fact, perhaps finding it easier to pretend that a failed marriage is still working. When either partner no longer finds what they are looking for, the relationship journey has come to its natural end, bringing you to a point of deep self-reflection. In most cases, the answer to the question you'll be asking yourself is indeed that you should leave, even if this is only to spend some time alone and discover yourself. The path of love ultimately brings you back to the source, back to you.

Love is an internal undertaking, so don't impose on others by expecting them to give it to you. Grant yourself some time in life during which you create a sense of distance between yourself and the familiar, clamorous world you know, give yourself permission to be totally selfish. Your quest to find love must be treated like a pregnancy: become a womb and let it grow within you. One day, you will feel reborn, even though no new life has really been brought into this world: you will only have shucked off the chrysalis that used to envelop the love that you are.

Biography

Khel Kalyan is a spiritual philosopher, modern mystic, and writer known for his piercing clarity on love, ego, and freedom. After experiencing a life-altering heartbreak in 2017, he began to question every assumption he held about relationships, romance, and identity. What followed was not a recovery — but a complete transformation.

Drawing from Eastern wisdom, non-dualism, and direct experience, Khel left behind societal roles and spiritual dogma to discover a truth both radical and simple: love is not something you find. It is something you *are*.

His writings do not offer comfort, but awakening. He speaks to those disillusioned with superficial answers and invites readers to explore the vast, often uncomfortable terrain of self-realisation. Khel's work blends poetic language with philosophical precision, offering not a map, but a mirror.

Make Love Not Marriage is his most intimate and provocative work to date — a guide for anyone who dares to break the rules in order to know what love truly is.

When he's not writing, Khel enjoys walking alone, sharing silence with strangers, and occasionally laughing at the absurdity of it all.

Printed in Dunstable, United Kingdom

72748473R10151

THE SILK MERCHANT'S SON

Peter Burke

FREMANTLE PRESS

For Auriol Jean Burke née Penrose (1930–2012)

Grew up in in Dalkeith, schooled at Loreto, married an Irishman whose sister was a nun, and raised five kids on the Canning River.

They're all in the book, Mum.

*There are few situations more unpleasant than when
two individuals are suddenly and unexpectedly brought
into collision, neither of whom is acquainted with one word
of the language of the other.*

George Fletcher Moore, Advocate-General of Swan River colony
Preface to his Noongar–English dictionary, 1842

The Twenty-Eight Missionaries

From Dom Rosendo Salvado's *Memorie Storiche dell' Australia*, (1851).

These are the names and nationalities of the missionaries who set out on Elizabeth *from England to Western Australia on 17ᵗʰ September 1845, with nationalities and approximate age.*

Priests	Bishop John Brady	Irish (45)
	Dom José Serra	Spanish Benedictine (35)
	Dom Rosendo Salvado	Spanish Benedictine (31)
	Don Angelo Confalonieri	Tyrolese Benedictine (32)
	Father Francis Thévaux	French Heart of Mary (25)
	Father Francis Thiersé	French Heart of Mary (28)
	Father Maurice Bouchet	French Heart of Mary (24)
	Father Peter Powell	Irish (30)
Subdeacon	Denis Tootle	English Benedictine (26)
Novice	Léandre Fonteinne	French Benedictine (26)
Catechists	John O'Reilly	Irish (20s)
	Nicholas Hogan	Irish (20s)
	John Gorman	Irish (20s)
	Timothy Donovan	Irish (20s)
	James Fagan	Irish (20s)
	William Fowler	Irish (20s)
	Martin Butler	Irish (20s)
	Terence Farrelly	Irish (23)
Brothers	Théodore Odon	French Heart of Mary (20)
	Vincent Eusbe	French Heart of Mary (21)
Layman	Nicola Caporelli	Count of the Papal States (29)
Nuns	Ursula Frayne	Irish Sisters of Mercy (28)
	Catherine Gogarty	Irish Sisters of Mercy (27)
	Anne Xavier Dillon	Irish Sisters of Mercy (27)
	Ignatia de la Hoyde	Irish Sisters of Mercy (41)
	Aloysius Kelly	Irish Sisters of Mercy (23)
	Baptist O'Donnell	Irish Sisters of Mercy (22)
Postulant	Kate O'Reilly	Irish Sisters of Mercy (21)

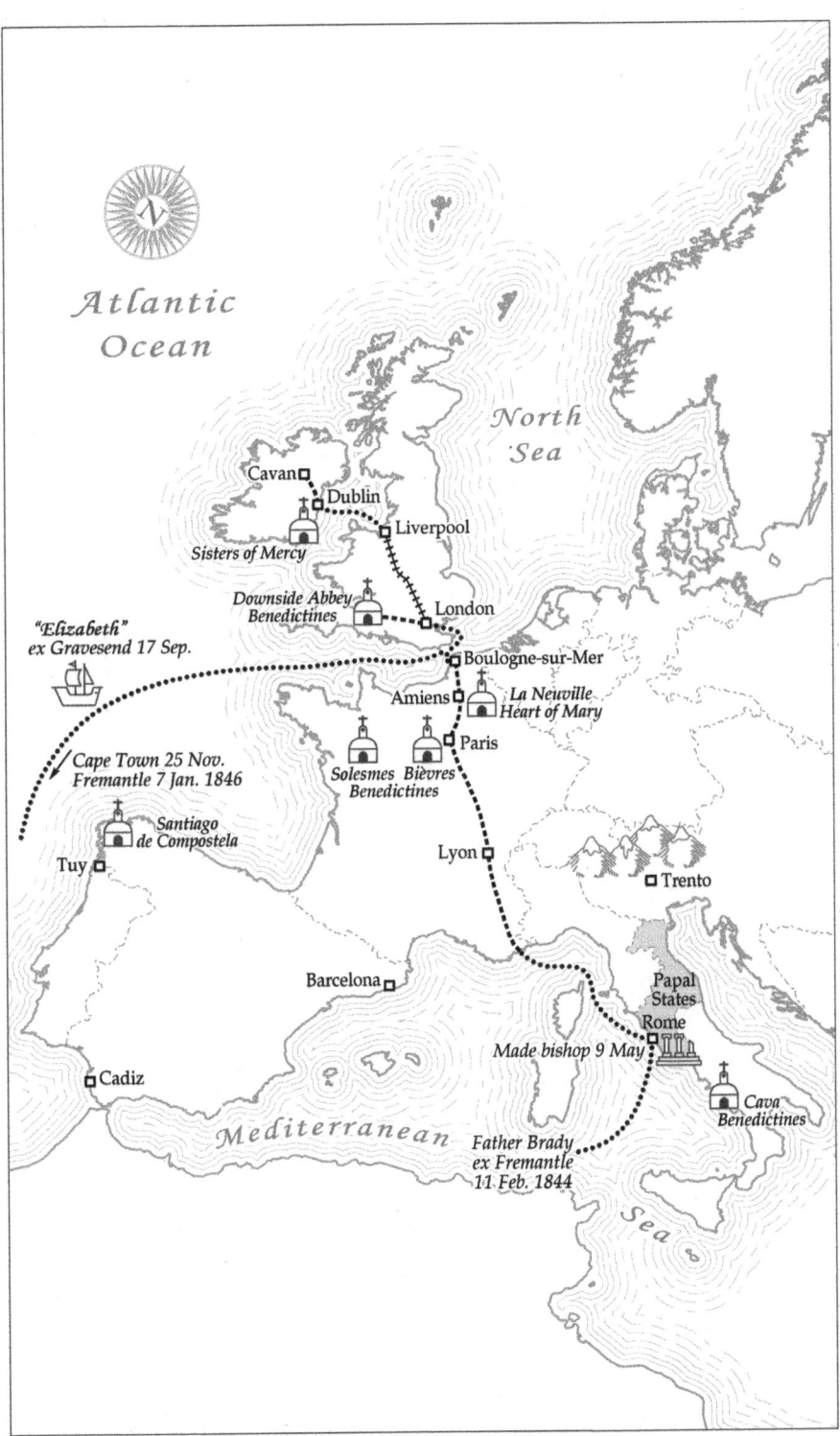

Atlantic
Ocean

North
Sea

Cavan

Dublin

Liverpool

Sisters of Mercy

Downside Abbey
Benedictines

London

Boulogne-sur-Mer

"Elizabeth"
ex Gravesend 17 Sep.

Amiens

La Neuville
Heart of Mary

Paris

Cape Town 25 Nov.
Fremantle 7 Jan. 1846

Solesmes Bièvres
Benedictines

Santiago
de Compostela

Lyon

Trento

Tuy

Barcelona

Papal
States
Rome

Made bishop 9 May

Cava
Benedictines

Cadiz

Mediterranean

Father Brady
ex Fremantle
11 Feb. 1844

Sea

BISHOP BRADY GATHERING THE MISSIONARIES, 1845

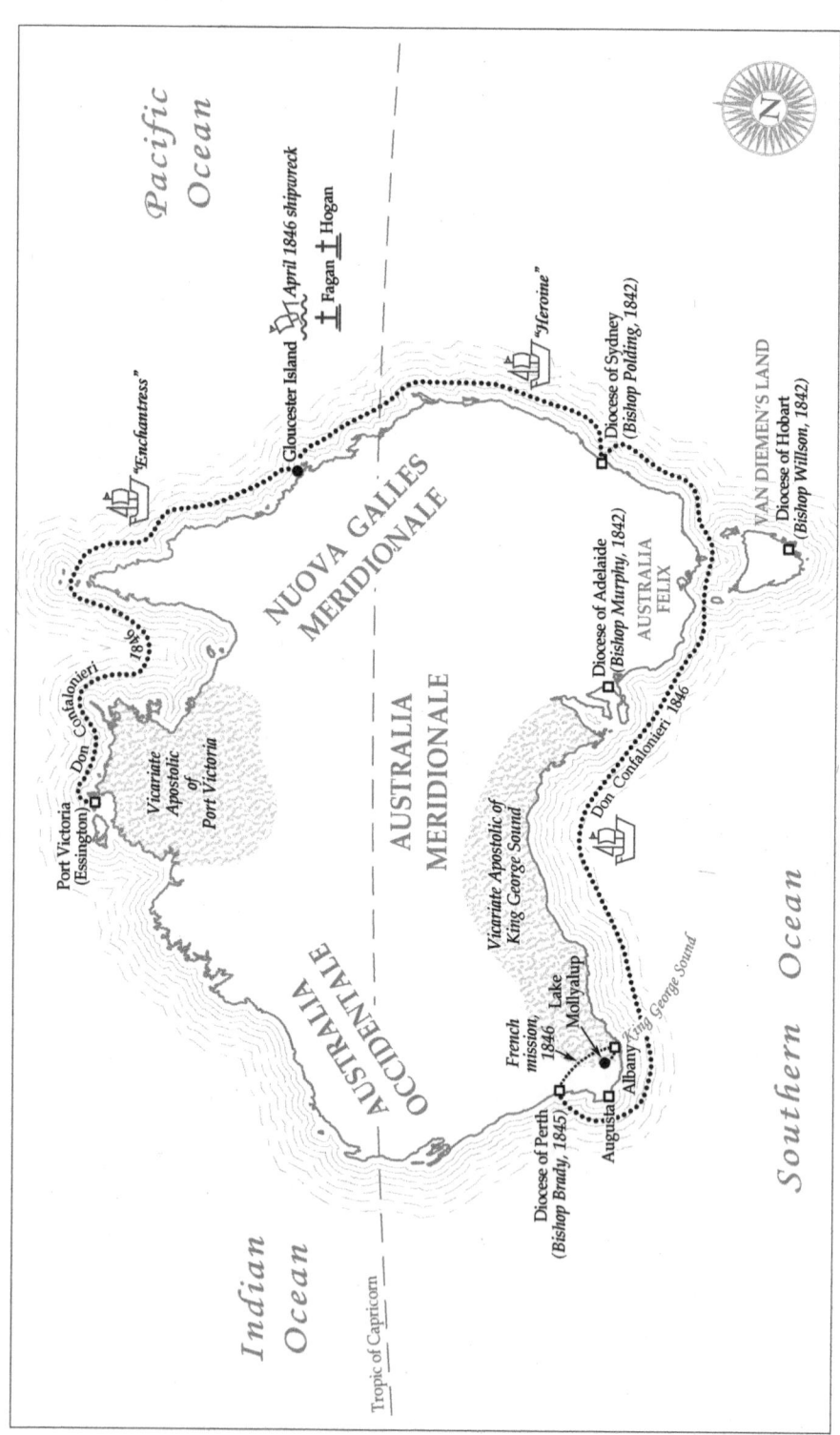

AUSTRALIA AS ENVISAGED BY BISHOP BRADY, 1846

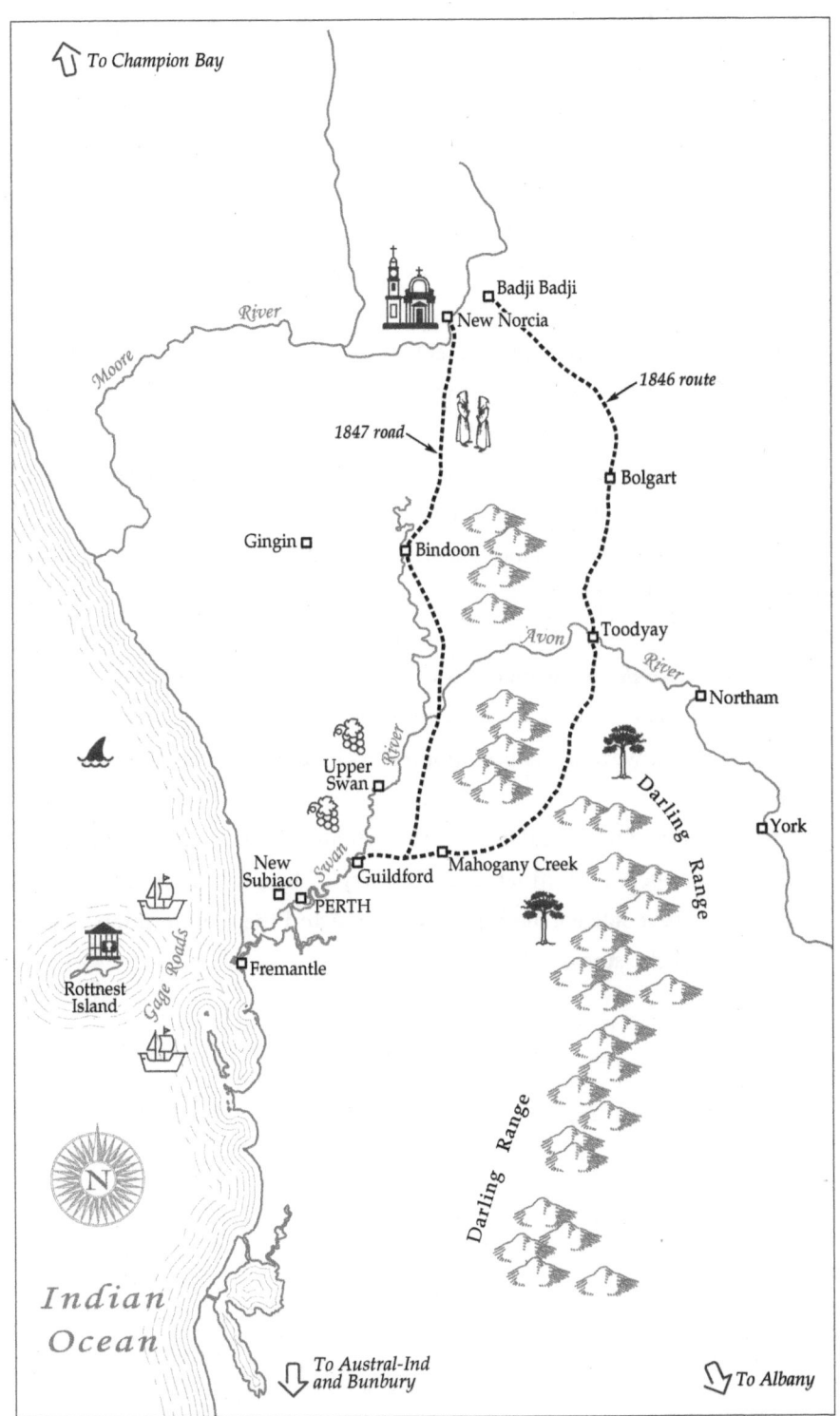

To Champion Bay

Moore River

Badji Badji

New Norcia

1846 route

1847 road

Gingin

Bindoon

Bolgart

Avon

Toodyay

Northam

Upper Swan

Darling Range

York

New Subiaco

Guildford

Mahogany Creek

PERTH

Fremantle

Swan River

Gage Roads

Rottnest Island

Darling Range

N

Indian Ocean

To Austral-Ind and Bunbury

To Albany

SWAN RIVER COLONY, 1846

Before the story starts

For an eternity before Spanish monks appeared on Victoria Plains, the land was home to the Yued Noongar people. So we start by acknowledging the Yued as the traditional custodians of the lands around New Norcia and pay our respects to their elders, past and present.

A word on language. This is a story about mutual miscomprehension. The Catholic missionaries had trouble enough communicating with one other, having seven different native tongues plus Latin, but not one of them spoke the language of the people they had set themselves to convert; not even Bishop Brady despite the Noongar–English dictionary published in Rome in his name. In this story we have a French linguist trying to understand the spoken Noongar word, and mostly failing; hearing, for example, *gouljacque* in place of *kooldjak* for the black swan, or *coumarle* for *koomal*, the possum. When the speaker is foreign, such errors are intentional. When the speaker is Aboriginal, however, a contemporary accepted spelling of the Noongar word is used.

This is a work of historical fiction. Though much of the material contained herein is connected to nineteenth century colonial history of Western Australia, creative licence has been taken here and there with timeframes in the interests of the story.

CHAPTERS

1. THE WRONG SCARF

There lived in Lyon an annoying young man by the name of Fabrice Cleriquot. Exactly where he was on this particular evening was a mystery to his father Claude, but he was definitely not at *Lorette* where he should have been. Being an idiot, the boy would be sauntering aimlessly along the *Montée St Barthélemy*, talking to someone or inspecting something that did not require inspection.

Claude Cleriquot did not feel charming this evening, and as a purveyor of fine silk it was his job to be charming. 'He won't be long, Pauline, I'm sure,' he said, trying to inject a little music into his voice. Few in Lyon would have addressed Mademoiselle Jaricot by her first name, for she was a living saint, but these two were old friends. Claude had been given his start in the silk industry by Pauline's father, who had thought that he was helping his future son-in-law.

They were standing on the porch of Pauline's pretty mansion, *Lorette*. She had named it after the Italian town of Loreto, where an angel had deposited the childhood home of Jesus. Years before, while on pilgrimage to Loreto, Pauline had almost died of fever but was saved by miraculous intercession for which she still thanked the Virgin Mary each morning, squeezing through a gap in her hornbeam hedge and walking up to the shrine of Our Lady of

Fourvière. This was her favourite place on earth; while standing on a wall built by the Romans, she could thumb her rosary beads, whisper her Creeds, Glory Be's and Ave Marias and, as the sun rose, inspect her own roof for damaged tiles or see what needed doing in her garden.

They had left the three black-cloaked visitors in her salon, each with a cigar and a balloon of cognac. Pauline could still hear them – clerical, male, argumentative. It was nice to escape into the fresh air to think. This new Bishop of Perth was a puzzle. Claude would have a reliable view.

'Should I trust this one?' she asked him.

But Claude was gazing into the distance, where he saw nothing. It was a lovely sort of nothing, of course. *Lorette*'s famous gardens glowed softly in the yellowing twilight. He saw Pauline's new gardener, another lazy Senegalese, and there were sparrows and a white peacock and so on. But no son. *Lorette at six o'clock, sharp* was the message Claude had sent to Fabrice. Too subtle, perhaps, for an assistant professor of linguistics to comprehend.

'Claude?'

'Yes, Pauline,' he answered dreamily.

'The bishop?'

'Oh. He is rather rough, is he not? Peasant stock, I would say.'

Claude Cleriquot looked just as a wealthy Lyonnais silk merchant should; dapper, silver haired with, of course, an immaculate silk tie and handkerchief. Pauline Jaricot by contrast dressed as she lived, simply and frugally. She wore a loose-fitting gown made of Indian cotton, not bourgeois silk. She wore no powder, no perfume. Having devoted her life to charitable works, Pauline was instinctively opposed to displays of wealth.

Pauline Jaricot had founded the most successful charity of the Catholic Church, the Society for the Propagation of the Faith, and had become known, to her chagrin, as 'The Saintly Virgin of Lyon'. Nowadays, most of the visitors to *Lorette* were Catholic missionaries seeking her money. Tonight, it was Bishop John Brady's mission to the natives of Western Australia.

Brady had pressed his case in an annoying manner. The more he spoke, the less inclined was Pauline to help him. He had trained as a priest in France, so he said, but could not tell her precisely where or under whom. His French was execrable. Perhaps they all spoke that way on the island of Bourbon, where he had run a parish for a decade. One source told her that the Pope may have consecrated the wrong priest; it was meant to be a Benedictine called Ullathorne. His Holiness' eyes were failing and such things could happen in Rome. So Pauline turned her thoughts instead to the poor natives whose souls were in peril. The Society for the Propagation of the Faith had to help them, of course. But once His Irish Lordship was off in distant Western Australia, how might the society monitor its investment?

Claude was still distracted so Pauline took his hand.

'Please, Claude. Stop worrying about Fabrice. He will arrive in his own time. I have known the boy since he was born and I know he is, you know …' She shrugged, unable to find quite the right adjective.

This had the wrong effect on the silk merchant. His aim tonight was to sell Pauline a bespoke product, the services of his only son. True, the boy was not easy to sell: he was of limited utility, demand for him was not great, and now he had failed to arrive on time. But Claude could not allow that the product was damaged.

'I assure you, he is usually very reliable,' Claude protested.

Pauline smiled at this lie. Everyone in Lyon had heard Claude Cleriquot complain about his disappointing son. 'He is merely typical of his generation,' he added.

This phrase Pauline had often heard, and always from silver-haired men who had lived through The Revolution, The Reign of Terror, then Napoleon and his endless wars. Adversity had given them character and backbone. Claude himself liked to brag that he had been born just as Marie Antoinette was beheaded, as if her execution had taken place in his very nursery. Their lazy sons, by contrast, had been coddled by their *mamans*, and only knew the peaceful, prosperous times of Louis-Philippe, the 'Citizen King'. They had fought for nothing, so they respected nothing, not the State, not the Church, not even their own fathers. Universities fomented such views. A decent war would correct them.

'Two million natives, he claims,' said Pauline, returning to the matter of the bishop.

'It does seem rather a lot.'

'His French is so poor, I thought perhaps he meant two thousand. I tried to help him, did you hear? *Deux mille*? I suggested. *Non, deux millions,* he grumbles!'

'Do such numbers really matter?'

'Good heavens, Claude!' Pauline was growing exasperated. 'Yes! Numbers matter a great deal to the administrators, whether one is counting souls or *scudos*.'

This rebuke restored Claude's attention. 'Of course. Let us think of it mathematically,' he suggested. 'The colony of Western Australia is about one million square miles, in the English measurement. Might there not be two natives to each?'

'I suppose,' sighed the hostess. Her instinct was always to help the Church establish itself in the New World, since this old one seemed at times beyond help. But this bishop. 'Just tell me your view, Claude, please, and smartly. Should I trust Bishop Brady with the society's money?'

Money! That lovely word fully restored Claude's attention. This was the moment in any business transaction that he would present the client with his solution to her problem. But tonight, where was the solution? A great opportunity seemed to glow in the cupped hands of the silk merchant, a firefly slowly dying.

Then the garden gate slowly opened and Fabrice Cleriquot appeared. He was not in a hurry. He saw them, began to stroll up the path, but stopped to talk with the Senegalese.

'Excuse me, Pauline,' said Claude, feigning as much good humour as he could manage. 'I will fetch him.'

Claude met his beloved son halfway down the garden path. As viewed from behind, a loving father warmly embraced his some-what tardy son. Fabrice, however, received a different view of the encounter. His father's face declared that he would rather have smacked the son's cheek than hug him. Strong bony thumbs pressed hard into the flesh at the front of his shoulders.

'Ouch,' yelped Fabrice Cleriquot.

'You are late, boy,' Claude snarled, while gently turning his dear son around to face the hostess and stroking his back with great affection. 'Kiss her hand. Say nothing stupid. Agree to every proposition. And do not ask questions.'

The expression on Fabrice's face was, like his father's, one of perfect calm. He had learned in childhood to rise above provocations.

'Naturally, Father,' said Fabrice, the perfect reasonableness in his voice calculated to annoy. He was not, after all, the callow youth of his father's imagination. He was thirty-one years old, and assistant professor of linguistics at L'Université Laïque de Lyon. 'But, Father, you do recall that I have become an Atheist? Why then would you ask me to meet ...'

'No questions!' replied the father, whose attempt to smile for the hostess made him grimace like a ventriloquist's dummy. 'Later. At home.'

At the top of the steps, Fabrice bowed low like a courtier and with theatrical extravagance kissed the slender hand of Pauline Jaricot. She smiled. She had a thin, pale, beautiful, rather sad face; a *saintly* face really, beatifically lit by the flickering porch lamp. Perhaps she blushed.

'I am sorry, Mademoiselle,' said Fabrice, 'but how should I greet a living saint?' He saw his father's jaw muscle tighten in the lamplight, which pleased him.

'Just like that, Fabrice!' said Pauline, laughing. She had not seen him for years, but his childhood naughtiness was still there. Most people watched their manners too well in her presence, which made life very dull. For the first time this evening, the eyes of the hostess sparkled.

'Let's get back inside,' she sighed, 'before these wretched priests finish off my cognac and fall asleep.'

As they entered the house, Claude pulled his son back by his coat collar and whispered in his ear. 'Do not upset the bishop. He is new, and very fragile.' It was only then, in the better light, that Claude realised the catastrophe of Fabrice's scarf. 'What colour is that?' he choked, but it was too late and besides, he knew the answer. It was amaranth, the colour reserved for bishops. Claude, good friend of Rome that he was, owned the only bolt of amaranth silk in Lyon. Earlier that evening, with some ostentation, he had presented Bishop John Brady of Perth with a new zucchetto and stole in that very colour.

Fabrice entered the warmly lit room to see three priests, all in black, each holding an empty glass. A pair sat together; one short and serious, the other broad shouldered and open faced. The hoods of their cassocks had been thrown back to reveal elaborate tonsury. Benedictine monks, Fabrice surmised. The third was standing with his back turned, seemingly caught in the act of refilling his glass. Atop this one's head was a round silk cap of similar hue to Fabrice's new scarf, and over his shoulders was a matching sash. Fabrice was a little annoyed by this sartorial clash. He had discovered one of his father's secret bolts and had rather hoped his new cravat would be unique.

'Do have another cognac, Your Lordship,' urged Pauline.

'Oh, no, I'd best not,' came the voice from under the pink silk cap. A foreigner, the professor of linguistics could easily tell, but whence, he could not say. His complexion, little red vessels bursting across the cheeks, suggested he had spent too long in the tropics and that he would have enjoyed that second drink even more than the first. 'I wished merely to inspect the bottle,' explained the pink-capped one, putting it back on the table. 'Sadly, we will not be enjoying the likes of this where we are headed.'

Claude made the introductions. The one with the silk cap was John Brady, Bishop of Perth.

'Your Eminence,' said Fabrice, with a low bow. He had learned in childhood the art of dissimulation.

Bishop Brady looked across to the father, back to the son and down to the bottle of spirits. 'Thank you, Monsieur Cleriquot,' he said, 'but 'Your Lordship' will quite suffice. Had I been made cardinal your father would have brought me a bright red zucchetto, rather than this one of mere … amaranth.'

At this last word, Fabrice noticed the bishop's eyes focus on his own neckerchief, then search his face for any clues that the offence had been intentional.

'I am sure one day you will be made a cardinal,' said Fabrice, loosening his cravat a little.

'Some would say I have already exceeded my capacities,' said Bishop Brady, attempting a smile. He was here to beg for money and this young fool was a distraction from the task.

The bishop was an Irishman, Fabrice decided, based as much on the self-deprecation as the awful accent. His robe looked new. It had sharp creases and all of its buttons. There were thirty-three black buttons on a bishop's soutane, Fabrice was surprised to recall – one button for each year of Our Lord's life. He was still rather new to Atheism, and could only hope that such religious knowledge would leave him eventually.

'Dom José Serra,' continued Claude Cleriquot, keen to move things away from the clash of silk, 'and Dom Rosendo Salvado.'

The monks were confirmed to be Spanish Benedictines and the artistic patterns shaven into their short-cropped hair a souvenir of their recent audience with the pope. Salvado seemed the more friendly, springing to his feet and greeting Fabrice in French. His accent suggested to Professor Cleriquot the province of Galicia, probably Santiago de Compostela. The linguist tested this theory by responding in Galician vernacular.

'É un pracer.'

Rosendo Salvado smiled broadly at these unexpectedly familiar words. Yes, he was a *galego*, he confessed, from the town of Tuy. He shook Fabrice's hand, embraced him like a brother, then held him by the shoulders at arm's length to inspect his new friend more closely.

The Galician had thick, muttony workman's hands; a labourer posing as a monk. He looked the sort who would survive not only in the religious world, but the real. A pleasant and expressive face, topped by bushy eyebrows which had somehow escaped the razor and seemed to act independently of their owner. They had jumped with amusement at first sight of the pink cravat.

The smaller monk, Serra, remained seated. He seemed intelligent and self-contained, and spoke like a Catalonian. His dark eyes seemed to be asking what evangelistic purpose this young silken fop could possibly serve, and Fabrice was not in the least offended by this posture, since he was asking the same question. Did his father refer to him as the missionaries' 'travelling companion'? What idea must the old fool have in his head this time?

Fabrice had known something like this was coming. Two weeks earlier, he had been summoned to his father's office to discuss 'a matter of grave importance to the family'. Fabrice was made to sit under a brass plaque which read *Cleriquot et Fils, Fournisseurs de Soie depuis 1826,* while pairs of rich women came and went. The enforced long wait was one of his father's favourite ways of asserting his authority.

The 'grave matter' turned out to be a triviality, a measure of his father's backwardness. It concerned a student from the university called Raphael whom Fabrice tutored in English and whose companionship he occasionally enjoyed outside the classroom. The boy's father was threatening all sorts of 'difficulties' with the Faculty.

Such things went on all the time in universities, explained Fabrice. Friendships between a student and his teacher had been known since the time of Socrates. The only problem was the boy's father.

'Silence, boy,' Claude had said, 'you will not make light of this.'

The Cleriquot name had *prestige*. One could bank on it, literally. Any damage to the name could destroy the family's silk business. Rome could never buy silk vestments from a family tainted in such a way. There was a need for decisive action, and so on. 'You will leave Lyon until this matter is forgotten,' his father had concluded.

So tonight's gathering of priests with their unfashionable *coiffure* and ill-chosen *chapellerie* must be his father's solution to an imaginary problem. Fabrice would play along for now; one could not altogether ignore one's need for money. Linguistics was alas not a very profitable pursuit, and Fabrice did enjoy a lifestyle rather in excess of his earnings. So he smiled at the priests, nodded, listened, and tried his best to avoid becoming part of their plans.

It seemed they intended to sail to some part of Australia called Perth, or perhaps Swan River. Endless dull details were being discussed. Nothing seemed to explain their need for a professor of linguistics, so finally Fabrice thought it sensible to enquire directly of the bishop.

'What is your mission to be, exactly?'

'To convert the natives, of course,' said Brady, brusquely.

'Why would you want to do that?' Fabrice pressed, deaf to his father's meaningful expectorations.

'Why would we not?' protested the bishop, his nose reddening further. 'We are missionaries!'

'Might the natives not be possessed of some special nobility, to be learned *from*, rather than converted by force or coercion?'

suggested Fabrice. To invoke Rousseau was usually a winning strategy in Faculty debates, but he was testing new waters here by invoking him before a prince of the church.

'The naïve sentiments of a theorist,' scoffed Brady. 'I presume you have never travelled, young man, and never met a dark man.'

These truths smarted. 'Well, your views sound like those of a colonist,' countered Fabrice.

'Colonist?' thundered Bishop John Brady of Perth. 'Are you mad? The Catholic Church is on the side of the poor native, protecting him *from* the English colonists.' He looked around the room for support, filled as it was with French and Spanish.

'But the church always sides with the rich,' suggested Fabrice, to silence, except for his father's angry sniffing. The Spaniards lowered their heads. They had heard this same argument from the so-called liberals just as they were thrown out of their monasteries.

'That may be so, in Europe,' conceded the Irish bishop, surprising Fabrice with his candour. 'Rome has done little for the poor in Ireland except build them huge cathedrals which they must pay for themselves. But in the new world, in Western Australia, I can tell you that the Church will be a friend of the poor, and especially of the poor natives.'

'Once there, I predict you will befriend the rich.'

'There are no rich there to befriend.'

Fabrice was flustered. An uneducated bishop had somehow outflanked him.

It took a Benedictine to ease tensions. 'Of Australia and its native population,' said Salvado diplomatically, 'we are all quite ignorant.'

'We are *not* all quite ignorant, Rosendo,' corrected his bishop. 'I have been to this colony, you may have forgotten. I have published a dictionary of the language of the natives.'

Salvado lowered his eyes once more. 'My apologies, Your Lordship. *You* are not ignorant, of course, but the rest of us are. That is why we shall follow your spiritual lead.' When tempers settled, it was the bishop who was left in his own corner, not the atheist.

The visit dragged on, even after goodbyes were said. Claude ingratiated himself to the new bishop with another amaranth-coloured gift, this time a *biretta* in an ostentatious box. Pauline gave Bishop Brady a handsome silver tabernacle and a pair of candlesticks. Once the priests had finally departed, Claude spent a long time on the porch with Pauline talking about francs while Fabrice sat nearby and smoked.

Pauline would advise the society to provide modest support to Brady, half the amount the bishop had hoped for. She felt guilty for doing so, and expressed an inclination to provide some additional support to the mission from her own purse. Claude whistled at this, but in truth he had expected and indeed hoped for it. In such a case as Bishop Brady, personal philanthropy would be risky, he explained. The solution was to entrust her money not directly to the bishop, but to Claude's very dependable son. Fabrice would accompany the missionaries to Western Australia and ensure any funds she gave were spent gradually and to good purpose.

'But I will *not* travel to Australia!' Fabrice declared as they walked home along the *Montée St Barthélemy*. Although the Cleriquot estate adjoined *Lorette*, so large were the respective grounds that it was a fifteen-minute walk from gate to gate. 'I cannot! I have students to teach!'

'No you don't,' countered the father, calmly. 'I have advised the university to reallocate them.' He handed Fabrice a purse. 'Feel the weight of my argument.' It was heavy. 'This is the Mademoiselle's own money. And there is much more to come, but only if you behave yourself.'

'How much?' asked Fabrice, in a tone noticeably more subdued.

'In total, one hundred and ten thousand francs.'

Fabrice fell silent. Great principles, he noted, made no sound as they collapsed.

His father continued. 'That matches the amount that the Bishop of Perth will get from the Society for the Propagation of the Faith. A more capable man than Brady may have received two hundred thousand from the society, rendering you unnecessary. But happily, there are many mysteries about this bishop and while mystery has its place in religion, it is not welcome where money is concerned.

'So, you have been given a task, my boy. You will travel to this Swan Colony or whatever the godforsaken place is called. There you will become the eyes and ears of Mademoiselle Jaricot, and disburse her funds precisely as she says, and when she says.'

'But I do not approve of proselytising natives,' objected Fabrice.

'Your view is inconsequential,' snapped his father. 'Just do as she tells you. Record for her the performance of this bishop and of his missionaries. Write regularly to her. Take perfect care of her purse. Dispense the funds only in accordance with her advice. Do you understand?'

'I understand,' repeated Fabrice, examining his fingernails. He permitted his father a few seconds to enjoy his complete surrender, before adding, 'but I heard her tell you I was to be allowed some discretion.'

'Discretion?' his father thundered. 'How can you exercise some-thing you do not possess?'

The Cleriquots, *père et fils*, walked the rest of the distance in silence, one contemplating the success of the evening, the other the disaster of it. Once home, Fabrice was bemused to find that Maman already knew everything and had even prepared one of her speeches.

'Our dear boy is starting his life again,' she announced, 'but on the right foot this time, we hope.' She presented him with an unusual tropical hat, dome shaped, made of woven leaf with a brass top. 'It is called a *salacco*,' explained Maman. 'They all wear them in the Far East.'

With a flute of champagne in hand, Claude softened. He had managed to turn adversity to profit this evening, and felt he also should say some kind words. 'I am quite sure,' he proclaimed, 'that despite all the past disappointments, our dear Fabrice will, if not triumph exactly, then succeed. Or if not succeed, then at least, ah … manage.'

Glasses were clinked, cheeks doubly kissed. Tears came to the eyes of Madame Cleriquot. It had suddenly hit her. Her only son was to travel to far-off Western Australia! And the poor boy was only thirty-one!

'It might not be so bad,' said Fabrice, almost resigned to the venture. 'I can still teach in the winter.'

'*This* winter?' said his father, exasperated, 'Three months will be barely enough time to get there, and only then does your job begin. You must stay until the mission is established. Besides, you must stay away from Lyon until this sordid matter at the university is forgotten.' Claude glanced at his wife, whom he had not told of any 'sordid matters', remembering as he did so to interrogate her later about her rôle in the scarf debacle. 'You will be gone for two years, boy, maybe more. Now go back to your apartment, pack your bags, and for your mother's sake do arrive on time for your farewell dinner tomorrow evening.'

Fabrice Cleriquot felt his face pale. 'When am I to leave?'

'When the priests leave. Tuesday.'

'In two days?' A cruel fist reached deep inside the chest of Fabrice Cleriquot as if to steal his heart. His very life had been snatched away. His friends at the university, with their intelligent wit. All the amusing parties. His comfortable apartment, gone. And now he remembered ... right now, probably asleep on the red velour sofa, the one who had triggered this difficulty would still be waiting for him.

Fabrice Cleriquot trudged disconsolately from his parents' mansion, the first sad steps on an unwanted journey. He was to sail in the unpleasant company of argumentative black-cloaked foreign priests, not to Tahiti or some such desirable place, but to a remote English-speaking outpost of which no one had ever heard, whose towns were populated, no doubt, by murderers, rapists and convicts, and then to venture beyond even that to live among the wild natives of Western Australia, all for no better purpose than to disturb their eternal peace in the name of a god in which he had no belief.

Alone, in the darkness, on the *Montée St Barthélemy*, Fabrice Cleriquot shed a silent tear for himself.

He returned to his apartment. As expected, upon the red sofa, still sobbing, lay Raphael. By some means the boy too had already learned that his *professeur* was to be exiled, like Napoleon, to some distant island. Instead of being consoled for his misfortune, Fabrice was wildly berated.

'You are utterly selfish and I hate you,' were the boy's last words before he slammed the door. Then from outside, 'I hope the savages get you and kill you and eat you.'

From: Pauline Jaricot, Lyon

To: Fabrice Cleriquot, Lyon

16th June, 1845

Cher Fabrice

I suspect it is against all your natural inclinations to travel to Australia with a group of monks and bishops. I understand. Even I sometimes tire of bishops, always grasping for something. I fear there may come a time on this journey where you are tempted to go your own way. I am writing this to explain why it is so important that you stay and succeed.

You and I are wealthy, educated and occupy an esteemed place in French society. Most of God's people do not have these advantages. Many are hungry, enslaved by their poverty, or dwell in far-off lands quite ignorant of Our Lady's love for them. We have a duty to these masses, we cannot deny it.

My sense of duty came upon me when I was fifteen. Before that, I was not a saint in miniature, I assure you! I was a pretty, rich, indulged girl living 'The Silk Life' as we called it. After dear Maman died, my father denied me nothing. I was quite the terror, really.

But one day I attended a dissertation by Abbé Wurtz. His subject was 'The Vanity of Women'. After that, I was done with girlish silliness forever. I dressed plainly, refused mirrors and went to work at the Hospital for Incurables. I grew up that day and threw off all desire for riches. I hope that you can do so as well.

In France, especially among the rich, the Church has become like a lamp without oil and I fear it will soon go out. Its best hope lies with the poor that suffer among us, and with those in distant lands who as yet know nothing of God's love for them. In such newfound places as Western Australia, the lamp is still full of oil and it is up to us to light it for them. Recently I had a vivid dream in which the New Lamp relit the Old.

The social ills from which France suffers fall mostly upon the working class who are destroyed by work, beaten down by it. But I am an optimist. I see in this downtrodden class the means of our Salvation. Improve their lot, and we all improve. The husband can be given back to the wife, the father to the child, and, through them, God to mankind.

I will share a secret with you Fabrice. I have bought a blast furnace! It will be run as a model of the Christian Spirit, as no capitalist would ever allow. The workers themselves will own the furnace, and run it, and profit from it. There will be a small village, with small neat cottages for the workers, a free school and a chapel. Your father would disapprove of the plan, seeing no possibility of profit. Please do not tell him or he will counsel me against it, and I always give in to your father.

You must ensure that the money I entrust to you is spent for the benefit of the native men, women and children of the colony of Western Australia, so that like my poor workers, they might prosper. They must be taught to read and write and add numbers, but above all, encouraged to grow in the knowledge of the Love of God. What I wish for these children of God, you see, is exactly as I wish for the working poor of Lyon.

Take the enclosed letter to M. Paracel, Manager of the Banque Lyonnais in Paris. He will arrange for you to collect some English currency from a London bank.

I have faith in you that your father may lack. Don't forget, my father was a wealthy silk merchant too. Such men have a certain way of looking at the world. My view is simple. For there to be true peace on earth it is necessary to correct certain imbalances, and I believe it is the will of God that we do so.

Bon voyage, mon cher Fabrice. Be assured I will pray to Our Lady of Fourvière every morning until your safe return to Lyon.

Pauline

2. THE LAST SWIM

Though they were still on the outskirts of Lyon, Fabrice Cleriquot already felt an overwhelming desire to escape the Catholic missionaries.

They had set off in high style, Bishop John Brady finding himself at last with a purse full of money courtesy of the Society for the Propagation of the Faith. Canal was the cheaper way from Lyon to Paris, but in a decision he would later see as profligate, His Lordship opted for carriage and chose a luxurious one, well sprung and polished. The carriageman looked like a well-fed Napoleon, an effect magnified by his green *chasseur à cheval* jacket. The postilion, a fourteen-year-old boy named Jean-Paul, was nimble and friendly and made sure that horses and passengers were kept well fed and watered.

Inside the cab sat four men, two in baggy black cassocks, one in a new black tunic topped by a pink cap, and a dapper layman in a navy jacket and a raffish silk necktie bearing the pattern of a peacock feather. On the seat beside Fabrice was the brass-tipped Siamese sunhat, which he had neglected to pack but had been discovered by Maman at the last moment and pushed through the window.

'You should know at the outset that I am an Atheist,' Fabrice Cleriquot told Dom Rosendo Salvado, speaking Galician so that Bishop Brady could not understand.

'How wonderful to be so certain,' said the Benedictine, his eyebrows seeming to tease the Frenchman. 'I can only admire your faith.' The monk smiled indulgently, a gentle father to a wayward son.

The Galician's lack of seriousness rather disappointed Fabrice, who wanted to explain that Christianity had been destroyed in the year 311 when Emperor Constantine converted, after which it was forever tied to the evils of wealth, power and property. Bishops, priests, monks, papal armies, Nicene creeds, Inquisitions, all these were the consequences of the Catholic Church having to protect its power and wealth. This was an enjoyable argument to recite during university debates.

Beyond the outskirts of town, Professor Cleriquot tried a different way to provoke.

'Why is it that all you Spanish priests now live in France and Italy?' he started. 'Could you no longer make enough money in Spain?'

'The regime closed all our monasteries,' replied Dom Salvado, looking very sad. 'They smashed our icons, beat our monks, banished us. Dom Serra and I saw many terrible things happen in Santiago de Compostela, but in the south it was much worse.'

'And why would they have done all that, I wonder?' asked Fabrice, feeling he knew the answer: it all emanated from Constantine.

'Because they were atheists.' Salvado waved a hand loosely at his companion's colourful shirt. 'Like you, I suppose, *Frère* Fabrice. But, ah, rather more compelling. They had guns, you see. Not silk neckties.'

Fabrice was stung by this barb. He came from money, it was true, but his heartfelt sympathies lay entirely with the workers.

'Perhaps they saw that the Catholic Church was really the friend of the rich and powerful,' countered the silk merchant's son.

'Possibly so,' conceded the monk, shrugging. 'The Church in Spain was seen by some as an oppressor. And it is true that some priests enjoyed too much the company of the rich and that some bishops enjoyed their influence in temporal matters. And there was the Inquisition, which, it must be admitted, endeared few to the Church.'

'*The Christian God is a father who cares more about his apples than his children,*' quoted Fabrice.

'Montesquieu?' guessed the Spaniard.

'Diderot,' corrected the linguist. 'It is irrefutable.'

Dom Salvado paused a moment in thought. 'It is *somewhat* refutable, I think. God the Father cares only about his children. It was his children who desired the apples. He warned them *against* apples, as I recall.'

Fabrice was flustered. Diderot had never failed him before.

'You are not from a poor family,' he said to the monk, to regain his momentum. 'Don't deny it. I can tell from your manner of speech.'

'True enough,' conceded Dom Salvado. 'The Salvados of Tuy were not poor. My father was not greatly wealthy like yours, but as a boy I got to take piano lessons, and so on. But if you mean to suggest that my brother and I entered the priesthood in order to increase the family wealth then, as you can see, it has proved a most unsuccessful plan!'

'What of your order?' Fabrice persisted. 'I will bet your monastery is the grandest building in the province.'

'San Martiño is indeed very beautiful. I miss it greatly, especially the organ I used to play. But I would just as soon chant my *Te Deums* in the wild bush.'

'Just as well, for in Western Australia you will have plenty of that.'

'Good!' replied Salvado, looking out the window, and they both fell silent. This meant the whole carriage was now silent, for opposite them Bishop John Brady from County Cavan and Dom José Serra from Catalonia had long since run out of conversation, each one annoyed at having to speak French when the other spoke it so poorly.

They came now to a small town and when the carriage was almost at a stop, a stranger on the road noticed it was full of Catholic monks. He stared at Dom Salvado with neither a smile nor a frown, and with his thumbnail made a slitting action across his own throat. Salvado looked back at the stranger with equanimity. In modern France, as in Spain, priests had become accustomed to such gestures.

'One of your fellow atheists,' observed Salvado calmly. 'But we will press on with Our Lord's work, regardless.'

Claude Cleriquot had told a story to the missionaries about the purpose of his son. Fabrice was travelling to Western Australia for purely mercantile reasons; *Cleriquot et Fils* hoped to establish itself in Perth ahead of its rivals, and the son was to report on the state of the silk market there. To support this fiction, Fabrice had been given a small slotted box containing ten cards of the highest quality Chinese silkworm eggs. He had it with him now in the carriage and showed it to the three priests, who exchanged looks of contempt.

'A pity your father didn't make his fortune selling farming equipment,' Salvado teased, using French so the amusement could be generally shared. 'Ploughs, yokes, iron nails; those are the sorts of things we will need. Silk is useless.'

'We all have our work to do,' replied Fabrice. 'Mine is silk. With two million new Catholics, think only of the robes you gentlemen will require.' Salvado fell silent. There was no answer to this without offending the bishop.

In Paris, Fabrice abandoned the priests to stay in a good *hôtel* where they knew the name Cleriquot. On the appointed afternoon, he went to the bank where the name Jaricot resonated just as well. He was greeted by Monsieur Paracel's personal assistant with a glass of champagne, and found himself sitting alongside Bishop Brady. The bishop had worn his silk cap and was nervously holding a letter similar to one Fabrice had folded inside his jacket. It seemed they were both there to collect more money – Fabrice from Pauline Jaricot's personal account, and the bishop from the Society for the Propagation of the Faith.

'I am here on an errand for my father,' Fabrice lied. 'The silk business, you see.'

'You must feel perfectly at home in a place like this, I suppose,' said the bishop, his scaly old hands trembling. 'Banks are a form of torture to me. Soon I will be interrogated by an insolent French banker who will disparage my accent and look down his nose at me. I hate the whole business of money. I am from peasant stock, and proud of it. I am not like those princes of the Church who enjoy mixing with the high and mighty.'

The bishop spoke fondly of his previous parish in New South Wales, where he daily rode his horse along rough tracks, minister-ing to an unusual constituency of Irish ticket-of-leave men, local natives, and troublesome French Canadians who had been shipped there by the British.

'Not a single penny was needed to run my parish,' boasted the Bishop of Perth, 'which was just as well, for there was not one to be had.'

'You must have a special affinity with the natives, *Monseigneur*,' said Fabrice, sipping delicately from his flute. He was thinking of Pauline Jaricot's letter, her instructions to direct her money to the benefit of the Australian natives.

'I am an Irishman, Cleriquot,' said the bishop with an endearing sadness in his voice. 'I know very well what English colonists do to the local inhabitants, and how they go about it. First, they starve them of property and of education. Poverty follows, then all the evils of begging, prostitution, the drink and so on. The poor black fellows in Perth will come to be despised for succumbing to the abuse inflicted upon them, just as we Irish are. I will do everything in my power to protect them.'

'How?' asked Fabrice. He should help this bishop after all, he thought, despite his excruciating accent. But then came the answer.

'Religion,' said Bishop Brady. 'Our Lord is the antidote. We will give them God, and education.'

What happened after that was just as Bishop Brady had predicted. An immaculately dressed *banquier* appeared, his cuffs pressed like blades ready to draw Irish blood. In scrambling awkwardly to his feet, the bishop dropped all his papers. He apologised ungrammatically, fumbled some more, and Fabrice saw all semblance of respect drain from the banker's face, replaced by Parisian condescension.

The silk merchant's son, by contrast, was greeted as a gentleman by Monsieur Paracel himself. Fabrice Cleriquot possessed all the qualities that brought one respect in a place of Finance: he spoke well, he dressed well, and he had the right surname. A second glass was poured by *Monsieur le Directeur* while his assistant counted and recounted the gold *Louis-Philippes*. Even this was not the full sum, the banker explained, and gave Fabrice a wax-sealed letter to take to a particular London bank. Monsieur Paracel did not generally approve of English currency but it may occasionally be of use, he admitted, in an English colony.

Two days later, the bishop told the Benedictines that he would be staying behind in Paris for a few days while they pushed on to Amiens; Monsieur Cleriquot would pay their fare. The first Fabrice knew of this plan was while enjoying a long lunch for two in the window table at Café Procope when, through the glass, he saw two unshaven fellows in black cassocks emerge from a waiting carriage and speak with the *maître d'hôtel*, who gestured inside.

Fabrice's laden fork froze an inch from his mouth. 'My god, I think I am about to be abducted by monks,' he told his friend, who was greatly amused. After that, all pleasure ceased as Fabrice journeyed across France in the company of a growing band of missionaries.

The first night was spent with yet more Benedictines at St Jean de Bièvres, a mercifully short journey from Paris. Their host was famous in France, explained Salvado. Dom Prosper Guéranger was the saviour of Solesmes Abbey, founded in the year 1010 and slowly decaying since, and restorer of the Gregorian chant in France. Now he was Abbot Guéranger of a thriving Solesmes Abbey, and from there had started some smaller communities such as this one at Bièvres.

The abbot had an intelligent, thin face and attentive eyes, and over liqueurs, was unexpectedly generous in his attention to Fabrice. Solesmes followed the ancient Rule of St Benedict, he explained, meaning its abbot had control over every aspect of the community, including the finances. No Benedictine community would ever countenance outside interference in its affairs, especially by a bishop. Dom Serra and Dom Salvado nodded in agreement, thinking perhaps of Bishop Brady.

'Our brother here is an atheist,' announced Salvado unexpectedly, causing the heads of couple of black-cloaked monks to turn toward Fabrice.

'Is that so, Monsieur Cleriquot?' said the abbot, with a hint of a smile. He seemed the sort to enjoy mild conflict. 'Like, ah ... Bertrand Barère, perhaps?'

Fabrice stiffened at this provocation. This was the most hated name in Lyon: in the worst days of the Republic, Barère had punished the city for being rich, Catholic, and uncowed. 'Lyon has made war on Liberty, so Lyon will be no more!' Barère removed the name Lyon from the map, renaming it *Ville-Affranchie*, Freed Town. He abolished the Catholic Church, enforcing instead the worship of a secular deity invented by the State, *le Culte de l'Être Suprême*, the Cult of the Supreme Being.

'No, abbot,' protested Fabrice, weakly. 'I am not like Barère, not at all.'

'I am so pleased to hear it, *frère*,' replied the abbot cheerfully, 'since you are our welcome guest.'

Salvado smiled and sipped, happy with his mischief.

A rare second glass was permitted to each man in honour of the visitors and there followed an interesting reading from *The Conferences of the Desert Fathers* regarding the lukewarmness of eunuchs. Then came the office of *Compline*, and by seven o'clock they were all in their freezing cells for The Great Silence. There were no blankets to be had. The ancient Rules of St Benedict did not condone blankets. To Fabrice's frustration, they were to enjoy three nights of Benedictine hospitality.

That the monks of Solesmes were devoted to their abbot, there was no doubt, but none could love him more than the novice, Dom Léandre Fonteinne. This was extravagantly confirmed on the morning that Dom Guéranger offered him up to the Spanish missionaries. Léandre did not want to leave his dear abbot, not at all. His soft sobs became loud cries, and then came a gush of such pleadings, such heartfelt oaths of devotion, that Fabrice could only find the whole display amusing.

'Why is he the only one?' Fabrice asked Salvado quietly, as they observed the performance.

'Is it not clear?' replied Salvado, carefully expressionless. 'But,' he sighed, 'it would be impolite to decline the offer.'

Eventually the little fellow did allow himself to be peeled from the cloak of his superior, dried his face on his scapular and climbed into the carriage, so becoming a missionary to Western Australia. They were again a travelling party of four, three black-cloaked Benedictines and one elegantly attired academic. Being two natural Spanish speakers and two French, they divided into conversational pairs.

'My dear abbot is a living saint,' the still-grieving Benedictine novice sobbed. 'I would not say it is *cruel* of him to send me away from my beloved brothers to this faraway terrible place, for Dom Guéranger knows nothing but love and is incapable of cruelty.'

Fabrice slowly grew accustomed to the novice's unusual cadence of speech; every utterance laden with self-pity, each thesis coupled with its antithesis. When not weeping, the novice loved to gossip, and could switch from one mood to the opposite in an instant.

By Beauvais, Fabrice had been told the secrets of every monk at Solesmes. When Léandre accused someone, he would always attribute the accusation to some other person and then add his personal disapproval of that view.

'Dom Bourgeteau must also come to Australia to join us!' he declared, speaking as if Fabrice knew who this Dom Bourgeteau was and loved him just as dearly. 'That he cannot be trusted even for an hour because of his interest in females, as they all say, I do not believe, even after what occurred in Le Mans between Dom Bourgeteau and the married parishioner.'

In every classroom in France there existed such a child, thought Fabrice, the type who dusted the chalkboards for the *professeur* and was despised by all the others. He felt sure Bishop Brady would come to deplore Léandre Fonteinne, and secretly delighted in the anticipation of it.

As they arrived at their destination near Amiens, tears appeared on the novice's cheek and he told Fabrice with great sincerity, 'Thank you, dear friend, for listening to my silliness. Please, tell me if ever I talk too much. But of course, a true friend would always listen.'

La Neuville was the house of the order of the Holy Heart of Mary, whose priests wore brown cloaks not black. The new arrivals were greeted by the superior, Father François-Marie-Paul Libermann, as well as Bishop Brady, who had arrived early from Paris, and a well-dressed handsome Italian; Count Nicola Caporelli, the bishop proudly announced, a nobleman of the Papal States.

'A prince!' gasped the novice, open-mouthed.

'I doubt it,' mumbled Fabrice, with a hint of jealousy. 'Look at his cuffs.'

It being a pleasant autumn afternoon, they all grouped outside in the courtyard, priests and monks cloaked in brown or black, plus the two well-attired laymen who kept their distance and eyed each other suspiciously.

'This must be your atheist,' said Father Libermann when introduced to Fabrice. The bishop blushed and looked hard at Salvado for an explanation.

'Merely one who has doubts,' said Fabrice, trying to soften the description. His colleagues at the university would have winced to see his conviction crumble before clergy.

'There is a special place reserved in Hell for you,' proclaimed Father Libermann smilingly, 'or so said Dante. But you are in good company, Monsieur Cleriquot, for there was a time when I too lost my faith. I was young, France was in troubled times, and I had taken to reading Rousseau. I was a Man of Reason, for a time. Rousseau led me to agnosticism, but there I had the sense to stop and turn around.'

This startling confession from the founder of a priestly order produced no reaction from those who listened. Perhaps, thought Fabrice, it was an oft-told story.

'I noticed what terrible things were caused by a *lack* of faith! It was even worse than faith, would you believe? The atheists enjoyed terrorising the Church, clergy and laypeople alike. So I rebelled once more, this time to join the Church. Now, as you can see from all these priests, I am forever cured of Rousseau!'

Father Libermann's eyes shone mischievously through his round glasses. 'I have even worse to confess, Monsieur Cleriquot. Before all that, I was a Jew!' He paused to give Fabrice time to assess his face for Jewish traits. 'You see, it's true, brother! My birth name was Jacob Libermann. My father was a rabbi.' Even this astounding news provoked no reaction from the other clergy.

'I like to think my journey has mirrored Our Lord's life on earth. I passed from Judaism, through great doubt, to this Holy Vocation. Do you see? You should try to remember this, Monsieur Cleriquot. Even Our Lord Jesus had His doubts. Even at the end of His time on earth, on the Holy Cross, He doubted. So please, do not feel badly about these doubts of yours. They will pass, you will see.'

The Heart of Mary order was devoted to saving the souls of black people in faraway lands. Father Libermann had some good news for the Bishop of Perth. He would provide five men for Western Australia, three priests and two young laymen. Before the evening meal, the bishop, impressive in pink biretta and stole, formally welcomed them and spoke enthusiastically about his evangelising mission to the two million natives on the far side of the earth. Even Fabrice, sitting among the clergy, felt within him a rising surge of oneness of purpose, and had to quash it.

Once Brady resumed his seat, Father Libermann addressed his men thus:

'Have no fear of the difficulties you are going to meet. Difficulties must never discourage you. It is after all not *you* who are doing the work, but the One who sent you. You are never alone. He will always be with you. Stop for a while in front of obstacles which seem to be insoluble and wait for God's moment with confidence. Be faithful, be patient, and that moment will surely arrive.'

He appointed Francis Thévaux, the younger of the Fathers Francis, to be the superior of the mission, but the missionaries would act at all times 'as if they had but one heart and one soul.'

Nonetheless, after Mass, three of those selected to go to Australia came to Fabrice seeking his advice and reassurance. He had been judged a useful Francophone with secret knowledge of the bishop's plans. First came the young laymen, Théodore and Vincent, who had some practical questions that they could not ask of a religious.

'This Swan River,' began Théodore, 'it is an English colony, correct?' Vincent, older but even shyer, listened intently for the answer.

Fabrice confirmed it and saw their shoulders relax.

'Good,' whispered Théodore. 'You see, we wish to avoid being conscripted into the French army.'

'Also, we love Jesus very much,' added Vincent, 'and wish to spread His Word.'

'Oh yes,' confirmed the younger man, seeing his error.

Father Maurice Bouchet also sought a private conversation. He was an anxious man and had heard nothing good about Western Australia.

'I was prepared to be sent anywhere, Monsieur Cleriquot, for our order is devoted to serving freed slaves. I had hoped for Haiti, perhaps, or to go to Senegambia to join my brother Marie. But this Western Australia fills me with fear. I am being punished for my thesis, I am sure.'

What terrible thing could he have written, asked Fabrice, trying to calm the poor fellow.

'I wrote about what Luke said of St Joseph,' Father Bouchet confessed to the atheist. 'What a mistake! As you must know, Luke never mentioned Joseph, not even once! So now I am to be sent to this Swan Colony or whatever they call it. It is the end of the earth, and English. Oh, *pauvre moi!*'

By the time the missionaries reached Boulogne-sur-Mer on the northern coast of France, their number had grown to eleven, a couple of whom struck Fabrice as mad or likely to soon go that way.

Next day they would sail to England.

Fabrice was content at last. He had found a table, a friendly waiter, a glass of wine and a smoke. Down below him on the beach he kept a vague eye on Léandre Fonteinne, the Benedictine novice disguised for the night in civilian clothes, and Nicola Caporelli, the so-called count to whom Léandre seemed to have transferred his love. Fabrice watched the little fellow performing for the Italian, who dared him to swim. Léandre took off his trousers, folded them too neatly and placed them carefully on the stone steps, his every action slightly odd.

The waiter's name was Henri. He had just been putting out the wicker chairs when Fabrice walked past, his first customer for the evening. Henri was an excellent waiter, anticipating Fabrice's every need. Without asking, he snapped down a red linen table-cloth, brought a carafe of white wine and a glass, then produced two small cigars and sat down with his only customer. Henri was probably not his real name, for he let it slip that he had recently abandoned the French army. He was not made for taking orders from idiots, he explained, nor waiting endlessly to no purpose, nor bayonetting strangers. The two men shared the sort of witty conversation Fabrice had not enjoyed since leaving Lyon.

Once the other tables started to fill, Fabrice was left alone to blow contented smoke rings and contemplate his future. He felt pleasantly detached from the myriad worries of these petty missionaries. Should Father Maurice Bouchet take a particular teacup to Australia, or the novice his blue vest? Everything these priests did seemed futile.

Fabrice was certain the natives of Western Australia were perfectly content in their ignorance of the dubious god to which these men were so attached. But he could not quite bring himself to ignore the money he carried, nor could he entirely disregard the letter from Pauline Jaricot, the sincerity of which had moved him. Nor could his father's view of things be fully ignored. Fabrice had no need of Jaricot money – indeed he wished it away – but Paris had reminded him that he did need Cleriquot money to live as he wished. It was, he had to admit, very pleasant to have important men in sharply pressed suits pour one wine.

From the darkness of the beach came the sound of Léandre ducking under the water and re-emerging with a small scream. The waters of *La Manche* were so *cold*, complained the novice, and so *salty*!

'Ah, young love!' smiled Henri, 'how sweet.' He was lighting the gas lamps, which came on with a popping noise and cast an arc of lovely yellow light upon the stony shore below, so that now one could again make out the two bathers. The novice's plump white orbs could be seen disappearing into a pair of trousers. That might be the last time he would ever bathe in the waters of France, Dom Léandre could be heard weeping, while Caporelli stood over him with folded arms, pretending to comfort the little fellow and calling him *Munaciello* after the midget monk of Naples.

When the swimmers joined Fabrice at the café, Henri reappeared unbidden with two extra glasses and a second carafe. Wet, freshly combed hair produced different effects on the two men; the Italian count appeared sleek and sharp while the Benedictine novice was a chubby child just removed from his bath. The three men touched glasses and bade one another *santé*.

The air smelt pleasantly nautical but it served to remind them of the long dangerous sea journey ahead.

'What a beautiful creation is the sea!' proclaimed the same novice who had just been heard professing his dislike of it. 'I will happily trust myself to the oceans. I am certain that it will not be terrible or harmful.' Then he looked up at Caporelli with his lips atremble. 'Will we drown, Nicola?'

'Most likely, *piccolo*,' said Caporelli, teasingly. He poured another full glass for the novice, who had decided to entirely abandon the Rule of St Benedict for this special night in protest against the cruelty of his abbot.

'I am not a missionary,' Dom Léandre said aloud. 'Not a priest, not even a proper monk.'

Fabrice's suspicions about Caporelli's wealth and influence had been proven earlier that day when Caporelli had asked him about 'the possibility of a small loan'. But in public the Italian was adept at singing his own praises. 'Once we are in Australia,' he boasted over the fish pie Fabrice had bought for him, 'I shall be Consul-General for the Papal States. Also, I will be headmaster of the main school.'

'*Are* there any schools in Perth?' asked Fabrice.

'Oh, yes,' the Italian reassured him, 'many.' Nicola Caporelli was trusting in bluff and bravado to get him through, just as the priests believed Latin incantations would buy them protection from their ignorance.

After the meal, as they took ports, a beautiful young woman in a brightly patterned silk dress appeared and stopped right next to the three men. The strap of her shoe required attention. It was Henri's girlfriend, Fabrice was unhappy to discover, waiting for him to finish work. The waiter soon appeared, threw his apron over a chair, kissed her twice, and off they walked, Henri's arm draped in a most familiar manner around his lover's waist. The three missionaries were silent for a while in their separate and private contemplations.

'I do so miss Rome,' said Caporelli.

'That silk is called organza,' Fabrice informed them, momentarily his father's protégé.

'It flows so beautifully,' observed Dom Léandre Fonteinne. 'How soft it must be against the skin.'

At two in the morning the bells rang for *Nocturns* and all the missionaries filed in to the pretty church of St Nicolas to celebrate their departure from France. Dom Léandre Fonteinne had become a novice monk again, head bowed and cloaked in black. At Léandre's insistence, Fabrice attended. The Benedictines filled the room with their incense so the altar could barely be seen. Led by the sweet-voiced novice they chanted their hypnotic Gregorian *Te Deums*, after which Dom Serra spoke a sentence and then allowed a long silent contemplation of the work ahead. The Heart of Mary priests, less accustomed to these hours, chewed peppercorns to stay awake.

Bishop John Brady, speaking in Latin, presided over a special exposition of the Blessed Sacrament, and there followed a candlelit procession during which Dom Salvado played the organ. He filled the little church with music of his own composition, a sound so compelling that the little novice without shame let his tears fall onto his black robe. Fabrice had to make an effort to appear unmoved.

'I saw you cry,' observed the novice, afterwards. 'How strange, for an atheist.'

'You were looking through your own tears, little man,' Fabrice insisted. 'My eyes were perfectly dry at the dullness of it all.'

Fabrice had had enough now of priests and monks and novices and bishops. The city of London was a very good place in which to get lost, so a friend at his university had told him. He had been given the name of an army officer who was *de l'autre bord*, but discretely so, in the English manner. It might be prudent, it occurred to Fabrice, to adopt a new name in London so as not to risk the precious Cleriquot cachet, nor the reputations of these fervent missionaries.

He would become Jean Martin. Even in London there must be dozens of Jean Martins.

From: Bishop John Brady, Downside Monastery, Somerset
To: M. Fabrice Cleriquot, possibly alias 'Jean Martin',
          c/o Horse Guards, Kensington

12th August 1845

Cher Monsieur Cleriquot

I trust your time in London has been restorative and that you have spent your leisure time in pursuits wholly consonant with the spirit of our mission. The rest of us have been doing work to prepare for Western Australia and are scattered in various locations across England. I am to depart in two days for Dublin to recruit our nuns. I require you to accompany me as translator since I will be travelling with two Italians. Also there are some documents from Rome I wish you to look at.

We depart Euston Station Wednesday at seven. The train fares and the ferry crossing from Liverpool will need paying for. You should know that I am in regular written correspondence with your father, who you must recall pledged his firm support for my mission, and with Mademoiselle Jaricot. I would not wish to have to mention to them the whispers I have heard about your conduct while in London. So please do not be late to the station, for the train will not wait.

Yours in Christ
John, Bishop of Perth

3. THE ROT SETS IN

Until the bishop's letter came to spoil things, Jean Martin had been greatly enjoying his anonymity in all the least reputable parts of London. What a wonderful city London was, if one had money: grimy, dark, cold and terribly hypocritical. Its most respectable citizens were also its naughtiest.

His Kensington apartment felt pleasantly familiar, the layout being similar to his lamented one back in Lyon. It had a balcony overlooking notorious St James Park with a view of its prettily curved avenues winding around trees and lakes. Around dusk it offered clandestine entertainment of which he never tired; watching the park's *habitués* on their naughty 'rambles', as the poet Wilmot had described them.

The knock at the door brought an end to all this. It was an English officer in civilian dress proffering a letter addressed to his real name.

'Might you know a Catholic bishop, at all?' the Englishman asked delicately. 'One called Brady seems to have sent this to our barracks. I could scarcely ignore a letter from a prelate, even a Catholic one, so I thought it best to deliver it in person.' The envelope had already been opened. Fabrice Cleriquot was, after all, French and could not be fully trusted.

Fabrice insisted the Englishman come in for a scotch.

'Glenlivet,' enthused the officer. 'I happened to enjoy one with Her Majesty this morning. Her mountain dew, she calls it.'

Fabrice read Brady's short letter. It was written in small shaky hand and left Fabrice no room for refusal. Feigning insouciance, he folded it and placed it on the bureau, wondering as he did so how the bishop had discovered him. Then he recalled; on the ferry he had told the little novice of his plans for London, in strictest confidence.

'Well, it seems I am to travel to Ireland tomorrow,' he told the officer, with more calmness than he felt. He had already calculated the cost of refusing. He could scarcely defy his parents, the Saintly Virgin of Lyon and the Bishop of Perth.

'Miserable luck, molly,' commiserated the officer, who already knew this information. 'That will rather put an end to your cater-wauling around the streets of London.'

'Yes, a great pity,' said Fabrice, trying his best to appear English in the face of disaster. 'I have only met half of your brigade.'

'And to Ireland, of all terrible places! They are all very hungry there, I understand.' The officer took a thoughtful sip, then bright-ened as an idea came to him. 'I will take you out tonight for your last good meal, Jean. Naturally,' he added, meaningfully, 'I will find you something sweet, for afters.'

Next morning at six, having had no sleep at all, Fabrice had the cab wait while he collected his bags from his apartment, then continued to Euston Station where he went straight to the ticket booth and bought four First Class fares to Liverpool. He handed three of the tickets to the waiting Bishop of Perth, whose gratitude was barely mumbled.

They made a picturesque quartet as they boarded the steam train. John Brady looked impressive in a black *douillette* double-breasted cloak with amaranth silk on view at his neck and atop his head. Count Nicola Caporelli still wore his only jacket, the collar and cuffs now clearly in need of repair. The new man, a small serious monk called Angelo Confalonieri, was dressed as if for the Dolomites in a smart green Tyrolean jacket with a fur-lined collar. Fabrice still wore whatever he had put on for dinner with the captain the previous evening. Recalling the clash of silk at *Lorette*, he checked which cravat he had thrown around his neck and was relieved to see it was one inoffensive to clergy – a rather beautiful blood-red, adorned with gold brocade in the Persian style.

First Class was not at all commodious. An attempt was made to serve biscuits and weak English tea, but the waiter had to stoop and the Tyrolean suffered a scalded thigh. Fabrice, suffering from lack of sleep, thought of the Café Procope and longed for proper strong coffee and brioche.

As a reward for paying for the fares, Fabrice found himself seated next to the bishop, who sniffed and pulled a face.

'Are you wearing perfume, Cleriquot?'

'Yes, Eminence.'

The prelate had no answer to this confession. The train whistle broke the awkwardness of the moment. 'Right, well. We are off to see the nuns,' Brady declared, and as the train took off, slapped his thighs with quiet satisfaction, for he would be going home a bishop.

Brady balanced a valise on his lap and started to peruse some important-looking papers through *pince-nez*. Every so often the bishop asked Fabrice to check a translation from Latin into English, for correspondence from the Prefect of *Propaganda Fide* or the

Evangelisation Congregation; or *vice versa*, for the bishop's written responses to these arcane entities. Fabrice was only permitted to view the particular passage in question, and not to hold the document.

It seemed Brady was advising Rome how best to divide up the island continent of Australia. On a map of Australia he had marked in boundaries for each diocese, ecclesiastical province and apostolic vicariate. Bishop Polding of Sydney owned the eastern third of the continent, he had conceded, and Bishop Brady the western third. The huge but sparsely populated central third appeared to be in dispute. There were only two towns marked in this vast area, 'Adelaide' in the south and 'Port Victoria' on the far north coast. All else was desert, the bishop explained. Brady was advising Rome that this central third be further divided into northern and southern vicariates to be called 'Port Victoria' and 'King George Sound' respectively, and that he be bishop of both.

'You would rule Adelaide from here, Your Holiness?' Fabrice asked, pointing to the port of Albany in King George Sound, three thousand kilometres to the west.

'Well, Rome is a long way from Dublin,' explained the bishop brusquely. 'And Cleriquot, it is Your Lordship, every time. The Holy Father is not on the train.'

Fabrice offered no more geographical suggestions, but felt compelled to correct the bishop's Latin syntax as delicately as he could. Cardinals in Rome, he imagined, would be just as snobbish in matters of language as were Parisian bankers.

In the seat opposite, Nicola Caporelli had thought to bring along a small bottle of red wine and a single glass. He chuckled occasionally as he read his missal which, Fabrice noticed, had a scandalous Italian novelette hidden within it. There was a hole in the toe of the right boot of the so-called Count of the Papal States.

'You do that to annoy, I suppose,' said Caporelli, mumbling in Italian, without looking up. He could have been commenting to himself on something he had just read.

'What?'

'Getting his honorific wrong.'

'Oh,' sighed the Frenchman, looking at his nails so as not to attract the attention of the bishop. 'I have no head for titles. I am a democrat by nature.'

The Italian sniffed. Possibly he was amused.

'Your purpose in Ireland?' Caporelli enquired, still fixing his gaze on the page before him.

'Translator,' said Fabrice. 'Yours?'

'Exotic ornament, I think. Why would he need a translator?'

'Because you speak neither French nor English very well, so it seems.' Fabrice knew Caporelli had taught both these languages at an exclusive school in Rome, and would be offended.

Caporelli did momentarily raise his head from his book at this. '*Ah bon*?' he said with great irony, and returned to his reading. An aristocrat, even one with a frayed collar, did not rise to the bait of mere clergy. But then he grumbled softly to his missal, in English, 'So says a man who cannot be understood in either tongue.' The bishop appeared to be safely asleep.

'And how goes our little friend?' asked Fabrice, with a bit more sincerity. He was speaking of Léandre Fonteinne.

'Badly, of course,' replied the Italian, licking his finger to turn the page of his secret pornography. 'Weeping for his abbot, and so on.'

The other priest was revealed to be another Benedictine, despite his dress. Don Angelo Confalonieri had the sad face and bulging eyes of a sickly child. Fabrice listened carefully to his accented Italian. The Tyrol was a linguistically complex region, falling between the Italians and the Austrians, but the professor of linguistics was fluent enough in Cimbrian, Mòcheno and one or two other of the dialects of the Dolomites to hazard a guess at what part this monk came from.

'Do all the priests dress so well in beautiful Trento?' Fabrice enquired, employing the vernacular of the better educated of that alpine town.

'Trento?' said Confalonieri, looking as if he had spotted a friend in a crowd. 'How on earth did you know?'

Fabrice smiled, happy with his detective work. 'I was not quite certain but your jacket helped. It is suggestive of Trento, I think, being lined with fox rather than ermine.'

Confalonieri was delighted to be able to hold a conversation in his native tongue. When away from home, he explained, he missed his language more than the hills or even the people. To occasionally wear his Tyrol jacket gave him some comfort. Also it was preferable these days to dress in civilian clothes, he explained, rather than the cassock. 'It results in fewer ...'

'... stones?' suggested Fabrice.

'Yes,' conceded the Tyrolean, smiling, 'and fruit. But I notice the English are generally less inclined to violence.'

'Your friend here rather gives you away when he dons his pink cap,' said Fabrice.

That Brady still did not rouse at this jibe gave Don Confalonieri the confidence to open up. He leaned forward conspiratorially. He was very unhappy with the bishop, who had got his hands on a large donation which had been mailed by his friends to Downside

Abbey, clearly addressed to him. The bishop was 'keeping it safe for me', the monk scoffed. Fabrice recalled Prosper Guéranger's words regarding the Benedictine's love of autonomy and their ancient resentment of bishops.

'I noticed your generosity at Euston Station,' warned Confalonieri. 'Be careful, or it will all vanish into a certain pocket.'

At Birmingham, it seemed that by some sort of magic the train had already arrived in Ireland. The navvies repairing the line were all Irishmen, as were the workers at the station where they changed lines. The sight of a pink-capped bishop on a train station was something, but the sensational discovery that His Lordship was an Irishman caused such joy as Fabrice had never witnessed at home at the sight of a mere cleric. Tough-looking men fell to their knees at the sight of one of their countrymen standing on a station platform in the miraculous form of a bishop. Workmen wept and knelt and grasped the hand of Bishop John Brady of Perth in order to kiss it. A queue formed.

His Lordship's mood on the next train was greatly improved by all this adulation as well as a small bottle of Irish whiskey which had been pressed upon him. When they finally pulled in to Lime Street yet more Irishmen appeared, the first thrusting his head through the window to pay his respects to the bishop.

Liverpool itself was full of Irish Catholics. Most of the men working on the docks seemed to be Irish and newly arrived Irish families were scattered all about, the mothers looking bewildered and the children barefoot even though summer was over and the ground was getting chilly.

The priests had work to do in Liverpool so the two laymen were permitted a day of leisure. At the Royal Institution they came upon a gruesome new exhibit from *The Remote and Exotic Colony of Swan River on the Coast of New Holland*. Here before them, in freezing Liverpool, was their first encounter with one of the souls that Brady's mission had set itself to save. It was the head of the son of a tribal king, impaled on a stick and decorated with a headband made from the fur of a native animal and feathers from a black-and-red bird called a 'cockatoo'.

The two observers fell sadly silent.

'In Rome, I helped Brady publish his little dictionary of the native language,' said Caporelli eventually. 'I used to practise saying some of the native words aloud, just to see how they fell off my tongue. Strange to say, even though this poor fellow's tongue is now dumb, I can hear his voice. He is not a savage, as the curators have dressed him, just a man full of rage.'

'Sadness, I think,' suggested Fabrice, peering into the glass case.

'Fear,' added the Italian.

From Liverpool the four men boarded an almost empty passenger steamer for Ireland. Their tickets read 'Kings Town' but everyone on board called the destination 'Dunleary'. On arrival at Dublin's port, the sign had been defaced with a scandalous comment about the English Queen.

The smell of Ireland assailed them first, then its inhabitants. Scabby-handed beggars were everywhere on the dock and the roads around it. It was clear that Dunleary wharf was no place for any man to wear amaranth. The bishop pulled off his silk zucchetto and emerald ring and became once more a humble priest.

There was nobody to collect them. As they struggled with their luggage, the missionaries kept an eye on three lean, shifty-looking young men who loitered nearby wearing dangerous expressions, but it was a beggar woman clutching an undernourished infant who cornered them.

'Mister, a few shillings,' she pleaded, tugging at the sleeve of the richest one. 'This child needs feeding. You've got money on you, man, I can tell.'

The hag was correct. In just one purse secured around his middle, Fabrice Cleriquot had enough to feed all of Dublin's hungry for a year, and such was the feeling that welled up within him that he almost gave a purse over to her to distribute at her discretion. This was after all a Catholic country and the local people were starving, so the Mademoiselle's conditions that it go to the benefit of the poor natives would be satisfied. The silk merchant's son guiltily recalled his lavish last meal in London. 'We *should* react slowly to these purported problems of the Irish,' the captain had smilingly advised over claret, 'since their supporters are so prone to exaggerating their troubles.'

The beggar agreed to guide them to Baggot Street for a penny. She knew the House of Mercy well. 'God bless those wonderful women,' she said. She went there daily for soup and bread and it was the nuns who dressed her babe against the cold. She lifted her shawl to better wrap the child for the journey. The little face that peered out with unblinking eyes belonged to an emaciated thing, looking old enough to walk but too weak.

When they reached the convent, Fabrice put a pile of coins in the mother's skinny cold hand.

'What's this?' she said, inspecting the strange currency. 'I'm not a fool you know.' She rebundled her child and hurried off, trailing a flurry of curses back to the foreigner whom she suspected of some sort of trickery.

Baggot Street was in the decent part of Dublin. Though they arrived at the convent just after dark, the gates were already locked tight. There was a high front wall with a small brick guardhouse at either end. Inside the grounds they saw a tiny nun having a coughing fit. The bishop, whose silk cap had reappeared atop him, called out to her in Irish language, but the poor woman could not hear him over the sounds of her own lungs. Fabrice offered to scale the wall but was firmly advised by the bishop that 'one does not climb into nunneries'.

Eventually a cheerful woman emerged from one of the guard-houses wearing a large black apron, from which she guiltily brushed off some ash. She was armed with a long stick, at the end of which was a soft round brush.

'I've been sweeping the spiders,' she explained. 'God, how I hate them!' She was either a cleaning woman dressed in the manner of a nun, or a nun who had been interrupted while cleaning. When she saw the amaranth zucchetto atop a familiar face, her expression changed to joy.

'My God! Is that Father John Brady?' said the face between the bars. 'I mean Bishop Brady. Is it true, Father, that you're a bishop now? Dear God! Look at you, with your actual cap on your head there!'

'It is me, Sister Anne,' said the bishop humbly. 'No need to fuss, now.' He had thought about this moment for a long time, and now here he was, back in Ireland, a prince of the Catholic Church.

Inside, Bishop Brady of Perth was greatly fussed over, but he was Humility itself. His three travelling companions were but minor players on his stage. Perhaps Caporelli was correct: these three had been selected because they were the most ornamental of the missionaries. That Fabrice was an atheist seemed to be of no importance, for his was not a speaking rôle.

Mother Superior Cecilia Marmion spoke acceptable French, as did one of the senior nuns called Ursula Frayne. They were joined by Catherine Gogarty, the thin one they had seen coughing outside the convent. A modest supper was provided by Sister Anne Xavier Dillon, the cheerful one who had opened the gates for them. She had put away her cobweb duster but still wore the black apron, for kitchens were messy places too. Then the four missionaries were sent around the corner to be accommodated at the cathedral presbytery, or in Fabrice's case, a cold one-roomed cottage just across the road from it.

The next night was His Lordship's grand performance. With great passion he spoke of the need for nuns to come to Western Australia where there were two million souls to be saved and five thousand existing Catholics 'for whom there was as yet no one to break bread'. Before such a willing audience, Brady surprised as an orator. A list would be compiled by morning, announced Mother Cecilia. An older novice named Ignatia had already volunteered.

Next day, the Bishop of Perth left for the country with Caporelli and Confalonieri. Fabrice's presence was not required, Brady informed him, but would he be good enough to pay the driver in advance?

The minute they departed, Fabrice was ushered down the corridor by Sister Ursula into the office of Mother Cecilia who was seated behind a desk covered in papers, alongside a serious priest. Both wore spectacles and neither deigned to look up at the

Frenchman. They were studying a document and making small changes to it. Fabrice sat in silence, intrigued by what possible rôle he might have in the proceedings. The priest, he noted, had a good knowledge of legal terminology.

Ursula whispered so as not to disturb Mother Superior. 'Mister Cleriquot, is it true you are a professor of language?'

He confirmed it.

'Would you be prepared to look at a document for us, then?'

He would be happy to.

Fabrice waited patiently for an hour until the document in question was dry and ready for his inspection. Only then did Mother Cecilia look up. Her questioning was unexpectedly sharp.

'Now, Mister Cleriquot, excuse me, but I need to ascertain your allegiances. His Lordship was not exactly clear about your connection to the mission.'

'My father made the bishop's hat,' Fabrice explained.

Quizzical glances were exchanged.

'Your father, he is a good friend of Mademoiselle Pauline Jaricot, of the Society for the Propagation of the Faith?'

'Yes.'

'That must be it, then,' Mother Cecilia said, and the others nodded. 'Mister Cleriquot, we would appreciate your view on something, in absolute confidence. The Sisters of Mercy have been greatly moved by Bishop Brady's appeal and feel compelled to help with his mission. Our founder, Catherine McAuley, made this a practical order. We are women of action, Mister Cleriquot, not cloistered nuns praying away in the dark, as some imagine. We dedicate our lives to the wellbeing and education of poor women and their children. Do you understand?'

Fabrice did not, but he nodded as if he did.

'Of course we cannot all go to Australia when so much work remains to be done here in poor Ireland. Sister Ursula will be the first superioress of the Perth house.' With that, Cecilia sat back and gave the floor over to Ursula.

Ursula Frayne interrogated him now. 'Might I ask, Mister Cleriquot, as a layman who has spent considerable time with His Lordship, what exactly is your assessment of him?'

'The pope?' said Fabrice.

'No, not the Pope.' Ursula looked at Cecilia, who looked sideways towards the priest, who paused in his writing and shook his head. 'The Bishop of Perth. Whatever you wish to say will be kept in complete confidence.'

'Ah,' said the Frenchman thoughtfully. Fabrice's opinion of the bishop had been adversely influenced by having to leave the infinite enjoyment of London for squalid Dublin, but he feared that too candid an opinion might get back to Brady. So he found a middle path. He expressed reservations about the character of the bishop, while taking care to look pained at having to do so.

'Has the bishop been respectful towards the Benedictines, would you say?' Ursula continued.

'Well, they are resentful of him at times,' Fabrice began, 'but only because he steals their money.' This had rather too much effect on the audience. Ursula stiffened and drew air sharply through her pursed lips in a nunly manner.

She came to her point. 'I have had prior experience with colonial bishops Mister Cleriquot, and I will not risk the sort of treatment to which I was subjected in Newfoundland at the hands of one called Michael Fleming. Bishops seem to think they can do no wrong, while we poor unlearned women should simply follow their every instruction, regardless of ...'

'Now, now, Ursula,' interrupted Mother Cecilia, 'we needn't bore Mister Cleriquot with all that.'

Sister Ursula sat back in her chair, took a deep breath. 'It would be best, I feel, for unity of purpose, that we sisters come to mutually agreed terms with this bishop before we leave this place. A proper legal agreement in writing, and signed by both parties.'

'We have a document we would like you to peruse from a semantic viewpoint,' explained Mother Cecilia, beckoning Fabrice to her desk. The priest gave up his chair, sighing with the effort. He could see no need for a second opinion, especially from this dandy.

'Make sure there is nothing in there he can use to wriggle out of it,' added Ursula, more bluntly. It was she who had to go to Western Australia with this bishop.

A document of three pages rested neatly on the desk, ready for signing in four places. The title, penned in beautiful font by the priest, read *Agreement for Sisters Leaving the Parent House on a Foundation*. It contained ten clauses, all to do with money and power. It bound the Bishop of Perth to provide sufficient funds for the nuns' accommodation and food; to bear the costs of their starting up a school; to respect the continued command of the parent house in Dublin; and to non-interference in their 'external government, usages or occupations'.

'That all seems very wise,' said Fabrice, uncertainly. He had no interest at all in the matter, but a few weeks travelling across France in the company of missionaries had taught him to feign a little concern. He especially did not want an argument with the priest standing behind him, who had the bearing of an attorney.

'The bishop may well sign it here in Dublin, Mother, but will he comply with it once out of your sight?' queried Ursula.

'Enough now, Ursula. Mister Cleriquot might begin to think you lack faith in the bishop, which could not be less true, could it?'

'Of course,' agreed Ursula. 'But in Newfoundland ...'

'Yes, yes. We all know what transpired in Newfoundland, Ursula. We need not go over it again, at least not while Mister Cleriquot is here.'

Six days later, the Bishop of Perth reappeared. Caporelli raised his hand and murmured the single word *orribile* as he emerged from the carriage, to save Fabrice the trouble of asking. Don Confalonieri invoked the Lord's name without context. A new man was with them, a serious-looking Irish priest who snatched his bag wordlessly from the coachman. This was Father Peter Powell.

'Were you able to communicate with the Italians, Holy Father?' asked Fabrice, within earshot of Caporelli.

'Yes Cleriquot, thank you for asking,' replied the bishop, looking over his shoulder. 'I understood them only too well, especially when they were mumbling about me.'

'And how was the Irish countryside?'

'The Irish countryside was dying, Cleriquot, that is how the Irish countryside was. There is no money for the table, much less for the missions. The eight catechists are coming behind us, on foot. Look out for them, get them some food. Take them into town, get them some suitable clothes and footwear.'

The mysterious catechists appeared very early the next morning at his front door. They had been instructed to look for a Frenchman in the cottage across from the presbytery.

'Are you awake there, fella?' came a voice so loud that Fabrice thought he had an intruder in his room. He pulled on his trousers. It was not yet six.

'Hurry up, would yer,' insisted the voice. 'We have men freezing out here. Are you up, man?'

Fabrice opened his door and reeled back. Filling the doorway was an *Illustrated London News* caricature of the Irish criminal class.

'Are you Clarico, the Frenchie?' the visitor demanded. His teeth were awful and he had a nervous straining of the neck muscles which seemed to suggest he was fighting against a natural inclination to strike. The men who loitered behind the fierce one were all underdressed against the bitter cold, with two of them actually shoeless. 'These lads are starving. The bishop said you'd feed us.'

The catechists were ragged creatures. The bishop's qualifications for the job must have been a desire to escape the cold and hunger of rural Ireland for a distant English colony where there was sunshine and food. To a man, these eight loved Bishop John Brady. Their intimidating spokesman introduced himself as Terry Farrelly. 'But this lot all call me The Terror, for some reason.'

Fabrice dressed and took the men in to Dublin Town for a cooked breakfast, then to a draper, then to another pub for a second breakfast, and then to a bootmaker. The proprietor of each establishment was very pleased to have made the dapper Frenchman's acquaintance. Soon each catechist wore a new woollen shirt, trousers, thick socks and leather ankle boots. They were grateful, but their gratitude was directed not to the Frenchman who paid the bills but to their bishop, John Brady, who was a living saint.

Over a pint of stout and a steak and kidney pie, The Terror gave an account of life in the west of Ireland, where the poverty was even worse than Dublin. The other men listened to him in silence, already grieving for the place they had fled.

At the end of his tale The Terror looked Fabrice in the eyes.

'In what regard do you hold the English, Frenchy?' Sixteen eyes waited on his answer. 'As a species, like.'

Fabrice answered honestly. His natural inclination as a Frenchman was to revile the English, but he had softened his views during his time in London due to the charming hospitality he had received there.

This was not the required answer. The Terror looked at Fabrice with renewed intensity. 'If you were to visit Cavan you would harden those views again, man. The English want every last aboriginal Irishman gone or dead.'

'So you will all leave?' asked Fabrice, innocently.

La Terreur glared at him and looked around at his mates, unsure if this fop had just accused him of cowardice. 'We *will* leave, Frenchy,' he said firmly, 'but under great sufferance and with heavy hearts for those we leave behind.'

There were twelve extra mouths to feed that night at the House of Mercy, and they were big, hungry mouths. Sister Anne, aproned as usual, banged things about in the kitchen with the stress of it all. Once she had fed all these blessèd Australian missionaries she would still have to find enough for soup to feed the poor women of Dublin and their ragged children. So she went out to the garden to pull up a few beets and spuds. The beets were looking good and plump and she threw a dozen into her bucket.

The leaves of the potatoes had been of concern to her the previous day, but now her heart sank. Overnight half the leaves had blackened and curled. She had seen frost damage which looked a bit like this, but it was August and there had been no frost. She pulled up a damaged plant, and gasped. The spuds were black and knobbly and when she cut them open, the flesh was dark and corky. Inedible.

Up and down the rows she looked, and the plants were all the same.

She called Mother Cecilia. The bishop and the serious Irish priest followed.

'Perhaps … I could maybe cut them up, Mother, and squeeze them through a wet cloth,' babbled Sister Anne, trying to put a brave face on it. 'They will still be good for soup, I think, or little potato cakes.' But then she looked at the fleshless spud in her hand, squeezed it, and wailed. 'Oh, but it is poisoned! Mother, with what will we feed the women and children?' Sister Anne had let everyone down by allowing this terrible thing to happen.

'It will be all right, Anne,' said Mother Cecilia, but even her voice wavered.

'It is a want of fertiliser, that is all,' diagnosed Father Peter Powell, walking off disinterestedly.

But His Lordship's roots were in the peasantry of County Cavan, and he could see exactly what Anne saw, and recognised the gravity of it. John Brady bent down, pulled up another sickly plant, ran a licked thumb across the ugly root to clean away the dirt and then looked up and away from the two nuns. He gave out an odd sad little cry, as if despairing at the uselessness of his new powers.

'Ah, dear God,' cried Bishop John Brady. 'If this disease goes west, they will all starve.'

The three Irish religious stayed in the garden for some time, inspecting the sad rows of dying plants and praying silently to the Loving God to whom they had dedicated their lives, that He would not let such a terrible thing happen to a God-fearing people.

From: Fabrice Cleriquot, Cap de Bonne Espérance, Afrique
To: Pauline Jaricot, Lorette, Lyon

25th November 1845

Chère Mademoiselle Jaricot,

I write from the floating monastery called Elizabeth, a representation in miniature of the Catholic world with all its internecine jealousies. The captain is an English Protestant by the name of Morrice, who has been very tolerant of all the Kyries, Glorias and Stabats emanating from the Benedictines. His crew weep and beg the priests to stop but to no avail. It is testament to the discipline of the English merchant seaman that the crew has as yet neither mutinied nor murdered a priest.

God did not want our boat to leave England, so provided an enormous storm that caused us to spend three days at the mouth of the Thames with every stomach churning. The French novice Dom Fonteinne begged the captain to put him ashore so he could return to the arms of his beloved abbot. Every passenger was prostrated except the bishop and the ugly fellow they call La Terreur.

But we have made it to Cape Town and this evening we sit at anchor in a beautiful bay, writing letters and looking longingly at the shore.

I am unofficial postmaster for twenty-seven missionaries who wish to hide their mail from He of the Amaranth Hat. The bishop, fearing any criticism reaching Europe, has made himself Supreme Editor. Each missionary has to present his letters for approval.

The Italian Caporelli, who says he is a nobleman but travels steerage and quietly begs me for money, laughed and ignored the bishop's instruction. The Tyrolean Don Confalonieri is livid at such impertinence from a priest 'of low birth' who he mumbles should be sleeping below decks with his shoeless catechists.

Only the French novice Léandre Fonteinne was perfectly calm about it, for he is the shrewdest. He quickly wrote two letters to his abbot at Solesmes and presented the first to the bishop, who read only flattering words about himself. The second, giving full expression to his feelings, is now hidden in my jacket. Soon, there will be a third, for the boy never stops writing, a flurry of words which come to the quill faster than he can think of them. The ink runs with salty water; not sea spray but his sad little tears.

The nuns, to my surprise, followed this example, each showing the bishop a slim, blandly worded letter to their Mother Superior, while a bundle of much thicker letters have somehow found their way into my satchel. You have allowed me discretion in such things, Mademoiselle, and one could not refuse these Irish nuns with their bony knuckles, pleading eyes, humble smiles and empty purses.

Mother Ursula Frayne has announced that she will not permit her Sisters of Mercy to disembark, not even their servant girl Kate, who has spent the whole voyage down in second class and barely seen the sun. The nuns have patients to attend to, Sister Catherine wasting away with consumption and a Heart of Mary priest by the name of Maurice Bouchet gone mad with fever. Quarantine rules do not permit the sick to go ashore. The Bishop of Cape Town came aboard to plead with Ursula to at least allow the younger nuns to go ashore to get a few nights' sleep in comfortable beds but she refused. Perhaps the nuns just want a respite from bishops.

The little novice Dom Léandre now says he will stay aboard with the nuns. He has dysentery, he says, but also he blurts, 'Africa frightens me.'

Emerging now from the hold with the goats are the eight penniless catechists Brady rescued from Ireland. They are all afflicted with mange, but nobody is to mention it. Caporelli says that their leader, 'Il Terrore', as he calls him, pushed him against a pole for threatening to tell the bishop about their feet.

I am travelling First Class along with the bishop, the nuns and the Spanish monks. They are all now convinced I am in the silk business because I have had some success in sericulture while at sea. Some of the eggs hatched in the tropics so I have now eighty hungry worms to care for. Our little novice has of course named each worm for a monk he is missing, based upon its personality.

Happily, there are some other passengers to talk to. I have be-friended an educated English blacksmith who declares himself to be a Humanist. Roger Smith is an idealist who wishes to set up a commune in a farming town near Perth of which he has heard favourable reports. I am tempted to assist him in this endeavour.

Bien à vous
Professeur Fabrice Cleriquot

4. IN FLEAMANTLE

It was dusk and the island continent loomed. If Africa had frightened Léandre Fonteinne, the prospect of setting foot on Australia
terrified him. In his anxiety, the novice had taken to quoting Isaiah
and imagining miracles. He had seen two white doves land upon
the deck of *Elizabeth*, and they had spoken to him.

'Seagulls, I would suggest,' said Roger Smith, the Humanist
blacksmith. He smiled indulgently at Fabrice Cleriquot, to whom
the novice clung tightly.

'*Non!*' protested the novice. 'Doves! They came to me and hovered
around the stern and let their gentle cooing be heard by me. They
had come out to thank the men of peace for bringing good news of
Salvation to the natives.'

'Talking doves,' mused Roger Smith, 'how jolly.' His big
blacksmith's arm was draped around the slender shoulder of Sadie,
the English maid who had been placed on the ship at Cape Town
in some sort of disgrace and had somehow come under his care.
Sadie, annoyed by his bullying of the timid French monk, peeled
his arm off her.

'I think it very sweet that you saw the little birds, Leon,' said
Sadie. At their first meeting, she had misheard Léandre's name as
'Leon'. Roger Smith had followed Sadie in this, partly because her

error amused him, and partly because he believed in anglicising foreign words whenever possible.

The pilot of the lighter looked at his four passengers with disdain as he swept the boat oar left and right, guiding them towards the landing. 'Nice and snappy when we get to shore, please,' he instructed. 'I have to get back to the ship before it gets too dark. If I have to use the lamp the old bloke will spot me and I'll be done for.'

Elizabeth had dropped anchor at eleven that morning but then came endless waiting. Their ship had not been expected. Mr Scott the harbour master piloted out to speak to the 'old bloke', Captain David Morrice, who then advised the bishop that nobody was permitted to disembark until approval came from ashore.

'Who has the authority, if not you?' demanded the bishop of the harbour master.

'Captain Irwin,' came the reply, to which the bishop thundered some unholy words. It seemed Brady and Irwin were not on friendly terms.

Fabrice could not bear the thought of another day listening to the Spanish monks' *Te Deums* and Roger Smith agreed, so they paid a boatman for the privilege of an early escape. To Fabrice's surprise, Dom Serra agreed to Fabrice's request to let the novice leave with them. It was not only the lay passengers that had grown tired of the religious.

So it was under cover of fading light on Wednesday the seventh of January in the Year of Our Lord 1846 that Fabrice Cleriquot arrived in Western Australia. There was no built port, so passengers had to get to the jetty by lighter, and since the jetty was occupied by a rotting whale carcass, the pilot advised his passengers that they would have to get their feet wet. He made the French dandy jump into waist-deep water among a thousand floating sponges to help push the boat ashore. This was unnecessary, and quite risky since the stinking slick of whale oil had attracted sharks, but the pilot was a democrat and curious to know what effect salt water might have on this silken foreigner.

Fabrice stood upon the grey sand of Arthur's Head, hands on hips, not quite knowing what to think. He was on the edge of a new continent, a new life, and though this journey was not of his choosing he had, during the long crossing of the Indian Ocean, often imagined this moment of arrival and expected a frisson of excitement. It did not come. He felt exactly the same in this new world as in the old.

When the novice clambered out of the boat, however, he fell to his knees; whether overcome by the occasion or feigning so, it was impossible to say. Kneeling on the beach, arms stretched and looking up in a pose of ecstasy, Dom Léandre Fonteinne cried aloud to this new land to whom his gracious God had safely conducted them.

'*Surge Jerusalem quia venit lumen tuum. Leva in circuiti oculos tuos vide.*'

Roger Smith's Latin was good enough to offer a riposte. 'I too am lifting my eyes, Leon, and looking around,' he said, 'but I'm afraid I don't see Jerusalem. I just see a rather dingy port town, and a lot of sand.'

The beach was cupped by limestone cliffs, on top of which was a substantial round building also made of limestone. A long dark tunnel had been cut under this structure, and through it they could glimpse the yellow lights of town. Someone had emerged from the darkness and was walking towards them – a stocky fellow with an odd gait.

'Look, Leon. An angel sent to help us,' said Roger Smith, drawing another whispered rebuke from Sadie.

The angel was, on closer acquaintance, a dishevelled guard whose boots were coming apart. An affable Scotsman, he greeted the new arrivals as if they had just stepped from a coach after a short trip across town.

'Trouble with my sole,' he explained.

'Leon here will be able to help you,' said Roger Smith, amusing only himself now.

It was only the accent that the guard understood. 'So you're Sassenachs after all,' he said, relieved. 'There was a rumour that you lot were French or Spanish or something. Half the town was thinking of coming down to beat you up! I shall call them off.'

'Don't do that,' said Roger Smith, seeing another opportunity for mischief. 'These two gentlemen *are* French.'

The guard looked closely at the two accused and could see it was true. But he was determined to be welcoming despite it.

'Ah, well, can't be helped now you're here. *Bon jornay,*' he said, proud to demonstrate his familiarity with the language, 'and, ah, *bienvenoo …*' He tailed off, having run out of ammunition.

The immigrants gathered up their possessions and followed the guard across the beach. There was a storehouse built into a cave in the limestone wall, containing two pointy-nosed boats with muffled rowlocks, oars, try pots, harpoons, lances and baskets of coiled line. Above it, on an angle, hung a sign saying *Western Australian Whaling Company.*

Fabrice pointed up to the round building which loomed ominously above them. 'Fort?' he asked the guard, in English.

'Oh, aye,' the guard replied, recalling another of his schoolboy

French lessons. '*Très forte,* lad, the old Round House. Has to be, to keep the buggers in!'

Fabrice had vaguely imagined that this bright new land would be free from all the ancient cruelties of Europe, but the first land they had seen from the deck of *Elizabeth* had been Rottnest Island, which Captain Morrice explained was a prison for the natives, and now the entrance to the colony was beneath another jail.

From the dark of the tunnel they emerged into lamplight. White sand was everywhere; the town of Fremantle was being reclaimed by the beach. Roger Smith disappeared with Sadie for lodgings which promised *clean linin & hot soapy bath.*

Outside the Round House, Fabrice and Dom Léandre met their first native Australians. Two men wearing wrist manacles were squatting on their haunches, talking softly together, while a guard stood nearby holding a rifle, but looking distracted. The younger prisoner looked no more than fourteen, and he wore arseless pants and a buttonless shirt, much like the catechists before Fabrice took them shopping. Across his chest was a series of linear scars or burns. The older prisoner wore a traditional tunic made of animal pelt.

Dom Léandre Fonteinne detected another biblical sign and blessed himself. 'Look!' he whispered in Fabrice's ear. 'The older one, in the hide. Is he not the very image of John the Baptist in Giotto's *Coronation of the Virgin*?'

The prisoners had been released from the ankle irons which were chained to the wall. Across the courtyard were the stocks, a form of punishment so ancient the Frenchmen only knew them from pictures in children's books. Some wag had put a straw-and-rag damsel in them, to lighten the mood of the prison yard.

The linguist was keen to test his knowledge of local words but never had he been so uncertain of a foreign tongue. He had never before heard a word of it spoken, and could only depend on a dictionary bearing the name John Brady, who did not speak the native language. The real author, being an amateur, would know nothing of phonetics, but it was a place to start.

'*Quaia*,' ventured Fabrice uncertainly, addressing the young fellow with the chest scars.

'*Wandjoo*,' replied the prisoner, looking across to the guard for an explanation of this odd behaviour from a *wadjala*. 'You got smokes?' he added, sensing this newcomer to be mad, or at least a soft touch.

'Don't stand too close,' warned the guard, seeing trouble in this unusual interaction. 'They're not chained, you know. They're off to Rottnest tomorrow, for their sins.'

'What have they done wrong, these poor fellows?' asked Fabrice.

'Johnny here attacked a white man.' He indicated the older man in the fur coat, Léandre's 'John the Baptist'.

'Just cut his nose a bit,' explained the prisoner.

'*Off*, Johnny. You cut it *off*.' The guard looked meaningfully at the newcomers, so they understood how dangerous his job was. 'Best stay back, Frenchy, or he'll take yours off, too.'

'That big nose done nothin' to me,' said Johnny.

'Well, if he sticks it in where it's not required,' said the guard, '*I* might have to trim it up!' All three grinned at that threat and Fabrice thought it best to smile with them.

Léandre shyly produced some tobacco from somewhere in his cassock, an action which surpassed the professor's efforts to be-friend the locals by linguistic means. Eager hands went out, black and white, manacled and free. The guard lit himself a pipe while the black men chewed.

Fabrice requested permission from the guard to touch the older man's shawl, which the bishop's dictionary suggested was usually made of kangaroo skin. '*Beauka*?' he asked. 'From, ah … *yongka*? He hopped a little to clarify his second question. Johnny chewed, looked at his toes and mumbled something.

'I am a linguist,' explained Professor Cleriquot.

'Righto,' said the prisoner, spitting out a plug of brown juice.

Just then a startling noise came from behind them. Someone on horseback. The guard dropped his pipe, stood up, and snapped to attention.

'Did I hear the sound of Frenchmen talking to prisoners?' These words came slowly, and with authority,

'No, sir. Not talking, sir,' said the guard. 'Just moving past, very swiftly.'

'It sounded very much like talking. Did I not hear this silken gentleman trying to speak the native language?'

Fabrice turned around. His accuser was jacketed and mounted on a fine white horse. He wore round myopic glasses which somewhat undermined his military bearing. An English officer, diluted with a bit of bookkeeper.

'Lieutenant-Colonel Frederick Irwin,' said the horseman, from above, 'but *Captain* Irwin will suffice in this egalitarian colony. And you are Monsieur …?'

'Cleriquot. Fabrice Cleriquot.'

'I presume you have received *permission* to come ashore, Monsieur Cleriquot?' The little monk, if he had been noticed at all, was ignored.

Fabrice sensed the threat implied in the question. 'Permission?' he blustered.

'Come with me, please,' instructed Captain Irwin, and then without looking at the novice, 'the little fellow as well.'

Fabrice feared they had been arrested, and this being an English colony there seemed no choice but to follow. He wished the prisoners a safe voyage to Rottnest, and the two immigrants shouldered their bags and followed the officer's white horse down the sandy track which was signposted 'High Street'. Dom Léandre pulled his hood over his head to retreat from the world and Fabrice could hear him breathing hard inside his cassock, on the verge of tears.

At an *hôtel* called The Commercial, the captain dismounted and removed his gloves. 'Do you Frenchmen drink beer at all?' he enquired, taking a bag from the struggling novice. There were only two tables in the pub and one was quickly cleared for them.

The publican came over and introduced himself as Paddy Marmion. He looked over the captain's unusual guests – a silk-tied gentleman and a monk. 'French?' he asked Irwin, as if they were a pair of exotic animals.

'Certainly we are French, *Monsieur*,' interjected Fabrice, keen to demonstrate his perfect English.

'Welcome to Fleamantle,' said the publican. 'What is it with your little friend here? Is he an actual monk, or just very shy?' The novice remained deep within his dark cape, worried that it may be the custom here, as in many parts of Europe, to beat monks.

'He is studying to become a Benedictine.'

'Well, well,' said the Irishman. 'The very first monk in Australia I would guess. First I've seen, anyway. I'm not sure I approve.'

Three lovely frothy ales appeared. The novice shuddered in his excitement at the sight, threw back his hood, and squeezed Fabrice's knee under the table as he lifted the pot to his lips.

'The first drink is free, lads, seeing as you are a guest of the captain. Just the first one, mind.'

Captain Irwin resumed control. 'Now, Monsieur Cleriquot,' he instructed, 'you will tell me about this ship, *Elizabeth*. I am told it is full of penniless Irish missionaries.'

'Yes, fifteen penniless Irish missionaries,' Fabrice confirmed, happy to assist a man of importance, 'counting laymen and bishops and nuns. There are some Spanish and Italian and French ones as well, also penniless.'

'Jesus, Mary and Joseph!' cursed the publican who had stayed put in case of gossip or further drink orders. 'I will have to board this place up.' The Irish always expected free grog, he explained, and religious ones were the worst. 'If my dear wife catches wind of all this,' he sighed, 'she will invite the damned nuns to stay and I will be going home to a convent.'

'You are the chief of the prison guards, Captain Irwin?' asked Fabrice.

'I am the chief of everything in this colony, as the need arises,' boasted the officer. 'I have been here since the start and know how things run, so I am frequently called upon to fill the gaps in authority. The guards, the military.' He brushed the sleeve of his jacket in imperious manner. 'The government, at times.'

Fabrice now recognised the name Irwin from the exhibit in the museum in Liverpool. 'Ah, you were the officer, I think, who shot the native chief.'

Captain Irwin's eyes narrowed. 'Wrong. I did not shoot him. I had him shot.'

'And his son too, I think?'

'Again, no. I merely put a reward on his head.'

'Yes. I have seen it in Liverpool, in a little glass box.'

Irwin was growing increasingly suspicious of this French dandy. He did not need a ship of meddlesome foreign Catholics turning every minor administrative difficulty into some sort of grand victory for themselves.

'You were not expected here,' he stated, a new hardness in his voice. 'I came down to Fremantle today hoping to greet the new governor and what do I get instead? A ship full of damned problems, as if I need more of those.'

The Frenchman shrugged.

'Is that red-faced turd John Brady on board?'

'Bishop Brady? Yes.'

'Bishop!' The captain sat up straight. 'Bishop of what? Of whom?'

'Of the Catholics of the colony, I suppose,' said Fabrice.

'There's no Catholics here!' said the proprietor, still eavesdropping.

'None?'

'Well, even I might be considered a cattle tick if looked at in the right light, but to advertise it would be bad for business. This is an English Protestant colony, Frenchy. Did no one tell you that?'

'Brady told the pope there are five thousand Catholics.'

'That's more than our whole population,' said Irwin.

'And two million natives awaiting conversion.'

Irwin scoffed. 'Well, that solves the mystery of how he got to be a bishop. As for conversion of the natives, it has been tried already and failed. I personally established the Western Australian Missionary Society, went to London, secured a willing minister and brought him out here. But we had to send him home.'

'He upset the natives?'

'No. *They* rather liked him. It was *us* he upset. Intemperate in his criticisms. Giustiniani was his name; foreign, you see.'

A second round of ales appeared and the proprietor hovered. Fabrice put a few coins in the hand of Paddy Marmion, who stared at them in disbelief. The colony had so few coins and suddenly there were half a dozen in his hand, half French and half English, but all sturdy looking.

Irwin turned his attention to the little robed fellow who had now fully emerged from his shell. 'Would your little friend here be the sort to make trouble for us, if my men were ever forced to take firm action against the blacks?'

'No, I would make no trouble,' said Dom Léandre. 'None at all, *Monsieur*.'

'Good,' said Captain Irwin, relieved to see the religious so easily cowed. 'We will not tolerate troublemakers in this colony, you see, whether they be religious or lay. And what about you, Mister Cleriquot? I take it from your elaborate dress that you are not a priest?'

'No, no. I am a Humanist, I think.'

Irwin narrowed his eyes. 'I am not familiar with that denomination. What then is your purpose of being here?'

'Silk,' explained Fabrice. 'My moths died crossing the Indian Ocean, but not before they laid many eggs. The climate here will suit sericulture, I think.'

'I would be unable to say,' said Irwin, looking toward the publican. 'So, to summarise. The colony has today acquired one Benedictine monk and a silk manufacturer, with two dozen penniless missionaries to disembark tomorrow, all of the wrong denomination. I cannot truthfully report to the new governor that the colony will benefit much by the arrival of *Elizabeth*, but I am confident neither is it much threatened.'

As they left the tavern, Fabrice piled more coins on the counter, telling the proprietor it was for beer for tomorrow's arrivals.

'You have given me over five pounds there, sir,' said Paddy Marmion, eyes glowing at the treasure.

'More?' said Fabrice.

Captain Irwin, noticing this exchange, became more helpful to the French newcomers. He arranged good lodgings for them and in parting, had some generous advice for Fabrice.

'You speak English reasonably well, Cleriquot, and you seem to hold acceptable views. You might fit in here. But that ship out there holds all the old enemies of England. If you say 'Spanish', I think 'Trafalgar'. Say 'French', I think 'Napoleon', whom I fought in the Peninsula Wars. And the Irish? Well, I was born in that country and know them only too well. Half are from the criminal class and hate the English, and their priests take instruction from Rome.' The captain looked out to sea as if spying an enemy armada. 'Frankly, a part of me wishes to set fire to that ship.' When he turned back, he smiled warmly to show he was speaking in jest.

'Bishop Brady thinks you are sworn by your queen to treat the Catholics equally,' suggested Fabrice. 'That your governor will give him money and help.'

'Good heavens,' smiled Irwin. 'Where did he get that idea?'

'New South Wales.'

Irwin chuckled. 'Look around. This is not Sydney.'

The captain bid the Frenchmen good night, in French.

'Oh,' he added, 'and Mister Cleriquot, Reverend Fonteinne, you are officially permitted ashore. May I welcome you to the Swan River colony.'

As first light fell upon the deck of *Elizabeth*, Bishop Brady looked from the poop deck across the sea passage called Gage Roads, to the sandy hamlet of Fremantle.

'It doesn't look much,' sniffed Father Peter Powell from behind him.

'That's my diocese you are disparaging,' snapped Brady. Powell was an annoyance and was probably after his job. The bishop had not slept. He had been thinking the whole night about money. He had less than two hundred pounds remaining to run a mission of twenty-eight members and a bishopric stretching two-thirds of the way across the continent. A proper cathedral would have to be built in the capital, and a monastery for the monks, a convent for the nuns. The feeling in his stomach had a name: despair.

He turned to the ever-reliable Farrelly. 'Get us off this feckin ship, Terry.'

'Right you are, John, I'll have another word to the captain. He'll pull his finger out all right, don't you worry.' The Farrellys and the Bradys went back a long way in County Cavan and it was not always easy to remember to say 'Lordship' to a man you had grown up calling 'Uncle'.

Hours passed, small vessels came and went with updates, but still permission to come ashore was not forthcoming. January was the middle of summer in this part of the world and it was hot and windless on the deck of *Elizabeth*. The missionaries all took turns peering at the flat nothingness of their destination and concealing from the others the empty feeling it gave them.

Salvado read aloud from a book he had found in a London store, intended for newcomers to the Swan River. It was good for his English to do so, and it helped calm the nerves of listeners.

'It is impossible,' he read, 'to maintain the right of civilised nations to establish themselves in the territory of native tribes without acknowledging that such intrusions will involve the settlers and the nation to which they belong in deep and lasting responsibilities. By our entry into their country, the natives will be gradually deprived of their hunting and fishing grounds and are so forced, unprepared, into new modes of life and new conditions of society.'

'Very true,' said the bishop.

'In other words, the English colonists are bound by the strongest ties of moral obligation to assist the natives in accommodating themselves to the great change they have to undergo.'

'Who is this excellent author?' asked Brady.

'The book is by Ogle,' said Salvado, turning to the cover, 'but here he is quoting a Captain Irwin.'

'Irwin!' spat the bishop. 'Hypocrite! Assist the natives, will he! He assisted them in Pinjarra all right. That same man is sitting there onshore laughing at us as we all bake to death in the sun. Close that stupid book, Rosendo.'

By late afternoon a hundred people had gathered atop the limestone cliff to watch the arrival of the Catholic missionaries. One monk had already come across the water as if by magic and was kneeling on the shore in the baking heat, singing. Viewed from above, Dom Léandre Fonteinne made a striking image, black cloak against grey sands, awaiting the arrival of his four confrères. Fremantle was hardly a religiously observant town, but everyone agreed this looked very holy.

Captain Irwin stepped ashore after visiting *Elizabeth* in order to inspect the passengers and humiliate the bishop. It had been an enjoyable trip and his boots were still perfectly dry. He gave permission to Mr Scott to allow the Catholics ashore, then ordered his men to dress for choir and assemble on the beach.

The first lighter to arrive carried the new bishop. John Brady was attempting to stand up, coat billowing in the sea breeze and left hand firmly upon his amaranth cap. He was flanked by four black-robed monks: Serra, Salvado, Confalonieri and the English subdeacon, Tootle, or Tottle, who looked ill.

The nuns were put one by one in a cargo basket which was lowered by rope into the second lighter. Sister Anne took a tumble in the process and her laughter could be heard from the shore. Next came a boat full of ragged-looking lads, their intimidating leader staring ahead to those gathered on the shore, as if daring any of them to step out of line. These ones looked like good drinkers, observed one in the crowd. Count Nicola Caporelli was wedged in among the ragged Irish, and looked most unhappy about it.

Last came the gentle French Heart of Mary priests with their dying confrère, Maurice Bouchet.

The Benedictines were chanting their *Te Deums* as usual, while onshore Dom Léandre, arms raised, chanted exquisitely in response, as if his voice would link with those of his brothers and pull them ashore. Even Fabrice Cleriquot, despite four months of suffering such noise, felt moved.

Captain Irwin's men were lined up on the shore. He believed songs of devotion to be very good for a soldier's morale and for discipline, and now seemed a good time. 'Hymn sixty-two!' commanded Irwin, and the military choir began, rather too slowly.

The Holy Ghost in part we know, for with us He resides
Our whole of Good to Him we owe, Whom by His Grace
  He guides

There erupted a musical competition for the ears of those assembled atop the limestone cliff. The Protestants had the advantage of proximity, but as the lighters brought the monks ashore, Irwin's men were overwhelmed by the low, strong voices of the Benedictines. Between the two was Dom Léandre's soprano – plaintive, sublime, a child calling his parents ashore. The combined effect, English verse and Latin response, was pleasingly ecumenical.

> *He doth our virtuous thoughts inspire, the evil He averts*
>> *Ora pro nobis*
> *And ev'ry seed of good desire, He planted in our hearts*
>> *Ora pro nobis*

The angel's voice melded with those of his brother monks, who chanted even as they helped pull the boat ashore. Those atop the cliff could see that these bearded monks, at least, were men of action, not just prayer.

The ceremony finished in pathos. Father Maurice Bouchet had been strapped to a stretcher with his arms bound so they could not flail, but no amount of gentle *chuts* from the two Fathers Francis could stop his screaming. Eventually, a sort of soft gag had to be employed. The rowdy cliff fell silent.

Fabrice wanted to stay ahead of the missionaries. One hundred and thirteen days at sea with them was enough. He toted his bags and took off in the direction, he hoped, of the Swan River and Perth.

Two fair-haired boys in short pants attached themselves to the oddly attired newcomer as he tried to find the ferry point. Nobody seemed to own them.

'Boat for Perth?' Fabrice asked them, in careful English.

'*Bôt ferpeu! Bôt ferpeu!*' mimicked the two boys, not once but over and over with no sign of tiring and much theatrical posturing.

Then, as if summoned by the gods, Louis Langoulant appeared. Louis was a fisherman, originally from Cherbourg. He had a tiny wooden rowboat with *Galilée* painted on the side. He insisted on rowing Fabrice to Perth, and would not be paid. Would Fabrice care to stay with him and Mary Ann until he got settled? They lived on the bank of the river, next door to the governor's house.

'*Oui*,' said Fabrice Cleriquot, and with that word all his problems were solved.

They rowed gently up the Swan River from Fremantle to Perth. The two skinny boys were still with them, giggling all the way at nothing in particular. The river here was wide and salty with pretty treed hills and rocky cliffs and occasional white sand moorings. Fabrice saw cormorants and pelicans, a sea eagle, but none yet of the famous swans, which he knew to expect would be black in this strange country.

Fabrice removed his shoes, sighed, and laid back to watch the enormous blue sky. Wet fishing nets felt nice under his bare feet. Upriver, Louis had caught a dozen silver fish he called *brème* but the two boys called *gilbert*. They would do nicely for tea, said Louis.

At Point Walter there was a canal through the sand bar, and at the end of the canal, a little wayside inn where they stopped for an ale. After that, the cooling sea breeze came in to help them towards the capital. Louis called it *le médecin* because, like the doctor, its arrival was always welcome.

'These are your apprentices?' Fabrice asked. The younger boy, still wet from the river, was lying upon him, feigning sleep.

'These two? No, they just hop in. Later, they will hop out.

Sometimes they help me fish. Sometimes they help themselves to my catch.'

'They steal?'

'No, *I* steal! These are their fish, really.'

Fabrice commented upon the unexpected beauty of the river, causing Louis to become serious.

'I love this country very much, the river especially. Mary Ann and I own nothing much. We do not need to. I try to live from what the river provides, just as they do. I try to learn from them.'

Just before The Narrows, at the base of Mount Eliza, Louis pulled in to the native depot so Fabrice could meet a man called Frank Armstrong. It seemed to Fabrice a dangerous place to stop: there were people moving in every direction, and lots of noise and arguments and laughter. The two boys recognised some aunty they were in trouble with, and scurried off to avoid her long arms.

Frank Armstrong was introduced as 'the governor's official interpreter to the natives'. He was busy handing out supplies of tea, flour and sugar to reward the 'better-behaved' native families, but despite the chaos all around him he greeted the French professor with an open smile.

'A professional linguist?' said Frank Armstrong, looking the dapper newcomer up and down. 'I am not one of those, mate. I am not even fluent, to be honest, even though I grew up around these fellas. The governor only gave me the job because I know more of their words than the next *wadjala*. I don't really get half of what they are saying. I just fill in the gaps with smiles and gestures.'

Fabrice showed the interpreter the bishop's thin dictionary, which was of great interest to him. Armstrong flicked through, shook his head, and laughed.

'Well, it seems you already have everything I know,' he said mysteriously. 'These look like the words I gave to Mister Moore.'

He disappeared for a minute into the store and returned with a well-thumbed dictionary of very similar appearance, but bearing the name George Fletcher Moore. The lists of words were identical.

'So, the bishop has stolen them?'

'Stolen?' smiled the interpreter. 'Not my words to steal, mate.'

These colonists were cryptic. 'You could perhaps give me some lessons?' asked the professor.

'Oh, it's not really the sort of thing you can learn that way,' said Armstrong, turning his back to dole out mealy flour to a sweet old aunty who held a small hessian sack and knew precisely what size a ration was meant to be. She shrieked, got more, laughed toothlessly, touched his hand in thanks. 'It's not like Latin or something. You just have to learn as you go.'

The interpreter dropped his scoop and wrapped his arms around a skinny boy, shielding his eyes, and extracting a scream with delight by telling him he was the *balyat*, of which every child was afraid.

'There, you see! We might have only one word in common, that boy and me, but now he thinks I speak his language. It is the *intention* that matters, I think.'

'And you make a living from this?' enquired Fabrice.

'A bit. I am supposed to help the government explain its intentions. The problem is, these people don't even have words for the things they want me to explain.'

'Ah, yes,' agreed Professor Cleriquot, nodding sagely. 'If there is no word for it, it does not exist.' A linguist's truism.

'I wish that was true,' said Armstrong. 'These fellas have no word for prison, but it exists anyway. It's left to me to explain to the young fellas that they are going off to the island to die. Breaks your heart, mate.'

They were now only a half *myriamètre* from home, Louis announced. As they rounded The Narrows, the town of Perth appeared, just two neat rows of white buildings dotted along the north bank of the Swan. There was a pier, but Louis continued on to his boatshed, where the two new friends pulled *Galilée* ashore. Mary Ann appeared and embraced her husband. She was Irish, and they conversed in English mixed with French. They had two little girls called Victoria and Emma.

The next evening they had a picnic on the riverbank and awaited the arrival of the missionaries. Chairs were brought down from the house, wine appeared, and they ate baked *brème* with their bare fingers while dipping their toes in the same water from which the fish had been pulled. The girls nuzzled into either side of Fabrice's coat as if he were a newly discovered uncle.

Just on sunset they heard the first voices, female, a quavering *Ave Maris Stella* coming up the darkening river ahead of the three ferries. As the first boat pulled in to the pier, Bishop Brady of Perth stood at the prow, arms apart, flanked by the Sisters of Mercy, and when the light from the pier flares caught his cap, His Lordship seemed to have become part of the natural landscape, touched by the same horsehair brush which had coloured the sky over the Swan a glorious pink.

On a still night, the sound of so many voices joined in the singing of ancient hymns was exhilarating. There was passion in those voices, and relief at having safely arrived. As the second and third boats pulled in, the voices of those already ashore joined with the new arrivals in a rousing *Magnificat*.

'God, it's too beautiful,' wept Protestant Mary Ann, and her two little girls agreed, though they could see nothing from deep inside Fabrice's jacket. The people of Perth gathered to watch, some to gasp at the joy of it, but some to glower, arms folded. There was even a catcall, some derisive laughter.

There was a pause in proceedings to get a raging Father Bouchet stretchered ashore, his mad protests bouncing across the water. Then the Benedictines resumed their chanting, and the Heart of Mary priests joined them, then the Irish for volume. Against a vivid sunset, twenty-seven silhouettes followed their bishop in unhurried manner up the Pier Street hill towards the newly built Catholic church. A *Benedictus* led by Dom Rosendo Salvado echoed now across the dark river, thundering at first then fading slowly until drowned out by the croaking of a million nesting frogs.

Fabrice, Louis and Mary Ann, though none of them very religious, were greatly moved by the holiness of what they had witnessed. They stayed down by the riverside for some time, talking together about Perth and France and Ireland and finishing off the wine, until the girls fell asleep and the mosquitoes became too troublesome.

'God knows where they will put those poor nuns,' said Mary Ann. 'Should we go up and offer?' She was a Protestant but hated the idea of these exhausted women being made to sleep on floorboards in a half-finished church.

From: Fabrice Cleriquot, Swan River
To: Pauline Jaricot, Lyon

31st January 1846

Chère Mademoiselle

We have not been here a month and the Heart of Mary priests
are already bereaved. Maurice Bouchet was 'blessed to be taken
to his reward', as they delicately put it. Poor Maurice was a sweet
fellow but full of anxiety. The bishop had nowhere to bury him, and
it being so hot here the matter became urgent. Fortunately the
new governor arrived, an Irish Protestant by the name of Andrew
Clarke, and his very first decision was to grant the Catholic bishop
a plot of land alongside the half-built Church of St John in the
Wilderness in which to bury the French priest.

Two others are very sick. An Irish catechist by the name of
O'Reilly has cholera, and the second superior of the nuns is dying
from consumption.

The colony is utterly broke. The colonists, all second sons of second
sons, have spent all their money on property and now lack the fare
to return home.

There are no convicts. That evil thing which stains the colonies of
New South Wales and Van Diemen's Land will never taint this one,
the colonists boast, and with their next breath complain there is no
affordable labour to be found. These English gentlemen must have
imagined that some creature called a 'worker' existed in a wild state
in Nature. Now a labouring class has to be created, they all agree.

They pin their hopes on the theories of a man called Wakefield, which they would not do if they had met him as I did once in London. An intelligent but unreliable man who freely admits he has never visited the colonies upon which he theorises.

The bishop has already spent all the Society's money, so says the fierce one called La Terreur, who came to me suggesting I contribute more. I told him I had spent all my father's money on unsavoury pursuits in Cape Town, which he was rather too quick to believe. Bishop Brady will never be able to raise any funds in this colony, whose population is small, Protestant and broke. The bishop's zeal cannot be questioned. He is, I think, genuine in his enthusiasm for evangelising his two million natives, but he seems no organiser of men or money.

La Terreur tells me all he knows, liking to advertise his importance as the bishop's lieutenant. To save money, he says, Brady will immediately send all the foreign missionaries off to the bush. Only he, the Irish nuns and a few of the Irish catechists will stay in Perth. Once out of the capital, the missionaries will need no money. Brady needed no money on the Hawkesbury River and so will it be for these poor priests. The grateful natives will help provide.

It transpires that there are only a few dozen Catholics here, and few are ardent in their devotions. Among them is my new friend Louis Langoulant. We went fishing today in his little boat. Everything was so beautiful. We saw many natives along the river. The children are sleek, athletic and very cheeky. On the river it seems they live much as they did before the English came, just seventeen years ago.

It is much sadder for the natives living in town, however. They beg for bread, sugar, tobacco and rum and unscrupulous white men take advantage in the usual ways. A government depot gives them some food and blankets but it has grown too popular say the colonists, who will support the missionaries if they promise to push the natives 'back out to the bush'. It doesn't matter to them if the missionaries are Catholic, Quaker or worshippers of the Egyptian sun god, if they can only achieve this.

How will the missionaries attract the natives, I wonder? By the same offerings which attracted them to town? Flour, sugar, tobacco? But in place of hard spirits, they will have to make do with the holy spirit I suppose. Matching the allure of rum will be a great test of their evangelistic powers.

You asked me, Mademoiselle, to above all look out for the welfare of the natives. I am not at all sure these missionaries will do so. Your purse strings have stayed mostly closed. There is anyway nothing to be bought here except land. An idea came to me that I buy the natives all their land back and spend the balance on fares home for the rest.

There is another possibility. I have decided to visit a farming hamlet called 'Two Jay', where I will help the English blacksmith and his maid build a commune which will be open to all hardworking, honest people, regardless of religion or hue. I think you would approve of Roger Smith, Mademoiselle. He is an admirer of the English socialist Robert Owen, the builder of utopian villages for the poor, an idea very close in spirit, I think, to your foundry village, and his views are those of a true Christian in every way, except for a firm disbelief in the existence of God.

Tonight there will be a full moon on the beautiful Swan River and Louis and I will try to catch a huge fish called a 'mulloway' which can only be caught from a boat at night in absolute silence. Louis is the most generous man I have met. Though he admits to having secretly enjoyed the absence of a church here until now, I feel this humble fisherman lives his life in close imitation of a more famous one.

Bien à vous,
Professeur Fabrice Cleriquot

5. THE THREE MISSIONS

The Benedictines had been camped long enough in bushland behind the rickety church of St John in the Wilderness that the place had become a Perth landmark and been given the name 'Spanish Camp'. Salvado and Serra had first constructed a simple hut with a tin plate roof, but it was not very good so they pulled it down and built a better one. This was good practice, Salvado declared, for they would soon have to build their mission in the remote wilderness and would improve on the design each time. Next to them had camped a family from the north who had drifted to town and found these strange black-cloaked fellows to be respectful, kind, and in the possession of food.

This February day was very hot, thirty-one *Réaumur* even down by the river. Fabrice Cleriquot walked from the fisherman's house up to the Spanish Camp in search of the novice. Dom Salvado was working alone, looking already the seasoned bushman, with a full black beard, broad hat and dungarees. He was pulling the tin roof off again and neatly stacking the building materials on the back of a dray. Any day now, explained Salvado, they would head off to found their mission.

'Where is Dom Léandre?' asked Fabrice.

Salvado shook his sweaty locks and nodded uphill. 'You will hear him before you see him,' he said, taking a long drink of water.

'You really should not work in this heat,' advised the Frenchman.

'Thanks for your sage advice, professor,' laughed the monk.

Fabrice followed the sound of sobbing and found the novice sitting on the ground behind the skirt of a huge old grass tree, holding a small paintbrush and a little pot of glue. The pot was steaming hot and Léandre was crying over it. His sleeves had stuck together.

In front of him was a wooden crate the size of a child's coffin. It was stuffed with straw and within it lay a Madonna, her veil the colour of the Perth sky, her cheeks as white as the drift sands of Fremantle. Her face was a picture of serenity, but there was something wrong. Her head seemed to tilt accusingly towards Léandre, a brightly painted corpse lying in its coffin. Mary's neck was broken.

The novice did not look up, though he must have noticed his friend's arrival. His shoulders shuddered and tears ran down his cheeks and fell wetly onto Mary's.

'She was a gift from my beloved abbot, Prosper Guéranger, the saviour of Solesmes Abbey,' said Léandre in a voice full of remorse and self-pity.

'Do not blame yourself,' Fabrice reassured him. 'Everything gets broken. The crew are so careless.'

'It was not the sailors,' sobbed the novice. 'Our Lady arrived here in perfect condition. It was I who broke her neck as I clumsily tried to take her from the box. Also, just now I allowed her to fall on her face and now her nose is slightly chipped. See?'

It was the resourceful Sister Anne, unable to stand any more of his wailing, who had heated up some *balga* resin on her stove and brought it up to the camp to use as glue. He would try to mend the Madonna's neck, the sad monk cried. He had already written to his abbot about the calamity, begging his forgiveness. This novice, thought Fabrice, had a regrettable propensity to confession.

He complained that Bishop Brady was punishing him for the disturbance he made at the funeral of Maurice Bouchet. *Consummatus in brevi, explevit tempora multa*, Léandre had wailed during Office and Mass of the Dead when contemplative silence was required; the soul of the deceased had so pleased the Lord that He plucked him from the midst of wickedness. Afterwards, he was unfairly reprimanded by the bishop, 'simply for loving dear Maurice so much'.

'Now as punishment he sends me to a place where he knows I will be speared.'

'Surely not, Léandre.'

'Surely so,' countered the novice. 'Captain Scully, Dom Salvado's new friend, whom I do not at all trust, has told me all about this place where he wants them to put the mission. It is called Victoria Plains.'

'It sounds quite benign.'

'Benign, you say!' the little fellow exploded. 'Everything is called Victoria, now, for their queen. Do not be fooled by that. It is in the most remote part of the colony and it is a desert, where only the strongest and most brutal natives survive.' Léandre was inventing facts as fast as he could speak. 'Some farmers moved their sheep there, but the land is entirely barren and the natives are very hostile and excellent hunters. Do you know what is a *kidji*, Fabrice?'

'Yes, I do,' said the linguist, pleased to recognise the word. 'A *kidji* is a native spear.'

'Sharp! Every native on Victoria Plains has one to repel intruders,' sobbed the missionary. 'Even the smallest of children.'

'Who told you all this, Léandre?'

'Captain Scully told me. He is a salesman for this Victoria Plains but Salvado cannot see through him as I do. He wants the mission located near his farm so he has told Salvado how wonderful it is. All of it is lies. I asked Captain Scully – do you want us all to be speared? *Chut*, he said, and don't tell Salvado about the *kidjis*. It will just upset him.'

The novice replaced Mary's head and looked at her expectantly, as if hoping she might thank him or bless him for his trouble.

'The Langoulants have instructed me to bring you to the river for dinner tonight, Léandre.'

'Oh?' said the novice sadly, still gazing down upon the boxed virgin. 'They are so nice. Mary Ann loves me so much. I have written to my abbot about Louis' kindness. Louis is as gentle and kind as *Jésus Christ* himself. Did you know, Fabrice, his full name is Jean Charles Louis Langoulant. He really is J.C., you see! But, no, I cannot come to dinner. I am much too depressed to eat.'

'You must come, Léandre. The boys from Amiens will be there too, so only French will be spoken. I will serve the fish that I myself caught from a boat, just like Jesus. Except, surely, he never caught one as large as my mulloway.'

'No, Fabrice. I cannot come. I would just weep and have to be comforted by Mary Ann.'

'Mary Ann loves to comfort you. And you must come, if only to see the size of my huge fish. You may not get fish for some time, if you are living in the desert. And Léandre, as your good friend, I would very much like to share a last meal with you before I leave for the town of Toodyay.'

'Oh, are you really going away, dear Fabrice?' the novice asked in dolorous tone, turning Mary's head a tiny bit to the left as if she too was saddened at the prospect. 'With the atheist?'

'Humanist. They are a bit softer, I think. Roger Smith has plans to start a commune.'

'I do not like him. But how I envy you, professor. While you will be enjoying such a *lovely* commune, I will be starving in the bush with my Spanish confrères and hiding from the hunters. Also, Dom Serra insists on the Italian version of the Rules of St Benedict, while I am accustomed to the Rules we had at Solesmes, refined by our dear abbot. Disputing with Dom Serra is useless. He does not understand French very well and just says *como? como?* whenever I talk. I suppose he thinks it a mercy to be unable to comprehend me, since I am so useless as a missionary.'

'Then come to tea, dear Léandre.'

The novice seemed on the verge of agreeing, but was not yet ready to utter the word. 'Have you ever read St Paul?' he asked, instead.

'No.'

'Nor have I. Not really. Who can read him? Every priest must be able to read St Paul, but I cannot. *Onus angelicis humeris tremendum.* So François Le Bannier says of the priesthood.'

'Angels carry great weight on their shoulders?'

'Angels, but not novices. Oh, I cannot be a missionary, Fabrice! Really, I can't. I know it, deep in my heart. Dom Serra knows it too. He is a short man, you see, which makes him angry. Me, I don't mind being so short. I expect no better of myself.'

In his sadness, Léandre gripped too firmly the Madonna's freshly glued head, which snapped off once more. His own head slumped to his chest, and his shoulders jerked. Fabrice squatted beside him and gently patted the back of his cloak, annoying the bush flies which had gathered there.

'You *will* come to tea at the Langoulants tonight, Léandre, so we

French can bid each other *adieu et bonne chance*. Will you promise?'

'*Oui*,' squeaked the novice, a sulky child compelled to give in. He did not look up as Fabrice stood to leave, but fingered the hem on Our Lady's skirt. 'Her blue dress is beautiful though, is it not?' he said. 'Look at the folds.'

There was to be a farewell Mass for the missionaries. Terry Farrelly, announcer of the bishop's encyclicals, went to the superior of each of the three missions to instruct them. All the missionaries were to gather at six on the dirt road outside 'the cathedral', as His Lordship had decreed the rickety church was now to be called. Full clerical dress was to be worn, no matter the heat. His Lordship had invited many dignitaries. Governor Clarke and his wife might attend.

Bishop Brady had divided them into Southern, Central and Northern missions and only the previous night had he advised each leader of his destination. The French Heart of Mary priests were to go south, the Spanish Benedictines north to Victoria Plains, and the lonely Tyrolean exiled to the distant tropics, weeks away by sea. Tonight they would be collectively fêted, blessed and bid *adieu* and within two weeks they were all to be gone from Perth.

Naturally, the three superiors wished to complain to Bishop Brady about the short time this left them to prepare and the absence of funds with which to buy supplies. They were directed to speak with Peter Powell, whom the bishop had elevated in order that his rival might enjoy the brunt of the missionaries' discontent. Father Powell dutifully listened to the complaints, advised them that he would pass on his concerns to His Lordship, but reminded each priest of his duty to his bishop. Leave Perth they must, and soon. Apart from the evangelistic imperative, it was far too expensive to keep them all in town.

Knowing the Tyrolean's reclusive nature, Fabrice sought out Don Angelo Confalonieri. He looked even thinner, paler and more troubled than usual, but brightened at an opportunity to converse in his native tongue with someone who was not a cleric.

'You have been sent north?' said Fabrice. 'I am confused. I heard the Spanish are going to the northernmost place in the settlement.'

'Alas, the continent goes on forever beyond even that. My beloved bishop has sent me beyond the bounds of the colony.'

'To New South Wales?'

'Alas, no. Sydney would suit me very well I think, the bishop there being a fellow Benedictine. I will sail to Sydney but from there I must continue on to a place called Port Victoria on the uninhabited north coast of the continent.'

Fabrice recalled having seen this remote place marked on Brady's map. The English had built a naval garrison there with a few dozen men, but he had heard it was to be abandoned. 'Does anyone still live there?'

'Nobody seems quite sure,' sighed the monk. 'I managed to find one man who has actually visited the place, a sea captain by the name of Blackwood who has been everywhere on this earth, all the way around Australia and to the jungles of New Guinea and Surabaya. He looked at me with great compassion. The one place to which he would never return, he told me, is Port Victoria.'

His fellow missionaries were to be two of the catechists, Fagan and Hogan.

'Irishmen?' said Fabrice. 'How will you converse, Don Angelo?'

'Latin, perhaps?' shrugged the monk. The two shared a smile, knowing this be a useless language for ordinary matters.

Fabrice sensed a disaster looming and felt in his breast pocket for a solution. He produced a note from a London bank for twenty-five

English pounds, flattened it out and placed it between them on the table. Don Angelo Confalonieri looked at the money and his eyes widened, but then averted them and shook his head.

'I cannot,' he said. 'You must give it to the bishop, who might give it to me.'

'He won't.'

'That is quite true. I would never see a penny of it, nor hear tell of it, but he is my bishop.'

'Angelo, I worry for you. You must obtain supplies for such a serious task. You can buy them in Sydney *en route* to this awful place.' Fabrice tapped the note, pushed it a little towards the monk. The note seemed again to have been rejected but as Fabrice went to withdraw it, a thin white hand shot out of a cassock and the paper disappeared up the sleeve. Both faces remained inscrutable and there came no word of thanks.

'Tell me, Don Angelo, will you wear your smart jacket in the tropics?' asked the linguist.

'I will wear it in Sydney, I think,' said the sad Tyrolean, 'for the last time.'

The 'Last Supper' for the French missionaries was a joyous affair. No one departing the cathedral could fail to envy the pretty lights on the riverside and the sweet sound of an Irish fiddle over the hubbub of French laughter. Next door, the new governor and his wife were also hosting a party, but the French soirée dwarfed it in sight and sound.

Léandre Fonteinne did, of course, come to tea. The minute the valedictory Mass ended, he rushed to find Fabrice. The little fellow's spirits had soared, for he had just learned that, on the suggestion of

Captain Scully, the Central Mission would travel to Victoria Plains via Toodyay.

'Now we can travel together!' the novice declared, squeezing his friend's hand with joy in the darkness.

'Still, we cannot leave together, Léandre.'

'And why not?' said the novice, a hint of anger rising in his voice.

'Roger Smith and Sadie have already gone to Toodyay to choose a site for our commune. I am to wait here in Perth until they return to collect the tools from Louis' boatshed.'

'But we *must* travel together,' Léandre insisted. 'We shall not part, dear Fabrice! Not yet! And with luck, our axle will break crossing the hills so I can remain even longer in Toodyay with you.'

The little Benedictine had further good news to report. Mary's head had held firmly. 'You cannot detect her broken neck much. She just looks just very slightly askance.'

Mary Ann had lit up the grounds with flares and sparklers so it looked like a fairy glen. The fiddler was one of the Irish catechists called Donovan. He stood beside the road so that his music, sad and cheerful at the same time, washed over the delighted guests as they walked in.

Léandre Fonteinne arrived at the Langoulants as a fat child might to a birthday party, with a whoop and a skip. He ran into the arms of the hostess, who laughed and kissed him tenderly. Already present were the two Fathers Francis, their two laymen, Théodore and Vincent, a friend of Louis named Charles Tondut, his wife Caroline and their six children of various ages, who were helping serve food, or playing, or crying. The serving table, really the hosts' back door removed from its hinges and laid upon on a trestle, was piled high with food. Seats were found for those that needed seats, but most were happy with blankets on the ground.

It was a perfect night to sit outside. The frogs were as noisy as ever. There was wine. Nico Caporelli, who had abandoned all reference to his title, brought along two generous casks marked *Sakild Burgundy for St John's Cathedral.* The Frenchmen agreed it was awful, but many *santés* were exchanged nonetheless. Charles Tondut had brought along a good cognac for later in the evening when the stars were out.

While Mass was being celebrated, Fabrice's giant fish was baking in Louis' outdoor oven. Fabrice proudly carved the steaming mulloway, and to anyone who would listen, he explained that he had captured it at night on this very river, at The Narrows, just out there, if you followed the line of his fork.

Léandre had been pressed into assisting the chef. For fun, Mary Ann dressed him in one of her flowery aprons, which looked most amusing draped over a Benedictine cassock. The mulloway was brought to the table with flourish. Léandre carried the large wooden tray upon which rested the fish, its great tail trailing artistically over one end while Fabrice, brandishing a large knife and spoon in theatrical manner, served each guest, the steaming white meat falling away from the bone in chunks fully three inches thick.

Léandre served himself an enormous plateful and sat beside the hostess. 'Why should I not enjoy a meal prepared in my honour,' he announced, growing more effusive with his second glass of wine. 'After this I have to renounce all the comforts of life. Dom Serra will inflict upon us a regime where everything points to abnegation and penitence.' He pouted sadly and proffered his glass. 'Might I have some more wine, dearest Mary Ann?'

The Heart of Mary missionaries had been staying with the Langoulants and spent a lazy afternoon by the river making plans while enjoying Mary Ann's lemonade under the peppermint trees. They had gone off to Mass quite happy with their destination of Albany, with the promise of a cooler climate, a settlement older than Perth, and frequent visits from ships, both steam and sail. But they returned in furore. Father Peter Powell had cornered the Fathers Francis after Mass to advise them that they would not be sailing to Albany after all, for the cost was too much for the diocese to bear. They were to go on foot. Furthermore, the bishop wanted the Southern Mission to be the first to depart. They were expected to leave Perth tomorrow.

'So we are to walk where there is no path, in this terrible heat!' complained Father Francis Thiersé. 'We will all perish.'

'He hasn't one *sou* to give us but wants to expand his diocese on the map,' complained Father Francis Thévaux, superior of the Southern Mission. 'I am flattered, of course, to be made his vicar general of King George Sound. But it is all a sort of fantasy. How can I care for the souls of Adelaide when my bishop cannot afford to pay our fare even as far as Albany?'

Léandre Fonteinne was not to be outdone in matters of adversity.

'But how lucky you all are to have a mission of French speakers and to enjoy the gentle, cool easy climate of the south. Poor me, I will be the only French speaker in the hot northern bush, where spearing white men is a common game. Apart from the Spanish monks, we only have that pale English one whom nobody likes, and an Irishman, who is … well, Irish.'

'But we are no longer free of them either,' Father Francis Thévaux interrupted. 'Peter Powell has decided to join us. To spy on us, I would guess. And the fiddler as well, I know not why.'

'To make us walk faster,' suggested Théodore.

'It is such a terrible thing to be born Irish,' explained the novice, nodding sadly to his fourth burgundy. 'To love them, you need to imagine they have been sent back to their own island so the high seas separate them from you.'

Mary Ann reached from behind around the novice's stomach. 'That's enough now about the terrible Irish, Leon,' she said, teasingly. 'What if Father Powell were to suddenly appear behind you, or His Lordship!' She smoothed his hair, which was still glued hard in places from his work on the Madonna.

'Oh, I did not mean *you* of course, Mary Ann!' whispered Léandre, ashamed of his outburst. 'I just meant the Catholics ones.'

'Well, that will be me soon enough.'

'No!' the little fellow gasped. 'You are converting? Why would you ever want to do that?'

She paused, uncertain of the answer. 'Because Sister Anne is so sweet, and she's travelled such a long way across the seas for so little purpose. It will make her happy to convert a terrible Protestant, I think, and if it lifts her spirits, then why not?'

The Langoulants were greatly loved by their guests, and Louis envied by the missionaries. As a layman, he was free to wear his religion lightly. He was married to a beautiful, cheerful girl and they had two sweet daughters to share their love.

It was dark now, the children had fallen asleep, and the conversation had grown more reflective. Cigars had appeared from somewhere, so that each speaker had his own ethereal glow, as if lit for the stage. One of the laymen, either Vincent or Théodore, asked Louis about life on the Swan River.

That he could make his living as a fisherman, Louis explained, was a wonderful piece of luck. One could learn so much from a river. Catching fish happened to be the thing he most loved to do. All he needed was his boat, his nets, his lines and hooks, and with these simple things he had perfect happiness, so long as he had Mary Ann and his two girls to come back to each night.

He sometimes fished downstream where the river was wide and salty and alive with ocean fish. *Brème* were plentiful upstream in the fresh water of the Canning River where it was narrower and had reedy banks. Mulloway could be pulled in where fresh met salt.

Sometimes in the heat of the day he would pull the boat ashore, lie flat on his back on the soft white sand under a shady paperbark, and shut his eyes for an hour. Some days he would not really fish at all, but just potter about repairing nets and pretending to work. If there was a particular tide or moon, or if the feeling came upon him, he might light a lantern and fish by night. If the oil ran out, he would lie on the wooden deck of his tiny boat, rocking upon the black waters of the Swan and look up at a night sky of such clarity he was sure it was matched nowhere on earth.

'Do you feel the presence of God at such a time?' said one of the Fathers Francis.

'Yes,' said Louis, after some thought, 'I suppose so.' He did experience a spiritual feeling at such times, but never analysed it too much for fear it would vanish. 'God' seemed the right word to use when speaking to a priest.

'What about the river natives?' someone asked.

That depended, said Louis. Some days, they might show an interest in his activities, but on other days, he would shout a cheerful *Allo!* and they would stay perfectly silent while he floated past. Sometimes the children might help him clean his catch, always keeping a few for themselves. On a good day, the older fellows might show him how to spear the bottom-dwelling *nyola*, a fleshy catfish, or how to build a trap. But the next day they might fill his boat with brown jellyfish while he was occupied, or help themselves to some rope or netting.

'What about the ones in the south,' asked one of the Fathers Francis, 'should we fear them?'

'Perhaps. They have had more time to know the white man down there,' said Louis, 'and they may have been punished for stealing flour or killing sheep, so they might fear you at first.' Louis knew the south well enough, for he had left a French whaling camp near Esperance and lived in Albany for a year before walking to Perth.

'So the distance to Albany can be walked?' asked Father Francis Thévaux.

'Well, it was not easy but I had to keep going.'

'You were being pursued?' asked Théodore or Vincent, and they all pressed in closer. 'By the whalers?'

'I was trying to escape a particular scoundrel by the name of Charles,' explained the host, 'but I could not throw him off.' He told them some amusing stories about this terrible fellow and then announced that this same Charles was present tonight: Charles Tondut, the father of these six bothersome children, and the bringer of the cognac they were all enjoying. This announcement brought a huge round of laughter, then applause.

The walk to the south coast would not be easy, Louis cautioned. Five hundred kilometres with few settlements on the way and no road. 'Charles and I walked it in July, when it was cool and there was plenty of water. You have been sent off in the middle of summer, a different proposition altogether.'

Fabrice spent the night in pleasant discourse with the lay 'brothers', *Frères* Théodore and Vincent, both optimists who refused to let life oppress them. Later in the night, with the Fathers Francis present, he posed a dangerous question. 'Tell me, why would the natives want to adopt the religion of their oppressors?'

'Because it is Truth,' explained Father Francis Thiersé with moving simplicity. 'Believe me, Fabrice, they will come to embrace Christianity more enthusiastically than the Europeans of this colony do.'

The other Father Francis expanded. 'Our order dedicates itself to freed slaves who were torn away by Christians from their African homelands. You may think they would be repelled, but no. Our confrères return from the Caribbean saying that they come to love God with an intensity never seen in France. It is the rich and educated in France that are spiritually poor, for want of adversity.'

Lying nearby on a blanket watching the night sky, Léandre Fonteinne had grown melancholy as he listened to the other Frenchmen making their wonderful plans together while he alone had been exiled to the terrible Victoria Plains with the Spanish. Mary Ann sat behind him, stroked his hair, held his sad head to her bosom and sang to him. The novice would have happily left his head resting there forever, had she not finally sat him up and kissed the top of his head.

'Enough, now,' she said at last. 'You had best wander home.' It was two in the morning, yet he was the first Frenchman to leave. There were many long embraces.

'Do not fret, Léandre,' the Heart of Mary men assured him as he tottered off. 'You will make a wonderful missionary.' Not one of the men from Amiens believed such words, but it was right that they be said.

Fabrice was worried the little monk might fall or go to sleep in a ditch so he accompanied Dom Léandre back to the Spanish Camp. All the way, in the darkness, the novice recited his many failings. He had been racked by doubt as he left St Jean de Bièvres six months ago, he sobbed, and every night in his cell at Downside Abbey. The feeling had only grown worse as he boarded *Elizabeth* at Gravesend. He was not a priest. He would never be a priest. He was always coveting. It was against the Commandments but he could not help it. The longings only grew stronger if he tried to push them away. He had become too close to Caporelli, who liked to lead him astray. Now Judgement Day was imminent. Within days he would leave with the Spanish for the wilderness. He was full of panic. He greatly feared the wilderness and the native men with their naked muscular chests and their sharp *kidjis*.

'Thank goodness you will come with me as far as Toodyay,' said Dom Léandre, throwing his arms around his friend's middle. Fabrice untied the bows at the back of Mary Ann's floral apron and pulled it over the novice's head. Surely Dom Serra would not approve of such a garment at morning prayers.

Fabrice lowered the novice onto his stretcher, took off his sandals and put his feet to bed with the rest of him. Still Léandre recited his many failings, as if in the confessional. Dom Salvado must have been awake in the darkness, for he laughed once, then said something about Vigils being in three hours' time. Fabrice Cleriquot pulled a blanket over the little fellow's shoulders, kissed his forehead and went back to the river to rejoin his countrymen.

From: Dom Léandre Fonteinne, Perth

To: Prosper Guéranger, Solesmes Abbey

16th February 1846

Most Reverend and Very Dear Father

We were supposed to have left Perth for Victoria Plains but a thousand obstacles have come across our path. What is holding us up now? First it is one thing and then another but Dom Salvado has the carts almost packed, so I suppose it must be soon that we depart. I shudder at the thought. But I still have a few moments left so I will pass them with you, my beloved Father.

While writing, I am distracted by seven natives who are in the act of doing themselves up as Europeans. Dom Salvado won their confidence using bread and grapes. They are a family group visiting from the Moore River, near to where our mission is to be located. They are afraid of the local natives so they stay close to our camp. This morning the old man came with great shyness to ask us for some breakfast. Dom Serra and Dom Salvado combed and bathed the children. I was too fearful to help this time but I assure you that the good natives of Victoria Plains are going to be very fond of us because we will take great care of them.

Would you believe it, dear Father, but just to get a pair of shoes from the bishop I had to go through an argument. He doesn't want to give us anything. It is a miserable situation here for us. He has too many debts to be able to satisfy his creditors and so he chooses to pay none of them. Already the tribunals have heard tell of him, so

I hear, but anyway it is not for the child to uncover the nakedness of his Father.

It is instead to you, my own true beloved Father, that I choose to speak, he who is so good and whom I love so fondly with all my heart, begging him as I tenderly embrace him, kindly to bless so beloved a child who is so very frightened of going on this mission to the dark bush so far from all those I really love.

I embrace you and love you with all my heart, as your entirely obedient and submissive child. I embrace you a thousand thousand times, as I do also all my Fathers and Brothers.

Your most lowly and most loving child
Br. Léandre

6. A SERIES OF DEPARTURES

'*C'est l'évêque!*' said Théodore, and he was right. Bishop Brady was indeed standing on the pier waving his arms and yelling at the three Frenchmen in the rowboat.

Sighing, Louis turned *Galilée* around. Last night he had enjoyed too much cognac and too little sleep. Twice already he had paddled up the Swan and Canning rivers as far as Canning Vale. He did not need any doubling back.

'Where is Father Powell?' demanded the bishop.

'Upriver with the *Abbés François*,' said Vincent.

'Take him this note.'

As soon as they were out of sight of the prelate, Vincent prised the letter open. It was written in English, in angry little letters. He held it in front of Louis Langoulant, who translated it for them as he rowed. His Lordship had new instructions for Father Peter Powell. He was to return to Perth and sail to Albany so he could arrive there ahead of the French priests, who would proceed on foot.

'*Quel bâtard!*' exclaimed Théodore. 'The Irishman gets to sail while we are forced to walk in this terrible heat.'

'*Bien sûr,*' spat Vincent, 'His Lordship always favours the Irish, and we French can go to hell.'

At Canning Vale, Father Powell was handed the bishop's note, and as he read it his face was closely surveyed by the four men from Amiens. There was no reaction. He simply grabbed his pack, climbed back into *Galilée,* and beckoned the Irish fiddler to do the same. Father Powell spoke to Louis only once after that, to instruct him to drop him at the pier so he could walk up to the Bishop's House, or 'Palace' as Brady had taken to calling it.

Louis Langoulant was exhausted, but at least the boat was empty and *le médecin* was behind him, for which mercy he thanked the Christian god and the *ouagil* in equal parts. Pain could give a certain pleasure, he noticed, if it was to a purpose, and he pulled the oars deeper and harder in order to feel it more profoundly. His palms were blistered and he sobbed with pain, but Louis Langoulant straightened his back for the last half *myriamètre* which would deliver him to the white sandy beach next to his boathouse.

Was this, he wondered, something like the Benedictines felt when they closed their eyes and chanted?

Galilée touched bottom and Louis staggered ashore, completely spent. He threw the oars into the bottom of his boat, took a few steps and collapsed on the grassy bank in blissful agony. An angel appeared above him.

'Dear God, you will go straight to heaven, Louis,' it said. He opened his eyes to look up Mary Ann's skirts.

'I am already in heaven, my beautiful girl,' he replied, dream-like.

Mary Ann tutted over her the state of her husband's hands. 'That will teach you to make offers to priests at two in the morning after a bottle of cognac,' she scolded.

Four feet circled his face now, tiny pink ones. Cherubs.

'Daddy's tired,' said Victoria, hovering above her father. A tear fell upon his face.

'Don't cry on Daddy!' scolded her little sister, 'he's too wet!' The offending teardrop was wiped away and a child's moist kiss replaced it.

A wonderful sense of peace came over Louis Langoulant. The last of the priests were gone, thank God.

The Langoulants had only one house guest remaining, and he was a Humanist, so no trouble at all. Fabrice was awaiting Roger Smith and Sadie's return from Toodyay. They appeared a few days later accompanied by Bob, a light-skinned native boy from the Avon. For a few nights they would occupy Louis' boatshed, where Roger Smith had stored all his tools for the Toodyay smithy.

'Our commune will be called The Garden,' Roger Smith announced over the evening meal; fish once more. He looked at Fabrice inquisitorially. 'You understand the reference, of course?'

'Eden?' guessed Fabrice, without confidence.

'Heavens, no!' said Roger Smith, shaking his head. 'In the Garden of Eden, anyone who sought knowledge was punished, quite the opposite of our philosophy. Our Garden is taken from Epicurus, of course.'

'Ah, yes,' said Fabrice, nodding; he was unfamiliar with Epicurus.

'Epicurus lived a simple life amongst friends on the outskirts of Athens,' explained Roger Smith. 'He and his followers forsook money and worked purely for the benefits work gave. They kept intelligent and lively company and drank wine made from their own grapes, broke bread which they baked and enjoyed cold meats and cheese which they themselves made.'

'They lived like monks,' suggested Fabrice.

'Nothing like monks!' protested Roger Smith, averse to any religious implications. 'They permitted themselves guiltlessly to enjoy pleasure, and of course they sensibly ignored the Greek gods with all their false morality and superstitions.'

'And how did they get on, these Epicurean lads?' asked Mary Ann, newly baptised a Catholic. 'I bet they upset people.'

'Indeed they did. They were widely resented for showing that a good life could be lived without money. Athens and Rome let them be until such time as Rome became Christian. The Christians invented all sorts of rumours of orgies and gastronomic feasts and prostitutes and so on, and forced the Epicureans to repent.'

At his university, Fabrice had heard plenty of theorists talk about starting a commune of equals, but they were all weak-limbed thinkers with wealthy parents. None were practical men like Roger Smith, just as intelligent and widely read, but with the strong arms and skills to turn such abstract concepts into reality. Roger Smith could actually build things.

'What of the native people?' Fabrice asked, thinking of Pauline Jaricot's instructions. 'Will they be allowed to join The Garden?'

Roger Smith waved a hand towards the newcomer Bob, as if his very presence answered the question. 'Man or woman, Athenian or Corinthian, white or brown, freeman or slave, these things were of no consequence to Epicurus, and nor shall they be to us.'

The Garden existed. Roger Smith displayed the freshly stamped title deeds to a property on the banks of the Avon River that he and Sadie had surveyed. They had left some materials there and a man in charge.

'A crook,' said Bob, his first contribution to the conversation.

Roger Smith was gentle in his rebuke. 'Now, now, Bob. You may not yet see eye to eye with young Eric but the two of you will get along in time. That is our way in The Garden, remember. We always believe in the goodness of others.'

Bob found something of interest to pick at between his toes.

'Bob's right,' said Sadie, firmly but without looking at Roger Smith. 'You don't know boys like that Eric. I grew up with them. Bit by bit, all our stuff will vanish.'

On the morning they were to leave, Fabrice rose early to take a walk along the river. Roger and Sadie had not yet emerged from Louis' boatshed.

He sat alone on the riverbank and watched the black swans glide among the reeds. A mature cob clambered up the bank and stood defiantly before him, a dignified bird with jet plumage, scarlet beak, and a sort of wisdom in its small eyes. It stretched its neck, raised itself up as if it were about to lecture him on some topic and then flapped its enormous wings, spraying river water on the Frenchman's face like a natural blessing.

'*Gouljacque*,' said Bob, or so it sounded to a French ear. The boy had been lingering nearby, unseen. That he anticipated the linguist's question made the Frenchman blush. With some guilt it occurred to Professor Cleriquot that when he spoke to a native it was only to demand a word from him in order to steal it and file it, like a botanist might a leaf, or a taxidermist a pelt.

'Come and sit with me, Bob,' he said gently, in English. The boy did not do so, but neither did he run away. He just stayed nearby pulling some paperbark off a tree. 'Please, tell me about yourself.'

The boy had nothing to tell him, so Fabrice told the boy about himself instead.

It was not easy to address issues of god and creation when they had so few words in common, but the linguist was determined to try.

'For you, Bob ... there is *l'ouagil*, I think. Louis told me of it.

That is how you say it? The *ouagil*?' The boy made no effort to help. Perhaps it was forbidden to discuss such things.

'Those priests, Bob, the ones you have seen dressed all in black despite the heat. They see god in everything, or say they do. They might see god in this tree here, perhaps.' The boy followed the Frenchman's gaze up to the canopy of a she-oak. 'Perhaps they see god in a cormorant or pelican, or in you, Bob, or even in me. I do not see god anywhere, but I am not a priest. Perhaps they have better eyesight and can see god all the time, while I can only sense it in this particular *gouljacque*, in this particular light.'

Bob had paused in his bark-stripping. Fabrice took this to mean they were making a connection on a philosophical level.

'Now, I cannot see your *ouagil*. I thought perhaps I felt its presence on the night I caught a mulloway, just out there, a very large one it was. Also, I cannot see the planet Saturn, but I have a friend in Lyon who has seen it through a lens: a very large planet he tells me, bigger than earth, surrounded at its waist by beautiful rings. Do I call him mad, Bob, *un fou-fou*? No. I believe that he has seen things that I cannot.

'So we are off to Toodyay, you and me, Bob, to form a commune. To my surprise, I find I am full of enthusiasm for it. I think perhaps we can create a new way of living together. And those priests in black, they think the same, except they see god, and do it for him, while I do not. Perhaps I am a missionary, after all, Bob, but a blind one. Do you understand?'

Bob was a good listener. Recalling Frank Armstrong's advice, Fabrice allowed his arm to fall over the boy's shoulder as they walked back to the boatshed. The sight of the black swan on the river at dawn had made the Frenchman feel very content, and the philosophical exchange with Bob even more so.

'*Merci, Monsieur Gouljacque*,' Fabrice sang back gaily to the swan, but neither the bird nor the boy seemed to understand his meaning.

When the sun was fully above the horizon, Roger Smith and Sadie appeared and enjoyed a cooked breakfast with Bob next to the boatshed, while Fabrice took his mug to a sunny spot on the grassy bank from where he could hear their conversations and heard his name mentioned.

Afterwards, the group was summoned for a briefing.

'We leave for Guildford this afternoon,' announced the leader of the Toodyay commune. 'We now have the strongest wagon axle in the colony, I would venture.' The previous afternoon, with Bob's assistance, Roger Smith had repaired the wagon. 'Fabrice, I am obliged to ask, are you still inclined to join us?'

'Of course,' said Fabrice, 'why would you ask?'

'Bob tells me you want to be a priest.'

Fabrice looked at the boy with annoyance. 'No,' he protested. 'Yes. I will join The Garden, if you will allow me.' Sadie unexpectedly threw her arms around him, as if she hadn't liked the idea of being alone with Roger Smith for too long.

'Very well, old chap,' said Roger Smith, with English reserve. 'You will no doubt be a most useful member, with your, ah, silk skills and so on. Now, to work. Our job for this morning is to empty the boatshed of my tools and pack up the cart.'

A blacksmith's workshop had been stored in Louis' boatshed in a hundred iron parts. As they stowed each piece on the dray, Fabrice and Bob received instruction as to its particular purpose. There were anvils, hammers and scrap. Plain tongs, pliers, farrier tongs. Handles and wedges. *Repoussé* hammers and chasing knives.

Cutters and punches. Cones, bickerns. Bending, scrolling and twisting forks. Punches and chisels. Bob could recall them all when tested. Fabrice felt no affinity for this language.

Dom Salvado appeared and came to admire Roger Smith's tools. The two talked at length about oxen and carts and axles and furnaces and such. It seemed to Fabrice that the monk and the Humanist agreed on almost everything.

'We plan to spend tonight in Guildford,' said the monk, leaning against the cart like an old farm hand.

'As do we,' said the Humanist.

'The second at Mahogany Creek.'

'Also my intention,' said Roger Smith. He had the start of a beard, though not as advanced as the monk's.

'We should wait for the sea breeze to arrive and cool things down.'

'Agreed. Three o'clock, then?'

'Perfect. Let us meet here at three,' said the monk

The two men shook hands. Fabrice Cleriquot, observing, imagined that the monk and the Humanist were thinking the same thing: what an excellent convert the other would make, if only the fool could be made to see the light.

A hundred well-wishers gathered on St Georges Terrace to see the popular Spanish missionaries head off. The Irish catechists were making a lot of noise because one of their lads, John Gorman, was leaving them. Nico Caporelli arrived with a Timor pony drawing a tiny box cart in which were squeezed Mother Ursula and Sister Anne, their knees drawn up and their faces acknowledging the comedy of it.

The Spanish monks had been lent two ox-pulled drays by Captain Scully of Bolgart. Salvado held the reins of the first and Gorman had control of the second. The monks had donned their black cloaks and crucifixes for the ceremonial departure, but beneath his cassock Salvado still wore his dungarees. The family living at the Spanish Camp had come down the hill to see the monks off, and soon Salvado was nursing the baby while the father of the group held the reins, impersonating him.

Léandre Fonteinne's disposition had been greatly improved by the news that his wish had come true; he would after all be travelling to Toodyay with his dear friend Fabrice Cleriquot. The novice had acquired a broad-brimmed hat and a long, gnarled stick for use as a staff, he explained, and to scare off wild dogs.

Finally, seated uncomfortably among the provisions on Salvado's dray sat the pasty-faced subdeacon from Downside Abbey, Dom Tootle or Tottle, who seemed to be in a sulk or perhaps unwell.

The bishop's lieutenant, Terry Farrelly, was posted a hundred yards up the terrace awaiting the signal that his bishop was ready. Now from his direction came a voice requiring no amplification: 'Right, enough of all that, lads! Silence for His Lordship's arrival!' Such were The Terror's persuasive powers that all those assembled on St Georges Terrace stayed pinned to where they stood, be they Catholic, Protestant or Humanist. Even the mangy dogs of Perth stood still and awaited the arrival of Bishop Brady.

The Benedictines climbed down, brushed the straw from their beards and stood beside their loaded wagons. At the first sight of smoke, they commenced a reverential *Te Deum*, led by the cathedral's cantor, Léandre Fonteinne. Roger Smith let out the tiniest of groans.

From the west, a holy cloud was approaching at slow walking pace. Farrelly, walking at the head of it, must have overloaded the thurible, such was the cover of incense smoke that proceeded from him. As the sweet-smelling mist dissipated John Brady himself was revealed, wearing an amaranth biretta, and in his right hand he carried the bishop's mitre, with which he struck the ground every second step. He was the Good Shepherd, this was his crook, and around him, his compliant flock moved not a muscle. On his right walked a stiff Father Peter Powell, a silver aspersorium in his left hand in order that the assembled might be sprinkled by His Lordship with holy water.

The bishop looked to have a deep and personal grievance against every man, woman and child assembled. He passed his mitre to Father Powell, took the silver aspergillum from the bowl and began to spray holy water over everyone and everything while muttering angrily in Latin. Many of the children thus blessed complained to their mothers about the violent actions of the grumpy old man.

When he came to the Benedictines, the men in black lowered their heads to allow the Bishop of Perth to bless them with water and then give them a cross of benediction. He asked for God's protection of these good missionaries who were about to venture into the wilderness in His name.

His Lordship then turned his attention to the matter of transportation and blessed the wheels of the Benedictine carts, then their oxen, invoking God's protection of them. He hesitated over Caporelli's dogcart, for he was greatly upset with the nuns. Still, he shook a little holy water on its wheels and then, after more hesitation, on the Timor pony, an animal entirely unmentioned in the Bible. He offered one final glare at the now silent Sisters of Mercy who, he had just been informed by Farrelly, were taking off to Guildford without his approval and were probably up to some sort of nunly mischief.

The atheists were invisible to him.

'Oh dear,' complained Roger Smith to Fabrice, loudly enough to be heard by the bishop, 'we are denied the magic water.' Brady braced, but walked on. He had had his fill of conflict and instead left, alone and without ceremony, trudging back up the terrace holding his pink hat in one hand and water shaker in the other – a worker carrying his tools home at the end of an exhausting day. Peter Powell took care of all the silverware.

With the bishop gone, the Irish laymen were again in charge of proceedings. It was a big occasion for the eight catechists. Gorman was about to leave with the Spanish. Tomorrow, Fagan and Hogan would sail off to the tropics. The remainder would stay in Perth and teach and help the bishop run the diocese. So there was singing, led by Terry Farrelly, who was revealed as a prodigious balladeer.

Then came the turn of the Benedictines, an inevitable *Salve Regina.*

> *Salve, Regina, mater misericordiae*
> *Vita, dulcedo, et ses nostra, salve*
> *Ad te clamamus*

When the Gregorian chant petered out, Roger Smith allowed silence enough to be respectful without risking a reprise, then raised his whip and shouted, 'To Guildford!' And off the ragged convoy took: a large oxcart, two smaller drays and a pony cart, between them carrying, besides the son of a Lyonnais silk merchant, a Humanist blacksmith of aristocratic origins, his companion Sadie, two Spanish Benedictine monks, a pasty English subdeacon, a frightened French novice, an Irish catechist, two Irish nuns, an Italian grape farmer and a slender boy called Bob who was returning to his home district. They moved off at such a slow pace that those on foot outpaced those on wheels.

Louis and Mary Ann Langoulant waved them off with a sense of profound relief at having once more regained their solitude. Louis had grown whiskers, was shoeless and wore a loose Indian cotton robe tied at the waist with rope, while Mary Ann was showing with their third child. Together, observed Roger Smith drolly, they looked like a couple in search of a stable.

The rowdy Irish catechists walked alongside their friend Gorman's cart, teasing him relentlessly until halfway down the Guildford Road, where with great emotion each one hugged his countryman and slapped his back and bade him a final farewell.

'That's the last we'll see of that poor bastard,' one of the Irish lads shouted after John Gorman as the last cart disappeared east, and they all laughed.

From: Anne Xavier Dillon, Perth
To: Cecilia Marmion, Baggot Street, Dublin

24th February 1846

My Own Loved Revd Mother,

Ursula's envelope is too full to include this, or so she tells me, so I am mailing it separately. It is a design I've drawn for our habits. The old ones are far too hot for this place. Every day is above a hundred degrees and Lord how we swelter. It is not pleasant for us nor I imagine for any poor people who have to come near us. This design would suit us much better and don't worry, we will still look like nuns. The round sleeves would free up our arms, since everything catches and sticks here. Might we also consider a lighter material, Mother? The serge we wear at home, sure it's grand for Dublin but awful in this furnace.

I hope I don't sound like the complaining one, I'm not, really.

Poor beloved Catherine Gogarty gets thinner and weaker but still not a word of complaint from her, just smiles and 'don't-you-worry-about-me's' and prayers thanking Our Lord for his Mercy. I know you hoped the fresh air would be good for her but we see no evidence of improvement. Each day it is in the other direction. Please have all our sisters pray for her, and have them write to her, Mother. Tonight, not next week. The boats are so slow to bring the mail, tell them they need to get on to it straight away, no dilly-dallying.

With dear Catherine fading I try to be of help to Ursula as best I can, but I am not Catherine Gogarty, not by a long stretch, and am probably more annoyance to Mother Ursula than assistance.

Please, please Mother do not fail to let all our beloved sisters know that we pray for you all and nightly recite a Divine Providence for you. Have them do the same Mother, and have them write letters, please. We so badly need letters from home.

Forever your own loving daughter and attached child in Jesus Christ, Sister M. Anne Xavier

7. A FIRESIDE CHAT

The missionaries' camp at Guildford had the air of a school excursion, except that whiskey was permitted. They had unhitched their wagons at Oakover, the property of Sam Moore, a generous Presbyterian who had told Roger Smith he was always welcome to camp there on his way to Toodyay. Mr Moore had a steam mill whose boiler was constantly bursting, so blacksmiths were always welcome. It was a secure dry plot on the banks of the Middle Swan. In the middle was a native mahogany tree fully eighty feet tall with a trunk that took four of them to encircle hand-to-hand.

'*Djaraly*,' said Bob, in anticipation of being asked by Fabrice 'your word for that big tree'.

'It must have been here before the flood,' quipped Sister Anne, meaning the Old Testament one. Anne was a country girl from a large family of Dillons and seemed perfectly at home here. She laughingly showed Caporelli the hole which his pony cart had inflicted on her black stockings.

Sam Moore came down from the house looking worried. His wife Dorothy had a fever and chills. Could the nuns go up and see her? Anne put together a little bag of useless things retrieved from Caporelli's cart, and she and Ursula followed the host up to the house. When they returned, they told the monks that Mr Moore had asked lots of questions about their mission and seemed to know everything about Victoria Plains. The Benedictines should speak to him. Also, he had given them some fresh mutton ready for roasting and a sack of potatoes.

They all ate together, the Humanists politely murmuring along with grace. Dom Serra suspended the Rules of St Benedict so the monks could eat late, in company, and continue to talk after dinner. There was only one member missing from the fireside, the English Benedictine having excused himself, saying he was feeling poorly.

For the nuns, tonight was a departure, for they rarely permitted themselves to be seen to eat. 'Our terrible secret is out,' joked Anne, 'and you thought I stayed this tubby through a special act of God!' Her superior was a bit stiffer in her manners, but both women were clearly enjoying a rare night of freedom from their convent, and especially their bishop.

Roger Smith, for whom controversy was a sport, decided to prod Ursula a little. 'Old John Brady seemed a little upset with you as we left,' he smiled. 'What terrible thing have you girls done to that poor fellow?'

Ursula easily took the bait, perhaps because Gorman had forced a small whiskey in her hand. 'His Lordship obstructs our every plan,' she complained, 'but that is a perfectly normal disposition for a bishop. He's not my first one you know.'

Fabrice could see the word 'Newfoundland' forming on her lips.

'You should move here, to the Swan Valley,' said Caporelli. 'There are lots of children, mostly Protestant, but never mind that, if their parents can pay. Tomorrow, I will take you to some people who might have a suitable building for your new school.'

All eyes turned to Ursula Frayne. None of them had heard about a school in Guildford, and they guessed the bishop knew nothing of it either.

'That information was not to be broadcast,' Ursula reprimanded the viticulturist. She looked thoughtfully at the play of light from the campfire through the amber spirit in her glass. 'We expect nothing but to be left free to teach. Some autonomy and a little money, that's all.'

Anne saw fit to join in. 'His Lordship comes and visits us at the convent every night, thinking we enjoy his company. Lord, we can't wait for him to leave!'

Ursula whistled her deputy to silence. 'His Lordship's heart is in the right place,' she said, smoothing things, 'but his actions can sometimes be otherwise.'

Roger Smith sensed another opportunity to provoke. 'Come with us to Toodyay, sisters. The children of the Avon Valley also need teaching and there will be no bishops there, I assure you. You could dress however you wish.'

Ursula sniffed in the Irish way. 'Things are not yet that desperate, Roger Smith, not by a long way.' In truth, Ursula Frayne had dreamt about starting a lay order. Catherine McAuley would have understood this inclination; she ran things that way herself in Dublin at the start and at times wished aloud she had kept it that way. Mother Cecilia, however, would see it as another act of wilful intransigence from a difficult nun, so for now Ursula would have to do as best she could and continue to pray to Our Lady that one day she might be granted that rarest of things, a good bishop.

Bob disappeared into the darkness for a while and reappeared just as quietly sitting alongside Fabrice. He waved a half-chewed chop bone in the direction of the canopy. 'Better *dadja* up there,' he said, mysteriously. He had taught Fabrice that word; it meant 'meat'.

After tea, Sam Moore rejoined them carrying two bottles and his own cane chair, or rather having the latter carried for him by his children. Caporelli relieved their host of the bottles, inspecting the labels carefully in the light of the fire; a light Tenerifi and a mixed Cape Madeira. There were still some very nice bottles tucked away in colonial cellars, he had learned. The two Moore girls gravitated to Anne to watch her darn her stockings, and the boys adopted the amiable John Gorman.

Dorothy had improved a little, said the host, and had sat up for soup. The nuns offered to go up and sit with her for the night. Sadie awkwardly joined them, taking up a letter she hoped Mrs Moore might post for her.

Fabrice, frustrated by a language which followed none of the usual rules, was thumbing once more through the Moore dictionary that Frank Armstrong had given him. The host asked to look at it.

'My brother wrote this,' said Sam Moore, handing it back.

'Your brother is a linguist?' asked the linguist.

'He would say so. George is the smart one of the Moore family. I'm afraid you have landed with his dullard younger brother.'

It was a black moonless sky with more stars than had ever been seen in Europe. Sam Moore had settled into his cane chair and was enjoying the dark sweet wine and the intelligent company. He had had a terrible time with the steam mill. First the boiler had burst, and been repaired with Roger Smith's help. Then all the wooden spindles broke due to excessive force. Then the driving cords snapped. He was thinking of going back to horse-powered. Horses never let you down.

'These are sort of troubles that wait for us on Victoria Plains, I worry,' said Dom Serra.

'Ah yes, Father Serra, the nuns told me you are headed there. Might I ask what possibly attracted you to that place?'

'We have been advised … many will be the black natives.' Serra struggled in English, especially if there was an audience. 'And pasture land too, naturally.'

Salvado helped his superior. 'We are hopeful that the two things we require await us in Victoria Plains. Firstly, the need. Secondly, the means.'

'The need?'

'We have dedicated ourselves to saving the souls of the original inhabitants of this colony. They live around the Moore River in large numbers, so we have been told.'

'Yes, I suppose they might,' replied the host, treading carefully. 'They may come and go a bit. And their numbers may have dwindled in the last little while, from measles and so on. And the means?'

'Farming,' replied Salvado. 'The most enterprising farmers from the Avon district have moved their sheep to Victoria Plains and greatly prospered. We shall join in their success.'

Sam Moore shuffled in his seat, swirled his glass. 'This advice you have received, the abundance of Victoria Plains, the number of natives, the enterprising farmers, and so on. Ah … John Scully was the source, I presume?'

Salvado sat up at this extraordinary piece of intuition. 'Yes, it all came from him,' he confirmed. 'He sought out our bishop, who quickly became enthusiastic. Captain Scully has been most generous. He supplied these drays, these bullocks and much of the provisions loaded upon them.' Salvado sensed some bad news coming. 'Have we been misled, Mister Moore?'

'No, no, not at all. Just, the optimism with which you ...' The host seemed to be weighing up the risk of speaking any further. 'Perhaps I should go up and check on Mrs Moore.'

It was Dom Serra who spoke now. 'Tell us your mind, Mister Moore, please. We are not little children, merely Spanish.' He smiled to show his good humour, and after a moment's hesitation the host sat back down. Salvado refilled his glass in order to anchor him to the chair.

Sam Moore was thinking how he might best relate a difficult story to these earnest Catholics, who most likely believed in the innate goodness of humans, and other improbabilities. He coughed, stroked some imaginary dust off his trousers and took on a carefully neutral tone.

'I can only tell you what little I know of Victoria Plains and the Moore River. It may well differ from what you have heard elsewhere. Of course, I do not profess to have the knowledge possessed by my brother.'

'Your brother?'

'George Fletcher Moore.' Everybody in the colony knew and admired his older brother, but tonight Sam saw only blank faces. 'Explorer, as well as linguist. He named the river you are headed to. The *Moore* River, you see.'

At that moment an enormous crack came from the big *djaraly* like a limb falling. Those near the tree jumped to their feet and ran a few steps away and looked up. Bob alone knew exactly what the noise was. He had been waiting for it. He raced towards the giant tree, leapt up, grabbed the rope that dangled from it, and when he pulled on it, a cat-like creature fell heavily through the canopy to the ground, where it tried to scamper away. Bob swiftly despatched it with a foot at the back of the neck and a jerk of the rope.

The missionaries gathered round the dead creature, half-repulsed and half-thrilled.

'*Coumarle*,' said Bob, or so it sounded to Fabrice. 'Better than lamb even.' This explained the riddle of the meat in the tree. Fabrice tried to call him 'good hunter' but there was no more recognition in Bob's eyes than if he had praised the boy in Latin.

The Moore boys were delighted by the dead possum. They asked Bob to show them how to skin it, which entertained them for the rest of the night. John Gorman remained with the youngsters for the gory lesson and was just as intrigued as they by the blood and fur and guts.

Roger Smith handed out stubby cigars and the men in the circle all lit up.

'Clever George,' continued the host, 'is also somewhat of a geologist. And a farmer, of course. And a judge, I should have mentioned, and a member of the Legislative Council, and so on. Pity for you he is not here. He would be the first to advise you that I am a poor substitute.'

'But he is not here, Mister Moore,' said Salvado, 'so we would appreciate your knowledge. We feel a little as if we are travelling blindfolded into the unknown.'

'Worse than merely blindfolded. Perhaps, a little deceived.'

Serra stiffened. 'You mean what, Mister Moore, by this word?'

Sam Moore sighed. 'Look, your friend Scully is a good man and a courageous one, I do think, for venturing out into Victoria Plains. But you must have your eyes open, fathers. Firstly, don't imagine the Garden of Eden. This is February, and the district will be as dry as straw. Not a blade of grass. Very tough country in summer. No water.'

Léandre Fonteinne, curled up next to Caporelli feigning sleep, was holding his breath so as not to miss a word of this bad news. It was all exactly as he had feared.

'Secondly, the natives. They are not, as it were, in a virgin state, never having before seen a white man. Their parents were that way, I suppose, but it will never be like that again.'

'There have been unhappy interactions?' suggested Serra.

'Euphemistically put, yes,' said their Presbyterian host. 'The native people naturally enough see the intrusions of any white men without their permission as a type of invasion. The rest you can guess at. It is much the same as on the veldts of South Africa or the prairies of America. Rifles, spears, rape, murder. Reprisals and so on. It's how it goes on any frontier, I imagine, no better, no worse.'

There was a prolonged silence. The host was sure he had now said too much.

'Murder, you say?' ventured Dom Salvado, after a while.

'Our host would be referring to the Johnston Drummond matter, I suppose,' said Roger Smith, stargazing from the darkness beyond the firelight.

'Well, yes,' said Sam Moore, 'he was murdered, that is true. But actually, I was thinking of the one that followed on from it.'

'What is all this murder?' said Dom Serra, 'and why am I the last to be told?'

The host paused, not wanting to inflame delicate matters.

'Scully. Drummond. Butler. Phillips. Two years ago, those were the only names you would find on Victoria Plains. The only other white men you would ever meet were their shepherds, cranky Scots of my denomination.'

The Spanish nodded, and sat stiffly.

'In this colony, only the workers prosper. Labourers earn more money than do their masters. This was certainly true in the first years on Victoria Plains. The squatters had to pay their shepherds well, and they used the money to buy their own flocks. Now the biggest farmers on Victoria Plains are the Macphersons and Mackintoshes. They in turn employ their own shepherds but, being canny, pay them less and so have attracted rough types who are inclined to treat the natives harshly. There are constant disputes with the blacks over sheep, water and, it must be said, women.'

There was silence as the monks absorbed this information.

'Where exactly does Scully intend to drop you by the way?'

'Some place called Mori,' said Salvado. 'Or Mora, perhaps. Murri Murri? Maurin? Something like that.'

'Yes,' said their host, amused, 'our family name appears to have been corrupted in a dozen ways up there. I trust it will have water. But here is the problem: if you are camped near good water in the month of February, there will be trouble. You may be attacked, if not by the natives, then by the shepherds, and believe me, those shepherds might be worse. They are armed and very wild.'

There came a tiny whimper from the novice, who was now concealed under a blanket but still listening silently.

'Who was this Johnston Drummond?' said Serra, still annoyed that an English atheist knew of this story while he did not.

Sam Moore sighed and swirled his madeira thoughtfully. 'Old Jim Drummond, or perhaps it was Sarah, must have been very fond of the letter J, naming their children Jane, James, John, and so on. Johnston was their youngest and was given the job of looking after their outstation on the Moore River. While living alone in the bush, he developed two hobbies. One was quite harmless, unless you were a furry creature. Zoology. He would trap or net as many hopping creatures as he could, dry them out and give them to my brother to send to buyers in London. It was quite a profitable enterprise, I believe, more so than sheep farming. But it was the other habit that brought him undone.

'Women?' guessed Salvado.

'Quite,' confirmed Sam Moore. 'His habits upset the local men, as I expect it would any of us. He was speared by a jealous husband.'

'Speared?' an alarmed Léandre Fonteinne said aloud. 'With a *kidji*?' All his secret fears were tonight being announced as facts.

'Indeed, with a *kidji*. The fellow's name was Kabinger. I met him, actually. Very nice chap, it seemed to me, always smiling. But the squatters were furious that he had killed a white man. A meeting was held in Toodyay, and retribution demanded.'

'There is a police force on Victoria Plains?' enquired Salvado. It had not occurred to him until now that there might be a need.

Sam Moore shuffled and rubbed his face uncomfortably, for this was a difficult story to get right. 'Well, no. Not a force, just a single officer. Constable John Drummond happened to be the dead man's brother. He patrolled the Toodyay district as well as Victoria Plains, and was popular for knowing how to quieten troublesome natives. Oftentimes he would sit down and talk with them, and explain the problems as the white men saw it, but sometimes he used firmer measures.

'So John Drummond went off to see the governor and got a warrant for the arrest of this fellow Kabinger. But when he caught up with his brother's killer, passions must have risen and he rather exceeded the terms of the warrant. No arrest was then possible. The governor was furious when he heard of it, fearing another Pinjarra.'

'So Constable Drummond was punished?' asked Salvado.

'Well, he has disappeared. Living wild with some friendly natives, I would guess, since he knows them and their ways and is pretty happy living in the bush. I expect he will reappear when things have settled down. What happens in remote locations like Victoria Plains is not much noticed in Perth, so awkward events like this can easily be brushed over with time.'

The monks pondered all this in silence until Salvado spoke. 'What will the natives make of us, Mister Moore, we who come to serve them?'

Sam Moore cocked his head as if the real answer was too difficult to explain to a missionary. 'That would depend, Father. It may not be the natives you have to be most wary of. The colonists may be your bigger problem. Perhaps you should stop by St Mary's tomorrow and ask the Reverend Mitchell what happened to his predecessor.'

'He also was speared?' croaked Léandre Fonteinne.

'No, no,' said Mr Moore. 'He was very friendly with the locals. He set up a farm for them, learned their language, and so on. But he liked to give homilies about the evils of retributive justice, so the colonists had him sent home. Giustiniani was his name.'

'Italian,' said Caporelli, who had been reading another of his short novels by the light of grasstree chips thrown on the embers, and only half-listening to the gossip. 'Troublesome people.'

Only now did Sam Moore remember that he was surrounded by Mediterraneans. 'I am so sorry, Father Serra,' he blustered. 'I did not mean to suggest that all foreigners are trouble.'

Serra waved a hand to reassure the host no offence had been taken.

'Tread carefully in your criticisms, that is all I am trying to say,' counselled the Presbyterian.

It was late, well past the usual time for monks to retire, but when Roger Smith had the floor, it was not possible to leave.

'It's all Rome versus Greece, you see,' he was explaining with an authority which only came with wealth and education. 'How should one treat those one has colonised? Rome was brutal, just as Greece was enlightened. But the Romans were smart enough to use both strategies. First they would vanquish a province, and only after they had broken it, could they turn Greek. A docile colony would be afforded every liberty, so long as its leaders agreed to remain passive and subservient. This is the reason that the Classics are taught to young English gentlemen. Not so they can recite Virgil, but to make them more successful colonists.'

'I think that does apply here in the Swan,' said Sam Moore, thoughtfully. 'Our first governor, Stirling, was a bit of a Roman, I would say. His true colours showed at Pinjarra and after that success he sent his Captain Bunbury to York to try to repeat the lesson to the natives there. His successor, Hutt, fancied himself a Greek. Tried to be agreeable to everyone and liked to berate the settlers. He sent the interpreter Frank Armstrong to York to talk to the natives, hoping perhaps to better understand things from their perspective.'

'An enlightened man,' said Roger Smith. 'And did Governor Hutt's approach work?'

'Yes, I suppose it did, for a while. Then poor Sarah Cook was speared, and her little baby, and one cannot help but turn a bit Roman when that sort of thing happens. Hutt had to look the other way while the resident magistrate led a shooting revenge on the native camp.'

Léandre was sitting up now, clutching his knees. He dearly wanted to be back at Solesmes with his beloved Prosper Guéranger.

'We are missionaries,' said Salvado, hoping to reassure himself and his confrères in the light of all this information. 'The *selvaggi* will understand we are not a threat.' Only the linguist noticed Salvado's use of that Italian word: not *nativi*, but *selvaggi*. Even Dom Salvado was frightened by this talk of spearings.

'But you *are* a threat,' countered Sam Moore, 'even with all your good intentions. You intend to farm? Then surely you will need their land and water and labour. You intend to dress their children, I presume, and have them sit down and sing your hymns and study arithmetic?'

Dom Serra braced at this Presbyterian insolence. Even Salvado had to breathe down his sense of indignation.

'We will encourage them to change in ways which will only benefit them,' explained the Galician, as calmly as he could manage. 'But we have no intention to profit from them, nor cause them harm.'

'Yes, well, nobody ever *intends* to,' the host persisted. 'The colonists who were enticed or tricked into coming to this faraway place were among the most genteel and enlightened folk of England. I dare say not one of them arrived here *intending* harm. But they have caused it, no doubt, and so have I, and so might you, Fathers. The question, and forgive my impertinence, is perhaps not how you see yourselves, but how you are viewed by others.'

Nobody spoke for an awkwardly long period, until Sam Moore stood, shook out his wine glass, and apologised.

'Now you see why I tried to decline offering you any advice.

I am not my intelligent brother. I am clumsy with words. George would support your ideals, I feel sure. He too has upset the colonists by advocating for Christianising the native population and compensating them for the loss of their lands. And he could have helped Mister Cleriquot here with his study of the local languages.'

Sam Moore received a warm embrace from Salvado.

'Thank you for your honesty, Mister Moore,' beamed the hairy Galician, an optimist at heart. 'But you will see. One day, we will run a farm as profitable as any on Victoria Plains.'

'I hope so, Fathers, really I do. And take my word on one thing, when the time comes to make flour, stick with a horse-powered mill. Steam will send you to an early grave.'

The Rules having been abandoned, Salvado and Serra spoke late into the night. One by one the others said their goodnights except for Roger Smith who was still in the mood for debate.

The novice remained nearby, eyes closed but listening to every word and sometimes trembling in his sack. Dom Léandre Fonteinne wished he could stay forever in the lovely Swan Valley making wine with his friend Nico Caporelli. He did not want to be a priest. He did not want to be a missionary. And he certainly did not want to go to the terrible Victoria Plains, where the grass was dead, the Scots hostile and where the police officer had made all the natives angry.

And he so greatly feared *kidjis*.

From: Sadie Markham, Guildford near Perth
To: Mrs Pilkington, Clayton Homestead, Cape Town

26th February 1846

Dear Missus P

First off please be kind about my writing. I cannot ask Mr Roger Smith to check it as I wish to write some things about him.

He is a queer man, like a minister of the church tho he says he cannot abide them. Much of what he says is of no understanding to me, but he has been kind and done exactly what he said he would when I was in that trouble so I cannot complain about him and would not ever. He has not tried anything and seems not interested in starting so that is something. I am like his maid but he says I am his equal, I am not quite sure which I am ment to be.

Perth is like Cape Town but with everything taken out of it. Now we move to a leser town called Toodyay. There is nothing there either. Even the water has been taken out of the river.

I would like to here by thank you for helping me when other mistreses would of chopped me off.

With every best wishes to you missus and also please kiss dear Lucy for me. This is my last letter to Africa now that I will stay here in this colony, which is much much further from Sydney Town than you said and cannot be got to from anywhere. So I am stuck here forever I suppose. Never mind it is doubtless all for the good.

Yours faithfully,
Sadie

8. TO TOODYAY

Early next morning, the nuns came back down from the Moore house looking ragged. They had been up all night attending to Dorothy. Three of the four Benedictines were already about. The English one, Dom Tootle or Tottle had taken his bedding up to the house where, according to Ursula, he had usurped Dorothy as the invalid of the residence.

'Mind you,' said Anne, 'your man does not look to be in any danger of dying. He said yes to a cooked breakfast and now has poor Mrs Moore bustling around as his servant.'

Salvado and Serra found their ailing English confrère taking breakfast on the front porch. He had his own pot of tea and a tiny jug for cream but pronounced himself 'stricken with the ague' and too ill to proceed. He would stay with Mrs Moore to convalesce and return to Perth when feeling strong enough to attempt the journey.

'So now we are four,' said Salvado as they walked back to camp.

'A very small loss,' said Serra.

Dorothy and Sam Moore came down to see the missionaries off, Dorothy bringing the nuns a basket of food and the latest copy of the *Inquirer*, which she thought might be of interest, since the dangers of Catholic schools were discussed in its pages. The Colonial Chaplain, Reverend King, considered it 'his sacred duty to forewarn his Protestant brethren against the evil which now threatens the souls of their children'.

'Dear me,' said Sister Anne.

'Oh, I wouldn't take it too seriously,' Dorothy explained. 'The people of this colony are not very sectarian.' The Protestants would readily send their children to a Mercy school without regard to such nonsense. 'The mothers are more concerned about the empty brains of their children, to be honest, not their souls.'

'What about the Wesleyans?' asked Ursula.

'The Wesleyans won't like you no matter what you do,' smiled Dorothy.

The nuns departed with Nico Caporelli, expected for lunch at the home of a Catholic family in the Upper Swan. It was an hour's travel if the track was dry and Caporelli assured them that, being February, everywhere was bone dry.

The other three carts took off east. Their destination for that night was Mahogany Creek atop the Darling Range, so today would be a long slow plod up Green Mount Hill. Dom Salvado's cart led the way, with Dom Serra seated alongside him. Gorman had the reins of the second, with Bob swapping wagons to sit with his new Irish friend, whom he had taught that morning to build a fish trap. Léandre Fonteinne, still cloaked but wearing his broad hat, sat glumly behind them among the supplies. He did not like the Irish generally and resented Gorman for his lightness of spirit. Roger Smith drove the Humanist's cart, with Sadie sitting alongside him and Fabrice Cleriquot behind, wearing his mother's *salacco* and reading Montesquieu.

They came to the octagonal church Sam Moore had mentioned. *St Mary's Church of England* said the little sign. To Roger Smith's annoyance, the Spaniards insisted it would be impolite not to call in. After a long wait the vicarage door was answered by a pale and nervous man, all whiskers and bluster, a music-hall caricature of an English parson. Mrs Mitchell was elsewhere, he apologised, and there were no biscuits.

Over lukewarm tea, Roger Smith could not resist the opportunity to tease. 'What became of your predecessor?' he asked abruptly. He had adopted an aristocratic tone, Professor Cleriquot noted, perhaps to remind the vicar of his inferior social rank. 'Italian fellow, wasn't he?'

'Left before I arrived,' said Reverend Mitchell, whiskers twitching. 'Upset the settlers, I believe.'

'Oh dear. Did he make the mistake of reminding them of the sixth commandment?' Sadie stiffened. She hated Roger Smith's habit of always arguing. They were the guests of a proper English vicar.

'The sixth?' began the reverend.

'Thou shalt not kill.'

'Thank you, I would not have known,' said the Reverend Mitchell, eyes set firmly upon the impertinent visitor. 'You are a religious man, then, Roger Smith?'

'Decidedly not.'

The vicar smiled insincerely. 'Oh dear.'

'Sunday school, as a child, but then I grew up.'

'You must think the three of us great fools, then.' The host waved his saucer at the monks, so as to include them in the offence.

'Not at all.'

'Kind.' Reverend Mitchell took an unhurried sip of tea, quite happy to let the bitterness sit in the air a little longer. 'Might I ask, Roger

Smith, in what capacity you are travelling with these good monks?'
He smiled at the Spaniards to ensure they noticed the flattery.

'In no capacity.'

'You are not a missionary, then?'

'Perhaps I am, of sorts.'

'Fascinating.' The vicar's expression was of pure empathy, as if he
were ministering to the unwell. 'Do educate me about your mission,
if that is the correct terminology.'

Roger Smith began to see that behind the whiskers was a Socrates,
and faltered. 'I am ... I will set up a commune in Toodyay,' he
stumbled. 'I will run a foundry, and other businesses, perhaps. Not
all the details are quite finalised. We will educate and employ any
who will come, regardless of colour or creed.'

'Ah,' smiled the vicar, detecting weakness, 'how democratic. And
God will be excluded, I imagine.'

'There is no need to exclude him.'

'Of course,' said the Reverend Mitchell, indulging a foolish child,
'because for you alone He does not exist, I suppose.' The Spanish
monks remained silent. This was not at all what they had expected
from visiting an English vicar for a cup of tea.

'You come from money, I can easily tell,' observed the Reverend
Mitchell, and Roger Smith did not deny it. 'Which will come first,
I wonder? Will you *lose* all your father's money on this folly? Or
will the locals run you from town?' This was delivered with another
display of English teeth, which in other circumstances might have
passed for a friendly smile.

Roger Smith was not the blanching sort, but he did so now. Both
of those dark possibilities had occurred to him but he had pushed
the thought of them away.

Morning tea with the vicar ended abruptly. As the visitors were ushered to their transport, Reverend Mitchell turned to Sadie, all charm.

'I regret I did not have the opportunity to speak with the lovely Miss ...?'

'Sadie Markham, Reverend. I am Church of England.'

Roger Smith froze mid step-up.

'How lovely, Miss Markham,' oozed the vicar. 'I do hope I will see more of you in Toodyay. We have no church there as yet, but we conduct a service from time to time in the home of one of the settlers, just as the early Christians did. We would be delighted to see you there.'

'How lovely that must be for the families,' said Sadie, putting on her best voice, 'especially the mothers.'

'Indeed it is,' said the chaplain, glancing up at Roger Smith to ensure his victory had been noticed. 'Why, in York last winter, I had the sad occasion to console a mother who had lost her little boy, drowned in the Avon.'

Sadie gasped and without thinking reached out and touched the vicar's shoulder in gratitude.

'Vernon was his name,' Reverend Mitchell continued, with great sensitivity. 'The sweetest little fellow you could imagine. I was pleased to be able to offer consolation to her in her grief.' He looked squarely at Roger Smith, as if to ask what solace an atheist could possibly have offered in the same circumstances.

He turned now to the Spaniards, not unkindly. 'Where exactly are you fellows off to, by the way?'

'Victoria Plains,' said Salvado.

'My goodness,' said the reverend, looking delighted but not meaning it, 'how adventurous! Presbyterian shepherds and some wild blacks, that will be your parish.'

'Yes,' said Dom Serra glumly, 'it seems so.' He had slept poorly last night, dreaming of exactly this scene.

'Do you proselytise the natives, reverend?' asked Dom Salvado, cautiously.

'Good heavens, no!' said Reverend Mitchell. 'I am here to serve Christians of the Established Church who live in my parish. I have no inclination to procure the souls of those who already have their own form of worship, and I certainly do not intend to roam the bush in order to do so. It is very *hot* in the bush, Father Salvado, and also *dry*, and *dangerous*. Snakes and so on. I have seven children to think of. Those who already have their own ways I will leave entirely in peace. Should a new parishioner wish to attend Communion, and are dressed appropriately for it, it is conducted here, at St Mary's, every Sunday at nine o'clock, in English.'

It was nearing midday by the time they started the slow climb up the western face of the Darling Range. It was hot and the mood of the caravan had changed for the worse. The Humanists' wagon at the rear was especially glum, its leader brooding after his encounter with the vicar. In the carriage ahead Serra and Salvado conversed in low tones. Only Gorman and young Bob in the leading cart seemed oblivious to the tension. They had wisely avoided morning tea and instead spent a productive hour together on the banks of the river collecting a basket of clicking black *djilki* to throw into the dinner pot.

Fabrice was deep in the pages of *Zadig*, but occasionally put it down to take in the surrounds. It was not a proper European forest, but still there was a kind of harsh beauty to it. It chirruped with unseen insects. He recognised the giant *djaraly*, which the English settlers all wrongly called mahogany. Bob helped him with the other tree names when he felt like it; the smooth-barked *warndoo*, the *mari* bleeding red gum like a knife wound, the candelabra-like *biyara*.

'That bright orange one,' shouted the linguist to leading carriage, 'what do you call that?'

'Christmas tree,' said Bob, and Gorman laughed with him.

'*Moodjar*, we Irish call it,' added Gorman, to the linguist's annoyance.

Halfway up the long climb, the Humanists' rear wheel hit a rock, the left wheel loosened and they had to pull over for repairs. An angry Roger Smith could contain himself no longer. He shouted ahead to the Catholics to carry on and pulled the wagon over into to the shade.

There had been, declared the first among equals, a betrayal.

'A betrayal?' said poor Sadie, frightened by his voice.

'A betrayal!' he thundered. 'We have no "Church of Englands" among us. No Church of Anythings.' Sadie froze guiltily, for these sounded like her words, but Fabrice kept his nose in Voltaire. He had grown up with a father prone to such outbursts. The first thing was to stay perfectly calm.

'In future,' continued Roger Smith, 'in such situations as we encountered this morning, it would be preferable if one person were to speak on behalf of the collective.'

Fabrice closed the book. 'You would answer as to *my* religious views?' he asked, calmly.

'Not necessarily on that particular question,' said Roger Smith, seeing the trap.

'But you *would* answer for mine?' came a surprising voice, Sadie's.

'Don't you start,' snapped Roger Smith. 'Remember the state you were in when I rescued you.'

'I do,' she said quietly, 'and I am very grateful, of course, but …' Sadie started to cry. 'But I *am* Church of England, Roger Smith,' she squeezed out. 'I like the songs. I think they are so lovely.'

'Oh, now,' said Roger Smith, an Englishman flustered by this unexpected show of emotion. 'There, there. Do not upset yourself. Stop your sobbing, please.' Her crying did help resolve the matter, for the time being at least, for it put Roger Smith again in charge of things. He advised the commune that the events of that morning were to be entirely forgotten.

'That's quite enough now, Sadie,' he urged, as they continued up the hill. 'At least *try* to be cheerful.'

The plod up Green Mount continued all afternoon. Happily, the sea breeze had arrived, so it would get no hotter. The bullocks proved reliable on the dry uneven track. No passerby could have guessed that these were missionaries. Salvado and Serra were dressed as farmers, only the wooden crucifixes hanging around their necks giving them away.

When they rejoined the caravan, Fabrice abandoned the Humanists to sit with the novice, coaxing his heavy black cloak off him. The little fellow was very pleased for the company. He was scared, he croaked, and gripped his friend's knee like a lover fearing abandonment.

'I am not so sure about the Spanish,' said Léandre Fonteinne.

'I am not so sure about the Humanists,' said Fabrice.

Near the top of the Darling Range the track steepened and they had to squeeze through a sort of ravine, causing the three carts to bunch up with sheer walls of red quartz either side and an ancient *djaraly* towering above, looking ready to crush them if it chose to. For some reason the insects had all fallen silent. In the late afternoon light it seemed an enchanted place and they all fell under the spell of it, until John Gorman stood up in the driver's seat of the leading dray, spread his wings and shouted.

'Jaysus, how I love this country!'

Bob laughed for a full minute at this. Occasionally thereafter, if it fell quiet, the boy would stand up, throw up his arms and mimic the Irishman. The lead oxen took these outbursts as instructions to move faster, so it was still good light when they made Mahogany Creek, where they set up camp alongside some sandalwood cutters.

They were not yet halfway to Toodyay, the sawyers told them, but they had done the difficult part. Tomorrow was long but mostly downhill into the Avon Valley, another twelve or fourteen hours.

A family of kangaroos, a rare sight nowadays in the capital, came close to their camp. John Gorman and Bob pretended to stalk them, using grasstree spears. Salvado, however, saw a genuine chance of a kill. He produced a handsome flintlock pistol, warned the two hunters to squat, and fired a shot at the buck, which looked calmly over its shoulder as if disappointed by the monk's behaviour, and hopped off.

'That thing's not much good for hunting, Rosendo,' observed the Irishman.

'It's for shooting blackfellas,' joked Bob. He could have easily hit that *yongka* with a well-aimed *boya*.

The missionaries lit a fire for dinner and the sawyers appeared with a can of water and extinguished it. It had not rained for some weeks, they warned, and the leaf litter beneath their feet was bone dry; a single cinder and 'they would all be goners'. You could not outrun a fire in this hill country. The sawyers had themselves failed to heed this advice last year, they confessed. Six months of stacked sandalwood was lost in the inferno.

'A thousand pounds in exports and a thousand hours of work all went up in smoke,' said one old hand, shaking his head.

'But it did smell lovely,' grinned the optimist among them.

With no fire, no moon and tall trees, it fell dark early and then there was nothing to do but sleep. When the last goodnights had been exchanged and silence had fallen, there came a belated 'God Bless you my Child', which sounded a lot like Bishop Brady and caused a ripple of laughter.

They awoke early to the smell of smoke, but could not detect its source. The sawyers had already decamped. They could see smoke in the sky above the treetops to the east and the rising sun burnt red through the haze. Léandre tied a wettened kerchief over his face so that he now looked like a sickly highwayman. It promised to be a very hot and windy day and they worried about getting trapped in a forest fire, but as the morning passed and they made their way east, the smoke gradually thinned and they never saw the source.

The Toodyay track was good on the flat stretches but rough in the low-lying parts where ruts had been eroded by winter rains then baked hard in summer. Every so often a cartwheel became stuck in a gully. Gorman managed to topple the leading cart on Jimperding Hill, throwing the novice to the ground and causing tears and delay.

They made Toodyay with an hour's light remaining. There was not much to see, just a few buildings scattered along a dry riverbed. The Avon was not like a perennial European river, Fabrice was depressed to see. It was dark clay baked hard as terracotta, and the last remaining waterholes were abuzz with midges, but at least there were places where the bullocks could be watered.

The Humanist's cart had taken the lead now. At a bend in the river Roger Smith loudly called out 'woah', climbed down, and proudly showed the missionaries a little wooden sign.

THE GARDEN

Stranger, tarry here, where our highest good is Pleasure.

They had arrived at the commune. It was a clearing in the bush by a dry riverbed, that was all. Fabrice's heart again failed to soar. Roger Smith used the occasion to flatter Sadie, who had painted the sign. He pointed out the pretty native flowers in the corners, a sprig of bright yellow wattle here and red bottlebrush there. The commune was lucky to have her as its foundress, he proclaimed, and he hoped she could forgive his occasional ways.

A surly white boy was waiting for them. He looked only sixteen or seventeen, and was introduced as 'Eric Hough, our Parkhurst boy'. Eric barely acknowledged the group, though he must have been expecting them, for he had a good fire going and dinner was steaming in the iron pot.

'Lamb stew,' he explained, without looking up. 'You said Monday, Roger Smith. Lucky I guessed.' And then he looked up at the leader of the commune and added, 'And I'm not Parkhurst no more, Roger Smith. You paid the governor, remember.'

'What is this Parkhurst?' asked Fabrice, and Eric stormed off, leaving Roger Smith to explain. A few better-behaved boys from this child prison on the Isle of Wight had been sent to the Swan River on a trial basis. It was hoped the change of climate would benefit the boys' morality, and that they would reform and stay. In the meantime, the colony would get cheap labour.

'Convicts?' said Fabrice, and Roger Smith drew breath through his teeth. This was a most sensitive matter in a free colony. The boys were correctly referred to as juvenile emigrants or apprentices.

'Or thieves,' interrupted Sadie, unable to contain herself. She had known lots of boys like Eric Hough and had never seen one change for the better. 'Let's see what's gone missing while we've been away,' she added.

But it did appear Roger Smith's faith in the boy had been vindicated. The Parkhurst boy had not run off. The camp had been neatly set up, with a new bushwood shelter built, fire pit dug out, wood stacked, water ported, and a hot dinner prepared and ready to ladle. Eric had even made salted damper to soak up the excellent gravy.

Bob avoided Eric Hough. There was a small incident between them after dinner. Eric explained the arrangements for the guests' ablutions, setting out warm water, bowls and soap. But it seemed there was not enough washing water for Bob.

'Eh you, put back that bowl, it's for the dishes,' said Eric Hough, giving Bob a sly shove, but not so sly that it went unnoticed by John Gorman, who had grown very fond of Bob.

'I don't think so, fella,' growled Gorman, handing Bob back the bowl, the kettle and a bar of soap. He ruffled the hair of the Parkhurst boy with mock affection and gave him a friendly pat on the back of his head, firm enough that it could be heard. For a moment, the Irishman thought the lad might throw a punch, so he placed a firm hand on the boy's shoulder his until he felt it relax in submission.

'Good lad,' he smiled. Then softly, in the boy's ear: 'Try that bullshit again, son, I dare you. See what happens.'

To Léandre's delight, the Benedictines would stay at the commune for three nights. Their oxen needed resting, feeding and watering and there were farming supplies to be bought and repairs to be made before they took off for Bolgart, 'the capital of Victoria Plains' as Salvado had taken to describing it.

'The capital?' smirked the depot keeper as he helped Salvado load a wheel of fencing wire onto the tray. 'Not sure it has a capital, mate. There was a bit of a rush to Victoria Plains a couple of years ago when word went around of wonderful pastureland and so on, but it's been pretty tough going up there in summer and a few have come back with their tails between their legs.'

'The land is no good?' pressed Salvado.

'Oh, I don't want to put you off, mate.' Pessimism was bad for commerce. 'Still plenty of sheep up there, I think. Just, don't expect it to be like back in Italy, if that's what you were imagining.'

Later, the shopkeeper put the word around town that these foreign priests had mad ideas and no chance of success. But they did have a little money in their pockets, and on that basis the town of Toodyay voted strongly in favour of Catholic evangelism. The missionaries were invited to the Royal Oak for a send-off. Nobody could recall ever having seen a monk in this part of the country before, much less one who could play a piano as Salvado could. Protestants, Presbyterians, even a couple of Wesleyans raised a glass to the success of the 'Italian' missionary farmers, while the French Humanist quietly paid the tab.

'You are a great source of encouragement to me, Roger Smith,' said Salvado. 'This garden of yours exists, at least. That is something. It tells me that it is possible for us to create something in the bush from nothing.'

Roger Smith took that as an invitation to educate the monks about his further plans. The Garden, he advised, would be run on Owenite principles. He had closely studied Robert Owen's ideal village of New Harmony in America, especially those things that went wrong, and felt sure he could improve upon it. The education system, when the children came, would be liberal in nature and based on Pestalozzi's theories. It was especially important, he explained, that everyone who came should contribute equally, in whatever way they could.

It happened that a couple of old men had wandered in to The Garden and were standing quietly outside the ring of firelight.

'They're after a bit of stew I suppose,' said Roger Smith to Salvado, watching them curiously.

But when Eric Hough spotted them, it was a different response. It was his job to keep these intruders out. He grabbed the poker from the fire and made at them with the hot end. There was shouting and the old fellows retreated into the darkness. Once again it was Gorman who intervened, grabbing the poker and kicking the boy's backside accurately enough that his bare feet lifted momentarily off the ground.

The leader of the commune seemed to have no policy for the treatment of such visitors. 'Perhaps you should allow them a little stew, Eric,' he suggested eventually.

'No,' replied Eric, knowing nothing of deference. 'The town folk will all be up here in a huff if you start feedin' 'em,' he warned. 'They ought to bugger off into the bush.'

It was left to Gorman to fill a couple of bowls and take them over to the visitors, patting their shoulders as if they were just old friends who needed feeding. Behind them in the shadows he discovered an older woman in a fur *booka*, then a couple of kids peering shyly from behind the women's legs until coaxed out. John Gorman emptied the pot for them.

'So, what is your policy to be?' asked Dom Serra of Roger Smith, later, over brandy. 'Will you allow the natives to stay in this garden of yours?'

The matter would need some thinking through, explained Roger Smith. 'And at your mission, how is it to be?' he countered. 'Will they come to you, or will you chase them through the bush?'

'We will follow them and camp where they camp,' said Salvado.

'We shall build a monastery,' said Serra. He was the superior and had held his tongue for long enough. 'The natives can come to us for instruction.'

Roger Smith was pleased to discover he had exposed a division. 'Which is it then, Fathers?'

'Both,' explained Salvado, ever the conciliator. 'We will of course permit them their roaming, should they wish, but provide a perm- anent place to come to, should they wish to come.'

'Perfectly clear,' said the Englishman, claiming the last word on the matter. 'You are nomads who will build another Santiago de Compostela in the bush.'

Late at night, Fabrice heard a whisper. It was the novice. His sadness could be seen in his face in the starlight and Fabrice was greatly moved by it.

'Wake up, Fabrice! I am so frightened.' Léandre still had a scabby nose from his fall from the cart, an accident caused by a lack of attention by the frivolous Irishman.

Fabrice placed his hand on the shoulder of the little fellow from Solesmes and could feel the shudders rippling across him, and then a convulsion as he started to sob. He took a blanket and steered Léandre away from the camp so they could talk. On the riverbank the only sound was the croaking of frogs and the only light was from the cloudless night sky. Fabrice kissed Léandre Fonteinne's face and waited for the whimpers to cease and his voice to return.

'I will not go to the bush tomorrow.'

'You must.'

'Why? I will never be a priest. Even Prosper Guéranger told me so, and he loves me so very much.'

'You have to go, dear Léandre.'

'Let the others leave,' he huffed. 'They do not want me. That Irishman *certainly* does not want me. I depress him, he says. I will remain in Toodyay with you and with Roger Smith, who has such noble plans.'

'Roger Smith is an Atheist, Léandre.'

'That is of no matter, so long as we do good in the world.'

'You are a monk.'

'I am *not* a monk. I am nothing.'

The two Frenchmen lay on their backs on the riverbank in silence. The night sky over the Avon Valley was hypnagogic. Gradually the novice's breathing slowed and the music returned to his voice.

'Why should we ever move from Toodyay, *Monsieur le Professeur*?' Léandre said, at last. Fabrice did not bother to answer but could hear the novice thinking. 'I could be with you. We could speak French together. Who will I ever speak to, out in the bush? The natives with their sharp *kidjis*?'

'You fret too much about that.'

'Are you deaf? Did you not hear? They speared a white man at Moore River and he had to be shot in return.'

'Salvado will have them put their *kidjis* away, I am sure.'

'I will die there, I think.'

There was a long, meditative silence. The novice sobbed and demanded to be kissed again. Fabrice consoled him as best he could.

It was Ash Wednesday when the Spanish left Toodyay. The wagons were packed by dawn and as the sun rose those who wished to be blessed were invited to kneel in a line. Dom Serra had prepared his mark using what ingredients he had to hand. The oil of chrism was from a can of Swan Valley olive oil supplied by Nico Caporelli. The ash was from the previous night's fire, crushed and roughly blessed.

It happened that this ceremony had been Fabrice's favourite as a child. He liked the mark, and the simple blessing. Roger Smith was not around yet, so Fabrice lined up with the others.

The little novice was blessed first.

Remember man, thou art but dust, and into dust thou shalt return.

'Amen,' replied Dom Léandre Fonteinne, thinking only of *kidjis*.

The Irish catechist was next.

Remember man, thou art but dust, and into dust thou shalt return.

'Amen,' said John Gorman, thinking of the famine in the old country.

Then Dom Salvado received the blessing from his superior, his thoughts profound for the work and trials ahead.

And last in the line, Fabrice Cleriquot raised his forehead to receive the blessing, just as he had as a child.

Remember man, thou art but dust, and into dust thou shalt return.

'Amen,' said Fabrice; such a beautiful word to utter, thought the linguist, even if absurd.

From: John Bede Polding, Bishop of Sydney
To: The Evangelisation Congregation, Rome

26th April 1846

Very Reverend Monsignore

At your request I have enclosed a corrected map of the ecclesiastical divisions of Australia.

The Apostolic Vicariates as suggested by the Bishop of Perth placed two-thirds of the continent under his precarious control. That the central third might be controlled from the west is an idea nobody who has visited here would ever seriously contemplate, even if the bishopric of Perth were solvent and administered competently.

That the Vicariate of Port Victoria in the distant north might come under the auspices of Perth is an idea close to madness. The sea journey alone is six thousand miles from Fremantle yet the Bishop of Perth has sent men there. Recently I was compelled to provide assistance to my fellow Benedictine, Don Angelo Confalonieri, who arrived in Sydney unannounced, having sailed from Fremantle with two Irish catechists. He was already sick, penniless and demoralised, with the most difficult part of the journey yet to come. He handed me a begging letter from the impecunious Bishop of Perth. From sympathy I had my Vicar-General give Don Angelo one hundred pounds, moneys this diocese could spend more wisely.

That South Australia might be administered from King George Sound is equally implausible and raises an additional problem.

There already exists a Bishop of Adelaide. In St Mary's Cathedral in Sydney on the 8th September 1844, with Papal imprimatur, I consecrated Francis Murphy to that rôle. John Brady was at that time a priest in my diocese and surely could not have so quickly forgotten. I would worry for his state of mind if he says he has.

You will see on the corrected map enclosed that I advise the suppression of the Vicariates of King George Sound and Port Victoria. The latter is a failure for the English, who talk of moving the garrison to the Gulf of Carpentaria, territory controlled by the Bishop of Sydney. The promising new settlement in the southern part of New South Wales called 'Australia Felix' should fall under the auspices of the Bishop of Sydney via a Vicar-General appointed by that bishop and subservient to him.

I have written to Dom José Serra, who might be called upon to lead the Diocese of Western Australia should it further decline into debt and chaos under its current prelate. Given John Brady's overstretched assessment of his own capacities, the dire financial straits of the Colony of Swan River, and the very few Catholics from whom he might raise funds for his inflated projects, this unhappy outcome appears to be inevitable.

I have the Honour to remain
Your Obedient Humble Servant
John, Bishop of Sydney

9. THE PIANO CONCERT

Rosendo Salvado perched over his instrument. The Perth Court House was packed and all was imminent. The room remained hushed, with just the occasional rustle of crinoline or creaking of boots on boards.

Salvado had been performing for thirty-five years. He knew how to draw gasps of delight from parents, classmates, aunties, bishops, confrères and parishioners. But all those previous performances seemed now to be mere preparation for this one, so much rode upon its success.

He made them wait a little longer. It was his favourite moment, the anticipation. He pointed his long unbrushed beard at the keys and appeared to study them with such intensity that some in the audience began to question the monk's ability to play. He was theatrically unkempt, draped in an enormous black cassock decorated with whatever it had picked up in the Western Australian bush. A wooden crucifix was strung loosely around his neck, and he was almost shoeless. Those near the front could detect straw in his beard. He was playing a role: a bedraggled hirsute holy tramp; a dishevelled ascetic dancing a jig and shaking a tin for Our Lord.

There came a mumbled comment from the back row, the start of a giggle, but then two great hairy arms burst dramatically from black sleeves and reached for the ceiling as if violence was planned, and then stillness again, his spade-like hands hovering once more above the keyboard.

His eyes were closed. Was he praying?

Then those heavy-looking paws crashed onto the keyboard and produced another surprise. The softest, gentlest sound one could imagine – an exquisite Spanish lullaby, played with such sensitivity that every breast in the room surged. Each heart wished the sound to go on forever, but longed for the last note to arrive so its owner could shout *bravo* and stomp the mahogany floorboards and thank this eccentric monk for bringing beauty to this damned colony which so often felt like an unwalled prison.

The concert would have been a great success even had Salvado then stood and bowed. The crowd was won. But he played for three hours and not for a minute of it did the admiration of the colonists dim.

He played no religious music. He knew what they wanted, popular tunes. There was a cheer and applause as the quickest in the audience recognised each one. Music took them back home. He played Chopin's 'Étude on the Bombardment of Warsaw', then foreshortened versions of classical numbers with amusing deviations, and, to finish, two melodies he had penned himself.

The finale was called 'Blackfellow Dance', at the end of which he raised his hand to prevent applause, closed the lid of the piano, faced the audience with eyes closed and continued to play on bush sticks while imitating the calls of the parrots with which Victoria Plains teemed. When the last parrot flew away, he was done.

Boots stomped. There were shouts of *encore*, but in truth everyone was exhausted. The popular new governor and his wife came and stood behind the performer. There was a whisper in the player's ear, a nod of black locks from the pianist, a gubernatorial wave for all to stand, and they all sang *God Save The Queen*.

Terry Farrelly, no royalist himself, took this opportunity to pass around the hat. It was a brave man who did not move his hand into his breast pocket when confronted by The Terror's toothless visage. His forceful pleading verged on extortion. 'Money in here, *sor*, thank you very much.' Fifteen pounds had been raised for the Central Mission in ticket sales. In just ten minutes twice that again was extracted from the thin wallets of the Protestant audience.

'Just keep the blacks out there in the bush and we will happily chip in,' said one, as he threw in a pound. 'It does become unsightly when they hang around town.'

Fabrice Cleriquot had enjoyed the concert from the very back, standing. He had arrived back in the capital from Toodyay the previous day to find every lamppost on the terrace plastered with bill notes advertising the great event to be held on the evening of the twenty-first of May. In this dull town, a piano recital by a Spanish monk was undoubtedly the social event of the year and tickets were impossible to obtain, unless you had money. Fabrice, sent to town by Roger Smith to buy supplies for the commune, was suffering an embarrassment of coins.

When the last congratulation had been made and the courtroom cleared, Terry Farrelly locked the doors and produced a bottle of whiskey. Salvado gulped his first glass, theatrically rested his beard on the piano keys and looked up at Fabrice, exhausted.

'Do not dare congratulate me, Monsieur Cleriquot. I could not take another.'

'I noticed you tripped up once on Chopin.'

More whiskey, and a great sense of relief on the part of Salvado that the thing was done.

'Twenty-seven pounds, four shillings,' declared Farrelly, having counted the money he had collected in the monk's broad-brimmed black felt hat. 'That's on top of the money from the door. Good work Rosendo. I will leave it with His Lordship.'

'You can leave it there on the piano,' said Salvado, a gentle hand on the hat's brim. Two hands remained on the hat for some seconds until the Irishman removed his. Fabrice once more recalled the abbot of Solesmes explaining the Benedictines' strong preference for autonomy.

'I couldn't see His Eminence in the audience tonight,' observed Fabrice. The bishop surely would have worn his amaranth biretta on such a public occasion, and there were none of those in the hall.

'His Lordship is out of town,' said Salvado, 'visiting some place called Austral-Ind, chasing money.'

'Austral-Ind? An excellent place to *lose* money,' said Fabrice. It was well known in the colony as an ill-starred horse-breeding project that had sent all its investors broke. 'Yours was a much better idea, to play piano for the Protestants.'

'I blush at the generosity of these Protestants,' said Salvado, sincerely. 'Governor Clarke gave me his court house at no charge. Reverend Wittenoom sent his verger across the road with all the chandeliers from the Anglican church. The posters were printed at no charge by a Protestant. Mister Lionel Samson, a Jewish merchant, personally sent out invitations to all the leading families and distributed the tickets. Families from the higher end of Perth society even offered me their pianos, but I decided to use this little square one I bought in London for the Sisters of Mercy. The piano at least had to be a Catholic, don't you think?'

The mission was saved, or so proclaimed The Terror as he left, though still plainly unhappy about leaving the cash behind. Fabrice could not feel the drama of it. Money bored him. He wanted to be rid of it. Earlier that day he even gave a bag of coins to the bank. It had not been his intention on entering; he presented a signed note from the manager of the Bank of London, intending to cash it, but the Western Australian Bank had run out of money so Fabrice supplied them cash in exchange for another promissory note which took the clerk a whole afternoon to prepare. It was a most attractive note, with a crest of a black swan in flight, and carried the elegant signature of the bank's chairman, Mr Samuel Moore.

The hat was still on the top of the piano and Fabrice reached inside his jacket thinking to grab the larger purse within and throw it in with the takings. But his hand remained there, fingers on the drawstrings.

'How goes my little friend, Léandre Fonteinne?' he asked. 'Has he emerged yet from under the blankets?'

'Ah!' sighed the monk, looking heavenwards. 'Our dear Dom Léandre. Our hunter and tracker! Our little explorer! We spent all of Easter Sunday trying to find him. We have left him at the mission with Gorman.'

'Was that wise?' said Fabrice. The novice did not like the Irish any more than he liked *kidjis*.

'It was *necessary*,' sighed the bearded giant. 'Until tonight, we were quite out of supplies and the funds to buy more. To be honest, we were almost out of the will to continue our mission. Dom Serra, I fear, has already lost faith in it. He has a new project in mind, a monastery near here that he wants to call New Subiaco.'

Fabrice's right hand was still inside his jacket, Napoleon-like. He removed it. 'In what terrible situation have you left poor Léandre?'

The monk ran a hand through his beard and stretched himself out, exhausted from thinking about such problems. 'A most *difficult* situation, Fabrice. Our supplies ran out and the natives, the women especially, can become quite unhappy if they think food is being denied them. It was very dry on Victoria Plains when we left. The rains are late. But yesterday it rained for the first time in many weeks, in Perth at least. I pray to God that some of it fell on our mission to relieve our two brothers of their thirst.'

'Are they protected?' asked Fabrice, surprised by the intensity of his feeling for the novice's safety.

The Galician looked downwards, ashamed. 'Just a bush timber hut, I am afraid. It is all rather makeshift. We had to move and rebuild, leaving behind a good source of water. The shepherds said we were trespassing on their masters' leaseholds. Mister Moore was right, I'm afraid, some of those shepherds are bad fellows. They molest the local women and enjoy upsetting the men, and us.'

'So, you have left my friend perfectly defenceless in the bush?' blurted Fabrice, the anger rising within him. 'With no food, no water and no defence.'

'I left him my pistol,' said Salvado, quietly.

'Your pistol? Are monks permitted to shoot their parishioners when attacked?'

Salvado sat forward now. 'To hunt for food,' he said firmly, but then added, more quietly, 'a warning shot, perhaps.'

'Can he shoot straight?'

'No,' laughed the Galician, stretching his tired arms and yawning. 'He is a terrible shot, of course. He would shoot his own foot off.'

So the two agreed to leave such difficult topics behind, and turned instead to lighter matters, reminiscences of life in Europe. Fabrice used his discretion. Piano concerts notwithstanding, the Spanish mission at Victoria Plains seemed to him doomed and any money spent on it would be squandered.

Once again, Fabrice stayed with the Langoulants. Mary Ann Langoulant was now a Catholic.

'How does it feel?' Fabrice asked her. His own attachment to Humanism had wavered during his three months in Toodyay with Roger Smith, whose certainty about everything had worn thin.

'Exactly the same of course,' smiled Mary Ann, 'but to baptise me brought such a smile to the face of my dear friend, Sister Anne.'

Nowhere in Perth did Fabrice feel more welcome than with Mary Ann and Louis. There was food and conversation and laughter. Their two little girls were a constant delight and Mary Ann was expecting her third very soon.

Late one afternoon during Fabrice's stay, Father Francis Thévaux staggered into the Langoulants without his Heart of Mary confrères. Mary Ann barely recognised him, and the little girls were frightened by his appearance and hid. The French priest looked terribly weary and his feet had fallen apart from the long walk back from the south. Fabrice sat him down in the same wicker chair he had occupied at the farewell party just three months earlier; he was aged just twenty-six back then, but now he was ancient, and gaunt from starvation and worry.

The French mission to Albany, Father Francis told them wearily, was a disaster from the start.

'I wanted to do what was right,' said the *abbé* sadly, 'but

I suppose I had neither the brains nor the holiness to prevail.' All his former good humour had evaporated, his every utterance an act of contrition. 'My miserable soul has been made desolate by all the difficulties we have undergone. I no longer know what we can possibly achieve for Jesus and Mary in that remote place. I cannot even take care of my own soul while my heart is so cold and lifeless.'

To help him tell his story, Father Francis received a glass of wine from Louis while Mary Ann rubbed his neck and Victoria and Emma, coaxed from under the bed, washed his feet with soapy water. The new visitor was not scary, they now realised, just very sad.

It had taken the Heart of Mary priests three weeks to walk to Albany, explained Father Francis. The days were hot, the nights chilly, and they often became lost. Their shoes fell apart, then their feet.

When they finally made it to Albany, the sight of King George Sound made the men from Amiens slap each other with joy. It was the most beautiful, wide, natural harbour imaginable. The southern sea air was fresh and cooling. Sparkling smooth granite rocks sloped dangerously down to white sand beaches pounded by the foaming ocean. The town itself was lively with American, English and French whalers who had over the years worked their way westwards from Van Diemen's Land chasing the humpbacks and sperm whales. The old Belgian, Father Joostens, greeted them warmly and arranged a place for them to sleep. For one blissful night in Albany, the men of the Southern Mission were happy.

But next day the Fathers Francis were summoned to a meeting with Father Peter Powell. The Irishman looked well fed, clean shaved, and his robe had sharp creases, for he had been allowed to sail down from Fremantle.

'I am to inform you that the arrangements for the vicariate have changed,' announced Father Powell, looking down at the papers which bore the bishop's treacherous mark. The Vicariate of King George Sound, he explained impassively, would not belong to the Heart of Mary priests after all, despite the agreement Brady had signed with their superior, Father Libermann.

'Who then?' Francis Thévaux asked the humourless Irishman. 'You, I suppose.'

'Well, it is not yet certain,' replied Peter Powell, enjoying himself, 'but that would be a reasonable expectation, I would think. I am after all the bishop's natural successor. It would be normal, therefore, that I take on the rôle of vicar-general.'

The Fathers Francis took care to conceal their anger, just as they had been taught by Father Libermann. 'Very well, Father Powell,' he smiled. 'I am sure we can still get along very well in Albany.'

'No,' replied Powell without hesitation, 'we will not get along in Albany, for you are not to stay. His Lordship was very clear on this. Only Father Joostens is to remain here with me.'

The Fathers Francis stared silently for a few moments, letting their anger subside. 'So what is to become of us?' asked Francis Thiersé, with perfect calm.

'You are to move inland and attend to the natives.'

'I see. Do we receive some money for food, at least?'

'Yes. Here.' Father Powell gave the superior of the Southern Mission a cheque for sixteen pounds, signed by John Brady, Catholic Bishop of Perth.

The cheque was worthless, such was the bishop's credit. The penniless missionaries were saved by the captain of a French whaler from Middle Island. When he heard the sad story of the Fathers Francis, Captain Cobrière bought them a hot meal at The

Ship Inn and gave them money to buy some food, seeds, tools and wire before their exile to the bush.

A week later, with limited supplies and just nine pence to their names, the four men from Amiens retraced their steps north in the direction of the only inland settlement, the guard post at Kojonup. Francis Thiersé limped along for nine miles but had to drag himself back to town with a septic foot. The other Father Francis pressed on with the two laymen in the direction of a lake called Mollyalup, where they had made a pleasant stop on the way down to Albany. There had been a fresh water spring there and some green grass even in the heat of summer.

Against all odds, the Heart of Mary men managed to build a little timber church at Mollyalup, calling it *Sancta Maria*. Native Australians were, however, few in number, and very shy. Occasionally a curious family would camp a little distance away, but they had no need of French missionaries. They came for their amusement, not to seek spiritual guidance, and left when the novelty of looking at starving Frenchmen wore off.

Without money to buy anything, or a store at which to spend it, they realised they would have to become self-sufficient. With the first rains in March, they sowed all their seeds, hoping for a crop of vegetables and corn. They sprouted, but there were no further rains and parrots ate all the seedlings.

Then a plague of frogs came. For two full weeks the four Frenchmen ate only frogs and rice, and gave thanks to God for the bountiful plague.

Finally, they could stand it no longer. Alone, the superior of the Southern Mission set off back to Perth, leaving the other Father Francis with Vincent and Théodore, starving and penniless at Mollyalup.

Father Francis Thévaux felt guilty for leaving the mission, he confessed, and angry. But he had come to Perth for one reason: to genuflect humbly before Bishop Brady and beg his support.

'He is not in Perth,' said Fabrice. 'He is away chasing money in a place that has none.'

Francis sighed. 'Perhaps that is just as well,' he said sadly, 'for I have had a long, long walk with painful feet and too much time to think. I confess I have had murderous thoughts.'

'You will have to line up behind Father Powell,' said Louis.

Father Francis looked at the fisherman, confused. 'What? The vicar-general of King George Sound is unhappy with the bishop who gave him the title he snatched from me?'

'But the vicariate did not go to Father Powell,' said Louis. 'Brady does not trust him, so *La Terreur* told me. He has been made the parish priest of Guildford.'

Father Francis nodded with satisfaction. 'So who is vicar-general? We hear nothing in the bush.'

'Old Father Joostens. He is very frugal, says *La Terreur*, so will not be constantly asking for money. Also, the Belgian is very frail and surely won't outlive the bishop, so Brady knows his job is safe.'

The Heart of Mary priest fell silent. There seemed nothing left now to further disappoint him.

'What will you do now, *Abbé Francois*?' asked Fabrice.

The French priest exhaled at length, shrugged, and smiled at the two cherubs who were now drying his feet. 'We have been left to die in the bush. I believe the bishop to be mad. He treats us like children; children he despises. If ever there were to pull in to Albany a steamer destined for Mauritius, we would take it.'

Fabrice once again found himself with the power to change the outcome of a mission. This particular mission was futile, it was clear, but still he could see a way that these four good Frenchmen could benefit, while satisfying Pauline Jaricot's requirement that the native population did also. It would just have to be the population native to a French-speaking island in the Indian Ocean.'

'Mauritius … would forty pounds cover the passage, for all four?' asked Fabrice, reaching within his jacket. 'Sixty?'

That night, Louis took them all fishing from the pier. Little Victoria caught her very first fish, which puffed up angrily to reveal scary spikes, making her little sister Emma scream and hide from it within Fabrice's jacket. Mary Ann also threw in a line but was permitted no exertion by Louis, who made her sit in a little chair he had carried down to the jetty. He constantly fussed over her, though she said not to. Their third baby was almost due, and Louis was given to worrying.

Early next morning, two bearded Spanish monks appeared at the Langoulants' door, looking worried.

'We have a favour to ask of you,' said Salvado, addressing Louis, Mary Ann and Fabrice equally. 'For the Church. For the Benedictine order. And for us, personally.'

'Whatever you need, Fathers,' said Louis. 'If we have it to give, it is yours.'

Serra looked furtive. 'What we tell you must be kept in absolute confidence, Louis, for the sake of the mission and the diocese.'

Something bad had happened at the mission, but it was not clear what. The news had been relayed by the parish pump, Farrelly, who had spoken to a wagon driver, who had heard it from someone in Guildford. Nothing was yet certain, but their grim expressions said they were very worried about the two missionaries they had left behind: John Gorman and Léandre Fonteinne.

'Are they dead?' asked Fabrice, a spear of ice running through him.

'Do not ask such questions,' scolded Serra.

The monks could not possibly leave Perth for at least two days. Serra had just barely arrived in Perth and Salvado had to buy a pair of oxen, a cart, and various supplies and provisions. Their trip back would be slow because the rain, now it had started, would not let up and the creeks were filling and there would be mud.

'We beg you, Louis,' pleaded Salvado, 'might you and Fabrice head up to Badji Badji as soon as possible? You two could travel lightly and get there quickly. Pack some food and a little wine. Take some succour to your countryman, if … if you can find him.'

'So Léandre is alive?' asked Fabrice. 'Is he lost?'

Dom Serra coughed. Salvado hesitated. 'We do not know the answers to those questions.'

Louis did not want to leave his dear wife in her condition. He looked across to Mary Ann, who looked up to heaven in resignation. She was a Catholic now, after all, and these were priests. Also, their beloved friend Léandre, poor frightened Léandre, was in some sort of danger. What choice did she really have?

'Of course, Fathers,' said Louis Langoulant. 'It is no trouble at all. Fabrice and I shall leave today. But this place you call Badji Badji. How will we ever find it?'

'Go first to Bolgart and find Captain Scully. Nobody knows Victoria Plains like Scully. If he cannot personally accompany you there, he will send you with a reliable servant.'

'We will take my boat as far as Guildford,' said Louis. 'With luck we can catch a ride from there to Toodyay with some timber men.'

Fabrice was still quietly turning over the possibilities. 'Léandre and the Irish catechist. Would they be inclined to assist one another in the event of difficulties?'

Salvado's eyes flickered towards his superior.

'It is best that you get up there as soon as you can,' said Dom Serra.

'We will depart today,' said Fabrice, his heart sinking.

Once the priests had gone, Louis knelt at the feet of his wife and kissed her belly.

'Our baby might come while I am gone,' said Louis.

'It probably will,' said Mary Ann, a voice of perfect calm, 'but Sister Anne is here. You must go up and see what has befallen poor Léandre.'

'Are you sure, my beautiful girl?' whispered Louis, a choke in his voice.

'Stop it now,' she countered. 'I am an Irishwoman, don't forget. We are raised to expect our men to be absent or drunk or useless. I can easily do without you for a while.' He would not release his embrace, so Mary Ann did it for him. 'Jesus, Louis, go.'

An hour later the Italian winemaker, Nico Caporelli, appeared. He happened to be driving back to the Swan Valley that afternoon and had room for two passengers. Actually, he admitted, he had not planned to leave until the following day, but *Il Terrore* had cornered him to advise him that his plans had changed. Farrelly wanted 'the two Frenchies' up at Badji Badji as soon as possible; he had seemed very worried about his friend, John Gorman.

'I'd planned to row to Guildford,' said Louis.

'Save your arms,' said Caporelli. He was no longer part of the mission, but he knew one should not defy Terry Farrelly in this town.

'Your little cart will cripple my knees,' countered Louis, recalling the poor nuns squeezed into the tiny dogcart.

'Ah, but times have improved!' said Caporelli, pointing to his new transport parked under the peppermint tree. Wine-makers, it seemed, were prospering in the Swan Valley. He now owned an elegant spring cart and a full-sized horse.

So they travelled down the Guildford Road together, these three men who professed to be sick and tired of Catholic missionaries, but who were helping them nonetheless, and whose conversation was mostly about them.

It rained all the way to Guildford, and then all the way to Toodyay, but Louis and Fabrice made good time thanks to the sandalwood cutters that worked the area. Where the Toodyay Road came close to the Avon River the Frenchmen could hear it, and when the river itself occasionally came into view, they could see it was flowing very fast, foaming where it crashed against rocks.

'How will we ever cross that?' asked Fabrice who had never seen it in flow.

'Is there no bridge at Toodyay?' said the fisherman.

'No bridge,' said Fabrice, and they both fell silent for a while, thinking of their friend, who they hoped was still alive in a remote camp on Victoria Plains, on the far side of this wild river.

From: Ignatia de la Hoyde, Perth
To: Cecilia Marmion, Baggot Street, Dublin

27th May 1846

Dear Rev. Mother

It is too late now Mother and I should have said so the very morning after the bishop's speech, but I was too hasty to volunteer for this place. I am the oldest of the sisters here and the least flexible in my ways, I confess. There is not a day that I do not awake with a heaviness in my heart for Ireland, nor a night when I do not weep silently in the darkness. I dare not cry aloud for fear of being scolded for drawing attention to myself.

Mother, I am compelled to tell you this, seeking neither solace nor pity. I am, every day, so very miserable in this place. But I will stay here, just as I vowed.

I am given the job of indoctrination of the adults. Sister Anne Dillon has divided them into four groups of her own invention. The Committed Catholics are very few. The Careless Catholics, who bitterly deplore their past conduct and hasten to repair it, are even rarer. The Concealed Catholics are those who deny their religion for the sake of Protestant patronage. And the 'OBs', as Anne likes to call them, are the 'Ought-To-Be' Catholics, including those who have suffered the sacrament of baptism at the hands of Wesleyan ministers. It is Anne's job to find all these and bring them to me. Sister Anne is an enthusiast for the task, I will give her that. Every evening the verandah is crowded with men, women and grown girls hoping to receive instruction for the sacraments.

The degree of religious ignorance here is hard to believe. This colony is like one great wilderness for all that its inhabitants know about Our Lord and Our Lady. I speak here only of the adults. The colonial children are equal in their utter ignorance whether they be little white ones living in the town with shoes on their feet or little dark ones running about barefoot in the bush.

Anne pulls me aside from time to time to tell me that I frighten her 'OBs' off with my seriousness and that we will lose them unless I feign cheerfulness. I have many deficiencies I know, but one thing I will never do Mother, is feign.

Your loving child and servant in J.C.
Sr M. Ignatia de la Hoyde

10. CROSSING THE AVON

Roger Smith's forge was dry, warm and occupied by Eric Hough, who was far too busy with hammer and tongs to acknowledge the arrival of two soaking Frenchmen. The Parkhurst boy had proved himself an excellent apprentice. 'Puffy', as the farmers and wagon drivers of the Avon Valley called him, was the town's blacksmith and wheelwright. Roger Smith concerned himself with loftier matters and was rarely seen at the hearth nowadays unless there was some filigree or other fine work to be done.

For Eric, one Frenchman had been bad enough. He didn't need two of them camped in his workplace. The Parkhurst boy did not say this aloud, of course; it was not yet his place to do so. Instead, he banged things noisily against the fireplace and used the bellows to fill the room with ash and waved red-hot work pieces dangerously close to faces and immersed them in the slack tub so they made an angry hiss on his behalf. No visitor to Eric Hough's smithy was left unclear as to the apprentice's feelings on the intrusion.

The rain had not let up, and the Frenchmen found themselves stuck on the wrong side of the Avon, watching it rise by the hour. Louis found Bob, and together they went out into the bad weather to look at the river and consider the options for crossing it.

Fabrice stayed in the warmth of the forge and attended to his *magnanerie*, as he called the ventilated wire cage he had built for his silkworms. His father's silkworm farms had been two-storeyed brick buildings with a dozen workers, but Fabrice's was just large enough for him to step in to. When he left for Perth two weeks earlier it had been full of fat hungry worms, and Fabrice had stuffed the cage full of mulberry leaves from the neighbour's tree. Now there were hundreds of ruined cocoons and as many flightless moths inside, all flapping their wings at high speed and mating.

'Annoying, that damned *zzz* noise they make,' opined Eric Hough, his first words to Fabrice. 'I would of smoked them dead if you weren't here. And they shit everywhere.'

This latter was true, and the cage had not been cleaned. Fabrice did so now, bagging the castings for Sadie's flower garden, then went next door to cut a couple of fresh branches from the neighbour's tree which he placed, tree-like, inside the *magnanerie*. The moths seemed grateful for the greenery. They fluttered and mated even faster, making best use of their remaining hours. This was their only job in life: to mate, lay eggs, and die. They had one week.

Eric Hough watched all this activity with arms folded. 'You said they don't eat once they got wings.'

'Yes. But still, it is nice for them to have leaves. Imagine you were a moth.'

The boy shook his head in the same disapproving manner that Fabrice's father would have done had he been present. A proper *magnanier* would never gather leaves for little moths to crawl upon for their happiness. The correct approach was to boil *les cocons* before they hatched.

Inside the cage, Fabrice noticed something suspicious, but not entirely unexpected. He had built a secret hatch in the back which could be opened only from within the cage and had secreted some of the money within it. He had anticipated the risk Eric might discover it and help himself to a few *sous*, so it was not too alarming to see the secret hatch was very slightly ajar. But a discrete inspection showed the three small purses to be still there, weighing about the same as he had left them. Perhaps the cage had just been bumped by the vigorous blacksmith.

Still it rained. A wet horse appeared in Eric's workshop. 'Oh good,' he blurted, 'my smithy is now a barnyard!' The reluctant grey was led in by the nose by the neighbour, Michael, who told Fabrice rather forlornly that he had 'agreed' to lend it to him for his journey to Victoria Plains. Michael was a soft man who spoke to his mare with great affection and stroked its nose. Turnip did not like water, not even puddles, explained Michael. She could never be made to swim across a river, not even a flat one.

Louis and Bob reappeared between showers, then Roger Smith and Sadie came up from the house, and now the smithy was full to capacity. The apprentice crashed hammer on anvil a few times, then angrily threw his tools aside and sat on a sack with his water bottle. 'No room to work,' he grumbled.

'Forget the horses,' declared Roger Smith, 'the river is too high.'

This pronouncement was to the great relief of the neighbour, who had only agreed to the loan under great sufferance. Michael was a bachelor, a simple man who knew his place in the world. He knew he was not an intellectual like Roger Smith, but he was, he hoped, a kind man. Sadie shared that view. She went over to Michael to help him soothe the mare, who had sensed from its owner's anxious hands that something bad was happening. Their fingers brushed on Turnip's muzzle.

Michael had taken to visiting The Garden most days, usually to help Sadie with some task or other. He was patient with her and handy with every kind of tool. Once a week he came reluctantly to dinner. Roger Smith had begun to refer to Michael as if he were a citizen of The Garden and to Michael's property as 'the back block', as if it were part of his own lease.

To Michael, Roger Smith was a man impossible to refuse. If Roger Smith requested a loan of something and Michael so much as hesitated, he would receive a lecture on the virtue of altruism. Famous philosophers were quoted against him.

Sadie helped Michael walk the mare home, for she liked Turnip, and she loved Michael. Something within her glowed when Michael spoke in his soft voice. It was a revelation to her that manliness could be mixed with softness. In Cape Town there certainly had been no softness in it. It didn't seem to matter what she and Michael talked about; the less important the better. Roger Smith would never have told her about such trivial things as his feelings for a horse.

Together, they returned Turnip to her warm stable where Michael's pampered chickens of various breeds scattered to safety. Sadie spent some more time stroking the mare's nose to settle her, as Michael towelled her dry.

'She loves you,' Michael told Sadie, smiling at his boots.

Sadie felt completely at home in this place. It was again raining heavily, which meant she could stay longer with no questions asked. They hung their wet coats to dry on Turnip's rail. Sadie's clothes had remained dry but not the very top of her. Michael cupped her face to warm her cheeks. So sweet did she look to him, soaking wet from the downpour. He found a clean cloth and gently towelled Sadie's hair, kissed her forehead and told her she looked like a drowned joey. Michael always meant things kindly, even if his words were wrong.

'Come on, my beautiful girl,' he said, taking her hand and leading her in familiar fashion to a particular spot in the corner of the barn where it was always warm and dry. He helped her out of her clothes and then had to close his eyes, dizzy at the strength of feeling that came upon him. Michael loved Sadie.

The rain bucketing down outside made the barn even cosier. Michael had made some additions that he was excited for her to see. He had thrown in fresh lucerne straw, sweeter smelling then plain wheat straw, he explained, and a clean blanket, and the little pillow that Sadie had requested. And there was his innovation, a bunch of her favourite flowers in each corner – red bottlebrush on the left and yellow wattle on the right, just like on the sign she had painted for The Garden.

'Oh! So pretty!' said Sadie, her hands on her cheeks, her elbows still held modestly against her breasts. 'Nobody was ever so nice to me.'

Michael gestured with his hand as if to royalty, and Sadie lay back. She sighed with happiness.

'The lucerne is a bit softer,' he explained, pushing it with the palm of his hand. 'It won't poke your arse so much.'

It was true. Sadie felt entirely at home in this particular place, with this particular man. He rested his wet woolly head softly on her shoulder and breathed and watched the miracle of her soft pink nipples rising and falling slowly, slowly, with her every beautiful breath, while Turnip looked approvingly across the rail, and whinnied. The rain had well and truly settled in for the afternoon.

Back at The Garden, Roger Smith was still dispensing fluvial advice to his French visitors.

'You should wait until morning to wade across,' he advised.

'Hold your swags above your head to keep them dry.'

'Wade?' said Louis. The water was white with foam. 'Would you attempt it, yourself?'

'Good heavens, no,' admitted the First Amongst Equals of the Owenite commune, 'it looks terribly dangerous.' Roger Smith was, he freely admitted, a theorist. The advice he dispensed had come from a camping trip to the Cotswalds in his youth. 'Could you perhaps locate a place where the river narrows and scramble across the rocks?'

Louis nodded thoughtfully while whispering, '*Ton ami anglais est un crétin.*' This was an unkind assessment, but Fabrice too had grown tired of the Englishman's sermons and had almost decided that Humanism was not all he had hoped. He had retrieved the three purses from the *magnanerie* with the intention of taking them to Badji Badji, without any idea what he might do after that.

Still it rained. Louis took Fabrice to a lookout point on the edge of Roger Smith's property where the river could be surveyed upstream and down. Bob – barefoot, short pants and an enormous borrowed rain jacket billowing around him – was amused by their dilemma.

'Bob and I have walked a good way in either direction,' said Louis, looking troubled. 'This will not be an easy river to cross.'

'I seem to recall we should look for the widest spot,' suggested Fabrice. 'The widest is the slowest, I think.'

Louis failed to respond. He led them down to the bank to examine the river from the water level where it looked even more fearsome.

Fabrice, recalling something, threw a stick in the water. 'If you can't walk faster than the stick, you should not go in the water.'

'See that big stick?' said Bob, pointing out a partly submerged tree in the middle of the stream. 'Get caught in that and you're dead.'

That ominous advice caused a moment of reflection, until, suddenly something unimaginable appeared.

'*Mon Dieu!*' gasped Louis, '*un bateau!*'

God had sent them a miracle, and it was approaching fast. A wooden boat, complete with oars, had appeared round the Z-bend and was wobbling rapidly towards them within a couple of metres of the near bank. Bob leapt up the bank and reappeared seconds later carrying Sadie's garden hoe, which served as a grappling hook. Within minutes the solution to their insolvable problem was displayed on the lawn outside Roger Smith's shingle-roofed cottage.

They all stared in disbelief. Every so often, they would laugh and embrace. In an Old Testament story, this would have been the work of a loving deity and their gratitude would have altered the course of civilisation.

'*Un miracle!*' repeated Fabrice, the lapsing Humanist.

'She must have come loose from a mooring upstream somewhere,' explained the fisherman.

Dinner was held in Eric's workshop, the only warm place in the commune. Bob had bagged a dozen parrots, pretty birds, with green plumage and a yellow ring around their necks.

'*Darmaluque,*' said Bob, or so it sounded to Fabrice's ear.

'Twenty-eights, in proper English,' Eric countered. 'Cos their screeching means twenty-eight in French,' he explained.

Fabrice doubted the etymology. He had Bob reproduce the sound such a parrot would make in its living state and its cry bore no possible resemblance to *vingt-huit*.

'I too shall call them *darmaluque*,' Fabrice announced. 'Such attractive birds; they would be served best, I think, roasted, followed by a creamy apple *teurgoule*. I have my mother's recipe in my head. We have green apples and rice and cream. It is the only thing my dear *maman* could cook.'

'Your *maaman*?' said Bob, confused. 'He did the cookin'?'

'It means mother,' explained Fabrice.

'Means father,' said Bob.

'Does it?' said Fabrice, wondering how much of the boy's advice could be trusted. 'The very opposite. How could that be?'

The forge became a stove on which were placed the wrapped birds and Fabrice's mother's pudding. Sadie added a couple of grainy loaves for the Frenchmen to take on their travels next morning.

Michael arrived unobtrusively, relieved to see Roger Smith fully occupied with the two Frenchmen, lecturing them on the risks of an unexamined life. This left him free to eat his bird quietly on a hay bale beside Sadie, their knees occasionally brushing. When occasionally he spoke, it was softly and about small matters. After the meal, when it came time for him to leave, Michael patted the miraculous boat, which had been dragged to the entrance of the workshop.

'I thought I had lost her,' he said quietly in the direction of the French fisherman.

'This is your boat?' asked Louis. All ears listened for the answer.

'Yes,' said Michael, as if ashamed. 'I tied it to a tree upstream but the bank subsided overnight and the tree half fell in. I climbed into the tree to try to undo the knot while perched above the foam, and I am not one who enjoys danger. As I freed the boat, the rope tried to drag me into the river, so I had to let go.'

'I didn't know you had a boat, Michael,' said Roger Smith, with a hint of indignation in his voice that a matter of such importance to the commune had been concealed.

'I do,' said Michael, looking at his feet.

'Well, tomorrow morning these Frenchmen require it to cross the river,' explained Roger Smith, who had an Aristotelian view of democracy, Fabrice had noted, his view counting for more than the rest of the *demos* combined.

'Of course,' said Michael, and patted his boat just as affectionately as he had Turnip earlier that day. *Pelican* was painted in small neat letters on one side. Already he was wondering how he might retrieve her; he would try to speak later to the smaller Frenchman who seemed to know about boats.

Sadie saw Michael to the gate, on which she had painted a pair of New Holland honeyeaters. 'I hope your little boat is not scared of the water too,' she smiled, pushing her face against his shoulder so he could feel her warm breath on his cold earlobes. 'I will have to tell him soon, you know. Before he guesses.'

Just before dawn, Roger Smith came into the forge. The two Frenchmen were curled up together like lovers. '*Il pleut beaucoup, boys*,' he proclaimed. 'Come and look. It is very swollen.'

The Avon had transformed into a great, angry, noisy, foaming monster set on destroying the banks of The Garden and washing away the commune. 'I am certain I did not leave the house this close to the river when I went to bed,' said Roger Smith. As an English gentleman he was obliged to wear adversity lightly, but it was clear he was worried.

Sadie had climbed down to a dangerous-looking ledge to inspect the damage to the bank and came back shaking her head. 'A big chunk has fallen away underneath,' she said. 'We'd best all stand back. The earth might collapse under us.'

Louis declared it unsafe to take a boat into the torrent. Besides, the Frenchmen could not set off in good conscience; they had to stay and help save the house from disappearing into the Avon.

Sandbagging kept six pairs of hands fully occupied all morning. Fabrice helped Sadie cut and stitch a roll of hessian into sacks and then he went around with a needle and yarn to those on spadework to close the mouth of the bags. It was the job of Bob and Eric to build the bags into a barricade, starting at opposite ends so they would not have to bump into one another.

About noon the rain stopped. 'At least your mad little friend in the bush will have water enough to drink,' observed Roger Smith, as they all stopped to inspect their work, 'and some more to cool his head.' He was glad for the elevated position of the block, he said, which he had chosen not for any practical reason, but because it was pretty.

Being perched on a bend in the river posed a different danger, however, the switch causing the swollen river to roar and chew at the banks. An enormous half-circle of earth was slowly subsiding just a few feet from their bedroom window and during lunch it all gave way as if a giant had taken a bite of it, lawn and garden and soil disappearing into the water at precisely the point where Sadie had done her inspection.

'I could have lost you forever, dear girl,' laughed Roger Smith, giving her a hug, to which show of affection Sadie smiled uncertainly.

Michael appeared after lunch, asking very shyly if he might per-haps borrow his own boat for a short while, since his neighbour's farm was flooded and the poor family were on their roof calling for help. Only now did the residents of The Garden appreciate the damage done to the properties that lay below them. On Michael's land and beyond, the river had widened into an enormous lake.

Louis the fisherman volunteered to undertake the rescue.

'Just be aware,' warned Roger Smith, 'they are Wesleyans. Very hard people to assist.'

His cynicism proved unwarranted. The grateful family was delivered by Louis Langoulant in twos and threes to the edge of Michael's block, for a total of nine. The father was the last to appear at The Garden, a ruined man. They would all stay, insisted Roger Smith, either in the house, if they felt it safe enough, or in the forge, which was dry and warm. The Wesleyan neighbour humbly thanked Roger Smith for his generosity, and opted for the forge.

'Don't mention it, dear chap,' said Roger Smith. Eric Hough protested at this latest intrusion by hammering loudly.

The Frenchmen helped the family retrieve what things they could, and shepherded what was left of their livestock up the hill to safety. Many of their sheep had drowned and were piled up together in a woolly muddy pile against a steep bank. The lovingly tendered fruit orchard was ruined. Louis paddled through stone fruit trees that were half-submerged and mature citrus that had been upended, their roots washed clean of soil. Six years of hard work had been ruined in one morning, said the Wesleyan without expression. God was not mentioned.

Fabrice and Louis stood on the shore of a vast new lake already populated by waterbirds. Their concerns for Léandre gnawed at them. They had made a promise to the monks and would have to cross this river the next morning, come hell or high water.

'On part d'ici,' said the fisherman. Here was the safest place to set off. The lake here was half a kilometre wide and in its middle the river could just be made out, flatter, wider and straighter than the foaming monster eating at the banks of The Garden. Tree branches and bushes were racing downstream. With Michael's help, they carried *Pelican* down and secured her for the night on some dry ground nearby. Michael coaxed Louis aside and they talked quietly together, pointing occasionally downstream. Michael threw in a generous length of rope to aid retrieval, and Louis embraced him and patted his shoulder many times and assured him that he would look after *Pelican* as if she was his own sister.

It was still dark in the smithy next morning when the Frenchmen roused, dressed, and stepped over half a dozen sleeping bodies to recommence their journey to Badji Badji. Sadie had left another loaf, still warm, on the top of the stove. Fabrice, fearful that his knapsack may end up in the water, secured the purses on a strap around his waist, and in so doing stumbled over the legs of the sleeping Parkhurst boy who emitted an English obscenity by way of farewell.

It was chilly outside but at least the rain had stopped. By lamplight the two men found *Pelican*, and as the first rays of sun appeared they were about to push off when Roger Smith appeared with an unhappy Eric Hough, steering a wobbling pushbarrow through the mud. Without consulting the captain, Roger Smith instructed Eric to tip the contents into the boat; a heavy length of metal chain.

'Never trust rope in such wild conditions,' cautioned the blacksmith. Louis shook his head, and kept Michael's rope handy. Chain was strong but was of no use in a hurry.

Another hundred pounds was added just as they punted off, in the form of Bob, who appeared from nowhere and stepped elegantly into the front. The Frenchies would never find the Bolgart track after these rains, he called back to Roger Smith.

'*Bonne chance, mes amis,*' said Roger Smith, pleased to put his schoolboy French to some utility.

'Don't drown,' said Eric, without much sincerity.

The crossing of the Avon began serenely. Louis stood up at the stern like a gondolier, using a single oar to negotiate their way through the Wesleyan's uprooted orange trees. Fabrice squeezed uncomfortably on the centre thwart alongside the unstable mountain of chain metal, while Bob was at the front on lookout, using his feet to push them clear of a submerged tree branch.

'Frenchy, Frenchy, watch out for that thing!' he warned. 'Don't kill us!'

Fabrice placed all his trust in his friend Louis, the expert boatsman. The new sun's soft light made the lake twinkle and all about them were blue-winged dragonflies, hovering with perfect stillness. He had no fear. If the dragonflies were not worried, why should he be?

'There seems to be no current at all,' said Fabrice, just moments before they reached it. A fast-moving river was hidden in the middle of the lake. *Pelican* abruptly changed personality and took off with frightening speed. Bob's shoulder muscles braced.

Fabrice Cleriquot crossed himself. They were fools for trying to traverse this river, and his friend Louis the biggest fool for not knowing his limitations. They were all going to die in a violent river in the remote Australian bush.

At the back, Louis kneeled down now and pulled in his oar. He told Fabrice, on the left side, to hold the other oar. Think of it as a canoe, he said. Wait, Louis instructed, wait until I say.

But Fabrice couldn't wait. The boat was racing now and straight ahead were rocks and noisy foaming rapids barricaded by tree branches. To their right it looked calm and lovely; it was obvious they should aim for that bank. So he dug his oar deeply in the water, his grip slipped, the pile of chain metal toppled towards him, Bob grabbed his pants and Louis yelled at the damned fool to pull his oar in and sit still as he had been told. Bob reached back and confiscated the oar.

Roger Smith's chain ballast could either save them, the captain briefly considered, or else sink them if it shifted the wrong way.

The three men were poised now like hunters while the boat went wherever the river wished it to go: to their very deaths, Fabrice felt sure. Too late had he realised that his friend Louis Langoulant was a fraud and a madman. He was not even *trying* to get them to the lovely calm bay on the other side of the torrent. The nose of the boat still pointed dead ahead to the rapids. Fabrice again advised the captain of the pressing danger but was abruptly told to shut his mouth.

Pelican brushed over another submerged branch, enough to again rock the boat and shift the pile of chain and throw water down Fabrice's throat – a taste of his imminent death by drowning.

A hundred metres ahead the river disappeared through a fence of trapped bushwood down a rocky staircase which led to hell. Any one of those jagged boulders would surely crunch the bottom of a rowboat. Fabrice picked out the precise spot where his life would end – just there, where the white water narrowed to a dangerous waist and it was all foam and spray and leg-snapping rocks.

He took one last look to their right, where the waters were flat and still and sparkled like a golden bay. The tranquil *gouljacque* was there, red beak luminescent in the morning sun. A gentle ray of sunlight flashed through the hole in the beak of the swan and met his eye – a sign, for sure, but of what?

Fifty metres now to the falls. Fabrice felt his body soften, yielding now to fate.

'Ready!' said Louis, the first trace of fear in his voice – then, 'Row!' Louis dug his oar in at the rear so the boat turned its nose and Bob pulled lazily two or three times on the left, effortlessly completing the task Fabrice had been given.

Pelican turned her nose towards the north bank of the Avon, where the mystic swan showed no interest whatever in the outcome. A dozen strokes took them beyond the current and suddenly all danger was gone. Louis rowed them gently to shore, like lovers on a resort lake.

Two metres from the bank the acrobatic Bob grabbed the rope and leapt from the boat, but lost his foothold and slipped back into the thick mud, laughing. Holding the bitter end of the line he dragged *Pelican* a little way along the bank to a drier landing where he secured it to the branch of a sturdy *bibool* under which he placed his skinny backside and sat, arms around his knees, as if nothing of consequence had just happened.

Fabrice Cleriquot stepped ashore. They had survived the Avon. His boots were barely wet but his knees were still trembling. He carried the bags of provisions onto dry land and sat next to Bob under the paperbark to recover, hat pulled down over his eyes to shut out the world. He heard, as if in a dream, Louis saying he was heading off with Bob to explore what things looked like downstream.

When Louis and Bob returned, there was another burst of action.

Louis told Fabrice to drag Roger Smith's chain out from *Pelican* so he could relaunch her.

'Your friend Roger Smith is a dangerous man,' grumbled Louis. Louis and Bob jumped back in the boat. 'Wait here,' said the fisherman. 'We should be back in an hour. '

'What?' exclaimed Fabrice, 'but we have to get walking.'

'I promised Michael I would get his boat back.'

'To the far side? You are mad, Louis!'

'Michael needs his boat. His farm is under water.'

'You really mean to paddle back across?'

'Not across. Down. Bob has cleared the branches away. We can do it, I think. If not, well, kiss Léandre for me. And look after Mary Ann.'

Fabrice watched from the grassy bank as, with just a few strokes, *Pelican* found the current again and took off sharply. In just a few seconds it went tumbling and scraping into the river and towards the same deadly rapids from which they had narrowly escaped. The oars were pulled inside. This was madness. Fabrice ran along the bank to observe the catastrophe and heard Bob whoop with excitement.

The two fools were heading straight at the middle of the cascade, Louis sitting on the rear boards gripping the thwart and Bob kneeling low in front, peering over the top with delight in his eyes. As *Pelican* was swallowed by foam, Fabrice saw them both brace for the crunch. He braced too, from the shore, but the feared crunch did not come, the water being high enough to protect the boat from the rocks below.

Then came two huge whoops, then laughter which echoed back

at him from down the river. 'Such fun, Bob!' echoed the voice of Louis, 'we should paddle back and do it again!' The boat vanished in the foam, but Bob's screams of delight could be heard as they approached the next rapid.

Fabrice sat alone on the riverbank for a long while. He threw pieces of Sadie's bread to the *gouljacque*. There was time now to contemplate the sign the swan had given him in that moment of great peril. It seemed incredible that a particle of light from the sun, which gave life to all things, had journeyed through the sky and via the nostril of this beautiful creature to land upon his eye, just so that he may perceive it.

There was no *necessity* for such beauty. Why did it even exist, this watchful black swan with its scarlet beak? It did seem a *godly* creation. More than that. There was god *in* the bird, and god *in* the light that passed through its beak. And Fabrice had strongly felt god to be *in* the cascade that had threatened to smash the life from him, as well as *in* the calm water near the riverbank which had saved them.

A revelation came to him, not from some fraudulent priest, but from his own pure observations of the natural world. Atheism, he saw now, was a sort of blindness. There was god everywhere, he now realised, but not a god that could intervene on his behalf or against it, not a god that required his worship or thanks. It was simply there in all things, for better or worse. That they had survived the river today was not due to a divine hand, it was simply because Louis was a good captain. Suddenly, everything seemed explainable this way.

In crossing the Avon, Fabrice Cleriquot had become a Pantheist.

An hour later, Bob reappeared, his short pants perfectly dry.

'Where's Louis?'

The boy snapped off a twig and inspected it carefully. 'Stuck in the river.'

'What?'

'Can't jump.'

The two adventurers had left *Pelican* at a place a kilometre downstream from which Michael could retrieve it, and then set off to return by foot over the rocks. Now, squatting on a dry boulder in the middle of the rapids was a forlorn Louis Langoulant, his knees drawn up to his chest like a sulking child. He had watched Bob leap across the narrowest spot and had very nearly copied him, but balked. Now his nerve for danger had completely left him.

'Come on, Frenchy,' said the boy. 'Jump!' To Bob, this was no crisis.

'I can't,' insisted Louis, ashamed, 'it is the devil's toilet bowl.' A strong vision had come to him of being wedged in the rock trap below with both legs broken, slowly drowning, and had sapped him of all power. 'Fabrice, find me a log to climb over.'

Fabrice had another idea. He went back and dragged down Roger Smith's heavy chain, threaded a sturdy branch through the second link to make it easier to catch, and threw it across to Louis. With the effort of the throw, he felt something snap inside his shirt; it was the leather strap onto which were attached three purses of the Mademoiselle's money. He watched the first disappear beneath the foam, then the second. The third purse he almost caught, but it hit the heel of his hand and it too disappeared beneath the foam with no possibility of retrieval.

The chain had fallen short. His second attempt was better. Louis caught the branch, looped Roger Smith's heavy chain around the back of the boulder, pulled half the length of it through and tossed the handled end back to Fabrice, who looped it twice around the trunk of a sturdy *bibool* and secured the end links with a twist of fencing wire. In just ten minutes an iron bridge had been constructed across the Avon River. Louis crossed it on his belly. It undid all his previous bravado, but he no longer trusted his feet.

Bob had trouble finding Drummond's Track. It had probably washed away, he suggested, or turned to mud. He led the Frenchmen west for a while, then a bit east, then west again. Then he took off and for a while could not be found. When they caught up with him, the boy was sitting under a tree, resting.

'Have you got us lost, Bob?' complained Fabrice. They were already hours behind.

'I seen a sign of it,' said Bob.

The Frenchmen guessed their guide had found some sign inscrutable except to those who had grown up in the bush. They followed him across a hundred metres of rough ground, watching him stop here and there to demonstrate his craft. He occasionally looked skywards, pulled some bark of a tree to taste it, inspected a termite mound. Checking the direction the ants were running, explained Louis.

When the two Frenchmen emerged from the bush, they found Bob standing in front of the sign he had discovered, so they too could read its flaking paint.

Bolgart Springs. 21 Miles.

It was noon. They might still get to Captain Scully's by dark.

From: Terry Farrelly
To: John Brady

6th June 1846

(Left on Bishop's desk)

Apologies for the mess you will come back too Lordship but I must leave in a hurry with the Spanish. Something has happened up at Central Mission and I fear for Johnny Gorman. Will let you know as soon as I do but I fear its not good. Very bad.

Hopefully something came of yr visit to Austral-Ind though it is not a Catholic stronghold and they are more likely to beg for money than give.

Yet more terrible news from our homeland. Could Ireland be made suffer anymore? The west coast is so very bad. Have them all pray for Ireland John there cannot be too many prayers offered.

Powell unhappy in Gilford so no surprise there. The carpenter rabbiting on again about debt so I dimmed his lights a little so he wont bother you while I am up at Moor River. Don't worry yrself with it that's why you have me.

Back in three weeks, D.V.
Please pray for Johnny Gorman.

11. TRAGEDY AT BADJI BADJI

The track to Bolgart, once they got away from the river, was a good one. It still drizzled, but the land here badly needed moisture and drank it in thirstily. The rains made it nice and soft underfoot. The bush smelled wetly beautiful and its myriad invisible inhabitants clicked away lazily.

They stopped for a late lunch of Sadie's bread, cold sausage and a swig of Caporelli's hock. The river crossing had energised the two Frenchmen and made them appreciate each other's qualities all the more. Bob listened in on their conversations and copied their favorite ejaculations. From time to time the white gum forest would echo with a *Mon Dieu!* or a *Merde!* shouted at the treetops by Bob for no purpose except to amuse them all.

They supposed they were in Victoria Plains now. It did seem good country to graze sheep in, not all dead flat plains, as Fabrice had imagined, but long gentle hills like folds in a blanket. They enjoyed shade for much of the time, and where the country opened up there were meadows of ankle-high grass dotted with rocky outcrops of granite boulders, all of which were covered on one side by pale green lichen.

There were few signs of white man's invasion into the country, apart from the track itself. They disturbed a flock of emus which raced away in a long wavy line only to regather watchfully at a distance like barnyard chickens with a fox about. Late in the afternoon kangaroos started to appear, the first being a muscular grey buck which had been napping until they startled it. It hopped just a dozen metres away, where it stood stock still, ears twitching, believing itself invisible.

They came upon a bough shed with a rough table and drying racks outside. There being no one around, the three went in to investigate.

Inside, it smelt like a museum and as their eyes adjusted, they saw a wonderland of native wildlife. Six dozen parrots hung from the roof, a few of the green and gold kind Fabrice had baked for dinner, pink-and-grey galahs, white corellas and one magnificent red-tailed black cockatoo, the late afternoon sunlight filtering through the slats of the shack at such an angle to perfectly backlight its rosy tail feathers. It could almost have been alive. There was a cold oven with six or seven black birds within it: ravens with upturned feet.

There were bags of salt, a box of shaven sandalwood and small trays of dried aromatic herbs, which the Frenchmen pinched to their noses to determine the scent. Cinnamon? Cloves, certainly, and pepper. Ginger, perhaps. The specimens had to smell sweetly when despatched to England. Fabrice found a dusty order book. The British Museum would like some koalas, which did not exist here, and a dozen emus, which did, though surely very hard to capture, the Frenchmen conjectured, and just as difficult to transport across the seas undamaged.

On one bench were arranged the creatures that jumped or crawled. A half dozen possums, a little family of potoroos placed amusingly in a circle as if convening, and a single echidna, its back having been sharply arched during the drying process with fencing wire to best demonstrate its vicious quills. A gentle slow-moving bobtail had had its mouth wired open to reveal its blue mucosa in an effort to make it seem fierce.

Little tags had been applied to the delicate legs of some of the wildlife, with descriptions in small neat hand.

Ring Necked 'Twenty-Eight' Parrot for Mr Gould.
Kangaroo Rat or 'Woylie' for British Museum.

'Johnston Drummond's old place,' explained Bob. 'He loved animals.'

Fabrice fell quiet. All these creatures from the natural world had had the spirit sucked out of them and their deaths felt like his too. The feeling came strongly upon him as they walked on that there was after all just one force, one immanent spirit that might as well be called god since it permeated all things.

There was no town where Bolgart was meant to be, but just on dark they arrived at Captain John Scully's property, which bore that name. 'This is it,' explained Bob as he walked into the house as if expected, 'the old man's place'. Scully was in the front yard loading freshly sawn timber onto a wagon. His greeting was perfunctory.

'French? Oh, you've come because of the business at Badji, I suppose?' he said, his back to them as he secured the load. 'Good timing. I'm heading there in the morning.' The timber planks were about two metres in length.

'Your countryman ...' said Scully, facing the Frenchmen now, dusting his hands and looking a bit awkward. 'Ah ... what was his name again?'

'Dom Léandre Fonteinne,' said the linguist.

'Yes,' nodded Captain Scully, 'that was him. How tall was he, do you think?'

'He was not tall,' said Louis, 'he was little.'

'Yes, yes,' said Scully, impatiently. Foreigners were impossible to deal with. 'But *how* little? Like this, or like this?' He offered two options. Louis shrugged and nodded at the latter.

'Right, so. I think what we have will be grand then. I have some longer ones cut but Helen was hoping for a table.'

The two Frenchmen looked at the cart and then one another to see if they had reached the same conclusion. A coffin was being loaded on the back of the cart.

'Is he dead?' enquired Fabrice, just to make sure.

'Yes,' said the Irishman, but then, seeing their Gallic faces drop, retreated from that firm position. 'Well, no, I don't know. Someone is. So the bush telegraph says, anyway. It could be wrong. It often is.'

'Speared?'

'Shot.'

'Shot?' Those wild Presbyterian shepherds, thought Fabrice. 'With a rifle?'

'Pistol,' said Captain Scully. 'Rosendo's, I presume.' The monk had brought from Spain an ornate ivory-stocked flintlock pistol, he explained. It was designed more for a duel with a love rival than hunting in the Australian bush, but Salvado had been practising on the local creatures.

Bob reappeared with a half-eaten jam scone. Fabrice introduced him to Captain Scully as 'their guide'.

'Your guide, is he?' said the host. 'Careful what he guides you into.'

'You know Bob, then?'

'Oh yes, Helen and I know Bob pretty well,' smiled Scully, not unkindly. It seemed to Fabrice Cleriquot that on Victoria Plains every clue contained within it another little mystery.

'I'm goin' with you to Badji,' said Bob with no hint of deference.

Only now did Fabrice realise why the boy had joined them: he wanted to see his Irish friend, Gorman.

When Helen appeared, Scully introduced her as his 'servant', but smiled and squeezed her intimately as he did so. Helen did not stand on formalities and, like Bob, she enjoyed teasing Frenchmen for sport. She was an inconspicuous but generous hostess, though unprepared for guests. A deep, hot bath was drawn and when the visitors emerged, the table was laden with an enormous lamb dinner with roast vegetables and red wine gravy.

In place of grace, their host bade them raise their glasses. 'To Bolgart, the farthest point from civilisation,' declared Scully. Once they had clinked glasses and said *sláinte*, he added, more seriously, 'I'm sorry about your friend, lads.' They should get an early night, he advised, for an uncertain day lay ahead of them and they would be setting off 'at sparrow's fart'.

'Captain,' asked Fabrice pensively, 'if there has been a death, should there not … should the police attend, perhaps?'

Scully smiled at the foreigner's naivety. 'Ideally they should, yes. This, however, is not an especially well-policed area. Victoria Plains barely exists as far as St Georges Terrace is concerned. If it's marked on their maps at all it is probably labelled *Terra Incognita*. We did have a chief constable here, a very effective one in fact, but he has not been rewarded by the government for his troubles.'

'Drummond?' said Fabrice.

Scully's smile melted away at this name, and he looked now at the Frenchman with suspicion. 'Yes,' he confirmed, his voice now slow and careful. 'I was indeed referring to Constable John Drummond. So who exactly have you been talking to, Mister ...' Suddenly names were of interest to Captain Scully.

'Cleriquot,' replied Fabrice. 'Mister Samuel Moore of Guildford mentioned some troubles that had occurred up here. His brother found the river, you know.'

'Oh, I know all about the older Moore brother, Mister Cleriquot. George Fletcher Moore is, you might say, my *bête noire.*'

Later, as they each disappeared into the darkness, the host pointed out the sign over the stone shed which read *VP Police*. 'That is Constable Drummond's station,' he explained. 'And, Mister Cleriquot, since you asked, don't worry yourself, I will see that the district magistrate comes along to Badji tomorrow.'

Next morning, the Frenchmen climbed aboard Captain Scully's cart. Once Helen had put in a heavy hamper of food supplies for the monks, there was no option for Fabrice and Louis but to sit on the makings of a coffin for their dear friend, Léandre Fonteinne. Two little ponies were hitched to the spring cart; Scully expected the going to be easy and flat and decided the bullocks wouldn't be needed. Bob opted to walk alongside, barefooted. He looked very handsome. Helen had made him have a hot bath the previous night and given him a new flannel shirt and pants, and in the pocket he had his own supply of jerky.

Everywhere was lush and green. They were in sheep country now. They saw a few lone fat ones, then the start of decent flocks, and then their first shepherd, who stared at them from a distance as if taking note. There was none of the expected exchange of pleasantries.

'Are we still on your land, captain?' asked Fabrice cautiously.

'Well, that is not the easy question it may seem,' replied the driver. 'Your friend Samuel Moore's wretched older brother holds the key to that one.'

'How so?'

'After three years in the district, I have yet to be afforded a depasturing lease.'

'So you are a squatter?'

'That's rather a pejorative a word for it, Mister Cleriquot. It is true that the government is yet to receive any revenue from me, but the grass grows free up here, so why should I pay for it?'

'That man back there, was he your shepherd?'

'A shepherd of my shepherd.'

'The Scots employ him?'

'Probably,' said Scully, growing wary. This Frenchman knew too much about other people's business. 'New ones keep appearing, each one younger and of worse character than the last.'

'Do the Scotsmen have leases?'

'Seems they may do,' said Scully, as if it pained him to say it. 'It's all up to the esteemed George Fletcher Moore, who doesn't seem to like me. I have just been told my salary is to be reduced. Moore will be behind that, somehow.'

'The government pays you to farm?' asked Fabrice.

'No,' barked Scully, 'of course not. They pay me to be the district magistrate. A hundred and fifty pounds per annum, currently. Moore feels I should do it for fifty.'

Behind him, the two Frenchmen looked at one another in surprise. Aside from being a pastoralist, coffin maker and wagon driver, was it possible that Scully was the district magistrate of Victoria Plains?

Sensing his passengers' disbelief, the driver reached back to grab a dusty leather satchel from under their feet. It bore the faded crest of the governor of the Swan River colony, and contained evidence of his official status – a leather-bound magistrate's notebook, a pencil and sharpening knife, as well as two-dozen heavy iron nails, suitable for hammering a large box together.

'Don't be fooled by all this green,' said the driver. 'It was not like this when my men dropped the Spaniards up here in February. The grass was dead, water was scarce and it was stinking hot. Stupid bloody time of year to try to get started.'

'Their lease did not have a water supply on it?' asked Fabrice.

'Well,' said Scully, hesitating. He forced a little laugh. 'There was a bit of confusion about exactly where their leasehold was.'

'Your servants took the missionaries to the wrong place?'

'Possibly.'

'Where they had no water?'

'Well, no water that they could get to without a bit of a fight.'

'They had to fight the natives, you mean? Or the shepherds?'

'Both, I expect. It would have been thirsty work for the Spanish lads, no doubt.'

Bob walked most of the distance alongside the cart, chewing and thinking.

'What do the local people call this place?' Fabrice asked him.

Bob shrugged. 'I dunno,' he mumbled. 'Nothin'. Just, *boodja*. They walk on it every day.' Bob appeared unusually thoughtful; worrying about the fate of his friend Gorman, so Fabrice presumed. He was wrong.

'You got to pay me now, Frenchy,' said Bob, a surprising interruption. 'Three days guiding at four shillings a day.' He climbed aboard now, palm up. 'Twelve shillings.'

'Three days?' asked Fabrice. 'We only left Toodyay yesterday morning.'

'I got to get home yet,' explained the mathematician.

Inside his jacket, Fabrice still had a few coins which had escaped drowning in the Avon, and he handed an approximate number to Bob, whose lips moved silently as he counted. It was too much. He mistrusted good fortune but shrugged and pocketed the money.

'That Parkhurst fella is a thief,' he advised Fabrice. 'Goes in your worm cage when you gone.'

Fabrice shrugged. With half of Pauline Jaricot's money now at the bottom of the Avon, the few *sous* Eric might have pilfered seemed to matter little.

They were now getting pretty close to Badji, Scully advised, at which information Bob jumped swiftly out of the cart and disappeared into the bush. Leaping across raging rivers was no challenge for this boy, but he greatly feared what he might see at that mission. He would watch and listen from a distance and perhaps take a look at things when it suited him, not a moment before.

Fabrice felt an urge to do exactly the same. It was shameful to admit, but in his thirty-two years, Professor Cleriquot had never encountered death. He tried to prepare himself to calmly accept whatever lay ahead. His feet were resting upon the timber for his friend's coffin. His beloved Léandre was dead, and when they got to the mission, Fabrice may be forced to look at his lifeless face.

Badji Badji wasn't much, just a rough hut in a clearing fringed by white gums. Someone else had just arrived. A bullock had been tethered to a tree where it was enjoying the new green shoots and near it was a rough sled made out of branches from the bush. There was no wagon to be seen. A large man was standing alone with his back to them, leaning on the largest tree.

Scully pulled the ponies up a respectful distance behind the fellow and called out something in Gaelic. He turned around, unsmiling; a familiar face, but not a friendly one. Terry Farrelly had somehow managed to get up to the mission ahead of them.

Farrelly dusted his hands sadly as he walked across to Scully. The two men clasped arms and spoke together in low tones in their own tongue. The linguist could understand barely a word the Irishmen exchanged – there had never been a reason to learn Gaelic – but confidences were being exchanged: short, serious sentences. Heads were shaken slowly. Scully patted his countryman on the shoulder as if in consolation, then Farrelly pointed toward the hut where two bearded men could be seen standing, one in a black robe, the other in dungarees.

Fabrice and Louis remained on the cart, quiet and seemingly invisible to Farrelly. Scully came back to them, explaining nothing. As quietly as he could, he geed the ponies a few steps so they could feed on the long grass at the base of the trees. There was going to be a wait, he said.

'What is happening?' asked Fabrice. The Irishmen had talked a lot and Scully must have learned about the fate of their friend Léandre.

'That's Salvado and Serra up ahead,' whispered Captain Scully eventually, as if at a funeral. 'They are trying to summon the courage to go inside the hut.'

The Frenchmen watched from the spring cart, hushed as if at the theatre. The hut was a forlorn structure, seemingly built from whatever materials the monks had retrieved from previous camps or could find locally. Outside it, the two Spanish appeared to hover like mystical beings.

A piece of bush timber had been wedged across the entrance, perhaps in an attempt to keep the dogs out. There was a pair of boots outside. Were they Léandre's? whispered Fabrice. Surprising nobody had stolen them.

The two monks on this gruesome stage were strong, practical men. They had seen death in Spain, even the death of confrères. They must know exactly what now needed to be done, Fabrice thought, but seemed unable to bring themselves to do it. Someone had to enter the hut and face Léandre's tragedy.

Salvado walked back to Farrelly to retrieve his cassock and sandals. Now both dressed in reverential black, the monks chanted a sad *Te Deum*, then paused together in silence, or else continued to chant so softly it could not be heard from the cart. Then they again adopted a pose of prayer, and stood together silently, then prayed aloud.

'*Jésus*,' whispered Fabrice harshly, 'just open it!' The district magistrate knocked him sharply with his knee.

Finally, Salvado shook his head, shrugged, and could be heard to utter a single word to his superior. '*Vamos.*'

'They will find a corpse in there, and it will be high,' whispered Captain Scully, clearly in possession of knowledge he did not deign to share. He blessed himself and the Frenchmen followed.

Salvado walked alone to the door of the hut, while Serra stayed and stared upwards towards the canopy of a nearby gum tree, suppressing all emotion. Salvado pulled on the flimsy timber barricade causing the whole door to come away from the rough frame. Averting his eyes from whatever lay within, he leaned it neatly against the brush bough wall.

The hut was finally open. Even from the cart the Frenchmen could hear a terrible buzzing noise coming from within.

Salvado paused one last time, lowered his head in silence, blessed himself, inhaled deeply and disappeared into the darkness.

The roof of the hut was not quite high enough for Salvado to stand upright. He stooped in the doorway, motionless, observing what had to be observed. The Frenchmen held their breath in sympathy, imagining the terrible thing that the monk was seeing: the week-old body of their confrère, dead by pistol shot.

'Dear God,' said Louis, feeling the reality sweeping over him, 'our beloved Léandre is dead.'

'He must have shot himself in despair,' whispered Fabrice. 'He was so very frightened of the bush.' The two Frenchmen again blessed themselves and cupped hands together.

Salvado remained in the darkness for a few minutes. The men on the cart thought they heard him praying or chanting, but it could have been weeping.

When he emerged, Salvado walked a dozen brisk steps away into the mild sunshine to Dom Serra, where he stopped as if to gather himself. He inhaled deeply, and could be seen to shudder. A few short words were exchanged.

It was now Serra's duty to enter the hut, but again he hesitated. Salvado followed him to the doorway and placed a brotherly hand upon the shoulder of his superior. Dom Serra did not quite enter but looked briefly inside the doorway, then walked away wailing like an animal in pain.

Terry Farrelly's reaction was much the same, though his pain louder and unconcealed. Some sort of Gaelic curse was uttered as he emerged and then the big man strode towards Scully's cart, head down purposefully.

The Frenchmen braced themselves for the news. In life, Dom Léandre Fonteinne had doubtless been an annoyance to many people, but he had a tender heart and had been a dear and loved friend.

'Right,' sighed Scully, jumping down from the cart, 'I have work to do. Grab me my satchel, would you.' The district magistrate strode off in the direction of the deceased, ignoring Terry Farrelly as they passed.

The Frenchmen were suddenly the focus of all Farrelly's attention. He swung upon them so closely they could feel his heart pounding. 'Have you seen your friend yet?' he choked. His face was red with rage or grief and so close he sprayed them with spittle.

'No!' said Fabrice Cleriquot, his chest rising in indignation, for he had expected commiseration on their loss, not this violence. 'We are not quite ready to see him.'

'Fool!' thundered *La Terreur*, more spittle flying. 'I am asking you, have you seen that murderous little shite, Fonteinne? Where the hell has he got to?'

Fabrice could not comprehend the meaning.

'Léandre?' said Louis. 'He ... he is alive, you say?'

'Sadly, yes,' said Farrelly. 'Unless he has fallen off a cliff and been eaten by the dogs. I beg Our Lord's forgiveness but I hope he has. Save me the trouble. If I were to see that little bastard right now, I confess he would not be alive for long.' And now the big man with the face of a failed show-fighter sobbed aloud and without shame.

Fabrice was now struck by the meaning of all this. 'You mean to say Léandre has ... he is not dead? He has killed the poor catechist?'

'Yes!' blurted Farrelly, distressed to hear the tragedy stated aloud and clearly for the first time. 'Your mad little friend has blown the top off poor John Gorman's head.' He coughed the last words and then the wailing became awful.

Fabrice could not believe what he was hearing. 'Suicide?' he suggested, without much conviction.

'The pistol is missing,' said The Terror. There was silence from the pony cart as the Frenchmen considered this evidence.

'*Un accident, peut-être*?' suggested Louis, softly, to no one in particular.

'Find that damned novice!' instructed Farrelly. 'We have a friendly magistrate here. There is the reputation of the diocese to think of. If Fonteinne is not found it will be much harder to resolve this problem quietly.'

The Frenchmen caught each other's eye, neither one knowing what to think. That their eccentric friend was, after all their days of worry, still alive, was surely a cause for celebration. But also, he stood accused of murder.

The Irishman, though full of rage, made a great effort in parting to soften his voice. 'If you do find him, lads, please, for God's sake do not let him anywhere near me for I greatly fear what I might do.'

The district magistrate inspected the tragedy in brief instalments. Frequently he staggered out into the fresh air to breathe, compose himself and to make forensic notes in his leather-bound notebook. In his secondary rôle as carpenter, Scully sized up the corpse, and frowned. Gorman was almost six foot. It would be a tight fit. He called Louis and Fabrice over to assist with the body. They had come all this way promising to help, he said. It was time they did so.

Fabrice forced himself over the threshold just as he had seen the others do. Inside the hut it was dark and hot and smelt of death. The cruel Western Australian sun shot in like a dagger, illuminating the green woollen socks of the dead man. The Irishman's feet were still crossed and his hands were behind his head, as if he were yawning.

It looked as if John Gorman was stretching out, relaxing, his head resting against a flour sack pillow when shot once, point blank, in the middle of the forehead. Talking, thought Fabrice. Gorman was Irish and they all liked to make a point. Now John Gorman's earthly body was a gruesome thing, the lower half in such natural repose, his head aswarm with bushflies.

Léandre must have been sitting directly opposite Gorman in this tiny hut, in the place where Fabrice now squatted. In what frame of mind had he been when he did this terrible thing? Angry? Frightened? Or had he simply been cleaning Dom Salvado's pistol and been careless? Any one of those seemed possible of Léandre Fonteinne.

With patterned silk scarves protecting their mouths and noses from the flies and stench, Fabrice Cleriquot and Louis Langoulant helped the district magistrate move poor John Gorman out of the shed to a spot under the trees. He was as stiff as a fallen branch and bent in the middle from dying while sitting up.

Bob could be seen watching the melancholy scene from a safe distance at the edge of the bush. The boy would recognise the green socks, thought Fabrice. Gorman had a bunch of them, knitted by his sisters, he had once laughingly explained, so that he would always be standing on Irish green.

Fabrice covered Gorman's face from the flies and The Terror kissed his friend's cheek for the last time through the silk shroud. Dom Serra, calmer now, came near to the body and looked at his own feet and recited some words in Latin, soothed by the repetition of long-memorised words.

The district magistrate made notes. He must have forgotten some detail of the head wound, for without notice he pulled back the shroud, at which moment Serra happened to look up, breaking his fragile calm. His voice broke and the Frenchmen, themselves still shaken from moving the corpse, saw the monk's shoulders jerk as he collapsed to the ground in grief.

José Serra stayed there kneeling. 'This mission has been damned by God,' he cried aloud, his voice full of anger mixed with grief.

Then, '*Se acabó*,' wept the superior of the Central Mission, his tears falling on the soft sand of Victoria Plains. It is all over.

From: Ursula Frayne, Perth
To: Cecilia Marmion, Baggot Street, Dublin

10th June 1846

My ever dearest Rev. Mother

After five months in this country I have been appraising our work in light of the three Objects of our Congregation: Education, Visiting the Sick, and Protecting Poor Women of Good Character.

As regards teaching, I aim for three schools – one for the rich, one for the poor, and one for the natives. So far we can claim some modest success in the first, though all but one of the children are Protestant. The absence of funds greatly limits our work with the poor. All the Catholics here are poor as mice, including our bishop, so who will fund it?

As for the natives, one cannot even make a start on the parents. What we really need is to get some little black girls from the bush. They would have to come to us at a young age for we must have them from the beginning.

I hope to get some from the missionaries, and the Spanish are our only hope. I have asked Dom Salvado if he might bring a little orphan girl back to us each time he comes down. I told Salvado, the younger the better, before they are set in their wild ways. It is just a matter of convincing the mothers of the benefits of giving them into our care.

Afterwards, it would be best I think that they be shielded from the parents, except for the shortest of visits. If they can be made to forget their native language they will be less inclined to try to rejoin their people, which would risk undoing all the work we have done on their behalf. Such are the necessary cruelties, for the orphans will no doubt by nature want to see their mothers again.

As regards visiting the sick, little Baptist O'Donnell comes with me each week to the hospital and the prison. Bishop Brady keeps pressing me to profess her, his real interest lying no doubt in the two hundred pounds that Baptist's brother promised to donate upon her profession. But she is not ready, and I told him so.

His Lordship persisted so I confess I went a little further. Forgive me, Mother, but I reminded His Lordship of the contract he signed not to interfere with our Order's Rules and Customs. Then the real shenanigans began. Even the Jesuits give up their customs when abroad on Missions, he roars, and so must we Sisters of Mercy. I said it would have been better had he mentioned these strong views before we all came to this place and not signed a written agreement knowing he would never act upon it.

The effect of these words upon him was rather frightening, Mother. Were he not a bishop I would have called him enraged. He said it was the greatest insult I could offer any man and that I was not to approach Holy Communion until I did penance. So for two days I was excommunicated.

In temperament, I would say His Lordship is more French than Irish. A true Irish bishop would never have spoken thus to a Mother Superior. It was all very upsetting to me, and I was trembling for some time afterwards, and even now still as I recount it. He repented next day, of course, coming round bearing gifts and was all sweetness and I am permitted again to receive Communion.

I would be grateful for your advice Mother as you are much wiser while I seem to be a provoker of things, though I really do not mean to. Is it all due to a lack of Humility on my part, Mother?

Begging a fervent prayer. Farewell dearest Rev. Mother, be assured of the heartfelt gratitude and affection of your fondly attached child in J.C.

Sr. Mary Ursula

12. A FUNERAL

When a man is shot dead in a remote place in the Western Australian bush, there are many practical matters to be taken care of in a short time. In the case of John Gorman at Badji Badji these tasks were welcome for they distracted each man from his personal grief. There were official reports to be made for the colonial secretary and the governor, a coffin to be assembled, a hole to be dug, a funeral ceremony to be arranged, and a hut to be dissembled, for this accursed place was to be abandoned.

Also, there was a French novice to be found.

'What shall we do, Louis?' said Fabrice Cleriquot, feeling useless amidst all the activity. 'Leave the camp to find Léandre or stay here and help Captain Scully with the body?'

'The body is busy enough,' said Louis. Scully, Farrelly, Serra and Salvado in their various capacities were all fussing over Gorman's mortal remains. 'Let's go and find poor Léandre.'

'We don't know this country,' protested Fabrice. 'We will get ourselves lost for sure.'

'He won't have gone far. Let's look along the riverbed. We can't get lost there. It's just one way there, one way back.'

So the two Frenchmen set off to search for their missing friend. Louis was wrong, it was quite possible to get lost because the river here was serpentine and in places split into a series of grass-edged creeks narrow enough to leap or wade across. There were many places for someone who didn't want to be found to hide from sight. For two hours they walked and waded and jumped and shouted out to the missing novice, trying to coax him out.

'C'est nous, Léandre!' they called. 'N'aie pas peur!'

'We'll never find him,' proclaimed Fabrice eventually. 'He may have taken off days ago.'

'Where could he possibly go?' said Louis. 'To the north it's wilderness until Champion Bay. To the east is desert. And he would not dare head back to Perth for fear of running into the bishop. He will still be nearby, I feel sure. I would bet the silly boy is listening to us now, even watching us, too scared to come out. We must reassure him.'

'Léandre,' they called, over and over, 'tu peux sortir!'

But by midday they had still found no trace of the novice so they trudged back to camp with hopes fading. Salvado's pistol had gone missing from the hut. Léandre must have taken it when he fled. Neither man would say it aloud, but both had imagined finding their friend slumped against the base of a blood-stained white gum.

The local people had started to reappear at the mission, attracted by all the activity and the promise of fresh provisions. There was a wiry, bearded older man, a few skinny children wrestling with one another, and two young mothers carrying babies.

A sort of normality seemed to have returned. The Frenchmen sat down with Salvado for a smoke and a billy tea and they talked about other less difficult things. The monk reassured them that, despite this disaster, life would go on and the mission would survive. He introduced them to the bearded fellow, whom he called N'yalbinga, 'a very reliable fellow'. N'yalbinga had seen Léandre Fonteinne, according to the Galician.

'What did he say to you, exactly,' said the linguist, dubiously.

'*On Lean, n'agna ciena, iei coli*,' said Dom Salvado. 'It means: I have seen Léandre, and he is on his way now.'

It seemed to Fabrice that N'yalbinga's words had been Latinised as they passed through the monk. So the professor addressed him directly, trying to piece together a sentence from the words he possessed. Had he *really* seen the little French monk?

N'yalbinga pointed back down to the place where they had just spent three fruitless hours. 'Yeah, I seen them blokes down there,' he replied, unhurried, in English, for it transpired that he had befriended a few *wadjalas*, farmers and police officers and shepherds. 'Plenty of 'em,' he added, nodding at the river. Fabrice remained unconvinced – they were not searching for 'plenty' of novices, just the one – but it was a clue, of sorts, where they had no others.

N'yalbinga was enjoying the attention. He indicated that a mug of sweet, milky tea would be very welcome. He was aged at least thirty, Fabrice guessed, tall and thin, and with a bearing suggesting he was accustomed to receiving respect. He was barefoot, but partly in colonial dress, with long pants and a fleecy jacket in place of a *booka*.

Salvado insisted the Frenchmen should trust his friend's word. He gave N'yalbinga a pinch of tobacco, which went straight in the jacket pocket for later use, and a mug of tea which he sipped at thoughtfully as he wandered off toward the remains of the hut. Salvado watched with interest as N'yalbinga walked around the structure seeming to observe things carefully, all the while keeping one eye on the location of the corpse for fear of bumping into it. The dead man's boots were of particular interest.

'He is checking the soles, I think, to match the prints to those he may find in the riverbed,' explained Salvado. Then the tracker walked away, staring for a while at nothing in particular, then shook out the remains of his cold tea. When he returned, he had an important question for Salvado.

'Can I have them boots, Father?'

'No,' Salvado told N'yalbinga, 'they belong to the deceased. But what about *Lean*, the little monk. Can you tell us where he is?'

'That *mamara* he's down there,' grumbled N'yalbinga, clearly annoyed about the matter of the boots. He waved a hand vaguely at the riverbed; that's where the dwarf man was.

After another hour or so, N'yalbinga reluctantly took off in the direction of the river and the Frenchmen followed him without much confidence. The leader of the search party was sighing and moaning a lot, complaining about his feet and how good it would be to have a decent pair of boots for this sort of terrain. Four skinny children had joined in the search but were not taking the task seriously. Every so often Fabrice asked the tracker the same question.

'You really saw him?'

'Little hairy fella,' said their guide, the description causing the Frenchmen's hearts to rise and then added, 'he got a goat on a string.' And sure enough, they saw there were ungulate prints in the river mud. Next, they heard the sound of a goat and then the voice of Léandre berating the goat for giving him away.

There was a white man sitting on the far bank, facing away.

He was hairy and dishevelled, but there was no doubting it was a feral Léandre Fonteinne. When he saw them approaching, he jolted upright like a hare spying hunters. Louis waded through the mud and grabbed him, the runaway schoolboy gone wild. Léandre whimpered for a while and then started talking.

'I had to rescue the goat,' he explained. 'It ran off.'

Then, 'Has he died, the Irish boy? He was getting weak after the accident. His skull was broken, I think. I was going for help to Mister Scully of Bolgart or to find the Scottish shepherds but it was raining and I would have got lost again in the dark so I went back to the hut.'

'Slow, Léandre,' said Louis, stroking the novice's matted hair. Louis was the one the little fellow trusted most. 'Scully is here with us. He is the local judge, and a friend of the mission.' The children came and took the goat away by its rope, a great game for them. Some brandy was found for the novice. 'Tell us your story, slowly, and then we can tell him in English.'

'*Un accident,*' blubbed the accused.

'Of course. But how?'

'Well …' The novice exhaled and sat up. He could see now that he was going to be believed, and loved Louis deeply for this, brushing his cheek against the fisherman's jacket.

'My beloved Father Superior, Dom Serra and my dear brother Dom Salvado left me all alone in the bush with the fine young Irishman. That they left us with no provisions caused no resentment in the two of us since it was our duty to sustain the mission. When we ran out of food, the natives lost all interest in Christianity, so the Irishman and I were quite alone in the desert but still we lived together in perfect peace, working hard and each day singing the praises of God and following St Benedict's rules.

'On Sunday after prayers the Irishman said he had a headache and I told him to rest up. I offered him a cup of tea. He asked if I had any sugar. I told him, no, we have no sugar. So he said, I do not drink tea without sugar. So I went out hunting and captured an eagle.'

'An eagle?' said Louis.

'Yes. It was well fattened, like chicken or rabbit and the claws can be chewed, but one must be careful.' His French audience nodded their heads as credulously as they could manage. 'Also I captured a small creature they call a *budi*.'

'You shot one?' asked Louis. 'Are they not fast runners?'

'Not run, leap. But I shot it right here, between ...' He stopped, sensing that to boast of his marksmanship might be incriminating. 'Very often, I miss.'

'The accident,' said Fabrice, resting a reassuring hand on the novice's fat hairy leg.

'I had been out hunting when a black cloud burst right above me and let out a torrent of water, so I returned to the hut.

'When I got back the Irishman was asleep, lying on his mattress with his head against a pillow. I went to clean the gun with a towel as it had got wet from the rain. Then the Irishman startled me by suddenly speaking when I thought him asleep. What was the time? About twelve, I answered, and at that moment the gun went off by itself and through no fault of mine.

'He uttered a terrible *Ah!* noise which will forever resound in my poor ears, and then he leaned to one side. Blood was pouring out in great gushes from a wound on his forehead. Poor me, the whole blast had lodged in the head of my unfortunate friend, knocking off the top of his head and scattering his brains. I called to him but he didn't answer me. I flung myself on my knees beside him and asked

God for forgiveness for so involuntary a crime.'

The fugitive monk paused for breath. Louis looked at Fabrice for guidance.

'Léandre,' asked Louis, gently, 'tell me, why did you hide?'

The little fellow's lip curled and then his face tightened and he howled as if in pain. 'I was frightened, Louis. Very frightened! I did not know what to do. I wanted to go to Captain Scully but it was still raining. I left the hut and hammered the door shut and put his boots outside to keep the wild dogs from getting to his corpse and then I didn't know where to go so I came here.'

'Dom Salvado's pistol?'

'Here it is.'

'Why did you keep it?'

'To catch food. And to keep away the wild dogs. They howl at night, Louis. Oh, how I hate the bush.'

They took Léandre back to camp. The first to spot him was Terry Farrelly, from a safe distance away, up on the hill, where he was digging a hole for Gorman. *La Terreur* stood stock-still, shovel on ground, following the novice with unblinking eyes.

'Keep him away from me,' the Irishman bellowed in a voice more pained than angry.

Bob showed no such restraint. When he spied the murderer of his friend he shot out from under the trees and ran straight at Léandre with eyes full of rage. He pushed the novice to the ground, grabbed his throat and punched him in his howling face – once, twice, three times – then hovered above his whimpering victim, watching impassively as the murderer's face grew purple.

Louis spoke softly to the boy, rubbed his shoulder and gently coaxed his hands off Léandre's neck. The novice sat up and coughed and spluttered until his breath returned. A tooth had gone through his lower lip.

Dom Serra came over in unhurried manner, hands in cloak, and looked upon the bloodied face of his confrère without pity. The superior of the mission did not directly acknowledge his novice but instructed Louis and Fabrice to take him off to the edge of the camp, well away from Farrelly.

There the three Frenchmen sat together quietly, Léandre still sniffling blood and looking about the camp warily. He saw that the hut had been pulled apart, opening his sins to the sunlight, and he saw the coffin on the back of Scully's dray.

'They will try to blame me, I think,' he said sadly.

The district magistrate came across to the French camp with his government satchel, a notebook and pencils. He had to interrogate the accused, he explained. But Léandre had lost all capacity to speak English, so it was left to the two Frenchmen to relay his account while the novice stared unhappily at his own dirty feet.

'Right, well, let's go with that then,' concluded Scully, to no one in particular. 'I shall issue a report to the governor.' He returned his notebook to his satchel, which was lighter now that all the iron nails were in the coffin. 'I'll let Serra know they can bury him.' He gave no indication how his letter to the governor might conclude and the Frenchmen could not guess from his manner; it was always hard to tell with the Irish, with all their fake bonhomie.

At sundown, the Irish catechist John Gorman, having escaped famine in his homeland, went deep into the ground in the remote bush of Victoria Plains. He wore his green socks but was bootless.

Terry Farrelly had chosen a dry place for him, well above the waterline, to avoid his being washed into the river should a bank subside in flood, and in case they should want to relocate him to a better gravesite at a later time.

It drizzled throughout the funeral. Four skinny local boys were pallbearers, chattering and laughing as they performed their funereal duties barefoot on slippery, uneven ground. Behind the wobbling coffin, the sad cortege walked mournfully. The monks, in black surplices and stoles, chanted their *Kyries*. After them, where usually would walk the catechist, came Bob bearing the cross and holy water. He looked solemn without trying. The deceased had been a good friend to Bob and they used to laugh at the same things.

As they reached the gravesite, a vivid sunset appeared, poetic in its symbolism of ending and renewal. A Benedictine funeral ceremony is a long thing, but the attention of the pallbearers was short. Having dropped the coffin beside the hole, the four boys clamoured for their reward from Salvado, who was known to keep treasure hidden in the pockets of his mysterious black cloak. Successful, they ran off to eat.

Absent was Dom Léandre Fonteinne, who remained down at the camp, alone. He had been asked by Salvado to stack the rest of the salvaged timbers on Scully's dray, and was doing so in very slow and meditative manner. Once the coffin had been lowered into the ground, Salvado went down, put an arm around the novice's shoulder and steered him up for the Office of the Dead. It was dark now and he sat Dom Léandre at the back, where Serra and Farrelly could pretend not to see him.

Afterwards, things grew more relaxed. There was whiskey and The Terror led the singing. He thanked Louis and Fabrice for their assistance, embracing them tearfully and with great feeling. They went across to sit with their miserable friend.

'Would you lead us in prayer, Léandre?' Louis said quietly, his hand gently upon the novice's shoulder.

Léandre trembled at the thought. 'I can't pray today, Louis. I have forgotten how. Let Fabrice do it.'

Fabrice had not yet learned any Pantheist prayers, was not even sure if such a thing existed, but he recalled something Epicurean from Roger Smith's library which he thought might sound nice if rendered in Latin.

'Non fui,' he began, and allowed a long pause. 'Fui. Non sum. Non curo.'

There was a prolonged silence.

'C'est tout?' whispered Louis.

'Oh,' said Fabrice, thankful for the prompt. 'Amen.'

'Amen,' said the other two, thinking their own thoughts.

'A very short prayer,' Louis whispered.

'At first, I was not,' explained Fabrice. 'Then, for a time, I was. Now, again I am not. It doesn't matter.'

'Such a lovely prayer!' said Léandre, who had managed to acquire a whiskey despite La Terreur. 'I feel better now,' he added, 'though I miss my late Irish friend so very much.'

Later, a stranger appeared from the darkness and startled Dom Léandre. He was a rough-looking fellow, bearded, and armed, but with slow deliberate movements, as if accustomed to being in control. The stranger sat on his haunches beside Léandre, looked curiously at him, and put a finger to the novice's lips to ensure he stayed quiet.

When the surprise was sprung, it seemed the visitor was known to every mourner except the Frenchmen. It was John Drummond, of whom Sam Moore had spoken, the constable who had taken retribution for his brother's spearing and had since been hiding in the bush. Once he came into the firelight, it could be seen that he still wore his police shirt, though it was much the worse for having been slept in under the stars.

John Drummond embraced Terry Farrelly for a full minute. The policeman said he understood the Irishman's grief, for the loss of his own dear brother was still raw. He offered his condolences to the two Spanish monks for the loss of their brother missionary. Then the police officer drew the district magistrate aside.

'It's official,' Fabrice heard him telling Scully. 'I'm back on the force. Docked a few quid a year, that's all.'

The two lawmen then retreated into the shadows and spoke seriously for a long while, with occasional glances toward the novice. There could be no doubt what they were discussing. The novice sat alone and motionless, a disgraced child awaiting his corporal penalty. Fabrice sat with Louis on the far side of the fire and tried to read his friend's fate from the men's gestures, but it was impossible to tell for sure, as they were Australian bush types and spoke in a flat tone with their hands in their pockets and eyes to the ground.

Eventually, Scully and Drummond shook hands and returned to the group. It seemed a determination had been made in the matter of the death of John Gorman. The constable whistled loudly for attention. The Frenchmen froze.

'When the hell are you going to feed me, Rosendo?' was Drummond's only proclamation. 'I've been eating like a blackfellow for a month.'

They all pulled in close to the fire to eat. Salvado had roasted the mission goat, together with the last of the mission's sweet potatoes and runner beans. St Benedict did not encourage the eating of red meat, observed Serra, but surely even he would have enjoyed this splendid meal. They toasted the deceased. Attracted by the smell of the stew and the firelight, the pallbearers reappeared, four skinny bottoms squeezed onto a single log, along with N'yalbinga and a few other parishioners who had drifted in from the bush.

The children were scared of the dark. In the really dark parts deep in the bush, there could be hairy *woordatji* who liked to grab kids and hide them away from their parents. They were laughing as they said it, but serious too. It was too great a temptation for Louis, who grabbed the biggest one and carried him out into the darkness, from where he ran straight back to his mates by the fireside, screaming with laughter. To be fair to all the pallbearers, the abduction had to repeated three times.

It was much later in the night, and only by accident, that the Frenchmen learned of the magistrate's decision. Fabrice managed to hear Scully explaining the verdict to Serra and Salvado, who looked greatly relieved.

The death of John Gorman had been an accident.

'It was not your fault, Léandre,' Fabrice whispered, embracing his friend. 'You are free.'

'*Bien sûr* it was not my fault!' snapped the novice, wounded by the implication it could be otherwise. 'Didn't I tell you? I have been the victim of a terrible misfortune. And did you notice, Dom Serra has no pity for me, none at all! I have twice asked him to hear my Confession so I can be relieved of my burden, but he ignores me. I shall write to my abbot of it.'

Some holy wine was found, and there followed some sad Irish

singing from The Terror, and many sweet tears for the deceased. There was an informal eulogy. John Gorman had been a very good man, wept Farrelly, and was already greatly missed. Letters would have to be written back home. The bishop would do it, knowing as he did all the families of the catechists.

'It looks like you're finished here,' said John Drummond to the monks.

'Yes,' confirmed Serra. 'We will move back to Perth where I have reserved some land. It will be called New Subiaco, after the place in Italy where St Benedict formed our first community.'

'But we shall also maintain a mission here, for the natives,' added Salvado. The matter had not yet been properly discussed between them and it was wrong of Serra to imply otherwise. 'Dom Serra and I solemnly committed to this mission many years ago when we were together at the abbey at Cava, near Naples, and we are men of our word.' He saw Serra stiffen. It was not proper to have this discussion in public. 'It will be named New Norcia,' Salvado added, 'after the birthplace of St Benedict.'

The bushman looked between the two monks with some amusement. 'So, where is your New Norcia to be located?'

'That is a question,' sighed Salvado, 'to which I do not yet have an answer.' The existing mission was neatly stacked on Scully's dray. They could not keep moving every few months. Each move consumed their energies and each collapse weakened their resolve. Here at Badji Badji they had planted vines, fruit trees and vegetables, even built a chicken coop, but while they were away in Perth, wild horses had got in. What they didn't ruin, the goat had eaten.'

The constable went quiet for a while, wondering whether he should make a particular offer of assistance. 'We have an outstation a few miles from here,' said John Drummond, eventually. 'It has a little hut. It would get you started at least. There is pretty good water all year nearby at Maurin Pool.'

Salvado's heart leapt. He knew of this property but would never have dared ask, knowing it was the place where the policeman's younger brother Johnston had lived. 'What of the Scots?' he asked, to disguise his elation. 'Will they dispute the water?'

'I think not,' said Drummond. 'My father has run sheep there since forty-one. And anyway, there has been some family news this week. It seems my sister Euphemia has got engaged to old Ewen Macintosh. So I suppose we are now all one family.' He did not look especially happy about the match. Nor did Scully, who sat up as if to sniff the winds of politics. The Presbyterians were grouping against him.

'Why did you not take the missionaries there in the first place?' asked Fabrice Cleriquot, and they all fell stony silent. Perhaps, he thought, it was his French accent, unpopular on this mournful evening, or perhaps he had said aloud what others had been thinking. 'Why did you not take the monks to this Maurin Pool, with its hut and its lovely water. Might it not have saved them a lot of trouble?'

'My brother had not yet been murdered,' explained Constable John Drummond. 'He required it still.'

Fabrice fell silent.

'I'll take you there myself tomorrow,' said Drummond, recovering from the impertinent Frenchman. 'It's not too far. Three or four hours allowing for mud. We will be there before dinner.'

The next morning was a new beginning. It had been a freezing night and there was frost and their breath smoked above their mugs. A cold night meant a cloudless day, or so declared Bob.

Everything had somehow disarranged itself overnight. Plans had to be remade. Three groups were departing Badji Badji in different directions: one returning east to Bolgart, one retracing its tracks south to the river crossing, and one heading across the Moore to found New Norcia.

Captain Scully left first, keen to submit his official reports 'before the wrong version of this event gets broadcast.' With the coffin gone he no longer needed the cart, so he and Drummond agreed to swap transportation. Scully took Constable Drummond's excellent black police horse, while the constable was given the whip for Scully's ponies and cart.

Bob chose to return to Bolgart with Scully.

'Will you not come with us to New Norcia?' coaxed Salvado, who saw great prospects in this intelligent native lad. 'We will educate you, and I know you would be of great assistance to us.'

'Nah,' said Bob, and hopped nimbly behind Scully for the ride home, his arm round the magistrate's waist, the government satchel slung round his neck. He wore green socks.

Farrelly had to return to the crossing at Walyunga to try to retrieve the supplies they had abandoned in their haste to get up to Badji Badji. They had tried the direct route, avoiding Toodyay. At the Avon, Salvado decided to unyoke the two oxen and force them across the river by application of a flaming torch to their switches. One did manage to get across but the other was last seen struggling downstream deep in foam. The new wagon Salvado had bought with the proceeds of the piano concert was left stranded on the far side and any provisions that they could not carry across were hidden nearby. There would be work for a week or two; firstly getting back to the river on foot with one bullock, then searching along the river for the lost beast, getting the dray and all the stores across the Avon, and then getting it all up to the new mission.

Louis and Fabrice felt obliged to help the Irishman. Since the funeral, they had grown almost fond of *La Terreur*, who they had discovered was sentimental enough to be a Frenchman. Farrelly gratefully accepted their offer. 'I do not hold you lads responsible for your countryman,' he declared.

A new fellow arrived from the bush and was embraced warmly by Salvado. 'Bilyagoro has been sent to us by God,' he told Farrelly, his arm proudly around the man's shoulders. 'Take him with you. He has rescued me more than once when I was lost on that track.' Bilyagoro was lauded as the mission's most loyal man and best guide. He had originally been brought to Salvado with his skinny legs all covered in sores from which he was expected to die. Every day, Salvado had cleaned and dressed the wounds, and within six weeks Bilyagoro was cured and expressing, by way of gratitude, his intention to kill six men in the event that the monk should ever die. Salvado asked instead that the patient merely commit to using his new strong legs for the benefit of the mission.

As Farrelly, the Frenchmen and Bilyagoro departed on foot, droving the lone surviving bullock, there was a final addition. Dom Salvado had acquired a skinny little girl whom he had dressed in a singlet cut short to make a slip. He placed the child on the shoulders of Louis Langoulant, where it seemed quite happy. 'Take this to Sister Ursula,' he said. 'Tell her I found it abandoned and starving, digging for yams. It will brighten her day.'

The party destined for New Norcia were the last to head off, packing and repacking Scully's cart and deciding who would carry what.

Constable John Drummond was to be their guide across the Moore River to the family's old outstation; a place already sacred in his mind for it was at the outstation that he had last seen his younger brother Johnston alive.

Salvado encouraged the local people to join in this pilgrimage, if only for the promise of an easy feed. Without the local people, Salvado told N'yalbinga, the monks would have no mission. Also, they needed extra hands, for there were many smaller things to be carried, including an angry caged cat which Farrelly had seen fit to carry across the Avon in flood.

The policeman kept his rifle on top of the building materials where he could easily reach it. The territory they were travelling across was perfectly safe, he assured Serra. He knew all the native people around here, and was on 'mostly friendly' terms with them. 'But you never quite know,' he added.

As the group started to move off, Léandre Fonteinne stood alone like a new boy at school. He approached his superior for instructions. Was he permitted?

'Come,' said Dom Serra, and did not speak again to the novice until they reached New Norcia late that afternoon.

A dozen or so of the local people walked with the Benedictines, with extras coming or going as interest in the project waned. This walk was nothing to them, explained N'yalbinga. This was their *boodja* and they knew every part of it, especially this river, which was really the track of the great serpent that made all things in ancient times – every water pool and the land and hills and springs either side of it. They were happy walking on their land, and proud to show it to the black-cloaked monks, who they could tell had no chance of surviving if left by themselves.

N'yalbinga however was not happy about the presence of Constable John Drummond or his rifle. He knew Drummond had killed Kabinger with that thing so he kept his eye on it. The mechanism looked simple. But he kept a smile on his face so the *manatj* couldn't read his thoughts.

'That big horse of yours get split up?' he taunted Drummond, with no response. 'Got two little ones now, eh?'

The children all hated the monks' new cat and teased it in various ways for the whole journey. They shook the cage and hissed at it, and it scratched them in return, so they poked it through the wires of its cage, and threw pebbles at it, and threatened to skin it and cook it.

The river in this place snaked about, and in getting to the new site they crossed and recrossed the Moore. As they left the riverbed and the Drummond outstation hut came into view, Rosendo Salvado felt his spirits soar. The depression of the previous day was entirely lifted and he felt his energies to be without limit. God Himself had willed New Norcia to be and would cause it to be built through many human hands. He put down the tins he was carrying, raised his arms skyward, pointed his great black beard to the heavens and prayed for divine guidance for the great work ahead.

Dom Léandre Fonteinne of course similarly fell to his knees in prayer, though the new mission looked just as barren and dangerous as the one they had abandoned and there was nothing in his heart but despair.

From: Dom Santos Salvado, Tuy, Galicia
To: Dom Rosendo Salvado, Swan River colony

5th July 1846

My Dearest Brother

Our beloved Father has gone to his Reward. He was eighty, but still this was not expected. He did not suffer, but was taken to the bosom of Our Loving Lord while sleeping.

How loved he was, and how respected. Every person in Tuy and half of Santiago de Compostela attended our father's funeral, spilling out from the cathedral onto the streets to weep.

Our mother is grieving of course but as ever is full of ideas as to how one must live a full life. Her current thesis is that she and I must travel to Western Australia to join your mission. She will teach the native women to spin yarn and to weave and knit and so on. I am to do whatever my brother instructs me to do.

Vittoria, Romana and Pedro all came home to help bury our dear Father and to be with Mother and they all of course wish me to send their love to you from so far away.

Your loving brother,
Santos

13. THE NAUGHTY MARYS

From Obduracy in Sin
  Deliver us O Lord
From all dangers of body and soul
  Deliver us O Lord

Every evening the nuns of the Convent of the Holy Cross chanted the Litany of Divine Providence and dedicated it to their sisters in Baggot Street, Dublin, that they be protected from typhoid, consumption, cold and starvation. Mother Ursula Frayne delivered the call in a thin, quavering soprano laced with a slight hint of threat, or so Sister Anne Dillon secretly thought, and the response from the other five came in shrill unison.

'Deliver us O Lord,' they had begged Him, over and over but, Anne noticed, rarely did He actually deliver them from anything. Consumption had taken Catherine Gogarty slowly and cruelly, and Our Lord did not intercede. Never once did Catherine complain about His failure, of course, but only thanked Him for his limitless Mercy.

From Thy well-merited chastisements
  Deliver us O Lord

From earthquake, pestilence, famine and distress
   Deliver us O Lord

Ursula's reedy voice seemed to render each word a personal accusation. She had been a bit angry ever since her dear friend Catherine died nine months ago. Now on cue, there came a little sob from just behind Anne's ear. Every night it was the same. It was the word 'famine' that always triggered it.

From disease, hunger and war
   Deliver us O Lord

Another sob. Anne coughed this time, on Ursula's behalf. It was of course Ignatia de la Hoyde, the elderly novice, drawing attention to her misery.

At Baggot Street, Ignatia's had been the first name on the list. She was the only nun to have volunteered to come to Perth, the rest had been nominated by Mother Cecilia. Ignatia had been greatly moved by the bishop's speech, but even the next morning she had started to regret her impulse. She had been miserable as *Elizabeth* left England, and from the day of arrival in this colony had been suffering from a dangerous temptation to return home.

These little displays of grief were the Sin of Pride artfully disguised, so Anne had decided. Ignatia was a performer. She had to show that her grief for Ireland was so much greater than that of the others. It had grown tedious, her relentless sadness. 'She should learn to wear her cross silently, as do the rest of us,' Ursula had declared after a previous performance, and Anne agreed.

They progressed now to the 'beseech thees'.

That Thou mayest pity all who suffer want
   We beseech Thee, hear us

That Thou mayest console and raise up all the abandoned
and oppressed
We beseech Thee, hear us

There came another sob from the usual source and this time Anne noticed Ursula's head lift ever so slightly in warning. If Ignatia's weeping did not quite stop after this rebuke, it at least quietened down.

With Catherine gone, Anne Dillon had been made Ursula's second superior. She knew how they would all laugh at this back in Dublin, where she was thought of as a mere cleaner and cook. But what could she do but her best? Catherine had gone to her reward and was buried alongside Father Bouchet. Anne was the only other fully professed nun, so that was that.

The rest of the convent were still young. There were two novices: Aloysius Kelly, a chirpy twenty-three-year-old Dubliner, and Baptist O'Donnell who had only received the habit a month before His Lordship came to Baggot Street. Kate O'Reilly, just twenty-one, had come out as a servant; whether to serve the Sisters of Mercy or His Lordship had been a point of contention until Ursula resolved it by declaring her a postulant. Anne liked Kate O'Reilly, she was the sort to stay the distance.

After the liturgy, the younger sisters packed away the chapel, turning it back into a bedroom, and took the sniffing Ignatia into the kitchen to help them make jam. Mother Superior and her second superior withdrew to the convent reception room, a journey requiring just a few steps. There was a comfortable sofa in 'the good room', and a writing desk and a good chair, as well as the square piano which

Dom Salvado had bought for them in London. Ursula was a good pianist but had given up playing.

This was the time of day, Anne knew, that Ursula most missed the wisdom and maturity of her late friend Catherine. The two of them had been through the trial of Newfoundland together and so understood bishops and one another. Anne knew herself to be a poor substitute. She had given up trying to be the intelligent sounding-board that Catherine had been, but found she could at least make Ursula smile despite all the responsibilities which weighed her down.

To prevent their conversation lapsing into *gravitas*, Anne turned to the latest shenanigans of the 'Naughty Marys'. The Sisters of Mercy had now acquired three little orphan girls, naming them Mary Christian, Mary Rose and Mary Catherine. Every so often a new one would appear on their doorstep, brought back from New Norcia by Salvado or one of the French laymen. The girls' antics provided good material for a storyteller, as Anne was. Their hilarious attempts to escape back to the bush. Their amusing battles with European clothes, even the simplest of shifts. Their infuriating inattentiveness to the learning of anything at all: prayers, or even basic English.

Little Mary Rose provided tonight's story. She had slipped away again and got as far as the other side of St Georges Terrace, turning up in the dark of Mary Ann Langoulant's wardrobe, half-hidden among the soft things, eating a stolen apple.

'Bless her,' said Ursula, smiling. 'Once they lose their native tongue, I expect the urge will stop.' The nuns called them orphans, but the Marys still had family somewhere in the colony. Occasionally Salvado would bring the parents all the way down to Perth so they could see the marvellous progress their little girl had made with the nuns. He meant it as a kindness but it was terribly disruptive for the Marys, and Ursula meant to put an end to the practice.

Anne sat on the sofa, unpacking her sewing kit and surrounding herself with garments that needed mending, while Ursula sat at her desk reading a letter she had started to write early that morning. Anne saw an opportunity to ask for a favour.

'Could you perhaps ask Mother Cecilia again about my design for our habit?'

'If it comes up,' replied Ursula, which seemed to Anne no answer at all. How could it 'come up' when a letter had only one voice?

'Only, I'll not survive another Perth summer in this old thing.'

'You will survive, Anne, if Mother decrees it.'

'And, might you perhaps ask Cecilia about my sister? Will she let her come out to join us?'

'Who? Your little sister?'

'Yes. Ellen.'

'The naughty one?'

'She's only a little naughty.'

'Is she even with the convent?'

'No. Not actually. Not yet. She would though, if Cecilia said yes.' Things were so desperate in Ireland, anyone would join a convent if there was a chance of free escape from the poor place. 'Could she not be made a postulant or something? Later on, with instruction, she would be a good nun, Ursula. Mother, I mean.'

Ursula breathed deeply through her nose. 'That would require quite a turnaround, from all I have heard.'

'Yes, it would. But Ellen would do so, Ursula. She would like to take the name Magdalene.'

'Well, that *would* fit I suppose.'

Anne sewed to hide her annoyance. The bossy eldest child in a big family, deference did not come naturally to Anne Dillon. None of the Dillons were made that way. Ellen would probably burst with the effort of it but Anne had to try to save the girl from Ireland.

'Could you not ask her anyway?' said Anne, very quietly.

'I am not writing to Mother,' said Ursula, pausing for effect. 'I am writing to Queen Victoria.'

Anne looked up from her sewing. 'The Queen of England?' She could not have understood correctly. 'You are writing a letter to the Queen of England?'

'Shoosh, Anne, please, settle yourself,' Ursula sniffed. Anne was a blurter of things, whatever came to her.

'But is she not, like …' Anne almost dared not say the word. '… a Protestant?'

Ursula placed her pen on the desk. 'That is immaterial, Anne. Money is non-denominational.'

'But you are a Catholic nun!'

'Thank you, Anne, I am fully aware of what I am. It is merely a financial proposal I wish to put to Her Majesty, not a religious one.'

'Her Majesty, is it? Oh right, then,' said Anne, smoothing her feathers. She was still annoyed at Ursula's dismissal of the matters of the habit and her sister. 'Grand. Well, I hope she coughs up. She has plenty of it, that's for sure. Much of it taken from the Irish.' Terry Farrelly had recently been indoctrinating Sister Anne on matters of English oppression.

Ursula sniffed her annoyance at this impertinence from her second superior. But she did fold the incomplete letter and guiltily put it away.

'His Lordship will want his hands on it, if she does,' added Anne.

'Now, you will be quiet,' warned Mother Superior. This was an especially sore point. 'I will not burden His Lordship at this stage. And nor will you, Anne. I shall not take you into my confidence, if I cannot trust you.'

'Oh, but you can, Ursula,' said Anne, chastened and very serious now. 'You can always trust me.'

There was a busy silence.

'Being a woman,' said Ursula, determined to have the final word on the matter, 'I think the queen might understand some of our difficulties. I would of course never write to a king.'

'Right, so,' agreed Anne, smart enough to know when to bite her tongue.

It was, of course, an act of desperation for a Catholic nun to write to an English queen, begging for money. Ursula half expected the paper to refuse the ink. But without money, the Sisters of Mercy could achieve nothing. Schools needed desks, chairs and books. The proposed Home of Providence for the orphan girls would need beds and blankets and clothing and food. Such things did not fall from the sky. They had to be purchased.

The bishop was quite useless. He had spent the thousands of pounds given to him by the Society for the Propagation of the Faith twice over and still had a drawer of unpaid bills. The nuns had done all they could, to the point of humiliation. They had held countless bazaars and raffles, and each time cheerfully collected a pittance. Nobody in this colony had a spare penny, least of all the micks.

'Could you not ask the French fella with the silk scarf?' suggested Anne. She had become good friends with Mary Ann Langoulant, who knew all the French Catholics. 'They say …'

'What, Mister Cleriquot? You berate me for seeking funds from a Protestant queen but you would have me embrace an atheist?'

'I suppose not,' said Anne, falling silent now. But inwardly, she did think a French atheist preferable to an English tyrant who wanted all the aboriginal Irish dead or gone. No atheist ever caused a famine, not that Sister Anne knew of.

Ursula did not confess it, of course, but she *had* stooped to asking Fabrice Cleriquot about money, and the terrible fellow had implied she was an abductress. Anyway, he had no money to give. Terry Farrelly confided to her that Cleriquot had lost it all in a bordello in Cape Town.

'Sure it's worth a try,' said Anne softly, the long silence having grown uncomfortable. 'You should send your letter off to the English queen.' There was no harm in saying so, she decided, because the old cow would never send the Sisters of Mercy a single penny.

Anne sewed busily. Ursula suggested she employ a pair of scissors to cut the cotton rather than use her teeth. Ursula set out the tools for her own pet project, a tiny shell house to send home to Dublin. The completion of the chimney required a pair of spectacles, jeweller's forceps, good glue and a steady hand.

The other sisters were in the kitchen making jam from the bucket of overripe apricots that Terry Farrelly had dropped off. There was a weekly visit to be done to the hospital, the lunatic asylum and the police lock-up, and jam was highly prized by the ill, the mad and the incarcerated. Also eggs, butter, cakes, wine, coffee, mutton and chicken: these were the things the inmates wanted the nuns to bring them. Solace, prayer, companionship – such abstract things came a poor second to food.

Anne was listening in to the goings-on in the kitchen and wishing she could take over. The young ones were fussing about getting rid of the skins. The skins were good in jam, chopped up. An older voice was insisting the fruit was rotten. Soon she darkened the door of the drawing room carrying a wooden spoon and bad news.

'Sure, they are alive with fruit fly,' moaned Ignatia de la Hoyde.

'They're just vinegar flies,' said Anne, briskly. 'Ladle them off the top if they're too silly to escape the pot.'

'Right you are,' grumbled Ignatia, turning her back. 'And have them all poison us.'

'They will add to the flavour,' Anne called after her, smiling at Ursula. She added, *sotto voce*, 'Lord, she is so very doleful.'

'Go and help them, for goodness' sake,' said Ursula eventually, and Anne leapt at the chance.

Alone in the drawing room, Ursula regretted the harshness of her own voice. She knew she oppressed these young women. She asked too much sacrifice of them. Their disappointments had been so many. The bishop had promised two million native souls awaiting the Holy Sacrament of Baptism, and the children of five thousand baptised Catholics awaiting education. None of it was true, they had learned, but still, here they were. These girls had given up so much to come to the ends of the earth, only to be rewarded with thwarted hopes and their mother superior's endless scolding.

Ursula called the pessimist in again.

'Did Mister Caporelli not leave us a gift, Ignatia?'

'Wine, Mother.'

'Open it, Ignatia.'

Ignatia's face opened up in a beautiful smile. 'Yes, Mother!'

'And Ignatia, I pray every day and night for your younger brother. I am sure you will hear good news of him soon.' The last survivor of Ignatia's family had boarded a ship for New York and had not been heard of since.

'Thank you, Mother,' gasped Ignatia, and fled.

A party of sorts could be heard to erupt in the kitchen when Caporelli's bottle was lifted from the ledge it had occupied for weeks. It was very sour but they all agreed they liked a hock exactly that way.

Later, two of the Naughty Marys, bathed and dressed in tiny nightgowns, were ushered in by Sister Baptist to kiss the superiors goodnight. Anne held them both tight for a full minute, singing to them all the while. Mary Christian, being the older and more sensible, was permitted to glue a cowrie shell in place on the roof of Mother's shell house, and her intense concentration to the task was charming to see.

'One day we shall take one of these little pets back to Dublin,' smiled Ursula, as the orphans were ushered off to bed.

'Oh, yes, yes!' urged Anne, 'can you imagine it!'

'They tell me little Mary Catherine has started wailing again.'

'Dear Lord, yes. It's terrible to hear. It was seeing her mother and father.'

'A mistake that I shall not permit to be repeated,' said Ursula.

Late at night, there was knock at the convent door. It was the Frenchman, Fabrice Cleriquot back from another of his trips to New Norcia. With him was a small child wrapped up in something that Mary Ann Langoulant no longer required for her little girls.

'Mary Ann dressed her for the cold,' explained Fabrice. 'She cried and cried all the way down. Greatly missing her people, I fear.'

'No,' Ursula corrected him. 'Just hungry. And needing a warm bed.'

'She keeps asking for her mother,' said Fabrice. '*Ngank, ngank,* she wailed, all the way down.'

'She is looking at her mother now,' said Ursula, and the child started crying again.

'She has a name,' said Fabrice.

'Her name is Mary Cecilia,' said Ursula, firmly back in the rôle of superioress. 'Good night then, Mister Cleriquot, we won't detain you.' The mother superior of the Sisters of Mercy disappeared inside with the crying child, cooing at it in a nunly way.

'Look who's arrived!' Mother called out to the younger nuns, who had retired early due to Caporelli's wine. One by one they came out to greet the wide-eyed thing, whose dark face was smeared with sweet apricot jam from the wooden spoon held in Anne's free hand. It was the only way she could get it to stop sobbing, she explained.

The Sisters of Mercy knelt in a circle around their new baby. 'Say welcome to Mary Cecilia, our new little daughter,' whispered Mother, joyously. 'Our fourth Naughty Mary!'

'How old is she, do you think?'

'Four I'd say. Or a skinny five.'

They fussed over the child until it relented and agreed to smile at Sister Baptist, proving how happy it was to be home at last. It was like a miracle, this new life in their midst. They so badly needed love, these young nuns, and now here it was, love itself, underfed and wrapped in borrowed clothes. The new Mary was an antidote to personal despair. The sisters could go back to their cots knowing that, despite so many hardships, they really were doing some good works in this difficult new land.

From: Mother Ursula Frayne, Convent of the Holy Cross, Perth

To: Queen Victoria

29th January, 1847
(extract)

To Her Most Gracious Majesty
Queen Victoria

Most Gracious Sovereign

... Encouraged by your Majesty's benevolence, justice and other Christian virtues, we, the Sisters of Mercy, must humbly beg to lay before Your Majesty a statement of our position in this most distant part of Your Majesty's dominion.

... but what can be said of the poor aborigines? They are wandering around in a wild land which affords them but a miserable subsistence, ignorant and unmindful of Him who died on the Cross for their redemption. Would it not be a glorious work to bring these poor beings to a moral and civilised life? To Christianity? To Heaven?

It is not impossible, it would not even be difficult. Some of the parents could easily be induced by kind treatment to give up the children into our care; these children, instructed first themselves, would in time draw others to share in their newly found happiness and thus hundreds of native children, as yet ignorant of every moral and social duty, could be brought to the knowledge, love and service of God, and consequently become faithful subjects of Your Majesty and useful members of society.

... Be assured, Most Gracious Sovereign, that the little children whom by Your Majesty's bounty we shall be enabled to snatch from ignorance and vice, shall be taught to bless your royal name and raise their young voices in supplication for their beloved Queen Victoria.

Your Majesty's most humble, most loyal, most affectionate servants The Sisters of Mercy of Perth

14. LIFE IN THE GARDEN

Roger Smith's white hairless buttocks shimmied in amusing manner with each blow of the axe. It was freezing in the Avon Valley on these winter mornings but Roger Smith insisted on chopping wood naked, except for the sandals; it was Sadie who had insisted on footwear, for fear of snakes and splinters. Every morning at seven she was carried from her warm bed, wrapped in a blanket and was required to watch this performance from the wrought iron table he had made for her, upon which he had placed a cup of sweet milky tea hot enough to make her breath smoke. The ritual no longer embarrassed Sadie, but still she did not understand it. It was something to do with Liberty, Roger Smith had said, but Michael explained it was an English eccentricity permitted to the wealthy.

Roger Smith had a centre of gravity like one of those novelty ornaments she used to dust on her lady's mantelpiece back in Cape Town; a porcelain man with red cheeks and oversized checked pants, you could push him down but he would always pop up again, smiling stupidly. Nothing could keep Roger Smith down. Sadie hoped so, anyway, for she could not hide things from him much longer. She had to tell him about Michael; that he had put a new life inside her, that she was going to marry him with that nice English vicar doing the ceremony, and that she would be his wife, forever and ever and ever, Amen.

Perhaps he would get angry because of all he had done for her. Or perhaps he would not mind at all, she really did not know Roger Smith well enough to guess. If he had any passion, it was only for one queer thing: knowledge. He had dozens of books, all serious ones without pictures. He was such an odd man, and very old. He must be sixty and seemed like a ghost to her already. Sadie thought only of her lovely Michael, and wished she were in his warm bed on this lovely cold morning, touching him.

Sadie Markham had found a safe shore in Michael. Her heart burst at every thought of him. She must remember to ask his surname, and whether she would be allowed to take it.

She stirred some gingered sugar into her tea. Michael had made it, of course, to treat her morning sickness. She moistened a finger, dipped it into the little bowl so it was covered in crystals, then licked them off. She sighed; half sad, half content. Springtime in this Avon Valley, she thought, was as lovely as anywhere on earth.

The Garden had grown lush after the heavy winter rains. The bottlebrushes were in flower, sending the birds mad. These were not gentle English songbirds, but cranky Australian ones: fidgety little greeneyes, flitting New Holland honeyeaters and assertive wattlebirds. Her favourite one arrived, her morning willy-wagtail looking for biscuit crumbs. *Jiddy-jiddy*, Bob called it.

Roger Smith put his hands on his hips to stretch his back and then, with all the lack of self-consciousness of a pantless two-year-old, bent down to stack the kindling into the wicker basket.

'You should leave that for Eric to stack,' said Sadie. 'Your back is bad and you pay that boy far too well.' That thieving Parkhurst boy would end up richer than his master, she had tried to warn him, but you could tell Roger Smith nothing.

Not much about The Garden was progressing as Roger Smith had hoped, except the forge. About ten o'clock, Terry Farrelly pulled up his wagon and started a loud conversation with Eric Hough. He was in town to buy provisions for New Norcia so the dray was heavily laden with sacks of rice, sugar and flour, and tins of meat, oil and tea. He produced a bent tiller and a cracked ploughshare, both of which needed mending 'quick smart'.

'Three days,' shouted the blacksmith.

'No good, son,' boomed the Irishman. 'I have to drive back to New Norcia tomorrow.'

'Cost you double,' shouted the Parkhurst boy, without hesitation. One man's problem was another's opportunity.

Such was the volume of The Terror's bargaining that the whole population of The Garden was soon attracted to the forge. Roger Smith was now dressed for a day's work in the vegetable garden, while Sadie looked sickly and Michael just happened to be passing. Bob was helping Eric in the forge but staying out of arm's distance.

Terry Farrelly turned to the First Among Equals. 'They want to turn the Swan River into a convict colony,' he told Roger Smith. 'We all need to go down to the pub at noon and shout the bastards down.'

The whole town was trying to squeeze into the Royal Oak. Officially this was a meeting of the Toodyay and Victoria Plains Agricultural Society, but anyone could join as an honorary member.

'Sign in here,' said the lady on the door, handing Farrelly the pen. 'And here, for the petition.'

'Petition to whom?' demanded the Irishman, awake to Orange trickery. 'And for what?'

'To the governor,' she said, 'for the labourers.'

'Labourers?' said Farrelly, looming over the poor woman. 'Is that what we are to call them? I will not sign.' And in he marched to take on these Tory proponents of convictism.

Eric Hough put his mark in two places, ignoring the woman's protest about apprentices being ineligible. Sadie did just as she was asked. Roger Smith hesitated to sign but, there being no one behind him to bear witness, did so. The commune badly needed more people, free or bond. Bob loitered near the entrance, but the woman looked at him a certain way so he decided to drift off somewhere else.

Inside, through a haze of smoke, the chairman was speaking to a full hall. The colony was struggling to survive, he declared, to a rumble of support. There was the real prospect of it being abandoned, not for want of pastures, nor fertile soil, but because of the cost of labour. Property owners took all the risks and went broke while labourers could demand twenty quid a year. If this were to continue landowners would end up enslaved to uneducated labourers.

'There are shepherds with larger flocks than their masters,' one voice yelled out.

'Perhaps they're better pastoralists,' suggested a Scot at the back, to a ripple of laughter.

'The solution is obvious,' said the chairman, restoring order. 'Cheaper labour. We demand the governor procure us a reliable supply of convicts.'

Only one man stood to argue against the proposition, and it was not Terry Farrelly, it was the Wesleyan from the orchard below The Garden. He sermonised about respect for all humanity, spoke of liberty and brotherhood, and was shouted down.

'You don't have to take any, Billy Boy,' someone yelled. 'Stay out of our business.'

But the Wesleyan gained some support when he talked about the *quality* of the convicts that might be brought to the Avon. They may well be Irish, he warned. English prisons were filling with Ribbonmen and the like; enemies of civilised society, renowned haters of the English.

'We need labour,' the Wesleyan shouted over the din, 'but at what price? Why risk having such types here in the Avon Valley?' There were soft murmurs of assent. 'And don't deceive yourself that they will suddenly vanish from our midst once the work is done. The Irish breed large. Bring in two and you will soon have twelve. And then, the criminal class will be among us forever. Is that what we want?'

'Yes!' boomed a voice from the back impossible to ignore. 'That is precisely what we want!' Its owner strode to the front. It was the big ugly Irishman from the Catholic mission at New Norcia. A murmur through the crowd predicted a diatribe about the terrible things suffered by the poor Irish.

'I came down from Victoria Plains yesterday on a rough track. There is no bridge. Nor is there a church in this town, of any denomination, nor a school. None of the things that a responsible government would provide in order that the farmers that produce the food to fill the bellies of his colony might prosper. We demand of the governor that these things be provided.' There was a muted *hear! hear!* The Irish were known for their ability to dodge and sway.

'Without food, the colony starves. Without the farmers of the Avon Valley and Victoria Plains, there is no food. To produce it, we require affordable labour and more capital. Becoming a penal colony would provide us with both. Or else, what is the future of this colony when the last landowner goes bust?

'It is a *patriotic* plea that we make, for the very survival of this colony.' The hall was now Farrelly's, but the pugilist held up one open hand for silence. 'We say to the governor: *Send us labourers.* Otherwise we will perish, and as we go, so will go Her Majesty's Colony of the Swan River. It's as simple as that. So sign up lads.'

The petition to the governor was signed by eighty-four citizens. Only the Wesleyan held out. On it being pointed out by Roger Smith that the colonial secretary was dead and Governor Clarke close to dying, the document was re-addressed for the attention of the acting colonial secretary, George Fletcher Moore.

Later, back at The Garden, the community gathered around the fire and shared a meal with their New Norcia guest. The whiskey stocks were growing low but Farrelly had been afforded a generous tumbler.

'You had rather a change of heart today, I notice,' said Roger Smith, warily. He was generally a lover of debate, but the Irish were given to speeches from the pulpit, which could be tedious.

Farrelly exhaled hard, causing the amber spirit in his glass to ripple. 'Nobody was more surprised than me!' he laughed. 'It was your Wesleyan neighbour that got my shackles up, talking about all those terrible Irish that may come here. It got me thinking, well, things are so bad back there, let the poor buggers come.'

'And the precious rights of the English landowners, on whose behalf you spoke so articulately?'

'Well, I wanted the bastards to sign. And they did. So.'

'But surely you don't really wish to see your countrymen arrive here in shackles?'

'They are already in shackles. Every Irishman, every Irishwoman, every Irish child born or unborn is already a prisoner of England on starvation rations. If Her Majesty is happy to send some of them here at her own cost, I am for it. Honestly, I'd tell them to burn down a barracks if it gets them on a boat.'

'Would that not empty Ireland of the Irish?'

'No faster than dying. Those are the only two choices left. Unless they can get themselves on a boat, they will starve. You should read the letters I get from home. Dear God, if we can save just a few ...' And now the big man was close to tears.

'We could use the labour,' contributed Eric Hough, as if he were landed gentry and worried about the cost of it.

'You *are* labour,' hissed Sadie, loudly enough that the Parkhurst boy could hear her, but not Roger Smith. 'That's all.'

'The gentry of Perth will be too proud to let this occur, I think,' mused Roger Smith 'It is a great point of honour for them. They disparage New South Wales for its terrible convict stain and will never allow it in. They would prefer to starve.'

'*Ráiméis*,' scoffed Farrelly, which sounded like 'rubbish' and meant much the same. 'The gentry of Perth will find a way around their consciences. The stain will become a mere blemish, you wait. They will invent a more genteel word for a convict. Every man bends his principles to his needs except, to his great credit, your Wesleyan friend.'

Later, Farrelly excused himself to pack for the morning journey back to the mission and Roger Smith retreated to a quiet corner of the fire to read a letter he had been handed in town. It had a crest and a wax seal, stamped in Edinburgh four months earlier. Sadie hovered nearby, wanting to say something. 'Please don't fidget,' he snapped, 'it is very distracting.' She walked off to speak with Michael, who just happened to be waiting at the gate with some eggs.

Then mayhem broke out in the shadows. There were screams and thumping and bellows and squeals. Punches were thrown. The little family had appeared again, looking for food. A little boy ran squealing past Roger Smith, tears and snot streaming down his face. He stopped and turned open-mouthed screaming for his *ngangk*, heard her let out an awful wail and then she appeared with a bloodied face and an eye already purpling.

Roger Smith got to his feet very slowly, hoping his calmness would smother the chaos. It did not. Eric Hough appeared now, leaping into the firelight with bloodied nose, followed by The Terror, who was bellowing that he was not yet finished with the boy. The Parkhurst boy tried to flee, but somehow became entangled with Bob's right foot. The Irishman picked the Parkhurst boy up by his neck hairs, turned him around and smashed out his upper teeth with a single punch.

'I really should kill you, you little bastard,' threatened Terry Farrelly, and seemed ready to.

'I warned them enough times,' spluttered Eric.

'Shut your stupid face,' said the Irishman, a tremble in his voice. 'Be very still while I decide.'

'What exactly has happened?' asked Roger Smith, a hand upon the Irishman's shoulder to discourage murder. 'It was all perfectly quiet, and then all of a sudden, this madness.'

'This boy of whom you're so proud showed his true colours,'

said Farrelly, loudly, right in the face of the offender. 'He attacked a woman and child with a hot poker.'

'I was just goin' for the old bloke,' protested the toothless apprentice.

'Quiet, you,' warned Farrelly. The boy sat still, but even in his stillness some insolence remained. A childhood spent in prison and you do not blink easily. Farrelly brought his face very close to the boy's. 'You have been farted from the arse of Mother England. That family you attacked are the owners of this land. You do need to learn your place.'

Something about this Parkhurst boy greatly offended Terry Farrelly. He was exactly the sort of heartless bastard to join the English army and enjoy a stint in Ireland, kicking the hapless locals.

'It's inbred in you English, isn't it?' continued the Irishman, breathing his words into the bloodied face of the apprentice. 'That overweening sense of superiority, even in the lowest of the low, even in filth like you.' He loosened his grip on the boy, who sulked off into the night, but not too fast, even in retreat.

Things settled down after that. The family was fussed over and left The Garden with full stomachs and on good terms with all its citizens, bar one. Roger Smith cut the seal off the last Balmenach, and the English aristocrat sat quietly with the Irish nationalist, each contemplating very different matters.

'My apologies for the ruckus,' said Farrelly, eventually. 'Oh, and for that bit about the old English superiority. I didn't mean to offend, like.'

'Not at all,' the Englishman reassured him.

Sadie and Michael were standing awkwardly nearby, hearts racing, awaiting an opportunity to tell their news.

'News from home?' asked Farrelly. He had seen the legal letter,

'Yes,' sighed Roger Smith. 'My father is dying. Or, more likely, he has died.'

'Very sorry to hear it.'

'Yes. It seems I may have to return to Scotland for a while to sort things out.'

Sadie looked at Michael. This was wonderful news.

'How long do you expect to be gone, Roger Smith?' asked a hesitant voice. Because Michael so rarely spoke, all heads turned his way. 'I … I could look after things here, if you like,' he added, to deflect attention.

'Well, it's rather hard to say,' said Roger Smith, turning things over in his mind. 'There is a property matter that will require my attention. Legal matters and so on. All rather a bother, really. A year or so, I suppose. Two?' Aloud, he weighed up the managerial qualities of his apprentice and his neighbour. Young Eric, he had to concede, may not yet be ready for the responsibility. 'Yes, Michael, I would be grateful if you could keep an eye on things for me while I am away.'

Sadie was furious. She alone knew what things needed to be done every day, yet Roger Smith considered the thieving Parkhurst boy as caretaker over her. No longer did she feel inclined to spare his feelings. 'Michael and I are to marry,' she blurted. 'I am carrying his child.'

'Ah,' said Roger Smith, his English equanimity stretched to breaking point. 'I see. Well … may I be the first to congratulate you both.'

Miraculously, English manners prevailed and there was no show of rancour at all. Roger Smith shook Michael's hand, then embraced him. Sadie, instantly ashamed of her outburst, melted into Roger

Smith's arms and thanked him for his understanding and told him she believed he had been truly sent by God, in order to bring her to Michael.

'I was most certainly not sent by any god, I can assure you of that,' said Roger Smith, keen to put a stop to all this show of emotion. Michael stammered that he felt exactly the same as Sadie. He was sorry if he had done the wrong thing, it was just that he loved Sadie more than he had ever loved anyone and could not help himself.

'Yes, yes,' said Roger Smith, looking at the ground. 'No harm done. Goodnight,' he mumbled, and the loving couple left together.

The two older men stayed and drank their whiskies in peace. Farrelly admitted the Scotch stuff was superior to the Irish.

'I'm sorry it has all turned out such a failure for you,' said the Irishman, 'your, ah, little garden experiment thing here.'

'A failure? Not at all,' objected Roger Smith. 'We have shown what might be done.'

'Your French friend seems to have abandoned you for New Norcia.'

'Cleriquot? Yes, a frivolous fellow really. He remains susceptible to religion. Has he actually joined the monks?'

'Only in body. There is a lot of work to be done up there and he has made himself useful to Salvado it seems.'

'In what possible way, I wonder? He is one of those university men with no practical skills.'

'He can cook all right, so Salvado says.' Suddenly an excellent idea occurred to Farrelly, triggered in part by the knowledge that after the beating he had just received, the Parkhurst boy would never get the rushed work done by his departure in the morning.

'You know what you should do, Roger Smith? Move this forge of yours up to New Norcia. Salvado could use a blacksmith ahead of any other occupation.'

Roger Smith reminded the catechist that as a non-believer he had no inclination to join a Catholic mission, but he did not entirely reject the plan. He liked Salvado and was curious to see what he had achieved in the bush. New Norcia could be an interesting diversion before departing the colony.

'Come up to the mission with me in the morning,' Farrelly pressed. 'Your experiment here is done with, but you at least achieved one thing. You taught the dullest and least personable boy in the colony how to run a forge. So, teach a few of the young native fellows to do it before you go off to your castle.'

'It's not a castle,' protested Roger Smith, 'just an old estate on the Highlands. Though there is an old fortress on the grounds.' He paused to make a decision. 'I suppose I could go up for a few weeks. Do the monks permit spirits?'

'It is almost compulsory,' The Terror reassured him, lifting his glass.

Next morning, Farrelly took delight in pulling the forge apart in front of the fat-lipped toothless Parkhurst boy who watched, arms folded, feigning disinterest. He would remain, he announced, and rebuild it.

'I'll pay rent,' Eric Hough advised the former proprietor, 'a pound a month.' He seemed as happy as Sadie to see the old man leave. The lad's confidence was a source of pride to the aristocrat. Due to the careful application of Owenist principles, a petty criminal had been rehabilitated in a mere ten months, and was now a business owner. Roger Smith agreed to the terms, without expecting to ever be paid. He left the lad a small selection of useful tools, and apologised for confiscating the furnace.

'There is an old one for sale in York,' shrugged Eric, a step ahead.

Bob helped pile all the bits on the cart, but declined Farrelly's invitation to come with them to New Norcia.

'Nah,' he told Farrelly, 'they try to boss you round too much, them monks.'

'Surely you don't want to stay here with that little prick Eric?'

Bob seemed unconcerned. 'He'll try to whack me, but I'm quicker than him. Long as he pays me, I'll stay. I'll just take off when I want.'

Before departing for the last time, Roger Smith took a last stroll around The Garden. It was like an idyllic colonial scene cut from the pages of the *Illustrated London News*: a pretty shingle-roofed cottage which had survived the largest river anyone could recall, a colourful garden alive with native birds, a poddy lamb tethered to a pole, a few ducks. True, there was no Owenite commune here to rival New Harmony and no children under the tutelage of Pestalozzian educators, but the idealist did not take these disappointments to heart. He was a dilettante in matters philosophical. Overnight, he had warmed to the idea of being an English gentleman on the Scottish Highlands where he could read his books and take long walks with his father's hounds, if they had not died with him.

With the last of the pieces of the dissembled forge stacked on the dray, the English aristocrat climbed alongside the bishop's acolyte. Three times Farrelly raised the whip and three times was detained.

First, Sadie and Michael came to bid them farewell. As he watched Sadie waddling across the mud, Roger Smith wondered how he could have failed to notice her belly. They were given permission to keep the sign Sadie had painted for The Garden; they both liked the words about 'strangers tarrying' and held it up like stallholders at a town fair.

Then Eric Hough surprised by handing Roger Smith something soft wrapped in brown paper. 'Give this to Frenchy,' he said. 'There's heaps of worm eggs stuck on the leaves. The mudlarks got in and ate all the ones that hatched yesterday but the grey ones are still good, I think.'

This necessitated another delay. Michael raced off to his farm, returned carrying an armful of cuttings from his mulberry tree, and wedged the lengths on the cart alongside the parts for the dissembled forge. 'Tell the Frenchman don't water them too much.'

The Terror would take no more delays. They were already more than an hour behind and would be lucky to make New Norcia by dark. Swearing something about French people generally and the uselessness of silk, he whipped the bullock across the soft riverbed northward bound in the direction of the Drummond Track.

From: Don Angelo Confalonieri, Port Victoria
To: Fabrice Cleriquot, Perth

Received Perth 11th February 1847

Caro Fabrizio

Back home in Trento, they would never be able to imagine Australia. Here, nobody understands my words. So it is to you I must write, knowing as you do both my language and this country. That you are not a priest is an advantage, in case I wish here to vent my true feelings.

So, I live alone in a tiny hut, surrounded by jungle, ten kilometres from the garrison of Port Victoria, or Essington as they call it here. There are just twenty-four Europeans living here. The captain is an English Protestant called Macarthur. He is amused that I am the only priest in the northern half of Australia, as well as the only parishioner. His men helped me build my hut at the very tip of the peninsula, which is called Coburg. I call it Castello del Buonconsiglio, after the grand home of the Bishops of Trento. I have been given a job, to maintain the signals which prevent ships from running aground. Possibly that is my only useful purpose here.

It is a steam bath here by day and night. The local mosquitoes possess more of my blood than do I. There are alligators three times my length. I am not well, Fabrizio. I was never a fat man, but am now decidedly a thin one. My missionary achievements are very modest. A few shy natives have sat and listened to my readings. They have even shared a few of their words with me. I will attempt to write a dictionary for you.

A catastrophe en route killed the two good Irish catechists, Fagan and Hogan. We had left Sydney on 9th April on the schooner 'Heroine', heading north. To avoid the treacherous reef which Captain Blackwood warned us about, our captain took the inner passage, sailing within sight of the mainland but in the middle of the night on the 24th we foundered on rocks close to Gloucester Island. Our ship sank in five minutes in complete darkness. There was panic. There were three lifeboats but no time to deploy them. A small boat was in the water being towed behind 'Heroine' so we clambered in and I cut the tow line before it could be dragged underwater by the sinking ship. There were twenty-four survivors. I prayed with them. In such circumstances, Fabrizio, everyone becomes a believer.

The Irishmen never reappeared, nor others including an English couple called Earl. When the captain floated past he was carrying a little white girl in his arms. She appeared to be dead but he would not give up.

We were rescued at daybreak by 'Enchantress' whose commander was an educated man named Essenhigh. I had but one possession left, a small wooden crucifix, which had miraculously stayed afloat. I took it as a sign from God that I must persist in my mission. You will say it was simply made of a type of wood which floats.

When I finally arrived at my destination, I wept, finding nothing here but a half dozen brick buildings. The English naval men and their sullen wives all want to leave. They all agree with the view expressed by a mad Prussian called Leichardt who departed declaring Port Victoria a worse place than the desert he had been lost in for a year. Captain Macarthur told me the garrison is almost destroyed every Christmas by a hurricane and if it happens just once more the place will be abandoned. Then he asked me to pray for a big storm!

I cannot leave, even if they all do. My bishop has sent me here and I expect to die here, Fabrizio, it is just a matter of by what means. At rare times, I allow myself to be nostalgic for the Dolomites, and for my family who live still in that beautiful place. I miss the hills, the faces, but most of all, I miss speaking my native tongue.

Enough of my misery. I shall close with something amusing. Bishop Polding of Sydney thinks Brady somewhat of a Napoleon Bonaparte, staring at maps with designs on expanding his diocesan territory. Keen to mark me down as an ally in this inter-diocesan war, Polding asked if would I like to become the Bishop of Port Victoria? Bishop, as well as its only parishioner! I told him I did not wish to find myself on the wrong side of Bishop Brady, in case he should punish me!

I continue to pray that you will rediscover your Faith, my dear Fabrizio. You will be very much happier in a serious sense when eventually you do. Kiss dear Louis and Mary Ann for me and tell them I will always remember their kindnesses to me. You may of course share this letter with my Spanish confrères, to whom I shall write separately of weightier things.

Yours in Christ,
Don Angelo

15. THE LADIES' LUNCHEON

The ex-monk, Léandre Fonteinne, was enjoying the attention of Mary Ann and her three friends as they worked on his face. He breathed in their beautiful smells and enjoyed the brush of their bosoms as they fussed over him. He had missed the company of women in the horrible bush of Victoria Plains. Even as a novice at Solesmes he had thought constantly of them.

What had started as a frivolous smear of colour to his cheeks had become for the women a work of art, and their canvas could not simply get up and leave the studio. So Léandre shut his eyes and let them perform their work upon him. A part of him wished to let go of all guilt and dissolve into the experience, but still alive within him was a stronger part preventing him from doing so – a part still mindful of the world which lay outside, with its hateful ruddy-faced bishops and disapproving Irish priests and tongue-clicking nuns. Leaving Holy Orders had not made the whole Catholic Church disappear.

After the sad event which had befallen him at Badji Badji, the Spanish monks had been terribly cruel to Léandre. He had tried to be useful but after three months Dom Serra declared him to be of no use at New Norcia and Léandre left for Perth. The Langoulants' home was his refuge. Never once had Louis or Mary Ann seemed to mind having him to stay, and never had they mentioned money. Most days he spent sitting, reading and regaining his strength. It gave Mary Ann pleasure to wait on him, and since Louis spent the days on the river, Léandre had grown accustomed to spending his days among women and little girls.

He rarely ventured anywhere else in this nasty little town. His friend Fabrice Cleriquot remained at New Norcia. The winemaker Nico Caporelli was still a dear friend, despite his teasing, and each Thursday they went to tea with one or other of the two Catholic families who had not yet shunned him.

He had been offered a teaching job in the government school but the bishop prohibited it; it would disgrace the diocese if an ex-monk were to take on a public rôle. Secretly, Léandre was relieved. He feared the English youngsters would ridicule his accent or else learn about the tragedy from their wicked parents and taunt him about the dead Irishman.

So Léandre Fonteinne was stuck in Perth with no money and no means by which to earn the fare home. His heart had fallen into despair. Neither the diocese nor the Benedictines who once called him a brother were inclined to help.

Today, however, a smile had come to his rouged cheeks thanks to the attention of the women friends of Mary Ann. They were being silly and fussing over him in a way that told him he really was loved after all.

The occasion was Catherine Mary's first birthday. *A Ladies' Luncheon by the River* declared Mary Ann's handwritten invitation. Léandre had two jobs: to serve the guests refreshments on arrival and to hold the baby while they showered her with grains of rice confetti.

But then, 'Leon, you look so dull,' the mischievous Maggie had declared. 'We will have to brighten you up!' First, they dressed him up to match the baby. The effect was hilarious to them, since he looked so glum. Then it was agreed he should become a Snow Queen. He objected to the glamorous gown they found for him but there was no denying it happened to fit him very well. A wide-brimmed sunhat was added, with a red hibiscus pinned to it.

'Oh my word,' said Maggie, 'you really are quite beautiful, Leon. Now we must paint your face!' Léandre let them do this, too. It was dizzying. His breathing was getting away from him, he knew not why. Without a cassock to disguise it, his ardour was noticed, first in a whisper and then to great laughter. It was even brushed against by Maggie's bottom, and after that he cared not. He laughed with the good-natured ladies of Perth, felt as if he were one of them. He pouted so they could crimson his lips.

The Langoulant home filled with shrieks of female laughter. How wonderful it was, thought Léandre, to be free now to do such a thing; yet he knew in his heart this must be a type of evil no churchman had ever yet thought to proscribe.

When their canvas was finished, the women stopped, settled their breathing and admired their work. Léandre Fonteinne was quite beautiful. He allowed them to inspect him as he really was, vulnerable and feminine. He looked at his cheeks in the glass and was enthralled. The new baby cried, but she was no longer the centre of attention. A little perfume was applied via a silk scarf wafted softly over the bodice.

'Shoes!' said Bernadette.

'Yes, get some shoes, Mary Ann,' urged another, 'and we shall all take the baby for a stroll!'

The group of five women took a stroll down St Georges Terrace, taking a baby's pram and two toddlers. Five-year-old Victoria held the hand of a rather stout woman who appeared to have rather overdone things with her morning toilet or perhaps made an early start on the brandy. As bad fortune would have it, they immediately encountered Dom Tootle or Tottle, the sickly English Benedictine from Downside Abbey, his alabaster complexion ghostly against his black cassock.

Léandre felt faint. This English monk despised him. Just last week he had bumped Léandre in the vestry and whispered the word 'murderer'. The Englishman was a weak man, *bien sûr*, but dressed as he was Léandre feared him as a rabbit might a fox.

The Downside monk had shown little curiosity as the ladies approached but then made a weak effort to lift his head and display his English teeth. To avoid scrutiny, Léandre tilted his lilac hat downwards and in the instant he did so he saw the English novice hold his gaze, stop in his tracks, then turn for a second look.

Léandre had been recognised. His heart pounded twice, very hard, and then seemed to stop altogether. His legs lost power, he stumbled, and he felt his visage change from carefree to culprit. The noisy women around him artfully confused the situation with a barrage of chirpy 'Morning Father's' and the group kept moving along.

'Home!' said Léandre to Mary Ann, his voice now snappy and masculine. 'I am going to be ill!' He was a vicious one, that pale subdeacon from Downside Abbey, a meticulous analyser of things. Terrible consequences would come from this, Léandre knew it.

The four women staggered their 'drunken' friend home down the grassy verge of St Georges Terrace. Passersby noticed the commotion and tutted at this latest confirmation of the gradual corruption of Perth society. But they got home.

'God, that was grand!' shrieked Maggie, pulling Leon's hatless head to her breast and planting a generous kiss on his heavily powdered temple. 'Did you see the looks we got? Oh, my beautiful wife, Leonie! *Ma chérie!*' The more startled and confused Léandre appeared, the more the women loved him.

'Stop it, you geese!' he snapped.

'Oh Leon, shoosh now,' said Mary Ann, playing mother to a child. 'Tootle or whatever he is called, he saw nothing but a bunch of dizzy women.'

'He saw *me*,' said Léandre, seriously and slowly, 'and he will tell the bishop.'

'That Tottle is always frowning, especially if he sees anyone having a bit of fun. Now sit there, Leon, stop being so serious, and hold the baby while we get lunch.'

Léandre did as he was told, but very miserably. His former prettiness was washed away by tears and he looked now like a miserable dowager.

God had provided a glorious spring afternoon on the grassy bank of the Swan, so Mary Ann declared. Louis had set up a table under the peppermint tree and Léandre covered it with a cloth of embroidered white linen. Cups of tea were poured and sandwiches and sugared teacake appeared. A proud pair of black swans joined the baby shower, bringing their new cygnets up from the water, for which they were rewarded by the ladies of Perth with cake crumbs.

Léandre, now hatless, sulked his way through luncheon, but managed to eat half a dozen sandwiches. Food, time, and the pleasant company of women combined to cheer him up a little, which was as much as he cared to be cheered up. But then a rowboat came near the shore.

'Well, well, ladies! What a lovely show you all make!' The voice was Italian, smooth. Nico Caporelli's.

'Oh, no! Make him go away!' gasped Léandre, pointing to his white gown with blue ribbon trim. 'This cannot be easily explained.'

'Come up and have a cup of chai with us, why don't you, Mister Capoli,' shouted Maggie, for the fun of it. The Italian immediately replied, yes, he would. He was another who loved female company. Maggie looked at Leon's face for a reaction. He looked back at her murderously, then retrieved his ribboned sunhat and tried to hide himself under it.

Caporelli strolled up the bank, barefoot, sleeves rolled up and shirt unbuttoned in the manner of a Venetian gondolier. His enjoyable new life among the vines in the Swan Valley showed. He had developed muscles, the luncheon party noticed, and seen the sun.

The viticulturist scanned the members of the tea party, lingering on the shy one in the lilac sunhat. He teased each with an Italianised version of her name, Maggie becoming 'Margherita Belladonna', and kissing the outstretched hand of each in the Italian manner. He fussed over the baby, asked Mary Ann if was she was getting enough sleep and kissed the two older girls, who called him 'uncle'.

'And this young lady?' Nico Caporelli offered Léandre Fonteinne his hand. 'I don't believe we have been introduced.'

The hat was flung off. 'Desist, Nicola,' came the gruff response from behind the white mask of powder. 'You know me perfectly well.' The cherry lips were now pursed in annoyance.

'Léandre!' exclaimed Caporelli, a bad actor in a pantomime. 'You look so pale! Are these invalid's robes? Quick, ladies, has the doctor been called?'

He happened to have a bottle of sweet wine in the boat and insisted they all wet the baby's head in the proper manner. Then he sat behind his friend, smiling, an arm over the Frenchman's shoulder in almost proprietorial manner. Occasionally, overcome by his own amusement, he would plant a great wet kiss on the little fellow's cheek.

A breeze blew a napkin off the table. 'God, the sea breeze is in already,' said Mary Ann. 'Louis won't be far off.' Lunch was over. With good humour, they all helped Mary Ann tidy up and started to take things inside.

Once the two men were alone, Caporelli's manner changed.

'There is a serious matter I need to speak to you about,' he whispered in Léandre's bejewelled ear. Then, at greater volume, 'I have a loose rowlock. Come down to the boat and help me with it.'

Léandre followed the Italian with a sickness gnawing at his stomach. Nico was never very serious and Léandre had a vague sense of what may be coming. Shoeless but still stockinged, he hobbled down to the water's edge.

Caporelli crouched and pretended to tinker with the boat. 'Did you try to make love to Liette, by chance?' he said, with none of the usual teasing in his voice.

Léandre's face blanched, though it could not be easily detected under the powder. 'What? Little Liette? She is only ten years old!' His painted lips quivered and his face grew serious. 'What has she been saying?'

'Her father has asked me to discover the truth of it.' Caporelli looked up, all mirth and charm gone from his face. 'You must tell me, Léandre. Is it true?'

'Why no! Of course not!' shouted Léandre in a whisper. 'We are all good friends, that is all. Me, the children, all of the family. You as well, Nicola.'

'So you did not touch her, or try to kiss her on the lips?'

'No! A thousand times no!' The little fellow from Solesmes trembled in his skirts.

'Good. That is all the father wished to hear.' Caporelli stepped back into his rowboat and punted it away from shore. The matter was dealt with. 'Don't worry, Léandre. She will not be believed. I will tell the father. We are still invited to dine with them on Thursday, as usual. It might be best if you could dress more ...' He gestured up and down Léandre's body.

'I shall wear trousers, of course,' protested Léandre, doing his best to look unconcerned by the accusations. He folded his arms and lifted his chin defiantly, but Mary Ann's cream tunic flapped prettily around his ankles in the breeze. 'Be more pleasant on Thursday, please.'

'Oh, but I think you are in my debt, little man!' the Italian replied, blowing a kiss to shore. 'However might you repay me, I wonder?'

After Caporelli had gone, Léandre's mind remained troubled. What could possibly have upset little Liette? Who else might have observed, and whom else might she have told of it? The silly girl had misinterpreted his kindness to her. It seemed that to suffer mis-understanding was his curse in life.

He really must escape this colony, which was so given to slander. He would have to write to his beloved Prosper Guéranger and explain everything. He had put the task off for months.

He sat in the shade. He mixed his ink. His pen hovered above the page. But, as on all previous attempts, the tragedy proved too difficult to put into writing. No matter what words he chose, he would look guilty on paper, and the effort required to explain it would bring back terrible memories of all he had suffered.

'A cup of tea for you, Leon,' said lovely Mary Ann. She stood behind him and stroked his cheek and hair. 'I am sorry that my friends are so silly. You were such a good sport to put up with them.'

Her kindness made the tears come, floods of them streaming down Léandre's still-powdered face. Spittle came from the corners of his mouth making the reddened lips look bloodied, and he wiped it on his white gown, ruining it in places. 'Sorry, my dear Mary Ann,' he blubbered. 'Only you and Louis love me. Nobody else in the world does, I think.'

Mary Ann held his hand. 'Who are you writing to, Leon?'

'My dear abbot at Solesmes,' he croaked, 'but I cannot. If only I could obliterate it from my memory, the blood-stained spectacle of my Irish brother, stricken by my own hand, his skull wide open, blood gurgling up in waves. I squeeze his hand, cover it with kisses, but ...'

'Bubby's crying, mummy,' came a sweet interruption. Little Victoria, hands behind her back.

'... his lifeblood pours in a flood over his face, which already bears the pale imprint of death. My eyes can peer into the very source of his life ...'

'Good God, Leon,' interrupted Mary Ann, 'that's enough now. I have to see to the baby.' She pulled out a sugared biscuit from her apron pocket and put it on the saucer, then brushed his balding pate once more. 'I don't think you need to write all that down for your friend.'

'He is my abbot. I tell him everything.'

Alone again, Léandre looked down at his soiled gown, realising what a pathetic sight he must be. He wiped his hand across his moist face but this only stained the paper with his rainbow tears. Prosper Guéranger had received many letters soaked with his tears, Léandre thought, but the addition of rouge and powder might confuse him so he discarded it, another failed draft, and moved indoors to clean himself up for tea.

Though a layman, Léandre was still permitted to attend Sunday Mass. His voice was such an asset that he was even permitted to pull on the cassock, climb the single step and perform the rôle of cantor. Thus was Léandre fully on display to the congregation when the bishop turned upon him.

'I regret to say,' began Bishop John Brady, casting his eyes about in a threatening manner, 'that a certain man who previously belonged to our mission has merited, by his own scandalous conduct about these streets of Perth in broad daylight, to be designated as an object opposed to good order. Our condemnation of his conduct is without limits.' Not one soul in any pew moved.

The bishop fixed his eyes unwaveringly upon the shaking Frenchman as he delivered his furious sentence, so all could see the shame.

'Each parishioner is to be aware that henceforth I do not wish to recognise *that person* in any way. I expect each one of you to do the same, and each of you to avoid his company. Any man who puts on the clothing of the other sex is *ipso facto* excommunicated from the Church, along with all persons who may have taken part in the despicable act of so disguising him.'

Then, as if it were an unconnected matter, Brady announced that the cantor, had, due to ill health, sung his last Mass.

As the parishioners filed out there was a skirmish in the narthex. The Irish teachers trapped Léandre with their knees and elbows and taunted him. Frightened of a beating, the little fellow panicked and called out to the nuns for help. They saw him but feigned deaf and walked past into the fresh air. Only one couple were sympathetic to his plight and steered him away from the Gaels. It was the parents of the little girl, Liette. They reminded Léandre about tea on Thursday.

Three nights after his excommunication, Léandre was summoned to the bishop's palace. He was to dress plainly, The Terror instructed, and enter through the side door.

'Come,' said Bishop John Brady. He was wearing tattered trousers, looking more a groundsman than a Prince of the Church. Brady wanted this supplicant to understand how low was the esteem in which he was held.

'Your Lordship, I am most grateful ...' began Léandre.

'Be quiet, Fonteinne,' growled the bishop. 'Listen to me. I want you out of my diocese. The fare is thirty pounds, which I do not have, and if I did, would rather send to the starving back in my own country, who are a thousand times more deserving than you. How much have you procured from Serra?'

'Only ten,' said Léandre Fonteinne, looking sadly to the floor-boards.

'Liar!' interrupted the bishop. 'He has given you half. Here is the balance.' From a drawer the bishop took a stack of tawny paper notes marked *Plymouth Dock Bank, Devonshire* and placed them upon the table. Note after painstaking note was transferred into an envelope by the bishop, his hands trembling at the injustice of it.

Léandre snatched at the money before it could be withdrawn, and it vanished inside his jacket.

'Might I kiss you your feet, Your Lordship.'

'Stand, you awful man and be silent. It is not a gift, but a loan. Sign here to indicate you will repay it, though I know of course you will not, because you are a leech and a liar.' Léandre signed at the bottom of the brief document, and Brady stared at the Frenchman's mark sadly.

'Now get out of my damned sight, and out of my diocese. May God bless you, if He so chooses. I will not pray for you, Fonteinne. I would not waste my breath.'

To: Prosper Guéranger, Solesmes Abbey
From: Bishop John Brady, Perth

14th April 1847

(Translated from Bishop Brady's imperfect French)

My very dear Venerable Father

The really unfortunate circumstances which made Dom Léandre Fonteinne decide to want to return are already well known to you. I fear your concerns about our mission will grow with his retelling of the story. Please, do not believe anything you hear that might diminish this mission that you have supported so well. The boy lies about everything.

I gave him fifteen English pounds, half his fare home, and in return only complaints that I had not provided for his other costs. I had him sign a deed to repay the loan to the Catholic Diocese of Perth. He will never do so, of course. He has disappointed me so many times for the bad. Nobody in this colony will ever wish him back.

I now ask you, my dear Father, for your influence with the members of the Central Council of the Propagation of the Faith. You know them well. We find ourselves in extreme financial difficulty and require their urgent assistance.

Your confrère in J.C.,
John, Bishop of Perth

16. NEW NORCIA BLOOMS

The wagon parked under a rusty salmon gum on the edge of a field of pink everlastings belonged to a farmer from York. He had offered to bring the merino ram up to the 'Italian priests' at New Norcia and brought the little fellow along for the adventure, or so he had told its mother.

George was the child's name and he sat there on the box boards peeking out attentively from under an old fleece shirt his father had thrown over him to keep the flies off. A monk approached, or so the farmer thought – a bearded fellow in workman's clothes and an unusual hat made of woven bamboo or some such material.

'Morning, Father.'

'I am not a father, I am a linguist. But I will take you to Father Salvado. He is busy with the hens. How old is your little boy?'

'One and a half, I think. Why are you here if you're not a monk?'

'My friend shot one. I came to help, but I've stayed a bit longer than I expected.'

'You're as good as a monk now, from the looks. Might as well sign up, mate. And by the way you've a couple of worms on your hat there.' A very odd fellow this, thought the farmer; rather than putting them under his boot, he dropped the wrigglers gently into his shirt pocket.

Fabrice led the farmer to Dom Salvado, who was grateful for the safe delivery of the ram, but even more interested in the child. He asked some questions regarding the child's provenance and detected in the farmer's eyes a look that could only be described as sheepish.

'Well, there's not much white women in the Avon,' he stumbled. 'No free ones, anyway.' Salvado knew this to be true. The colony had just published its first census and he had studied it with care, mindful of Bishop Brady's wild estimates. There were one thousand, eight hundred and four European females in this colony of a million square miles, counting children. Salvado prided himself as a man of the world: a brown baby was a natural consequence of this demography.

Salvado picked the child up. George stared back, wondering who the bearded one in the tattered cassock might be.

'He's pretty fair,' explained the farmer, watching the monk's eyes warily.

'He's paler than me!' joked Salvado, pulling back a sleeve to reveal arms baked brown behind the plough. He patted the farmer's back to reassure him there would be no sermon. In fact, Salvado was delighted. He needed reliable parishioners who would not disappear into the bush on a whim. That this farmer, a good man, would travel all the way from York to bring the Benedictines such a gift seemed to be a sign that God was happy with all He saw at New Norcia. The Pope badly wanted native priests. This boy could be the future of the mission.

Salvado pulled the little fellow up onto his feet. Sturdy, not even a sway. 'Look at those legs,' said the monk, a broad grin interrupting his black beard. 'Farmer's legs!'

'Will you take him then, Father?'

'What of the mother?'

The farmer looked at his boots. 'Best we keep her out of it, for now.'

Salvado propped the little fellow on his left hip and let him pull something from his beard.

'Prudencio,' said the monk thoughtfully. 'He looks like a Prudencio.'

'We call him George ...' started the farmer.

'We shall baptise him anew,' Salvado explained. 'Is he to retain your surname?'

The farmer blew out hard, uncertain. The Avon was a small district, and though he was over thirty he had not quite given up all hope of one day marrying.

'There would be no shame in his having it,' Salvado reassured him 'Look how well you have cared for him.'

Still no certain answer came. The father was having doubts. 'You talk Italian here?'

'Spanish, for general conversation. Latin for prayer.'

'And the black fellows, you make them talk Spanish? Or the other one?'

'We use both. And we try to learn their language, as best we can.'

'Why not just teach them proper English?'

'Not all the monks speak English very well.'

'Sorry, Father,' said the man from York, to give himself time to think. 'Not my business what you talk. Let's get this ram into your barn. And show me around, mate. Your success is the talk of the Avon, you know.'

First, the farmer was shown inside the only stone structure, the Church of The Blessed Trinity. His own design, explained the monk; he had studied architecture as a young man in Spain. Forty-two feet by sixteen by fourteen high. Half a dozen men had come up from Perth to build it, including an Italian, two Frenchmen and three non-Catholics. Denomination did not matter to Salvado if they were hardworking men and handy with a saw or trowel.

The first stone had been laid on the first of March: the Feast of St Rudesindas, after whom Rosendo was named. The two monks had slept inside the roofless church just seven weeks later, the twenty-eighth of April, 1847. A very special night, Salvado told the farmer. Watching the night sky from the floor of the altar was the first time he truly believed that the mission would succeed.

'Next, we build the mission house.'

'You're lucky to have good stone close by,' observed the farmer, looking at an outcrop which he could see had been quarried to build the church.

'The monastery will need even more than that hill can provide. It will be on a Spanish scale.'

'Why?' said the farmer. 'It's not Spain here.'

'Our Lord deserves good walls and a roof.'

'The blackfellas won't like being in the dark, you know.'

Salvado gave an enigmatic smile. 'Well, we have tried the nomadic approach, and failed. We will go back to what we know works.'

The farmer winked as if in agreement. A Spanish monastery in the bush. The rumours about these foreign priests being a bit mad were true.

'Come,' said the monk, sensing a lack of enthusiasm for matters religious. 'Let's look at the farm. You can tell me all the things I am doing wrong!'

Salvado looked at his brass pocket watch; it was just after ten, so they had an hour before Angelus. Everything at New Norcia ran according to the Rule of St Benedict, he explained. They rose every morning at five for Vigils, then came time for private prayer, and then a small breakfast. Lauds were sung at half past six, Mass at half past seven, then there was a second breakfast and the farm work began.

'I wonder all that praying leaves you time to run a farm,' observed the man from York.

'It makes us more efficient!' smiled Salvado, leading the farmer down the path. '*Ora et Labora* is our motto. Prayer and Work. The one helps the other, I am sure. When all the physical work is done, we treasure quietness. Vespers are at half past six, then dinner, at which wine is permitted. Then Dom Serra allows us time to read and write before Lectio. Compline is at eight, followed by the nine hours Great Silence.'

'Such discipline,' said the farmer, without apparent irony.

The monk grinned. 'I need discipline, you know! There is still something of the wasteful youth in me.'

'I doubt that,' said the farmer, looking ahead to the collection of sheds and workshops. A lot of work to knock them up, he thought, but they were made of bone-dry timber and would burn to the ground in a minute.

They stopped at a wooden sign on which was painted, in shaky hand: *I was a strangler and you welcome me. Matt 25:35.*

'That's Benedict's good work!' explained Salvado, provoking a shy grin from the artist, who had the obstinate ram on a rope. Benedict Upemara was a handsome boy of nine or ten whose wavy dark hair had been partially tamed with olive oil and comb. 'New Norcia exists not for our benefit, but for these Australians,' said Dom Salvado, his hand upon the boy's head. 'All are welcome here.'

'Even stranglers,' said the farmer, nodding at the sign.

'Of course!' said the monk, enjoying the joke. 'We have not come to this place just for the righteous, but to call sinners to repentance.'

As it always did when farmers in this colony walked together, the talk turned to pastoral leases. The future of his mission depended on having secure depasturing leases, Salvado explained. The acting governor had promised him twenty acres but he would like a thousand times more.

The farmer blinked. 'Twenty thousand acres?'

'At least,' said the monk. 'Each family is to be given their own plot of land, but only once they have learned to farm it.'

The man from York looked dubious. 'Are blackfellas even permitted to own land?'

'Of course not,' said the monk. 'The leases will stay officially in our names, held on their behalf.'

'And you, are Italians allowed to own land?'

Salvado balked at this, for the problem had not occurred to him. 'We are Spanish,' he protested. 'Though that may be worse. But there is a way around every rule. Perhaps I will have to become British. I have learned all about colonial bureaucracy. Did you know, it is the same fee no matter how many leases you apply for? If I write in small, neat letters I can fit ten lease applications to a page, and only pay for one!'

It was springtime, and swathes of pink, orange and yellow wildflowers fringed the green fields of New Norcia. They went down to look at the condition of the new livestock. Salvado and Bilyagoro had shepherded them all the way back from York.

'Not one did I lose,' boasted Salvado, 'despite having the worst sheep dog on Victoria Plains.'

'You really are the good shepherd,' observed the farmer, dryly. 'But you'll start losing them if you let them eat this stuff.' He snapped off a piece of prickly bush which had just come into orange flower. 'York Road poison. It gives the little ones the shits.'

'Is there treatment?'

'They say you cut off an ear to let the poison out.'

'Does it work?'

'I've never known it to,' said the farmer, 'but it is what they all say.' He nodded his hat brim towards the ram who had been left by Benedict in grass up to his twist. 'You'll kill that big fella too if you're not careful. Pen him over there in the dirt or he'll keep eating till his guts burst.'

There was an olive grove, cuttings from the governor's trees. There was a new vineyard where a couple of older fellows were tying young vines to wooden crosses. Salvado went across to yell at them and pace things out. The idiots had managed to plant them too close together, he complained, despite all his explanations. There was a vegetable patch with healthy cauliflowers in head, and the start of a fruit orchard, with a dozen young apricot and plum trees struggling to get established but not yet dead.

They came to a working forge, full of heat and noise and activity. The aproned blacksmith could have been Salvado's twin brother, except that he spoke with a cultured English accent. He had two native apprentices who seemed to be enjoying the work.

'Meet our newest brother, Dom Prudencio,' smiled Salvado, pulling the child from atop his shoulders and placing him on the sand floor of the smithy.

'Dear me,' said the blacksmith, looking down with mock sincerity, 'run away, little fellow, while you still have a chance.' George looked up with great seriousness.

'You're Roger Smith,' said the farmer, recognising him from the workshop at Toodyay. 'You've worked on my wagon, or that Parkhurst boy of yours did.'

The hairy blacksmith confessed to it.

'Everyone thinks you've gone back to Scotland to be a baron. Or else that that convict lad of yours has buried you up the back of your block.'

'The latter is quite untrue,' said Roger Smith, dryly. 'But I still intend the former. I would have left already, if these dull lads would just learn their lessons.' The accused boys looked adept enough, one holding the glowing work piece steadily with the tongs while the other worked it with the hammer. 'Soon I shall escape these papists and retire to my estate, where I shall read the pre-Christian Greeks in peace until I die, after which there will be nothing, by the way. Nothing at all.'

Salvado patted his friend firmly on the back. 'Roger Smith never misses an opportunity to taunt me,' he explained, with great affection. 'But we will convert him yet, I have faith. In the meantime, I would settle for the repaired coulter I was promised three days ago.'

'Patience,' counselled the atheist blacksmith. 'You monks really must learn some patience.'

'So you're a Christian now?' asked the farmer. Everyone in the Avon knew the English blacksmith was a strident non-believer.

'I am like Erasmus of Rotterdam,' announced Roger Smith. 'I see religion as a useful folly. I am not strongly opposed, so long as it is not taken seriously. Some of the English hymns, I am forced to admit, are quite lovely.'

Salvado was making use of the fireplace for a small project of his own. Benedict fetched him a bashed-about tin pot and a delicate wooden box and a brush. The monk heated some water, extracted a few blue crystals from the gauze and dropped them, wizard-like, into the warm water, which turned indigo.

'Sheep got sores?' suggested the farmer, who knew bluestone.

'Not the sheep,' said Salvado, mysteriously, 'but members of my flock with a similar affliction.'

'So you are a doctor as well, Father?'

'A monk must be everything! St Benedict taught us to be apothecaries and herbalists and to minister to the infirm. I am trying to learn about the healing properties of local plants, as they would be much easier to obtain than these crystals, which have to come from Switzerland. There is an old medicine fellow round here they call *mabarn* and he must know such things, but won't tell me.' He stirred the solution with a stick, and carried the steaming pot of blue tincture down the path and across the field to the privacy of the riverbank where his patients were secreted.

In a wet corner of the farm were four young mulberry trees almost stripped of leaves, and a sort of cage, in front of which was the odd fellow with the oriental hat. The farmer asked him what secret thing Salvado was doing down at the riverbank.

'The shepherds are syphilitics,' explained Fabrice.

'He is treating the shepherds?'

'Of course not. He treats the sores of the women they have raped. So, George is your boy?'

The farmer did not reply, unsure if he had just been accused of something.

'Those shepherds are nothing but trouble,' Fabrice continued.

'They take the women, intimidate the men, and kill a dozen of their kangaroos just for sport with the help of their horrible dogs. But if even one of their sheep is missing, they threaten to have the men sent off to Rottnest.'

They were standing in front of an elaborate wooden structure covered in fine mesh.

'A beehive?' guessed the farmer.

'No. A *magnanerie*,' explained Fabrice Cleriquot, son of the famous Lyonnais silk merchant. He led George in. The cage was alive with dull white moths which did little except mate and shoot jets of green liquid. 'Come, help me gather *les cocons*,' he instructed, giving the boy a small bowl to hold. George quickly learned not to put the delicate fluffy objects in his mouth.

When the *magnanier* emerged, his assistant carried a bowl full of golden cocoons. The farmer inspected one up close.

'These look spoiled, mate. Are you meant to let them hatch?'

'No,' said Fabrice. 'You should boil them alive, but I cannot.'

'Waste of effort,' scoffed the farmer.

'True,' agreed Fabrice, 'but so much kinder, and I can still retrieve some thread.' A spoiled cocoon might still produce two hundred metres of silk thread, he explained, but even so he would need five thousand to produce a pound of raw silk.

'And then?' asked the farmer.

'Well, my father would have machines to spin it into thread, and then looms, and dyes and designers and artisans of various sorts, to turn it into beautiful garments.'

'But out here, in the bush?'

'Here, I would just have a pound of silk.'

The farmer shook his head at the futility of the project. 'No one needs silk, mate,' he said, unkindly. 'Muslin, calico, burlap, those materials we could use. Silk is useless. Is that really all you do in this place, make silk?'

'Oh no,' said Fabrice, thinking hard, for he had never been sure of his purpose. 'I also study the language of the natives but they are not very helpful. I have learned to cook on the open fire. And there is the garden. I have planted marigolds.' He knew this list sounded thin. In fact, Fabrice had been learning a lot of unexpected things in this quiet place, much to his surprise. He had learned that it was in the doing of many small things, each unimportant in itself, that he gained a sense of purpose; that he felt best when connected to nature; and that, ever since his encounter with the *gouljacque*'s beak, he had sensed god in every little thing that lived. Perhaps he was meant to be a gardener, like the Senegalese at *Lorette*. Also, he had grown to greatly miss his dear Maman and it was possible he had forgiven his father; they would have to meet again for him to be sure. But he could not find the words to explain such things to the farmer from York.

A man of impressive physique appeared from the bush with half a kangaroo dripping blood across his shoulder. He glanced dismissively at Fabrice then let the gift flop at the feet of the farmer. He was lean, about the same age as the farmer but without any fat round his middle, and adorned with two spears and a knife slung around his waist. He pointed to the carcass and told the farmer something important.

'*Kwenta libras*?' said the farmer. 'What's he mean by that?'

'*Cinquenta*,' explained Fabrice. 'Fifty pounds of meat.'

'*Para Salvado*,' the hunter expanded, now addressing the Frenchman, who was not as stupid as he had first seemed. '*De Dwergan*,' he added, tapping his own chest.

'*Se lo diré*,' Fabrice reassured him, and the hunter took off, still dripping blood, to collect the other half from whatever cool place he had hidden it.

'You do speak the local lingo,' said the farmer.

'Spanish,' explained Fabrice. 'We are to tell Salvado the gift came from Dwergan.'

The Frenchman had claimed to be a cook but he looked pretty useless so the farmer went back to his cart to retrieve a hessian bag which he soaked and wrapped the meat in before taking it up to the kitchen. The blowflies were in a frenzy. He would clean it and butcher it properly for the pot.

Benedict Upemara wanted to help. He was pretty good with a knife. With boys, the farmer knew, it was best to talk while they were busy. What was the mission like? he asked Benedict. Was he allowed to see his family much, and to go bush? What about sitting in the dark saying all those prayers? He was really asking for George.

When Salvado returned, the farmer told him of his decision. He would be taking George back home to York after all. The mother would get distraught if he went back without the boy. There would be wailing and the waving of arms, and then she might get a stick. Maybe later he would bring the mother to look at the place herself and decide. There might be two littlies by then, he mumbled at his shoes. She seemed to be carrying their second.

Salvado, hiding his disappointment, said he thought that an excellent plan. He would get a house ready for them. He picked Dom Prudencio up and brought his face close so the boy might better remember him. This young man definitely had the makings of a priest, beamed the monk. The farmer stayed diplomatically silent on the matter, but no son of his was going to become a Catholic priest.

As the sun got low, the farmer and the monk walked down to the Moore River. The farmer was curious to know what the shepherds were up to. Everyone knew the shepherds in these new districts were wild men. Perhaps they needed to be; it was as lonely a job as you could ever get and in other districts one or two had got speared.

Salvado took him to a spot in the riverbed where they could observe the shepherds in their camp just across the river. They were just young blokes. All seemed quiet, just mumbled conversation and the odd ring of laughter.

'These the ones disturbing the local women?' ventured the farmer in a low voice that would not carry.

'Yes,' said Salvado, thoughtfully. 'And they intimidate the men, threatening them with the chain and the island. That island terrifies them, it means death to them. And they make up all sorts of terrible stories about us. Some good people have left the mission because they believed the stories.'

As they emerged from the riverbed they came upon a wild-haired old man performing some sort of ceremony. There was smoke and sticks and singing.

'The *mabarn*,' whispered Salvado. 'Very important fellow. Their doctor, and priest. His medicine is very much stronger than mine. We should leave.'

Salvado touched the farmer on the shoulder and took off in the direction of the ridge, beads in hand. There was a special spot up on the hill where he liked to be alone and pray.

The farmer stayed a while in the bottom field to inspect things. Dusk was a sort of prayerful time for him too, a time to reflect alone on a day's work. The soil was quite rich here, he noted, and soft underfoot. Someone needed to run the harrier over it.

In York, he was known as a water finder. He could see the trouble that would come in the dry months when the surface water dried up and Maurin Pool shrunk to a puddle. Then the monks would have to compete with the shepherds and the natives. There might be enough for the humans but not for the hundreds of sheep, all tramping and dirtying the water. That's when all niceties would end and the shepherds would try to push the missionaries out.

He cut a forked branch suitable for divining. It gave a good result. If Salvado was prepared to dig twenty feet in this place, he could have a good well, come rain or dry.

The farmer looked up the crest to see where the monk had got to. The black cockatoos had gathered in numbers, noisy and playful, and when they perched in the gum trees and spread their red tail feathers, the low sun shone through like a Chinese lantern. Salvado was walking up the hill, dark against a huge orange sun, arms behind him, deep in thought. He seemed a wise enough sort of fellow, thought the farmer, and quite practical, despite his religion. Atop the hill he could be seen to stop and stand motionless. The silhouette blessed itself, bowed its head and pressed its hands together in prayer, holy beads suspended.

Black against a reddening sky, cassock and beard blown around by the westerly, the monk in his prayers seemed to the man from York to belong in this place, almost as if he had been here forever, no less than the old *mabarn* down in the riverbed making smoke and singing ancient words through his nose and just like the monks when they chanted away in their little stone church.

From: Fabrice Cleriquot, New Norcia Mission
To: Pauline Jaricot, Lyon

17th January 1848

Chère Mademoiselle Jaricot

The simple thing you asked me to do has proved impossible, to support an enterprise which is to the benefit of the native people of this colony. I had high hopes for the Humanist commune but it fell apart, the only beneficiary being a juvenile prisoner hostile to the blacks. The Heart of Mary priests have left for Mauritius in hope of finding a better bishop. Poor Don Confalonieri was banished so far north we cannot even be sure if he is still alive.

Only the Spanish mission survives. New Norcia is three days from the capital along bush tracks and over wild rivers. At first the Benedictines tried living like the natives. Now Dom Salvado aims to build a grand Spanish monastery like he knew in Galicia, while Dom Serra wants to build another one at a place near the capital he has called New Subiaco, well away from troublesome natives.

In Perth, the Irish nuns have persisted despite everything. They have started two schools and do good works in the prison and hospital. You have contributed anonymously towards the building of a Benevolent Institution where they will house the little girls they confiscate from their mothers.

What good will finally come from all this effort and tragedy? Two million souls gained for the church? Of course not. Dom Salvado has a grand plan to send native boys from the bush to Rome to be trained as priests. The long journey at sea would most likely kill them, but why would a priest care? The church has killed so many of those who love her that the death of a few dark boys from the Australian bush will hardly be noticed, or if noticed, will more likely be celebrated than regretted.

I have produced some Australian silk, so that is something, I suppose. Father may be proud of me for it. Nothing can be done with it here, of course, and the material is anyway despised in this place because of its beauty.

I want to be surrounded by loveliness again. I find I am more and more thinking of Europe, Mademoiselle, and of dear Maman and others that I love and miss. I think I have done almost all that I can possibly do in this dull place; by which I do not mean I have been successful, for I have not, but that your purses have almost been emptied, or else drowned in the Avon River. I shall explain when next I see you in Lyon.

Affectueusement,
Fabrice

17. THE SYNOD

It was a hot January day and the two Irishmen took turns cursing as they bumped along Salvado's new track. He had got a group of men and boys from the mission to clear a line all the way from the Brockman property at Bindoon, but the road to New Norcia had not been used much and it kept disappearing.

'That damned Serra is a conniving bastard,' said Brady, speaking of the monk who would be their host for the next three days. 'He has been writing again to the Bishop of Sydney, doing his level best to undermine me.'

No one overhearing the conversation between these two Irishmen on the bullock cart would have guessed them to be the Catholic Bishop of Perth and his newly appointed subdeacon. Nor would appearance have given them away as clerics. A single night in the Western Australian bush will quickly dilapidate an Irishman, and they already looked like they had been living rough for weeks. In the back, old Father Joostens dozed.

'Of course he writes to Polding,' said Farrelly. 'They're all Benedictines and those fellas always look after each other.'

'Polding is a bigot,' the bishop growled. 'Very much in love with his own image. He thinks New South Wales *is* Australia.'

'Power and money, John. That is all they think about, the monks.'

'Indeed. Mammon, didn't Jesus call it on the Mount? A great evil, did He not say? Turned the tables over in the temple, did He not?'

'He did,' agreed The Terror, 'but you can bet they turned them back up the minute he was gone. Only Ireland listened and stayed poor. If Serra were to go back to old Spain and shake the tin, he'd get a thousand pounds. Do the same in our poor homeland and there would not be a farthing to be got.'

They were heading up to New Norcia for the inaugural General Synod of the Perth Catholic Diocese. Farrelly had the whip hand. The rivers were dry, so there had been no delay at the crossings and they would save a whole day by avoiding the Toodyay Road. Barring a broken axle, Farrelly promised his bishop, he would be sleeping on a mattress in New Norcia this night.

'Mattress?' grumbled John Brady. 'Bed of nails, if I know Joseph Serra.'

The previous week, the two Irishmen had been allowed to visit the native prison on Rottnest Island. Acting Governor Irwin, in granting permission, personally cautioned the Catholic bishop not to create dissent among the native prisoners.

Brady and Farrelly still burned with fury at what they had witnessed. The young age of the prisoners was what struck them first. An English strategy to weaken the race, the Irishmen agreed, to take the young, fit and sturdy. The troublemakers had been stolen from all directions – from Pinjarra in the south, from Champion Bay in the north, and from the Avon Valley to the east of the capital. The buggers all seemed to want to escape, so the guards complained, and when they finally worked out they could not, were apt to curl up and die.

'God damn the English race,' Farrelly had declared aloud on the prison sloop sailing back to Fremantle. The guards all heard this sedition but The Terror did not have the sort of face to invite correction, even by a prison guard.

'English colonialism is theft, pure and simple,' added the bishop, knowing his words would be reported back to Irwin. Let the bastard hear it. It was the truth.

Certain images from the island had imprinted themselves upon John Brady's imagination. Iron bars, manacles, bolts, locks and keys – none of these things existed in the bush. The bishop wept at the memory of miserable creatures wrapped up in blankets in the heat of summer, rocking back and forth trying to sing their way back to their own country. There was something familiar and personal in those downcast eyes, in the shame, the despair, the suppressed anger. He had seen it before, in another land appropriated by others. He could do nothing about it back then, and though consecrated by the Pope, still could do nothing.

'If I was starting again, Terry, I would bring out only Irish,' declared the bishop, ignoring any possible offence to their Belgian companion, Father Joostens, who was still half-asleep. 'The French were useless: all emotion and no practicality.'

'What of Salvado?' said Farrelly.

'Well, he's Galician, that almost counts as Irish. There's something of the Irish poet about him.'

'And he's good with his hands,' agreed Farrelly. 'I look forward to seeing what progress he has made up there.'

'If you can find the place this time.' This was a friendly provocation. On a previous attempt, Farrelly had got lost and they had to turn back.

'Sit tight, Your Lordship,' said the subdeacon. 'I'm a man of my word. I'll have you in New Norcia before dinner.'

'Are you sure?' said the bishop. 'Do you know how early those bloody Benedictines eat?'

A dozen bumpy miles ahead of them, New Norcia was in readiness. Salvado had lined up the four married couples and their freshly bathed and dressed children. Four little houses had recently been given to those men who had shown the greatest inclination towards hard work and monogamy. These were N'yalbinga, the mission's best tracker; Takencut, whom Salvado admired as a steady fellow; the mission's best hunter Dwergan; and Salvado's most loyal man Bilyagoro, who had wandered down to the riverbed this morning to avoid all the fuss. All four wives had been renamed Mary, but were permitted by the monks to keep their native names as a surname.

Each couple had to promise to learn useful skills: fencing, shepherding or ploughing for the men; cooking or cleaning for the women. They were to be paid for their farm work, but since coins were scarce and quickly lost, Salvado put the money for them away, or else payment was provided in kind. Just this week Dwergan had been given his own calf and allowed to brand it with a *D* as proof of ownership.

Houses, farming, cleaning, money, ownership: all these were new concepts to the local people, and only partly embraced. The four wives, all noisy and assertive women, thought their new rôles a comedown from being boss of the camp. The husbands could not be made to understand what Dom Salvado meant when he offered them their own piece of farmland. They failed to see the incentive in that proposition, no matter how carefully he explained it. They seemed to believe that the country they walked upon was already theirs.

The parents given houses had to allow their sons to stay with the monks in the new Mission House to start their education. On this special day, the houses were to be swept and cleaned, and the children similarly swept and cleaned and lined up ready for inspection by the Bishop of Perth.

Noon came and went, still no bishop had appeared, and interest in the matter had greatly waned. Salvado realised he was fretting.

Bilyagoro reappeared from the river carrying a lamb across his shoulders in biblical manner. Salvado guessed it had become trapped in the mud and Bilyagoro was carrying it to the barn to recover. He allowed himself some satisfaction at this. Kindness could be learned: just a year ago Bilyagoro would have broken the poor creature's neck without hesitation.

Then, from the direction of the shepherds' camp, came a horse-man and then a gunshot. Bilyagoro dropped the lamb and ran towards Salvado. He arrived in distress, his bare chest heaving and face smeared with river mud. There was no blood to be seen.

'Mad bugger shot me!' he declared, eyes red. Bilyagoro looked back to the river, still a warrior but a fearful one. Courage was no match for a smoking rifle. The horseman had reshouldered his weapon and was riding up toward the mission. Salvado recognised him vaguely. There had been three shepherds camped at Maurin Pool for the last week, taking advantage of the long grass there, and they seemed an especially bad lot.

'Go inside and see Kiara,' said Salvado, using the name the locals used for Serra. 'He will give you a smoke.' Bilyagoro made off, but the group of children in their smart mission clothes ignored

Salvado's instructions to run off. They wanted to stay and watch the excitement.

'Don't let him shoot your head off, Father,' was Bilyagoro's final advice, 'make all these little kids cry.'

'Seventeen sheep,' were the shepherd's first angry words as he pulled his horse up almost on top of Salvado. He was young, but his teeth were much older. A Brunswick rifle was slung over his shoulder.

'Did you fire at my man?' demanded the monk.

'He was carrying off a sheep. That's seventeen we've lost in two days.'

'That lamb is his own property.'

'Don't talk nonsense,' grinned the shepherd. Natives stole sheep, they didn't own them.

'It is perfectly true,' protested the monk. 'The native men of this mission are farmers. Shepherds just like you.'

The shepherd shook his head. These Italian priests were every bit as mad as everyone said.

Salvado tried appeasing. 'I am sorry if your sheep have been speared.'

'Last couple had their throats cut. As if some whitefella had taught them how to butcher.'

That information took Salvado aback. He might have to have a word with Dwergan.

'You better warn them. We've got just one job, to protect the flock. We'll do whatever is needed.'

'I will tell your boss of your threats,' Salvado retorted. The Scots were tough men, but had always been polite and reasonable in their dealings with the monks.

The young shepherd spat on the ground, then winked at one

of the little girls who was looking up at him, bare-bellied, hands behind her back. 'There's laws in this country, you know. Tell your blacks if they touch any of our flock, just one, they will be off to the island in chains.' Then for effect, without taking his left hand off the reins, he aimed the rifle over the tops of the rivergums and let loose a single bullet. The horse reared. 'I'm the soft one,' he said, touching the stirrups, 'my mates aren't so forgiving.'

Salvado, because he was shaken, made a show of being unaffected by the encounter. He pointed skywards. 'He was trying to shoot that eagle,' he joked. But the children understood perfectly well where power lay. Benedict Upemara, being the favourite among the boys, had spent a lot of time standing beside Father Salvado and to see his hands trembling was an entirely new thing.

By late afternoon there was neither a bishop nor any remaining interest in one. Even Salvado was barefoot, clipping his nails on the wooden steps of the church. 'Benedict, my sandals, quick!' he instructed, when the wagon finally appeared. Of all the boys, only Benedict could be relied upon to retrieve both of them.

His Lordship climbed from the cart rubbing his rump but in better humour than the old Belgian. 'I have brought you some whiskey, Rosendo,' were his first words. The Terror sprang from the driver's seat, embraced Salvado and began admiring what improvements he could make out in the dimming light.

Dom Serra emerged eventually from the mission house, seeming in no hurry to greet his bishop. His rôle in this synod was administrative: to have the church ready for the welcoming Mass, the papers prepared, and to find a place for three extra bodies for three nights. Brady followed Serra inside, both men stiff in their manners, but Farrelly said he needed to stretch his legs before dark so Salvado took him to inspect the ground pegs for the new monastery.

Mass was held. The church was full, and beautifully candlelit. Benedict sang his line quite well. The women had been taught to sing some of the *Kyrie*, their full-throated voices sounding unexpectedly well against the Benedictine's deep chanting. The bishop, understanding the importance of the occasion, had thought to wear his amaranth biretta, the sight of which brought tears to Salvado's eyes. This place had so recently been wild bush and now, through his efforts and the guidance of Our Lord, there was a church, an altar, and now a bishop's head saying Mass over it.

'What is this thing?' Brady demanded, as they exited. He was looking at a statue of Christ crucified. A miniature wooden spear had been glued to the wound in His side.

'A *kidji*,' explained Benedict Upemara.

Bishop Brady glared at Dom Salvado. 'Our Lord has a *kidji* glued upon His person?'

'He *was* speared,' said Salvado. 'And it helps them to imagine Christ as one of them.'

'You shall remove it,' said Brady, 'just as the Roman soldier was good enough to do.' Then he peered closely at the Lamb of God and again looked at Salvado for explanation. 'And this graffiti?'

'Wool, Your Lordship. I allowed Benedict to ... it was to help them understand that it is, after all, a common sheep, just as we have in our fields.'

'It is a symbol of God, Rosendo, not a child's toy. Have it cleaned up.'

Next morning, Dom Serra formally declared the Rules of St Benedict suspended for three days in deference to those visiting clergy who were not of their order. Breakfast was served by Fabrice Cleriquot, who had made a flamboyant chef's hat for the occasion and produced crêpes from fresh eggs and smoked ham.

Father Joostens was especially appreciative. *'C'était un petit déjeuner digne d'un pape,'* he whispered to the chef as the plates were cleared, wiping his eggy jowls on the white linen. Though Flemish, Joostens spoke perfect French, a legacy of his time as a chaplain in Napoleon's army.

The breakfast table was wiped clean and reappointed for business. Chairs were pulled in, documents appeared, and the Bishop of Perth declared the inaugural Grand Synod of the Diocese of Perth to be open.

The bishop called the roll. There were just four priests and subdeacon Farrelly as scribe. The number of clergy in the colony had thinned, Brady confirmed. The Heart of Mary priests had left for Mauritius, and Peter Powell for Calcutta; 'and very welcome to it he is,' His Lordship added. The sickly English monk had gone back to Downside Abbey 'for reasons of his health', and the French novice had been sent home, necessitating a loan of fifteen pounds. The bishop looked hard at Dom Serra as he said this and instructed Farrelly to include that debt to the diocese in the minutes.

'Soon, we shall lose another,' continued Brady. 'Our eldest and most respected confrère, Father Joostens, is to retire to Batavia. I am personally indebted to him more than I can express. Though not an architect, he built our cathedral during my absence in Rome, and a grand job he made of it, even if the walls were finished before the windows were thought of. So soon we will have to struggle on with just three priests.'

'Two,' announced Dom Serra, to silence.

For a terrible moment, the bishop thought the devious Benedictine had used his influence in Rome to have him replaced. 'How so?'

'I am shortly to travel to Rome, *ad visitanda limina*,' said Serra.

'When?'

'I leave in two weeks.'

'For how long?'

'Some months. A year, perhaps.'

The prelate's relief turned to annoyance, for Serra's public announcement of this without first seeking approval was surely designed to undermine his authority. Publicly, he feigned disinterest. 'In that case, Dom Salvado, you become my vicar-general.'

Salvado braced. Was he to be sent to Albany to replace Father Joostens as vicar-general of King George Sound?

The bishop sensed his alarm. 'Be calm, Rosendo. It will not interfere with your work here. But even a faultless bishop such as I must offer his Confession from time to time.'

The synod had not yet properly begun and already there had been three changes in personnel.

'Now. Let us plan these three days ahead,' said Brady, moving his chair closer to the table to regain control of proceedings. 'The first two Acts of this synod regard diocesan affairs in general. The next three Acts will consider our Missions, including here at New Norcia and Port Victoria.'

'Ah! How fares *Le Tyrolien*?' An unexpected voice from behind the bishop. It came from the waiter, who was pouring tea and

303

delicately placing sugary biscuits on saucers using tiny silver tongs. 'He is still alive?'

The bishop stared straight ahead. Such an interruption was not permitted. The Northern Mission was a painful catastrophe, with two good Irish lads lost *en route*. Terry Farrelly guided Fabrice from the room. There were firm noises off.

The bishop continued. 'We will also discuss matters to do with the Sisters of Mercy, who are under my control, and the matter of the orphan girls they receive from this mission. And finally, we shall come to the matter of the mission I propose to establish for the prisoners of Rottnest Island, for whom our hearts break.'

The agenda set, there was a shuffling of papers and sips of tea before His Lordship began with a direct assault on his host.

'To diocesan matters. Dom Serra, you will explain what exactly has been the nature of your recent correspondence with Bishop John Polding of Sydney.'

Serra demurred. There had been nothing of special significance.

'I am your bishop,' Brady reminded Serra. 'All mail comes through me. I know that you correspond with another diocese. Upon what matters do you correspond?'

There seeming no way to avoid the matter, Dom Serra took his time choosing his next words. He looked intently at the loveheart-shaped *palmier* that the waiter had placed on a dainty plate before him, and when he spoke it was as if addressing the biscuit, rather than the bishop.

'Bishop Polding asked me to sail to Sydney.'

'Has he indeed? And at whose expense has he proposed you do this?'

'His.'

'And to what purpose?'

'I believe he has some concerns about this diocese.'

'*My* diocese, you mean. And what sort of concerns might those be?'

'Financial.'

There was a silence as the bishop's face reddened.

'The financial matters of this diocese are solely my responsibility.'

'Not solely,' said Serra, still regarding the sugary biscuit with great intensity. 'They affect us all. The Bishop of Sydney is of the view, I think, that the diocese might benefit from the appointment of a coadjutor.'

'A coadjutor!' thundered Brady. 'And who is that to be? You, I suppose!'

'I do not yet know,' said Serra.

'But instead of Sydney, you have now decided to sail to Rome. What mischief have you planned there?'

'No mischief, Your Lordship.'

'Are you to see the Pope?'

'I would certainly hope so.'

Brady looked up to the scribe. Farrelly had been dead right, these Benedictines were too well connected. Bishops here. Popes there. Brady was the outsider.

'Do your best, Joseph,' sulked the bishop. 'You are every bit as bad as the nuns. You lack respect for ecclesiastical structures. You monks respect neither your diocese, nor your bishop. Autonomy is more important to you than fidelity. Well, go and get yourself appointed coadjutor, if you can. Try for bishop, if you like! But be warned, I too have friends in Rome. I am the Bishop of Perth, consecrated by the Pope, and I will remain so until the Lord takes me.'

There was a lengthy silence while the bishop's anger died down. Papers were shuffled. Things needed reading.

John Brady continued. 'Deacon Farrelly, read the report on the works required on the cathedral.'

The rest of the day was kept very business-like, allowing tempers to cool. Serra was kept separated from the bishop at all times by one other body. The diocesan budget was quickly dealt with and no questions were permitted.

'So the dapper Frenchman has joined you,' said the bishop, accepting another *vol-au-vent*. The day's meeting had mercifully come to an end and Fabrice had set out *apéritifs* and cold ales in the garden. Brady had not forgotten the Frenchman's earlier intrusion, but did appreciate his work in the kitchen. 'Is the fellow not an avowed atheist?'

'Merely a lost Catholic, I like to think,' replied Salvado, dryly. 'Ours is a mission, after all, devoted to converting heathens. If we can win souls from the bush, we may yet have success with the Frenchman. In the meantime, he tends the garden, cooks some good meals and makes silk.'

'Of course, silk,' said the bishop, almost allowing a smile. 'You must always maintain a good supply of silk up here in the bush.' His Lordship had had his fill of anger for one day and was glad for the Galician's constant good humour and openness, which contrasted with the furtive nature of his scheming superior.

Benedict Upemara, hair oiled and combed severely across his head in a manner that made him barely recognisable, appeared from the kitchen carrying another plate of small French things for the priests to nibble. When he got to Dom Serra, he was asked if he would like one day to see Rome.

'Yes, Father,' replied the boy, not knowing what was meant by 'Rome'.

'Then you shall,' said Serra. 'Rosendo, I will take this little one to see the Pope. He will be a great asset, I think.'

Salvado wished to object, but he was the most junior priest in this company, flanked by his bishop and his superior. Dom Serra wanted a trophy to display to His Holiness. Everything the boy knew about the Church had been put in his head by Salvado alone. If anyone were to take Benedict to Rome, it should be him. It felt like a type of theft.

The same table at which the synod had convened was carried outside and placed next to the campfire for dinner. It was a lively evening for the visitors to enjoy. A new family group had wandered in during the day, and were not entirely welcomed. The newcomers had built their own fire on ground well away from the incumbents, but minor arguments were constantly breaking out, especially among the women.

Things came to a head when the soup was ladled out. Nudity was not permitted at dinnertime, so the newcomers were not being served. Offence was taken. There was screaming, then punches. Salvado intervened to restore peace. *Bookas* were thrown over bare shoulders in desultory fashion, but then more squabbles broke out over the size of servings.

The Irishmen were delighted by all this rowdiness. 'What a shindig,' said The Terror. 'It makes me feel quite homesick.'

After dinner, the niggling degenerated into open conflict. There was screaming and shouting, women's voices carrying on the night air. One belligerent among the visitors waved a *wana* in a threatening manner and a couple of mission women who knew her ways retaliated, and then a proper *mêlée* started.

Salvado again excused himself from the synod and went across to speak with the mission men who were sitting on the other side of the campfire, ignoring the noise. He urged them to intervene but they laughed at him so the Galician went across to the women and tried to reason with the main troublemaker. He wrenched the digging stick from her hand with some difficulty and struck her once on the back with it, loud enough to be generally heard. Everything quietened down after that.

'I admire your methods, Rosendo,' said Farrelly, upon the monk's return. 'I had imagined you to be a negotiator.'

The monk, seeming ashamed of his actions, settled back to his meal.

'The men always do nothing,' he said, after a while. 'They just say, let them finish, don't get in their way. If I took that approach, there would be split heads and speared legs every week.'

Dinner was traditional bush fare. Earlier in the day, Fabrice had offered the bishop a choice of kangaroo or lamb pie, and His Lordship had opted for the indigenous meat. To accompany it, N'yalbinga put an emu egg on the fire, balancing the enormous object in the ashes. When it had warmed up a bit, he cracked a little hole in the top, and gave His Lordship a stick with which to stir the egg every so often in order to distribute the heat. Brady took his job seriously and spent much of the evening watching the egg and asking N'yalbinga how to start a fire from scratch in the bush, and how to catch an emu. N'yalbinga shook his head at the red-faced old fellow, who was only just learning to cook an egg and must not know how fast those things could go.

The second day of the synod concerned New Norcia. Salvado had prepared a list of needs. What he really wanted was for the mission to be declared a diocese unto itself – in a word, autonomy – but he had seen the effect of that word upon the bishop, who had a tendency to see conspiracies everywhere. So he lowered his aim. The achievable thing, he decided, was to have the synod officially acknowledge the primacy of Benedictine Rule at New Norcia.

In the third Act, when Salvado was permitted to speak, he approached it as he would a musical recital, slowly and with charm, reading the audience's mood as he went, and adjusting his performance accordingly.

'The plan for evangelising the natives is understood by us all,' commenced the Galician. 'We have two generations of natives here, and the two must be treated quite differently. The parents are mostly dissolute and set in their wild ways. At best, the women may be taught to sing a *Kyrie* and the men taught a trade. It is the children we must focus on, especially the boys. The more promising ones shall be separated from their parents in the mission house, educated under our care and taught to farm.'

'No mention of God, Dom Salvado,' interjected the bishop. 'Does He not come into it?'

'My fault, Your Lordship, for not coming to it more quickly. Those two things must go together, the practicalities of life and their spiritual education. But the latter is a long journey. Even we old men are still learning. So we must be patient, especially when we feel we are getting nowhere.'

Brady shuffled papers impatiently. 'That's all understood, Dom Salvado. Do you have something to ask?'

'Nothing to ask,' declared Salvado, then asked it. 'Only that the Acts of this synod confirm our plan for evangelising of the natives and that the Rule of St Benedict is recognised as being uniquely well adapted to the needs of the native people of this land.'

'Very well,' began the bishop, but Salvado had not finished.

'And that the way of life of the Benedictines, occupied as we are with prayer, preaching and working in the fields, be the *only* one, according to the verdict of experience, to inspire confidence and secure the conversion and proper civil formation of the natives.

'Yes,' said the prelate, barely listening now. 'Speak with Farrelly and get the wording right in the minutes. Whatever you wish.'

Salvado was delighted at this response. The Rules of St Benedict included a strong insistence on the autonomy of the community and freedom from any external interference in its affairs, even by a bishop. The details could be more clearly stated in the written record. Farrelly being no writer, Salvado would offer to write it for him.

'Thank you, Your Lordship. And it follows that we will wish to purchase more land.'

'Does it now?' said the bishop, looking up and wondering whether he had really just agreed to that.

'Naturally. The most helpful natives must of course be rewarded with their own property, which they will themselves farm and profit from. We currently have only twenty acres, allowed us by Governor Irwin. We will need very much more than that to put into effect the plan that the synod has just approved.'

'Acting governor,' interjected the bishop. Any mention of Irwin raised Brady's temperature. The man offers twenty acres to the Spanish, no doubt to encourage them to keep the Aboriginals out in the bush, while in the capital he does all he can to obstruct all Catholic endeavours, even objecting to St John's being called a cathedral, since 'cathedrals encourage popery'.

'There are two thousand, six hundred and fifty acres adjoining this property currently up for sale,' Salvado was saying, 'with no competitors bidding. I have received an understanding that I might receive it for half the going rate. That is, ten shillings an acre.'

The bishop looked flustered. How had they moved so swiftly to matters of real estate and finance? He looked to his loyal scribe for help.

'In whose name?' asked Bishop Brady, 'and with what money?'

'In my name, for practical reasons, since I alone will be remaining here to sign documents.'

'Only British subjects can own land. I qualify. Are you a British subject Dom Rosendo?'

'Not quite yet, but the acting governor has indicated I shall be made so within a short time.' The bishop sniffed and even Serra looked up at this news. 'As for money, no diocesan funds will be required. I have been advised that the amount can be paid in instalments in London at seven, eleven and fifteen months. That would allow Dom Serra enough time to raise the required funds from our supporters in Italy and Spain.'

Again Serra was surprised: he was now being allocated duties by his second. But he nodded assent, quietly impressed by how much better a negotiator Salvado was, using charm and bluster.

'Yes, yes. Very well,' said the bishop, sensing it had all been arranged, whether he approved or not. He already had enough battles to fight and did not wish to start a new one with Salvado. 'Anything else up your sleeve there, Rosendo?'

'Perhaps one thing. I seek the advice of the synod on how to proceed with the problem of the shepherds.'

'Advice' proved a good choice of word, for it threatened no one and flattered them all. The priests leaned in, apart from Joostens, who was asleep.

'They deny us access to water and abuse our people in many ways. They tell the men that we are poisoning them with the altar wine. They threaten to have the men sent to the prison island. They invite the women, even little girls, down to the river, and inflict their wickedness upon them.

'The women develop disease from the incontinence of these men and then give the sores to their little babies, some of whom are born quite fair-skinned. The mission men are frightened away for weeks at a time, or else threaten to retaliate for the rape of their women, which will sooner or later lead to murder. Just yesterday, while we awaited your arrival, a shepherd fired a shot at Bilyagoro, my most loyal man, for carrying his own sheep across our field.

'My question to the synod is, what action should I take?'

'Whose men are they?' asked the bishop.

'The Scots, I presume, the Macphersons and Mackintoshes. They are reasonable men and have done us many kindnesses.'

'Then that is how we shall address the problem,' said the bishop, enjoying the opportunity at last to provide a sensible solution to an earthly problem. 'Through the Scot landowners. Might Scully not have a word with them?'

'I have asked, Your Lordship, but without success as yet. I wonder, with your greater authority ...?'

His Lordship was flattered to have his powers acknowledged, for there were times recently when he thought he had none. 'I shall send a representative to Captain Scully,' he said. 'Deacon Farrelly would be the man for the job.'

This was precisely the outcome Salvado had hoped for. Scully was sympathetic, but he was too close to old Jim Drummond, who had become too close to the Scots, his daughter having married one of them. Some pressure on the district magistrate from the bishop may trickle down to the shepherds and improve their behaviour.

Though he said nothing at the time, the scribe had devised a more direct approach towards the problem. That evening, a little before dark, Terry Farrelly took Bilyagoro down to the river to find out more about the previous day's shooting incident. The two had got to know each other well from their eventful trip down to Walyunga to retrieve the runaway ox and cart.

'Show me where, Billy,' laughed The Terror, trying to make light of the event. 'Where exactly did you come out from the river with the lamb?' Bilyagoro was reticent because he had already been shot at once and didn't want any more trouble, but Farrelly wanted to know everything about these young shepherds. 'Was it about here, Billy? Or further down, was it?' He coaxed the frightened Bilyagoro all the way down to the now dry riverbed, and as they emerged from the vegetation, the shepherds' camp came into view, along with their latest wickedness. Farrelly watched for half a minute, until he had seen enough.

'What's that big burnt thumping stick of yours called, Billy?' he said quietly. 'Your *do-whacker*, is it? Go back and fetch it could you, there's a good lad. I'll keep watch here.'

From the riverbed, in silence, Terry Farrelly sat unobserved for a while and planned his move. There were three young fellows, none looking older than twenty. He was close enough to see their yellowed teeth and hear their filthy words and beastly noises. There were two female voices, the older one at first angry but now sobbing, the younger one childlike and badly distressed.

Billy took his time coming back. Perhaps his fear of rifles had overwhelmed him. Finally the Irishman could watch from the shadows no more. He stood at full height and strode straight into the shepherds' camp, unarmed.

There were two girls in the camp, their mission dresses pulled off. The little one had blood trickling down her ankle. The three shepherds, young fellows, froze at the unexpected intrusion. An enraged Terry Farrelly was an intimidating sight, even for men who had rifles nearby. The guns must be in their swags, Farrelly guessed, because that was where their eyes flicked. He held one very large paw threateningly above the three of them, daring them to move. He could take any one of them individually, he was quite sure of that, but he would be in trouble if all three acted at once.

'Stay right where you are, lads,' The Terror warned with calm authority. Two remained perfectly motionless, while the youngest, exposed in his ardour, risked trying to pull his pants up. 'Leave your flies alone boy. Sit up, that's a good lad, hands up high where I can see them.'

With his eyes fixed firmly upon the three rapists, he bid the two girls dress themselves and head back to the mission. The little one was sobbing and said she was sorry. Farrelly spoke softly to her and reassured her that she had done nothing at all wrong.

'It's only these fellas here that are in trouble,' he said, patting her head as she passed. 'I will stay behind and have a little chat with them, don't you worry.' His eyes remained fixed on the three half-dressed men. 'Go wash yourself in the pool then go up and see Father Salvado.'

One of the shepherds made a dart for his weapon, but since his pants were still around his ankles he was easily restrained with a boot upon the crutch of the garment. Down he went, face to the dirt, hairless white arse to the moon. The accent in which he then pleaded for the Irishman's mercy seemed to be from some southern corner of England. It was important that an example be made of this one, Farrelly thought, 'to encourage the others' as they said in the military. The strategy worked well. Once they saw their mate's bent nose streaming gore, the other two dared not move, so the deacon could impart his lessons to each offender in a measured and unhurried manner.

When, during the lecture, The Terror heard a branch snap behind him, he did not flinch.

'Come on out Billy,' he called to the shadows, 'help me teach these young fellas some manners.' Bilyagoro emerged tapping a short heavy *dowak* against his own leg. 'Oh, yes, that will do the job nicely, son.'

When the Irishman arrived back late for dinner, his fists needed treating. He had stumbled across a stump in the darkness. It was lucky, observed Salvado as he dressed the subdeacon's knuckles, that he had sustained not a single scratch on his face.

'Well, when you've a pretty face like mine to protect,' explained Terence Farrelly, 'you learn how to fall.'

The shepherds were gone by morning. There was no longer a need for the bishop's representative to discuss the problem with Captain Scully. Thus ended the synod.

From: Léandre Fonteinne, Tours
To: Prosper Guéranger, Solesmes Abbey

29th March 1848

Dear good Father

As expected, I have been unjustly dismissed from my work at the train station at Tours and soon I will be back on the pavement. I am at the mercy of Providence and it would not take much for blasphemy to rise from my mouth against her. When thus will I find a stable rock under which I may shelter? I think my life is cursed. There is a remedy to all these evils. It is death. Let us try that.

Where will I go? You ask me, dear Father, to come and be near you. Your affection calls me, believe me. But as much as I wish to, I fear the world we live in now is too mad and dangerous to risk visiting a monastery. All existence is under threat. The sword hangs over the head of the clergy, whatever they do. I am not sure I wish my neck to be so close to yours when the rioters come crashing into Solesmes to carry the heads of all the brothers away on pikes. But, what choice do I have? My finances are not strong. So I suppose I shall come. If I die at the hands of the rabble, at least I will die with my beloved Father.

I will leave Tours on Sunday evening and go through Le Mans. You know why, I am weak. I will arrive by the evening carriage. By Monday evening at the latest I will be in your arms! If I did not so greatly fear imposing, I would ask you to send me one of the novices to fetch me from the station, for it will be dark and I have no money for the fare.

You will notice my changed appearance. You must promise not to tease or reject me. I have grown older and fatter and with my greying beard I regret that I now look like Proudhon. We are almost twins, he and I, another joke that God has played upon me. The only difference is that Proudhon always wears a white hat and I a black one. That is how you will know it is really me, my black hat. On the other hand, beware if I arrive wearing a white hat, for that means I am the revolutionary come to kill you all!

Farewell, therefore, until Monday. I love you and embrace you with all my heart, as my own true dear Father.

Your child,
Léandre.

18. THE SHIPPING NEWS

The streets of Fremantle were full of tearful farewells and bewildered new arrivals.

'Never seen it so busy,' said Mr Scott, the harbour master. 'Three ships waiting in Gage Roads.'

'Business is grand,' declared Paddy Marmion, proprietor of the Commercial Hotel, placing two frothing tankards in front of the French pair. One was Cleriquot, the dapper wearer of silk scarves, the other his latest sailor friend, who declared he had last enjoyed an ale seven weeks ago in Port Louis. Paddy quite liked the French, despite their dubious ways. At least they were generous with the old *gratuités*. There was never the risk of a tip from the English, and his fellow Irish were the worst, always on the scrounge for free drink.

Fabrice had started visiting Fremantle more frequently. The port town was decrepit in comparison to neat Perth but at least there was activity there. The newly arrived and soon-to-depart tended to be more honest in their words and braver in their actions. He had become a regular at a guesthouse which had two important attributes – a deep bath and an incurious owner.

But something else drew Fabrice to the ships: he craved the latest news from Europe, even though it was always three months stale. In May, he learned that France had been in revolt in February. Louis Philippe, the beloved Citizen King, had been chased all the way to Honfleur, the monarchy abolished and a Second Republic declared. The mob attacked the rich, not for the first time in France, and the Catholic Church was again being punished for its closeness to power.

In June, Fabrice got his hands on some English newspapers from March. Paris was ablaze. The future of the country was in the hands of radicals. Fabrice interrogated every intelligent new arrival. Of Lyon, he could get no particular news, but an English officer told him, 'The lowlife are marauding everywhere, why would Lyon be spared?' Fabrice's parents, being Catholic and wealthy, were natural targets for the swarming ochlocracy and dear Maman would always open the door to anyone.

With each ship that arrived, Fabrice learned a little more, but no two versions quite aligned. Continental Europe was on fire, said the officers; the baying mob had been unleashed. Ordinary sailors put it differently. Today he had met one called Jacques and as they enjoyed their third pot at the Commercial, the young sailor from Le Havre effused about the wonderful new freedoms that were sweeping their country.

'France is not burning, *cher* Fabrice, unless you are a banker or a landowner or some other thief,' Jacques explained. Previously, only one percent were permitted to vote, now everyone could. Beer and optimism caused the young man's cheeks to glow attractively as he gripped Fabrice's wrist for emphasis, causing his lager to spill. '*C'est le printemps des peuples!*' he declared. The year 1848 would be remembered as The Year of Freedom. France had even freed its slaves.

Fabrice saw many dangers in this enthusiasm but had no wish to reduce the flame of passion within the young idealist. One part of him shared the sailor's longing for democratic change, but a greater part feared for his dear Maman.

One of Jacques' attributes was his collection of radical newspapers. The masthead of *Le Représentant du Peuple* revealed its editor to be none other than Pierre-Joseph Proudhon. Fabrice knew Proudhon, who had once worked for his father as an office clerk. He was an intelligent autodidact and young Fabrice had spent some enjoyable lunchtimes talking to him. Now, in his newspaper, Proudhon urged the workers to rise up against such exploiters as the Cleriquots and destroy them. The revolution now sweeping across Europe could not be stopped. The Austrian people had forced Metternich to flee. Berlin had erupted, led by university professors demanding freedom for the press and freedom of assembly – that they were slashed and shot at only further stoked their anger. All kings were doomed: Denmark, Hungary, Wallachia, Moldavia, Romania, the Habsburgs. The pope would go too, just another corrupt king with massive wealth and an army.

Fabrice was both seduced and repulsed by what he read in *Le Représentant*. He detested the mob, yet in his dreams he was a part of it, marching down the *Montée St Barthélemy* with his old friends from the university, while watching from the balcony his father, the king, nod to his general to start the shooting.

One morning while Fabrice was poring over the tiny print of an English paper, his sun was extinguished. 'What news of the Crime and Outrage Bill?' came a voice from the corpus which had caused the eclipse. *La Terreur*.

'Ireland?' asked Fabrice.

'Of course, Ireland,' said Farrelly, as if they had been engaged in a long conversation on the matter and the Frenchman had not been paying sufficient attention. 'They dare protest the crime of their own extermination, so now protests are declared illegal. The English would prefer the Irish to starve like gentlemen, politely, and in silence.'

Farrelly had recently taken to dressing in black, in a manner more becoming a subdeacon, but the face above the Roman collar was still very much that of a boxer.

'There is slaughter everywhere on the continent,' said Fabrice, folding the paper away for later. One could never read with an Irishman present.

'No country suffers as Ireland suffers,' insisted Terry Farrelly. 'But these three girls at least are saved.'

Only now did Fabrice see Farelly's companions. He jumped to his feet, ashamed of his deteriorating manners. Pale and thin, the three Irish maidens smiled shyly and curtseyed for the dapper French gentlemen. He responded elegantly and they giggled with relief; after weeks in the dark at sea they finally had solid earth beneath their feet, and the locals seemed friendly.

'These three are all good Catholics, and good needlewomen,' Farrelly explained, sounding like an agent. 'God knows we need more Catholic children.' He saw his charges blush at this prediction. 'Not quite yet, of course. First, we will take them off to the nuns for a good feed and a warm soapy bath.' More embarrassment came from mention of a bath, so he clarified his role in the matter. 'I won't be staying, like.'

Terry Farrelly had become a man of some influence in the Swan River colony, but he had always one eye over the horizon to poor, suffering Ireland. He wanted to see every boat arriving at Fremantle filled with young Irish Catholics, whether free or not. These single Irish women were a good start; 'orphans of the famine' he called them. This colony could feed them, protect them and give them a new start in life. The new colonial secretary, Dr Madden, was a great supporter of the scheme and Farrelly could not speak highly enough of him: a Dubliner, a physician and an abolitionist.

Fabrice watched the Irish girls in their pitiful shoes dragging their own bags towards the river jetty. Wagon drivers circled but Farrelly waved them away, determined to protect his charges from any male attention. Fabrice felt compelled to intervene, whistling over two reliable-looking drivers, one to carry the waifs and the other to share with Farrelly.

'A cab was not required,' insisted Farrelly, ungraciously.

'Think of their little feet. They've been at sea for months.'

Irish women were known for having the toughest feet in the world, Farrelly sniffed. 'Why are you in Fremantle so much nowadays,' he asked, 'or is it best I don't ask?'

'It is the closest point to home,' Fabrice replied.

'Ah, now. I know what you mean there,' said the subdeacon, meaningfully. 'It was the first place we set foot, old Fleamantle, and it's a mangy place really, but I too feel closer to the Old Sod here. Whenever I see the ships, I dream about heading home.'

'Will you, one day?' asked the Frenchman.

'God no, I will die here. I said goodbye to my old ma, and that's it. Wouldn't want to upset her twice.'

The ferry from Perth arrived late carrying a flustered Dom Serra. With him was Benedict Upemara, his wavy hair shaved short and cloaked like a Benedictine novice. They were off to Rome, Serra confirmed curtly, in response to the The Terror's interrogation.

'While there, you will not discuss the running of this diocese,' warned Farrelly.

'Who are you to say that?' retorted Serra. 'I remind you that I am a priest.' He had tolerated enough insolence from this illiterate Irish layman.

'You are a traitor to your bishop,' whispered Farrelly, close to the monk's face.

'Move out of my way!' spat Serra, pulling the boy's arm sharply.

Fabrice felt for little Benedict. He offered to help with their bags, then walked slowly. He assured Serra he need not rush as his ship had been delayed. He had to put the bags down at intervals to stretch his arms while Serra hovered impatiently.

'You don't really mean to take this little boy to Rome?'

'I will do exactly that,' said Serra, annoyed by the meddling of this French dandy who, he noticed, had reverted to wearing his fancy silks. 'He dearly wishes to meet His Holiness.'

'Does he understand the journey required?'

'Of course,' said the monk. 'These people have more intelligence than you seem to allow.'

The wagoneers were circling again, running departing passengers to Arthur's Head. Serra, always short of money, glanced at Fabrice for assistance, but Fabrice shook his head at the cab driver so Serra, mistrusting the Frenchman's knowledge of the shipping timetables, strode on ahead.

Fabrice walked with Benedict and talked to him in his own language.

'*Windja noonook koorliny yeyi*?' asked the linguist. Where are you off to now?

'*Ngana karlak,*' said the boy. Back home.

'*Noonook wort-koorl koomba kebarak-al?*' Aren't you going on a big boat?

They had already been on the boat, explained Benedict, meaning the river ferry. Now they were going home.

What about Rome?

This was Rome, the boy explained, right here. It was too noisy for him. It had been fun to have a look, but he wanted to get back to the bush now.

Unfortunately, they did not miss the ship. When they got to the cliff above Arthur's Head, it was moored in Gage Roads, sails still furled, and the last two lighters were waiting at the jetty, pilots impatient for the stragglers.

'Look, Benedict,' explained Fabrice. 'That's your boat. That great big one. This here is not Rome. Rome is nights and nights and nights away.'

'No!' said the boy.

Fabrice tried to explain the misunderstanding to the Benedictine monk.

'The trip will kill him, Dom Serra. Please, leave him here with me.'

'He could not sleep last night for the excitement of it.'

'I will take him back to New Norcia for you.'

'You will not!' snapped Dom Serra. 'Cease your interference, Cleriquot. This boy is baptised, and he wishes to meet the Pope. Come, Benedict.'

The boy allowed his hand to be taken by the monk, but as he was pulled along the jetty, the black-cloaked Benedict turned his face back to the last person who might have been able to save him from this terrible journey.

Soon after their ship set sail, another monk appeared, also in a fluster. He had hoped to farewell Dom Serra and especially to kiss his beloved Benedict Upemara, the first Western Australian child to be baptised in the Church. With heavy heart, Dom Salvado stood alongside Fabrice on the cliffs above Arthur's Head watching the ship head out to sea.

'My heart is a little broken,' Salvado admitted, making a cross over the water in the direction of the ship. 'May God protect them both, and deliver them safely to Rome.'

This, thought Fabrice, was the Galician's foolish solution to every problem, even those of his own making: to ask his imagined god to solve it for him.

'They might arrive in Rome to discover your pope is no longer there,' said Fabrice, feeling unfriendly.

'What do you mean by that?'

'All the kings of Europe are being dethroned,' explained the Frenchman.

'The Pope of Rome is not a king,' insisted the monk.

'Yes he is,' said Fabrice Cleriquot, exhilarated to proclaim the truth aloud. 'That's all he is, a rich and powerful king. All the rest is subterfuge.'

Salvado spat something unusually terse and left. Fabrice almost went after his friend to apologise, but stopped himself. He had read too much of Proudhon and was too upset by Benedict's abduction to listen to any more priestly nonsense.

The new governor finally arrived, a naval man who carried certain written instructions from the third Earl Grey, Great Britain's Secretary of State for War and the Colonies, regarding the contentious matter of convicts. On his first day, Captain Irwin showed him the state of the Treasury, and Fitzgerald announced that he would be putting a bold proposal to Westminster. That it was immediately approved was unsurprising, since England had run out of places to export its excess prisoners.

Continental Europe was having its Year of Freedom, and even New South Wales had determined to become a free colony, but against the tide of history the Swan River had elected to become a penal colony. To reassure the genteel colonists, the governor made much of the conditions upon which he had insisted. There would only be small numbers of 'indentured emigrants', mostly well-behaved men from Pentonville, and for each one, London had promised to send one free man or woman, mostly Pensioner Guards and their families, who could be easily attracted to Perth from the less salubrious parts of the empire by the offer of good pay and free housing and land.

One day in October, it happened that two ships arrived, one carrying two dozen more Irish needleworkers and the other, thirty Parkhurst boys. Fabrice was again in Fremantle seeking news from Lyon, and Terry Farrelly was there to collect the Irish girls. Also in the port was Eric Hough, the Toodyay blacksmith, dressed smartly for the city and leaning elegantly on a fence rail, accompanied a few yards away by his assistant, Bob.

'What brings you to Fremantle?' asked Fabrice of Eric, raising his nose as he did so. The Parkhurst boy had developed airs and needed deflating.

'Business,' replied the blacksmith, looking away. He had taken to carrying a cane and twirled it for effect. 'I require one of each.'

'One of each of what?'

'A boy for the forge and yard work,' Eric explained. 'A girl for the rest of it, indoors.'

Fabrice was indignant. 'Are you even permitted … what is your age?'

Eric feigned not to hear this provocation. The first of the new Parkhurst arrivals were shuffling along the beach and he moved along the cliff to get a better view of their condition.

'Have you completed your sentence?' persisted the Frenchmen.

His timing was bad: they were alone, standing at the gates of the Round House. This place held bad memories for Eric, for it was the exact spot where he had watched his mate Johnny Gavin hanged just a few weeks after they arrived. The idiots in this stupid colony didn't know how to hang a boy so it was a botched job. He was too skinny so when they moved the wagon from under his feet he just choked and went *ga-ga-ga* until the sheriff pulled down on his feet to finish the job. That's what they all meant, these gentle colonists, when they spat the words 'Parkhurst boy' at you. It meant they thought you were good for hanging, and nothing else. Eric grabbed the insolent Frenchman by his silk-scarfed neck. It was scarlet, and the dandy let out a scream, thinking for a moment his neck had been cut.

'*Never* speak that way to me again, Frenchie. I have turned eighteen. I owe not one penny to no one, not even the damned guv'nor, he's got his ten quid back. I am a free man and a landowner.' Air from the horrible boy's nostrils puffed onto Fabrice's cheek. 'And unlike some, at least I am an *Englishman* in my own country.'

With that firm advice, Eric Hough let loose the Frenchman's neck, dusted himself off, and walked away twirling his cane, as if nothing of consequence had happened.

Bob reappeared, having seen the assault, but unbothered by it. He showed Fabrice two silver coins in the palm of his hand.

'Who's this?'

'Louis Philippe, in better times.'

'Scottish king?'

'French.'

'How much is it in real money?'

Fabrice explained what one could buy in Lyon for five francs – a chicken perhaps, or a couple of fish. Its likely source occurred to him. 'Have you been digging in the riverbed, Bob? At that place where Louis got stuck?'

'No diggin',' shrugged Bob, 'just pick 'em up.' Bob announced a plan to buy a farm like 'old man Scully's'. Ten pounds for ten acres was his budget, but he needed an Englishman to buy it in his name. Eric had agreed to help him with the paperwork.

The Toodyay blacksmith also seemed to be flush with funds. Over at the barracks he had already chosen a Parkhurst boy, the least affable looking, spoken with the guard, handed over some documentation and a generous consideration, and had his name pencilled alongside the boy's. He had to pay at the office in Perth, the guard advised, then come back next day with the receipt to collect his apprentice.

Eric next turned his attention to the group of young Irish women who had been gathered together at the top of High Street.

'Which of these are unclaimed?' he enquired of the one who seemed to be in control of things.

'None of them, you piece of piss,' said Terry Farrelly, softly. He had seen the Parkhurst boy coming down the Round House steps and did not even look up from his notebook, so that nobody out of range of hearing could have been guessed that they were in dispute.

'I doubt that,' said Eric. 'The red-haired one, anyone got her yet?'

'It is not a market.'

'Is she free or not?'

'Mend your own shirts, you little arse rag,' growled The Terror, all the more menacing at low volume. 'Did they not teach you to mend your shirts in prison?'

Recalling a previous belting from this Irishman, the blacksmith chose not to hear that last barb. 'I'll speak with the government man then,' he said and, with his back turned, added, 'I guess you are only here to touch them up for free.'

Farrelly found his right hand had moved to the boy's shoulder and was squeezing it very tightly. Every fibre of him wanted to smash this lad, but he was a subdeacon now, wearing a clerical collar, and any violence done in public might reflect badly on his bishop. A quiet trip to the Avon Valley might have to be in order.

Instead, Terry Farrelly leaned forward and left the boy with something to ponder, an old saying from the west country, where the English had done their murderous worst.

'*Go dtachtar le d'anáil thú,*' he whispered. May you choke on your breath.

From: Raphael Ledoux, Lyon
To: Fabrice Cleriquot, Swan River, Australia

16th June 1848

(Marked: *Dead Letter. Addressee has departed colony.*)

Mon très cher ami

After three years I have found the courage to write to you and I do so only because our city is on fire and I fear I will die or you will die and I will not have spoken to you simply because I was sulking like a child.

The marauders here nightly set fire to buildings and attack the rich and undertake acts too hateful to be permitted to drip from my pen. Nobody dares wear nice things anymore.

I want simply to tell you that I love you, dear Fabrice, and I am so frightened. You are still the only one who could console me, were you only here. You would kiss me and make me laugh, despite all this. I hope there will come a night soon, or ever, when I am again in your arms. But perhaps with the world as it is now, either you will die or I will before that can happen. If it is I that dies first, I hope you will feel terrible.

I tried to cure myself with poetry. Useless. Though we two are apart, the poet says, I should think of the distance between us not as a 'breach' but rather an 'expansion', and our love 'like gold plate beaten to airy thinness'. Oh, pauvre-moi! I just want you here, Fabrice, though you should be warned I am still very angry with you for leaving me.

Je t'embrasse tendrement mon très très cher Fabrice.
Je t'interdis de m'oublier!

Ton Raphael pour toujours

19. MEETING PIO NONO

'*Possiamo sapere cosa portano i ragazzi in questi sachetti bianchi?*' asked Pope Pius IX. What did these two lads from Western Australia have hidden in their little bags?

Kneeling before the seated pontiff, heads bowed, John Dirimera and Francis Conaci each grasped a white linen bag. They did not answer the Pope because they did not understand Italian and had been firmly told by the scary red-capped Father not to speak, but only to look downwards at the centre of a particular marble tile until red-cap told them otherwise.

Francis glanced sideways and the boys exchanged shy smiles. This Pope really was very funny, a bit like the Bishop of Perth, only fatter and richer.

It was Dom Salvado who answered on the boys' behalf. 'Inside the bags are their monastic robes, Your Holiness,' he announced, slowly and proudly, for this was momentous. These two wild boys, rescued from the bush, were to be delivered to his old monastery at Cava where they would begin their noviceship.

'Ah!' said the Pope, feigning surprise. He had seen hundreds of such linen bags, and every one of them contained robes. 'Australia's first dark monks!'

'Australia's first monks of any colour,' Dom Salvado corrected him.

Cardinal Fransoni coughed meaningfully. One did not correct Pio Nono.

His Holiness went to stand, stopping to massage a painful knee on the way up. He took the bag from the taller boy, bade him stand too and dressed him in his new habit. John Dirimera's eyes remained dutifully fixed on the stone floor of the fort. Francis Conaci hiccuped.

'What are your name?' asked the Pope, attempting English, since the boys had come from an English colony and seemed not to understand Italian.

'His name is John,' said Dom Salvado.

'Now I give you the name John Mary,' decreed the Pope. Confusion followed. Mary! John looked to Salvado for an explanation, and the still-kneeling younger boy was unable to suppress a giggle.

The Pope, sensitive about his English, reverted to Italian.

'And this other boy?'

'His name is Francis.'

'Very good. Australia needs another Francis Xavier; may the Lord bless him and turn him into one!'

The Pope rewarded each novice with a silver crucifix, placed a firm hand upon the two shaven heads and spoke many dark and unintelligible words. It was a blessing but, as the bejewelled hand hovered near his left ear, Francis braced for a smack.

'And this must be your convert?' said the Pope, shifting his attention down the line by one place. He was speaking to the air above the head of Fabrice Cleriquot. Fabrice had chosen a simple white silk blouse for the occasion. That it happened to match the white robe worn by *Pontifex Maximus* annoyed the linguist a little.

It annoyed him further to be described as a 'convert'. That would be Salvado's doing, no doubt. Fabrice had been reading the Greeks and had almost settled into Pyrrhonism, allowing him to suspend judgement on the existence of god. He thought to explain this distinction to the white Pope, but feared upsetting the other one in the blood-red zucchetto.

A short silence ensued. Disappointed, the Pope took this to mean his attempt at humour had missed its mark and had caused offence.

'I joked, of course, Monsieur Cleriquot,' said Pope Pius. 'Blame Dom Salvado for it was he who dared me to say it, and now I feel ashamed for obliging him. Of course, I know the Cleriquots of Lyon are devout. Your father was always welcome here in Rome, for he always dressed us so well. This white cap upon my head, these very robes, all were gifts from Rome's favourite silk merchant, Monsieur Claude Cleriquot.'

Unexpectedly, Fabrice felt his breast surge to hear such praise from the lips of a pope. At last he was starting to understand his father, even to forgive him; perhaps, with time, he could even learn to love him.

'I was very sorry to hear of his terrible death,' added Pio Nono.

There was a pause while Fabrice took in this last bit of information.

'My father is dead, Excellency?'

The cardinal gave another of his educative coughs, meaning Fabrice should remain silent. Cardinal Fransoni was not a force easily ignored: his black soprana robe had red buttons that gave the appearance of his having been stabbed thirty-three times by a very neat assassin, and a vindictive burst of scarlet ran the length of his lapel. But surely, Fabrice thought, his father's death was a subject of sufficient *gravitas* to justify his speaking aloud, so despite the cardinal, he looked up to do so.

He was surprised by what he saw. The pope was gesturing

urgently to his cardinal for advice. The boys from New Norcia, sensing the rules had softened, also looked up at the bejewelled king of the church, and bumped shoulders in amusement.

'I am so ... my sincere apologies, Monsieur Cleriquot,' said the pontiff, greatly flustered. 'I thought you knew of your father's awful ...' His hand rolled as if to pluck a word from the air but none came, so he glanced to Fransoni who stared straight ahead and sucked air through his nose. 'And your dear mother, as well, of course, in a gruesome manner beyond all human comprehension. *Tragico! Atroce!* But it was not my place to have told you. I am sorry.'

To retrieve his composure, the pontiff blessed and prayed over Fabrice. '*Et parentes euis in pace,*' said Pio Nono, touching the back of the head of the newly bereaved. He shut his eyes for a very long time after this, possibly deep in prayer, but when they blinked open His Holiness seemed momentarily surprised by the presence of an audience.

Pius IX turned his attention now to the Galician. 'Tell me, Dom Salvado, how fares the mighty port?'

Salvado, uncomprehending, nodded sagely. 'Quite well, I suspect,' he answered, as confused by his own response as he was by the question.

'I speak of your Port Victoria, near Adelaide,' Pio Nono explained, and smiled, knowing he had surprised Salvado with his geographical knowledge of the central third of Australia. 'I have told the family of Don Angelo Confalonieri that I will not let his mission die with him.'

The cardinal gave another of his cautionary coughs, a very discrete one, since it was directed at the Pope. It meant: 'Your Holiness, we discussed the Port Victoria debacle, and you may recall I made the suggestion that the place never be mentioned again.'

'Garibaldi!' shouted the Pope, angrily. He was still looking at Salvado, who stiffened, unsure what His Holiness could possibly mean by such an utterance. Cardinal Fransoni leaned in towards the pontiff and whispered some cautious advice.

'*Ego. Sum. Papa,*' the pontiff growled in reply, spacing the words evenly. I am the Pope. He blessed the four missionaries from Western Australia rather roughly, and the audience was finished.

As Cardinal Fransoni ushered the Western Australians out of the His Holiness' presence, Pio Nono called Salvado back. He wished to speak with the Galician alone.

Salvado's heart leapt. A private audience! He had one request of the Pope, should the opportunity present itself: that New Norcia be declared *Abbacy Nullius Diœceseos*, a community without a diocese. That would finally free him from the incompetent Bishop of Perth and allow him to complete his life's work.

Fransoni groaned under his breath. Whenever the Pope departed from the order of things, it created a problem for him to put right. What would it be this time? He tersely instructed Fabrice and the two boys to remain in the corridor, and was about to re-enter the audience room when an angry shout came from within. The corridor jumped, then froze as one. The Red Pope exited, his face the colour of his buttons, and waited outside the door with all the common folk, while sniffing and looking furious.

Outside at last, the boys could talk. John Dirimera wanted to know why the Pope had called him Mary. Francis gave a sly impersonation into the sleeve of his cloak of His Holiness doing so. There were inappropriate giggles, including from Fabrice Cleriquot, despite his newfound grief.

Two powerful-looking men in tail coats looked down at the dark novices disapprovingly; whether they disapproved of the boys' light hearts or their race, Fabrice could not tell. The two were conversing in French, so Fabrice listened in. They were not discussing the boys at all. They were French military officers in civilian dress and were debating the pope's request that they invade Rome on his behalf.

When the door reopened, Salvado looked bewildered.

'So?' said Cardinal Fransoni, turning on his heels and beckoning the four to follow him down the corridor. 'What thing has now happened that I will have to fix?'

'Well,' said Rosendo Salvado, flustered. 'It seems ... I am to be a bishop.'

Fransoni stopped still and looked hard at the Spaniard.

'What?' declared the cardinal, his manner accusatory. 'His Holiness has made you Bishop of Perth?' Among Cardinal Fransoni's many responsibilities, he was Prefect of the Congregation for the Propagation of the Faith and, in that capacity, he was to be consulted before any such appointment.

'Not Perth,' said Salvado, feeling the need for fresh air. 'Port Victoria.'

'Oh, no!' gasped Fabrice. 'That awful place where poor Don Angelo died?'

'The same,' said Salvado, unhappily.

'Hasn't Dom Serra been made bishop of it?'

'He has,' said Salvado, shaking his head, 'by this same Pope, one year ago to this day. But His Holiness feels he erred in making that decision. He has changed his mind.'

'His Holiness does not *err*,' growled Cardinal Fransoni. 'The Pope of Rome does not *change his mind*. He determined, following my advice, that Bishop Serra be moved from Port Victoria to Daulia.'

'Daulia?' asked Fabrice, who knew his geography well. 'Where is that place?'

'It *is* nowhere. It *was* in Ancient Greece, on the road from Orchomenus to Delphi. It is, as we say, a bishopric *in partibus infidelium*. Bishop Serra will actually return to Perth as coadjutor to Bishop Brady, who will be grateful to be relieved of the burden of managing the finances of his troubled see, in order to refocus on matters spiritual rather than temporal. As for Port Victoria, I thought I had given clear advice that it be left vacant, the diocese being somewhat diminished in size.'

'Abandoned,' said Fabrice Cleriquot.

The cardinal ignored the pagan. 'It seems my advice was not clear enough.'

'Might His Excellency have confused the Victorias?' suggested Fabrice. 'There are rather a lot of them. Perhaps he meant Bishop of Victoria Plains?'

'His Holiness is never confused,' said Fransoni.

'Cardinal Fransoni is correct,' said Salvado glumly. 'Pio Nono was perfectly clear. He wished by this gesture to pay tribute to both the courage of Don Confalonieri and the wisdom of the last Pope, who specifically instructed Brady to send missionaries to that place.'

'It seems a lot of bishops for so few Catholics,' observed Fabrice. Salvado would be the third of *Elizabeth*'s passengers to be consecrated, and these three bishops could have no more than four hundred Catholics between them.

'His Holiness has greater wisdom than we,' suggested the cardinal, but then shook his head and mumbled something altogether different in Latin.

The party of four was led to a quiet side-room and told to sit. A very young acolyte, not much older than John Mary, came in carrying a silver tray of four brightly coloured liqueurs, spilling one in his nervousness. The two novices looked at Salvado and he shrugged. Why not? They could have one glass each.

'His Holiness says He needs half an hour to wash His hands before seeing the French officers,' said the acolyte, earning a terse reprimand from the cardinal for saying such mundane things aloud.

Cardinal Fransoni looked back through the doorway to the throng of supplicants lined up to see the Pope, and turned back to Salvado. 'Let's go outside, Rosendo,' he sighed. 'The French will need this room soon and believe me, they will not want any ears. We can escape out this way. I badly need to smoke.'

They followed Cardinal Fransoni through a heavy door into bright sunshine. Gaeta was a medieval fort perched on a small peninsula whose steep jagged cliffs led down to the Tyrrhenian Sea. The New Norcia boys were delighted by the sense of danger: it was clear that anyone who slipped or threw themselves from these cliffs would be impaled and die. There was a natural grotto at the bottom, the cardinal told them, which they could go and look at if they liked. The novices discarded their clumsy robes and raced down.

Outside, with pipe in hand, the cardinal was more relaxed. Rome, he explained, had become a bloody place. Last November, on the steps of the *Palazzo della Cancelleria*, the mob had cut the throat of his friend Pellegrino Rossi, the Minister of the Interior. Pio Nono surely would have been next, so Fransoni dressed him up as a priest, bundled him into a carriage and drove him in darkness to this old fort, a hundred and fifty kilometres to the south. Now the Pope was in hiding from his own people.

'Italy is a bloodbath,' the cardinal explained. 'The people have gone mad. They say they want a united Italy with a secular government. They place nationalism ahead of the Church! Garibaldi utters terrible profanities about the Pope, and the people believe him. They declare His earthly powers to be a historical lie, accuse Him of political imposture, religious immorality. Outrage. Sacrilege. Profanity.'

There was a strong breeze and the cardinal caught his red cap just before it blew off.

'Surely the Pope can regain Rome,' said the bishop-elect of an abandoned naval garrison. 'He possesses a powerful army.'

'No longer.' The cardinal exhaled a long stream of white smoke. 'Garibaldi has disarmed them. His mercenaries control Rome and the Papal States.'

'Then you will ask the Austrians to assist,' suggested Salvado.

'You have been away too long, Dom Salvado! The Italian people want the Pope to go to war *against* the Austrians for their meddling in the Tyrol.'

'So what will you do?'

'We will invite the French.'

'What, again?' interrupted Fabrice. Every French schoolboy knew that Napoleon Bonaparte had rescued the Pope in similar circumstances fifty years earlier. Now it was Bonaparte's nephew who had control of the French army.

'They are our only chance,' said Fransoni.

'And how will the people of Rome see that?' asked Fabrice. His parents had been massacred and he no longer saw the need for diplomacy. 'The pope re-entering the city behind a parade of French bayonets?'

The cardinal glared at the impudent dandy in the white silk shirt. 'It is not an ideal alliance, for sure, but only Louis Napoleon controls an army large enough to thwart the Italian nationalists and intimidate the Austrians. If he wishes to retain the votes of the *ultramontane* Catholics in his own country, he will have to come to the aid of the Pope. It is neither good nor bad. It is *necessary*.'

'And then?' Fabrice persisted.

'And then,' said the cardinal, speaking very deliberately, 'previous errors will be corrected.' This whole state of affairs had been caused by the Pope's naïve embrace of liberalism against the advice of his cardinals. He made accommodations with the nationalists, released political prisoners, refused to declare war on the Austrians. To the enemies of Rome, this looked like weakness. But a few weeks in hiding at Gaeta had already hardened his thinking.

Once they were back in Rome, Pio Nono would reform his ways. He would reimprison dissidents; the cardinals were preparing a list. He would restore capital punishment, scandalously banned by the Republic. Never again would the Pope hesitate to put military force to good use. He would restore the power of the Church over the state, banning all forms of religious unorthodoxy, except for the Jews.

'And these measures will cause the people to love him again?' asked Fabrice, as innocently as he could.

'Love?' The cardinal pondered the word as if he were reading it etched on an ancient Sumerian tablet. 'First, the people must fear and respect Him. They must be cured of their infidelity. His Holiness will declare Himself to be infallible. Then all dissent will cease.'

Salvado's heart sank. It followed that the Pope would be unable to reverse any rash decision he might have made, such as the appointment of bishops to abandoned ports.

'Did I hear the Pope shout the name of his enemy?' asked Fabrice.

The cardinal shook his head, exasperated. 'It is His queer way of berating me for insolence, should I dare to offer advice, even with the utmost tact. He calls me in private, and occasionally in public, 'Cardinal Garibaldi'. Like Garibaldi, he jokes, I wish to usurp his power or replace him as *Pontifex Maximus*.'

A howl of pain rose up from the sea grotto. The red cardinal, the black monk and the white silk merchant raced to the cliff's edge to see John Dirimera reappear, protesting that he'd done nothing at all to harm the younger boy. Francis clambered up with a badly skinned knee, but once on flat ground was quite able to run after John, smack his head and remind him of the effeminate holy name the Pope had given him. Salvado reached into one of the many pockets of his cassock and produced some medical spirit and a dressing.

With trepidation, Fabrice asked what more the cardinal may have heard about his parents' demise. Fransoni had none of the Pope's reticence. He confirmed that they had died awfully, especially his dear Maman.

'Tragic, of course, but you should not particularise your grief,' the cardinal calmly advised. 'In these times it is quite normal to lose one's parents in such a manner. Civilised life in Europe is gone. All that was good or noble has been smashed. What happened in Lyon last year was unpleasant, no doubt, but worse things have happened in Rome, I assure you.'

Fabrice doubted that there was much worse that could be done than what he had just learned of his dear Maman. It brought back memories of the church stories that had frightened him as a child: the tales of the ancient martyrs like Blandina of Lyon, tied to a stake to be gored by a steer, then burned on a red-hot grate and stabbed to death with a dagger. When the Church of Rome appeared in his childhood dreams, it was always like this, smeared with the blood of good people. It was why he had left. It had so frightened and repulsed him. Now his own parents had become martyrs, just like in those horrible stories.

They travelled south next day to deliver John and Francis to Salvado's old monastery. The boys wore plain suits. Salvado had trimmed his beard to look like a working man and borrowed an old jacket. From the carriage window they saw military men everywhere, some in proper uniforms, but also gangs of ragged mercenaries.

The Benedictine monastery at Cava de' Tirreni made Fabrice shudder: an ancient, cold, dark, place, founded in the eleventh century by Alferius of Pappacarbone. Salvado alone seemed to think it warm and cheerful, having only happy memories of the years he spent there after being thrown out of Spain. It was at this very place, he told the two boys, that he and Dom Serra had conceived the idea for an Australian mission.

John and Francis stared miserably at the vast stone walls of their new prison, despaired at the crypt containing the body of some queen from antiquity, and were frightened by the huge ancient books, unreadable even to an assistant professor of linguistics.

'Where is the bush?' John asked Fabrice, guiltily, once Salvado had left them alone.

'We are just *koorlangka*,' Francis explained, 'bush kids, not priests.'

Fabrice felt a pain in his heart at the sight of these two sad boys and determined to do what he could to protect them from the monks.

Their newly appointed teacher was Father Bernardo Gaetani. He seemed to Fabrice an overly serious man – not unkind, perhaps, but entirely lacking sympathy for the boys' plight. Only Italian and Latin were to be spoken, for what other languages could serve any purpose here? He disparaged the boys' ugly sounding native tongue and any communication by that means was strictly forbidden, even whispered words in their cells. If they continued to gabble together in such a way, they would never learn God's word. God spoke only Latin. Fabrice was instructed to explain this to the boys, but he told them something altogether different, something about their tutor, who wondered why they looked at him and laughed.

It fell also to Fabrice to explain to them that they were to be left alone in this strange place for three years. They were too young to know what a year was, but they understood what it meant to be left.

'No, Father, no,' the boys protested to Dom Salvado, but their hands were peeled away from his habit and they were made to stand some distance away from him alongside Father Gaetani, who made no motion to console them. Salvado told the boys to stand up straight and reminded them of the commitment they had made. The Pope's blessing would give them powers they could not yet appreciate. Remember, said Salvado, back at the mission, when they had begged him to take them to Rome?

'Yes, Father,' the two boys wept.

Fabrice wept too as he later confronted the Galician. 'You tricked them,' he told Salvado, with anger in his voice. 'They thought they would be away for a night or two. Not for years, learning your priestcraft.'

Salvado stiffened at this word. He had last heard it a decade ago in Santiago de Compostela, from the mouths of the atheistic soldiers who came to evict the monks from their beloved monastery.

'They will adapt, with time,' said Salvado, speaking evenly in order to calm himself.

'No. They will die,' said Fabrice. 'And what became of little Benedict, by the way, the one you loved so much?'

'I believe he is in Rome still.'

'In bloody Rome? Whence even the pope has fled?'

Salvado looked momentarily ashamed at this confession of abandonment, and Fabrice knew exactly what foolish invocation would come next.

'Our Lord will protect him.'

With that, Fabrice's friendship with this foolish monk ended.

Late the next day, at the port of Naples, the two men parted company forever. Salvado was now officially Bishop of Port Victoria, having been consecrated that same morning by Cardinal Fransoni who murmured his annoyance during the ceremony. Bishop Salvado would now sail to Spain where still he hoped to recruit men to build New Norcia. The linguist in the meantime would return to Lyon, where his parents had been murdered.

Fabrice Cleriquot and Rosendo Salvado walked wordlessly along the dock and when they reached the steamship, shook hands for the final time. There was no embrace, for both men were stubborn by nature. Salvado was the first to board, and Fabrice felt appeased to hear the ship's captain being rude to him: he could board, but they were not yet ready for passengers so he should stay out of the way and not ask for anything. Black habits were sufficient reason for abuse in these torrid times.

Alone on board, Salvado had time to think. What Cleriquot had said about the boys was impertinent, but true. Benedict Upemara was not living in Rome, as he had pretended. He had died a few months after Serra had taken him there. Now he had left his beloved John and Francis with strangers who did not understand them. They might well die at Cava, he could not deny it. Certainly they would never be happy there. They would weep every night for their lost country and people and language.

Salvado tried to convince himself of the greater good. Countless martyrs before them had suffered for the sake of the Holy Catholic and Apostolic Church. The boys' pain would be worth it in the long run. They might even survive the ordeal and return to Perth as the colony's first black priests. But if not, they would make a path and perhaps the boys after them would prevail.

It did not work. Such rationalisations required a deep love for the Catholic Church, and Salvado realised this love had left him. In truth, a foolish Pope had made him bishop of an abandoned place an eternity away from his true life's mission at New Norcia. Certain things could no longer be denied. This wealthy Church of which the Pope was king was too often an enemy of the common man, too often a friend of the rich, a lover of armies.

The thought that came to him next made Rosendo Salvado feel seasick, even though the ship was still at anchor. Perhaps the Church of Rome was an encumbrance to his mission in Western Australia. For the first time, alone and guiltily, Salvado considered whether he might better serve the natives of Western Australia in a purely pragmatic way, without the Catholic Church and all its ancient dictates. Fransoni knew nothing about the people of Moore River. The Pope could not stab his bejewelled finger at the boys' home on a map, not within three thousand kilometres. The Australians needed practical skills if they were to resist the English invasion; the men needed to learn to grow crops, the women to sew, the boys to herd sheep. But Rome was of no use in any of that. And what even of Kindness, Forgiveness, Gentleness? The Greeks had spoken eloquently of them long before Christ.

Roger Smith had been right in his aims. Even Cleriquot was justified in some of his criticisms. The natives of Moore River should be allowed to keep their own sacred spirits and their own ways of seeing the world. The Christian God was unnecessary.

Alone on the deck of a motionless steamship, Dom Salvado removed his habit, scapula and wooden cross and bundled them up ready to throw into the stinking water of the Bay of Naples. It was only a voice from the dockside that stopped him. '*Monsignore*! Your men are here!'

Eight men had come to help him build New Norcia. They were lined up on the dock and behind them, their mothers and sisters waved their arms and wailed at their imminent loss. There were no robes: they were not theologians, these men, but carpenters, glaziers, stonemasons and smiths, exactly the sort of men Salvado needed. But he knew that not one of them would have volunteered were the works not to be done in the name of God, so he pulled his cassock back over his head, replaced the crucifix and prepared to greet each volunteer as he boarded.

The men's arrival was of course designed by his loving God to rescue Bishop Salvado from his hour of great doubt. His faith had been tested and was now restored, even stronger than before. As the new men boarded, he closed his eyes and chose to push away all his anger with God. For Salvado was a mystic, no less than the old bearded *mabarn* on the banks of the Moore River. As *Blasco de Garay* steamed up, he let the sea air blow on his face, chanted

347

the rosary, and with eyes closed he saw himself walk through the fertile fields of New Norcia and then through the doors of the grand monastery which had been built there by these worthy men, sent by God as a reward for his fidelity.

Eight would not be enough, however. He would need forty tradesmen to build the New Norcia he had designed in his mind: forty skilled men motivated by a shared love of God. He would find them in Spain.

In Barcelona, Salvado learned that the workforce he dreamt of had already been assembled by Dom Serra. His old friend greeted him coolly, though they had been apart for more than a year. Dom Serra seemed changed. He was furtive, humourless, and flashed a heavy gold ring with an enormous purple amethyst at its centre. By his side was an unlikable Irish priest by the name of Urquhart, who seemed already to have formed an unfavourable view of Salvado.

'Have you a trade?' demanded Urquhart of the new bishop. This unpleasant priest, a Cistercian from the looks, appeared to have usurped Salvado as Serra's second. Wanly, he thanked Salvado for the Neapolitan recruits. 'Metalworkers,' said Urquhart, as he perused the list, 'that is what we really needed.'

The work of gathering men and treasure was complete, Serra explained. Alone, he had recruited thirty-two tradesmen from across Spain – skilled stonemasons, carpenters, artisans. He had also solved their financial problems by extracting moneys from *Propaganda Fide* and various societies and philanthropists from Rome to Paris to Barcelona. Prosper Guéranger of Solesmes had contributed generously by way of apology for the defective novice. The coffers were full. The problem of transport had been solved by Bishop Serra too, through the generosity of Queen Isabella, who had granted the missionaries free passage from Cadiz to Fremantle on her warship *La Ferrolana*.

The Galician tried to look delighted at the news of all this activity of which he had not been a part. How swiftly the fortunes of the Church in Spain had changed, he smiled. A decade ago, monks were being dragged down the street by their feet. He praised his old friend aloud, but in his heart, he felt the victim of a sort of theft. He knew Serra lacked his enthusiasm for New Norcia. As coadjutor of the diocese of Perth, his old friend could divert all these men and funds to build New Subiaco if he wished. Salvado even allowed himself to wonder if Serra had somehow connived to have the Pope send him to the hated Port Victoria in place of himself.

'Oh, my dear brother!' said Salvado, remembering an official letter he had secreted in his cassock, 'For your eyes, from Cardinal Fransoni.'

Serra handed it wearily to Urquhart to be read. The Irishman looked disparagingly at the contents and handed it back.

'From the Pope,' said Urquhart, as if he had read too many such letters to be bothered.

When Serra looked up, it was with no particular expression. 'So you have been made a bishop, Rosendo?'

'It is an annual sport for this Pope to make some fool the next Bishop of Port Victoria,' laughed Salvado, but Serra saw no humour in it. He left with Father Urquhart; they had forty men to organise.

Dom Serra, a Catalonian by birth, enjoyed celebrity here in Barcelona, where the Catholic Church was resurgent. After Mass in the cathedral, hundreds flocked around the missionaries to bid them farewell and especially to praise Bishop José Serra of Perth.

In the port of Cadiz, Bishop Salvado fully realised he was super-fluous to Serra's plans. Father Urquhart in his every utterance and gesture made sure he understood it. So Salvado left the dock and strolled around the town attempting to reflect on the inscrutable ways of Divine Providence which foresees all things and brings all things sweetly to their appointed ends, but such ponderings failed to calm his inner fury so he lit a pipe and repeated the journey, this time allowing his rage to burn at the deceit of his erstwhile dearest friend, at the stupidity of this church, with its plotting cardinals and its ignorant Pope. Heads turned at the furious monk stomping down *Calle Virgen de la Palma* with unbrushed beard and billowing cassock, but he did return feeling lighter.

On the night before departure, Bishops Salvado and Serra dined with royalty at Sanlúcar de Barrameda. The sister of the queen, Infanta Luisa Fernanda, hosted a lavish farewell dinner for the departing missionaries and insisted Salvado play the piano for her. He had decided to regain his humour and was especially charming, causing Her Highness to laugh aloud at his silliness at the keyboards. A courtier whispered in his ear that such frivolity was not permitted. Her Highness was just sixteen and her baby might come at any time.

After dinner the Bishop of Port Victoria fell into a philosophical conversation with the host, Antoine, Prince of Montpensier. Antoine was the youngest son of the dethroned King Louis Philippe of France, now in exile, and the Spanish royal family into which he had married was precarious, but it greatly amused him to discover in Salvado, whom he called Bishop of the Jungle, someone with an even worse situation than he. So cheered was the royal consort by Salvado's adversity that he made a generous contribution for

New Norcia. Serra ordered the money be immediately passed on to Father Urquhart. '*En totalidad*,' he felt the need to add.

At the port next morning, the captain, Señor Quesada, sought out Bishop Salvado. He waved a document.

'I am afraid you are not permitted to board, *Monseñor*.'

'What do you mean? My belongings are on board.'

'I have received a written instruction from Rome. *The Cardinal Prefect of Propaganda grieves to be obliged to transmit this notification that it is deemed not expedient that His Lordship the Bishop of Port Victoria should depart Europe without the previous pleasure of His Holiness to that effect.*'

Father Urquhart, standing alongside, searched Salvado's face unkindly for signs of defeat.

'Well,' said Bishop Serra, taking hold of the letter and carefully inspecting Cardinal Fransoni's signature, 'it seems you are to stay in Europe until passage can be arranged to your bishopric.'

Salvado was forced to retrieve his bags and watch all the activity from the dockside. This was his last opportunity to ask Serra about his intentions for all the men and treasure he now possessed.

'Dom José, my dear brother, I must ask you this, since it seems I will not be there. Which will you support: New Norcia or New Subiaco?'

'Both are required,' said Serra, after a pause, 'but a community in the wilderness should naturally be the more modest.'

Benedictine monks being experts at dissimulation, no hint of disapproval showed on either face. If these friends of twenty years were to part, there was no reason for them to do so on bad terms.

'It is exactly as we planned at Cava all those years ago,' said

Salvado, 'except that God, in the unsearchable depth of His counsel, has decreed that I am no longer needed at New Norcia. He requires me in some other place. Please tell the people of Moore River that I love them still, that I have not abandoned them, but merely handed the task over to my betters.'

With heavy heart, the Bishop of Port Victoria watched from the quay as one by one the forty missionaries boarded the corvette *La Ferrolana* bound for Fremantle, each man shaking the hand of Captain Quesada. The last to board, his oldest and most loved confrère Dom Serra, did not turn back to look at him.

Cardinal Fransoni's written instructions could not have been more clear: Bishop Salvado was to return to Naples. But he set off from Cadiz alone, on foot, and in the opposite direction. He had no plan. He followed the coast, and saw signposts to Huelva. He walked for days, turning over his thoughts and feeling his anger start to dissipate. On and on he walked, westward and northward, away from Italy. He crossed into Portugal, stopping at Coimbra, Aveiro and many small places.

After Oporto, he found he was walking in the ancient footsteps of Iago, the Apostle James, brother of John, son of Zebedee. He started to meet other pilgrims and talk with them. They all had their own troubles, but were sure that to walk where Santo Iago had once walked would ease the burden. The depth of faith of these honest lay men and women made the bishop ashamed to recall that just three weeks earlier he had been ready to throw his cross into the Bay of Naples.

At the river Minho he crossed the bridge into Galicia and visited his parent's house in Tuy, where he was not immediately recognised by his own sister. He spent a blessed week there with his mother, who was ailing. He removed his sandals after that and, barefoot, in tattered black cassock, with long black beard and wooden cross, he walked the rest of the pilgrim's path towards Santiago de Compostela, stopping whenever he wished, for as many nights as he wished.

The blue sky, the limestone terrain and the sunburnt faces of the simple farmers – all of these once familiar things he had quite forgotten. To experience Galicia anew reminded to him why Western Australia, though on the other side of the world, had felt like home from the first day.

In a forgotten pocket he found some eucalyptus leaves and gumnuts from Victoria Plains, and he rubbed them under his nose for the nostalgia of the lemony smell. He turned the pocket out and found it lined with tiny seeds, which he picked out as he travelled, scattering the seeds in spots by the roadside where it was dry and sandy and they might thrive. Perhaps one day there would be some Western Australian gum trees by the *camino* to provide shade for the pilgrims. On a later trip, he might bring some red-tailed black cockatoos to sit in them.

The more ragged he became, the more pilgrims stopped to talk to the wise ascetic. Occasionally someone would try to kiss his feet or press a coin into his hand, for it was still rare in this part of the country to see a monk in holy robes. Not once was he attacked or spat upon. Spain had had too much of that sort of abuse, and grown tired of it.

The Camino de Santiago took him finally to the monastery of San Martiño Pinario where, at fifteen, Rosendo had become a novice, and later taken his vows. The church had been long boarded up by the republicans and become home to vermin, and anything of value had been long stolen, but its baroque interior had not been vandalised and he knelt in darkness before the altar.

As his eyes adjusted, he felt his way through the choir stalls and found his beloved instrument. Miraculously, it had not been destroyed by the mob. Over a month of days and nights by lamplight, Salvado took it apart, cleaned each of a thousand pipes, put them carefully back together, repaired the manuals, pedal board and stops and finally played a *Gloria* to an empty church. In slowly doing that purposeful task, through myriad tiny steps, each one by itself of no importance, Rosendo Salvado recovered his Faith, if not in the Church, then at least in God.

He would never see Victoria Plains again. New Norcia was not, after all, to be his life's work. He had paved the way, but it was not he who was to build it. Rather, by way of great mystery, God needed him to serve in the same terrible place the devout Angelo Confalonieri had achieved nothing and died a miserable and lonely death. Thus had it been decreed by Infinite Wisdom as part of His Divine and Inscrutable Design, as understood by an infallible Pope unburdened by any knowledge at all of Australian geography. This was his fate and he was reconciled to it, almost.

For the next few days, Salvado stayed in the lateral, seated in front of his beloved organ. He prayed a lot, giving thanks to God for His Wisdom, and he silently meditated, but mostly, he played. By the third day he had grown tired of religious music. For his own amusement, he performed '*Maquialó*', the Western Australian native dancing-song he had composed for his piano concert in Perth. It sounded particularly well in the empty church, with a natural echo descending from the half-dome to the nave.

On his last day he noticed an old couple, dressed for Mass,

kneeling in the dusty back pew, their grey heads bowed. They had heard the church organ for the first time in a decade and had crept in silently past the barricade to witness the miracle for themselves. They were greatly moved, if a little surprised, to hear not the sacred *El Cant de la Sibilla*, as they had hoped, but Bach's robust *Toccata and Fugue in D Minor*.

From: Ursula Frayne, Perth
To: Cecilia Marmion, Dublin

11th January 1850

My own dear Rev. Mother

So I am now a 'contumacious malcontent', berated by the three powerful men of the diocese of Perth, two of them consecrated bishops and the third thinking himself one.

His Original Lordship, our John Brady, is about to sail to Rome to fight for his See. Since we simple nuns are not permitted to travel alone, Anne Dillon and I have had to accept him as our chaperone on our journey home to see our beloved Sisters. Our ship Arcadia will be like Elizabeth in reverse, except we go this time via Ceylon, and our bishop no longer deigns to talk to us.

Dr Brady plans to take along a sweet little fellow called Placido. It is expected in Rome nowadays that Australian priests should bring a black child to show around the place. We will bring to Dublin the best-behaved of our orphan Marys, if she does not run away in the meantime.

It will be a great relief to escape Perth for a while Mother for there is a war between the two bishops and we are caught in the crossfire. Bishop Serra can talk only of money. He claims that precisely 144,710 French francs were given to Bishop Brady by Mademoiselle Jaricot's missionary society and that only eleven thousand are accounted for. Brady keeps no records. He may well have lost the money but to visit the bishop's palace is to confirm that he most certainly has not spent any of it on himself.

There is a third problem for us now. Father Urquhart was brought here by Serra. They boarded the ship in Spain as allies and disembarked as enemies. This fellow Urquhart will be Bishop Brady's attorney while he is away. Forgive me Mother, but I cannot speak mildly of him. Rumour says he was rejected by four different monasteries of Trappists.

His Other Lordship Joseph Serra arrived at Fremantle with forty men to build New Norcia and another monastery he calls New Subiaco. It seems he has bags of money with which to do it. No talk of course of a more comfortable convent for we poor nuns, or of improvements to our Benevolent Institution. On the contrary, last week Father Urquhart showed me what I thought to be a new storeroom, only to learn he intended this tiny space to be the Home for our orphan girls. Somehow I found the good grace to smile and thank him for his thoughtfulness and only after I had walked home did I allow myself to scream.

Mother, I confess at times I almost give in to despair. Surely the strongest evidence of the divinity of the Catholic Church is its continued existence after all these years despite all the blunders and faults of its clergy.

Perhaps the solution to the problem of the two bishops is to get a third. It seems that Dom Salvado too has been consecrated. It seems to happen routinely to every priest that visits Rome. Perhaps Salvado could still the waters that have been stirred by these three experts. I certainly cannot begin to do it, nor could you Mother, for we are mere women and our views disparaged.

Anne and I hope to arrive on your doorstep with little Mary Catherine Palamira before Easter Sunday. Please have a warm bed ready for our darling sweet girl, who will not be at all used to the cold of Dublin and could easily fall ill.

Give to each of my dearest Sisters my fondest love,

Your devoted child in J.C.
Sister Mary Ursula

20. RETURN TO LORETTE

From Naples, Fabrice sailed to Marseille where a queer thing happened. He spotted his old friend Léandre Fonteinne sitting outside a café in plain clothes and wearing a white hat. The disgraced ex-monk had put on weight and had a new air of importance about him. Fabrice waved from the far side of the street, but was ignored, so he teasingly called out something about Léandre being too proud to speak to him. Léandre's new friends, thuggish types, took offence at the interruption and carted the silk-tied provocateur off, while Léandre watched the fracas impassively, sipping at his coffee.

As Fabrice sat, bruised and angry, on the pavement, a well-dressed stranger passed. Without stopping and with his head turned away so he could not be seen talking to the troublemaker, he said, 'A complete bastard, that Proudhon. He would happily cut all our throats.' It had been a case of mistaken identity.

From Marseilles, Fabrice took the ferry to Port St Louis at the mouth of the Rhône, where he spent the last of Mademoiselle's money on a comfortable berth upriver to Lyon. As he drew closer to home, his heart grew heavier. At each port he sought and received ever more vivid accounts of what had transpired in his home town in that so-called Year of Freedom.

It took the *éclusier* at Givors to provide the really awful details that even the cardinal had withheld. He knew all about the Cleriquot murders, so he claimed, and his being a slow-filling lock, had plenty of time in which to relate the story. After the tragedy, as the *éclusier* recalled it, the Cleriquot mansion was occupied by their murderers. Fabrice, white as a ghost, reboarded and lay in his cabin, staring at the underside of the bunk above.

It all seemed impossible to imagine. Tomorrow he would arrive in Lyon, he would walk along the *Montée St Barthélemy* as he had done so many times, but his dear Maman would not run to hug him and soak his shirt with her silly tears. Nor would his father be standing there, three steps behind her, ready to express his disappointment at his son's latest failure.

But when he arrived in Lyon next day it was all exactly as the *éclusier* had said. His parents were gone, the family home abandoned and everything inside defiled. Grieving and discombobulated, Fabrice walked the scarred streets of Lyon. Everyone he knew had disappeared or gone into hiding. Strangers flinched as he approached.

The buildings near his apartment had all been wrecked and few had yet attempted to repair things in case the mob returned. There was one miracle, however: Fabrice's little apartment was untouched. Having an inauspicious façade and a concealed entrance, it had been overlooked. Fabrice found his key in the usual place, and to his surprise it still turned the lock. He dusted down his favourite red sofa, lay upon it, and did not leave it for two days.

He finally emerged to seek out old friends. He went first to the family home of his favourite student and stood for a while outside with a great anxiety burning within. He even walked to the door, but could not bring himself to knock. They had parted on bad terms.

The disapproving father might be violent. And a terrible feeling washed over him that dear Raphael would have been a natural target for the mob, being young, wealthy, educated, and so very elegant in manner and dress. Fabrice was not yet strong enough to hear such news.

Everyone on the streets of Lyon was trying to be grey. Perhaps there were still religious people and wealthy people living here, but nobody let it show in their dress. All silk had vanished. Pauline Jaricot's simple manner of dress had become the norm. And what had happened to her, he wondered? Had these lovers of freedom also killed the saintly virgin of Lyon?

It was a week later, and with great trepidation, that Fabrice walked up the familiar white pathway of *Lorette*, but this time he did not have to find the courage to go to the door, for he found Mademoiselle Jaricot deep in the overgrown garden. The Senegalese gardener was long gone, she explained, and now she had to do it all herself. She was wearing a broad hat, it being twenty degrees *Réaumur*, and her hands were dirty from digging up bulbs. She had aged a lot but did not appear distressed. Indeed, she seemed quite detached from the horrors which had taken place all around her. In a certain light, Fabrice thought he saw her glow.

Pauline Jaricot only vaguely recognised Fabrice. Once reminded of the work she had asked him to do in Australia, she responded as if he had just been away on an errand, perhaps to the market to buy her some seedlings. He embraced her and consoled her about the terrible things that had happened.

'What things, dear?' she replied, as if the violence of 1848 had been a trifle. 'Oh, all that. They did not kill me, dear, nor molest me as they did your poor mother. Merely, they took all my things.'

'Your money?' asked Fabrice gravely. He had come to dislike the sound of this word. Soon he would have to confess to the saintly Pauline Jaricot that he had spent all she had given him to no good effect, and explain the circumstances in which he lost the balance in a foaming cascade in the Avon River.

'Don't worry,' Pauline reassured him, 'I only had a little left. Fortunately, I had already lost most of it in the furnace.' There seemed no hint of regret. She was merely relating a fact.

'The furnace?'

'Yes, the hot blast furnace. The very modern sort.' Her voice was sadder and more frail than he recalled, but then she smiled, recalling the humour of the failed project. 'It was as if I threw all my money into the flames! What the investors did not take, the bank helped themselves to, so ...' A black spot on a jonquil bulb distracted her.

'It all turned out exactly as your father predicted,' she laughed, seeming to have finally placed Fabrice in the scheme of things. 'Claude warned me against such philanthropy, so I kept it all secret from him. Unscrupulous types will circle, he warned. Your father was always so correct on everything, I wished to defy him just this once.'

It was a great blessing that she was bankrupt by the time the mob came, smiled Pauline. 'I think the poor boys felt a little sorry for me actually, a destitute old lady living in a poorly heated mansion.'

'Who were these villains?'

'I am not sure they were *villains*, Fabrice. Just simple, lower-class boys without education or refinement. Some of them stayed on here at *Lorette* and they were not very bad boys, really. One of them, Thierry, liked to call me *maman* for he had none. He was very sad to leave at the end, but the officers had bayonets.'

'The men who killed my parents stayed with you, here at *Lorette*?'

'I think so, dear. *Perhaps* they were the ones. I did not think to ask them. And I never *invited* them to stay. One does not *invite* revolutionaries into one's home. They just liked the grounds, I think. It was peaceful here, Thierry said, after all that was going on in the town.'

'I expect they have since been shot or imprisoned.'

'I suppose they have,' sighed the saintly virgin. 'How sad to think so, Fabrice. It is necessary to suppress riots and restore order, of course. But it is even more necessary to remove the causes of disorder by giving those who suffer the two things that no one can do without. Bread and Hope.'

Fabrice finally confessed that he had squandered all the money she had given him.

'I gave you money, dear?'

'Yes, for the natives of Western Australia.'

'How lovely. Did they have need of money?'

'Not really. Some of it I lost in a flood.'

'A flood?'

'In a town called Toodyay.'

'How much did I give you?'

'One hundred thousand francs, Mademoiselle. A bit more.'

She sat thinking for a little while, trowel held in the air. 'Oh well,' she said, and kept digging. 'One fortune drowned, one burned.'

Fabrice suddenly felt very tired. 'Might I stay with you here for a while?' he asked, looking at her with very sad eyes.

'Of course you may stay. If I allowed revolutionaries, I must allow you, the son of my dear stubborn Claude.'

She put down her little spade now, brushed a lock of hair back with a grubby hand and suddenly looked the fifteen-year-old maiden again.

'Do you know something, Fabrice? I will tell you a secret. Had I not given my heart to Mary at such a young age, before I knew anything of the world, I would certainly have given it to your dear father. The larder is quite empty, by the way.'

'My father said that all his wealth and success in silk was due to the generosity your father showed him, many years ago.'

'Is that so?' she said dreamily. 'He never told me that.'

'That has disappeared, too,' continued Fabrice, for there seemed nothing he could not tell Pauline Jaricot, 'all my parents' money.' He had been up to Paris to finalise their affairs. Monsieur Paracel was gone, he was kept waiting for an hour, offered no champagne, and was finally greeted with insincere sympathy by a lowly manager who told him that all the assets of *Cleriquot et Fils* had been consumed by its debts. The bank had been forced to take possession of his father's factory, his several *magnaneries* and all the silk stock. The staff was dismissed without final pay. But the bank had not acted without a heart, said the unctuous banker. It had forgiven some unpaid loans on compassionate grounds, knowing the distressing manner of his father's death, and, unmentionably, he winced, his mother's.

Afterwards, Fabrice had felt the need to visit his father's once-grand offices for the last time. Outside still the brass sign declared it to be the premises of *Cleriquot et Fils, Fournisseurs de Soie depuis 1826* but inside it had been vandalised, perhaps by the hateful acolytes of Proudhon, who had himself once worked there. The windows were smashed and boarded up and when Fabrice peeked through a crack in the pinewood, a rat peered back at him from within.

Fabrice and Pauline were still in the garden when it started to rain. They walked up the steps together, the same steps he had climbed to kiss her hand on the night that the new Bishop of Perth had come to beg her for money. Back then, Fabrice recalled, the verandah had been as immaculately presented as the hostess, with polished boards and ranunculi in matching pots. Now the boards were lifting and there were gardening tools and buckets scattered everywhere. As the rain grew heavier, water started to pour in through a hole in the roof, under which an already full bucket was in position.

'Perhaps I can help with some of the things that need fixing,' suggested Fabrice.

'Oh, can you fix things now? I thought you were an academic.'

'I have acquired some useful skills from working with the monks.'

'Oh good. I always saw you with the monks, once you settled down.'

Six pleasant months passed at *Lorette*, much of it in the garden, until one morning Fabrice saw, from his favourite garden chair, over a mug of tea, a procession of Western Australian missionaries. They had come quietly through the gate, which no longer shut properly, and were walking hesitantly up the path towards the house. They had not spotted him, so Fabrice raced indoors.

Bishop John Brady strode ahead of the women, proclaiming aloud that the place had greatly declined since he was last here. The boxwood hedges were unclipped and the citrus unpruned. He was wearing his amaranth cap – an indication, Fabrice guessed, that he was looking for money.

The two nuns, Mother Ursula Frayne and Sister Anne Dillon, looked disgruntled and footsore and there was a thin little dark girl with them. She would no doubt be called Mary, thought Fabrice, now bearded and dressed like a provincial farmer. The garden was lovely, the nuns countered. The bishop shook his head. These little women were always inclined to say everything was 'lovely' even when patently it was not. He could barely wait to be rid of them. It would happen after Paris, just three days hence. Then he could go back to his beloved Ireland and see how 'lovely' that poor place had become.

For the nun's part, the feeling was double. They had whispered about the problem in their cots last night. To travel with this man any longer was intolerable. No longer did they refer in their letters to 'their bishop' or 'His Lordship' but merely 'the prelate who travels with us' or 'Dr Brady'.

Yesterday he had demanded money from them. The Sisters of Mercy had shaken the tin at each port *en route* to Rome, he recounted. They received sixty-nine pounds in donations at Colombo, though Ursula had to suffer the shame of standing on a garden balcony to be adored by those gathered below, like a sort of female pontiff. They got thirty-nine pounds at Malta, another thirty-three in Rome and twenty-nine in Florence. That would be one hundred and seventy pounds the nuns would hand over when they got to Paris, Brady announced. Despite what the Pope had said aloud at their audience in Rome, John Brady *could* add up a simple set of numbers.

The nuns would not hand a penny of it over, they had secretly decided. They would follow in the steps of their founder Catherine McAuley, who had started with her own money and understood the power it gave, but only if kept in the right hands. Having nursed Catherine in her last months, Ursula felt she knew what their founder would have to say on the matter. Obedience, humility, poverty: these were all very good things, in balance. But with too much of them, nothing could ever be achieved. In Paris they could find a cloistered order to stay with, Ursula was thinking, or undertake a silent religious retreat from which they could not possibly be disturbed, even by an avaricious bishop.

The Church of Rome was designed for men, the nuns agreed, which was why violence was always breaking out within it and without it. Christ Himself had not been that way. He always had his Marys about him, his beloved Mother Mary and Mary Magdalene, rescued from sin. In Alexandria, the Holy Virgin had caused them to bump into Florence Nightingale so that they may learn from her vigour and determination. Now Our Lady had led them to *Lorette* so that they may be inspired by Pauline Jaricot, foundress of the Society for the Propagation of the Faith, instigator of the Devotions of the Living Rosary and supporter of the Society of the Infant Jesus for the Rescue of Chinese Infants Abandoned by their Parents.

A warm tea cup discovered by Anne on the garden table suggested Pauline was at home. It was decided by Dr Brady that the nuns should try the door while he waited at the foot of the stairs in the sunshine. He did not wish to appear mendicant. Sister Anne was given the honour of knocking. The door half opened and a male voice came from within.

'I am sorry, sisters,' a manservant told them from the darkness, 'but Mademoiselle Jaricot is out. She is … visiting.' He spoke excellent English for a Lyonnais, thought the nuns. 'You will have to go away,' he added through the crack in the frame.

Anne looked at Ursula for advice. The fellow's voice seemed to have a familiar ring to it. 'Might she be back later today, do you think?' she asked, bending her neck and trying to peep inside for further clues.

'She might. But, no. She will not be back for ...' (Anne thought she heard a soft instruction from within) '... one week. She is on retreat, you see.'

'How sad,' said Sister Anne. 'We have come a very long way to meet her.'

'Bad luck,' said the servant, almost closing the door against the toe of Anne's black shoe.

Anne Dillon tried another tack. 'Could we perhaps ... we would like to walk up to the shrine, Sister Ursula and I, with the little black girl. Might we be allowed to freshen up?'

There followed a long pause. It was impossible in Catholic Lyon to refuse ablutions to a pair of nuns with a small child. The manservant emerged into the daylight and showed himself.

'Fabrice!' said Sister Anne, giving him an Irish hug. 'Jesus, Mary and Joseph, look at you there with the big bushy beard! Are you trying to become a Benedictine? And what on earth are you doing at the home of Pauline Jaricot?' Behind her, much less cheerfully, the reddening face of the bishop wordlessly demanded the same information.

'Staking the delphiniums,' explained Fabrice.

With Anne's help, Fabrice Cleriquot brought out glasses of water and a sweet treat for little Mary Catherine Palamira.

'We have not seen you since you left Fremantle last year with Dom Salvado and little Francis and John,' said Ursula. 'We suspected you would not return, didn't we Anne?'

'We missed you,' added Anne. 'You may not be much of a Catholic but you were a breath of fresh air in that stale place.'

Fabrice had relaxed now and felt he could tell them his story.

'Well, a lot has happened, not much of it for the good. We arrived to find that Europe had fallen apart. In Rome, lovers of freedom had taken over the city and disarmed the Swiss Guard and turned the army of the Papal States against the pope, so he fled to Gaeta. He seemed quite sad there in his lonely castle on a rocky promontory.'

Brady's eyes widened. 'You are not telling me you met the Pope, Cleriquot?' he demanded.

'Oh, yes!' said Fabrice. 'But not for very long. He had to speak with the French generals.'

'You? An atheist?'

'I am a Pyrrhonist now, I think,' Fabrice explained.

'I am sure it will pass,' mumbled the Bishop of Perth.

'Pio Nono was grateful to my father for making his little white hat,' Fabrice continued. 'He was quite nice, but very anxious about Garibaldi and so on. It was he who told me that my parents had been slaughtered. And he made Salvado a bishop, you know.'

'Of Port Victoria,' gloated the Bishop of Perth. 'May God spare him from the alligators.'

'His Holiness was lovely to us, too,' reminisced Sister Anne. 'And what a humble man! We had kneeled to kiss the crosses embroidered upon his Papal slippers, but he insisted we rise and kiss his hand instead.'

Fabrice asked why the bishop had not brought a child along with him, fearing he knew the answer.

'Placido remains in Rome with a bad chest,' said John Brady. 'We will get him across to Ireland when he recovers.'

They sat out on the lawn on chairs that did not match, before a table that wobbled. Fabrice, helped enthusiastically by Sister Anne, managed to put together a modest afternoon tea. Neither did the teacups match, but nobody minded. The sun reappeared. A friendly goldfinch flitted onto the table to steal crumbs and observe the exotic visitors.

In a far corner of the garden, partly hidden by an untamed climbing rose, an old woman in a broad hat sat on a plank supported on house bricks. She was very slowly pulling up thistles and shaking the soil from the roots. She was, Fabrice explained, a local eccentric who liked to garden, but did not have one herself, so Mademoiselle Jaricot allowed her free access. Little Mary Catherine, bored with sitting, wandered off to help the old lady.

'Things here have deteriorated greatly,' observed the bishop. 'Is there no proper gardener anymore?'

'No. Just us,' said Fabrice. 'Mademoiselle lost all her money in a blast furnace. She can no longer pay for a gardener. And anyway, she has decided she prefers it to be wild. The birds prefer it that way, too.'

'I think it is so lovely here,' said Sister Anne, dipping a stale pastry in cold tea. 'Lord, how I miss the beautiful green!' And then she sobbed unexpectedly, and Ursula brushed the back of her hand to comfort her, for she knew Anne was thinking again of poor Ireland.

Next, Ursula excused herself on the pretence of checking on little Mary Catherine, who had disappeared deep in the wild garden. Fabrice watched the nun approach the old lady and instead of standing to talk with her, fall on her knees and bow her head and seem to pray before her. The old lady put down her little spade for a minute and her lips moved too. The bishop had not noticed the scene at all, and Sister Anne was pretending not to, so Fabrice distracted them with stories of the ill fate that had befallen everyone he had once known in Lyon. Merchants, priests, academics, they had all suffered at the hands of the unlearned.

'Anarchists,' spat the bishop.

'Perhaps they were right to rise up,' proposed Fabrice.

'Good God!' said the bishop. 'They murdered your parents!'.

'Well, nothing stays the same forever. 'All things must be examined, debated, investigated without exception and without regard for anyone's feelings. So said Diderot.'

'Whomever he might be,' concluded John Brady of County Cavan.

'How are things in the colony?' asked Fabrice, hoping to buy more time since Ursula was still kneeling in the garden.

'It is now a convict colony,' said the bishop, 'so things are looking up.'

'You are looking forward to the convict ships arriving, Excellency?'

'Yes, I suppose I am,' said Brady, seeing opportunity where others might see despair. 'Irish Catholics will fill those ships, wanting nothing more than fresh air, a new start and the blessing of Our Lord Jesus Christ. I have worked with such men before, French Canadians exiled by the English to New South Wales. They are very tractable, loyal to the Church. I may even scour the prisons back home for such men. We would be very pleased to receive them in Perth.'

Ursula returned to the table now, her knees rich with garden soil.

'Mary seems perfectly happy helping pull up weeds,' said Mother Ursula. 'I think she would live here if she could, like a wild little black.' And they all laughed.

After lunch, the nuns asked to leave a few belongings on the porch while they took a walk up the hill to the Marian shrine. Fabrice showed them the gap in the hedge through which they could find the start of the path. It had not been accessed for a while. Mary Catherine had no problem sneaking through a gap at the bottom, but the nuns had to push their way through the soft branches. The bishop declared no interest in visiting shrines to Mary and departed for other business in town; a clandestine meeting with a potential donor, Fabrice guessed.

'Peace at last,' said Pauline Jaricot, carrying a wicker basket of gladioli bulbs she had dried over the autumn and were ready for replanting.

'Mother Ursula prayed with you?' Fabrice enquired. 'I saw your lips move.'

'Is that who she was?' said Pauline, addressing a bulb.

'Might I ask, what did you say to her?'

'I prayed that she might leave me alone. I told her I don't want to see any more missionaries with their little black children stolen from their own lands. It just makes me sad. Leave the natives where they are, I told her. Leave them to their own gods.'

'Did she reply?'

The saintly virgin had bad knees so to reach the soil she had to bend down at the waist, legs splayed. She remained in this awkward position, but managed to pull away her draping apron, look up at Fabrice and smile. 'She was a little unhappy with me, I think. But I don't care.' Her words came slowly nowadays, in thoughtful bursts. 'Not like I once did. My older brother went off to Cochin China as a missionary. I was fifteen and so very proud of him. That was before I understood much. Now, when they try to rid themselves of troublesome priests in Danang, we French send naval ships and shoot them all. It makes one not so sure.'

Fabrice dug a little trench in front of Pauline's knees to help with the planting. The lunchtime goldfinch reappeared accompanied by his mate, hoping to find worms in the upturned soil.

'I too think I have learned a lot, Mademoiselle,' Fabrice reflected. 'It occurs to me how different was my conversation today with the bishop compared with the last time he was here. I find I am not as opposed to the church as I once was, but I do not take it so seriously. Perhaps at the nub of it there is even some good. Look at the nuns, they are without doubt good people. And Dom Salvado, even though we parted on bad terms, is a good man in his heart, though he may do as much harm as good. And to my surprise I find I am quite in favour of monasticism. To be a Benedictine is quite a purposeful vocation and not so very far removed from Epicurus, were it not for the matter of God. When I look back now on my time in the university, it was much like a monastery, everyone sharing the same opinions and saying the same thing. But real monks make their own bread, which is excellent, and they farm and they drink wine. And monks appreciate silence. There is much to be said for silence, I have learned. Do you agree, Mademoiselle?'

'Oh yes,' said the saintly virgin, though it seemed she had not been listening very closely. She positioned the last bulb, looked at it approvingly, and briskly filled the trench, seeming to delight in the chocolatey dirt which covered her apron. Then Pauline Jaricot stood upright, a slow and deliberate process, looked up as if she were about to pray, but then winced and put her hand to the small of her back.

'Lord, I have to stretch every so often, nowadays,' she explained.

As Pauline looked skywards, and the sun caught her hair a certain way, Fabrice again imagined her as a young woman, full of earnest optimism. Perhaps this was the girl his father had once seen, and loved all his life. She shook her apron and picked up the basket of bulbs to move to the next row.

'How wonderful it feels to be with you again at *Lorette*,' said Fabrice, 'at the very place where my own spiritual journey began.' He was feeling sad and nostalgic, for his parents were dead and so much had happened. 'It seems to me there is a chain of events in this world, linked in ways we cannot know. In truth, I did not wish to come to your mansion that evening, but had I not, I would never have travelled with the missionaries to Western Australia, or lived in a commune with a Humanist, or helped build a monastery in the middle of the bush, or learned to speak some words of the native tongue, or seen the sun's light shine through the beak of a *gouljacque*, or rediscovered that after all god does exist, in some form, even though he is powerless to influence anything we do. I would instead have simply stayed here in Lyon, lived selfishly with my friends at the university and been butchered with my parents.'

Pauline Jaricot was inspecting one of the bulbs. That black discolouration on the skin might be a fungus. She had to be more careful in future to dust them while were they in the drying drawer.

'How interesting,' Pauline replied, 'but, Fabrice, let us leave all that please. There is gardening to be done, and that is all that matters today.'

NOONGAR WORDS

The spoken language of the Noongar people is over 45,000 years old and the relatively recent spellings of the oral tradition vary considerably depending on dialect and region. Quite a few Noongar words have been adopted, slightly corrupted, into the vernacular of English-speaking Western Australians.

balga		grass tree, xanthorrhoea
balyat		cheeky little spirit man
bibool		paperbark tree
biyara		banksia tree
boodja		ground, country
booka	(*beauka*, Fabrice)	kangaroo skin cloak
boodi	(*budi*, Léandre)	woylie, brush-tailed bettong
boya		rock, 'boondi'
dadja		meat
darmoorlook	(*darmaluque*, Fabrice)	'twenty-eight' parrot
djaraly		jarrah tree
djidi-djidi	(*jiddy-jiddy*, Sadie)	'willy-wagtail' wren
djilba	(*gilbert*, Fabrice)	bream (fish)
djilki		small freshwater crayfish, 'gilgie'
dowak	(*do-whacker*, Farrelly)	short heavy club, throwing stick
kaya	(*quaia*, Fabrice)	hello
kebarak		boat
kidji		spear, 'gidgee'
koorlangka		children
kooldjak	(*gouljacque*, Fabrice)	black swan

koomal	(*coumarle*, Fabrice)	possum
koomba		big
maaman		father
mabarn		medicine man, sorcerer
mamara		hairy dwarf man
manatj		policeman
mari		marri tree, which 'bleeds' red kino
moodjar		Western Australian Christmas tree
ngangk		mother
nyola		catfish, cobbler
wadjala		white man
waugal	(*ouagil*, Fabrice)	mythical rainbow serpent, 'wagyl'
wana		woman's digging stick
wandjoo		welcome
warndoo		wandoo, white gum tree
woordatji		mischievous little men
yongka		kangaroo

HISTORICAL FIGURES AND PLACES

Listed in approximate order of appearance. Note that the Cleriquots, Roger Smith, Sadie, Bob, Michael and Eric are all fictional characters.

Pauline Jaricot

The youngest of seven children of a wealthy silk-maker, Pauline lived a privileged life in Lyon until her teens when, following her mother's death, she took a vow of perpetual virginity and devoted her life to supporting Catholic missions. Her older brother Philéas was a missionary in Vietnam. At twenty-two, she founded the Society for the Propagation of the Faith, which grew to become the most valuable charity in the Catholic Church. The society provided generous financial support to Bishop Brady's mission after Pauline met with him in Lyon. In 1845 she invested most of her own money in a philanthropic project centred on a community blast furnace, but due to the unscrupulous behaviour of others, she lost everything and died destitute. In 1963 Pope John XXIII declared Pauline Jaricot 'Venerable'. In 2020 Pope Francis recognised a 'miracle' caused by her intercession, clearing the way for her to be beatified as a Catholic saint.

John Brady

Brady's early biography is uncertain. He was born 'of peasant stock' in Corratober, County Cavan and educated in a French seminary, perhaps the *Seminaire des Colonies* in Paris. He is said to have served as a priest on the island of Bourbon (Réunion) before coming to Australia. In the Hawkesbury district of New South Wales he was known for his good work with the local

Aboriginal people and convicts. Late in 1843, Bishop Polding of Sydney appointed Father Brady his vicar-general for Western Australia, whose small Catholic population were crying out for a priest. Brady came to Perth with Father John Joostens and catechist Patrick O'Reilly, but only stayed for ten weeks, laying the foundation stone for the new church before sailing off to Rome. There he befriended the well-connected 'fixer' Father Jean-Félix-Onésime Luquet and to everyone's surprise, especially Polding's, returned to Perth as a bishop nominally in charge of two-thirds of the continent and with twenty-seven missionaries in tow. Brady was terrible with money, eventually resulting in Bishop Serra being given control of the diocesan purse strings. Perth split into Irish Bradyite and European Serraite factions, the two feuding bishops filing suit and countersuit until Bishop Polding sailed across from Sydney to end it. On 19 October 1850, Brady left Fremantle on the *Eugene*, never to return. However, he was allowed to remain nominally Bishop of Perth until 1871, when he died at Amélie-les-Bains, France. In 2011 His Lordship's exhumed remains were flown to Perth, brought up the Swan River on a boat, and reinterred in a ceremony at St Mary's Cathedral in which an actor appeared as Bishop Brady, resplendent in amaranth.

José Serra

Orphaned at eleven, Serra was schooled in Barcelona and at the age of sixteen was sent to Santiago de Compostela in Galicia to become a Benedictine monk. Soon after his ordination, in a savage process called the Ecclesiastical Confiscations of Mendizábal, church property was taken by the Spanish state and all the monks were thrown out of their abbeys. Serra fled to southern Italy and joined the Abbey of Trinità di Cava de' Tirreni, or 'Cava', where he and Salvado made their pact to go to Australia as missionaries. In 1848 he was made Bishop of Port Victoria but he never actually visited that place, and exactly one year later the dubious honour passed to Salvado. Although never officially made Bishop of Perth, Serra ran the diocese from Brady's departure in 1850 until 1862.

Rosendo Salvado

Salvado was from the Galician town of Tuy, the first Spanish town pilgrims come to when walking the Portuguese Camino from Oporto to Santiago de Compostela. His family was moderately wealthy and very musical. As a young man he studied music, architecture, liberal arts and philosophy. With Serra, he was thrown out of Spain soon after his ordination and fled to Cava. Like Serra, he was made Bishop of Port Victoria, but never visited the place. Instead, he remained in Italy for four years, writing his memoirs about the early days of New Norcia, raising money for the project and winning approval for his grand plans. He returned to Western Australia in 1853 and devoted the rest of his life to the mission. In 1867 Salvado was made Lord Abbot of New Norcia 'for life'. He had been naturalised as a British citizen as early as 1848 and was deeply involved in secular political life, such as being a member of the inaugural Victoria Plains Road Board. Salvado died in Rome just three days before Australian Federation, having devoted fifty-four of his eighty-six years to New Norcia. His remains were brought to Perth and reinterred behind the high altar of the church at New Norcia.

Francis Libermann

Born Jacob Libermann, the son of the Chief Rabbi of Saverne discovered Rousseau in his teens and became an agnostic for some years before converting to Catholicism, as did two of his brothers. He began studying for the priesthood, but was held back due in part to epilepsy. At age thirty-nine he was finally ordained and at *La Neuville* near Amiens formed the Missionary Society of the Heart of Mary, an order of priests especially devoted to proselytising freed slaves in Réunion, Mauritius, Haiti and West Africa. The order was a predecessor of the Spiritans.

The Fathers Francis

The Heart of Mary priests, François Thiersé and François Thévaux, together with the younger lay brothers Vincent and Théodore, were ill-equipped for success in the Great Southern region of Western Australia. It did not help that the bishop failed to provide them with funds or equipment and then locked them out of Albany. They somehow managed to build a little church at Lake Mollyalup near present-day Mount Barker, but in 1847 a letter came from Father Libermann instructing them to abandon Western Australia for Mauritius. This French colony proved a much happier mission, both priests living out their long lives there, Father Thévaux dying in 1877 and Father

Thiersé in 1888. An excavation of their Lake Mollyalup site in 1997 unearthed cooking pots and two pairs of rosary beads, one with a metal crucifix bearing the words *Mère de Dieu, Priez Por Nous* – 'Mother of God, Pray for Us'.

Maurice Bouchet

The third of the Heart of Mary priests died soon after arriving in Perth after developing fevers and delirium on board *Elizabeth*. He was only twenty-four. His death was attributed by the unreliable Léandre Fonteinne to his failure to wear a hat at night when crossing the equator. He is buried in a marked grave in a quiet corner of what is now St John's Pro-Cathedral, alongside Catherine Gogarty.

Prosper Guéranger

Born in Sablé and ordained a priest at age twenty-two, Dom Prosper Guéranger was a bishop's secretary who became known as the Saviour of Solesmes Abbey when he rescued the ancient building from ruin and restored a thriving Benedictine congregation. He is credited with reviving Benedictine monastic life in France after it had been wiped out in the French Revolution. He also brought back the Gregorian Chant, sending his monks to old libraries across Europe seeking out old chant manuscripts.

Léandre Fonteinne

A novice from Solesmes Abbey, and the only monk Abbot Guéranger offered to Brady's mission, Dom Fonteinne proved disastrous. He was responsible for the accidental shooting death of John Gorman and was subsequently excommunicated by Brady for alleged offences which included, according to Fonteinne's own account, public transvestism and indecent dealing with a young parishioner. *The Correspondence of Léandre Fonteinne*, translated by Peter Gilet, is a compelling read. Dom Fonteinne is revealed as an intelligent writer, a meticulous observer of things, funny, gossipy, emotionally manipulative and completely self-obsessed.

Nicola Caporelli

Caporelli was the only layman to join Brady's mission. His father was a prominent lawyer and the Caporellis an influential family in the Papal States, but older brother Antonio had ruined the family financially and Nicola was said to be 'subject to fanciful obsessions'. His purpose in coming to Perth was nominally to set up a secondary school, and to act as 'Consul-General of the Papal States', a rôle which existed only in theory since there was no trade and no diplomatic ties between the crumbling Papal States and any colony in Australia. Rome withdrew the honorary consulship after Brady wrote a letter of complaint about him. Instead, Caporelli made wine in the Swan Valley, before leaving for Adelaide where he set himself up as an 'Agent and Professor of Languages'. He later followed his fortune to the Victorian goldfields where he died in Castlemaine aged thirty-six.

John Wilmot

The Right Honourable Earl of Rochester was a seventeenth-century poet whose works are not on any high school curriculum. 'A Ramble in St James's Park' still warrants a strong language warning.

Angelo Confalonieri

Young Angelo was a sickly youth who put himself through rigorous training in the Dolomites, spending nights alone in the mountains and undergoing extreme tests of endurance, temperature and fasting. Ordained a Benedictine monk (the Italians tended to the honorific 'Don' while the Spanish preferred 'Dom') he was personally nominated by Pope Gregory XVI to join the mission to the Swan River. He soon clashed with Bishop Brady over financial matters and was despatched to the English naval garrison of Essington, or Port Victoria, on the tip of the Coburg Peninsula north of present-day Darwin. *En route* he survived a shipwreck in which the two Irish catechists accompanying him drowned, but he dutifully continued on to Essington where he lived alongside the local people, whom he referred to as 'the Iwaidja'. He was called by them 'Nagoyo' which he took to mean 'Holy Father', and learned enough of their language to publish a dictionary and to translate prayers into their language. He died in that awful place, aged thirty-five, of some sort of tropical fever.

Sisters of Mercy

Catherine McAuley founded this order in Dublin in 1831 with the aim of protecting and educating impoverished women. She was in her fifties and quite wealthy, having inherited a fortune from a childless Protestant couple who loved her like a daughter. At first she had run the House of Mercy with laywomen volunteers and was reluctant to convert it into a religious community, fearing a loss of independence, but managed to get a special papal rule ensuring her order would be protected from meddling bishops. They became known as the 'walking nuns' because, unlike like the cloistered Carmelites, they could readily be seen around the streets of Dublin, providing practical help to poor women.

Catherine Gogarty

Catherine was chosen by Cecilia Marmion as Ursula's second superior because they were so close. The two young women had together survived a difficult posting to freezing windy Newfoundland, and had nursed Catherine McAuley in her dying days. Catherine was suffering from tuberculosis and it was hoped that the change of climate might be therapeutic, but she faded away within a few months of the nuns' arrival in Perth and was buried alongside Maurice Bouchet.

Ursula Frayne

Ursula's father was a prosperous businessman so she probably knew more about financial management than her bishop. The obstacles to her success in Perth were many, starting with Bishop Brady and the parlous state of the colony. She really did write to Queen Victoria begging for money. After Brady was sent home, there was even worse friction with his successor Serra and the irascible Urquhart. Meanwhile, on the other side of the continent, it turned out that Irish Catholics were very good at finding gold. The booming new colony called 'Victoria' suddenly had a desperate need for teachers and plenty of money to build schools. In 1857 Ursula and Anne accepted an invitation to move to Melbourne from Bishop Goold, a Corkman described by Ursula's biographer Catherine Killerby as 'young, energetic, decisive, orderly and down-to-earth'. Suddenly the nuns had everything they had been denied in Perth; a lovely bluestone convent opposite Carlton Gardens in Fitzroy, financial support and administrative autonomy. Their first fund-raising bazaar alone raised 950 pounds. Ursula remained in Melbourne working tirelessly in education, care of the sick and the welfare of poor women, especially orphaned Irish girls, until her death in 1885. She was buried in the convent with 'her best friend and lifelong companion, Anne Xavier Dillon, standing alone at the foot of the grave'.

Anne Dillon

Anne had to step up when Catherine Gogarty died, as she was much less experienced and a mere 'lay nun' not a full 'choir nun', as they were then categorised. She proved a great surprise to herself and Ursula, and their relationship survived difficult times and many decades. Anne did manage to get her wayward younger sister Ellen to Perth, only for them to part again when Anne moved to Melbourne. She too died there in 1894 and was buried 'in a vault beside Ursula, with a memorial stone to her carved and placed under Ursula's Celtic cross'.

Kate O'Reilly

A County Cavan girl brought out as a servant, Kate was the only one of the Sisters of Mercy group not to travel First Class on *Elizabeth*. Once in Perth she was made a postulant and she really did 'last the distance' as Sister Anne predicts. She was ordained Sister Evangelista, eventually became mother superior of the Perth convent, and died in 1899, having provided fifty-three years of unpaid service to the Swan River colony.

Terence Farrelly

The man everyone called 'The Terror' was a valued ally of Bishop John Brady during the mission's difficult early years in Perth. From Fonteinne's descriptions, Farrelly was the natural leader of the eight lay 'student catechists' that Brady brought out from Ireland on the eve of the Great Famine. There is an occasional reference to him as a 'nephew' of the bishop. He married a Caroline Gresswell in St John's 'Cathedral' in 1849 and is described at various times as being a schoolmaster of the Catholic boy's school, a director of the Swan River Steamboat Company and, following the arrival of the first convicts, a prison officer. That his conversion to convictism may have been driven by Irish nationalism is mere speculation by the author. He died in Perth in 1883, leaving three daughters and a son. His descendants were present at Brady's reinterment ceremony at St Mary's Cathedral in 2011, the family link between the Bradys and the Farrellys having survived 140 years since the bishop's death.

John Gorman

In June 1846, just after Salvado gave his famous piano concert, the young Irish catechist John Gorman was shot dead by Dom Léandre Fonteinne at a place on Victoria Plains the monks called Badji Badji. The Frenchman then fled, so when Serra and Salvado returned to Victoria Plains, they found the mission abandoned and Gorman's days-old body in the hut. According to Salvado's memoirs, John Gorman was laid to rest at this forgotten place. Dom Fonteinne provided graphic accounts of the 'accident' in his later letters to Prosper Guéranger, many of his words making their way into this novel.

Father Peter Powell

Contemporary reports suggested Powell left Perth for Calcutta, but his name soon after appears in the eastern colonies of Australia, where he served as a priest in various locations. He was the inaugural Catholic priest of Penola, South Australia from 1854, and then in Adelaide, St Leonards, Penrith and Melbourne, where he died in 1872.

Robert Owen

Robert Owen was a Welsh textile manufacturer, philanthropist and social reformer. A founder of utopian socialism, he established a number of experimental socialist communities including New Harmony, Indiana in 1825. It failed after two years.

Frederick Irwin

A veteran of the Peninsular War in Spain fighting Napoleon's forces, Irwin came to the Swan River in 1829 as the officer in charge of the detachment sent to protect the new colony. He was a cousin of the first governor, James Stirling. He was reprimanded by the Secretary for the Colonies for his mishandling of the case of the captured Midgegoroo, whom he had executed by firing squad in front of the Perth Police station, and for the reward he placed on the head of Midgegoroo's son, Yagan. Upon the death of the popular young governor Andrew Clarke in early 1847, Irwin became acting governor until Charles Fitzgerald arrived eighteen months later. His tenure was broadly unpopular with the settlers, the colony being at that time in dire financial straits and Irwin being of very unyielding character. He left the colony in 1856 and died in England four years later.

Louis and Mary Ann Langoulant

Jean Charles Louis Langoulant was from Cherbourg, France and came to the colony with a French whaling crew operating off the south coast. He abandoned the whaler or, according to one account, simply went ashore for a drinking session and missed the departing ship, and lived the rest of his life in the Swan River colony. Once in Perth, he married Mary Ann King, who had arrived with the first colonists in 1829, and they raised twelve children. Louis was at various times a fisherman, a lime burner, a drover, a horse breeder and a gold miner. The Langoulants were very helpful to the missionaries, and Mary Ann converted to Catholicism. Louis appears to have been a relentlessly energetic man to the last. Though he was seventy-two when Mary Ann died, he remarried a twenty-one-year-old, with whom he had another three children.

Frank Armstrong

That the early colony had such a position as Interpreter to the Natives might come as a surprise. Armstrong's rôle was diverse. He was required to be present at all trials and court proceedings involving Aboriginal people, ran 'the depot' (Perth Natives Institution) at the bottom of Mount Eliza, policed 'troublemakers' in the capital and acted as 'moral agent' to the prisoners held at Rottnest. Armstrong had come to Perth from Edinburgh as a teenager with his widowed father, who invested in the ill-fated Thomas Peel project south of Perth. When that failed, his father found a pleasant riverside block which he named *Dalkeith* after his childhood home; the Dalkeith landmark now called Gallop House started life as the Armstrong residence. His contribution to G.F. Moore's 1842 dictionary was acknowledged by Moore in the foreword. He was also a bird lover, which unfortunately in the nineteenth century involved a lot of taxidermy.

E.G. Wakefield

A prominent theorist on British colonial settlements, Wakefield was heavily influential in the new Australian colonies of the mid-nineteenth century, and later New Zealand and Canada. The Wakefield Scheme aimed to keep land prices high while making the colonies more attractive to workers, tradesmen, artisans and capital. Adelaide was largely established on Wakefield-ian principles. He wrote as an expert *in absentia*, never having visited an Australian colony, partly because he was imprisoned for long periods due to his tendency to abduct underage heiresses. He wrote his famous 'A Letter from Sydney' while in Newgate Prison.

Captain F.P. Blackwood

British naval officer in command of the sloop *Fly* who from 1842 to 1845 undertook a comprehensive hydrographic survey of the Australian coastline from Sydney to Perth via the Barrier Reef, Torres Strait and Port Victoria, which he didn't think much of. A town in Victoria was named after him. The Blackwood River south of Perth was named after his father.

Samuel Moore

Samuel followed his older brother George to Perth, initially running a barge between Fremantle, Perth and Guildford, and rising to be inaugural chairman of the Western Australian Bank. With his wife Dorothy and their six children, he lived at *Oakover* in Middle Swan, where Salvado sometimes stayed *en route* to the mission. In 1848 they suffered bad debts, family illness, poor crops and the wreck of *Vixen*, with heavy loss of their goods. He died in 1849, aged forty-five.

George Fletcher Moore

A Protestant lawyer from Derry who was a prominent citizen of the Swan River colony from the outset. He was the first advocate-general, a member of the Legislative and Executive Councils, and a successful farmer in the Swan and Avon Valleys. He was an early explorer of rivers, confirming that the Avon River fed into the Swan and, in 1836, 'discovering' the river which he named for himself. He acted as an agent for the Drummonds, getting Jim's plants and seeds and young Johnston's bird and animal specimens safely transported to England and into the hands of prominent collectors. In 1842 he published in London *A Descriptive Vocabulary of the Language in Common Use Amongst the Aborigines of Western Australia.* When colonial secretary Peter Broun died in late 1846, it fell to Moore to act in that position, alongside Irwin as acting governor. He kept an entertaining diary, an invaluable record of life in the early colony from a settler's perspective.

Luis Giustiniani

An ex-Catholic Anglican minister brought out to the Swan River colony in 1835 by the Western Australian Missionary Society to establish a Moravian-style mission. It was Frederick Irwin's project, but he would come to regret his choice. Giustiniani had an unusually enlightened approach for the time, establishing a small mission employing Aboriginal people at Guildford, and his advocacy for equal application of the law caused him to fall foul of the settlers, the government and the Anglican ministry. He was declared a troublemaker and sent home, in a case which, in the words of religious historian Lesley Borowitza, 'reveals much about the prevailing culture and prejudices of the early colony'.

William Mitchell

Anglican minister who was appointed by the Western Australian Missionary Society to replace Giustiniani as clergyman for the residents of Middle and Upper Swan. He arrived in 1838 aged thirty-five with his second wife Frances, four children and a governess. Three more children would be born in the Swan River colony. Mitchell proved a much more acceptable choice to the conservative settlers. He built an octagonal church called St Mary's in Middle Swan in 1840, replaced in 1868 by the rectangular St Mary's which still stands in Yule Avenue today. He remained as rector, chaplain and prominent citizen in the colony until his death in 1870. The acerbic character the author has inflicted upon him is for dramatic purposes only. He was probably a perfectly sweet man.

Austral-Ind (now Australind)

One of several failed enterprises which broke the hearts and emptied the wallets of early investors in the Swan River colony. Based on Wakefield-ian principles, the idea was to build an idyllic English-style settlement on the Leschenault Inlet north of Bunbury. The business plan was to breed Australian horses for the British army in India, hence the original name *Austral-Ind*, but it failed, in part due to poor soil and climate, apart from the enormous logistics of shipping horses across the Indian Ocean. Still, its leader Waller Clifton and his wife Elinor left an enormous legacy to the colony: they had a dozen children, many of whom became prominent members of colonial society.

John Scully

An Irish Catholic who arrived at Fremantle on the *Hindoo* in 1839 and took up land at York. Together with James Drummond, Scully explored the lands they named Victoria Plains and first opened it up for sheep in 1841. Scully settled at the tiny town of Bolgart and was made resident magistrate of Toodyay and Victoria Plains. It was Scully's influence on Bishop Brady that caused Victoria Plains to be chosen as the site of the Central Mission, and his early support was crucial. Some of his early advice, however, seems to have set the monks up for failure. He directed them to a location where the Scots were already running sheep, ensuring conflict over the lease and water, rather than to the Drummonds' outstation at Maurin Pool, where they moved after John Gorman's death. Scully ran into financial difficulties soon after and returned permanently to Ireland in 1847.

James (Jim) Drummond

Previously Curator of the Cork Botanical Gardens, Drummond was an original pioneer, arriving on the *Parmelia* in 1829 with wife Sarah and six children in tow. He was appointed Government Naturalist and Botanist and was prodigious in his classification of new plant species throughout the breadth of the colony, many receiving the epithet *drumondii*. Less commendably, he was an enthusiastic 'collector' of native fauna in the rather destructive manner of his day, which was to catch, kill and stuff the native wildlife for private buyers or European museums to display. Along with

Scully, Drummond opened up Victoria Plains for sheep farming, but was not granted an official depasturing lease from the government. His youngest son, Johnston, was speared by Kabinger and his second youngest, John, was the police constable who tracked down Kabinger and killed him. His youngest child, Euphemia, married Ewen Macintosh, previously one of his shepherds.

The Scots

By the time the Spanish monks arrived, the Scottish shepherds had usurped their bosses to have the largest flocks on Victoria Plains. Prominent among them were the three Macpherson brothers (Donald, Duncan and John) along with Ewen Macintosh. In partnership, they were by July 1842 running sheep 'in an area of 12000 acres which included Murra Murra (later Glentromie Station), Badji Badji and Noondagoonda'. Salvado's diaries hint at an uneasy relationship between the mission and some of his neighbours, including infections in women and their babies 'brought about by the incontinence of the white man,' but he is careful not to attribute such difficulties to the Scots, 'from whom we had received many kindnesses'. Badji Badji was the ill-fated early site of the mission where Gorman was shot by Fonteinne. If the Scots were already running sheep at that location, it is a mystery why Scully directed the Benedictines there in the heat of summer, ensuring dispute over property and water.

Ludwig Leichardt

This extraordinary Prussian explorer arrived unexpectedly in Port Victoria, or Essington, on 17 December 1845 with six skeletal men on equally gaunt horses. The party had left Jimbour Homestead on the Darling Downs on 1 October the previous year, and had long been presumed dead; poems and songs had been written in their honour. Leichardt wasn't as disparaging of Port Victoria as this narrative suggests. In fact he wrote, 'I was deeply affected in finding myself again in civilised society.' The explorers sailed home from Port Victoria on the *Heroine*, arriving in Sydney on 29th March 1846. Eleven days later the same vessel left Sydney on its return voyage, with Don Confalonieri and the two Irish catechists on board.

Bilyagoro

Occasionally referred to by Salvado as 'Guillermo Bigliagoro', he was a Yued man who seemingly spent a lot of time with Salvado in the early days of the mission. According to Salvado's memoirs, Bilyagoro had been brought to the mission 'by his four wives' covered in sores, and once cured became a fierce supporter. Salvado refers fondly to 'my friend Bilyagoro', or 'my old and faithful companion in the bush'. In one scene, Salvado and Bilyagoro go hunting for ducks and kill thirteen by disguising themselves behind a screen of branches, then clubbing them with their *dowaks*. It was usually Bilyagoro who guided the missionaries through the bush between the mission and Perth.

Benedict Upemara

'The first native boy to be baptised on our mission', Benedict was taken to Rome by Dom Serra in February 1848. As Salvado tells it, Benedict 'asked me to arrange with the bishop to let him go', and the boy's father, 'backed up his son's request', a version of events suggesting an understanding of the journey that neither father nor son could possibly have possessed. According to Salvado's own memoirs, the father angrily confronted him a few weeks later, having heard rumours that his boy had died at sea and his body thrown into the sea. It transpired that Benedict did make it to Rome and was taken to see the pope, but soon after became unwell and was deposited by Serra at the Propaganda College in Rome where he died a few months later, probably from pneumonia.

John Gavin

A Parkhurst 'apprentice', this fifteen-year-old boy was the first European to be executed in Western Australia, having confessed to using an adze to murder his employer's eighteen-year-old son at Dandalup. He was publicly hanged outside the Round House, Fremantle, on 6th April 1844 and, after phrenological casts had been made for scientific purposes, buried in the sand dunes nearby.

Richard Madden

Colonial Secretary of Western Australia from 1847, Madden was an Irish Catholic surgeon and an enlightened man who had travelled the world. He was an anti-slavery campaigner, the author of the seven volume *Lives of United Irishmen*, and was greatly concerned with the suffering of the Irish peasantry during the Great Famine. He saw echoes of this in Western Australia, writing home to the Catholic vicar-general of Dublin that 'the colony is administered by Irish Orangemen in the interests of Orangemen … unprincipled astute bigots are in authority'. He was godfather to Francis Conaci and John Dirimera.

Francis Conaci

Aged about seven, Francis was the younger of the two Aboriginal boys from New Norcia who were taken to Rome by Salvado in 1849 and deposited with Father Gaetani, the Novice Master at Cava. At first, Francis coped better than did John with the cultural and climatic shock. A poignant document still held at New Norcia provides testament to this boy's resilience. It is a letter to Salvado written in neat but slightly wobbly copperplate, dated 18 July 1851. 'It is with great pleasure that we received your welcome letter, by means of which we learnt that you are in good health, and we assure you that we are, too.' The letter has been annotated by Father Gaetani, who disparages the boy's writing, saying it 'shows how little attention he pays'. Francis soon after became unwell and died in Rome in October 1853, probably from pneumonia.

John Dirimera

John was aged about eleven when Salvado took the boys to Rome. Understandably, he found it very hard to learn anything, the only permitted languages being Italian and Latin. He persisted even after Francis died but then he too became unwell. He was brought back to Fremantle by Serra in May 1855, but sadly did not make it back to his own country and family around Moore River, dying three months later in Perth. Salvado's hagiographers have pondered the question of his ill-fated decision to take these two boys to Rome, and drawn conclusions quite at odds with contemporary views. Two jarring examples follow.

Thus did these two young aboriginals, in the fresh ardour of their self-offering, pass through the portals of eternity to plead God's blessing on the Mission's labours.
John McMahon, *Bishop Salvado Founder of New Norcia*, 1943

Had Salvado acted too quickly with these aboriginal boys? It cannot be said that he did. They probably would have died young of white men's diseases had they remained at the mission, as others had done. It was not going to Europe that killed them. The very presence of the white man among them was to do so. Salvado and his helpers merely softened the harshness of the contact with white civilization, so destructive of the aboriginal.
George Russo, *Lord Abbot of the Wilderness*, 1980

Mary Catherine Palamira

An 'orphan' girl probably taken from around Moore River and adopted by the Sisters of Mercy, baptised and raised in their 'Benevolent Institution'. In 1850, aged about nine, she was taken by Ursula and Anne to Europe. On the way she got to see elephants in Ceylon and meet Florence Nightingale in Alexandra. She was presented to Pope Pius IX and then travelled with the nuns across France and then to Ireland. She was subsequently left by Ursula at an exclusive private school in Isleworth which was funded by an aristocratic Catholic philanthropist, the Earl of Shrewsbury, and run by the widow of a French viscount. She died there a year later, probably from pneumonia or tuberculosis.

Placido

In 1850 Bishop John Brady took a young boy referred to only by this name to Rome on the same trip as the nuns and Mary Catherine Palamira. In her *Sketches of Conventual Life in the Bush* Ursula records that on the long sailing trip 'Placid hardly ceased day or night crying out in the most doleful tones' that 'the ship was bad' and he wanted to return to the bush, because 'the bush was good'. His name does not appear in accounts of their subsequent journey across Europe. Perhaps he died at sea or was left by Brady at a monastery in Rome and died there.

Florence Nightingale

En route to Europe, Ursula, Anne and Mary Catherine Palamira met with Florence Nightingale in Alexandria, Egypt, and were given a tour of the understaffed hospital where she was working. This was six years before Nightingale's work in Crimea made her famous, but this highly educated, urbane, spiritual and fiercely independent woman must have made quite an impression on the nuns, who were travelling under the disapproving eye of their troublesome bishop. In her diaries, Nightingale records her admiration for the nuns' work in Western Australia, and favourably compares the manners of little Mary Catherine with those of a bored daughter of a wealthy Egyptian family with whom she met later that day. Later, she wrote admiringly of Salvado's work at New Norcia.

Pope Pius IX

Pius IX, or Pio Nono, reigned for thirty-two tumultuous years from 1846. Initially he was the darling of Enlightenment liberals, promising reforms and freeing political prisoners, but 1848 changed all that when rampaging republicans fired cannon upon the Quirinal Palace and murdered his Minister of the Interior. The pope fled Rome for the fortified town of Gaeta, south of Rome. It was in Gaeta that Salvado, Francis and John had an audience with Pio Nono, who presented the boys with their robes. When in 1850 he returned to Rome, it was under cover of the French army, and he was transformed into an ultra-conservative 'prisoner of the Vatican', which he was never able to leave until his death. Rome itself and the Papal States were forever lost under his papacy. He was the pope who declared the office 'infallible'.

Cardinal Fransoni

Giacomo Filippo Fransoni (or Franzoni) was Prefect of the Congregation for the Propagation of the Faith (*Propaganda Fide*) which controlled Catholic missionary activity all over the world. Appointed by Pope Gregory XVI in 1834, he held the position for twenty-two years. Every foreign bishop was answerable to Fransoni, and his position was so powerful during this period of rapid global expansion for the church that he was sometimes referred to as 'The Red Pope'.

Pierre-Joseph Proudhon

The first person to describe himself as an anarchist, Proudhon was an influential theorist in the 1848 Revolutions in France and elsewhere. His best-known quote is 'Property is Theft'. Karl Marx was an early admirer but they fell out when, in response to Proudhon's *The Philosophy of Poverty*, Marx responded with a critique he stingingly called *The Poverty of Philosophy*. In a later letter to Prosper Guéranger, ex-Benedictine Léandre Fonteinne writes that he had come to look exactly like Proudhon (short, tubby, bearded, bespectacled) and could only be distinguished by his hat; Léandre always wore a black one, while Proudhon's was white.

Dominic Urquhart

An argumentative Irish Cistercian monk from Mount St Bernard's Abbey in England who seemed to wreak havoc wherever he went. Bishop Serra brought him out to Perth at the end of 1849 thinking him an ally, but they quarrelled *en route* and on arrival Urquhart switched allegiances to the Irish side to become Brady's attorney. Ursula Frayne and Salvado wrote excoriatingly of him. After the Irish side lost the battle of the bishops, *Propaganda Fide* ordered Urqhuart to leave the colony. He asked Rome's permission to go to Peru and when this was refused, he went anyway. He was last heard of having a feud with the Archbishop of Lima, for which he was imprisoned.

Queen Isabella II of Spain

Isabella, contemporary of Victoria, came to the throne two weeks shy of her third birthday, was officially crowned at aged thirteen and was married off at aged fifteen in a double ceremony along with her younger sister, 'the Infanta', Luisa Fernanda. Isabella survived as queen for thirty-five tumultuous years despite fierce opposition from the Carlists, supporters of her uncle Carlos. She depended on the support of the army and of the parliament or *Cortes Generales*, dominated by the so-called Moderate Liberals. Though she was a Catholic queen, the church came under great political attack during the early part her reign. She survived the turmoil of 1848 but came to be known as *La Reina de los Tristes Destinos* – the Queen of Sad Mischance.

The Cathedral of St John the Evangelist

Happily, given the fate of so many early colonial era Perth buildings, the church whose foundation stone was laid by Father Brady on 16th January, 1844 still stands in Victoria Avenue. It has been sympathetically restored and renamed St John's Pro-Cathedral. Next door is Mercedes College for Girls, still run by the Sisters of Mercy, and in the convent grounds lie Catherine Gogarty and Maurice Bouchet.

Toodyay

Prettily situated on the banks of the Avon River, Toodyay has been very nearly washed away a few times by floods. The original town was situated where West Toodyay is now, but was so prone to inundation that in 1860 the town proper was relocated to its current location on higher ground a few kilometres east. Nowadays, Toodyay boasts the country's best bakery and every weekend the main street is full of Harley-Davidsons. The Avon River Descent, held every August, is one of the world's premier white-water events, but in summer the river runs dry.

New Subiaco

Serra's project ran from 1851 to 1867 but has faded from memory. The extensive monastery lands were south of Lake Monger and Herdsman Lake, corresponding to most of the current suburb of Wembley. The Benedictine monks ran livestock there and grew lemons, figs, almonds, grapes and olives. Only the stables have survived the years, beautifully preserved in the grounds of the MercyCare aged care facility. The adjacent suburb of Subiaco took its name from the monastery Serra built, but the road in which St Joseph's Catholic Church and St John of God Hospital are now located was named for his more popular confrère, Salvado, who disparaged the New Subiaco project and shut it down once Serra was gone.

New Norcia

To view New Norcia for the first time still makes an impression. As you drive through featureless farming country, a hundred and thirty-two kilometres north of Perth, there suddenly appears Australia's only monastic town, built in the Spanish style.

When Salvado returned there in 1853, the rest of the colony was struggling to survive, but under his control, New Norcia grew. Salvado's fundraising in Europe allowed him to buy more land, to build and to acquire religious art, books and objects, while also buying the equipment needed to establish a farm, foundry, bakery, post-office and so on.

In the 1860s the Aboriginal population was decimated by disease, especially measles and pneumonia, and after that Bishop Salvado's commitment to sustaining Yued culture seemed to evaporate. New Norcia became a receiving place for 'orphaned' children from all corners of the colony, different family groups being thrown together with children whose fathers were white men.

His successor Abbot Fulgentius Torres made New Norcia more like a traditional European monastery. Torres built two of New Norcia's most impressive buildings – *St Gertrude's for Ladies* and *St Ildephonsus for Boys*. At its territorial peak, New Norcia reached an area of seventy-five thousand square kilometres, the size of the three Benelux countries combined, including thousands of acres of farmland, a bustling Spanish monastic village and seventy monks, most of them Spanish. Still, Torres was an expansionist and he journeyed three thousand kilometres north to the Kimberley coast to establish Kalumburu Mission.

After World War II, New Norcia steadily contracted. The Aboriginal Schools closed in the 1970s. New Norcia's *abbey nullius* status was gradually revoked and it came back under the control of the Perth archdiocese. New Norcia Catholic College closed in 1991. All the farmland has been sold. Even the beloved New Norcia Hotel has ceased operations.

New Norcia faces an uncertain future. Its newest buildings are now over a century old and in need of expensive repairs. But it continues to serve as a popular place for spiritual retreats. The Camino Salvado, starting from St Joseph's in Salvado Road, Subiaco, and finishing in New Norcia, offers a week of quiet reflection combined with bushwalking. And the New Norcia archives are a historical treasure trove, especially as Spanish, Italian, French and Latin sources are gradually translated into English.

Questions abound as one walks through New Norcia:

Why is it there, really?

What should one feel about the monks?

Was their mission ultimately a force for good, or ill, or some mix of both?

In the iconoclastic twenty-first century, New Norcia has the sort of history ripe for reinterpretation, and this author has no special wisdom except to suggest that we should all be judged in the context of the times in which we live. Salvado's writings over many decades indicate a lifelong desire to protect, lift up and encourage Aboriginal people, and in the latter years of the nineteenth century, New Norcia was widely lauded as the template for achieving this. Salvado was a 'leftie' of his time, for sure. But it is also easy to see that as much harm was done to Aboriginal people in colonial times by misplaced good intentions as by evil or malice.

For Western Australians, the very name New Norcia is evocative, and in more recent years, provocative. Mention the place to any ex-student of a Catholic school and you are sure to receive a smile, or a groan, and then an oft-recounted story about what happened on a religious retreat or music camp back in Year 10. There are said to be ghosts at night. New Norcia does look like a place that would have ghosts.

BIBLIOGRAPHY

These are some of the books the author depended on for historical context, or especially enjoyed. It is not a comprehensive list of sources. If the reader has got this far and wants more, start with the Fonteinne book; you won't be able to put it down.

Bérengier, Dom Théophile, *New Norcia: History of a Benedictine Colony in Western Australia 1846–1878*. Gilet, Peter (trans.), Abbey Press, Northcote, Vic., 2021.

Brady, John. *A Descriptive Vocabulary of the Native Language of Western Australia*. T. Bryan Printer, Perth, 1899. (This version, with a 'new' introduction not written by Brady, can be viewed online at nla.gov.au/nla.obj-26250201. The original was published in Rome in 1845 and all the content appears to have been copied from Moore.)

Byrne, Geraldine. *Valiant Women: Letters from the Foundation Sisters of Mercy in Western Australia, 1845–1849*. Polding Press, Melbourne, 1981.

Cromb, Alison. *The Road to Toodyay: A history of the early settlement of Toodyay and the Avon Valley of Western Australia*. Self-published, Dianella, WA, 2016.

Erickson, Rica. *Old Toodyay and Newcastle*. Toodyay Shire Council, 1974.

Gilet, Peter (trans.) & Charles Leen (additional material). *The Correspondence of Léandre Fonteinne*. Abbey Press, Northcote, Vic., 2014.

Girola, Stefano (trans.). *Report of Rosendo Salvado to Propaganda Fide in 1883*. Abbey Press, Northcote, Vic., 2016.

Girola, Stefano (trans.). *Report of Rosendo Salvado to Propaganda Fide in 1900.* Abbey Press, New Norcia, 2020.

Killerby, Catherine Kovesi. *Ursula Frayne: A Biography.* University of Notre Dame / Fremantle Arts Centre Press, 1996.

Máiz, Ramón and Tiffany Shellam. *Rosendo Salvado and the Australian Aboriginal World*, Consella da Culture Galega, Spain, 2016.

Moore, George Fletcher (ed.). *A Descriptive Vocabulary of the Language in Common Use Amongst the Aborigines of Western Australia: With copious meanings, embodying much interesting information regarding the habits, manners, and customs of the natives, and the natural history of the country.* Wm. S. Orr & Co., London, 1842. Moore acknowledges in the foreword his special debt to three men: 'Mr Symmons' (Charles Symmons, Protector of Aborigines, later retitled Guardian of Aborigines and Protector of Settlers), an anonymous 'friend' of Symmons (perhaps Peter Barrow, Guardian of Aborigines for York) and Frank Armstrong. He also cites the explorer George Grey, 'Bussel (sic) of Vasse River', and a mysterious Mr Lyon who he says published the very first known list of Noongar–English translations in the Perth newspapers in 1833. These names from the early colonial period remain important today in the re-establishment of the Noongar spoken language.

Ogle, Nathaniel. *The Colony of Western Australia: A manual for emigrants.* James Fraser, London, 1839.

Stormon, E.J. (ed. and trans.). *The Salvado Memoirs: Historical memoirs of Australia & particularly of the Benedictine Mission of New Norcia & of the habits & customs of the Australian natives.* UWA Press, Perth, 1977. (Rosendo Salvado's memoirs were originally published in Rome in 1851 by the Society for the Propagation of the Faith with the title *Memorie Storiche dell' Australia.*)

Wiltgen, Ralph M. *The Founding of the Roman Catholic Church in Oceania, 1825 to 1850*, Pickwick Publications, Oregon, USA, 2010.

ACKNOWLEDGEMENTS

Thanks to John Hall and the WA Historical Society Writing Group for their early encouragement. To my late mother-in-law, Jennifer Robertson; to John Webb and John Nash for their many helpful suggestions, and Ron Lloyd for his smiley faces. To Candy Aubry for her gentle correction of my pidgin French, and so on. And to all at Fremantle Press, especially Georgia Richter and Rachel Hanson, for their enthusiasm, attention to detail and excellent judgement.

First published 2023 by
FREMANTLE PRESS

Fremantle Press Inc. trading as Fremantle Press
PO Box 158, North Fremantle, Western Australia, 6159
fremantlepress.com.au

Cover images: unsplash.com (Josh Applegate, David Clode, Annie Spratt)
shutterstock.com (Alexander Sviridov, AzureJasper)
Designed by Carolyn Brown, Tendeersigh.com.au
Maps by Chris Crook, Country Cartographics, ccarto.com.au
Printed and bound in Australia by Griffin Press.

 A catalogue record for this
book is available from the
NATIONAL
LIBRARY National Library of Australia
OF AUSTRALIA

ISBN 9781760991678 (paperback)
ISBN 9781760991685 (ebook)

Department of
Local Government, Sport
and Cultural Industries

Fremantle Press is supported by the State Government through the Department
of Local Government, Sport and Cultural Industries.

MIX
Paper from
responsible sources
FSC® C009448

Fremantle Press respectfully acknowledges the Wadjak people of the Noongar
nation as the traditional owners and custodians of the land
where we work in Walyalap.